LINGUISTICS

for Students of Literature

LINGUISTICS

for Students of Literature

Elizabeth Closs Traugott
Stanford University

Mary Louise Pratt
Stanford University

HARCOURT BRACE JOVANOVICH, PUBLISHERS
San Diego   New York   Chicago   Atlanta   Washington, D.C.
London   Sydney   Toronto

ISBN: 0-15-551030-4

Library of Congress Catalog Card Number: 79-91194

Printed in the United States of America

To our parents:

August Closs

Joyce Pratt

McGillivray Pratt

And in memory of Hannah Closs

Preface

This book is intended primarily for upper-division undergraduates and beginning graduate students in English departments. It is also addressed to education students studying language arts and to students of linguistics who wish to explore practical applications of linguistics in one field—literature. Each chapter starts with linguistic analysis of some aspect of the English language and then moves to applications of the linguistics in analyzing specific literary texts in English. In this respect our book differs from most others on linguistics and literary analysis, which usually start with a critical discussion of literary texts and then bring linguistics to bear on these texts. Our own emphasis stems from the conviction that a broad grounding in linguistics must be achieved before linguistic concepts can be applied usefully and systematically to any field, whether literature, pedagogy, or speech therapy.

We have chosen to cover briefly a wide number of topics in linguistics, rather than a few in depth, because we believe the beginner needs to survey the field in general before selecting a particular area for deeper study. This does not mean that all aspects of contemporary linguistics are covered; there is simply too much for one book or one course. Nor does it mean that we have restricted ourselves solely to those topics in linguistics that appear to be particularly illuminating in reading and interpreting literary texts. Rather, we have made a broad selection of topics central to contemporary linguistics, and within those we have further selected a number of topics that have proved, or could potentially prove, to be of considerable interest in literary criticism. Our general approach is that of "generative" linguistics, but we apply the term in the broadest sense, as the branch of linguistics devoted to accounting for our abilities as language-users both to utter and to understand new sentences. For students who wish to pursue the topics further, we have provided Suggested Readings at the end of each chapter. Footnotes are used to acknowledge sources or to provide references for instructors and students who want to delve into the materials at considerably greater depth than they will be able to in the chapters or Suggested Readings. Since the focus of this book is linguistic, the references are nearly all linguistic; the few works of literary criticism that are cited all emphasize language study. Each chapter concludes with a set of exercises that can be used as the basis for discussion in class, as homework, or as food for further thought.

A great many literary texts are analyzed or presented for analysis in this book. While some will be recognized as familiar mainstays of stylistic analysis, many, perhaps most, will not. We have deliberately sought sample texts not widely known and studied, in the hope that our readers will encounter them fresh and not find themselves retracing already established critical paths.

This book would not have existed without the endurance of many hundreds of students, especially those in Elizabeth Traugott's course on the structure of English, taught in various forms over the years at the University of California at Berkeley, Princeton University, and Stanford University. From those classes the idea for this book gradually emerged. Our students have plied us with questions, criticized ideas, suggested examples and topics to expand or drop. To all we give our thanks, and especially to Kevin Dungey, W. Anne Garvey, and Marthe McCulloch for their helpful criticism of an earlier draft. Thanks also to Rebecca LaBrum and Patricia Porter for their invaluable editorial assistance, to the Department of English at Stanford University, which financed some of this assistance, to Barbara Kao, who did a magnificent job of typing, and especially to Sandy Lifland at Harcourt Brace Jovanovich for the pleasure of working with a really fine editor.

To Edmund L. Epstein, Donald C. Freeman, William Golightly, Richard Ohmann, and Donald A. Sears, our gratitude and appreciation for many valuable comments on the prefinal draft. We alone are responsible for what errors of fact, interpretation, and omission remain.

And above all, our thanks to John Traugott and Toni Guttman for their patience while these pages multiplied and for their wisdom as our readers and critics.

Elizabeth Closs Traugott
Mary Louise Pratt

Contents

7 ESTABLISHING A UNIVERSE OF DISCOURSE   272

I

Language, Linguistics, and Literary Analysis

Of all the aptitudes and behaviors which characterize human beings, language is the most uniquely human, and quite possibly the most important. It is around us everywhere, in speech, writing, sign language, or simply in our minds as we dream, remember a conversation, or quietly think out a problem. It is a vehicle of power, a means by which we control, create, and preserve. The question "What is language?" has been asked from remotest times, yet its answer is still far from clear. The more we discover, the more mysterious and complex language appears to be. One thing seems certain, however: Language is a capacity that distinguishes human beings from other creatures. Many myths bear witness to this. For example, according to the Mayan sacred book, the *Popol Vuh*, after the Creators had made the earth, carved it with mountains, valleys, and rivers, and covered it with vegetation, they created the animals who would be guardians of the plant world and who would also provide food for the gods and praise their name:

> And the creation of all the four-footed animals and the birds being finished, they were told by the Creator and the Maker and the Forefathers: "Speak, cry, warble, call, speak each one according to your variety, each, according to your kind." So was it said to the deer, the birds, pumas, jaguars, and serpents.
>
> "Speak, then, our names, praise us, your mother, your father. Invoke then, Huracán, Chipi-Caculhá, Raxa-Caculhá, the Heart of Heaven, the Heart of Earth, the Creator, the Maker, the Forefathers; speak, invoke us, adore us," they were told.

1

> But they could not make them speak like men; they only hissed and screamed and cackled; they were unable to make words, and each screamed in a different way.
>
> When the Creator and the Maker saw that it was impossible for them to talk to each other, they said: "It is impossible for them to say our names' the names of us, their Creators and Makers. This is not well," said the Forefathers to each other.[1]

As a punishment, the birds and animals were condemned to be eaten and sacrificed by others, and the Creators set out to make another creature who would be able to call upon them and speak their praises. This creature would be man.

As the Mayan myth suggests, many animals have rudimentary communication codes, but in no case does the communicative capacity of other animals even remotely approach our own. Efforts to teach sign language to our closest relative, the chimpanzee, have had only moderate success. Moreover, language is different from all other forms of human behavior. We speak of "body language," "computer language," and the "language" of music and painting, but in all these cases, "language" is used in a metaphorical or extended sense, extended from "human language" to fields of human endeavor and experience where certain characteristics of language can be found. None of these senses, however, combines all the aspects of language—its symbolic nature, its systematic internal structure, its creative potential, its ability to refer to abstractions or imaginary objects, and its ability to be used in talking about itself—and none plays the central role in human affairs that language does. All but the most rudimentary forms of social organization depend on language, as do all but the most rudimentary technological achievements. It is chiefly through language that human communities control and change their structures, and create institutions which embody community aspirations and shape community life. Without language, the accumulation of shared knowledge and customs which we call culture would be impossible. Thus, when you use your knowledge of language to read a story from the *Popol Vuh*, you become a new link in a chain of human communication stretching back into the distant past, a chain that only language can create.

The power of language is dramatically attested to in one of the oldest stories of Judeo-Christian mythology, the story of the Tower of Babel in the Book of Genesis. According to this story, some generations after the Great Flood, the descendants of Noah decided to settle down in "a plain in the land of Shinar." There, instead of setting up a society subordinate to the will of God, they challenged God's authority by deciding to build a tower which would reach heaven. Recognizing the implications of this defiance, God regained control through a linguistic stratagem. He caused all the people to speak different languages, so they could no longer understand one another. Then he scattered them across the face of the earth.

The story of the Tower of Babel is no longer used to explain the diversity of languages in the world, but it does demonstrate rather dramatically where the power of language lies. As God saw very clearly in the story, the people's ability to build their tower rested on their capacity to communicate with one another, to agree on a plan, to delegate and coordinate labor, and to give orders. Language enabled the people to pool their energies in a construction effort so ambitious as to threaten the power of God himself. To meet this challenge, God destroyed not the tower itself, but the linguistic unity which made the collective effort possible. A wise move indeed, for as long as the unity was there, the tower could always be rebuilt. In fact, God concluded that as long as the people had one language, "nothing will be restrained from them, which they have imagined to do."

Despite the importance language has in our lives, we tend to take little notice of it, at least not until something goes wrong, as when a person grows up deaf, or experiences speech loss of one kind or another, or simply tries to communicate in a foreign country. We think of language, too, when it becomes a political issue, as in Belgium or Quebec or the southwestern United States, or when it becomes a cause of bloodshed. And we think of it when we become involved in using it to create special effects, as in poetry, or in the construction of particularly difficult messages, like letters containing bad news.

Even when language has been studied in the past, it has been studied mainly as an adjunct to other disciplines, such as philosophy, psychology, religion, literary criticism, or the art of persuasion. Only over the past 150 years or so has language been studied consistently as a discipline in its own right. During this period, considerable advances have been made toward an understanding of the internal structure of linguistic systems, that is, of the processes by which smaller components like words are combined to form utterances. Not as well understood is the way language functions in the lives of its speakers. This area, language use, has come to the forefront only in the past ten or fifteen years.

This book introduces most of the major questions a linguist asks when investigating the structure and use of contemporary English, and shows how the linguist's observations can be brought to bear on the study of literature and the phenomenon called "style." Many of the questions the linguist asks can be considered as parts of a single question: "What does it mean to 'know English'?" The linguist who poses this question is chiefly interested in making explicit the internalized knowledge which English speakers possess that enables them to speak and understand the English language. Another important area of linguistic investigation can be considered in the question: "How did English come to be this way?" This question, a historical one, is much too large to be introduced thoroughly in a book of this kind, although we will be frequently touching upon it in passing.[2]

Before turning to the structure of English, we will devote the next few

pages to discussing some of the basic characteristics of human language in general, and of the linguist's approach to it.

WHAT IS LANGUAGE?

Symbols

We have said that language is symbolic. What exactly does this mean? First of all, it means that language involves signs, that is, entities which represent or stand for other entities the way a plus sign (+), for instance, stands for a certain mathematical operation, or the way a black armband is a symbol of mourning. In language, the signs are sequences of sounds, though these can be transferred into visual signs, as in writing or the gestural sign language of the deaf. According to one theory, the relationship between an object, whether real or imaginary, and the sign which stands for it can be of three types.[3] If the two are associated by a physical *resemblance*, like an object and a photograph of it, the sign is called an icon. If the relation is one of physical *proximity*, as between smoke and fire, thunder and lightning, spots and measles, then the sign (smoke, thunder, spots) is called an index. If the relationship is one of *convention*, that is, one which has to be learned as part of the culture, like the relation beween a black armband and mourning, then the sign is called a symbol. Of course, these classes are not completely distinct. Some culturally learned information is needed to interpret an icon like 🚺 on the door of a toilet, or ⊽ beside a road. The three types of signs are basically on a continuum, with a sign like a skull and crossbones toward the iconic end, and ♀ , =, 𝄞 , ✡ , or a national flag toward the symbolic end.

Language is mainly symbolic in that the relations between the sound sequences and their meanings are conventional and have to be learned. There is no natural connection between the sound sequence f-o-r-k and the pronged utensil we eat with; we could just as easily use the sequence k-r-o-f as the sign for this object, or the sequence t-e-n-e-d-o-r, as in Spanish. Some words can be thought of as iconic or indexical, but even these are at least in part conventional. For example, the words we call "onomatopoetic" are partly iconic, in that their sound in some way resembles what they refer to. One obvious example is **cockadoodledoo**. But if this word were truly iconic, we would expect it to be the same or virtually the same in all languages; yet even in languages as closely related to English as French and German there are significant differences in the consonants and vowels and even the number of syllables: French **cocorico**, German **kikiriki**. In Japanese it is **kokekoko**.

Similarly, **ouch** is in part an indexical sign for pain, in that it is normally uttered only in response to pain. But if it were completely indexical, that is, if its relation to pain were as natural as the relation of smoke to fire, we might expect the identical form to occur in many languages. But it does not. For instance, the French expletive with the same meaning is **aie** (pronounced like English I). In Japanese it is **aíta**, in Russian **okh**.[4] In language, all signs are ultimately arbitrary, that is, conventional in form.

With icons and indexes, both the sign and the object it signifies have concrete reality. With symbols, the concrete sign can be used equally well to represent things that exist and things that do not, which is why we can use human language to lie, mislead, exaggerate, and create imaginary worlds in novels, poems, or tall tales. We can even speak of impossible worlds as in science fiction, or of nonexistent ideas, or of phenomena like black holes whose existence we have hypothesized but not proven. None of this would be possible if the signs of language were not symbolic. This is another important difference between human language and the communicative codes of animals.[5] Some animals are able to make quite complex indexical messages, but as far as we know, they can only use their signs in the presence of concrete stimuli. An example is the dance of the bees, an elaborate indexical code by which bees indicate the place where nectar can be found. We know that the dance is indexical because the bees do not perform it unless they have actually made recent forays for nectar. In other words, they cannot lie about the presence or position of nectar, nor can they invent it.

No one knows how the symbolic linguistic code of humans came into being. Some have argued that the origin of language lies in onomatopoeia, that people began talking by creating iconic signs to imitate the sounds heard around them in nature. This theory, sometimes called the *bow-wow* theory, is unlikely to be right, because language in fact makes very little use of iconic words. (**Bow-wow** itself is conventional. In French, dogs bark with **oua-oua**, pronounced "wa-wa.") Another theory is that language was originally indexical, arising out of cries of fear, pleasure, and so forth. This theory leaves as much to be desired as the iconic one. Neither theory explains how symbolic signs came to be. We do know that at this point in our biological history our ability to use symbols and learn language is genetically built in, an innate capacity of the human brain. But we know practically nothing about language over ten millennia ago, and very little indeed about language over five millennia ago. That is a tiny fraction of the biological history of man, and until we know far more about the neurophysiological aspects of language, we can only speculate about the origins of signs as symbols.

System

In general terms, a system is a whole made up of smaller units which stand in particular relation to each other and perform particular functions. For instance, a family can be viewed as a system in which each member is related by particular blood or marriage ties to all the others, and has specific roles and responsibilities. In much the same sense, language is a symbolic system made up of units, functions, and relations. For instance, sounds are units which combine to make words or parts of words like **un-** and **-tion,** and these in turn are units which can be joined in systematic ways to form larger meaningful sequences, like complex words, phrases, or sentences. In these larger sequences, each of the smaller units has a particular function and particular relations to all the others. Just as the basic sound-meaning combinations are conventional, so these larger sequences are highly conventional. For example, in Modern English we say **I saw them,** whereas in Old English the equivalent sentence was **Ic hie geseah,** "I them saw," employing not only different-sounding words, but also a different word order. At any particular time in a language one will find agreed-upon sound-meaning relations and agreed-upon orders. Often there are options—as a system changes from the **I them saw** to the **I saw them** order, for instance, both structures will exist side by side for some time, with different frequencies over time. They will probably also develop different functions in a speech community, being used for different styles or for different topics. Thus in the sixteenth century, the older word order was largely restricted to poetry. In short, even where there are options in a linguistic system, they are not random, but are restricted according to context.

Personal pronouns provide another example of the systematic character of language. In any language, the personal pronouns form a set of interrelated members, each with a different function—a little subsystem, in short. This system is always internally organized, but the way it is organized varies a lot from language to language. In English, for example, we have three third person pronouns (**he/she/it**) whose function is to distinguish sex. In the second person, English used to distinguish a single addressee (**thou**) from more than one (**ye**), but this distinction is no longer part of the system. Indonesian makes some rather different distinctions. For instance, **we** in Indonesian is distinguished according to whether it excludes or includes the addressee. This is a distinction we can make in English only by using rather clumsy constructions like **John and I, we're going to the movies tonight** (exclusive of the addressee), or **We, and that includes you, are going to the movies tonight** (inclusive of the addressee). In the Indonesian system no distinctions are made for sex, but distinctions are made according to degree of familiarity. For all three persons there is both a familiar and an unfamiliar (or polite) pronoun in the singular. Thus the Modern English and Indonesian pronoun systems look very different when set side by side (F stands for "familiar," P for "polite," Ex for "exclusive," In for "inclusive" in the chart at the top of the next page). However, the differences between the sets are not random. Each set functions as a system, that is, as a set of units held together by a network of relations.

The set of organizing principles that control any system can be called a set of "rules." In linguistics, we speak of language as being "rule-governed," and we say, for instance, that English has a rule specifying **I saw him** as the

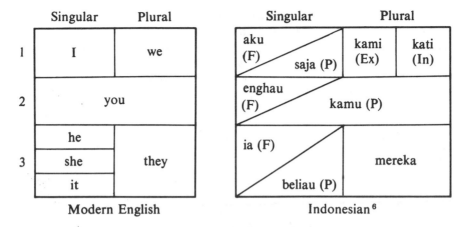

	Singular	Plural
1	I	we
2	you	
3	he / she / it	they

Modern English

	Singular		Plural	
1	aku (F) / saja (P)		kami (Ex)	kati (In)
2	enghau (F) / kamu (P)			
3	ia (F) / beliau (P)		mereka	

Indonesian[6]

normal word order for sentences, and a rule specifying that sex is distinguished in third person pronouns. But this term "rule" may be misleading. In linguistics it does not mean that language is controlled by notions of what ought to be said. Rather, it means that everything that is said is organized systematically according to a set of principles internalized in the brain of the speaker. In this sense, "rule" simply means a *pattern observed or observable by the investigator of language.* Another common way of making this point is to say that the rules of language are "constitutive" rather than "prescriptive." The rules of etiquette are prescriptive; they prescribe how one should behave. The rules of language, on the other hand, constitute language, the way the rules of poker constitute poker. The linguist's rules describe how a language is; they do not prescribe how it should be spoken. Learning to talk involves internalizing the system of a particular language at a particular time, something every child normally does spontaneously. Each of the next eight chapters in this book deals with a different aspect of the linguistic system of English. Chapter 2 deals with the sound system, Chapter 3 with the system of sound-meaning relations at the level of the word, Chapters 4 and 5 with sentence structure and sentence meaning, Chapters 6 and 7 with the structure of discourse, Chapter 8 with how the English system varies from dialect to dialect. Chapter 9 examines what happens when the English system comes in contact with other linguistic systems.

Language Universals

As we have seen, much of language, including the basic sound-meaning relations, is arbitrary and conventional. But not everything is. Linguists have been puzzled for a long time by the fact that the languages of the world are actually much more similar to each other than one might expect. For example, though some languages like Modern English, Yoruba, and Thai favor the word order **I saw them,** and other languages like Old English and Japanese favor **I them saw**, and yet others like Welsh and Hebrew favor **Saw I them**, very few languages favor the other three logical possibilities: **Saw them I**, **Them I saw**, or **Them saw I**. This does not mean that the last three orders are impossible; indeed, they all occur, given special circumstances such as emphasis, repetition, and so forth. But rarely are they basic word orders. It seems, then, that there is some kind of general restriction or "constraint" on what can be a basic order in a language. Pronoun systems exhibit similar restrictions. For instance, in the languages of the world, we do not find a system that distinguishes familiar versus polite in the first and third person forms but not in the second person forms. Nor do we find a system which uses the same term for **I** singular and **you** plural.

Facts like these indicate that not all of language is purely conventional or culturally imposed. Languages are partially shaped by universal constraints on what combinations of elements occur, what historical changes occur, even on what meanings are distinguished in languages.[7] Some linguists argue that the universal constraints on language must be genetic, part of the human capacity for language with which one is born. Others seek an explanation in very general cognitive structures such as our tendency to perceive dualities more readily than three-part structures. Still others argue that the universal constraints are explicable in terms of the functions language serves, such as self-expression and manipulation of others. (What would a language be good for if it made no distinction between **I** and **you**?) The issues once more concern the origin of language and are essentially unanswerable at the moment. What is important is to recognize that by no means everything in a particular language is arbitrary and unique. The universal tendencies in the structures of languages are so widely attested to that at the present time it seems justifiable to claim that part of our cognitive capacity is specifically linguistic.

Creativity

Recent experiments with chimpanzees suggest that certain animals can not only learn individual symbols (in this case manual rather than vocal signs), but can also learn to combine them in ways reminiscent of sentences like **Give me key**.[8] However, as far as we know, they cannot do certain things which all human speakers can—they do not appear to be able to learn sign language without specific instruction, and they cannot, on the basis of a small number of elements and relations between them, create an infinite number of messages.

When linguists speak of the "creativity" of human language, they are usually referring to these two characteristics. Anyone who knows a language is able, without specific instruction, to produce and understand utterances which have never been heard before but which are possible within the system. You are using this ability right now to read this book, and you rely on it nearly every time you talk. Certainly, language does include some fixed routines like greetings, farewells, toasts, and a wide variety of other relatively fixed utterances which function in the society as gestures of group solidarity, somewhat like the mutual grooming of monkeys. But obviously, humans are not limited to such routines. The number of sentences possible in a human language is infinite in principle, for there is no limit on how long a sentence can be. It makes no sense to say, for example, that the longest sentence in English (or any other language) is a thousand words long, since, for any longest sentence, someone can propose another even longer. The easiest way to lengthen a sentence is to add parts introduced by **and**. More complex, but equally infinite structures can be created using subordinating relations, as in **I expect you to force Bill to leave**. Structures of this sort can be recycled, as in this line from Thom Gunn's poem "Carnal Knowledge," which theoretically could go on forever:

You know I know you know I know you know.[9]

To sum up, the creativity of language consists in this fact: The number of elements and rules in the system is finite, while the number and length of utterances the system can produce is infinite. In this respect, linguistic systems are somewhat like the number system. Given any number, one can always construct a larger number by addition or multiplication. In practice, we are limited, of course, by space, time, memory, interest, and many different factors, so that no actual sentence will ever be infinitely long. But what is important is that the system has this potential.

Ambiguity

Creativity is a linguistic universal, that is, a characteristic shared by all human languages. Ambiguity is another, and is of particular interest to linguists. Ambiguity in language results from the fact that there is not always a one-to-one correspondence between expressions and meanings. For instance, the single sound sequence **pale** is a sign for a color quality, a kind of stick, and (with the same sound though different spelling) a bucket. Sentences too can obviously be ambiguous, like **I speak to you as a mother**. Language differs in this respect from mathematics, which is carefully constructed so that each symbol or sequence of symbols has only one meaning.

Teachers and writers often frown on ambiguity, seeing it as a hindrance to communication and a symptom of unclear thinking, as indeed it sometimes is. Poets and literary critics often deal with ambiguity as a creative device that concentrates meaning in few words, and it can be this too. Linguists are not interested in evaluating ambiguity, but they are interested in its presence, in the kinds of ambiguity language permits, and in the knowledge speakers have about ambiguity. For instance, taken out of context, the following sentences in English are ambiguous and can thus be interpreted in two or more ways: **You may go, All of the members weren't present, Eleanor took Bill's coat off, Sam almost killed Pete**. Most importantly, linguists are interested in the fact that speakers know sentences such as these are ambiguous and are usually able to explain the ambiguity through paraphrases that "disambiguate" the meanings. For example, for **Sam almost killed Pete**, one might distinguish the two meanings as follows: **Sam nearly killed Pete but decided not to** and **Sam nearly killed Pete, his driving was so reckless**. Secondly, linguists are interested in the fact that when ambiguous sentences are uttered in context, language-users are nearly always able to tell which meaning is intended. Accounting for abilities like these is a major task in linguistic theory, and we will return to this point throughout the book.

An important distinction needs to be made between ambiguity and vagueness. Ambiguity involves two or more distinct meanings for one word, phrase, or sentence. Vagueness has to do with lack of specificity—**I know some French** is vague because it specifies nothing at all about how much and what sort of French the person knows. But it is not ambiguous. **I neither confirm nor deny the report** and **It's sort of exciting, but not really** are also vague and lacking in specificity, but they are not ambiguous. There is no more than one distinct meaning for each of them, however vague that meaning may be.

LANGUAGE AS ACTION IN CONTEXT

Knowing a language means a great deal more than simply knowing how to produce sentences; it also means knowing how to use them. When people speak, they intend things. They speak in order to accomplish something in what has recently come to be called the "linguistic marketplace," the inter-actional situations in which language is used to explain, describe, criticize, amuse, deceive, make commitments, deliver opinions, get others to do things, and so forth. From one point of view, sentences like **Answer the question** or **Let's go to the movies** are instruments for producing action in others. From another point of view, the sentences themselves are actions performed by the speaker. To explain something is to do something verbally; to ask somebody a question is to request that they answer. All utterances can be thought of as goal-directed actions or "speech acts" as linguists call them. Some of the many different classes of speech acts include utterances whose goal is getting people to do things; contractual speech acts, such as promising, betting, agreeing on a plan; and describing, informing, and explaining, which, along with criticizing, judging, and evaluating, play an important role in education. The speech act of greeting illustrates yet another important function which language serves, that of expressing and establishing social relations between people. A less obvious function of language, perhaps, is the way it is used to establish shared worlds between speakers and hearers. Suppose you and a friend are arranging furniture and the friend, facing you, says **Move the chair a little to the left**. You are probably intended to move it to the speaker's left, which is your right. In other words, you are being asked to enter into and share the speaker's perspective. Expressions like **this, that, here, there,** or like **come, go, bring, take, left, right** usually require the addressee to share or at least interpret the world in the same way the speaker does, and thus they establish a shared world of discourse. In a later chapter, we will be examining more closely the importance of this language function in communication.

Another basic function of language is that of giving names to concepts and things. Naming is often seen as a way of getting control over things. For example, the small child's incessant naming of objects is usually understood as an effort to establish a kind of naming control over them. This same impulse is reflected in many creation stories, like the first chapter of Genesis where Adam names the beasts of the earth and so becomes their master. Another way of gaining linguistic control over an object is to describe and define it. A language used for definition and description is called a "metalanguage." Terms like "experiment," "entropy," "chi-square" are part of the metalanguage of mathematics, psychology, and other disciplines. "Sentence," "sound," "rule," and "ambiguity" are all terms belonging to the metalanguage of linguistics. Language is unique in that it is not only the medium for describing everything else in the universe, but also for describing itself.

The fact that language can be a metalanguage for itself sometimes causes difficulties, for we often fail to sort out the metalinguistic meaning of a term from its other meanings. In the case of "subject," there is no real problem since "subject" as a linguistic term is now so far differentiated in meaning from its usual meaning of *matter or topic* that most people think of it as one word with two meanings. But in the case of a term like "cause," we have more difficulties. In the metalanguage of linguistics, all of the following sentences are "causative": **I had her go, I made her go, I got her to go, Bill lightened his load.** One could certainly argue whether these sentences really involve causation in its usual sense. A philosopher might claim that such usage is too loose; a layman might find it too abstract or implausible. But in calling these sentences causatives, the linguist is using the word metalinguistically, separate from other usage, to refer to the fact that all the sentences involve an agent manipulating something or somebody for a certain purpose. In reading this book, it is important to be able to recognize when language is being used metalinguistically, because we will obviously be relying heavily on the metalinguistic function of language, and will be introducing many terms probably familiar to you, but with different meanings.

When language is used, it is always used in a context. What gets said and how it gets said is always in part determined by a variety of contextual factors. One such factor is "channel," the medium of expressions being used. Face-to-face speech, telephone speech, and writing are all different channels, and each constrains choice of expression in particular ways. For example, English has a different range of greeting expressions for each of these channels. On a larger scale, a lecture that is truly appropriate to a live audience that can respond immediately is not appropriate to print, or vice versa, for print is visual and allows the audience to go back or ahead and impose their own temporal scheme on that given by the writer. Without gesture and tone of voice, the written word must be far more explicit than the spoken. Both the spoken and the written word are governed by another contextual factor, namely the degree of formality of the speech situation. In speech, **I'm going to leave** and **I'm gonna take off** represent different degrees of formality, and each corresponds to a different range of speech contexts. Similarly, in writing, formal **You are requested to reply immediately** contrasts with less formal **Please answer right away.**[10]

Another set of contextual factors that intersects with those already mentioned has to do with the identity of the participants in communication. What gets said and how it gets said is partly governed by such factors as the age and sex of speaker and hearer. For instance, **What a darling pair of shoes** is more likely to be spoken by a woman than a man. Men have been shown to interrupt and use direct command forms of the type **Do that** or **Do that, please** to a greater extent when addressing men than when addressing women.[11] Age differences can be just as important. Speakers of different generations often tend to be more formal with each other than speakers of the same generation.

The regional, social, ethnic, and educational backgrounds of speaker and hearer are another set of contextual factors that can come into play. A person from a rural town in Kansas may choose to use the Kansas dialect only when in Kansas, or only to those he or she considers inferior in Kansas, or only with non-Kansans to affirm regional identity in the face of the social demand for a "standard" pronunciation. Use of distinct regional forms, as of socially or ethnically distinct markers like **ain't, bad** (meaning "outstanding, powerful"), or **schlepp** (meaning "drag"), to persons not in the same group often establishes social distance from the addressee and strong affiliation with the regional, social, or ethnic group implied. From the linguist's point of view, any language is best viewed as a conglomeration of language varieties which differ with respect to the regional, social, ethnic, sexual, generational, and educational groupings within the society. "Standard" languages—like Midwestern in the U.S. or Received Pronunciation in England—are simply seen as one variety among many.

In sum, all utterances are to some degree determined by a complex set of contextual factors including who is talking, who is being addressed, what is being talked about, and others. If speakers did not take these factors into account, all kinds of communicative misfires would result. Imagine, for example, a person exclaiming **Look at the mess in here!** over the telephone, or a lawyer addressing a jury with **Look, you guys gotta give my client a break**, or a citizen claiming **To be or not to be, that is the question** at a town meeting on garbage collection.

THE TASK OF THE LINGUIST

Linguists study the ways in which the sound-meaning correlations of languages are structured and how they function. As with all other fields of study, there are a variety of ways to do this. Suppose a linguist were asked to analyze the sound-meaning correlation **You may go**. One possibility would be to take a historical view and to show that while this sentence is ambiguous in Modern English, the equivalent sentence in early Old English some twelve hundred years ago was unambiguous and meant "You have the strength/physical power to go" (**may** is related to **might**, "strength"). You might show that a weaker meaning of "have the capacity to" developed from the sentence, and that this meaning in turn allowed for the development of the "maybe" meaning, and eventually, some six hundred years ago, of the "permission" meaning. A historical study would, of course, be concerned with the ways in which these new meanings could arise and the reasons for the changes. Another, rather different possibility would be to consider **You may go** from the point of view of production—under what circumstances would a contemporary speaker select **You may go** over **You have my permission to go**, **You can go now**, or even some nonlinguistic act like getting up and shuffling papers for one meaning of this sentence? Under what circumstances would **Maybe you'll be going** be selected for the other meaning? This is a task involving the encoding of messages and is a task to which computer-simulation of language production is addressed. Another approach is to consider the sentence from the point of view of the hearer: By what means does a hearer know how to disambiguate the sentence in a given context? This is a task of decoding. Yet another approach, the one we will take in this book, is to consider the sentence from the point of view of the code that makes either production or perception possible. In the metalanguage of linguistics, the description of the code that the linguist produces is called a "grammar." [12] As might be expected, a variety of ways of constructing grammars have been proposed.

Some linguists undertake to construct grammars on the basis of what is found in specific utterance samples, for example, a body of elicited texts provided by informants. [13] This is an easy sounding task; but in practice it is actually so difficult that no one has been able to achieve it satisfactorily, at least where sentence structure as opposed to sound structure is concerned. This is because sufficient examples of any particular structure simply do not occur in any piece of running text.

Other linguists, and we share their view, consider that concrete utterance samples are not enough in themselves without access to the intuitions of users of the language in question. These linguists argue that the role of utterance samples is simply to illustrate and test intuitions. For example, any native speaker of English knows by intuition that there is something odd or wrong about the expression **her obviousness to dance**, and nothing at all odd about **her eagerness to dance**. On the basis of this intuition, the linguist extrapolates that **obviousness** and **eagerness** do not occur in the same range of positions, and goes on to explore this difference further. A corpus of real data could never have revealed this difference, however, because it would contain only actual English utterances, and not impossible or ill-formed ones like **her obviousness to dance**.

In the view that we are adopting, intuitions about what is and is not possible in the language are the data of main concern to the linguist. Sample utterances are viewed simply as illustrating the knowledge and intuitions of speakers. Linguists who share this view consider it their ultimate task not only to describe what is found, but also to explain it in terms of internalized knowledge and innate (genetic) capacities for language, as was suggested earlier in connection with language universals. These capacities are inferred not only from contemporary languages but also from what we know about how and why languages change. Part of the ultimate task is to distinguish that which is universal in language from that which is unique to a particular language or language-group.[14] The question about universal features of language inevitably draws the researcher further into the question of how it is that language-learning takes place in the way that it does, partially independently of input, and in steps that resemble each other across languages to an extent far too great to be merely random.[15]

Whatever approach they adopt, linguists are in fairly general agreement about the basic subdivisions of linguistic investigation. There is "phonology," the study of sound systems (from Greek **phono-**, "sound"), "syntax," the study of phrase and sentence structure (from Greek **syn**, "together," and **tassein**, "arrange"), and "semantics," the study of meaning (from Greek **semainein**, "to signify"). Many also recognize the area of "morphology," basically the study of word formation (from Greek **morphe**, "form"). Of more recent date is "pragmatics," the study of language use (from Greek **pragma**, "deed, affair"). Often each of these subdivisions is seen as constituting a separate component of the grammar of a language.

Many linguists are interested not only in describing languages, but also in constructing theories, that is, well-organized hypotheses about how language works. Like all theories, whether of physics, biology, or literature, linguistic theories can never be proved right, but must be judged by how much data they can account for, that is, by how many questions they can answer and to what extent they can show relationships that hold the systems under investigation together. One theory that has proved particularly successful in addressing the problems of what is or is not universal and what makes language a specifically human phenomenon is the theory known as "generative grammar" developed initially by Noam Chomsky in 1957 in his book *Syntactic Structures*, and substantially modified since then. Generative grammar is a theory of language that aims to characterize what a language-user knows about his or her language, that is, the knowledge that a language-user puts to use in producing and understanding sentences.[16] (Note the metalanguage here—"generative" grammar does *not* mean a grammar that produces anything. It is simply a means of describing a system.)

Generative grammar forms the basis for a significant portion of what follows in this book; however, we will also be exploring some of the alternative hypotheses that have been developed in answer to questions that Chomsky raised. More important, we will be exploring a number of questions Chomsky did not pay much attention to, notably the areas of language use and linguistic interaction. In the next few pages, we will outline some of the basic concepts in the approach to language that we are adopting. They are introduced here merely to provide an orientation and frame of reference for thinking about language and about the language of literature. If certain issues are not fully understood from this necessarily condensed outline, this should be no cause for concern since they will all be elaborated on in the course of the book.

Competence and Performance

One of Chomsky's most important theoretical claims is that we need to distinguish our "competence," which is what we know about language, from our "performance," which is what we do when we speak or listen.[17] As language-users, for whatever language (or languages) we speak, we have a kind of linguistic blueprint in our heads, an internalized code, or system. As we have seen in the discussion of **You may go**, this internalized system is to be distinguished from the activity we engage in as speakers producing messages, or from the activity we engage in as hearers receiving messages. Chomsky sees the linguist's task as primarily describing competence, and only secondarily performance, because performance is impossible without competence. In other words, the linguist's grammar describes competence first and foremost.

As originally formulated, Chomsky's idea of competence encompassed only people's ability to produce and understand sentences of their language out of context, and to distinguish those that conform to the code of the language from those that do not. In other words, it encompassed the issues discussed earlier in the section entitled "What Is Language?" Others have argued, however, that competence also encompasses the ability to use language to accomplish particular communicative goals in particular social and linguistic contexts.[18] In other words, they argue that competence also encompasses the issues we discussed in the section entitled "Language as Action in Context." This is the view that we are adopting here. An example will illustrate some aspects of competence and help distinguish it from performance. Let us suppose that we are told to analyze the sentence **Can you bug the office of the head of HEW?** As regards the internal structure of this sentence, any English speaker knows such facts as the relation of the two **of** phrases to each other, and the significance of the inverted word order **can you**, which marks the sentence as a question. These observations would therefore be included in our account of the sentence. Our account would also point out that the sentence is potentially ambiguous. English speakers know that, depending on the circumstances, this sentence can be a question about the addressee's physical ability or about the addressee's administrative power, or about the physical layout of the HEW office. Alternatively, it may be a question about the ability of people in general (**you** = "one"). Or yet again it may function as a command to actually do the bugging. We will also have to point out that if it is to be used as a command, it is "well-formed" (to use some linguistic jargon) only if the speaker has authority to command such things. If we were accounting for a particular performance of this sentence, on the other hand, we would have to ask such questions as whether, in this particular case, it was being used as a question or a command; and if it was a command, we would have to ask whether the particular speaker actually did have the authority to make such a command. Clearly, performance takes competence into account, but it is not the same thing.

Just as clearly, we do not have direct access to competence. We make hypotheses about it from indirect evidence, such as available utterances and intuitions. Some of the pitfalls of this procedure are considered in Chapter 8. For the moment, suffice it to say that a particularly useful procedure for arriving at aspects of linguistic competence is the deliberate manipulation of language to create not only sentences that conform to the rules of the language but also sentences that do not. For example, we can construct the set **He is an entomologist, isn't he?**, **They are entomologists, aren't they?**, **He is an entomologist, aren't they?**, and **She is an entomologist, isn't he?**, and verify that English speakers find the last two peculiar and the first two not. On the basis of such intuitions we can formulate a rule which in essence says that in the grammar of English the pronoun in the **isn't** phrase must be the same as the subject of the sentence. Thus, rather than excluding ill-formed sentences from the inquiry, the generative grammarian uses them to gain access to competence. In the metalanguage, sentences that are in accord with the system internalized by the language-user are called "grammatical"; sentences that are not in accord with that system are called "ungrammatical" or "deviant." Ungrammatical sentences are starred, as, for example, ***He is an entomologist, doesn't he?**

The notion of "grammaticality" that linguists use is descriptive, not prescriptive. A "grammatical sentence" is one that occurs in the system and is accepted as a norm by the speech community in which it is used. In this sense an utterance like **I ain't goin'** is ungrammatical for some English-speaking speech communities (mainly those which use what is known as "standard" English), but grammatical for many others. The descriptive concept of grammar is quite different from the prescriptive notion of "what you ought to say" that you probably came across in school. Prescriptive grammars suggest how to speak and write in order to become a well-accepted member of a certain community. Most prescriptive grammars are conservative and tend to uphold at least some notions of linguistic good behavior that have long ceased to exist in everyday language, even of the "best speakers." For example, **It is I**, insisted on in the eighteenth century on the model of Latin, is still sometimes insisted on in the schools, although practically no one, including the teacher, actually says **It is I**, but rather **It's me**. An example of a contemporary change that has not yet been recognized by prescriptive grammars is the use of **good** for the adverb **well**, as in **You sang good**. While the prescriptive grammarian would insist on **well**, the linguist would recognize that **good** is often used instead, and would note that **well** is, for many speakers, restricted to writing or formal speech.[19]

Underlying and Surface Structure

As we have seen, there are many types of grammar. But every grammar must account for the fact that there is no direct one-to-one correspondence between meaning and sound. The sound **a** means nothing in itself, but conventionally combined with certain other sounds it can be part of a sign, as in **pat, lamp, at**. Equally inescapable is the fact that a language is not a dictionary. Signs alone do not make up language—they are arranged in sequences, and these sequences involve a hierarchic structure or grouping. Thus we divide up **The box on the table is mine** into **(The box on the table) (is mine)** and not into **(The box) (on the table is mine)** or **(The box on the) (table is mine)**. We divide up the ambiguous sentence **I ran into the girls with the flowers** into **I ran into the girls (with the flowers)** and **I ran into (the girls with the flowers)**. This hierarchic structuring, or "putting together," is somewhat similar to the bracketing of math: $2 \times 2 - 1$ is understood by convention to be grouped hierarchically as $(2 \times 2) - 1$; the other meaning of this sequence must be indicated by parentheses—$2 \times (2 - 1)$. In a grammar, we need to distinguish at least between sounds, words (and word parts), groups of words, or "phrases," like **on the table**, and sentences.

Describing sound-meaning correlations is not always a straightforward task of dividing sentences into various kinds of groupings. Ambiguous sentences present one kind of problem. Consider, for example, **The fish is ready to eat**, which is ambiguous as to whether the fish is going to eat or to be eaten. Do we say in this case that there is one sentence with two meanings or two separate sentences? How does the grammar correlate this sound sequence with each of its two meanings? Generative grammar answers this question by positing two levels of sentence structure: "surface structure" and a more abstract structure which we will call "underlying structure." The underlying structure unambiguously specifies the basic meaning and categories of the sentence[20]; this structure is modified in various ways to become a surface structure, which is the linear arrangement of words and phrases which will be pronounced. **The fish is ready to eat** is a surface structure. In one of its interpretations, this surface structure corresponds to an underlying structure something like **The fish is ready (for someone to eat the fish)**. In the other interpretation, it corresponds to the underlying structure **The fish is ready (for the fish to eat something)**. These two underlying structures can be modified to give the same surface structure; linguists call the rules that account for these modifications "transformations."

The distinction between surface and abstract or underlying structures is one of the most basic and innovative concepts of generative grammar. While this distinction is accepted in most current linguistic thinking, there is disagreement on what the underlying structure should look like, how abstract it should be, and what information about the sentence it should include. In the course of this book, we will be looking at a number of different views of underlying structure. For the moment, let us repeat only that it includes both the basic meanings and the basic syntactic categories of the sentence, so that the underlying structure of a sentence looks something like an extended paraphrase of the surface sentence. Surface structures are said to be derived from underlying structures by the application of transformational rules. As we shall see in Chapter 2, a generative grammar also includes a set of "phonological rules" which modify surface structures into sentences as they are actually pronounced.

A Model of Grammar

In linguistic metalanguage, a grammar is seen as consisting of various components. The underlying syntactic/semantic structure forms one component, the surface syntactic structure forms another, and the surface phonetic structure yet another. Sets of rules state the relation of one component to another. For example, rules relate the underlying structure **The fish is ready (for someone to eat the fish)** to the surface structure **The fish is ready to eat,** and rules relate the latter to the actual sounds (consonants, vowels, rhythm, rise and fall of the voice) that represent this sentence in speech.

As we mentioned earlier, in the approach we are adopting, and in accord with much current linguistic thinking, a model of competence must also account for the language-user's ability to use language in relation to specific contexts and specific communicative goals. These are described in what is called the "pragmatic" component of the grammar.

The relations between various components of the grammar can be modeled as follows:

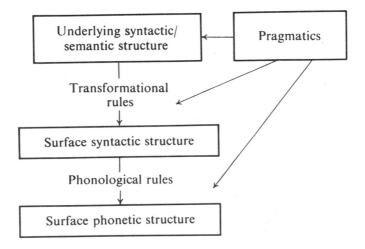

The arrows indicate dependency relations—some phonological facts, especially pitch patterns, for example, depend on syntactic structure. In turn, choice of sentence structure and pronunciation as well as choice of what is said at all depend on contextual factors specified in the pragmatic component.

In subsequent chapters, each of the four components will be discussed in considerable detail, starting with the phonological one because it is in some ways the simplest to describe and because it can be used to introduce nearly all the basic linguistic concepts. To set the scene for our dual purpose of discussing both what the study of the English language involves and also what it can contribute to analysis of English literature, first we must describe in a general way how the broad linguistic hypotheses introduced in this chapter can be relevant to literature.

APPLICATIONS TO LITERATURE

"Applying" Linguistics

When people talk about "applied" fields, like applied linguistics or applied physics or applied anthropology, they usually refer to the use of the discoveries, the frame of reference, and the terminology of one discipline to serve the ends of another area of endeavor. The discoveries and methods of the social sciences are often applied to the solution of concrete social problems. Many applications of linguistics are practical in this way. The study of speech sounds and the physiology of speech, for example, have been of use in therapy for the deaf or those with impaired hearing. Semantics and discourse analysis have contributed to the understanding and treatment of aphasia (loss of speech through brain damage). Contemporary phonology and syntax have markedly influenced methods of language teaching, both of first and second languages, while the study of discourse and linguistic interaction has provided new insights for workers in psychotherapy. Research in dialects, bilingualism, and the interaction of language and class structures is applied by governments in formulating their national language policies and conducting the language planning so important to the many multilingual nations of the world. At the same time, computer scientists rely heavily on linguistic insights in their work on machine translation and on computers which can produce and recognize speech. Pragmatics and the study of speech acts have recently come to the fore in the area of language and the law, where they are applied to such questions as truth in advertising, definition of libel, and interpretation of the law itself.

The study of style and the language of literature is one of the most traditional applications of linguistics, one which has been given new impetus by the rapid new developments in linguistics since the development of generative grammar. At the present time, linguistic analysis of literature is one of the most active and creative areas of literary studies. As is the case with its other areas of application, linguistics is not essential to the study of literature. Certainly one does not need to know linguistics in order to read and understand literary works; and critical analysis has long been carried out without formal linguistic apparatus.[21] However, linguistics can contribute a great deal to our understanding of a text. It can help us become aware of *why* it is that we experience what we do when we read a literary work, and it can help us talk about it, by providing us with a vocabulary and a methodology through which we can show how our experience of a work is in part derived from its verbal structure. Linguistics may also help us solve problems of interpretation by showing us in rigorous ways why one structure is possible but not another. Above all, however, linguistics can give us a point of view, a way of looking at a text that will help us develop a consistent analysis, and prompt us to ask questions about the language of the text that we might otherwise ignore. Since texts are the primary data for all literary criticism, adequate means of textual description are essential if any criticism is to be properly founded. Linguistics helps ensure a proper foundation for analysis, by enabling the critic to recognize the systematic regularities in the language of a text. In fact, we can use linguistics to construct a theory about the language of a text in the form of a "grammar of the text." In this sense, although linguistics does not encompass literary criticism, it is relevant to all criticism.

Literature as a Type of Discourse

Though we sometimes tend to think of literature as a realm of free, individual expression, it is in many respects highly conventionalized, like everything else in language. One important set of conventions are those governing literary genre. In linguistics, the term "genre" is used to refer not only to types of literary works, but also to any identifiable type of discourse, whether literary or not. In this sense, the lecture, the casual conversation, and the interview are all genres, just as the novel and short story are. This broader view of genre is valuable in that it helps us conceptually to bridge the traditional gap between literary and nonliterary discourse. It enables us to view literature as a particular range of genres or discourse types, that is, as a particular subset of the repertory of genres existing in a given speech community. In our own culture, there is some disagreement about exactly which genres constitute literature. There is little consensus, for example, on the status of the limerick or the nursery rhyme; the distinction sometimes drawn between literature and folklore is dubious at best; a religious poem might be considered literature when it appears in a poetry anthology, but not when it appears in a hymn book. For the purposes of this book, we will be using "literature" in the sense that it usually has in the phrase "modern English literature," that is, novels, poems, short stories, and so forth.

Among characteristics of literature as a range of genres is that it is generally public, not private, discourse. In addition, written literature is discourse that may be read at a far distance in time and place from its origin. This means that the relationship that holds between speaker/author and hearer/reader in written literature is of a very special sort and one that is a particularly important aspect of what can be called "literary pragmatics."[22] Furthermore, literary discourse is often fictional. One of the pragmatic conventions of fictional narrative is that the speaking *I* of the speech act is understood not to be the author of the work, but an intermediate narrator or addresser who has been created by the author. Within the fictional world of the story, the narrator (or addresser), not the author (or speaker), is held immediately responsible for what is said. Thus we speak of reliable and unreliable *narrators*, not authors. The author is responsible as speaker, however, when the fiction comes to be judged by the external world, as in criticism, libel suits, censorship cases, or Pulitzer Prizes.

Aside from genre conventions, literary discourse has many other general linguistic characteristics for which the linguist can provide tools of analysis. Certain kinds of phonological, syntactic, and semantic phenomena occur with much greater frequency in literature than in other kinds of discourse. For example, "poetic" devices like metaphor, alliteration, and archaism are commonly associated with literature, although they are, of course, not unique to it. The conventions of rhyme and meter constitute elaborate formal constraints on phonology, syntax, and vocabulary, and the study of grammars can help show exactly what these constraints are. One of the most important characteristics of literary discourse is its recurrent linguistic patterning, or "cohesion," a patterning which may be found to operate at all levels of the grammar; and it is here especially that the linguist can throw light on the language of a text, demonstrating both what the linguistic system in the work is and how it operates in that particular text.

Cohesion

The idea of cohesion was first developed in detail by Roman Jakobson, one of the leading linguists of the twentieth century and a pioneer in the application of linguistics to literature. In 1960 Jakobson characterized, with reference to poetry, a notion basic to the analysis of literary texts: that they have cohesion or internal patterning and repetition far exceeding that of most non-literary texts.[23] Cohesion in poetry is usually discussed in terms of repeated refrains, regular stanzas, rhymes, alliteration, meter, and similar devices. Jakobson's interest lay not so much in these well-known features but in rather less frequently discussed linguistic features, especially linguistic cohesiveness created between elements at different levels of the grammar, such as parallels between meaning and sentence structure, or between sentence structure and sound structure (and, of course, their interplay with other specifically poetic features, such as meter).

Jakobson describes the phenomenon of cohesion as follows: "The poetic function projects the principle of equivalence from the axis of selection into the axis of combination."[24] A difficult sentence, but probably the one most often quoted in linguistic approaches to literature. What he means by this is that, in poetry, structures which are roughly equivalent in sound, or sentence structure, or grammatical category, or some other aspect tend to be combined in a linear order or sequence. Poetry, in other words, involves partial repetition, whether of metrical patterns, rhymes, or sentence structures. Jakobson cites Caesar's famous **veni, vidi, vici** as an example. This sentence combines in sequence three words of the same grammatical category (verbs), same inflection (first person singular past tense), same number of syllables, same stress pattern, and very similar sound structure (rhyme and alliteration). This extraordinary cohesiveness is what makes the sentence so memorable. In the English **I came, I saw, I conquered**, some of the effect is lost because of the **s** versus **k**, and the two syllables of **conquered** versus the single syllables of the other words, but the sentence is still strikingly cohesive. At the semantic level, the cohesion has a particularly interesting effect. By seeming to equate the acts of coming, seeing, and conquering, Caesar's sentence implies that the last act was as easy for him as the first two. Hence, the impression of majestic arrogance it produces.

Political slogans and advertisements thrive on the principle of cohesion, in part because it makes them easier to remember. For example, among advertisements we find **Turn on Schick, turn out chic** for a Schick hair styler and **Silk and Silver turns gray to great** for Silk and Silver hair coloring. These both involve cohesion in phonology, vocabulary, and meaning associations. In poetry the principle is usually exploited in a more subtle way; but cohesion is present at least to some degree, except in some experimental poetry that deliberately rejects it.

A relatively simple literary example of cohesion is provided by Robert Browning's well-known song from "Pippa Passes":

> *The year's at the spring*
> *And day's at the morn;*
> *Morning's at seven;*
> *The hillside's dew-pearled;*
> *The lark's on the wing;*
> *The snail's on the thorn:*
> *God's in his heaven—*
> *All's right with the world!*[25]

Patterning is evident at every level in this poem, and at the same time we can see how patterns are varied to avoid monotony. One of the most obvious cohesive patterns here is the syntax—each line is a single clause consisting of noun + 's + X, and X consists of a prepositional phrase everywhere except in lines 4 and 8 where the pattern is varied. (But note that this variation itself is cohesive, in that it occurs at the same point in each pair of four lines, and involves an adjective in both cases). The syntactic cohesion coincides with semantic cohesion among the nouns. In the first four lines, we find a series of time nouns in order of increasing specificity: **year, spring, day, morn, morning, seven,** joined by the preposition **at**. This extremely tight patterning is loosened and played upon in the second four where **lark** and **snail** are linked both by semantic likeness (two animals) and contrast ("higher" versus "lower" animals). With **on the wing** and **on the thorn**, syntactic and lexical likeness interplay with semantic difference (**on** has the same form but different meaning in each case). In line 7, **God** is forcibly incorporated into the pattern and thus unexpectedly placed on the same level of existence as **lark** and **snail**, while the change of prepositions from **on** to **in** keeps the parallelism from being complete.

Metrical patterning in the poem interacts rather subtly with lexical and syntactic patterns. In each part, the first, second, and fourth lines have the pattern $\smallsmile / \smallsmile \smallsmile /$ (where / means a stressed syllable and $\smallsmile$ an unstressed one), while the third line has the mirror image $/ \smallsmile \smallsmile /\smallsmile$. Thus, though the last line of each part breaks syntactic and lexical patterns, it does conform metrically, while metrical variation is used in the third and seventh lines and helps counteract any monotony arising from the syntactic and lexical cohesiveness.

At yet another level, the internal regularity of this poem is itself counterbalanced by the fact that, with respect to normal spoken English, many of the poem's expressions are decidedly "irregular." We do not say that years are "at the spring" or days "at the morn." These expressions illustrate the fact that literature often uses expressions that are not, or are no longer, common in spoken conversational language. Moreover, in this poem, the fictional singer, Pippa, is a young Italian woman, and the song, fictionally, is being sung in Italian. Doubtless, Browning wants to remind us of this by estranging us from the English in the text.

The phenomenon of cohesion in literature obviously has everything to do with the fact that literature is art, that literary texts are constructed to produce in us the kinds of experience we speak of as "aesthetic," in which symmetry and interplay of sameness and difference play a major role. A complete understanding of cohesion will depend on further understanding of aesthetic experience and perception.

One of the secrets of good poetry is to be cohesive, and yet not too much so. Too rigid an equivalence leads readily to doggerel. While the literary critic may want to evaluate the cohesiveness in a text, the linguist's task is not so much to evaluate as to demonstrate exactly what is present and what is not. It is also the linguist's task to show where there are differences as well as similarities, or where there is some variation in a pattern or some kind of opposition between surface and underlying patterns. We will be examining several more examples of cohesion from a linguistic point of view in this and the next two chapters.

The Idea of the "Grammar" of a Text

From the point of view of generative grammar, discovering the systematic regularities in the language of a text is only a partial step toward a full account of the text's linguistic structure. Rather than limiting an account of a text to observed regularities, we can go on to make generalizations about the text's phonological, syntactic, and semantic structure and its pragmatic characteristics, generalizations which will reveal the text's stylistic traits and tendencies and the principles on which it is structured. Such generalizations resemble those that constitute the grammar of a language. It has therefore become customary to extend the term "grammar" from "grammar of a language" to "grammar of a text." Constructing a grammar of a text, then, is a way of hypothesizing about its overall internal structure. It enables the critic to make stylistic observations in an organized way about the most detailed facts of language.

One of the most interesting ways to use a grammar of a text is to compare it with the overall grammar of the language in which it is written. Such comparison can reveal, for example, what grammatical categories and options have and have not been used, and in what ways the text departs from normal usage. Indeed, a grammar of a text provides the only rigorous basis for comparing the language of an individual text with "the language as a whole."

An example should clarify the broad outlines of what might be done with the grammar-of-a-text approach. The details can be filled in as you read the following chapters. The text is T. S. Eliot's "Rhapsody on a Windy Night," one of the Prufrock poems, published in 1917. Here the speaking "I" describes a long late-night walk and the inner, mental experiences that accompany it.

RHAPSODY ON A WINDY NIGHT

Twelve o'clock.
Along the reaches of the street
Held in a lunar synthesis,
Whispering lunar incantations
Dissolve the floors of memory
And all its clear relations
Its divisions and precisions,
Every street lamp that I pass
Beats like a fatalistic drum,
10   And through the spaces of the dark
Midnight shakes the memory
As a madman shakes a dead geranium.

Half-past one,
The street-lamp sputtered,
The street-lamp muttered,
The street-lamp said, "Regard that woman
Who hesitates toward you in the light of the door
Which opens on her like a grin.
You see the border of her dress

20   Is torn and stained with sand,
And you see the corner of her eye
Twists like a crooked pin."

The memory throws up high and dry
A crowd of twisted things;
A twisted branch upon the beach
Eaten smooth, and polished
As if the world gave up
The secret of its skeleton,
Stiff and white.

30   A broken spring in a factory yard,
Rust that clings to the form that the strength has left
Hard and curled and ready to snap.

Half-past two,
The street-lamp said,
"Remark the cat which flattens itself in the gutter,
Slips out its tongue
And devours a morsel of rancid butter."
So the hand of the child, automatic,
Slipped out and pocketed a toy that was running along the quay.

40   I could see nothing behind that child's eye.
I have seen eyes in the street
Trying to peer through lighted shutters,
And a crab one afternoon in a pool,
An old crab with barnacles on his back,
Gripped the end of a stick which I held him.

Half-past three,
The lamp sputtered,
The lamp muttered in the dark.
The lamp hummed:

50   "Regard the moon,
La lune ne garde aucune rancune,
She winks a feeble eye,
She smiles into corners.
She smooths the hair of the grass.

The moon has lost her memory.
A washed-out smallpox cracks her face,
Her hand twists a paper rose,
That smells of dust and eau de Cologne,
She is alone
60   With all the old nocturnal smells
That cross and cross across her brain."
The reminiscence comes
Of sunless dry geraniums
And dust in crevices,
Smells of chestnuts in the streets,
And female smells in shuttered rooms,
And cigarettes in corridors
And cocktail smells in bars.

　　　The lamp said,
70   "Four o'clock,
Here is the number on the door.
Memory!
You have the key,
The little lamp spreads a ring on the stair.
Mount.
The bed is open; the tooth-brush hangs on the wall,
Put your shoes at the door, sleep, prepare for life."

　　　The last twist of the knife.[26]

In "Rhapsody on a Windy Night," the "I" of the poem experiences, as he walks, a mental struggle between two views of the world, one active, focused on the moving present, and one passive, focused on the inert past. This struggle is expressed through two images, that of the street lamp and that of memory. The poem alternates between their two perspectives, so that stanza 2 deals with the lamp, stanza 3 with memory; lines 33–37 with the lamp, lines 38–39 with memory; lines 46–61 with the lamp, lines 62–68 with memory; and stanza 6 with the lamp. The rest of the poem, stanza 1, lines 40–45, and the final one-line stanza, consists of direct commentary by the "I" of the poem. (It is surely no accident that these sections occur at the beginning, middle, and end.) A detailed look at the language can show that within the overall grammar of the poem there are two sub-grammars, that is, two linguistic systems which, although not entirely complementary, are nearly so. The language used in connection with the lamp is radically different from that used in connection with memory. The linguistic structures of the two parts combine in the sections of commentary by the "I."

What is important in the lamp's grammar is that action verbs and directional adverbs are so frequent that everything seems to be in motion, especially individual parts of the body: **the corner of her eye twists like a crooked pin** (21–22), **she smiles into corners** (53), **her hand twists a paper rose** (57). In the memory's grammar, however, there are static pictures expressed by nouns coupled with place adverbs: **a twisted branch upon the beach** (25), **a broken spring in a factory yard** (30), **dust in crevices, smells of chestnuts in the streets** (64–65). Even those few verbs in the memory part that are usually action verbs have no action meaning here. Thus, in **the reminiscence comes of sunless dry geraniums** (62–63), memory does not really come in any active sense, but just happens. The two grammars are complementary, each using the vocabulary of the other in terms of its own structure: **smell** is a verb in the lamp's grammar (**that smells of dust and eau de Cologne**, line 58), **smell** is a noun in the memory's (**female smells in shuttered rooms**, line 66); the lamp's grammar has **twist** and **smooth** as verbs (22 and 54), while memory's has **twisted** and **smooth** as adjectives (24 and 26). The fifth stanza provides a highly consistent example of the contrast between the two grammars, the lamp's expressing the world of action and the present, the memory's expressing the world of stasis and the past.

The same contrast is apparent in the pragmatic aspects of the two grammars. In the lamp's grammar, direct speech is possible. The lamp's descriptions of the world come as speech acts addressed directly to the "I" by the lamp. Moreover the speech acts performed by the lamp are predominantly commands in which the lamp directs the "I"'s attention to immediate details. In the grammar of memory, there is no direct speech and no imperative speech-act function. Language is used only for description, not direction, and the perceptions of memory are presented as purposeless, random, and non-verbal in origin. Language is used to describe memory, but language does not exist within the world of memory. Hence there is no metalanguage in memory's grammar, while the lamp's grammar is full of it (**sputtered, muttered, said**). As a verbally active entity, the lamp is able to use the language to establish a shared world with the "I" of the poem, and its grammar includes many expressions with this function. For instance, in **Regard that woman who hesitates toward you in the light of the door** (16–17), **that** requires the addressee to share the lamp's spatial domain, in which the woman is distant; in **toward you**, the lamp adopts the "I"'s spatial perspective to describe the direction of the woman's movement. By contrast, there are no pointing expressions establishing an immediately shared spatial world between the "I" and his memories. We do not get, for example, **that twisted branch up on the beach over there**. Paradoxically, then, the "I"'s own memories seem to engage him less than the external and social world pointed out to him by the lamp.

Despite what one might expect, the two contrasting sub-grammars in "Rhapsody on a Windy Night" do not rule out the possibility of cohesion in the poem as a whole. The regular alternation between the lamp and memory is, in itself, a source of cohesion, as is the regular pacing by clock time (**twelve o'clock, half-past one**, and so on). In addition, there is a great deal of syntactic cohesion, such as repetition of sentence patterns as in lines 14–16 and 47–49. The basic structure here is article-noun-verb (**The street lamp muttered**), with an added adverb, **in the dark**, at line 48, to prevent monotonous over-repetition. Similarly, there are patterns parallel to **She winks a feeble eye** (52–53) and to **dust in crevices** (64–68). More complex examples of syntactic cohesiveness can be found throughout the poem. For instance, there are patterns involving directional adverb . . . subject-verb-object in the first stanza. **Along the reaches of the street . . . incantations dissolve the floors of memory** (2–5) parallels **through the spaces of the dark midnight shakes the memory** (10–11). Cohesion in the vocabulary is very clear both within stanzas, for example, **Held in a lunar synthesis** (3) and **Whispering lunar incantations** (4), and between stanzas (cf. especially **street lamp, memory, dark**). Semantically, we have a great many words denoting destruction or decay: **torn, stained, crooked, broken, rust, rancid**. Phonologically, we cannot miss echoes. For example, in the first stanza there are **incantations . . . decisions . . . precisions; reaches . . . street**.

Of course, constructing a grammar of a simple text is not exactly the same thing as constructing a grammar of a language. Grammars of languages have to account not just for the available data in a language, but also for the potentially available data, the infinite number of sentences that *could* be produced in the language. Because they have this predictive power, grammars of languages can always be tested against new data in the language. With individual text grammars, there are no other potentially available data against which the analysis could be tested. Still, in theory, a grammar of a text would enable us to characterize a text specifically enough to produce another text stylistically indistinguishable from it. In practice this is seldom completely possible, because literary works are often highly individualized and because their internal structure depends on factors other than purely linguistic ones. But the possibility that one can know the structure of a text well enough to produce something similar is one on which pastiche and caricature operate, and the idea that a grammar can characterize the language of the text in full detail underlies computerized poetry, since the program which produces such poetry is a grammar of the text it produces.

Describing a text in terms of its grammar involves viewing it as a single whole in which certain structures are simultaneously present. Likewise, to speak of cohesion as the presence of internal patterns is to treat the text as an object possessing certain properties, rather than as a temporal progression. Such a view is necessarily incomplete, for a text is also a temporal sequence. A written text is laid out in space because expressed language is a temporal thing. The act of reading takes time; the experience of a literary work is temporal. So of course is the author's act of writing. There are critics who maintain that the only valid way of approaching a literary text is through description of the temporal experience of reading.[27] Others claim a text must be viewed as a dynamic structure constantly transforming itself as the work progresses.[28] In fact we need all these perspectives.

Style as Choice

It is customary not only to talk about the language of a text or author, but more specifically about the "style." People speak of racy, pompous, formal, colloquial, inflammatory, or even nominal and verbal styles. How can such generalizations be characterized linguistically? One way is to say that style results from a tendency of a speaker or writer to consistently choose certain structures over others available in the language. With this view, we can distinguish between "style" and "language" by saying that language is the sum total of the structures available to the speaker, while style concerns the characteristic choices in a given context.[29] In this sense, in writing a grammar of a text, we will probably be more concerned with the style than with the language, for it is not so much that every possible structure available is interesting, as those which dominate a text, or part of it.

To claim that style is choice is not, of course, to claim that it is always conscious choice. Indeed, if one had to make all phonological, syntactic, semantic, and pragmatic choices consciously, it would take a very long time to say anything at all. In literature, as in all discourse, a sense of the "best way of putting something" can be intuitive or conscious; the result as far as the reader is concerned will be much the same.

Stylistic choice is usually regarded as a matter of form or expression, that is, as choice among different ways of expressing an invariant or predetermined content. But this view is misleading, for writers obviously choose content too. In our grammar, with its semantic and pragmatic components, both content and expression can be viewed as matters of choice. Choice of content involves choice of semantic structures; choice of expression involves choice of pragmatic functions and contextual features (such as what relation a speaker adopts toward the hearer, what inferences are to be conveyed, what assumptions made). Choices in both these components of the grammar are in turn the basis for phonological, syntactic, and lexical choices. This approach provides us with a new way of thinking about whether there is or is not a duality between form and content. This issue has been discussed in philosophy and aesthetics for centuries. A large number of critics and stylisticians acknowledge such a duality, saying that given some particular content ("meaning") a variety of surface forms are possible. In this view it is possible for there to be sentences that are synonymous, even though they have different forms. The opposing position is that every difference in form brings a difference in meaning and that synonymy is therefore impossible. Now it is clearly useful to say that **My twenty-three year old brother is a bachelor** is synonymous with (has the same meaning as) **My twenty-three year old brother is unmarried**. Yet they are not exactly equivalent. For example, one would scarcely say the first sentence to a child because **bachelor** is a technical term, while one might say the second. The difference is pragmatic, not semantic. In terms of our grammar, in choosing between these two sentences, the speaker makes a pragmatic, contextually motivated choice between two semantically equivalent surface forms. Thus the grammar allows for synonymy (thereby maintaining a form/content distinction) and at the same time accounts for the fact that synonymous surface forms are not exactly equivalent.

The interplay between semantic sameness and pragmatic difference is exploited by Samuel Beckett in the following passage from his novel, *Murphy*. In the climactic scene of this novel, the ill-adjusted and alienated protagonist, who works as an orderly in a mental hospital, looks deep into the eyes of a singularly withdrawn patient, Mr. Endon, and encounters nothing but his own reflection. Endon's complete unawareness of his presence profoundly shakes Murphy's confidence in his own existence. We read:

> Kneeling at the bedside, the hair starting in thick black ridges between his fingers, his lips, nose and forehead almost touching Mr. Endon's, seeing himself stigmatised in those eyes that did not see him, Murphy heard words demanding so strongly to be spoken that he spoke them, right into Mr. Endon's face, Murphy who did not speak at all in the ordinary way unless spoken to, and not always even then.
>
> > "the last at last seen of him
> > himself unseen by him
> > and of himself"
>
> A rest.
>
> "The last Mr. Murphy saw of Mr. Endon was Mr. Murphy unseen by Mr. Endon. This was also the last Murphy saw of Murphy."
>
> A rest.
>
> "The relation between Mr. Murphy and Mr. Endon could not have been better summed up than by the former's sorrow at seeing himself in the latter's immunity from seeing anything but himself."
>
> A long rest.
>
> "Mr. Murphy is a speck in Mr. Endon's unseen."
>
> That was the whole extent of the little afflatulence. He replaced Mr. Endon's head firmly on the pillow, rose from his knees, left the cell, and the building, without reluctance and without relief.[30]

Here Beckett gives us several different formulations of the same rather complicated content. The first, highly elliptical, is set out like a poem; the second is an explanatory paraphrase of the first using complete sentences and no pronominalization; the third, reminiscent of nineteenth-century novelistic style, adds some emotive content (**the former's sorrow**), which is removed in the final aphoristic summary of the situation, where a metaphor (**a speck in Mr. Endon's unseen**) is introduced. Notice too the way this passage dramatizes the process of choice of surface form. The four versions seem to be a series of (pragmatic) attempts on Murphy's part to arrive at a shortest, clearest formulation. Alternatively, Murphy may be (equally pragmatically) providing several versions to meet the needs of a variety of hypothetical hearers, so that they may do the choosing. Incidentally, this passage also provides a novelistic example of cohesion, being based on the linear sequencing of equivalent units.

A further concept of style, one that has been favored by the generative frame of reference, is the concept of style as deviance, the idea that style is constituted by departures from linguistic norms. Like the concept of style as choice, the concept of style as deviance is by no means new. One of its chief proponents in this century was Jan Mukařovský, a leading linguist and literary critic in Prague in the 1930s. He speaks of style as "foregrounding," bringing to attention, making new: "The violation of the norm of the standard, its systematic violation is what makes possible the poetic utilization of language; without this possibility there would be no poetry."[31] Everyday usage, according to Mukařovský, "automatizes" or conventionalizes language to the point that its users no longer perceive its expressive or aesthetic potential; poetry must de-automatize or "foreground" language by violating the norms of everyday language. As an example of what this means, consider the Eliot poem once more. The language certainly differs from standard spoken English. For example, rhyme is a rare phenomenon in normal speech, whereas it occurs frequently in the poem as in **sputtered . . . muttered** (14–15, 47–48) which also rhyme elsewhere with **shutters** (42), **shuttered** (66). The **sputtered . . . muttered** sequences are odd in another way, which is that they are highly repetitive and redundant. In speech as a rule, it would sound strange indeed to begin a sentence by giving two or three slightly different versions of the opening phrase, though this might occur as a mistake or false start like **Well, then he said—no, I said—no, he said that we were late.** In Eliot's lines, the repetition imitates the sputtering of the lamp, adding a note of humor. Other examples of this rhyming redundance are **that cross and cross across her brain** (61) and **la lune ne garde aucune rancune** (51), where excess of rhyme again adds a playful note. This latter line is even more foregrounded in that it is not English at all, but French. Rhyme couples with meaning to make a rather complicated pun in **I could see nothing behind that child's eye. I have seen eyes in the street** (40–41). The language of the poem also differs from the spoken norm in that it uses the simple present tense as in **the memory comes** (not **is coming**). Most of the time we use the "present progressive" forms to say what is happening. In answer to **Are you busy?** we would say **I'm cleaning up my room**, not **I clean up my room.**

Notice that while Eliot's use of the present tense differs from ordinary usage, it nevertheless seems absolutely natural and expected for poetry. Indeed, it is often difficult in classes to get students even to notice that the present tense **comes** differs from conversational usage. As a convention of poetry, this device is automatized. The same is true of many of Eliot's other foregrounding devices mentioned above. Rhyme, repetition, archaic and foreign words de-automatize the spoken norm and mark the language as literary, but at the same time they are conventional or automatized features of literary language. In applying the idea of foregrounding, we must carefully distinguish these levels of analysis. Of course such automatized literary conventions are themselves subject to de-automatization. Indeed, for Mukařovský, it was essential for literature to continuously rejuvenate itself by violating its own norms. Thus Eliot's abandonment of traditional metric regularity is, within literature, an act of foregrounding even though it in some respects brings his text closer to the spoken norm.

At another level of analysis, any structure, particularly a highly cohesive one, may be said to automatize the language within the work, however deviant it may be from the standard. This is the case in the poem "love is more thicker than forget" by e. e. cummings (as he spelled his name):

> love is more thicker than forget
> more thinner than recall
> more seldom than a wave is wet
> more frequent than to fail
>
> it is most mad and moonly
> and less it shall unbe
> than all the sea which only
> is deeper than the sea
>
> love is less always than to win
> less never than alive
> less bigger than the least begin
> less littler than forgive
>
> it is most sane and sunly
> and more it cannot die
> than all the sky which only
> is higher than the sky[32]

There is obviously a very real sense in which this poem startles us into seeing the conventional side of love in a totally new light. But if we understand it, it is largely because there is a pattern so consistent that we could venture to set up a mathematical formula for it. Cohesion within this poem is based on the pairing of antonyms.

Stanza 1 is based on the lexical antonyms **thicker-thinner, forget-recall, seldom-frequent**, and made syntactically cohesive by a **more-than** construction. Stanza 3 is structured in the same way by the antonyms **always-never, bigger-littler**, and is made syntactically cohesive by a **less-than** construction. This **less-than** construction is antonymous to **more-than** in stanza 1 and so completes the parallel between them. Stanzas 2 and 4 have no antonyms within themselves, but are antonymous line by line with each other. The first, third, and fourth lines of stanzas 2 and 4 are antonymous in their nouns and adjectives (**mad-sane, moonly-sunly, sea-sky, deeper-higher**), but not in their comparatives and superlatives. **Most-less** and **most-more** contrast, but are not opposites, and therefore are not antonyms. The second lines break the pattern, but less so than might appear at first sight. The difference is that here the auxiliary verbs **shall** and **cannot**, not the main verbs, are antonymous. The main verbs are synonymous. Since **un-**, when attached to a verb, indicates reversal (as in **undo, untie, unscrew, unscramble**), **unbe** must mean "cease to exist," which is essentially the same thing as **die**, except that it emphasizes dying as a reversal of state.

Texts like the cummings's poem, in which deviant language is automatized, are especially well-suited to the grammar-of-a-text approach. If we take a deviant text (and cummings is often a target of such analysis, since he is so overtly interested in language and creating a deviant language) and treat its deviance simply as a *lack* of internal structure, we are left with no way to explain how the text (a) is comprehensible to us, (b) is consistent, (c) sets up its own world in which structures can be deviant. If, however, we try to establish a "grammar" of a deviant text, we can show how it is internally consistent and exactly what is deviant and, therefore, how we understand it.

The study of style as deviance helps us to clinch the idea of a grammar of a text and to keep in mind that the language of literature is not always entirely that of everyday usage. It helps us focus on cohesion and on recognizing that what may be perfectly automatic and normal in one text, or for one author, or even one period may be abnormal in another. However, the idea of style as deviance has the disadvantage of encouraging the linguist to look at the language of grammatically highly deviant authors like cummings at the expense of relatively nondeviant ones like Eliot or Wallace Stevens. More generally it tends to undervalue all nondeviant language, both within literature and without. The theoretical claim that aesthetic effects can only be achieved through deviance assumes that normal usage is somehow in principle un- or anti-aesthetic, and even suggests that linguistic systems themselves are by nature hostile to poetry. This is certainly not the case. In the end, the idea of style as deviance always leads back to the broader view that style is choice, where choice includes selecting or not selecting deviant structures. Style as choice subsumes style as deviance, for deviance is only one aspect of the language of literature.

To speak of style as choice, one must recognize not only that there is freedom of choice, but also that there are constraints on choice. In our approach, linguistic choice is made on the basis of the total options available in the grammar, that is, the total options available in the syntactic, semantic, phonological, and pragmatic systems. The first three systems specify the range of structural possibilities which can be chosen from or deviated from. The fourth specifies in part the contextual basis for choice, including such factors as intended audience, topic, genre, channel, degree of formality. Some people might think that a view of style as choice given a preexisting range of potentialities is incompatible with our usual view of the artist as a creator, or that it undervalues the originality of the artist. But this is not the case. If anything, the view of style as choice enables us to appreciate artistic creativity more fully by understanding better wherein it lies. As we discussed at the beginning of this chapter, though the linguistic system is finite, the range of actual utterances possible in language is infinite even at the level of the single sentence, to say nothing of the possibilities at the level of longer discourse. The more one understands the linguistic system, the more one appreciates the infinity and variety of possible choices and combinations of choices available, and the more one appreciates the genius of an artist who, by making and combining choices, creates structures that are deeply meaningful, imaginatively fulfilling, and expressive of our most fundamental concerns as human beings.

SUGGESTED FURTHER READINGS

Studies of particular topics will be cited in the relevant chapters. The readings mentioned here are all of a very general nature; those on linguistics and literature are all either from a strictly linguistic point of view, or are strongly oriented toward linguistics.

Among general introductions to linguistics, Fromkin and Rodman's *An Introduction to Language* and Akmajian et al.'s *Linguistics: An Introduction to Language and Communication* are both the most introductory and the most comprehensive. They include chapters on animal communication, language and the brain, and language change. Excellent books emphasizing the enormous variety of language are Bolinger's *Aspects of Language* and Falk's *Linguistics and Language*. Much briefer than any of these, but an outstanding introduction to language and its use in social context is Greenberg's *A New Invitation to Linguistics*. Bloomfield and Haugen's *Language As a Human Problem* provides a series of papers on a variety of topics, emphasizing the interdisciplinary nature of language study. Lyons's *Introduction to Theoretical Linguistics* is an ideal reference book but more advanced than the title suggests. Sapir's *Language* is now one of the classics of linguistics. Although published in the early 1920s, it focuses on many areas of vital interest in contemporary linguistics, especially language and mind, and language and varied social and cultural groups. Another classic, Jespersen's *Modern English Grammar on Historical Principles*, gives one of the most detailed accounts of English available, with extensive examples from literature of the sixteenth century on.

A general philosophical overview of the main theoretical concerns of generative grammar can be found in Noam Chomsky, *Language and Mind*; backgrounds to Chomsky's thinking are discussed in Leiber, *Noam Chomsky*, and Lyons, *Noam Chomsky*. A good foundation in generative grammar and general linguistics can be gained from Langacker, *Language and Its Structure*.

Among more specialized books, the following are particularly interesting: Brown's *Words and Things*, which focuses on language and thought; Clark and

Clark's *Psychology and Language*, which provides a thorough introduction to linguistics as well as psycholinguistics, especially recent advances in the study of language acquisition; Burling's *Man's Many Voices; Language in Its Cultural Context*, which stresses meaning and use of language in various cultures; and Farb's *Word Play*, a book written for a very general audience, drawing on a large number of linguistic sources to develop a fascinating overview of the function of language in context. Useful introductions to alternate ways of doing linguistics can be found in Gleason, *Linguistics and English Grammar*, Part I, and in Herndon, *A Survey of Modern Grammar*.

There are several valuable collections of readings on linguistics and literature, but all of them precede the period of extensive work on language in context. The first major collection was published in 1960—Sebeok's *Style in Language*, which contains the difficult, but by now classic paper by Roman Jakobson entitled "Closing Statement: Linguistics and Poetics," alluded to earlier in this chapter. Probably the best collection for the beginning student is Freeman, *Linguistics and Literary Style*. Others are Fowler, *Essays on Style in Language*; Chatman, *Approaches to Poetics*; Chatman and Levin, *Essays on the Language of Literature*; Babb, *Essays in Stylistic Analysis*; and Love and Payne, *Contemporary Essays on Style*. The latter compares several different approaches, both literary and linguistic, to the definition of style. An important series of papers, some of them fairly advanced, is to be found in Chatman, *Literary Style: A Symposium*.

Among studies in linguistics and literature that are primarily linguistic rather than literary are Chapman, *Linguistics and Literature* and Cluysenaar, *Introduction to Literary Stylistics*. Cluysenaar's book is an in-depth study of many of the issues discussed cursorily in this chapter, as also are G. W. Turner's *Stylistics*, Epstein's *Language and Style*, and the older book, *Linguistics and Style* by Enkvist, Spencer, and Gregory. More devoted to literary criticism than the other works, Culler's *Structuralist Poetics*, Lodge's *The Language of Fiction*, and Nowottny's *The Language Poets Use* are mentioned here as outstanding examples of the way in which literary criticism can benefit from linguistics or at least from a strong focus on language.

There are many linguistic journals, some devoted to particular subfields of study. The latter will be mentioned in the relevant chapters. The major American and British journals covering the field of linguistics in general are *Language* and *Journal of Linguistics*, respectively. Among journals concerned with linguistics and literature in general are *Language and Style*, *Poetica*, *Style*, and *Poetics*. Many articles in the latter are highly formal and theoretical.

Exercises

1. Select six signs that are not mentioned in this chapter and discuss whether they are primarily iconic or primarily symbolic, and why.

2. Paraphrase the following to disambiguate them:

    a. It's too hot to eat.
    b. There are many men to fight.
    c. He wanted them to study.
    d. I decided on the boat.
    e. Bill left Joan with the children.
    f. The bank was the scene of the crime.

State in each case whether the ambiguity arises from homonymy (same word for two different meanings) or from different possibilities of syntactic grouping. Which sentences can be disambiguated by stress (rhythmic emphasis) alone?

3. People often make slips of the tongue in speaking. The following are some (real) examples:[33]

skitty school	for	city school
thrink through	for	think through
a phonological fool	for	a phonological rule
heft lemisphere	for	left hemisphere
fart very hide	for	fight very hard
threw the window through the clock	for	threw the clock through the window
a hole full of floors	for	a floor full of holes
tay the plop note again	for	play the top note again

Discuss in a few sentences how slips of the tongue reveal a difference between competence and performance. Why would you not expect anyone to err by saying, for example:

skty schloo	for	city school
nkith outhr	for	think through
the threw clock window through the	for	threw the clock through the window

4. We used **It's I** versus **It's me** in exemplifying the difference between prescriptive and descriptive approaches to grammar. Take three examples of linguistic rules that you have been told to use but that in fact you rarely follow, except perhaps in formal writing. Then suggest:

    a. Why the prescriptive rules you have chosen might exist.
    b. Why a descriptive linguist might choose not to include them in a grammar of your speech.

5. Find three advertisements that are cohesive, and discuss what is cohesive in each case.

6. The following poem by Ralph Pomeroy involves several different kinds of cohesion. Identify them as specifically as you can:

CORNER

The cop slumps alertly on his motorcycle,
Supported by one leg like a leather stork.
His glance accuses me of loitering.
I can see his eyes moving like fish
In the green depths of his green goggles.

His ease is fake. I can tell.
My ease is fake. And he can tell.
The fingers armored by his gloves
Splay and clench, itching to change something.
10   As if he were my enemy or my death,
I just stand there watching.

I spit out my gum which has gone stale.
I knock out a new cigarette—
Which is my bravery.
It is all imperceptible:
The way I shift my weight,
The way he creaks in his saddle.

The traffic is specific though constant.
The sun surrounds me, divides the street between us.
20   His crash helmet is whiter in the shade.
It is like a bull ring as they say it is just before the fighting.
I cannot back down. I am there.

Everything holds me back.
I am in danger of disappearing into the sunny dust.
My levis bake and my T shirt sweats.

My cigarette makes my eyes burn.
But I don't dare drop it.

Who made him my enemy?
Prince of coolness. King of fear.
30   Why do I lean here waiting?
Why does he lounge there watching?

I am becoming sunlight.
My hair is on fire. My boots run like tar.
I am hung-up by the bright air.

Something breaks through all of a sudden.
And he blasts off, quick as a craver,
Smug in his power; watching me watch.[34]

7.   The following is a poem by Peter Davison:

1. JULY

The afternoon is dark and not with rain.
Intent on conquest, the sun presses its attack
Harder as the blunt day closes in.
Swallows like knives carve at the thickening air.

I swab the sweat from my blistering hide and walk
Burnt, unblessed, my brain inert as alum.
I stagger beneath the weight of the day
Like a three-legged dog howling curses at the climate
Until, defeated by the weather's bludgeon,
I lift my hands to half a god
And stammer out a portion of a prayer.[35]

Comment on cohesion in the poem. This poem is the first in a longer sequence of poems titled "The Breaking of the Day" and accompanied by the epigraph "Genesis 32: 24–30." Look up this text from Genesis and comment on how it is cohesive with the text quoted above.

NOTES

[1] *Popol Vuh*, Delia Goetz and Sylvanus G. Morley, trans. into English. *Popol Vuh: The Sacred Book of the Ancient Quiche Maya*, trans. from Spanish by Adrián Recinos (Norman: Univ. of Oklahoma Press, 1950), p. 85.

[2] For the history of English, see Albert C. Baugh and Thomas Cable, *A History of the English Language*, 3rd ed. (Englewood Cliffs, N.J.: Prentice-Hall, 1978); Thomas Pyles, *The Origins and Development of the English Language*, 2nd ed. (New York: Harcourt Brace Jovanovich, Inc., 1971); and Barbara M. H. Strang, *A History of English* (London: Methuen, 1970).

[3] The theory of signs was developed primarily by Peirce, cf. Justus Bucher, ed., *Philosophical Writings of Peirce* (New York: Dover, 1955); for discussion, see John Lyons, *Semantics*, Vol. I (London and New York: Cambridge Univ. Press, 1977), pp. 99–109.

[4] For these and many other examples of differences between "onomatopoetic" words in various languages, see Axel Hornos, "'Ouch!' he said in Japanese," *Verbatim*, 3, No. 1 (1976), 1–5.

[5] See Adrian Akmajian, Richard A. Demers, and Robert M. Harnish, *Linguistics: An Introduction to Language and Communication* (Cambridge, Mass.: MIT Press, 1979).

[6] From J. C. Catford, *A Linguistic Theory of Translation: An Essay in Applied Linguistics* (London and New York: Oxford Univ. Press, Inc., 1965), p. 45.

[7] See, for example, Joseph H. Greenberg, *A New Invitation to Linguistics* (Garden City, N.Y.: Anchor Books, 1977), Chapter XI; and, in more detail, Joseph H. Greenberg, Charles A. Ferguson, and Edith A. Moravcsik, eds., *Universals of Human Language*, 4 vols. (Stanford, Ca.: Stanford Univ. Press, 1978).

[8] See Ann James Premack and David Premack, "Teaching Language to an Ape," *Scientific American*, 227, No. 4 (1972), 92–99. A valuable summary of chimpanzee research and evaluation of the degree to which chimpanzee signing does and does not resemble human language can be found in Victoria Fromkin and Robert Rodman, *An Introduction to Language*, 2nd ed. (New York: Holt, Rinehart and Winston, Inc., 1978), pp. 46–51. See also Akmajian et al., *Linguistics*, Chapter 14.

[9] Thom Gunn, "Carnal Knowledge," in *Fighting Terms* (London: Faber and Faber, 1962), p. 20.

[10] In much of the literature on variation in speech, degree of formality is called "style," as when linguists speak of "casual style" or "careful style," cf. William Labov, *Sociolinguistic Patterns* (Philadelphia: Univ. of Pennsylvania Press, 1972), Chapter III. For many linguists, "style" in this sense means degree of attention paid to speech. Since we will be using the term "style" for choice of form regardless of degree of attention to speech, we will use "formality" for the latter.

[11] Don H. Zimmerman and Candace West, "Sex Roles, Interruptions and Silences in Conversations," in *Language and Sex; Difference and Dominance*, eds. Barrie Thorne and Nancy Henley (Rowley, Mass.: Newbury House, 1975). For additional studies see other chapters in Thorne and Henley, *Language and Sex*.

[12] Note that "grammar" is used to cover the whole of the linguistic system, including phonology. In other contexts, for example, high school grammar classes and also traditional language study, "grammar" usually refers to sentence and word structure, but not to sound structure.

[13] For example, Leonard Bloomfield, *Language* (New York: Holt, Rinehart and Winston, 1933); and Charles C. Fries, *The Structure of English* (New York: Harcourt Brace Jovanovich, Inc., 1952). For further discussion of this approach, see Jeanne H. Herndon, *A Survey of Modern Grammars* (New York: Holt, Rinehart and Winston, Inc., 1970).

[14] See Noam Chomsky, *Aspects of the Theory of Syntax* (Cambridge, Mass.: MIT Press, 1965), pp. 27–30; Noam Chomsky, *Language and Mind*, 2nd ed. (New York: Harcourt Brace Jovanovich, Inc., 1972), especially "The Formal Nature of Language"; and Greenberg et al., *Universals of Human Language*.

[15] Catherine E. Snow and Charles A. Ferguson, eds., *Talking to Children: Language Input and Acquisition* (London and New York: Cambridge Univ. Press, 1977).

[16] Chomsky, *Aspects of the Theory of Syntax*, pp. 4, 8–9.

[17] See especially Chomsky, *Aspects of the Theory of Syntax*, pp. 3–5.

[18] The theoretical validity of postulating "communicative competence" as well as "grammatical competence" is well argued in Dell Hymes, "Competence and Performance in Linguistic Theory," in *Language Acquisition: Models and Methods*, eds. R. Huxley and E. Ingram (New York: Academic Press, 1971). See also Labov, *Sociolinguistic Patterns*; and Charles J. Fillmore, "May We Come In?," *Semiotica*, 9 (1973), 1–15.

[19] An excellent discussion of the difference between prescriptive and descriptive grammars can be found in Harry A. Gleason, Jr., *Linguistics and English Grammar* (New York: Holt, Rinehart and Winston, Inc., 1965).

[20] Chomsky, *Language and Mind*, pp. 28–29.

[21] For example, Ian Watt, "The First Paragraph of The Ambassadors," *Essays in Criticism*, 10 (1960), 250–74; and Winifred Nowottny, *The Language Poets Use* (London: The Athlone Press, 1972).

[22] Richard Ohmann, "Speech, Literature, and the Space Between," *New Literary History*, 4 (1973), 47–63.

[23] Roman Jakobson, "Closing Statement: Linguistics and Poetics," in *Style in Language*, ed. Thomas A. Sebeok (Cambridge, Mass: MIT Press, 1960); rept. in *Essays on the Language of Literature*, eds. Seymour Chatman and Samuel R. Levin (Boston: Houghton Mifflin Co., 1967). See also Samuel R. Levin, *Linguistic Structures in Poetry* (The Hague: Mouton, 1962). Recently Shapiro has argued against the Jakobsonian interpretation of cohesion as symmetry, pointing out that poetry is based on contrast rather than exact similarity and parallelism, see Michael Shapiro, *Asymmetry: An Inquiry into the Linguistic Structure of Poetry* (New York: North-Holland Publishing Co., 1976). In our view, since contrast cannot exist without shared similarity (that is, contrast depends on two aspects of the *same* thing), whether parallelism or contrast is involved in any literary work, either can be considered an example of cohesiveness. For a full length study of linguistic cohesion, in both literary and nonliterary discourse, see M. A. K. Halliday and Ruqaiya Hasan, *Cohesion in English* (London: Longman, 1976).

[24] Jakobson, "Closing Statement," p. 358.

[25] Robert Browning, *The Poetical Works of Robert Browning*, Cambridge Edition, with a new introduction by G. Robert Stange (Boston: Houghton Mifflin Co., 1974), p. 133.

[26] T. S. Eliot, "Rhapsody on a Windy Night," in *Collected Poems 1909–1962* (New York: Harcourt Brace Jovanovich, Inc. 1963), pp. 27–30.

[27] For example, Stanley Fish, "How to Do Things with Austin and Searle: Speech Act Theory and Literary Criticism," *Modern Language Notes*, 91 (1976), 983–1025.

[28] For example, Wolfgang Iser, "The Reality of Fiction: A Functionalist Approach to Literature," *New Literary History*, 7 (1975), 7–38.

[29] See especially Richard Ohmann, "Generative Grammars and the Concept of Literary Style," *Word*, 20 (1964), 423–39; rept. *Contemporary Essays on Style*, eds. Glenn A. Love and Michael Payne (Glenview, Ill.: Scott, Foresman and Co., 1969); rept. *Linguistics and Literary Style*, ed. Donald C. Freeman (New York: Holt, Rinehart and Winston, Inc., 1970). Ohmann's view of style as choice makes a sharp separation between choice in what one has to say (this is choice of content or underlying structure, not style, according to him), and choice of how one says it (style). This view is strongly upheld by Hendricks, see William O. Hendricks, *Grammars of Style and Styles of Grammars* (New York: Elsevier North-Holland Inc., 1976). As will be discussed in later chapters, there is considerable disagreement about exactly what kinds of choices are made available in underlying structures. At least for the preliminary stages, we adopt a fairly broad view of style as choice, one that does not exclude choice of underlying structure, but emphasizes choice of surface realization.

[30] Samuel Beckett, *Murphy* (New York: Grove Press, 1957), pp. 249–50.

[31] Jan Mukařovský, "Standard Language and Poetic Language," in *A Prague School Reader on Esthetics, Literary Structure, and Style*, trans. and ed. Paul Garvin (Washington, D.C.: Georgetown Univ. Press, 1964), rept. in *Linguistics and Literary Style*, ed. Donald C. Freeman (New York: Holt, Rinehart and Winston, Inc., 1970), p. 42. By "standard language" Mukařovský means "the language of science with formulation as its objective" (p. 43).

[32] e. e. cummings, "love is more thicker than forget," in *Poems, 1923–1954* (New York: Harcourt Brace Jovanovich, Inc., 1954), p. 381.

[33] Data based on Victoria Fromkin, *Speech Errors as Linguistic Evidence* (The Hague: Mouton, 1973); and the authors' speech.

[34] Ralph Pomeroy, "Corner," in *Stills and Movies* (Gesture Press, 1961).

[35] Peter Davison, "The Breaking of the Day," in *The Breaking of the Day* (New Haven: Yale Univ. Press, 1964), p. 57.

CHAPTER 2

The Sounds
of English

Each language, indeed each subvariety of a language, has its own unique "sound," yet the number of possible sound distinctions that can be made in any language is quite limited, and all languages share at least some sets of sounds. What makes English sound like English or, more realistically, what makes the various varieties of English identifiable as such, is not so much the inventory of sounds (or "phones"), but the ways the sounds are put together, the ways in which they influence each other, and especially the rhythm, stress, and pitch patterns. These patterns of combination are highly restricted in any given language variety, but are not completely fixed. As different speakers enter the community, or as social groupings change, the sound system may change too.

In this chapter we will explore some of the facts about the sounds of English and some of the ways in which linguists analyze and interpret these facts. We will also suggest ways in which knowing about the sound code of a language can help one to come to grips with how sound patterns are created in written, especially literary, texts. Since speech and writing are really very different, we will start with a brief discussion of the nature of writing as opposed to speech.

SPEECH VERSUS WRITING

Differences in Information Conveyed

One of the greatest difficulties many people have in thinking about the sounds of a language is in separating sound from spelling. It is part of the high cost of

41

literacy that many of us cease to hear ourselves and others accurately; instead we rely heavily on the visual image we have of words in their written form. This is particularly true of academic communities and even more so of students of literature. Those of us who can remember or concentrate on a lecture only by writing copious notes, or can organize our thoughts only by writing them down are particularly likely to find the separation of sound and spelling hard to make.

Writing is a symbolic way of representing speech, and as such it is secondary to it. However, writing has enormous cultural importance as it gives a permanence to language, allowing a society to record its literature, its history, and its technology. In some ways, writing gives less information than speech, in others it gives more. It gives less insofar as, being highly conventionalized, it does not readily indicate variations in pronunciation. Writing systems which use an alphabet segment the stream of speech without showing that there is a phonetic continuum. Only the grossest characteristics of pitch rise and fall are indicated in writing (by punctuation marks such as question marks, commas, periods, and so forth). Very often writing does not reveal stress (emphasis and rhythm). Vocal qualifiers such as hoarseness or clipped speech are not represented at all and have to be compensated for by descriptive commentary if considered important information. That is why a transcribed tape that adds no pitch and stress cues can be totally misleading.

On the other hand, writing can give more information than speech. For one, writing systems are nearly always somewhat conservative, though most are not as conservative as English spelling, which, for the greater part, goes back to the late fifteenth century. Writing can therefore reflect the history of a word and provide a link with the past. Those who argue against spelling reform always make much of this point—**knight** spelled just that way rather than as **nite** provides us with a reminder of Old and Middle English, when the word was actually pronounced with a consonant cluster at the beginning and ending (as in Modern German **Knecht**), and reminds us of its Germanic origin. Another way in which writing also provides more information than speech is that it allows us to distinguish homonyms (words with the same sound but different meaning) such as **meat, mete, meet**, or **knight** and **night**. In Old English these words were originally **mete** and **metan** with short vowels, **mētan** with a long vowel, **cniht** and **niht**, respectively. For historical reasons they later came to sound the same. Hence, although these forms are potentially ambiguous in speech, they are not so in writing. Likewise, writing allows us to relate together synonymous parts of words that for historical reasons have come to sound different, as in **serene-serenity, human-humanity, real-reality**, and many other similar pairs.

In literature, the gap between speech and writing makes itself felt in a number of ways. Many of the oldest works of literature in our possession were originally composed and executed orally, and only later committed to writing. This is the case, for instance, with many classical and medieval epics, and with much Old English poetry. Such works are problematic for literary scholars because in cases like these, the written text which has come down to us cannot really be considered to *be* the work. Once the oral tradition is lost, the actual work is in part unrecoverable, and we can only hypothesize about it on the basis of the incomplete written facsimile. In the case of living oral traditions, film and recording equipment have made it possible to preserve much more complete "texts" of oral works.

By contrast, with a literary work which was composed in writing and intended to be read rather than heard, the printed text can be considered to be the complete work. Here too, however, authors confront the gap between speech and writing whenever they try to represent speech. It is very difficult to write what would actually be said in an oral situation and be understood. The most conversational written dialogue is still stylized when compared with the spoken language, simply because for the medium of writing, an enormous amount has to be "edited in." Cues are put in, sometimes ad nauseam through a kind of metalanguage, such as **he asked, he explained, she commanded, she apologized**. These are standard trappings of literary conversation, even where the only actual information provided is that the speaker has changed. For example, **"Did they stop?" I asked** is obviously a question, as the word order and the question mark make clear. **Asked** is redundant, but **I** is not, as it identifies the speaker. Too much of such metalanguage may become tedious, or, in the right context, comic:

> "Thank you, Pooh," answered Eeyore. "You're a real friend," said he. "Not like Some," he said.[1]

Often, especially when representing nonstandard speech, authors use "eye dialect," attempting to represent nonstandard pronunciation phonetically, as in **Ah'm goin' down to th' crick fer water**. We will be discussing this kind of "editing in" further in Chapter 8.

Because speech styles are so laden with social content, they are often explicitly discussed in written narratives, as clues to a character's background or personality, for instance, or as signs of the social meaning of a situation. A particularly good example is to be found in John Updike's novel *Marry Me*. At this point in the novel, Sally and Jerry are having an affair. Their language is the key to the kind of relationship they adopt:

> He had grown to affect with her an adolescent manner of speech, mixed of hip slang and calf-love monosyllables.[2]

They meet in the dunes one day. He has arrived late and has been looking for her, slightly alarmed at finding she is not waiting for him in her car. Finally he catches sight of her.

> She had been sunbathing. Her heart-shaped face was pink. "Hey? I'm glad you're here?" She was slightly panting and her voice excitedly lifted each phrase into a question. "I've been waiting in this dune with a pack of

horrible boys without shirts whooping and yelling all around me; I was getting quite frightened?"

As if his manner of speech kept shifting around an unsayable embarrassment, he momentarily lapsed from hipsterism and spoke in a courtly way. "My poor brave lady. The dangers I expose you to. I'm sorry I'm late; listen. I had to buy the wine . . . ."[3]

Notice how much explanation and paraphrase Updike has used here to communicate facts about the characters' speech which would have been self-evident in an oral situation.

At the other extreme are authors who break away from the tradition of using metalanguage about speech cues. Particularly consistent in his avoidance of metalanguage about tone of voice or even who is speaking, is William Gaddis in his novel, *J.R.* We learn to recognize speakers first by the way they are addressed, and before long by what they say or how they say it. In these first few lines from the beginning of the book, Gaddis carefully distinguishes Anne, with her strong visual and auditory perceptions, from Julia, who always insists on facts and the reasons for them.

—Money . . . ? in a voice that rustled.
—Paper, yes.
—And we'd never seen it. Paper money.
—We never saw paper money till we came east.
—It looked so strange the first time we saw it. Lifeless.
—You couldn't believe it was worth a thing.
—Not after Father jingling his change.
—Those were silver dollars.
—And silver halves, yes and quarters, Julia. The ones from his
10   pupils.
I can hear him now . . .
Sunlight, pocketed in a cloud, spilled suddenly broken across the floor through the leaves of the trees outside.
—Coming up the veranda, how he jingled when he walked.
—He'd have his pupils rest the quarters that they brought him on the backs of their hands when they did their scales. He charged fifty cents a lesson, you see, Mister . . .
—Coen, without the h. Now if both you ladies . . .
—Why, it's just like that story about Father's dying wish to
20   have his bust sunk in Vancouver harbor, and his ashes sprinkled on the water there, about James and Thomas out in the rowboat, and both of them hitting at the bust with their oars because it was hollow and wouldn't go down, and the storm coming up while they were out there, blowing his ashes back into their beards.
—There was never a bust of Father, Anne. And I don't recall his ever being in Australia.[4]

Have you figured out who the first speaker is?

In terms of the gap between speech and writing, drama occupies an interesting position between oral and written literature. As a rule, dramas in the modern period are composed in writing and intended to be executed orally. Yet it is also considered legitimate to read plays, much as we read novels, and there are plays, such as Vonnegut's *Happy Birthday, Wanda June*, which are intended only to be read. The text of a drama consists primarily of represented speech, so that reading drama requires a huge amount of "editing in," not only of staging, costumes, and so on, but also of the sound of speech itself. As with written narrative, there are conventions in dramatic texts for indicating who is speaking and how a thing is to be said, but these tend to be even sparser than in novels. Ultimately, the gap between speech and writing in drama is filled by the performers themselves, and this is one of the main reasons why no two productions of a play will ever be alike. Part of the richness of drama as a genre lies precisely in its openness to interpretation in this regard.

While we often find writers going to great lengths to overcome the gap between speech and writing, it is also possible to exploit this gap. We noted earlier that, unlike speech, writing tends to reflect earlier forms of a language, and is able to distinguish homonyms. James Joyce was one of the first writers to exploit these potentials of the writing system, as well as the multiplicity of spellings for one sound. He carried this to such a degree that he used the visual form of words to create whole levels of meaning in addition to those normally derived from sound and sentence structure. In the following passage from *Finnegans Wake*, for instance, the spelling of **kennot** insists on the Old English meaning of **can** "to be intellectually able, to know"; **exlegged** puns on no legs and bandy legs (x-shaped legs) as well as **exile**; **phatrisight, psing,** and many other words suggest Greek vocabulary and, by implication, Greek culture and mythology:

> And this is why any simple philadolphus of a fool you like to dress, an athemisthued lowtownian, exlegged phatrisight, may be awfully green to one side of him and fruitfully blue on the other which will not screen him however from appealing to my gropesarching eyes; through the strongholes of my acropoll, as a boosted blasted bleating blatant bloaten blasphorus blesphorous idiot who kennot tail a bomb from a painapple when he steals one and wannot psing his psalmen with the cong in our gregational pompoms with the canting crew.[5]

Notice that in this passage Joyce also exploits the fact that writing does not always distinguish homonyms. The word **canting** in the last line, for example, obviously alludes to Latin **cantare**, "sing," from which we get English **chant** and the literary term **canto**; but in conjunction with **kennot** and **wannot**, **canting** also alludes to Modern English **can't**, as well as to **cant** as a derogatory term for "jargon," as a verb meaning "whine," as a verb meaning "lean" (especially with ships—hence the word **crew**), and possibly to Irish English **cant** meaning "to sell at auction."

More recently, a new genre of poetry, often known as "concrete poetry," has deliberately sought to combine this visual aspect of writing equally with the verbal. A brief example is the following, which combines verbal cohesion (the word **like** preceding and following the verb, and the repetition of **like attracts like**) with typographic cohesion (matching one meaning of **attracts** on the one hand, with reduction of spaces until attraction involves merger, and on the other, with an arrow-like trajectory across the page, symbolizing the kinetic nature of attraction):[6]

Representing Speech in Writing: The Phonetic Alphabet

We pointed out earlier a number of ways in which writing does not fully capture speech. For English, we noted in particular the vast difference between the way words are spelled and the way they are now pronounced. Yet for a linguist studying the sounds of languages, it is important to have some way to write down sounds unambiguously. In other words, linguists need an alphabet allowing for a one-to-one correspondence between sound and written symbol. Such an alphabet is equally important for the literary critic interested in the sound texture of a work, and the way it interrelates with the written form. Political history, custom, meaning relations, all of these are important for understanding how writing systems are used, but they are irrelevant when one wants to find out what sounds are used in which variety of language. That is why the International Phonetic Alphabet (IPA) was developed in the late 1880s, based on the conventional Latin alphabet but with many additions, especially from the Greek alphabet.[7] Its purpose was to provide a writing system that could be used by anyone with the appropriate training, to record the speech of any language of the world in such a way that any other person who could read the alphabet could interpret the transcription unambiguously.

In this system, the famous *ough* of English spelling cannot exist, since the combination of sounds o-u-g-h does not occur in English. Instead, we find the following transcription of the English words (square brackets [ ] indicate that the alphabet used is phonetic):

through	[θru]
though	[ðo]
cough	[kaf]
bought	[bɔt]
tough	[təf]
bough	[baw]
hiccough	[hɪkəp]

Since "silent letters" are not pronounced, they do not appear in a phonetic transcription. Thus **rid** and **ride** are differentiated according to their vowels, not according to whether silent **e** is present: [rɪd], [rayd]. Since the **b** of **limb** and the **g** of **ring** are not pronounced, they, too, are not transcribed (except for some dialects where they are pronounced): [lɪm], [rɪŋ]. On the other hand, where distinctions in pronunciation are made that are not reflected in traditional spelling, the distinctions are recorded in phonetic transcription. Thus **use** in **I use it often** and **I have no use for it** is spelled as [yuz] and [yus], respectively.

For our purposes in this book, a detailed phonetic alphabet giving all possible sounds of English is unnecessary. Instead we will use what is called a "broad phonetic" alphabet. This alphabet characterizes the most basic set of sounds in English, namely those that can be used to distinguish one word from another. For instance, the words **clamp** [klæmp] and **cramp** [kræmp] are identical in sound except for their second consonant. Thus the distinction between these two words depends on the distinction or contrast between [l] and [r], and we say that [l] and [r] are "distinctive" or "contrastive" sounds in English. Though the actual sound of [l] and [r] may differ from speaker to speaker in English, these sounds are nevertheless distinctive for any speaker of English. There are languages, such as Japanese, in which [l] and [r] are not distinctive, that is, they are not used to distinguish one word from another. Likewise, [s] and [z] are distinctive sounds in English, as shown by pairs such as **loose**/**lose** and **rice**/**rise**. In the section on phonology that follows, we will be discussing at some length the concept of distinctive sounds (more technically called "phonemes"). For the moment you should keep in mind that the broad phonetic alphabet we will be using characterizes only the distinctive sounds of English.

Below you will find a list of the consonant and vowel symbols which make up our broad phonetic alphabet, along with examples of words in which the sound in question occurs. In examining the list, you will find that the sound illustrated is not always completely identical in all the examples given. This is because sounds vary according to their environment. For instance, the sound **r** tends to retract and lower the tongue, so that a given vowel will sound different before an **r** than before other sounds. Contrast, for example, the sound of the vowel in **beer** and **beet**, where the basic **ee** sound is modified before **r**.

People speak differently depending on their regional and social backgrounds. Because we have chosen "Standard Midwestern American" as the basis for description in this book, you may find that our sound list does not accurately represent your pronunciation. For example, English dialects differ a lot in the use of the "back" vowels, those often spelled **aw**, **augh**, **ough**, and **o**. You may distinguish **caught** and **cot**, or you may not, depending on where you come from. However, if you do not distinguish them, you probably do distinguish **core** and **car**. Go through the examples of consonant and vowel symbols, listening to your pronunciation of the relevant sounds very carefully. If a sample word does not match your pronunciation, cross it out and add it to the appropriate class of sounds elsewhere.

Consonants

p   pin, spin, simple, zip, zipper, hiccough

b   bin, amble, nib, nibble

t   tin, stick, cater, bit, latter,[8] walked, Thomas

d   din, laden, did, shoved, ladder, fiddle

k   kin, quick ([kwɪk]), crock, creek, critic, crackle, scheme, mechanic, fix ([fɪks]), plaque

g   goat, fig, giggle, guest, fugue, ghost, Pittsburgh, exact ([ɛgzækt])

f   fin, trifle, if, sniffle, snuff, tough, philosopher

v   veal, evil, eve, of, nephew (*for some speakers*)

θ   thin, pithy, bath

ð   then, father, bathe

s   sin, psychology, scion, whistle, pussy, nurse, democracy, receive, descent, bus, fuss, pats, piece, fix ([fɪks])

z   zip, xerox, visor, roses, crescent (*British English*), fuzz, pads, peas, horses, houses, maids, scissors, exact ([ɛgzækt])

š   shin, sure, fashion, glacial, passion, nation, fish, machine, mansion, conscious, special, ocean, luxury ([ləkšəri] *for some speakers*)

ž   treasure, precision, azure, beige, luxury ([ləgžəri] *for some speakers*) h   hen, who, rehash

č   chin, pitcher, righteous, rich, nature, fixture

ǰ   judge, gin, midget, region, residual ([rəzɪǰuəl] *for some speakers*), suggest, adjacent

m   mum, impossible, mummy, intercom, come, comb

n   nip, gnat, knee, pneumatic, mnemonic, skinny, sin, sign

ŋ   finger, sink, singer, sing, anxious ([æŋkšəs])

l   little, silly, salt, call

r   rip, girl, furry, fairy, fur, right, rhythm

w   win, which, Qantas ([kwantəs]), queen, sewing, grow, language, won, choir, sweet

y   you, few, buying, spaniel, feud, beauty, muse, *and for some speakers*: suit, new, due

Vowels: Simple Vowels

i   meet, meat, mete, be, been (*British English*), reprieve, receive, key, aureola, people, Caesar, ravine, city

ɪ   bit, impossible, been (*American English*), rhythm, pretty, women

e   abate, bay, steak, bear, air, bain, vein, freight, gauge, feign, they, bass (*not the fish!*)

E   met, obscenity, says, quest, let, lead, friend, said, many

æ   mat, laugh, comrade, plaid

u   moot, do, due, duty, rude, through, to (*stressed*), too, two, move, chew, juice, shoe

U   bull, put, would, foot, wolf

o   moat, mow, beau, doe, dough, go, soul

ɔ   bought, taught, ball, stalk, jackdaw, awe, auto, water, (*Santa*) Claus; boar, bore, floor (r *will sometimes radically change the quality of the vowel; however, it will still be back and in the mid range*)

a   bottle, father, balm, harmonic, car, heart, cough, knowledge, sausage, yacht ə   *the stressed vowel in* sun, putt, does, son, love, tough, flood, bird, herd, heard, turd, word (*again,* r *affects the quality of the vowel considerably; in a more detailed transcription the symbol for the central vowel before* [r] *is* [ɜ])

the unstressed vowel in Rosa, alone, tuna, telegraph, harmony, difficult, melodious, fainted, possible ([pasəbəl]), gentleman, woman, suppose (*in fact, most vowel letters and their combinations*)[9]

i   *the unstressed vowel in plurals with a full syllable, e.g.,* roses (*as opposed to* Rosa's, *which has* [ə]); *also, for many American speakers, the stressed vowel in the adverb* just *as in* **I'm just coming**, *which contrasts with* [jɪst] "gist," [jəst] "fair," *and* [jɛst] "jest."

In many dialects, especially, in Britain and the Eastern U.S., there is no **-r** after vowels, so that **car** is pronounced [ka], and **card** is pronounced [kad]. Most speakers of these dialects distinguish **caught, cot,** and **cart** as [kɔt], [kɒt], [kat] (the [ɒ] of **cot** is a very back, slightly rounded a-vowel). So-called **r**-less speakers also distinguish **hut** and **hurt** not by **r** but by a lower, backer vowel in **hut**, symbolized as [ə], and a higher, fronter vowel symbolized as [ɜ] in **hurt.** In Southeastern U.S. dialects which contrast **fire, far,** and **for,** an additional symbol for **fire** is needed, one that symbolizes a sound between the vowels of **fat** and **father.** You will not be able to use the [æ] symbol of **fat,** since **fat** and **fight** will contrast. The usual solution is to use [æ] for **fat,** [a] for **fight** and **fire,** and [ɑ] for **father** and **far.**

Vowels: Diphthongs

Vowels followed by an upward glide to the front (**-y**) or back (**-w**) in the same syllable are called diphthongs. There are three main ones in most varieties of English:

ay   bite, fight, sign, by, dye, aisle, choir, island, height, die, eiderdown, **eye, buy**

aw   bow, down, doubt, sough

ɔy   boy, foil

Phonetically, [i, e, u, o] are diphthongs in many English dialects. [i, e] have glides to the front, [u, o] have glides to the back. However, they are not treated as diphthongs here, since nobody makes a contrast between, for example, [se] and [seɪ] (but many speakers do make such contrasts as [pa] "pa" and [paɪ] "pie"). To tell how much of a diphthong a particular speaker makes in pronouncing any so-called simple vowel or diphthong, it is useful to make a tape recording of one syllable words like **say, so, sue, sow** (the pig), **sigh** and play them backward at a very slow speed. Some speakers' **say** will sound somewhat like **yes** (in other words, there will be a strong diphthongal element), others' will be more like **ess** (with little or no diphthong).

CHARACTERISTICS OF SPEECH SOUNDS: PHONETICS

The production of any speech sound involves the projection of the air stream from the lungs through the mouth and/or the nose. In its passage, the air stream is shaped in various ways by tongue and jaw movements. It may be momentarily interrupted or not interrupted at all. It may be made to vibrate a lot or a little by the vocal cords. Phonetics is the branch of linguistics concerned with the physiological and acoustic bases of speech, and with such questions as how speech sounds are produced and perceived. Some knowledge of these bases is essential to an understanding of linguistic patternings of sameness and difference. Here we will touch on a few aspects of articulatory phonetics, that is, the study of how sounds are produced. In particular, we will discuss some of the basic articulatory features of consonants and vowels.

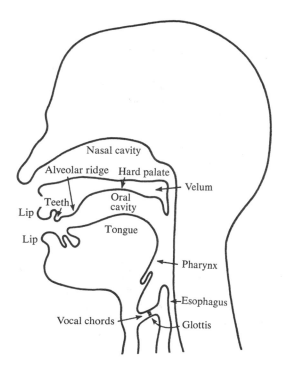

POSITIONS OF ARTICULATION IN THE MOUTH

Figure 2-1 [10]

The Articulatory Characteristics of Consonants

It is customary to classify consonants according to place of articulation and manner of articulation (degree of obstruction of the air stream). The places of articulation should be clear from Figure 2-1. Sounds may be produced that involve both lips ("labials": [p, b, m]), or the lower lip and upper teeth ("labiodentals": [f, v]). Other sounds are produced by the tongue between the teeth ("interdentals": [θ, ð]), by movement of the tongue toward the hard ridge immediately behind the front teeth ("alveolars": [t, d, n, s, z]), by movement of the tongue toward the hard palate behind the alveolar ridge ("palatals": [š, ž, č, ǰ]), by movement of the tongue toward the soft palate ("velars": [k, g, ŋ]), or by constriction of the glottis or vocal cords ("glottal": [h]).

Manner of articulation involves presence or absence of voicing and of nasality, as well as degree of obstruction.

Voiced versus voiceless sounds: These differ according to whether or not the vocal cords of the glottis (Adam's apple) vibrate when the air stream moves through it. Vibration produces voicing. The main difference between [s] and [z], for example, is that in the latter, the vocal cords vibrate, while in the former, they do not. When we whisper, all sounds are voiceless.

Nasal versus nonnasal sounds: The difference between nasal [m] and nonnasal [b], both of which involve lip closure and voicing, is that in [m], the velum ("soft palate") is open, allowing air to pass through the nose as in Figure 2-1. In [b], it is closed (the velum is raised against the back of the nasal cavity), preventing air from passing through the nose. When we have a cold, and the nasal cavity is blocked, our [m]s, [n]s, and [ŋ]s sound more like [b], [d], and [g], because the air cannot pass through the nose, even though the velum may be open.

Stopped sounds: Consonants pronounced with the air completely closed off or stopped at some point in the oral cavity are called "stops" ([p, b, m, t, d, n, k, g, ŋ]). Nasals are fully stopped in the oral cavity although they are not obstructed in the nasal cavity. Because of this, nasals are usually listed separately from stops in articulatory charts.

Fricatives and affricates: If the air stream passes through a narrow passage without being totally stopped, friction results. Sounds articulated in this way ([f, v, θ, ð, s, z, š, ž, h]) are called fricatives. Another term for these is "spirant," from Latin **spirare**, "to blow." If a stop has a fricative release, we have what is called an affricate. The only affricates in English are [č] and [ǰ]. [č, ǰ, s, z, š, ž] are all "hissing" sounds and are sometimes classed together as "sibilants."

Liquids and glides: These are sounds with very little obstruction of air. In English, the liquids are [l] and [r], and the glides are [y] and [w]. Glides are produced with so little obstruction that one might think of them as vowels. However, they are not vowels in that they do not carry pitch or stress. Rather, they are glides to or from vowels. For these reasons, they are sometimes called semivowels.

PLACE OF ARTICULATION

	Labial	Labio-dental	Inter-dental	Alveolar	Palatal	Velar	Glottal
Vl. stops	p pit			t tip		k kit	
Vd. stops	b bit			d dip		g get	
Vl. fricatives		f fat	θ thigh	s sip	š ship		h hip
Vd. fricatives		v vat	ð thy	z zip	ž measure		
Vl. affricate					č church		
Vd. affricate					ǰ judge		
Nasals	m mat			n nip		ŋ thing	
Liquids				l lip	r rip		
Glides	w wet				y yet		

MANNER OF ARTICULATION

CHART OF ENGLISH CONSONANTS
Figure 2-2

The classifications given here are summarized in Figure 2-2. The chart gives only crude distinctions concerning place of articulation. For instance, [r] is actually pronounced by curling the tongue back (retroflexing it) just behind the alveolar ridge. Strictly speaking, it is therefore alveopalatal rather than fully palatal.

The Articulatory Characteristics of Vowels

As we have seen, consonants typically involve obstruction of the air stream as it flows through the mouth. By contrast, vowels involve not obstruction but shaping of the air stream in its passage. To characterize vowels in general, we therefore need slightly different terms of reference, even though we will still be referring to the criteria of manner and position of articulation. For vowels, manner of articulation involves voicing, lip rounding or spreading, length, and degree of muscular tension. Place of articulation for vowels involves gross generalizations relative to the front and back of the mouth, rather than the particulars necessary for consonant identification; it also involves tongue and jaw height relative to the roof of the mouth.

All languages have voiced vowels. Some, like Japanese, also have voiceless ones. While voiceless vowels can occur in English in special conditions of rapid speech between voiceless consonants, they are not structurally important in the language. Lip spreading versus rounding is typical of all languages. In Modern English, the vowels [u, ʊ, o, ɔ] are rounded. Some languages, like Old English, French, or German, distinguish meanings according to this feature alone. For example, in Old English there were **i** and **u** as in Modern English, and also a front rounded vowel **ü** pronounced like *i* but with lips rounded instead of spread. Three-way contrasts were possible, such as: **fild,** "level like a field"; **fyllan** ([füllan]), "to fill"; and **full,** "full." In Modern English [ü] has been lost, and no distinction of meaning depends only on rounding. Other differences of articulation have to do with vowel length. Long vowels are marked by a following [ˑ]. As we shall see, this distinction is predictable in English depending on the voicing of the following consonant. In some other languages it is distinctive. Finally, there is the criterion of tenseness (tension of the muscles) or laxness (relative relaxation of the muscles). When you pronounce the [i, u, e, o, æ, a] of **beet, boot, bait, boat, bat,** and **father,** your tongue muscles will be tenser than when you pronounce the [ʊ, ɪ, ɛ, ɔ, ə] of **full, fill, fell, bought, but,** and **Rosa.** The degree of tenseness of [æ] and especially [a] depends on the dialect and word involved. All stressed word-final vowels in English are tense, for example, the vowels in **bee, buy, bah, bow, boo.**

Place of articulation for vowels involves gross generalizations relative to the front and back of the mouth, as well as tongue and jaw height. We speak of high, mid, and low vowels. If you start with your tongue forward and fairly close to the roof of your mouth, and slowly lower your tongue and jaw, you

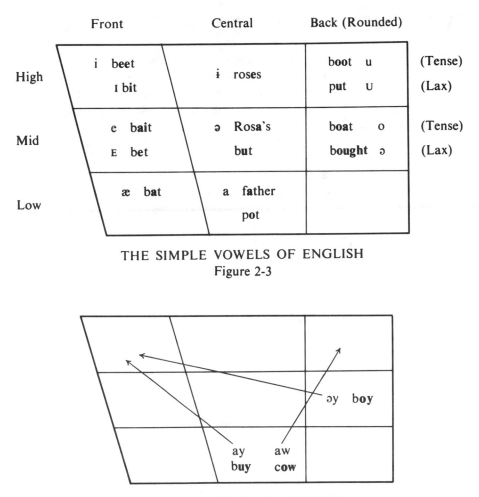

THE SIMPLE VOWELS OF ENGLISH
Figure 2-3

THE DIPHTHONGS OF ENGLISH
Figure 2-4

will pronounce [i, ɪ, e, ɛ, æ], and finally, with the tongue and jaw in lowest position, [a]. Because of the shape of your mouth, your tongue will be considerably further back than it was for [i] by the time you reach [a]. Move it further back still, round your lips and raise your tongue toward the roof of the mouth, and you will pronounce [ɔ, o, ʊ, u]. This pattern is the basis of the so-called vowel triangle. In a central position, roughly between [e] and [o], but higher or lower, fronter or backer for various people and in various positions in the word, are the vowels of **sun, hurry,** and **Rosa** (final syllable).

These facts are summarized in Figure 2-3, which gives a schematic presentation of the mouth, spacious in front, more contracted in the back. The articulatory positions involved in pronouncing diphthongs are given in Figure 2-4.

SOUNDS AS SYSTEM: PHONOLOGY

Although an enormous number of minute variations occur when we speak, all speakers in a speech community agree that certain utterances are "the same" or "different." It is knowledge of the systematic ways in which sounds are put together in a language that enables a speaker to make such judgments, to form meaningful utterances, to invent new words, to recognize "accents," and so forth. The branch of linguistics called phonology is concerned with identifying those groups of sounds that can be distinctive in a language and with establishing how they can be put together to form a sequence. That is, phonology is concerned with the ways in which the phonetic elements of the language are grouped and exploited by speakers of that language to effect communication. Such patterns function as the framework of literary expression and control an author's choice of words as well as the invention of new words, and therefore are of importance to textual criticism.

Distinctive Sounds versus Predictable Variants

Basic to a speaker's phonological knowledge is the ability to know which sounds in the language are distinctive and which are not. As explained earlier (see page 47), distinctive sounds are those that may be used to contrast meanings in the language. One interesting example of the difference between distinctive and nondistinctive sounds is the case of fricatives in the history of English. In Old English the difference between voiced and voiceless fricatives was not distinctive. Roughly speaking, voiceless fricatives [f, θ, s] occurred at beginnings and endings of words, voiced fricatives [v, ð, z] occurred between vowels. More formally put, voiced and voiceless fricatives were "complementary," that is, they never occurred in the same phonetic contexts and could never be used to distinguish meanings. Pairs like **wife-wives**, **path-paths**, **house-houses** still reflect this situation (the plural originally consisted of a vowel plus a consonant). For a variety of historical reasons, the distribution of voiced and voiceless fricatives changed in late Old English so that both could be used in word-initial position. Now words starting with [f] were distinct from those starting with [v], and so on (cf. **feel-veal**, **thigh-thy**, **sip-zip**). Thus, although the phonetic sounds [f, v, θ, ð, s, z] occur in both Old and Modern English, they are part of different phonological systems. In Old English no new word could have been invented beginning with [v, ð, z], but in Modern English speakers can invent words beginning with [v] and [z]. We would have no hesitation in accepting [væks] as the name of a new product. Curiously enough, we still cannot invent words beginning with [ð] and have them sound English. An advertiser who invents a name of a soap powder spelled **Thax** knows that the product will be pronounced [θæks] and not [ðæks], despite the potential spelling ambiguity. The reason for this is that the only words beginning with [ð] in English are pronouns or grammatical words like **this, that, the, these, those, there,** and **then.** [ð] is not available as an initial sound for a noun, verb, or adjective. This indicates that part of our phonological knowledge includes knowledge of what kinds of sounds go with what kinds of grammatical elements.

Sounds that are contrastive in a language are called "phonemes"; sounds that are predictable phonetic variants are called "allophones" (**allo** comes from Greek **allos,** "other"; **phone** is Greek for "sound, voice"). Thus, in Modern English, where [θ] and [ð] are contrastive, we say there are two interdental phonemes in the sound system. In Old English, there was one interdental phoneme with two predictable phonetic allophones, [θ] and [ð]. A phoneme is not really a single sound or entity. Rather it should be thought of as a sound class consisting of at least one, and usually more than one, member. In transcription, to clarify the distinction between phonetic, that is, actually pronounced sounds, and phonemic sound classes, we enclose the former in square brackets [ ] and the latter in slashes / /. Thus, in Old English there was one phoneme /θ/ with two predictable phonetic variants, [θ] and [ð], whereas in Modern English there are two interdental phonemes, /θ/ and /ð/.[11]

We now turn to consider some predictable sound relationships in contemporary English. Our first example is the relationship that holds among stop consonants. Voiceless stops ([p, t, k]) may be aspirated or nonaspirated. This means that there may be a short period after the stop is released, often accompanied by breathiness before a voiced sound is articulated, as with **p** in **pit** (in detailed phonetics [pʰɪt]), or there may not, as with **p** in **spit** (in detailed phonetics [spɪt]). Voiceless aspirated stops occur at beginnings of words, voiceless unaspirated ones after /s/. [pɪt] sounds distinctly foreign, as does [spʰɪt], although the latter is heard in speech involving loud or careful enunciation. Indeed, in English, [pʰ] and [p] never contrast, nor do [tʰ] and [t], or [kʰ] and [k]. While English would never distinguish the meaning of two words on the basis of the aspiration of the voiceless stop, other languages such as Thai make this distinction. For example, Thai [pʰaa] "to split" contrasts with [paa] "forest." In English aspirated and unaspirated stops are in complementary distribution; in Thai they are distinctive. To put it yet another way, English has only three voiceless stop phonemes, while Thai has six.

The facts of the relationship in English between aspirated and unaspirated stops can be formalized as follows:

$$/p/ \rightarrow [pʰ] \text{ word-initially}$$
$$[p] \text{ after } /s/$$
$$/t/ \rightarrow [tʰ] \text{ word-initially}$$
$$[t] \text{ after } /s/$$

$$/k/ \rightarrow [k^h] \text{ word-initially}$$

$$[k] \text{ after } /s/$$

These "rules" are statements in shorthand about relations that hold between phonological classes (phonemes) and their phonetic realizations, and read as follows: The phoneme /p/ is realized phonetically as the allophone [p^h] at the beginning of a word and as [p] after /s/ (the arrow means "is realized as"), and so forth. Notice that the conditions for the occurrence of the aspirated and nonaspirated versions of a stop are the same, whether we are dealing with a labial, an alveolar, or a velar. This shows that our knowledge of how sounds can be grouped is not limited to individual sounds, but to whole sets of them. We will return to this point shortly.

Another set of predictable variations or allophones in English concerns vowel length. All vowels are slightly longer when they precede voiced consonants than when they precede voiceless ones. If we mark length by [·], we will notice:

[bit] versus [bi·d] beat versus bead

[bɪt] versus [bɪ·d] bit versus bid

We can say that in English there are two phonemes /i/ and /ɪ/, each with a lengthened variant before a voiced stop.

Distinctive Features

Linguistics always aims at making significant generalizations. Such generalizations can be made in phonology by referring not to individual sounds or even classes of sounds (phonemes) but to shared articulatory characteristics. For example, we can say that all voiceless stops are aspirated in initial position in the word, unaspirated after /s/. Rather than list /p, t, k/ separately, we can refer to their relevant characteristics, specifically, voicelessness and stopness (position of articulation is irrelevant for this particular phenomenon). Each distinctive sound of the language can be considered as consisting of a bundle of sound characteristics or features. These sound features may be arrived at by a principle somewhat similar to factoring in mathematics:

	3	is to	5
as	6	is to	10
as	9	is to	15
	3n		5n

So we can extract, for example, features of voicing (plus or minus voicing) and nasality (plus or minus nasal), as in:

	p	is to	b
as	t	is to	d
as	k	is to	g
as	f	is to	v
as	θ	is to	ð
as	s	is to	z
as	š	is to	ž
	[−vc]		[+vc]

	b	is to	m
as	d	is to	n
as	g	is to	ŋ
	[−nas]		[+nas]

Factoring out the three articulatory features [±voice], [±stop], and [±alveolar], we can produce the following array for labial and alveolar stops and fricatives:

	p	b	t	d	f	v	s	z
voice	−	+	−	+	−	+	−	+
stop	+	+	+	+	−	−	−	−
alveolar	−	−	+	+	−	−	+	+

This way of describing distinctive sounds differs from the articulatory classification presented earlier, in that sounds are described not positively in terms of characteristics they have, but both positively and negatively, as either plus or minus a given feature. Notice that each sound in the array above appears as a unique bundle of features, different from each of the other sounds in the array. At the same time, the feature system enables us to relate sounds to each other, in terms of their similarities and differences. If we were to add more sounds to the array, we would need to include more features to distinguish the sounds. For instance, the feature [± stop] distinguishes stops from fricatives above, but if the affricates /č, ǰ/ were added, they too would be [+stop], so we would have to add another feature to distinguish them from stops.

Description in terms of features lets us draw relations not only between sounds, but also between the sound systems of different languages. The individual sound features are often viewed as members of a hypothetical universal set of possible distinctions in the languages of the world. According to this view, individual languages select certain components and certain combinations out of which to construct their sound system. Thus, the inventory of some languages, for example Arabic, includes sounds produced by the pharynx (called "pharyngeals"). English does not include such consonants in its inventory of phonemes. As we saw, Old English had fricatives, as does Modern English, but the combination of voicing with fricativeness was not distinctive in that language, whereas it is in Modern English. Since voicing was distinctive for Old English stops, we must say that (in respect to the sounds discussed here) Old English had the same inventory of components as Modern English (stopness, fricativeness, voicing) but used them in different combinations.

Various feature systems have been proposed for languages, some based on articulatory principles, some on acoustic ones. For our purposes, articulatory features like those already illustrated will suffice. One of the advantages of the feature approach to sounds is that it enables us to capture similarities in the way sounds behave. Sounds sharing specific features are likely to have similar variants in similar environments, as we saw above with English stops, all of which have an aspirated variant word-initially. With features, rather than write individual rules for each stop, as we did above, we can write a single rule for the relevant shared features: *Sounds that are [+ stop] and [− voice] acquire the feature of aspiration word-initially*. In what follows, we will be seeing more examples of the kinds of generalizations that can be captured by feature analysis.

How do the phonological rules we have been discussing fit into the grammar as a whole? However it is formalized, a grammar must include a statement about which members of the universal grammar are used distinctively in the particular language under discussion. It must also include a list of words or parts of words that correlate meanings with specific sequences of sounds. As will be discussed at length in Chapter 3, this list is a kind of dictionary, called a "lexicon," and in it words or parts of words will be represented as specific bundles of features in specific sequences (there will be syntactic and semantic features as well as phonological ones). The phonological rules will give the proper surface phonetic forms to the lexical entries. This relation between lexical entries, phonological rules, and phonetic manifestations can be modeled as shown at the top of p. 61.

What we learn, then, is the particular set of distinctive features associated with each word or part of a word, and some general ways of expressing these. We learn, for example, that the word for a soft cushion to sit on (**pad**) is

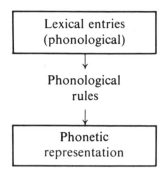

associated with a voiceless labial stop, a low front vowel, and a voiced alveolar stop. We also learn a general rule of expression whereby any voiceless stop at the beginning of a word is aspirated before a vowel, and any vowel is lengthened before a voiced consonant. We thus derive the phonetic form [pæ·d] from the phonological representation /pæd/. In a grammar using these features this is expressed as follows:

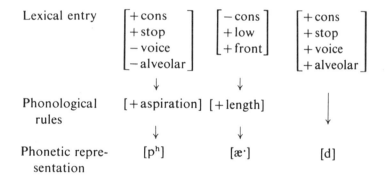

Constraints on Sound Sequences

No language permits all its possible distinctive sounds to combine in any order. For example, not all distinctive sounds of English can occur word-initially. Specifically, /ž/ and /ŋ/ are excluded. This has a historical explanation: /ž/ derives from /zü/ in borrowed French words like **measure** (Fr. /mezür/), a sequence which does not occur word-initially in French. /ŋ/ originally occurred only before velars and was a predictable variant of /n/. In late Middle English, /g/ was dropped in final position after /n/ (e.g., [rɪŋg] → [rɪŋ]), and also in medial position before -er meaning "one who does the action designated by the verb" (e.g., [sɪŋgər] → [sɪŋər] for most speakers

of English), while [ŋg] remained before other -er's, as in **young-younger,
finger**. As a result, [ŋ] became a distinctive phoneme in the language, instead
of being a variant, and contrasted with [m] and [n], as in [rən], [rəm], and
[rəŋ]. Even if we knew nothing about the history of English, we would know
that no new product is likely to be named /ŋəmp/ or /ŋɪp/. How would we
even spell them?

Consonant clusters are even more constrained in English, especially at
the beginning of a word. Such combinations as the following do not exist
word-initially in any but foreign words:[12] stop + stop (e.g., /pt, gb/); stop +
nasal (e.g., /dn, pm/); stop + fricative (cf. Yiddish **kvetsch**); nasal + stop
(cf. Bantu names like **Mbutu, Nkruma**). The only two-consonant clusters
permitted word-initially in English are: stop + liquid or glide; voiceless
fricative + liquid or glide; and /s/ + voiceless stop or liquid or glide or
/m/ or /n/. But even this is too general, as the following array shows (* signals a nonexisting combination):

pl	bl	*tl	*dl	kl	gl
pr	br	tr	dr	kr	gr
py	by	ty	dy	ky	gy (*almost obsolete*)
*pw	*bw	tw	dw	kw	*gw
plank	blank	—	—	clank	glean
prank	brink	trinket	drink	cream	grease
puny	beauty	tune	dune	cute	gules
—	—	twice	dwarf	quick	—
fl	*θl	sl	*šl	*hl	
fr	θr	*sr	šr	*hr	
fy	θy (*obsolete*)	sy	*šy	hy	
*fw	θw	sw	*šw	hw	
flee	—	sleet	—	—	
free	three	—	shrink	—	
few	thews	sue	—	hue	
—	thwart	sweet	—	which	

The nonoccurrence of /pw, bw, fw, tl, dl, θl/ can be explained as a constraint that two labials and two alveolars cannot co-occur (the interdental /θ/
behaves like alveolars in this and other respects). /w/ is quite limited, and so is
/y/; in many American dialects the latter has almost disappeared except after
labials, with the result that **due** and **do**, which are regularly contrasted in

British English as /dyu/ and /du/, are both pronounced /du/; when /y/ does occur, the following vowel must be /u/.

The relation between the /s/ and /š/ series is interesting. /s/ does not occur with /r/; only /š/ occurs with it. There is, therefore, a complementary relationship between /s/ and /š/ with respect to a following /l/ or /r/. One can either consider this fact as a peculiarity of English and think no more about it, or one can look for a possible reason for it. Since /š/ does not combine with anything else, can it be regarded as an underlying /s/ modified for some reason? In thinking about this problem we can use feature analysis. It is common in languages for one of two adjacent sounds to modify toward the other; this is particularly true when the second is palatal (consider, for example, rapid speech modification of [ay mɪs yu] to [aymɪšu]). If /r/ is defined as a palatal, it is possible to think of the existence of /šr/ as resulting from the modification of alveolar /s/ to palatal /š/ because of the palatal /r/, in other words, as an instance of a very common modification in the languages of the world.

In discussing any kind of gap in the system we must distinguish between real and accidental gaps. **sr**, **tl**, and **dr** simply do not occur in words that are part of the system of English word formation, that is, such consonant clusters are not part of the rules that are used, however unconsciously, in inventing new terms. If enough borrowing were to occur from languages with sounds like **tl** (e.g., the Alaskan language Tlingit), we might expect our system to change and to permit **tl** initially (just as the influence of French helped introduce **v** into word-initial position in Middle English), but such extensive borrowing into English is not occurring at the present time. In contrast to the systematic absence of any word beginning with **tl**, consider the absence of a word like **blick**. This is an accidental gap in the system, since other words with **bl** occur, such as **black, blind, blue, blandish, blimp**. A sequence like **blook** could easily be used and could well serve as the name of a new product. Creative writers (and advertisers) make great use of such accidental gaps. They rarely use systematic gaps except when deliberately borrowing or appearing to borrow a foreign word. We will return to this issue in the next chapter.

Our phonological knowledge comes into play not only when we are dealing with sound combinations, but also when we are combining elements of meaning. For example, the so-called -s plural in English has three possible phonetic forms: [s, z, ɨz], as in **cats, dogs, horses**. But we do not have to learn individually which words take which of these three forms in the plural. Rather, we have internalized the systematic variation here, and know that the plural is:

[ɨz] after sibilants (/s, z, š, ž, č, ǰ/)

[s] after other voiceless consonants (/p, t, k, f, θ/)

[z] after voiced sounds (/b, d, g, v, ð, m, n, ŋ, l, r, w, y/ and vowels)

In other words, the form of the -s plural can be partially predicted in terms of sameness of features (voicing and sibilance). Words which do not form their plurals according to this system, such as **foot/feet, phenomenon/phenomena**, do have to be learned individually, of course.

This rule for "adding s" in English does not apply only to plural formations. We know that the same rule applies to the -s possessive (cf. **the horse's** [hɔrsiz] **hoof, the cat's** [kæts] **tail**, and the **seal's** [silz] **coat**), as well as to the -s third person singular of the present tense (cf. **she kisses** [kɪsiz], **she hates** [hets], **she loves** [ləvz]). In other words, we know that there is an underlying sibilant which is the manifestation of each of the three meaningful elements—plural, possessive, and third person singular present tense—and that it has different phonetic forms according to the preceding sound. This is somewhat similar to claiming that a voiceless labial stop /p/ has different surface manifestations, aspirated and nonaspirated, according to context, except that in this case the sibilant has specific meanings attached to it.

Pitch

People vary considerably in the actual pitch (melodies or "intonations") they use. Compare, for example, the actual pitch of males with that of females—without seeing a speaker, you can usually tell from pitch alone what sex the person is and whether he or she is a child or an adult. What is significant in the linguistic system, however, is not actual pitch, but the patterns of relative steps up and down.[13]

In some languages, like Chinese, Burmese, Yoruba, and to a small extent Swedish and Norwegian, word meanings are distinguished by pitch. For example, in Mandarin Chinese the following distinctions can be made: **ma₁** "mother" (1 indicates high level pitch), **ma₂** "hemp" (2 indicates high rising pitch), **ma₃** "horse" (3 indicates low fall-rise), **ma₄** "scold" (4 indicates high falling pitch). Languages such as these that distinguish words by pitch as well as by consonants and vowels are called tone languages.

English is not a tone language, but like other languages of the world, including tone languages, it uses pitch to distinguish meanings of sentences (as opposed to words). Think of all the ways in which you can change the "tune," and thereby the meaning, of **yes**. Among the forms you think of, there will probably be:

(1) ỹes   (2) yes   (3) yes   (4) yes   (5) yes

Speech communities differ somewhat in interpreting such utterances, but many English speakers would agree that (1) is a straightforward agreement, (2) is a question, (3) implies agreement, but with reservation, (4) is annoyed, and (5) querulous. Pitch, then, in part signals the speech-act function of the utterance and also signals various emotive attitudes, such as contempt, hesitation, surprise, disgust, and so forth. The attitudinal patterns vary dialectally and may be the cause of much misunderstanding. British English

Please hand me those files

may seem preposterously arrogant to the Midwestern American who uses

Please hand me those files

but the two have the same function for the different speakers. Within any one speech community, the patterns are highly consistent and are basic cues in communication. Children learn to distinguish intonation patterns well before they master words, both in perception and production. Such patterns are far more important than one would think from our writing system, which has little more than . , ? ! and — to indicate intonation.

Although the written representation of intonation is inadequate, it nevertheless characterizes the basic system. Statements are characterized by a fall at the end of the utterance, symbolized by the period. Questions, at least those called "truth-questions" which demand a yes or no answer, are characterized by rising intonation, symbolized by a question mark. Breaks within a sentence, such as between items in a list, hesitations, suggestive pauses, and so forth, are characterized by a level intonation. In writing this is symbolized by a comma, or in the case of a pause, by a dash:

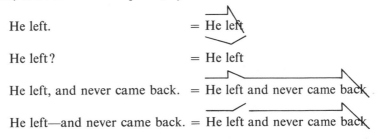

He left.   = He left

He left?   = He left

He left, and never came back. = He left and never came back

He left—and never came back. = He left and never came back

The attitudinal function of intonation is largely reflected by modulations of the beginning of the utterance, or shades of grading (relative size of the step up or down). For example:

Pick some flowers.

suggests a command. It would usually be inappropriate as an answer to "What can I do next?" In such a context:

Pick some flowers

would be expected. Compare also the accusatory:

Nobody told me

with the statement:

Nobody told me

Such distinctions cannot be made in writing except by grossly inadequate symbolization such as capitalization or italics for emphatic speech.

Stress

In some languages, including English, word meanings may be distinguished by stress, that is, by the degree of emphasis on the vowel. For example, the main phonological distinction between **ímport** (the noun) and **impórt** (the verb) is the amount of stress assigned to the first and second vowel. In other languages, stress may not be significant at the word level. For example, it might always occur on the first syllable of the base of a word, as it did in the old Germanic languages, or it might occur on the penultimate syllable of the word as it does in Swahili. That is, in some languages stress is predictable, in others it is distinctive at the level of underlying phonology.

Some very general rules apply at the word level in English that assign stress to final or nonfinal syllables.[14] There is some variation, however, because English once had word-initial stress, being a Germanic language. With the influence of French in Middle English times, the so-called "Romance stress rule" came to supersede the Germanic rule. The Romance rule assigns stress from the end back through the word according to (a) the type of vowels and consonants present in the final syllable, (b) the syntactic category of the word, and (c) the number of syllables.

Consider, for a start:

Group I	Group II
collápse	admónish
exíst	éxit
repént	ímage
revólt	cáncel
adópt	elícit
contórt	práctice

In Group I, the stress is on the final syllable; the common factor among all the forms listed is that the final syllable ends in two consonants (sounds, not letters). In Group II, the stress falls on the penultimate syllable; the common factor here is a single consonant word-finally. Now consider:

disdáin
eráse
delíght
alóne

These all have only one consonant in word-final position, yet the stress falls on the final syllable. Here the common factor is the diphthong or tense vowel of the final syllable.

This is not all, however. There are many verb-noun pairs in English in which the verb follows the rules just mentioned, while the noun does not.[15]

Verb	Noun
impórt	ímport
tormént	tórment
compóund	cómpound
subjéct	súbject
suspéct	súspect
convért	cónvert
recórd	récord

We can say that the noun is formed from the verb by moving the stress one syllable back from the end of the word.

Rules for words of more than two syllables are very complicated and cannot be gone into here. They are the result of massive phonological changes during the Early Modern English period, starting in roughly 1500, changes which affected not only vowel height but also stress. For example, there are regular correspondences of the type:

harmónious	harmónic	hármony	[harmóniəs	harmánɪk	hármɵni]
melódious	melódic	mélody	[məlódiəs	məládɪk	mɛlədi]
symphónious	symphónic	sýmphony	[sɪmfóniəs	sɪmfánɪk	símfɵni]

In all cases, variations between forms are a matter of surface realization. In the underlying dictionary entry, the skeletal phonological structure is the same for each of the three forms of the word in question. Phonological rules assign the correct stress and the correct vowels to give a phonetic surface form.

So far the stress patterns we have looked at operate on words. They do, however, also operate on phrases. For example, stress distinguishes compound nouns like **bláckbìrd** from adjective plus noun sequences like **blàck bírd** (` represents a stress intermediary between full stress and unstress). In addition, there is sentence stress, a separate stress which, in the most neutral case, falls on the last noun, adjective, or verb of the sentence or clause. This is the stress that shifts depending on what information the speaker assumes is new to the addressee. Thus in the pair

I bought the físh

I bóught the fish

the second sentence sets **bought** apart as the new information, while in the first, either **fish** is the new information or the whole sentence is new. This kind of information structuring will be discussed at length in Chapter 7.[16]

PHONOLOGY AND LITERATURE

As was mentioned earlier, the sound patterns of language constantly influence an author's choice of words, as well as influencing the sound composition of the words available to choose from. Linguists are particularly interested in the ways in which constraints on linguistic structures in a specific language affect the forms literature takes in that language. Especially clear examples can be found at the level of phonology. For instance, it seems possible that the sound patterns of a language in part determine the kind of verse most likely to be favored in the language. Old English poetry, for example, favors alliteration, whereas later Middle English and Modern English poetry does not. The following example is typical of Old English poetry, with several stressed syllables starting with the same consonant.

> Over breaking billows, with bellying sail
> And foamy beak, like a flying bird
> The ship sped on.[17]

It cannot be a coincidence that in those traditions where alliteration is preferred, the language has stress on the first syllable of the word, while in those traditions where rhyme is preferred, the language has stress either on different syllables in the word, or in a fixed position other than the first syllable.[18] Particular languages can also be seen to favor particular types of rhyme. For example, English favors "strong" rhyme, that is, rhyme ending with strong (usually fully stressed) syllables, as in **life-knife**, whereas other languages, like Swedish, favor or at least readily allow for "weak" rhymes, that is, rhymes ending on a weak (usually unstressed) syllable, as in **divisions-incantations**. Languages favoring strong rhyme appear to have many monosyllabic words like English; those favoring weak rhymes tend to have many multisyllabic words, or else words with stress near the beginning. Again these facts are surely not coincidental. A further example is provided by restrictions on rhyme and alliteration. Nearly always, consonants are required to be identical for both rhyme and alliteration (in rhyme the final consonants are in question, in alliteration the initial consonants). Vowels, however, do not need such close identity. This is exemplified by "slant rhymes" like **come-plume-room, possessed-dust-last** found in Dylan Thomas's "Love in the Asylum."

The question that has traditionally been of greatest interest to critics regarding the sound structure of a text is the reverse of the one raised in the preceding paragraph: To what extent does a particular author exploit the phonological possibilities available in the language? Neither question can really be answered without considering the other, since all creative language use involves choices among limited possibilities, in other words, both constraint and exploitation. Here we will exemplify how the knowledge of the phonological facts of English, combined with certain linguistic concepts, particularly those of underlying and surface structure, can suggest ways of thinking about aspects of the particular phenomenon of sound texture called "cohesiveness in sound." We will discuss the issue in general first, focusing on the concept of sound matching sense, and will then discuss metric and rhythmic cohesion in particular.

Phonological Cohesion

Phonology alone can be a source of cohesion in a text, as with alliteration, assonance, and rhyme, all of which involve textual patterning created by repetition of same or similar sounds. In the Joyce passage quoted earlier, for example, the cohesion created by the repetition of [f], [b], [bl], and [p] is made so excessive as to achieve a comic or parodic effect. Extreme phonological cohesion is the basis for tongue twisters like **Peter Piper picked a peck of pickled peppers.**

Rhyme, assonance, and alliteration are among the most obvious and easiest ways a poem can be made phonologically cohesive. Therefore this cohesion is often very superficial. More complex is a kind of cohesion created by interaction of phonological patterns with meaning patterns. Even though sounds in themselves have no meaning, and even though the associations between sounds and meanings in language are arbitrary and conventional, there are ways of using sounds to complement meaning. This kind of cohesion is both discussed and exemplified in the following famous passage from Pope's "Essay on Criticism" (the italics are an eighteenth-century convention for emphasis; nouns are capitalized, as in Modern German, because they were considered to be names for things, just as Alexander is the name of a person):

> True Ease in Writing comes from Art, not Chance,
> As those move easiest who have learn'd to dance.
> 'Tis not enough no Harshness gives Offence,
> The *Sound* must seem an *Eccho* to the *Sense*.

Soft is the Strain when *Zephyr* gently blows,
And the *smooth Stream* in *smoother Numbers* flows;
But when loud Surges lash the sounding Shore,
The *hoarse, rough Verse* shou'd like the *Torrent* roar.
When *Ajax* strives, some Rock's vast Weight to throw,
The Line too *labours*, and the Words move *slow*;
Not so, when swift *Camilla* scours the Plain,
Flies o'er th'unbending Corn, and skims along the Main.[19]

Pope's key dictum here is that "the sound must seem an echo to the sense." To see how his passage illustrates this principle it is useful to transliterate part of the text into the phonetic alphabet so that we can talk about classes and combinations of sounds without being distracted by the spelling.[20] Although not all word boundaries would be observed in any spoken rendition of the lines, they are retained here for convenience of reference.

1. ðə sawnd məst sim ən ɛko tu ðə sɛns.

2. sɔft ɪz ðə stren hwɛn zɛfər ǰɛntli bloz,

3. ænd ðə smuð strim ɪn smuðər nəmbərz floz;

4. bət hwɛn lawd sərǰiz læš ðə sawndɪŋ šor,

5. ðə hɔrs, rəf vərs šud layk ðə tɔrənt rɔr.

6. hwɛn eǰæks strayvz səm raks vast wet tu θro,

7. ðə layn tu lebərz, ænd ðə wərdz muv slo;

8. nat so, hwɛn swɪft kəmɪlə skawrz ðə plen,

9. flayz ɔər ðənbɛndɪŋ kɔrn, ænd skɪmz əlaŋ ðə men.

In line 2, the idea of the softness of a breeze is reinforced by the repetition of the midvowels /e, ɛ, o, ə/, the repeated fricatives /f, s, z, ǰ, ð/ (an affricate is partially fricative), and the repeated nasal /n/. Line 3 continues the fricatives and has a repeated vowel /u/ and nasal /m/ this time, echoing the idea of smoothness. In both these lines, it is important to note that the sounds suggest meaning only insofar as they are associated with the meaning of key words. In line 2, **soft** and **gently** are the cues; in line 3, the key word is **smooth**, which here allows association of **str** not so much with a gentle strain but with an everflowing, stable rhythm as heard near a stream. In lines 4 and 5, the word /lawd/ cues us in to the significance of the low vowels, especially the diphthong /aw/, intended to echo the roaring of waves. In these lines, the palatal fricatives /š/ and /ǰ/ contribute not to softness but to harshness and hoarseness, and the ordering of like fricatives in sequences such as **rough verse should** makes the line difficult to pronounce smoothly. Here, as elsewhere, it is not only the sound but also the syntax which is matching sense. Adjectives preceding nouns normally carry stress somewhat lighter than main stress, but considerably heavier than prepositions or articles. In line 2, **soft** and **strain** are carefully separated by two unstressed syllables, and all the other stressed syllables are likewise separated by an unstressed one. From line 3 on, by contrast, we find increasing use of adjective-noun constructions like **loud surges, hoarse rough verse**, in which no unstressed syllables intervene between stressed ones. The result is that the monosyllabic adjectives with following pause actually acquire increased stress, so that the smoothness of alternating stressed and unstressed syllables is replaced by a harsher, pounding rhythm. By the time we get to line 6, we have **some rock's vast weight**, a sequence of determiner, noun, adjective, noun, in which every syllable has some stress. (**Some**, meaning "certain" as opposed to "not many," always carries a certain amount of stress. Compare relatively stressed **Sòme bóy came by selling the Tribune** with unstressed **Some bóys came by this afternoon**.) In fact, the only unstressed syllables in line 6 are **when** and **to**. In addition, in line 6 as in line 5, virtually no smoothness of flow is possible—/ejæks strayvz səm raks vast wet/ requires separate articulation at the beginning of each word, since, in the case of /ejæks strayvz/, the consonant is repeated, and in the others the voicing is changed. Contrast the consistent voicing in line 2 of /ɪz ðə . . . hwɛn zɛfər ɟɛntli/ or the juxtaposition of consonants and vowels as in /sɔft ɪz . . . ɟɛntli blɔz/.

To continue would be repetitive. The point to keep in mind in dealing with this kind of cohesion is that the sound alone will not usually create the meaning. A key word gives the semantic cue which triggers the sound-symbolism associations, and the syntax contributes further to the total effect. This is what Pope presumably meant when he said the sound must "seem an echo" to the sense. Its role is that of supporter, not creator, of meaning. As Pope's use of the verb **seem** acknowledges, sound-symbolism of this kind is based on somewhat vague and subjective impressions rather than on any systematic feature of the language.

Pope's example was consciously exaggerated since it was intended to illustrate a theoretical claim. However, it is by no means atypical. A more modern example is provided by Carl Sandburg's "The Harbor":

> Passing through huddled and ugly walls
> By doorways where women
> Looked from their hunger-deep eyes,
> Haunted with shadows of hunger-hands,
> Out from the huddled and ugly walls,
> I came sudden, at the city's edge,
> On a blue burst of lake,
> Long lake waves breaking under the sun
> On a spray-flung curve of shore;
> And a fluttering storm of gulls,
> Masses of great gray wings
> And flying white bellies
> Veering and wheeling free in the open.[21]

Transliterated, this is:

1. pæsıŋ θru hədəld ænd əgli wɔlz,

2. bay dɔrwez hwɛr wɪmən

3. lʊkt frəm ðɛr həŋgərdip əyz,

4. hɔntəd wıθ šædoz əv həŋgərhændz,

5. awt frəm ðə hədəld ænd əgli wɔlz,

6. ay kem sədən, æt ðə sıtiz ɛǰ,

7. an ə blu bərst əv lek,

8. lɔŋ lek wevz brekıŋ əndər ðə sən,

9. an ə sprefləŋ kərv əv šɔr;

10. ænd ə flətərıŋ stɔrm əv gəlz,

11. mæsəz əv gret gre wıŋz

12. ænd flayıŋ hwayt bɛliz

13. virıŋ ænd hwilıŋ fri ın ði opən.

Crudely, the poem concerns the contrast between the constraints of the man-made city (lines 1–5) and the freedom of nature (lines 6–13). This contrast is expressed at all levels of the poem. We may note how the poverty and confinement of the town are reflected by the repetition of the phrase **huddled and ugly walls**, and by the use of the invented compounds **hunger-deep** and **hunger-hands**, in which parts of the body are bound to hunger by an artificial hyphen. Syntactically, too, we may note that the whole description of the city is subordinate to the main clause **I came sudden**, and is located before the main clause, as a preliminary to the main action. The poet passes **through, by,** and **out,** but **and** is noticeably absent; everything in the city is tied spatially to everything else, giving a sense of compression and organization. By contrast, in the second part, few words are repeated, and the different elements of the open are coordinated to each other in a kind of loose, cumulative structure. Phonologically, /hədəld/ is the key word of lines 1–5, with /h/, /ə/, and /d/ repeated in various combinations in each of the lines. Of these three sounds, /ə/ predominates, since it carries the main stress in the central words **huddled, ugly, hunger.** /ə/ recurs in the second part of the poem, in **sudden, sun, flung, fluttering,** but its combination with a different semantic set and a different set of consonants (/fl, s/ not /h, d/) gives it a totally different function in the second part of the poem.

Among other things to notice in the second part of the poem are the sets of alliterating consonants which overlap wave-like from line to line: /s/ in line 6, echoed in 7–10, /b/ in line 7, echoed in 8, /l/ in line 8, already present in 6 and echoed right to the end. There is also an increased use of front vowels, most noticeably in lines 11–13. Indeed, the description of the lake (lines 7–9), with its alliteration and /ə/ vowel, appears to form a world itself relatively distinct from the world of the gulls (lines 10–13). The description of the gulls includes only one alliterative line (11), but makes extensive use of assonance (/flətərɪŋ gəlz/ (10), /gret gre/ (11), /flayɪŋ hwayt/ (12), /virɪŋ, hwilɪŋ fri/ (13)) and suggests a structure as follows:

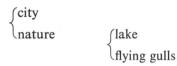

where the lake, though sharply contrasted with the city, is more constrained than the sky.

The function of the sounds, then, is very subtle. /ə/ in lines 1–5 contrasts by its semantic and phonological associations with /ə/ in lines 6–10; this suggests that sound is by itself totally independent of meaning. Yet the association of /ə/ with constraint is not lost entirely in lines 6–10; rather, along with other devices like alliteration, it helps one to see lines 6–10 as partly transitional. And understandably so—a lake is after all an enclosed piece of water, bound by the city's edge.

It is interesting to note that the kind of sound-sense matching we find in the Pope text and in "The Harbor" is especially typical of poems celebrating nature or the harmony of the natural world. One can think of sound-symbolism as a device to make the relation between sound and sense in language itself appear natural rather than purely conventional.

Meter

So far we have ignored the discussion of meter, that is, patterning of stressed and unstressed syllables in a poetic line. The subject is vast and can only be touched on here. The emphasis will be on how the phonological analysis of English proposed above may contribute to an understanding of metrical problems, and especially on the way in which meter can contribute to cohesion and to the axiom that "sound must seem an echo to the sense."

Meter is essentially a conventionalized type of stress pattern. Stress is a perceptual phenomenon, internalized by the child with the linguistic system. Meter, on the other hand, is an abstract construct imposed on language; it is learned separate from stress. Everybody agrees that stress and meter are not the same, but are nevertheless somehow related. There is, however, considerable disagreement about the exact nature of the relationship. One of the most obvious differences between stress and meter is that meter is based on a binary stressed-unstressed contrast marked ′ ˘ (strong, weak), while English has at least three noticeable degrees of stress, and many other fine shades of differences. Furthermore, in English the strong-weak metrical combinations are highly controlled in number and sequence, and recur in "feet," whereas there are no such rigid controls in the language itself.

The most common metrical types in English are:

Iamb: ᵁ/   The Sound | must seem | an Ec|cho to | the Sense

Trochee: /ᵁ   And be|fore the | Summer | ended

Stood the | maize in | all its | beauty²²

Anapest: ᵁᵁ/ Not a sound | hath escaped | to thy ser|vants,

of prayer | nor of praise²³

Dactyl: /ᵁᵁ   Lulled by the | coil of his | crystalline | streams.²⁴

The differences between stress and meter have led to the view that meter is a phenomenon which exists independently of other phonological, grammatical, and lexical phenomena within a language, and that the relationship between meter and stress is essentially one of tension.²⁵ Meter is viewed as being imposed on the language, independent of anything else. But there are obvious points of contact between meter and stress, beginning with the simple fact that metric stress and normal word stress do coincide a good deal of the time, as the examples just quoted indicate. This points to some deeper similarities in the way stress systems and metric systems are set up. In normal spoken English, there is a constant alternation of syllables with different degrees of stress, simply because of the way word stress works (one main stress per word, some words always unstressed, no consecutive stressed syllables within a word, and so on). In fact, word stress in language normally tends to occur at roughly equal intervals. Moreover, word stresses participate in larger patterns of sentence stress, the way feet participate in the larger pattern of the verse line. In fact, verse lines commonly form syntactic units ending with a normal pause (comma or sentence break), and thus tend to conform to the intonation system of normal speech. One of the most important indications that stress and meter are related is the fact that languages with certain kinds of stress patterns seem more suitable for certain kinds of meter. English, German, Modern Greek, and Russian all favor iambs, and all have largely noninitial stress. Swedish favors dactyls, and has primarily initial stress. All these considerations have led to the suggestion that there is a basic parallelism between stress and meter, and that meter actually imitates the stress and intonational structure of the language.²⁶

Parallel or not, there is a basic difference between stress systems and metric systems in that meter constrains the language more than the language constrains meter. In a line like:

The hŏarse, | rŏugh vérse, | shŏuld líke | thĕ tŏr|rĕnt róar

the meter requires stress on *like* and nonstress on *rough*, while normal speech would probably place middle stress on *like* and *rough*. But the meter is not compatible with just any sentence. We could not accept a verse line like:

Thĕ róugh | vĕrse shóuld | rŏar líke | thĕ bíg | tŏrrént.

Just as we find it useful to contrast an underlying word like **melody** with its different surface forms in **melodic, melodious, melody**, so it can be useful to contrast an underlying meter with its different surface manifestations. A variety of linguists have indeed hypothesized that there exist underlying verse patterns, such as iambic pentameter, that can be distinguished from a given "verse instance."[27]

According to one such generative theory of metrics, originally proposed by Morris Halle and Samuel Jay Keyser,[28] a given meter can be described as a system of potentials for stress, somewhat like a musical beat that may undergo various modifications in particular contexts. For example, for iambic pentameter, the basic metrical line in English poetry, Halle and Keyser propose an underlying structure consisting of ten positions, the odd positions (1, 3, 5, 7, 9) being weak and the even positions being strong. Also, according to this view, iambic pentameter has at least three "stress maxima," that is, strong beats with weak ones on either side—there can be no stress maximum in the last position since there is no following weak one. Given this view, **The Sound must seem an Eccho to the Sense** is, in underlying metrical structure:

Thĕ Sóund mŭst séem ăn Éccho tŏ thĕ Sénse

   W   S   W   S W   S W S W   S

This particular verse illustrates the basic iambic pentameter line, in which the underlying and the surface structures are metrically the same. However, surface structure modifications can occur, indeed must occur if monotony is not to result. These modifications are conventional and can change over time. Among typical modifications are the following:

a. In an individual line the first two positions may be reversed, resulting in a strong-weak beginning:

Sóft ĭs thĕ Stráin whĕn Zéphyr gĕntlý blóws.

   S   W   W   S   W   S   W   S W   S

b. Two syllables may be "run together" to fill one position in a process called "elision." In Middle English, elision involving the deletion of a consonant could only occur if the vowels of the two syllables in question were separated by a nasal or a liquid, as in:

to Caunterbury they wende "to Canterbury they go"[29]

w   s   w   s   w   s   w

In the sixteenth century this set of conditions was extended to allow elision of syllables with intervening voiced fricatives, as in **over (o'er), ever (e'er), prison,** and so forth.[30]

c. Stress maxima may be neutralized by a process called "stress neutralization." A weak position may be realized by a stronger stress than normal; this is usually effected by using a medium stressed syllable in this position, for example, an adjective preceding a noun as in **blàck bírd** (**black** has far more stress than, for example, **the** or **a,** and thus obliterates or neutralizes the basic strong-weak contrast).

We may now return to Pope's passage on sound matching sense, to show more precisely what is slowing down lines 2–6. We have already mentioned the consonant clusters as a factor. Even more important is the stress neutralization resulting from the syntactic choice of adjective-noun and other sequences. Using the rules a–c for iambic pentameter verse outlined above, the passage may be interpreted metrically as follows (⌢signals stress neutralization):[31]

The Sound must seem an Eccho to the Sense.

w s   w s   w s   w s w   s

a. Soft is the Strain when Zephyr gently blows,

s w w   s   w   s w s w s

a. And the smooth Stream in smoother Numbers flows;

s w   w s   w s   w s   w   s

c. But when loud Surges lash the sounding Shore,

w   s w   s w s   w s   w   s

c. The hoarse, rough Verse shou'd like the Torrent roar.

w   s   w   s   w   s   w s   w   s

c. When Ájax strives, some Rock's vast Weight to throw

    w s w   s   w   s   w   s   w   s

c. The Line too labours and the Words move slow;

    w s w s w   s   w   s   w   s

Not so, when swift Camilla scours the Plain,

    w s   w   s   w s w s   w   s

a, b, c. Flies o'er th'unbending Corn, and skims along the Main.

    s   w   w s   w   s   w   s   w s   w   s

Particularly striking in this and other verse where stress neutralization occurs, is the coincidence of the neutralization with the key word that cues semantic-phonological cohesion (**smooth**, **loud**, and so forth).[32]

Rhythm and Meter

Meter inevitably produces rhythm in a text, but a text does not have to be metrical in order to be rhythmic. Free verse and prose are discourse types which by definition do not make use of any fixed metrical scheme; but in both, rhythm is often a source of cohesion and of sound-sense connections. One of the most rhythmic prose writers in English is Virginia Woolf, from whose novel *Mrs. Dalloway* the following passage is taken:

> What a lark! What a plunge! For so it had always seemed to her, when, with a little squeak of the hinges, which she could hear now, she had burst open the French windows and plunged at Bourton into the open air. How fresh, how calm, stiller than this of course, the air was in the early morning; like the flap of a wave; the kiss of a wave; chill and sharp and yet (for a girl of eighteen as she then was) solemn, feeling as she did, standing there at the open window, that something awful was about to happen. . . .[33]

In the absence of any verse line, we often find that rhythm in prose is organized according to syntactic phrase groupings, identified in speech by pauses and in writing usually by punctuation marks. Indeed, the syntactic phrase can be considered the basic unit of analysis for prose rhythm. In the following rendering of the Woolf passage, the syntactic phrases are numbered, sentence pauses are marked by a double bar, sentence-internal phrases by a single bar.

As in our verse analyses, unstressed syllables are marked with ᵕ, syllables with middle or heavy stress with ´:

> What a lark!‖ What a plunge!‖ For so it had always seemed to her,|
>   1   2   3
>
> when,| with a little squeak of the hinges,| which she could hear now,| she had
> 4   5   6
>
> burst open the French windows| and plunged at Bourton into the open air.‖
> 7   8
>
> How fresh,| how calm,| stiller than this of course,| the air was in the early
> 9   10   11   12
>
> morning;‖ like the flap of a wave,| the kiss of a wave,| chill and sharp and
>   13   14   15
>
> yet| (for a girl of eighteen as she then was)| solemn,| feeling as she did,|
>   16   17   18
>
> standing there at the open window,| that something awful was about to
>   19   20
>
> happen. . . .

Much of the rhythm in this passage comes from the repetition of similar stress patterns either within a phrase or between consecutive phrases. The pattern of repetition is introduced in the first two sentences, each consisting of a single phrase identical in syntax, syllable structure, and stress. The fourth and fifth sentences each likewise begin with paired parallel phrases (**how fresh, how calm,** and **like the flap of a wave, the kiss of a wave**), in which likeness of stress pattern accompanies virtually identical syntactic and syllabic structure. Most of the other phrases in the text also show interior stress patterning based on pairing. Phrase 3 is highly symmetrical, consisting of two occurrences of ᵕ/ᵕᵕ separated by the stressed syllable of **always**. This stress structure would encourage a reader to give the first syllable of **always** heaviest stress in this phrase. Phrase 5 is a mirror image of 3: two occurrences of ᵕᵕ/ᵕ separated by **squeak**, which carries heaviest stress in this phrase. At another level, phrases 3, 4, and 5 taken together likewise exhibit a tripartite structure of two parallel groups separated by a one-syllable peak:

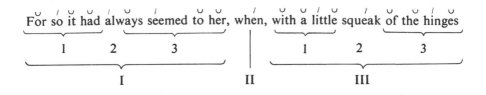

Notice that the heavy stress on **when** is the consequence of the unusual syntax, involving a prepositional phrase placed at the beginning of the **when**-clause.

With normal word order, **when** would have little stress as in **so it seemed to her when she had burst** . . . .

Phrase 7 consists of alternating pairs of unstressed and stressed syllables; phrase 8 has an equally regular alternation of single unstressed and stressed syllables, that is, iambic feet. No one familiar with English verse can miss the iambic rhythm in phrase 8, or the fact that the phrase is a line of perfect iambic pentameter, with routine elision of unstressed **the** with stressed **ópen**. Like phrase 8, phrase 20 is also a line with iambic meter. Just as phrases 3–5 form a tripartite structure in which phrase 5 is a mirror image of phrase 3, so phrases 19–20 form a tripartite structure, this time with an unstressed syllable separating the equivalent groups (**was** elides with **about**):

standing there at the open window, that something awful was about to happen

1	2	3		1	2	3
	I		II		III	

Comparison of phrases 3–5 with phrases 19–20 shows that the first tripartite structure not only contains mirror images within itself, but also that the two sets of phrases are themselves partial mirror images of each other: Phrases 3 and 5 start on a weak syllable, 19 and 20 on a strong one; the links between the two rhythmic groups are strong in 3–5 (**always, when, squeak**), but weak in 19–20 (**the, that, was**).

Those who have read *Mrs. Dalloway* will recognize the relation between these alternating rhythmic patterns and one of the novel's main themes: life as an alternation between a joyous "lark" and a "plunge" into despair. The search in the novel for a point of equilibrium between the two is echoed perfectly in the tripartite rhythmic pattern which recurs here, in which a single syllable appears as a point of balance between two equal groups.

SUGGESTED FURTHER READINGS

For detailed studies of writing and the history of writing, the most useful books are Diringer, *Writing*, and Gelb, *A Study of Writing; the Foundations of Grammatology*. Among excellent introductory books on phonetics are: Denes and Pinson, *The Speech Chain; the Physics and Biology of Spoken Language*, and Ladefoged, *A Course in Phonetics*; on phonology: Hyman, *Phonology: Theory and Practice*, and Sloat, Taylor, and Hoard, *Introduction to Phonology*. Gimson's *An Introduction to the Pronunciation of English* provides an invaluable account of British pronunciation in different dialects, along with historical comments and extensive examples of the various kinds of spelling used for different sounds. There is nothing comparable in breadth and depth for American pronunciation, but Kenyon's *American Pronunciation* provides sound background materials for a limited number of dialects.

While no important journals are devoted exclusively to phonology, there are several on phonetics, the most important among them for the beginning student being *Journal of Phonetics* and *Journal of the International Phonetic Association*.

Studies of metrics should begin with the sections on meter in Chatman and Levin, eds., *Essays in the Language of Literature*, and especially in Freeman, ed., *Linguistics and Literary Style*. A detailed application of the Halle-Keyser theory of metrics to Hopkins's famous poem, "The Windhover," can be found in Scott, "Toward a Formal Poetics: Metrical Patterning in 'The Windhover.'" A modification of the generative metrics outlined here is being developed by Paul Kiparsky in a series of articles in the journals *Language* and *Linguistic Inquiry* (see, for example, Kiparsky, "The Rhythmic Structure of English Verse"); but these presuppose fairly extensive knowledge of linguistics, and make advanced reading. A key introductory article on rhyme and alliteration is Kiparsky's "The Role of Linguistics in a Theory of Poetry." Nager's "A Selective Annotated Bibliography of Recent Work in English Prosody" provides a useful survey of linguistic and literary studies of metrics and prose rhythm, and includes some references to rhyme and assonance.

Exercises

1. Transcribe the following in the phonetic alphabet (this is a warming-up exercise):

peace	point	pit	pet	pour
pace	pert	pint	peat	poor
pose	port	put	paint	pause
pot	pout	putt	past	pear
poop	price	part	pant	peer

2. Transcribe the following in the phonetic alphabet.

psychic	quick	fear	conquer
devastate	thunder	philosophy	anxious
salmon	lose	mnemonic	butcher
thanks	loose	acre	although

pigeon	newt	bathe	grudge
bath	measure	rhythm	handplough
think	incongruous	depth	pumpkin

3. Phonetically, there are three l sounds in some varieties of English: a clear [l], with relatively front resonance, dark [ɫ] with relatively back resonance, and voiceless [l̥]. These are in complementary distribution. Using the following data, write a rule showing precisely in which contexts the phoneme /l/ is realized as [l, l̥, ɫ]. To simplify this exercise, all sounds other than the l's are written phonemically. (An asterisk indicates that the form is ungrammatical, i.e., does not occur.)

lɛt	glin	daɫ	pl̥aw	*gl̥in	*hɛlp
liv	gled	puɫ	kl̥in	*gl̥in	*hɛl̥p
læk	blak	pərɫ	kl̥aym	*pɫe	
lʊk	blənt	hɛɫp	sl̥ɪp	*ple	
let	fɪɫ	mɪɫk	*ɫɛt	*fil	
lawd	fuɫ	əɫðo	*l̥ɛt	*fil̥	

4. In rapid speech [y] after [t, d] often combines with the preceding consonant and palatalizes it. The result is an affricate. This phenomenon is particularly common if the [y] is the first sound of the pronoun **you**, but is not restricted to such environments. The question [hwerzðəstyudənčunyən] "Where's the Student Union?" was asked of one of the authors.

    a. Write in the phonetic alphabet the slow and fast speech varieties of:

        Did you hear about Jill's nomination?

        Could you do me a favor?

        I want you to go.

    b. Two other consonants often combine with an underlying [y] and are replaced by their palatal neighbors in the articulatory scheme in rapid speech. Which consonants are they? Give examples.

    c. Give as formal a rule as you can to account for the palatalization illustrated in a and b.

5. On pages 62–63 we outlined constraints on two-consonant clusters occurring word-initially. What consonants can occur initially in three-consonant clusters? What systematic relationship does this three-consonant set show to the two-consonant set?

6. In the section on sound sequences, it was pointed out that the forms of the -s plural, possessive, and third person singular are predictable. The -ed forms of the past tense are also predictable, as for example in:

    walked   lugged   started

finished   huddled   excited

worried   preserved faded

gnawed   booed   complicated

    a.   Transcribe these data in the broad phonetic alphabet.
    b.   List the different forms of the past tense in these data.
    c.   Describe the phonological environments for the different past tense forms.
    d.   What other inflection has the same three **-ed** variants? Give examples.

7. Mark the intonation patterns you would expect in each of the following utterance sequences. (Q = question, A = answer: Where Q and A are involved, two speakers, questioner and answerer, should be assumed.)

    a.   Let me give you a piece of advice. Get a haircut.
    b.   Q. What do I have to do to look respectable? A. Get a haircut.
    c.   (Speaker comes into the room and puts a package on the table.) I'm putting this down here. Please leave it alone.
    d.   Q. Did you remember to get the coffee? A. I'm sorry, I forgot.

8. Many varieties of children's secret languages, such as Pig Latin, can be characterized by one or two phonological rules which convert a conventional underlying structure into a deviant surface one. Select a secret language familiar to you, give some examples, and write a phonological rule (or rules if necessary) that will derive these examples, and others not listed in your sample, from ordinary English.

9. A lot of fun can be derived from writing a language in a way that makes it look like a different one. In this poem by Jonathan Swift, English is made to look like Latin:

TO SAMUEL BINDON, ESQ.

> MOLLIS abuti
> Has an accuti
> No lasso finis
> Molli divinis
> Omi de armis tres
> Imi na dis tres
> Cantu disco ver
> Meas alo ver.[34]

    a.   Transcribe the poem in English orthography (you'll have to redivide the words in some cases).
    b.   What added meaning(s) does Swift's written version have that yours does not?

10. Writing and speech typically occur in different contexts. Sometimes the same event cannot be described the same way in spoken and written language.

Discuss the ways in which the sentence **Velma was here** illustrates the potential difference between speech and writing (consider the use of **Velma** rather than **I**, the use of **was** rather than **is**, **here** as opposed to **at the west door of Grace Cathedral**, and any other points of interest to you).

11. Using the concepts developed in the section on sound matching sense, comment on the following discussion of Milton's use of **s**.

> . . . all our poets love their consonants; even **s** is not despised of (= by) any of the great ones save Tennyson; it reminds Milton neither of geese nor of serpents. Not even when the final **s** meets the initial **s** does he squirm:

> > His goary visage down the stream was sent,
> > Down the swift Hebrus to the Lesbian shore.

> Thus does water whisper among the reeds as it slips towards the roaring gulf of sea-sounding "shore."[35]

12. The following is an excerpt from a poem by Robert Bridges entitled "November." These are the final lines of the poem, which describe the countryside on a late fall afternoon (we will be examining the poem in its entirety in the next chapter):

> And here and there, near chilly setting of sun,
> In an isolated tree a congregation
> 30 Of starlings chatter and chide,
> Thickset as summer leaves, in garrulous quarrel:
> Suddenly they hush as one,—
> The tree top springs,—
> And off, with a whirr of wings,
> They fly by the score
> To the holly-thicket, and there with myriads more
> Dispute for the roosts; and from the unseen nation
> A babel of tongues, like running water unceasing,
> Makes live the wood, the flocking cries increasing,
> 40 Wrangling discordantly, incessantly,
> While falls the night on them self-occupied;
> The long dark night, that lengthens slow,
> Deepening with Winter to starve grass and tree,
> And soon to bury in snow
> The Earth, that, sleeping 'neath her frozen stole,
> Shall dream a dream crept from the sunless pole
> Of how her end shall be.[36]

a. Transcribe the text in the phonetic alphabet.
b. State the major theme of the excerpt.
c. Show how the sound patterns contribute to the theme and the meaning. Include general comments on meter and rhyme.

13. Reconsider Peter Davison's poem "July" (Chapter 1, Exercise 7) in the light of what you have learned in this chapter. Are any new patterns now apparent to you? Or can you be more precise about those you noticed before? The first and last lines of the poem are in iambic pentameter. In what way do the deviations from this pattern foreground aspects of meaning in the rest of the poem? Consider line length as well as distribution of stressed and unstressed syllables.

14. The following is a poem by X. J. Kennedy:

A WATER GLASS OF WHISKY

Through the hill by the Rite Nite Motel
Not a picture unbroken can reach:
An old famous head in the screen
Facelifted, falls halt in its speech

As if no line cast from the set
Could fix with a definite hook
Into any live lip going by.
There is no good book but the Good Book.

No use. Try the window instead
But the near-beer bar's sign is no more.
As far as the breeze stretches off
Only outer space answers your stare.

You don't die for want of TV
But even so, here lies a lack
As though more than night or a hill
Had walled you in, back of its back.[37]

    a. Comment on the use of rhyme, alliteration, and assonance in this poem. How are they used to stress the sense of superficiality and lack of meaning the poet is trying to convey here? (Note especially the role of rhyming pairs of monosyllables and their effect on meter.)

    b. Comment more carefully on meter in the first two stanzas. How does it contribute to the meaning? How and where does it work against our expectations?

NOTES

[1] A. A. Milne, *The World of Pooh* (New York: Dutton and Co., Inc., 1957), p. 48.

[2] John Updike, *Marry Me; A Romance* (New York: Alfred A. Knopf, 1976), p. 4.

[3] Updike, pp. 4–5.

[4] William Gaddis, *J.R.* (New York: Alfred A. Knopf, 1975), p. 3.

[5] James Joyce, *Finnegans Wake* (New York: Viking Press, 1958), p. 167.

⁶ Emmet Williams, untitled poem, in *Concrete Poetry; an International Anthology*, ed. Stephen Bann (London: London Magazine Editions, 1967), p. 181.

⁷ *Principles of the International Phonetic Association; Being a Description of the International Phonetic Alphabet and the Manner of Using It, Illustrated by Texts in 51 Languages* (London, 1949).

⁸ Some speakers may have a sound here more like **d** than **t**. However, a distinction is usually still made between **latter** and **ladder** and similar pairs of words.

⁹ In some grammars, the stressed vowel in **sun**, etc., is symbolized as [ʌ], while [ə] is reserved for the unstressed vowel in **Rosa**, etc. Since the distinction is predictable in terms of stress, we will ignore it here.

¹⁰ Reproduced from Herbert H. Clark and Eve V. Clark, *Psychology and Language: An Introduction to Psycholinguistics* (New York: Harcourt Brace Jovanovich, Inc., 1977), p. 181.

¹¹ For a more detailed definition of "phoneme" and discussion of alternate definitions, see Larry M. Hyman, *Phonology: Theory and Analysis* (New York: Holt, Rinehart and Winston, Inc., 1975), Chapter III.

¹² The following discussion of word-initial consonant sequences is based on Archibald A. Hill, *Introduction to Linguistic Structures; from Sound to Sentence in English* (New York: Harcourt Brace Jovanovich, Inc., 1958), pp. 70–77.

¹³ A good account of the nature and function of pitch can be found in Dwight Bolinger, *Aspects of Language*, 2nd ed. (New York: Harcourt Brace Jovanovich, Inc., 1975), pp. 46–52. For a longer discussion, see Dwight Bolinger, "Around the Edge of Language: Intonation," *Harvard Educational Review*, 34 (1964), 121–93.

¹⁴ Noam Chomsky and Morris Halle, *The Sound Pattern of English* (New York: Harper and Row, 1968).

¹⁵ Fred W. Householder, *Linguistic Speculations* (London and New York: Cambridge Univ. Press, 1971), p. 268. Householder lists 135 entries of verb/noun alternates of this type. Half of them are explicable in terms of rules different from those discussed here, and a few are very unusual words. But a large number of pairs remain that can be accounted for like impórt/ímport.

¹⁶ While a detailed study of stress and pitch and their relations to rhythm, especially to phenomena such as caesura and run-on lines, is of great interest, especially for the interpretation of poetry, it is so subject to dialect variation, and so relatively problematic for analysis, that the topic is only mentioned here.

¹⁷ From Charles W. Kennedy, *Beowulf: The Oldest English Epic* (London and New York: Oxford Univ. Press, Inc., 1940), p. 10. This translation captures both the alliteration and the meter of Old English poetry.

¹⁸ See p. 66 on the shift from initial stress in Old English to noninitial stress in Middle English.

¹⁹ Alexander Pope, "Essay on Criticism," in *Alexander Pope: Pastoral Poetry and An Essay on Criticism*, eds. E. Audra and Aubrey Williams (New Haven: Yale Univ. Press, 1961), pp. 281–83, lines 362–73.

²⁰ Pope's pronunciation was not exactly the same as that of any modern dialect. It is doubtful that he pronounced **r** following a vowel, as in **hoarse**. The modernized, Americanized transcription does not, however, change the significant sound-meaning matches in this passage, although some differences of importance occur elsewhere, as evidenced by rhymes like **tea-obey** and **oil-isle**.

²¹ Carl Sandburg, "The Harbor," in *The Complete Poems of Carl Sandburg* (New York: Harcourt Brace Jovanovich, Inc., 1970), p. 5.

²² Henry Wadsworth Longfellow, "The Song of Hiawatha," in *The Complete Poetical Works*, Cambridge Edition (Boston and New York: Houghton Mifflin Co., 1893), p. 125.

[23] Robert Browning, "Saul," in *The Poetical Works of Robert Browning*, Cambridge Edition, G. Robert Stange, Introd. (Boston: Houghton Mifflin Co., 1974), p. 179.

[24] Percy Bysshe Shelley, "Ode to the West Wind," in *The Complete Poetical Works of Percy Bysshe Shelley* (London: Oxford Univ. Press, Inc. 1934), p. 578.

[25] For example, Seymour Chatman, *A Theory of Meter* (The Hague: Mouton, 1965).

[26] See, for example, Roger Fowler, "'Prose Rhythm' and Meter," in *Essays on Style and Language: Linguistic and Critical Approaches to Literary Style*, ed. Roger Fowler (London: Routledge and Kegan Paul, Ltd., 1966).

[27] See, for example, papers on metrics by Kiparsky, Halle and Keyser, and Freeman in Donald C. Freeman, ed., *Linguistics and Literary Style* (New York: Holt, Rinehart and Winston, Inc., 1970).

[28] The theory is best expounded in Morris Halle, "On Meter and Prosody," in *Progress in Linguistics*, eds. Manfred Bierwisch and Karl Erich Heidolph (The Hague: Mouton, 1970).

[29] Geoffrey Chaucer, *Canterbury Tales*, in *The Works of Geoffrey Chaucer*, ed. F. N. Robinson (Boston: Houghton Mifflin Co., 1957), Prologue, line 16.

[30] Morris Halle and Samuel Jay Keyser, "Chaucer and the Study of Prosody," *College English*, 28 (1966), 187–219, rept. in *Linguistics and Literary Style*, ed. Donald C. Freeman, 1970; and Donald C. Freeman, "On the Primes of Metrical Style," *Language and Style*, 1 (1968), 63–101; rept. in *Linguistics and Literary Style*, ed. Donald C. Freeman, 1970.

[31] Based on Freeman, "On the Primes of Metrical Style."

[32] The generative metric approach just outlined does not make use of the term "foot," and speaks instead of "positions." Several linguists since the 1930s have argued that the traditional "foot" is neither linguistically nor poetically significant. See, for example, Otto Jespersen, "Notes on Metre," in *Linguistics* (Copenhagen: Levin and Munksgaard, 1933); rept. in *Essays on the Language of Literature*, eds. Seymour Chatman and Samuel R. Levin (Boston: Houghton Mifflin Co., 1967). For a defense of the foot see Chatman, *Theory of Meter*, p. 1; rept. in *Linguistics and Literary Style*, ed. Donald C. Freeman, 1970, pp. 320–24.

[33] From Virginia Woolf, *Mrs. Dalloway* (New York: Harcourt Brace Jovanovich, Inc., 1925), p. 3.

[34] From Joseph Horvell, ed., *Poems of Jonathan Swift*, vol. I (London: Routledge and Kegan Paul, Ltd., 1958), p. 335.

[35] Katharine Margaret Wilson, *Sound and Meaning in English Poetry* (London and Toronto: Jonathan Cape, 1930), p. 248.

[36] Robert Bridges, "November," in *Poetical Works of Robert Bridges, with The Testament of Beauty but Excluding the Eight Dramas* (London and New York: Oxford Univ. Press, Inc., 1953), pp. 344–45.

[37] X. J. Kennedy, "A Water Glass of Whisky," in *A Controversy of Poets*, eds. Paris Leary and Robert Kelly (New York: Doubleday, 1965), p. 193.

CHAPTER 3

Morphemes and Words: Introduction to the Lexicon

In Chapter 2 we saw that every language has a phonological system of phonemes and rules about how those phonemes combine in sequence. We also saw that the sounds in a language rarely have any immediate correlation with meaning, and certainly no systematic or predictable one. For instance, observing that the English words **this, that, then,** and **there** all contain the sound /ð/, a person learning English might think that the sound /ð/ in English represented some notion of pointing to time or space. But this would be plainly wrong, since /ð/ has no such association in words like **though, than, bathe,** or **either**. If sound and meaning were directly correlated in language, you would be able to determine the meaning of a word just from hearing it, and poets would not have to work to make the sound seem an echo of the sense—they would have to work to avoid it.

How is it, then, that strings of sounds have meaning? In language, sound and meaning are associated by virtue of a large and complex set of relations internal to the linguistic system. In English, the string of phonemes /pɪg/ is conventionally (and arbitrarily) employed to refer to a certain type of domestic animal. For the string /θem/ "thame," on the other hand, the system specifies no such relation, which is just a more technical way of saying that **thame** has no meaning in English. However, since **thame** is perfectly possible phonologically in English, it could be assigned a meaning tomorrow and thus become part of the system.

Words represent only one level of the complex bridge between sound and meaning in language. As we shall see in a moment, words are not the smallest building blocks in this bridge, nor are they the largest. Words are combined in structured sequences to make meaningful phrases and sentences. Chapter 4 will be devoted to the levels of phrase and sentence structure. In this chapter we will be discussing sound-meaning relations below the level of the phrase and sentence, and we will be introducing you to the part of the grammar in which most of these sound-meaning relations are specified: the "dictionary" of the grammar, usually called the "lexicon" (from Greek **lexis** "word," **lexikon** "inventory of words").

We can get some valuable clues to the way the bridge between sound and meaning works by looking at texts where it has been interrupted. One famous example is Lewis Carroll's parody, "A Stanza of Anglo-Saxon Poetry," later to become the first stanza of his poem "Jabberwocky." Here, real English words are used alongside sound sequences which, like **thame**, are phonologically possible in English but have no meaning associated with them in the system:

> Twas bryllyg, and the slythy toves
> Did gyre and gymble in the wabe:
> All mimsy were the borogoves;
> And the mome raths outgrabe.[1]

Despite the fact that half the "words" in the text have no conventionally associated meaning in English, any speaker of English readily interprets the text as a description of an outdoor scene with creatures of various sorts frolicking or moving about. To see how we understand even this much, we can begin by taking out all the nonsense words:[2]

> Twas —— and the —— ——
> Did —— and —— in the ——
> All —— were the ——
> And the —— —— ——

All the familiar words in the text are words whose primary function in English is to show how other words and sentence parts relate to each other. These are called "grammatical" or "function words." In any language, they comprise a small and relatively stable class. Languages rarely invent new grammatical words or borrow them from another language. Other examples of English grammatical words are **which, but, so, of, some.** The unfamiliar words in the stanza, on the other hand, belong to the class of so-called "content" words. These are words whose primary function is to name objects, concepts, qualities, processes, events, and actions in the world. This set is very large and is continually being enlarged by borrowing or invention. Much of the meaningfulness of Carroll's stanza, then, derives from the fact that real grammatical words are used, and used in the right places (**in the**, not ***the in, **were the**, not ***the were). Now let us take out the grammatical words in the text:

> —— bryllyg —— —— slythy toves
> —— gyre —— gymble —— —— wabe
> —— mimsy —— —— borogoves
> —— —— mome raths outgrabe

These words are almost nonsense, but not quite, for certain elements set associations working. Some of these associations are grammatical. For example, the final **y** on **slythy** and **mimsy** suggests they are adjectives, after the pattern of **happy, gory**; the **s** on **toves, raths**, and **borogoves** suggests either a plural noun or a third person present verb (**runs, dives**). These elements which suggest grammatical categories function in the passage in much the same way as do words like **the** and **did**. They may be thought of as grammatical subparts of words, which are adjoined to content subparts. Other associations here are semantic, inviting hypotheses about the content of words or subparts of words. **Bryllyg** suggests a meaning associated with **brilliant** and **bright**; **slythy** suggests **slimy, slithery**, and so on. Carroll makes fun of these semantic associations or "sound-symbolisms" in the glossary he made to go with the poem. Here are some of the definitions he provides:

> *Bryllyg* (derived from the verb *to bryl* or *broil*): 'The time of broiling dinner, i.e. the close of the afternoon.'
> *Slythy* (compounded of *slimy* and *lithe*): 'Smooth and active.'
> *Tove:* A species of badger. They had smooth white hair, long hind legs, and short horns like a stag; lived chiefly on cheese.
> *Gyre*, verb (derived from *gyaour* or *giaour*, 'a dog'): 'To scratch like a dog.'
> *Gymble* (whence *gimblet*): 'To screw out holes in anything.'
> *Wabe* (derived from the verb *to swab* or *soak*): 'The side of a hill' (from its being *soaked* by the rain).
> *Mimsy* (whence *mimserable* and *miserable*): 'Unhappy.' . . .
>
> Hence the literal English of the passage is: 'It was evening, and the smooth active badgers were scratching and boring holes in the hillside; all unhappy were the parrots; and the grave turtles squeaked out.'[3]

Only the second of Carroll's definitions corresponds to semantic associations we might be likely to make. The others are deliberately outrageous, to emphasize the arbitrariness of the relation between sound and word meaning. Notice, though, that Carroll's definitions do corroborate some of our grammatical intuitions about the poem. **Toves** is a plural noun, and **slythy** an adjective.

MORPHEMES

We have said that grammatical words like **the** and grammatical subparts of words like **-s** perform the same kinds of function in the linguistic system. For the linguist, this means that at some level of analysis, **the** and **-s** must be viewed as elements of the same type, despite the fact that one is a word and one is not. The same is true for content elements. For instance, the sequence **tove** is a complete word in the phrase **the tove**, but only a subpart in **toves** or **tovely**. So we need a level of analysis which identifies **tove** as a unit, whether or not it appears as an independent word. At the level of analysis we are talking about, **the, -s**, and **tove** are all called "morphemes." (**Morphe** is the Greek word for "form"; -eme as in "phoneme" means "class of.") The and -s are grammatical morphemes, while **tove** is a content morpheme, or more simply, a "root." Words, then, can be made up of one or more morphemes. **Tove** has one, **tove** + **s** and **tove** + **ly** have two, while **un** + **tove** + **ly** has three. Morphemes are the smallest units forming the bridge between sound and meaning in language, and they are as important in linguistic analysis as words.

Every morpheme in a language has (a) a characteristic phonological make-up (although there may be variant forms, as will be illustrated below), and (b) restrictions on the positions it can occupy with respect to other morphemes (the plural -s in English, for example, occurs only after the noun). Most morphemes also have a meaning, but a few are simply carriers of other meaningful elements. For example, **did** in **He didn't enjoy linguistics** serves no function other than to carry the past tense and the negative markers of the verb; this type of "empty" morpheme will be discussed further in Chapter 4. When morphemes combine to make words, they combine in layers. Take, for instance, the word **fatalistic**. We do not view this word simply as a linear sequence **fate** + **al** + **ist** + **ic**, but as a set of layers: **fate** + **al**, **fatal** + **ist**, **fatalist** + **ic**. This can be shown by a display such as:

> fate
> fatal
> fatalist
> fatalistic

or, equivalently, by use of brackets as in:

$$[[[[fate]al]ist]ic]$$

This kind of description also captures the fact that the order in which morphemes combine is crucial and fixed. We cannot have either *fatistalic or *fatistical instead.

Classes of Morphemes

We have already made a distinction between content morphemes on the one hand and grammatical morphemes on the other. Within the class of grammatical morphemes, it is useful to distinguish a number of subclasses. As we have seen, some grammatical morphemes are words, like **the, all, and**; others are affixes, that is, elements that attach to roots. In the case of affixes, it is customary to distinguish between (a) prefixes, which precede roots, as in **un** + **cola**, **im** + **mortal**, and Carroll's **out** + **grabe**, (b) suffixes, which follow roots, as in **quick** + **ly**, **beat** + **nik**, **rose** + **s**, and (c) infixes, which are inserted into roots. The latter are rare in English except in swearwords such as **fan-damn-tastic** or literary coinages such as **manunkind**, coined by e. e. cummings to suggest not only man who is unkind but also man without true kin.

We can also group affixes according to function. The word **fatalists** has a root **fate** and three suffixes, **-al, -ist, -s**. The first two suffixes serve to assign the root to a certain grammatical category: **-al** makes **fate** into an adjective; adding **-ist** turns the adjective into a noun once again. But **-s** does not affect the syntactic category. It takes something that is already a noun and pluralizes it. Notice, too, that **-al** and **-ist** modify the meaning of **fate** significantly so that **fatal** does not just mean "having to do with fate." On the other hand, **-s** does not alter the basic meaning of the noun at all. Furthermore, only a few nouns can have **-al** attached to them, but most can be pluralized. On the basis of these differences in function, we can distinguish between "derivative" morphemes (such as **-al** and **-ist**) and "inflections" (such as **-s**).

Inflections in English are all suffixes and all occur at the very end of a word, after any derivative suffixes that might be present. Examples include the plural marker (trees, child**ren**), the possessive marker (children**'s**), the comparative and superlative markers for adjectives (long**er**, long**est**), tense markers for verbs (he walk**s**, walk**ed**), and others. The tense marker **-s** is called "non-past" while the tense marker **-ed** is called "past." These morphemes are linguistic categories that overlap only to a limited degree with the meanings of past, present, and future. For example, non-past can signal either present or future time as in **He is here** and **He leaves tomorrow** respectively; it can even include past time in such expressions of habit as **He leaves at eight every day**, since this ranges over past, present, and future. The future is not represented in English by a distinct inflection, but rather by a separate verb as in **She will leave tomorrow**. Contrast French, in which the future is an inflection attached to the verb. Some languages, including Old English, have a great many more inflections than Modern English has. For example, if you know Latin, Greek, German, or Russian, you are familiar with the "gender, number, and case" inflections these languages have for nouns. Like the inflections of English, these are primarily markers of grammatical relations among words in a sentence. They do not alter either the syntactic category or the basic meaning of the roots to which they are attached. The main importance of inflections lies at the level of sentence structure and sentence meaning, rather than at the level of word structure and word meaning. They will therefore be considered more fully in the next chapter.

Derivative morphemes are so called because they are used to derive new words and meanings. In English they are of two kinds, those that change syntactic categories and those that do not. Most suffixal derivatives affect both the syntactic category and the meaning of the root to which they attach. The "agentive" **-er**, for example, changes a verb into a noun with the meaning "one who does" the action or activity the verb denotes, as in **singer** or **philanderer**. On the other hand, prefixes only change the meaning of the root without affecting the syntactic category, as, for example, **mal-** in **maladjusted** or **a-** in **asexual**.

The largest class of category-changing derivative suffixes in English are "nominalizers" which make nouns out of adjectives or verbs. They include

-acy, -ance, -ician, -ism, -ist, -ity, -ment, -ness, -ship, and -ster. You can easily think of hundreds of nouns formed with these suffixes. Adjectivalizers include -able, -al, -an, -atic, -ful, -ic, -ine, -ish, -ory, -ous, and -y (as in pithy). Verbalizers include -ate, -en (as in lighten), -ify, and -ize. Adverbializers form the smallest set, and are chiefly -ly and -ward. Of course, in English, words can change syntactic category with no indicator of the change at all, as in the case of run, balloon, kill, hog, man (noun or verb), black, right (noun, verb, or adjective) and bare, dirty, empty, narrow, weary (verb or adjective).

Most derivatives that are prefixes in English affect only the meaning of the root, not its syntactic class. Meaning-changing prefixes include a- (as in amoral, asymmetric), anti-, arch-, bi-, circum-, co-, crypto-, de-, dis-, en-, ex-, in- (as in insurmountable, inadequate), inter-, mal-, re-, semi-, sub-, and un-.

A root plus one or more derivative morphemes is classed as a "stem." While inflections, as we have seen, are suffixed to roots and stems in English according to strict, but very general principles, the affixing of derivative morphemes to roots is highly idiosyncratic and unpredictable. For example, from probable we derive probability, probabilism, and probableness, but not probablehood, probablicy, or probablance. The verbalization probabilize is now coming into the language, but not probabilify, probabilate, or probabilitate, though these are all conceivable. In other words, there are gaps in the system; for example, not all roots which by their meaning could allow agentive derivations actually do so.

Identifying Morphemes

Morphemes cannot be identified by their surface form and location alone. Your intuitions tell you that -er is a morpheme in longer, runner, and eraser, and that it does not mean the same thing in each case. The -er in longer indicates the comparative form of the adjective; in runner it indicates an animate agent or doer of the running; and in eraser it indicates that the thing is used as an instrument or means of action. What we have here is not one morpheme with three meanings, but three different morphemes, that is, three different sound-meaning combinations, which happen to have the same phonological form. We say the three morphemes are "homonyms." Other homonymous morphemes are to, too, and two; the three different inflections signaled by -s (noun plural, noun possessive, and verbal third person singular non-past); and also pairs like roe-row, pale-pail. Because of homonymy, we cannot always determine from surface forms what morpheme is present in a given case. Perhaps even more obvious is the fact that we cannot determine from surface forms alone whether a morpheme is present at all. For example, -al and -ist are separable units in the word fatalist, but obviously not in coral or mist.

Like phonemes, morphemes are classes. The members of the class of phonemes are allophones in complementary distribution; similarly, the members of the morpheme class are "allomorphs" in complementary distribution. However, while most phonemes have several variants with similar phonetic characteristics, many morphemes, especially content and derivative morphemes, have only one variant. By contrast, most noun and verb inflections in English have several phonological variants. For example, here is a list illustrating the main surface manifestations that the plural inflection can have in English:

Plural = vowel alternation, as in **man-men, foot-feet, mouse-mice**

       = additions, as in **ox-oxen**

       = vowel alternation and addition, as in **brother-brethren**

       = alternation with a marker of the singular, as in **phenomenon-phenomena, formula-formulae, cactus-cacti** (these are nearly always words borrowed from Latin or Greek; many have also been given -s plurals.)

       = unrealized (∅), as in **deer-deer, sheep-sheep**

       = [z, ɨz, s] as in **dogs, horses, cats**

The -s plural represents the commonest form of the plural, and the one most likely to supersede the others. That is why it is specified last in the rule—it applies to all nouns other than those listed above it. It is also the one that will be added to any new noun invented in the language, with the possible exception of some technical terms derived from Latin or Greek. Only one underlying sibilant need be specified, the particular sounds [z, ɨz] and [s] being predictable in terms of the final sounds of the preceding morphemes, according to regular phonological rules that have already been discussed in Chapter 2.

The ∅ form of the plural as in **deer** and **sheep** is perhaps more difficult to understand. We cannot just say that **deer** and **sheep** "have no plural" or "have no singular" because in a very clear sense they do. Specifically, they affect other morphemes in the same way that regular singulars and plurals do, as is illustrated by:

1. a. The cat is pouncing.
   b. The cats are pouncing.

2. a. The deer is running.
   b. The deer are running.

3. a. There are two cats on the hot tin roof.
   b. There are two deer on the hot tin roof.[4]

It is essential for an understanding of linguistic formalism and method to recognize that this ∅ is not nothing—it is a linguistic element of any size (not just a morpheme) that is unexpressed. In more formal terms, it is a unit that, while present in underlying structure, is not present in surface structure. Ø can range in size from an unpronounced consonant or vowel (typical of rapid speech, as in [ðədɔrposaratɪŋ] "the doorposts are rotting" for the slower form [ðədɔrpostsarratɪŋ]), to an unexpressed morpheme like the plural of **deer**, to a part of a sentence consisting of several morphemes (**Go!** can be analyzed as the surface form of **You will go**, as discussed in the section on imperatives in Chapter 4).

Another more radical kind of phonological variation in morphemes is of a type called "suppletion." Suppletion occurs when a single morpheme is realized in different contexts by sound sequences that have no phonological similarity at all. One example is the pair **go** and **went**, where **went** is **go** + past tense. Historically, this alternation is the result of a merger of two separate verbs, Old English **gan** "go" and Old English **wendan** "turn" (cf. **wend one's way**). **Wen-** is now the form that **go** takes before the past tense marker. Another instance of suppletion is provided by the adjective **good**, which alternates with **bet-** before the comparative inflection **-er**.

The notion of suppletion has even been extended to refer to such cases as the predictable alternation between **some** and **any** in certain negative contexts, as in:

4. a.   I caught some fish yesterday.
   b.   I didn't catch any fish yesterday.

5. a.   Bill saw some anteaters.
   b.   Bill didn't see any anteaters.

THE LEXICON

How do we capture in a grammar the kinds of facts we have been discussing? Most sound-meaning relations are given in the dictionary or "lexicon" of the grammar. One possible way of constructing a lexicon would be simply to make a list of all the morphemes in the language, specifying their sound and meaning. This would reflect part of the speaker's knowledge, including the ability to create and understand new combinations of morphemes. But such a list would be far from adequate since it would fail to describe the speaker's knowledge of what combinations of morphemes are currently available in the language. Derivational morphemes, as we have seen, are unpredictably restricted in their combination, and are unpredictable in their effects on meaning. Hence, not only do speakers have to learn the meanings of all morphemes individually, they also have to learn what combinations each morpheme enters and what each of these combinations means. The grammar has to capture these idiosyncratic facts.

On the other hand, it is not necessary to list all the morphemes and combinations of morphemes in the language, because some, namely inflections, are for the most part predictable in form, meaning, and distribution. Generally speaking, any verb can have past or nonpast inflections attached, any noun can have plural or possessive. It would be enormously redundant to list in the lexicon all possible plural, past tense, possessive, or other inflected forms. Only the unpredictable exceptions need be listed. For the regular cases, inflections are introduced by general rules in the syntactic component of the grammar rather than in the lexicon.

Forms listed in the lexicon are called "lexical items" to distinguish them from morphemes and words, with which they have a lot in common but with which they are not identical; not all words and morphemes are lexical items; not all lexical items are words or single morphemes. Chiefly, lexical items will include roots, derivatives, and combinations of roots and derivatives. But it is also possible for two or more roots to combine into a unit which functions as a noun, verb, adjective, adverb, and so on. These, too, will be lexical items. There are two main kinds of lexical items involving two or more roots: "compounds" like **horse-manure** and "idioms" like **throw in the towel**.

Compounds

A compound is a lexical item in which two roots combine to make one unit, for example, **redneck**, **dogfish**, **whitewash**. Many such compounds derive historically from syntactic phrases, e.g., **black board** (adjective + noun) became **blackboard**. There are a great number of syntactic sources for compounds, among them noun plus an adjective or a describing phrase, as, for example, **blackbird**, **goldfish**, **numbskull**, **bedfellow**, **bagpipe**, **birthright**. Other compounds derive from verbal phrases, as, for example, **skyscraper** (something which scrapes the sky) and **pickpocket**, both of which involve a verb and an object. There are also compounds derived from a verb and an adverbial like **sharpshooter** (one who shoots sharply), **turnout**, **leftovers**, **dugout**. Of more recent origin are such verb-adverb compounds as **sit-in**, **laugh-in**, and **love-in**. A particularly large number of compounds are formed with adverbials in initial position, for example, **aftermath**, **background**, **bystander**, **downpour**, **forthcoming**, **inroad**, **offspring**, **onslaught**, **outrage**, **overweight**. Some compounds derive historically from stems or other compounds by a process of redivision of component parts. A recent example is **hamburger**, which meant a kind of meat from **Hamburg** (**-er** here is derivative) and was redivided as **ham** (without reference to pork) and **burger**. The new root **burger** was compounded with still other roots such as **fish**, **cheese**, and **chili**.

Whatever their syntactic origin, nominal compounds can usually be identified by the stress pattern—**stòne wáll** is a phrase, not a compound, while **to stónewàll** is a compound.[5] Another criterion is semantic—usually a phrase has the literal meaning of its parts, whereas a compound does not. However, there are unclear boundaries here. Thus, while **offspring** means something rather more specific than one who springs off from someone, a **bartender** is certainly one who tends bars.

The criterion of stress applies only to nominal compounds, and the distinction between compound and idiom becomes much more fuzzy for verbs and other nonnominal categories. However, in addition to the semantic criterion, we may also use one involving order. In a verb plus adverb compound like **be forthcoming**, there is a clear difference in order between the phrases from which they derive (e.g., **come forth**) and the resultant compound. Similar examples are provided by verbs, adjectives, and nouns like **outmaneuver, backpedal, jet-propelled, underpass,** and **upkeep**. By contrast, such a phrase as **look out for**, which is usually considered an idiom rather than a compound, involves no modification of the underlying word order.[6]

Idioms

Phrases like **bring to light, take into consideration, kick the bucket, take off,** and **man-of-war** are idioms insofar as they have semantic unity and function as noun, verb, adjective, and so forth. Nominal idioms differ from nominal compounds in that they retain the stress patterns of the phrases from which they derive, as in the case of **blàck márket**, but they share with them the property of semantic unity. Idioms differ from compounds in that they, for the most part, allow a certain amount of internal modification. The nominal idiom **man-of-war**, for example, pluralizes as **men-of-war**, not **man-of-wars**. In verbal idioms the tense of the verb is usually modifiable, as in **bring to light/brought to light**, even though the tense change is internal to the structure of the whole idiom. Idioms, in other words, are structurally looser units than compounds.

Verbal phrase idioms like **dig up** consist of a verb and what is usually termed a "particle." Although homonymous with both adverbs and prepositions, these particles clearly have a different function from these two in their meaning, their syntactic behavior, and also their phonological behavior. Consider, for example, the difference between the particle **up** and the preposition **up** in **run up a bill** and **run up a hill** in:

6. a.   I ran úp two big bills in the same week.
   b.   I ran them both úp in the same week.

7. a.   I rán up two big hills in the same week.
   b.   I rán up them both in the same week.

In 6 we have an idiom, in 7 we do not. Example 6 cannot be the answer to a question of the type:

8.   Where did you run?

but 7 can be. The **up** in the idiom clearly belongs to the verb preceding it; in the phrase it belongs to the noun following it.

Verb-particle idioms have become extremely common in English during the last three centuries or so.[7] Such constructions are more common in American than in British English. Those consisting of three rather than two parts are almost exclusively American in origin, as, for example, **miss out on, meet up with, boogie on down**. Some of these verbal idioms add a time-dimension to the action named, especially those formed with **up**. For example, **drink up** and **burn up** mean "to completely drink/burn" or "drink/burn to the end." Note also the time-dimension with **on** in **drink on, burn on**.

These examples of idioms show once again that a lexical item does not coincide with a word. In the case of derivative morphemes, a lexical item may be less than a word. In the case of idioms, it may be considerably more than one word, as in **bring to light**. Speakers of English tend to assume that words are the basic units of language: Our dictionaries are based on them; we write and read in units called words. Nevertheless, "word" is hard to define consistently in English. Isn't it chiefly just the convention of writing that leads us to think of **the table** or **look out** (in the sense of "beware") as two words rather than as one word of two morphemes, like **something** and **lookout**? This is not to say that words have no place in English grammar. They do, for they have significant linguistic consequences. For instance, in English, stress patterns, breaks in pitch patterns, rhythm, and insertion of hesitation markers like **uhmmm** or fillers like **you know** depend in part on word units (and also to some extent on phrasal ones).

THE FORM OF LEXICAL ENTRIES

For each lexical item in the language, a lexical entry is made in the lexicon, containing four main types of information about the item: (a) its underlying phonological representation, (b) the possible sequences of morphemes into which it enters, given (c) its syntactic properties (as noun, verb, and so forth), and (d) its semantic representation. All this amounts to a great deal of highly detailed information which speakers of a language have to learn, information which, as we said earlier, makes up the basic level of sound-meaning correlation in the language.

The kind of information included in lexical entries resembles in many respects that provided in a regular dictionary. In one area, however, there is a radical difference between the treatment of lexical items in a grammar and in a dictionary—in the descriptions of the meanings of the lexical items. Semantic description is the most controversial and least developed aspect of lexical description (and indeed of the theory of grammar as a whole). Even the fundamental question: "What is lexical meaning?" is a matter of debate. In the 1930s some linguists and psychologists tried to interpret meaning entirely in terms of reference to phenomena outside language. For example, Bloomfield, one of the most important American linguists of the time, said that:

In order to give a scientifically accurate definition of meaning for every form [i.e. morpheme] of a language, we should have to have a scientifically accurate knowledge of everything in the speaker's world.[8]

Bloomfield acknowledged that at the present time human knowledge is very limited, but to him the task did not seem hopeless—a day would come, he felt, when physics, chemistry, psychology, anthropology, and all the fields of behavioral research would be sufficiently advanced for linguists to show exactly how the morphemes of language referred to the real world.

There is, however, another school of thought, deriving its basic tenets from the work of the nineteenth-century philosopher Frege. This school states that in language the meaning we should study is not that which refers but that which is the "sense," in other words, the meaning relations that hold internally within language.[9] Linguists of this school (generative grammarians and indeed the majority of linguists since the late 1960s) argue that we have an internalized conceptual system as well as internalized phonological, morphological, and syntactic ones. Linguistic forms must be analyzed in terms of the sense they have within this conceptual system, rather than in terms of their referent in the real world. This conceptual system is organized in such a way that two forms may have the same referent, but express different concepts. For example, **the fat woman** and **my neighbor across the street** may refer to the same person, but they express different concepts. It is those concepts, insofar as they are formulated by language, that the linguist is interested in, not who is being referred to. Conversely, a single form may be used with any number of referents, while it actually expresses the same concept. For example, every time anyone uses the word **I**, it expresses the concept of "speaker," but it refers to different people at different times. The linguist is not primarily concerned with who the speaker is on any occasion, but with the contrast between speaker (**I**), addressee (**you**), and a third person (**he, she**).

Dictionaries mainly give definitions in terms that capture the sense rather than the reference of a word, but they also often give definitions that rely primarily on knowledge of the world (reference). Pictorial illustrations are always referential, but verbal definitions may be too. A dictionary definition of **left** is a well-known example of the difference between the way a dictionary and a lexicon can handle meanings. **Left** has been defined as:

> Pertaining to, designating, or being on the side of the body that is toward the north when one faces east, and usually having the weaker and less dominant hand, etc. . . .[10]

This definition is incomprehensible unless one knows where north, south, east, and west are, and which hand tends to dominate. A lexicon would make no such reference to geography or physiology, but rather to relative locations expressed in the language. It would have to show that **left** is a term which locates something relative to some other object, as do other terms like **front** and **back**; it would have to show that unlike **front** and **back**, **left** and **right** involve position at the side of the object relative to which they are located. Also, although in many cases the two terms are symmetrical (that is, if A is to the left of B, then B is to the right of A), there are certain properties of **left** that are semantically negative—in many languages the term for **left** acquires a meaning of dubiousness, while **right** acquires a meaning of justice. For example, Latin **sinister** "left" came to have the meaning it now has in English, while **human rights**, **doing right**, and so forth come from locational **right**. All these definitions are internal to language and make no reference to the human body or any other object in the nonlinguistic world.

More generally, since dictionaries are meant to be consulted by people who already know the language, they can tolerate a certain amount of looseness of definition. Since they are not formal systems, they need not require that every item be defined with respect to the system rather than to knowledge brought to bear by the reader. The lexicon must be structured far more rigorously, because it sets out to model knowledge of the language.

How can meanings be specified in a lexicon without reference to the outside world? One proposal is that lexical meanings can be specified by "semantic features" similar in function to the distinctive phonological features discussed in the preceding chapter—components can make up the meaning of a lexical item. For example, "male" is part of the meaning of **man**. These components are ideally "primitives" in the sense that they cannot be broken down further and are the givens of the semantic system. The primitives (or rather the near-primitives that linguists have analyzed so far) are thought to combine in bundles, just like phonological features. As far as semantics is concerned, then, lexical items are labels put on bundles of semantic features.

Like phonological features, semantic ones are established on the basis of oppositions significant in language in general, such as male-female, adult-young, movement-stasis.[11] For example, we can factor out male-female as the opposition that holds between the noun pairs:

man	woman
boy	girl
rooster	hen
bull	cow

To capture this generalization in the grammar, we can establish a binary feature [±MALE] (the capital letters indicate that this is a metalinguistic term not necessarily exactly identical with the homonymous word **male** in English). With the same list we can factor out an opposition between human and nonhuman:

man	rooster
woman	hen

boy   bull

girl   cow

and the opposition adult-young, as in:

man   boy

woman   girl

We can thus set up three binary semantic features: [±MALE], [±ADULT], [±HUMAN]. Using these terms we can characterize **man**, **woman**, **boy**, **girl**, **bullock**, and **cow** semantically as, among other things:

man   [+MALE, +ADULT, +HUMAN]

woman   [−MALE, +ADULT, +HUMAN]

boy   [+MALE, −ADULT, +HUMAN]

girl   [−MALE, −ADULT, +HUMAN]

bullock [+MALE, −ADULT, −HUMAN]

cow   [−MALE, +ADULT, −HUMAN]

Needless to say, it would take a great many such features to fully characterize almost any lexical item semantically, and we are very far indeed from having a full set of semantic features. In what follows, we will present only some of the more obvious and general semantic features that would be used in a lexicon.

The nouns listed above will be distinguished from others like **book**, **chair**, **dictionary** by the feature [±ANIMATE]; we will also need a feature [±VEGETABLE] to distinguish plants. The feature [±MALE] would not be relevant for many [+VEGETABLE] nouns, but [±ADULT] would be, as in **tree/sapling** (and **nursery** for both plants and humans). Nouns are further subcategorized according to whether they are [±ABSTRACT]. **Boy, table, book** contrast with **hope, thought, problem** in this feature. Nouns are also subcategorized according to the feature [±COUNT]. This feature distinguishes countable nouns (**one dog, five dogs, many dogs**) from so-called "mass" nouns (*****one gravel, *****many gravels, **much gravel**).

Different features are relevant for stems involving other syntactic categories. A distinction relevant to verbs is whether they are primarily action verbs or state-of-being verbs. Action verbs are those that can be used in reply to questions like **What are you doing?** Most verbs are of this kind, but some, such as **know** and **like**, are not. **I knew the answer** and **I liked that story** may not be used in reply to **What did you do?** As we have seen in connection with verbs like **burn up** and **drink up** as opposed to **burn on**, verbs can also be subcategorized for completiveness versus duration. Other features for verbs will produce other subcategorizations, such as verbs of motion, verbs of perception, verbs of mental process, verbs of judging, and a great many others.

Adjectives illustrate some rather different kinds of semantic oppositions. Consider, for example:

long	good
short	bad
tall	well
narrow	sick
wide	

All the words in the left-hand column have something to do with measurement, and therefore can occur with such measurement phrases as **two inches**, as in **This is two inches long**. All the terms in the list share the property of being relative terms. A tall person is small relative to a tall building, a good person or an honest person is not good in any absolute sense but is good relative to a certain set of morals or other criteria of behavior. However, the measurement terms listed above are not only relative. They also involve a norm of comparison. A good person is not necessarily good-er than any other person, a bad person is not bad-er. But a tall person is tall-er than the norm, and a small person somehow misses the norm. Thus a person who is two inches short is missing some criterion of height that has been established (for example, by the police department for recruits). Similarly, a long pencil is longer than the expected norm, and a pencil that is two inches short again misses some needed length.[12]

The set of adjectives we are discussing can be regrouped in another way:

long	short
tall	short
wide	narrow
good	bad
well	sick

Here we can factor out a negative meaning in the right-hand column. This negative meaning is obvious for **bad** and **sick**, but perhaps not quite so obvious for **short** and **narrow**. However, if we consider that **short** in some locutions means "lacking/missing" the expected length or height, we can readily understand it as a negative word. Similarly, **narrow** can be used in negative ways, as, for example, **narrow-minded** or **narrow-fisted**.

You may be wondering how we decide which member of an opposition should be plus and which minus. In contrasting **man** and **boy**, for example, should we establish a feature [±ADULT] or a feature [±YOUNG]? Sometimes the decision is arbitrary, but most of the time it is not. With **man** and **boy**, for example, one reason to select [±ADULT] and thus make **man** the basic term is that **man** in some uses includes **boy**, as, for example, with **men** on the outside of a washroom. When **man** means "mankind" it includes boys and also women and girls. For this same reason we establish [±MALE], not [±FEMALE], for the **man-woman** distinction. However much we may wish male and female to be equal members of an opposition, they do not work that way in the linguistic system, at least not at present. This is reflected also by the fact that **man** is the term to which **wo-** is attached (in Old English this word was **wif-man** "female person"). Similarly, it is **male** to which **fe-** is attached. **Man** also has the greater number of extensions of meaning. For instance, it has been made into an intensifying expression, as in **Man, that's good**, whereas **woman** has not. **Man** has also been made into a derivative morpheme as in **cháirmăn**, where absence of stress on **-man** indicates that it is no longer a compounding element. By contrast, words like **cháirwòman** and **cháirpèrson** have the stress pattern of compounds, indicating that **woman** and **person** are still compounding and not derivative morphemes. We find similar asymmetric relationships between words in nearly all "antonymous" pairs.

When the included member of a pair also happens to be negative in some way, its distribution is apt to be particularly restricted. It has often been observed that positive terms can have negative morphemes added, as in **happy-unhappy**, but that semantically negative ones rarely do, because **un-** is deprecatory as well as negative.[13] We do not find **sad-unsad**, for example. The absence of **ungood** appears to be an accidental gap in the lexicon of English (or was until George Orwell coined it in his novel *Nineteen Eighty-Four*), but the absence of **unsad** is not accidental, given the semantic structure of English.

Study of semantic systems of a wide number of languages strongly suggests that primitive semantic features, like phonological features, are not restricted to specific languages but are universal. If so, it seems reasonable to hypothesize that primitive semantic features reflect part of the basic cognitive and perceptual structure of the human organism. And if that is the case, one presumably does not have to learn the primitives but has an innate disposition toward them. As one linguist has put it, such meanings

> ... have to be actualized or released by experience during the process of language acquisition, but as a possible structure they are already present in the learning organism. Hence what is learned during the process of language acquisition, is not the semantic components, but rather their particular combinations in special concepts, and the assignment of phonemic forms and morphological properties to these concepts.[14]

This view remains a hypothesis but suggests exciting possibilities, especially for the study of new languages such as pidgins and creoles.

SIZE AND VARIABILITY OF THE LEXICON

The size of the lexicon varies a good deal from language to language, but in no language do we expect to find individual speakers who know the whole lexicon. You can open a major English dictionary at almost any page and find entries unfamiliar to you. One reason for this is that most languages have specialized vocabularies that relate to particular fields of knowledge or activity in the culture, like medicine, law, sports, weather, or trading, and that are mainly used by people with special expertise in the field. Thus, when we list in the lexicon all the lexical items in a language and the principles on which new ones can be coined, we are not representing the competence of any real speaker. Rather, we are representing the competence of a hypothetical and idealized speaker. Moreover, in the lexicon of a real speaker, we will find a marked difference in size between the speaker's "use" vocabulary, that is, the lexical items that he or she uses in composing utterances, and the speaker's "recognition" vocabulary, that is, the lexical items that he or she understands in deciphering utterances. In any real speaker, the latter is by far the larger; however, the lexicon of the grammar does not reflect this distinction.

The lexicon of English is very large; indeed, it is now probably the largest of all languages. There are some 450,000 entries in *Webster's Third New International Dictionary* (1961). The reasons for the size of the English lexicon are many, but two are of particular importance. First, from the very beginning of the Old English period, English has constantly borrowed vocabulary from other languages. English vocabulary was heavily influenced by Latin, both under the influence of the Church in the early period of Christianization in the late sixth century and under the influence of classicism in the Renaissance. It was also heavily influenced by Scandinavian languages owing to large settlements in eastern and northern England in the eighth to tenth centuries, and especially by French after the Norman Conquest in 1066. While foreign words sometimes supplanted native ones, more frequently they were simply added to the vocabulary, with the result that we have native **hound** from Old English **hund** "dog," beside **dog** from Scandinavian; likewise, we have native **fatherly** beside Latinate **paternal**. Even though they may have been basically synonymous at the time of the borrowing, native and borrowed words soon differentiate in meaning, as in the case of both pairs cited above. Sometimes they come to be associated with different levels of formality, as is the case with **help** and **assist**, or **fatherly** and **paternal** (note also the pejorative **paternalistic**). Not all languages have tolerated borrowing as much as English has. In German, for example, until recently there had been a preference for coining new words from native bases, rather than borrowing.

Another reason for the size of the English lexicon is the rapid expansion of knowledge and technology that English-speaking countries have experienced in the last few hundred years. As a result of this expansion, specialized vocabularies in English are relatively numerous and relatively large—every scientific discovery or technological innovation, every new theory or methodology gives rise to new vocabulary. Much of the technical vocabulary in English is actually not from native word stock but rather is coined from Greek and Latin morphemes. This, in part, reflects the longstanding tendency in the West to select Latin and Greek for erudite subjects, but also a deliberate policy to create a relatively international vocabulary that is not markedly English.

Of all the components of the grammar, the lexicon is the one which varies most over time. New lexical items are being added to the language every day, and old ones are being lost. Changes in the phonological and syntactic systems are much rarer by comparison. To some extent, changes in the lexicon over time are simply the result of an unsystematic but constant turnover in vocabulary, motivated by people's desire for originality and by changes in their linguistic habits. This turnover is particularly rapid and evident in slang, but it manifests itself in other areas as well. For instance, in some areas of contemporary English usage, we see a preference for word formations using the derivative suffixes **-able** and **-ability**. Words like **affordable, saleable, drinkable, beddable** and their analogues **affordability, saleability,** and so on have a decidedly contemporary ring, and we can easily create other combinations along the same pattern—**writable, takeable, climbable, paintable**. Speakers of English 150 years ago would have been much less likely to come up with such terms and would have found them much less acceptable in the language than we do. Indeed, such items are even now considered undesirable in many quarters. Within the grammar, however, they are viewed simply as products of a currently productive word-formation process.

Changes in vocabulary can also be motivated by verbal taboo, that is, the tendency to avoid making reference to certain things. What is considered taboo at one time or by one group varies enormously, but verbal taboo is present in all cultures. Many people in Britain and America have taboos about matters such as sex and excretion, so that a term like **toilet** is avoided and replaced by **bathroom**, whether or not there is a bathtub, and both **bathroom** and **toilet** are in turn replaced by ridiculous euphemisms like **powder room** or **little boy's room**. Such verbal taboos arise from general cultural taboos which define sex and excretion as private matters. In some cultures, one's personal name or the names of one's dead relatives are private matters, not to be mentioned in the presence of strangers or outsiders. Verbal taboos are also often associated with subjects considered unpleasant, whether private or not. Death may be unmentionable, and direct reference to it substituted by idioms such as serious **pass on, go to our reward**, and jocular **kick the bucket, throw in the towel**. As these examples suggest, one of the verbal consequences of taboo is that terms for taboo subjects tend to increase in number far more readily than terms for neutral subjects. Also, such terms group into two main sets: On the one hand, we find euphemisms which are polite or formal (for example, **be under the influence of alcohol, be in a family way**). They express delicacy, reserve, and respect for taboo, in sum, verbal decorum. On the other hand, we find slang, often obscene terms which may be seemingly cute (like

have a bun in the oven) or downright aggressive or sadistic (as, for example, **knocked up** in the sense of "pregnant"), all of which deliberately violate decorum and call attention to the taboo.

Because the lexicon is the part of the grammar most susceptible to change, it is also the part at which attempts to control linguistic development are most often aimed. For example, in the interests of cultural or national integrity, language groups sometimes try to reverse the effects of borrowing, requiring that foreign borrowings be replaced by lexical items made up of forms native to the language. One contemporary attempt was that of French authorities in the 1960s to replace recent English borrowings like **hot dog, parking** (in the meaning of "parking lot"), **weekend**, and **drugstore** with French equivalents.

Another example of lexical change motivated by social change is the attempt in some countries with active feminist movements to "desex" the language. In English, this undertaking involves the elimination of those agentive morphemes which refer directly to sex, such as **-man, -ess,** or **-tress.** The objection to these derivatives is not simply that they refer to sex, but also that the male and female terms function asymmetrically, with the male terms being inclusive in the ways we have already discussed. **Author** and **poet** are basic terms. No extra marker is added to refer to males, but it is sometimes added when referring to females; moreover, the female marker is usually understood to be pejorative. An **authoress** or **poetess** is not only a female writer but, by innuendo, one who need not be taken seriously.

Possibly the most difficult problem in desexing English, and many other languages as well, lies in the pronoun system, specifically in the so-called "generic he," as in **Before he registers, each student consults with his advisor, who adds his signature to the study list** or **Anybody who cares about animals will see that his pets are vaccinated**. To get around this problem, some have proposed that new sexually neutral pronoun forms be added to the language, such as **thon, hiser, co,** and **E,** but these have not caught on. Even the attempt in the United States to use **one** in a way long customary in British English has been rather unsuccessful. The British usage requires the use of **one . . . one** instead of **one . . . he,** as in **One does one's work as best one can** versus American **One does his work as best he can.** In America, the **one . . . one** usage is apparently felt to be too impersonal. There have also been attempts to standardize **they/their/them** as singular as well as plural forms, as in **If a customer doesn't pay their bill, what do you tell them?** This usage, though common in informal speech,[15] continues to be viewed as nonstandard and has not been accepted for formal or written discourse. In writing, the form **s/he** has been adopted by some, but since this form has no oral counterpart, it does not provide a satisfactory solution.

Part of the opposition to desexing the language derives from cultural attitudes. Part of the opposition to change in the pronoun system may also be primarily linguistic, since pronouns are in most languages highly resistant to change, except where sound changes cause forms to become potentially ambiguous. It is important to note, however, that there is no need to alter the pronoun system in order to eliminate the generic **he**. Language-users need only adjust their speaking and writing habits. A great many people are now doing so and are finding it increasingly easy to get around these forms. This can often be done, for example, by using plurals as in **People who care about animals**, or by rephrasing as in **Before registering** instead of **Before he registers**, or by using articles instead of possessives as in **After taking the** (instead of **his**) **preliminary exam, the student begins work on a** (instead of **his**) **dissertation**, or by using the combined **he or she, his or her**.

THE WHORFIAN HYPOTHESIS

Deliberate efforts to change vocabulary presuppose that language must in some way affect thought—desexing the language is meant to promote a change in attitude to males and females, not simply to reflect a change that has already occurred, regardless of language. Likewise, calling people "underprivileged" rather than "poor" is meant to direct people's thinking to questions of privilege rather than to the fact of poverty. The question "How far does vocabulary control thought?" is an ancient one. It is part of the larger question concerning how far language in general influences thought. In this century it was given special attention through the work of Edward Sapir and, more importantly, Benjamin Lee Whorf. Working on American Indian languages, especially Hopi, the language of the Pueblo Indians of Arizona, Whorf became acutely aware of the inadequacies of traditional grammatical techniques built on Indo-European languages, especially Latin, Greek, and Sanskrit, for dealing with non-Indo-European languages. Experience of American and Hopi culture suggested to Whorf that the cultures and thought processes were different *because* their languages were so different. This led him to establish:

> . . .what I have called the "linguistic relativity principle," which means, in informal terms, that users of markedly different grammars are pointed by their grammars toward different types of observations and different evaluations of externally similar acts of observation, and hence are not equivalent as observers but must arrive at somewhat different views of the world.[16]

A more succinct version of this claim: "We dissect nature along lines laid down by our native language,"[17] came to be known as the "Whorfian hypothesis."[18] Language influences thought, it was claimed; mind is in the grip of language.

Whorf is perhaps best remembered for his claim that the Hopi language does not make space-time distinctions such as are characteristic of English and other Indo-European languages. Rather than being concerned with the time of an event, the Hopi, he argued, are interested in the validity that the speaker intends the statement to have (report, expectation of an event, generalization about events, and so forth). He suggested that had they developed a physics of their own, the Hopi would therefore have developed a kind very different from European and American space-time physics. His hypothesis came under attack for a variety of reasons. One is that he compares Hopi and English surface structures—comparing words and morphemes, rather than the components of meaning that underlie them. For example, he says that where English has a future time expression as in **He will run**, Hopi does not, because there is no exact equivalent to **will**. Instead, Hopi has an expression which translates into "expectation of running." Nevertheless, Hopi does have time categories; while in English anyone who says **John will run** is understood to hold the expectation that he will run. Furthermore, if we were as bound by language as the Whorfian hypothesis suggests, we would not be able to translate Hopi into English, since we would not be able to understand any time reference not given by the surface structure of our language.

In all fairness to Whorf, the "Whorfian hypothesis" reflects only part of his thinking—he does acknowledge that language "is in some sense a superficial embroidery upon deeper processes of consciousness."[19] Even so, he did not call these deeper processes "thought"; this he regarded as dependent on language. However, in the forties and fifties, a very strict, deterministic interpretation of "we dissect nature along lines laid down by our native language" arose, and led to some interesting pedagogical and literary experiments. If language does in fact determine thought, and if it does so primarily through morphology rather than syntax or phonology, then, it was argued, teachers should be able to improve the thought processes of their pupils by teaching certain kinds of words and morphemes, especially grammatical ones. For example, as will be discussed in more detail in Chapter 8, many speakers of Black English do not use the connective word **if** to join sentences. Thinking that a surface word must be used if the thought **if** is to be possible, some teachers concluded that speakers who did not use **if** did not understand the concept it expresses. Some attempted to teach the concept through teaching the use of the word **if**.[20] However, further study would have revealed that the speakers in question do express the *if*-concept, not by a word but by a rising pitch pattern; the concept is as much present as in speakers who use **if**. Only the expression is different. Too ready an attempt to associate meanings exclusively with surface words (or morphemes) led many who were inspired by Whorf into considerable misunderstanding about what it is that language-users know or must learn.

If one could increase possible strategies in thinking by increasing vocabulary, one might also expect to be able to decrease thought by restricting vocabulary. Another issue of concern in the fifties was whether language could be so manipulated for political purposes that people would be totally tyrannized or "brainwashed" by it. This idea was explored by George Orwell in an appendix to his famous novel, *Nineteen Eighty-Four*. Convinced of the power of language to influence thought, Orwell was horrified by the prospect of a society that sought to control thought by controlling its vehicle, language. He envisioned a totalitarian society, called "Ingsoc" (from *English socialism*), in which the authorities attempted to repress thought by reducing vocabulary. For this imaginary society, Orwell devised a vocabulary of extremely limited resources, exploiting basic principles of English word formation, especially compounding and the use of one morpheme in several different syntactic categories. The appendix is worth quoting at some length since it represents one of the clearest statements we have of the "Whorfian hypothesis" taken to its most literal conclusion:

> The purpose of Newspeak was not only to provide a medium of expression for the world-view and mental habits proper to the devotees of Ingsoc, but to make all other modes of thought impossible. It was intended that when Newspeak had been adopted once and for all and Oldspeak forgotten, a heretical thought—that is, a thought diverging from the principles of Ingsoc—should be literally unthinkable, at least so far as thought is dependent on words. Its vocabulary was so constructed as to give exact and often very subtle expression to every meaning that a Party member
> 10 could properly wish to express, while excluding all other meanings and also the possibility of arriving at them by indirect methods. This was done partly by the invention of new words, but chiefly by eliminating undesirable words and by stripping such words as remained of unorthodox meanings, and so far as possible of all secondary meanings whatever. To give a single example. The word *free* still existed in Newspeak, but it could only be used in such statements as "This dog is free from lice" or "This field is free from weeds." It could not be used in its old sense of "politically free" or "intellectually free," since political and intellectual free-
> 20 dom no longer existed even as concepts, and were therefore of necessity nameless. Quite apart from the suppression of definitely heretical words, reduction of vocabulary was regarded as an end in itself, and no word that could be dispensed with was allowed to survive. Newspeak was designed not to extend but to *diminish* the range of thought, and this purpose was indirectly assisted by cutting the choice of words down to a minimum. . . .
> The grammar of Newspeak had two outstanding peculiarities. The first of these was an almost complete interchangeability between different parts of speech. Any word in the language (in
> 30 principle this applied even to very abstract words such as *if* or *when*) could be used either as verb, noun, adjective, or adverb. Between the verb and the noun form, when they were of the same root, there was never any variation, this rule of itself involving the destruction of many archaic forms. The word *thought*, for example, did not exist in Newspeak. Its place was taken by *think*, which did duty for both noun and verb. . . . Adjectives were formed by adding the suffix *-ful* to the noun-verb, and adverbs by adding *-wise*. Thus, for example, *speedful* meant "rapid" and *speedwise* meant "quickly."[21]

Is Newspeak a real human possibility? Probably not, for the view of language with which Orwell is working in this passage overlooks many central aspects of human language. In particular, Ingsoc here overlooks the creative nature of language that makes the uttering of new sentences in new contexts possible and thereby opens up the possibility of new ranges of meaning. It denies any notion of semantic features that can be reused in different groupings of sound-meaning correlations. It denies the possibility of saying one thing and meaning another, as in puns and in ironic statements like **You are being nice today**. And it begs the question of how languages get to be as complex in vocabulary as they do. In reality, people are always having new thoughts and seeking out new words to express them. In short, Orwell's discussion presents an incomplete view of what human language is, and to the extent that this is so, Newspeak is not a real possibility. To give a specific example, the society of Ingsoc imagines that using content words as grammatical words will undermine the fundamental organization of language whereby thoughts are expressed in terms of relationships. People will not be able to think logically if unmistakable grammatical words are not available (this is the same sort of argument as was mentioned in connection with pedagogy). However, in actual fact, many grammatical words derive historically from content words, for example, **while** (originally "long time" as in **stay a while**), **shall** (originally "to owe"), **may** (originally "to have the strength to"), **very** (originally "truly"), and so forth. In other words, it is common for content words of suitable meaning to become grammatical words, that is, to change their hierarchical status in the sentence. The static kind of system the proponents of Ingsoc believe in simply has no reality, although strict attention to the idea that language determines thought might lead one to conclude that it does.

Chomskyan grammar, as we have seen, emphasizes linguistic creativity, and stresses language as a psychological entity with universal characteristics, rather than as a culture-specific entity. Given these concerns, we might expect Chomskyan grammarians to deny the "Whorfian hypothesis" entirely. Indeed, many transformationalists have done so. However, transformational grammar can actually suggest ways of accounting both for the undeniable fact that language influences the way we think, and for the equally undeniable fact that this is not the whole story. It can do this because of the two levels of analysis—one underlying and one surface. Consider, for example, the idea of semantic features. Insofar as a grammar refers to universal semantic features, and insofar as we claim that these features are part of a basic cognitive system, we are in fact claiming that certain inbuilt cognitive structures, including thought processes, determine what language is like. What is similar among languages and renders them translatable one to the other is precisely this universal organization that we try to define when we seek to characterize the nature of human language. In this respect all languages are similar. On the other hand, insofar as particular languages select certain bundles of features to express as lexical items, and no other bundles of features, and insofar as particular languages select certain syntactic categories to express certain concepts, particular languages do foster preferences for certain thought processes rather than for other ones. For example, in Old English, the equivalent of **to be thirsty** and **to be hungry** were "to thirst" and "to hunger." Similarly, in Chinese, grass **greens** rather than **is green**. In each case, the verb implies more active participation in the state of being thirsty, hungry, or green than does the **be** + adjective expression.

Interest in language functions, especially language as a tool of power, has recently sparked new interest in the Whorfian hypothesis, though in new form, and under the name he originally gave it: linguistic relativity. An important distinction that was not so obvious in Whorf's days as it is now must be made between the nature of language systems and the uses to which they are put. It is true that languages tend to give us categories. But that does not mean that we necessarily suppress or ignore anything that does not fall into those categories, as the Whorfian hypothesis suggests. We have terms like **blue** and **green**. Some people will call a color that falls between the two **green**, others will call it **blue**, because we usually select an existing term even if it doesn't quite fit the context. We can, however, talk about it, and decide whether it is bluish green, greenish blue, or between blue and green. We can even make up a name for it if we need to, or borrow one, like **turquoise**. The language itself allows us, in other words, to invent new categories, or to acknowledge the fuzzy boundaries and hedge (**Well, it's sort of this and sort of that**).

People tend to think that it is the fault of language that it can be used to brainwash people. But we must be careful not to lay the blame in the wrong place and not to shirk our own responsibility. Language does not force people to think of someone who has been labeled as Jew, Negro, WASP, Communist, racist, or sexist only in terms of that category. Language may be abused, but it can potentially lead us away from our tendency to categorize by allowing us to make new combinations of meanings and to qualify every semantic distinction we make.

MORPHEMES, THE LEXICON, AND STYLE

Lexical Cohesion

As we have seen, literary texts are particularly likely to exhibit cohesion at levels beyond the basic logic of the sentence. Here, cohesion among content morphemes is especially important. For instance, phonological patterning is done almost exclusively through content morphemes—they are almost invariably the primary carriers of alliteration, assonance, and rhyme, partly because they tend to be stressed, unlike grammatical morphemes. Furthermore, as in the examples from Pope and Sandburg analyzed in Chapter 2, it is through key content words that sound-meaning correlations are established.

Apart from their sound patterns, content words may be associated in a text through shared semantic features. For instance, in the passage from Pope's "Essay on Criticism" discussed in Chapter 2, lexical cohesion is created by repeated use of content words whose semantic description involves water or liquids: **stream, flows, surge, shore, torrent, main** ("ocean"). Another set of terms in the text involves sound: **harshness, sound, echo, soft, strain** ("tune"), **loud, hoarse, roar**; a third lexical set involves air: **Zephyr, blow, fly, skim**; a fourth involves motion of various kinds: **move, dance, blow, flow, surge, move, scour, fly, skim**, and this set ties in with other action verbs like **lash, roar, strive, throw**, and **labor**. Even the proper names, **Eccho, Zephyr, Ajax**, and **Camilla**, referring to figures in classical mythology, contribute to the lexical cohesion of the text. Notice that all these lexical classes overlap to some extent, so that there is cohesion between as well as within them. In Eliot's "Rhapsody on a Windy Night," discussed in Chapter 1, over and above the contrast between the two grammars in the poem, lexical cohesion is created by a concentration of items whose semantic description involves the concept of decay and destruction.

Robert Bridges's poem "November," already quoted in part on page 83, exemplifies several kinds of lexical cohesion typical of traditional nature poetry. Here is the poem in its entirety:

NOVEMBER

The lonely season in lonely lands, when fled
Are half the birds, and mists lie low, and the sun
Is rarely seen, nor strayeth far from his bed;
The short days pass unwelcomed one by one.

Out by the ricks the mantled engine stands
Crestfallen, deserted,—for now all hands
Are told to the plough,—and ere it is dawn appear
The teams following and crossing far and near,
As hour by hour they broaden the brown bands
10   Of the striped fields; and behind them firk° and prance
The heavy rooks, and daws grey-pated° dance:
As awhile, surmounting a crest, in sharp outline
(A miniature of toil, a gem's design,)
They are pictured, horses and men, or now near by
Above the lane they shout lifting the share,
By the trim hedgerow bloom'd° with purple air;
Where, under the thorns, dead leaves in huddle lie
Packed by the gales of Autumn, and in and out
The small wrens glide

20   With a happy note of cheer,
     And yellow amorets° flutter above and about,
     Gay, familiar in fear.

     And now, if the night shall be cold, across the sky
     Linnets and twites,° in small flocks helter-skelter,
     All the afternoon to the gardens fly,
     From thistle-pastures hurrying to gain the shelter
     Of American rhododendron or cherry-laurel:
     And here and there, near chilly setting of sun,
     In an isolated tree a congregation
30   Of starlings chatter and chide,
     Thickset as summer leaves, in garrulous quarrel:
     Suddenly they hush as one,—
     The tree top springs,—
     And off, with a whirr of wings,
     They fly by the score
     To the holly-thicket, and there with myriads more
     Dispute for the roosts; and from the unseen nation
     A babel of tongues, like running water unceasing,
     Makes live the wood, the flocking cries increasing,
40   Wrangling discordantly, incessantly,
     While falls the night on them self-occupied;
     The long dark night, that lengthens slow,
     Deepening with Winter to starve grass and tree,
     And soon to bury in snow
     The Earth, that, sleeping 'neath her frozen stole,
     Shall dream a dream crept from the sunless pole
     Of how her end shall be.[22]

---

10 firk: frisk   **11 grey-pated**: grey-headed   **16 bloom'd**: bright
21 amorets: love-birds   **24 linnets and twites**: small English song-birds

The poem begins and ends with the cold. But the ending is much more positive than the beginning. In the opening stanza we find a concentration of terms with negative meanings. These include not only the obvious negatives **nor** and the derivative **unwelcomed**, but also the adverb **rarely**, and the spatial terms **low** and **short** which, as discussed earlier, are negative with respect to their counterparts **high** and **long**. Furthermore, the meaning of **lonely** includes not only "absence of others," but also, unlike **alone**, "unwanted absence." Of the two motion verbs in the stanza, **flee** involves motion away from something desirable, while **stray** involves motion along the wrong path (though here in the poem it is negated, **nor strayeth** meaning simply "does not move"). All these negative terms set the initial view of November as a time of lacks and absences. This view is modified in the course of the poem, so that in the final summing up (lines 41–47), it is the positive spatial terms **deep, long,** and **lengthen** which appear (**long night** in line 42 instead of **short days** in line 4), balancing off the negative terms **sunless** and **starve.**

What produces this modification from negative to more positive are the birds, who throughout the poem are portrayed as lively and vigorous in the air, in contrast with the earth and its creatures, which are approaching death and immobility. Thus the birds are subjects of many verbs of motion, including **firk, prance** (10), **dance** (11), **glide** (19), **flutter** (21), and **fly** (25). By contrast, the things of the earth appear as subjects of many nonmotion verbs, such as **stand** (5), **be told** (7), **appear** (7), **be pictured** (14), **lie** (17), and **sleep** (45). Accompanying the difference in verbs is a difference in spatial prepositions—static locational terms are used for the earth, such as **out by** (5), **far, near** (8), **behind** (10), **above** (15), **by** (16), **under** (17), **'neath** (45). Directional terms are used for the birds: **in and out** (18), **across** (23), **to** (25, 36), **off** (34), **from** (37), and **about** (21). **In** is static for the earth (17), directional for the birds (18). The bird lexicon does have the relatively static locational **above** (21); but this term contrasts explicitly with a set of earth terms whose meaning involves static **under**, such as **under** (17), **'neath** (45), **bury** (44), **stole** (45), **mantled** (5). Moreover, **above** is associated with action (**flutter**) and **about** (21).

Metaphors heighten the contrast even more. In line 17, we find **dead leaves** lying **in a huddle,** which suggests they are animate (though dead). In exact contrast is the simile in line 31, where the birds are compared to living leaves in summer. But the birds are more lively than the summer leaves, since, rather than fall, they leap upward into the air (line 33, **the tree top springs**). This same contrast reappears in line 39: The birds **make live the woods**— again adding life—while, in line 43, approaching winter prepares to **starve** ("make dead") **grass and tree.**

In lines 37–40 we find grammatical rather than content morphemes used to create cohesion. In these lines, the vocabulary used to describe the sound of the birds displays a noticeable concentration of affixes and inflections: **un**seen, runn**ing**, **un**ceas**ing**, flock**ing**, **in**creas**ing**, wrang**ling**, **dis**cord**antly**, **in**cess**antly**. This accumulation suggests the complexity and discordance of the birds' chattering, both at the phonological level, where the many unstressed syllables create an uneven rhythm, and at the semantic level, where roots are surrounded by various kinds of modifications and qualifications.

The subject matter of "November"—nature and the changing seasons— is reminiscent of the calendrical pictures that were so popular in medieval manuscripts, depicting seasonal activities, and also of sixteenth-century "genre" paintings like those of Breughel, in which scenes from rustic life were depicted. The stock-in-trade of such pictures for fall and winter are haystacks (**ricks**), harvesting machines (**the mantled engine** of line 5), and teams of oxen ploughing the land. However, it is not only the things selected for mention, but also the choice of words which conjures up associations with such pictures. For one, the archaic forms and, especially, **strayeth, amorets,** and **firk** all point to the late sixteenth or early seventeenth centuries (in *The Oxford*

English Dictionary, entries for **firk** in the sense of "dance, be frisky" all date from 1596–1679). More obviously, the lexicon itself includes a set which involves painting. Within two lines we find **miniature** (13) (which is a pun between "a small representation" and "an illustration in a manuscript"), and **are pictured** (14). Cohesion in "November" is therefore not only internal within the text, but also external, with another form of art.

Lexical Foregrounding

As the above examples suggest, examining a text in terms of its lexicon can often reveal sources of cohesion that we might not otherwise notice and can help us discover the recurrent themes and images of a text. Sometimes, however, this approach may seem singularly unrevealing. For example, looking at the lexicon of "November" (on pages 111–112), we find it contains a large number of terms referring to objects and processes in nature, and to agriculture. Hardly an interesting observation, we might think. Since the changing season is the subject of the poem, a concentration of such terms cannot surprise any more than a concentration of zoological terms in Darwin's *Origin of the Species*. What is at issue here is a question of levels of analysis. In any discourse, lexical choice is intimately associated with, and partly limited by, choice of subject matter. Lexical choices which result most directly from choice of subject matter are likely to be the least striking stylistically. What is of more basic interest in "November," then, is the choice of subject matter itself, rather than the vocabulary associated with it. This does not mean that the nature terms in "November" or the zoological terms in *Origin of the Species* contribute nothing to the cohesion of those texts, for they certainly do. What is does mean is that these choices, to the extent that they are likely in the context, are not foregrounded.

"November" does illustrate a number of traditional kinds of lexical foregrounding. To begin with, a number of words in this poem stand out by virtue of their rarity of occurrence. These include **ere** (7), **firk** (10), **pated** (11), **awhile** (12), **amorets** (21), **chide** (30), **'neath** (45), and the idiom **all the afternoon** (25). These items along with the **-eth** inflection on **strayeth** (3) are "archaisms," that is, old forms that have passed almost completely out of the language and are used now only in extremely specific contexts such as poetry and religious ritual. Other items in the poem are familiar to us in form, but are used with archaic or unusual meanings. **Familiar** (22), for example, is used in the older sense of "family-like" or "intimate" rather than its current sense of "well-known." **Gain** (26) and **surmount** (12) are used as verbs of motion, the former meaning "arrive" rather than its more usual sense of "acquire," the latter meaning "come over" rather than its more usual "overcome"; the idiom **tell to** (7) with a following noun is archaic; the adjective **thickset** (31) applies nowadays only to bodies, but is used in the poem with reference to leaves; **bloom** (16) is used in its rare sense of "glow."

Another type of lexical foregrounding is the opposite of archaism, namely, the invention of new lexical items, or new meanings for old lexical items. Such inventions are called "neologisms." Carroll's **jabberwocky** and Orwell's **newspeak** are neologisms that have made their way into the lexicon of English. One of the richest sources of lexical invention lies in the creation of new compounds, some of which can be very striking, like Sandburg's **hunger-hands** and **hunger-eyes** ("The Harbor," lines 3 and 4). Compounds like these juxtapose morphemes in new ways and challenge the reader's imagination by suggesting new and concentrated meaning or casting a new light on the conventional meanings of the components. In colloquial discourse, creative compounding serves as a source of vivid insult epithets, of which **four-flusher, bootlicking,** and **motherloving** are some of the less obscene examples in the language.

Homonymy gives rise to another kind of lexical foregrounding and cohesion, the pun. Puns are often described as involving double or multiple meanings, or intentional ambiguity. What puns usually do is introduce more than one lexical item by means of a single phonological sequence. One example mentioned in Chapter 2 is Joyce's use of the morpheme **cant** in **with the canting crew** (see page 45). As already discussed, there are quite a number of morphemes and morpheme sequences in English with the phonological form [kænt], and several of them are plausible in the particular context of the Joyce text. The multiplicity of possible meanings for **cant** in the context creates layers of unexpected cohesion. As "cannot," [kænt] is cohesive with **kennot** and **wannot**; as "jargon" and "whine," it is cohesive with other references to verbal activities (**psing, psalmen**), and so on.

Because written English often distinguishes homonyms, puns occur somewhat more readily in speech than in writing. For instance, the familiar riddle **What's black and white and [rɛd] all over?**—**The newspaper** puns on [rɛd] as a color term and as the past participle of **read**, so that [rɛd] in the sequence is cohesive both with **black and white** and **newspaper**. But this pun is lost in writing because of the spelling difference **red/read**. In literature, it is partly because of this speech/writing difference that the pun tends to be associated especially with drama. One way people do make puns in writing is by manipulating spelling to suggest multiple lexical items by a single word. This is the main punning technique Joyce uses in the passage quoted in Chapter 2 where, for example, **painapple** suggests the **pain** of a prickly **pineapple**, as well as **pineapple** in the slang meaning of "hand grenade" (cohesive with **bomb** and **pain**). This same kind of punning creates the humor in the following excerpt from a story by John Lennon called "The SinguLARGE Experience of Miss Anne Duffield." The text is intended to be a parody of a Sherlock Holmes story narrated by Doctor Watson:

> I find it recornered in my nosebook that it was a dokey and winnie dave towart the end of Marge in the ear of our Loaf 1892 in Much Bladder, a city off the North Wold. Shamrock Womlbs

had receeded a telephart whilst we sat at our lunch eating. He made
5   no remark but the matter ran down his head, for he stud in front
of the fire with a thoughtfowl face, smirking his pile, and casting
an occasional gland at the massage. Quite sydney without warping
he turd upod me with a miscarriage twinkle in his isle.
    'Ellifitzgerrald my dear Whopper,' he grimmond then sharply
10   'Guess whom has broken out of jail Whopper?' My mind immediately recoughed all the caramels that had recently escaped or
escaped from Wormy Scabs.[23]

Lennon's specific procedure in this passage is to create multiple meanings by
replacing lexical items or parts of lexical items with others which resemble
them phonologically: **ear** for **year** (line 2), **fowl** for **ful** (6), **ellifitzgerrald** for
elementary (9), **caramels** for **criminals** (11). Particularly funny are the sub-
stitutions that introduce taboo words: **telephart** (4), **turd** (8), **stud** (5); or
taboo subjects such as excretion: **bladder** (3), **pile** (6); childbirth: **miscarriage**
(8), **Womlbs** (3); or simply the body: **gland** (7), **recoughed** (11), **scabs** (12).

    In general, we find that morphological experimentation in literature tends
to focus primarily on content morphemes, less on derivatives, less on inflections, and even less on relational expressions like **and, but, this**. This tendency
is as apparent in the passage from Joyce's *Finnegans Wake* quoted on page 45
as in Carroll's "Stanza of Anglo-Saxon Poetry." (However, as we shall see in
Chapter 8, when dialects are being represented, this hierarchy tends to be
reversed.)

Diction

In literary criticism the term "diction" is often used to refer to the lexical
aspect of style. Diction can simply mean the totality of lexical choices found
in a given text or group of texts, but more often it refers to patterns of lexical
choice, as when we speak of a writer's diction being "abstract" or "lofty."
Traditionally, stylisticians and literary critics have been interested not only in
describing diction, but also in evaluating it. Thus diction may be used to
refer to correctness of lexical choice, as when people speak of "good" and
"bad" diction, or of "learning proper diction." As we have seen in the discussion of taboo words and jargons, not all morphemes and lexical items are
equally appropriate in all contexts. Knowing what forms are associated with
what contexts is an important part of competence. For example, knowing the
lexical items **commit homicide**, **blow away**, and **murder** involves knowing not
only that all three include the meaning "cause to die," but also that the first
belongs to legal discourse, the second to slang, while the third is unspecialized
contextually. A great many morphemes and lexical items in the language
are unspecialized, and these are probably the ones that get used most.
Nevertheless, it is surprising how many are specialized to some degree.
For instance, as we noted earlier, many forms which are synonymous or

nearly synonymous semantically are differentiated pragmatically in the language, according to such factors as degree of formality, as with **happen/ occur/come down** (in one of its slang senses); degree of technicality, as with **bruise/contusion, opening/aperture**; attitude conveyed, as with **government/ regime** (the latter being pejorative) or **thin/svelte** (the latter being positive); genre of discourse, as with the **-eth** third person present inflection (associated with religious or poetic discourse); or addressee, as with the **thou** pronouns used to address divine beings. Because many lexical items are associated with particular contexts, it is important in analyzing the diction or lexical choice in a text to consider how particular choices interact with the kind of choices that one might expect in the context. A psychiatrist might well describe a patient as **off his rocker** in a casual conversation, but this expression will have rather different effects if used by the same speaker in a formal diagnosis.

Is there a specialized vocabulary for literature? In literary studies, it is customary to speak of "poetic diction," a phrase which would seem to suggest a specialized lexicon, for poetry at least. To explore this idea, let us return to the lexicon of "November." The majority of items in this text are fairly unspecialized ones that could be appropriately used in any speech context. There are quite a few, however, which would stand out in casual conversation. We have already discussed some of these, namely the archaisms, and the forms used with archaic or unusual meanings. Other less obvious ones are the idioms **as one** (32), **dispute for** (37), and the derivatives **unseen** (37), **unceasing** (38), **discordantly** (40), but not **incessantly** (40). We recognize these items as belonging to formal discourse, and in some cases can even pinpoint what the informal lexical counterpart would be, such as **all together** for **as one**, **fight over** for **dispute for**, **invisible** for **unseen**. Even **flee** (1) has the less formal counterparts **escape** and **run away**; **gem** (13) is more specialized than its synonym **jewel**. In addition to being formal, many of these items are of the type people often describe as "poetic." To say that an expression is poetic, however, is not to say that it is appropriate only in poetry. Rather, it usually means that the expression conveys an attitude of solemnity or emotional intensity on the part of the speaker. "Poetic diction" is above all diction that is both formal and "emotive" (that is, it conveys strong emotion). Again, we can find pairs of synonyms illustrating the contrast between neutral and poetic forms, such as **incessant/unceasing, branch/bough, girl/maiden, sleep/slumber, room/chamber, problems/woes** or **cares**, and a great many others. Sometimes a single form will have both a neutral and a poetic meaning. For instance, in "November," **land** (1) is used with its poetic meaning as a [+count] noun meaning "region"; **tongue** (38) with its poetic meaning of "language"; and **above** (21) poetically as an adverb (neutral usage has **up above**). Metaphor is also traditionally considered characteristic of poetic diction, and so is archaism, which conveys a high degree of formality and solemnity. The appropriateness of this kind of diction in "November" is indicative of the fact that the lyric is a formal and emotive context. By contrast, a meteorological report that said **It was sunless and rained ceaselessly at**

elevations of 5000 feet or beneath yesterday would be perceived as lexically deviant because "too poetic"—it seems to suggest that the meteorologist is undergoing a personal emotional crisis provoked by the weather, and this kind of information is inappropriate in a weather report.

The concept of poetic diction has its origins in the belief that some words and morphemes have greater inherent beauty and aesthetic potential than others, and that only those of sufficient inherent beauty should be used in poetry. In some periods in the history of English literature, it was felt that poetry required a special lexicon of its own since the lexicon in general use lacked intrinsic beauty and was inadequate for achieving the effects poets are after. In other periods, it was felt, on the contrary, that the greatest beauty lay in the vocabulary of "common speech," a view commonly associated with the Romantic poet Wordsworth. Nowadays, we no longer think of words and morphemes as being inherently beautiful or ugly, or of beauty as residing intrinsically in the language itself. We see it as a matter of tradition and convention that specific forms are considered poetic or formal or colloquial while others are not. Nevertheless, these conventions are very real indeed— real enough to be used as the basis for some very rich and intricate kinds of lexical foregrounding. A dramatic example of this type of lexical foregrounding can be found in Gregory Corso's poem "Bomb," from which the following lines are taken. The poet is singing a sarcastic song of praise to the atom bomb:

> O Bomb in which all lovely things
> moral and physical anxiously participate
>
> . . .
>
> I bring you Midgardian roses   Arcadian musk
> Reputed cosmetics from the girls of heaven
> Welcome me   fear not thy opened door
> nor thy cold ghost's grey memory
> nor the pimps of indefinite weather[24]

What strikes us in these lines is a clash between the terms **reputed, cosmetics, girls, pimp,** and the diction in the rest of the passage. Content words like **rose, musk, ghost, memory,** the relational words **thy** and **nor,** the historical present inflection (**I bring,** not **I am bringing**), the archaically inflected imperative **fear not** (versus formal **do not fear** and informal **don't be afraid of**), the archaic spelling **O,** and the erudite allusions of **Midgardian** and **Arcadian** exemplify the kind of diction we are accustomed to seeing in lyric poetry, and which we associate with the formality and emotiveness of the genre. The derogatory slang term **pimp,** the informal term **girl** (meaning **woman** as opposed to **child**), and the commercialese of **reputed cosmetics,** on the other hand, are felt to violate this norm and are thus foregrounded in the poem. These examples give us an idea of the kinds of vocabulary that are felt *not* to belong in poetry, namely items marked especially as informal or colloquial or as belonging to a jargon. Corso's foregrounded lexical choices tie in with his choice of topic, the atom bomb, a subject which in itself departs from the traditional range of subject matters for the lyric. The effect seems to work two ways. On the one hand, the horror and obscenity of the bomb is emphasized by its clash with the traditional diction of the lyric song of praise; on the other hand, a criticism of the traditional diction is also implied—how can a poetry of roses and Arcadian musk pertain to the urgent contemporary threat of the bomb?

The conventional diction of prose fiction is much the same as that of poetry, with the exception that archaisms play a much smaller role in prose. Just as in Corso's poem, prose writers can exploit our knowledge of this conventional diction, as Ken Kesey does in this passage from his novel *Sometimes a Great Notion*, in which an old boltcutter overhears a group of townsmen in a smalltown bar discussing their community's economic troubles and internal strife:

> The old wino boltcutter has seen them all, has heard all the talk. He has been listening over his shoulder all afternoon, hearing the younger men talk about the trouble nowdays as though their dissatisfaction is a recent development, a sign of unusual times. He listened for a long time while they talked and pounded the table and read bits from the *Eugene Register Guard* blaming the despondency on "these troubled times of Brinkmanship, Blamesmanship, and Bombsmanship." He listened to them accuse the federal government of turning America into a nation of softies,
>
> 10 then listened to them condemn the same body for its hardhearted refusal to help the faltering town through the recession. He usually makes it a rule on his drinking trips into town to remain aloof from nonsense such as this, but when he hears the delegation agreeing that much of the community's woes can be laid at the feet of the Stampers and their stubborn refusal to unionize, it is too much for him to take. The man with the union button is in the middle of explaining that these times demand more sacrifice on the part of the goddamned individual, when the old boltcutter rises noisily to his feet.
>
> 20 "These times?" He advances on them, his bottle held dramatically aloft. "What do you think, everything *used* to be apple-pie 'n' ice cream?"
>
> The citizens look up in surprised indignation; it is regarded as something of a breach in local protocol to interrupt these sessions.
>
> "That bomb talk? All horseshit." He rears over their table, unsteady in a cloud of blue smoke. "That depression talk and that other business, that strike business? More horseshit. For twenty years, thirty years, *forty* years, all th' way back to the Big War, somebody been sayin' oh me, the trouble is *such*, oh my the trouble
>
> 30 is *so*; the trouble is the *ray*-dio, the trouble is the Re*pub*licans, the trouble is the *Demo*crats, the trouble is the *Commy*-ists . . ." He spat on the floor with a pecking motion of his head. "All horseshit."[25]

The diction in this passage reflects a state of affairs that arises almost inevitably in any realistic novel, namely that the language that is the norm for novels differs markedly from the language that is the norm for the characters in the situation being represented, particularly as regards vocabulary. One way writers deal with this state of affairs is to approximate the characters' actual speech only in dialogue while observing the novelistic norm everywhere else, including in summaries of the characters' words and thoughts. In this passage, Kesey takes a slightly different tack. In describing the words, thoughts, and actions of his characters, he mixes conventional novelistic diction with the diction the characters would actually use. Thus, when the boltcutter is focused on, informal and colloquial expressions are interspersed with formal diction: Contrasts are made between informal **make it a rule** (12), **drinking trips** (12), **into town** (12), **too much to take** (15), **in the middle of** (16) and more formal **remain aloof** (12), **rises noisily** (18). In the summaries of the townspeople's arguments, the slang terms **softies** (9) and **goddamned** (18) signal that, to some extent, their speech is being quoted directly (our knowledge of novelistic diction lets us know not to attribute these terms directly to the voice of the author/narrator). But the language used to summarize the townspeople's arguments is distinctive in another way: It is riddled with formal clichés like **hardhearted refusal** (10), **faltering town** (11), **community's woes** (14), and **lay at the feet of** (14). Now these clichés do not primarily characterize the real speech of the townspeople. It is unlikely that they would actually use terms like **faltering, woes,** or **body** (meaning "institution") (10) in the situation. Here Kesey uses this formal clichéd style primarily in order to characterize their thoughts as being conformist, unreflective, and narrow-minded, a view which is corroborated by the content, since we, through the boltcutter, see them arguing contradictory positions (lines 9–11). The clichés do, however, characterize the actual speech of the union man (quoted in lines 16–18) and the editorial style of the newspaper (quoted in lines 7–8). By applying this language to the townspeople as well, Kesey suggests their tendency to conform to the views advocated by these outside voices rather than attending to the local wisdom of people like the boltcutter.

When the boltcutter actually begins to speak, the divergence between him and the townspeople is dramatized even more acutely. Naturally enough, his diction is colloquial—the nouns **talk** (25) and **business** (meaning "matter") (26), the taboo word **horseshit** (25), the idioms **apple pie 'n' ice cream** (21), and **the Big War** (28) all suggest this. The colloquialism and the representation of spoken language are further stressed by spelling—**'n'** (21), **Commy-ists** (31) to indicate regional uneducated pronunciation. In contrast, the townspeople's response to his remarks, set apart in a separate paragraph (23–24), are given to us again with a deluge of formal clichés.

There is a third kind of diction which emerges in this latter part of the passage, one that we can associate directly with the narrator/author. In contrast to the colloquialism of the boltcutter's speech, the language used to describe him as he speaks is solemn and emotive. The formal verbs **rise** (18) and **advance** (20), the archaism **aloft** (21), the metaphors in **rears** (25) and **pecking motion** (32) combine with the image of the **cloud of blue smoke** (26) and the dramatic spitting gesture (32) to give a kind of authority and emotive intensity to the boltcutter's words. Thus both the boltcutter's speech and the language the narrator uses to describe him contrast in different ways with the stale, colorless clichés associated with the townspeople, ratifying his viewpoint as the authoritative and sincere one.

The townsmen in the Kesey passage are associated with a "jargon," the patriotic rhetoric of the union man and the newspaper. Jargon is language specially designed for certain people and certain subjects in certain contexts. It mainly involves specialized vocabulary. Jargons perform important and useful functions for members of the ingroups who design them, but to others, they can sound contrived and pretentious—precisely because they are the "property" of an ingroup. Hence in literature, jargon is sometimes used, as by Kesey, to make characters and societies unsympathetic. This device is also one of the most memorable stylistic characteristics of Cyra McFadden's novel *The Serial*, a humorous critique of life in the upper-middle-class suburbs of Marin County, near San Francisco. Both the narrator and the characters in this work use a jargon which, though partly regional and partly generational, is primarily associated with a particular socioeconomic class:

> Harvey agreed to meet Bill at Ethel's because Bill said on the phone that he had something heavy to lay on him and thought they ought to get together in a nurturing environment. Ethel's did a mind-blowing minted trout. Minted trout was nurturing. And
> 5   evading Ms. Murphy for one evening, Harvey thought, might just be the saving of his sanity or at least his lower back.
>   He was a little spooked, though, because he didn't know where Bill was coming from, and so he fortified himself on a couple of Heineken's at the *no name* before he made the funk-and-fern scene
> 10   at Ethel's. Beside him at the bar, an advertising type was coming on strong with a chick in the rich-peasant look, complete with the jewel-studded babushka Ms. Murphy had flipped over in Joseph Magnin's Christmas catalogue. "I want to get together some loving, seeking people so we can put together a really altruistic portfolio,"
> 15   he was saying earnestly.[26]

A great many of the jargon terms in this passage refer to psychological states and processes—these being one of the main concerns of the social group being described and parodied. We have the terms **heavy** (2), **nurturing** (3), **seeking** (14), **altruistic** (14), **flip over** (12), **come from** (8), **lay** (something) **on** (someone) (2). Called "psychobabble" by some of its critics, this vocabulary arose out of the interest in psychology, psychotherapy, and consciousness-raising which developed in the United States in the 1970s, especially among the young upper middle class. Part of what makes this jargon ridiculous in the text is the association of the abstract psychological terminology with banal concrete realities—**mind-blowing** (4) and **nurturing** (4) to describe a minted trout; **altruistic** (14) to describe a portfolio. Other instances of this class jargon in the text are not associated with psychology, such as the intensifier **really** (14), the nouns **environment** (meaning "setting") (3), **look** (meaning "style of dress") (11); the expression **an X type** (10) to characterize a person.

One of the ways the text gives us a critical perspective on this kind of language—and the values with which it is associated—is by attributing it to characters other than the main character, Harvey. For instance, the first three sentences, jargon-packed, are a summary of Bill's phone call. Sentence 4 (lines 4–6) gives Harvey's own thoughts—he will go to Ethel's not to have his mind blown in a nurturing environment, but to get away from Ms. Murphy, whose demands on his body are as much of a burden as those on his mind. In sentence 5 (lines 7–10), this distinction is made within Harvey's own thoughts. In connection with Bill, he thinks in jargon (**where Bill was coming from**); in connection with himself, he uses the outmoded slang **spooked** and the colloquialism **couple of**; in connection with Ethel's, he returns to jargon (**made the funk-and-fern scene**).

Why is this jargon so alienating to the outsider? By definition, jargons exist by contrast to the spoken norm, however vaguely defined that may be. In the presence of a jargon, outsiders are likely to feel that there are other words that could be used which are equally good and more widely shared. This is particularly likely with the jargon in the McFadden text, since the most commonplace facts of everyday life are being discussed—food, clothing, love, sex, friendship. In addition, jargons are, as a rule, acquired by people as adults, long after the more spontaneous language-learning of childhood is over, and their acquisition is usually part of an effort to gain access to a specialized group or subject. Hence their impression of artificiality and exclusiveness, the more disturbing in literary works where, it is supposed, the writer is interested in achieving a wide audience.

SUGGESTED FURTHER READINGS

Two major studies of word formation in English are Marchand's *The Categories and Types of Present-Day English Word Formation* and Adams's *An Introduction to English Word-Formation*. Mencken's *The American Language* is a classic study of the American language and especially its vocabulary. In her book, *Our Own Words*, Dohan provides a lively and up-to-date account of the development of American English, with emphasis on coinages and borrowings in the twentieth century. In *All-American English*, Dillard focuses on the influence of other languages on the development of contemporary American English. More detailed studies of considerable interest are to be found in Brown, *Words and Things*, Chapter 4 (on sound symbolism), and Leach, "Anthropological Aspects of Language: Animal Categories and Verbal Abuse." The latter is a study of taboo from a Whorfian point of view.

A traditional account of lexical semantics, with extensive material on meaning-change, is to be found in Ullmann, *Semantics: An Introduction to the Science of Meaning*. In Chapters 9 and 10 of his *Introduction to Theoretical Linguistics*, Lyons provides a critical overview of traditional semantic research and then proposes a theory of semantic features (he calls them "components"). Current issues in lexical theory are well illustrated in Farkas et al., *Papers from the Parasession on the Lexicon*. The majority of generative studies on lexical semantics deal with sentential as well as lexical semantics; some are cited in the Suggested Readings for Chapter 5.

Diction has, for the most part, not been studied seriously by linguists. Among the many studies written by literary critics are Davie's *Purity of Diction in English Verse* and Josephine Miles's *The Vocabulary of Poetry*. The latter is an excellent example of in-depth analyses of more particular aspects of diction. The book contains three studies, one on Wordsworth, one on the "pathetic fallacy" in nineteenth-century poetry (that is, the assignment of animate, largely human, vocabulary to things in nature), and a third on the adjectives used in poetry from the sixteenth to the twentieth centuries.

Most studies of diction must rely heavily on information about various aspects of usage from innovativeness to archaism, from formality to slang. While contemporary rhetorics are an invaluable source of such information for literature of the past, the student would do well to start investigations with the help of a major dictionary, preferably one that provides historical information about word meanings and appropriateness of usage. Most important among such dictionaries is *The Oxford English Dictionary*. The *American Heritage Dictionary* can also be used profitably, although, unlike *The Oxford English Dictionary*, it does not have extensive quotations from earlier literature. There are also a large number of specialized dictionaries of underworld language, slang, and so forth. Among them, Harold Wentworth and Stuart Berg Flexner's *Dictionary of American Slang* is one of the most up to date. Eric Partridge's many books on slang, bawdy language, and other topics have delighted several generations. His *Slang Today and Yesterday* is particularly useful for studies of the language of literature. A rich source of various types of current specialized vocabulary, including slang, jargon, and regional vocabulary, is the journal *American Speech*.

Exercises

1. The following passage is an excerpt from a novel that is truly, as its title says, "A Story of Over 50,000 Words Without Using the Letter E."

> Upon this basis I am going to show you how a bunch of bright young folks did find a champion; a man with boys and girls of his own; a man of so dominating and happy individuality that Youth is

drawn to him as is a fly to a sugar bowl. It is a story about a small town. It is not a gossipy yarn; nor is it a dry, monotonous account, full of such customary "fill-ins" as "romantic moonlight casting murky shadows down a long, winding country road." Nor will it say anything about twinklings lulling distant folds; robins carolling at twilight, nor any "warm glow of lamplight" from a cabin window. No. It is an account of up-and-doing activity.[27]

To write even one paragraph like this without using the letter e is quite a feat, let alone a whole novel. Try writing a story of about a hundred words without using the letter e. Then discuss what caused more problems: avoiding grammatical morphemes or content morphemes? If English spelling were phonetic what problems would be eliminated?

2. In the mid-sixties several new words were coined with **-in**, for example, **love-in, teach-in, be-in**. Many of them are now obsolete. How many can you think of? What sorts of constraints are there in the derivation? In other words, if you were coining new words with **-in**, why would **lecture-in** not fit the extant pattern very well?

3. How many three-part verbs like **put up with** and **boogie on down** can you think of? Do you know any four-part verbs? Do the particles **up, down, on,** and **with** keep part or none of their original meaning? Are these verbs restricted in use to particular ways of speaking (e.g., colloquial language), or do they have a wider range? In what kinds of written texts would you expect to find them?

4. Some words are coined through the process of "blending." Here are a few:

motel	= motor hotel
Amerindian	= American Indian
beefalo	= beef and buffalo
smog	= smoke and fog
ballute	= balloon and parachute
brunch	= breakfast and lunch
bit	= binary digit
positron	= positive electron
fantabulous	= fantastic and fabulous

There is no way of predicting whether the first one or two syllables of the first word will be selected, or whether the last one or two syllables of the final word will be selected (e.g., there is no way of predicting **bit** from **binary digit** rather than **binit**). Nevertheless, the phonological relation between the first and last words is regular in these data. Whatever part of the first word is selected, it always ends in the same way, and whatever part of the last word is selected begins in the same way (**bite** would be impossible from **binary digit**). Say as precisely as you can what the phonological constraints are on blends in these data, and give some more examples. (Note that not all blends in English follow the pattern here; ignore those that do not.)

5. Which of the following contain verb phrase idioms? For each idiom, provide a paraphrase with one word instead of the idiom. (Note that some of these sentences may be ambiguous.)

> a. Cindy went in for stamp collecting.
> b. Cindy went in for a check-up.
> c. Grandpa came down with the guns.
> d. Grandpa came down with the flu.
> e. Grandpa came up with the guns.
> f. Elizabeth dropped a brick at the party.
> g. That music doesn't exactly turn me on.
> h. I didn't turn on the tap.

6. Think of as many expressions as you can meaning **fat** (e.g., **overweight, plump, husky**). Rank the words in each set from the most unpleasant (and taboo) to the most innocuous, and discuss the effect of the euphemistic terms. Is meaning lost or distorted? Are the terms cute, jargonistic, or really neutral?

7. Given the set:

father	mother
son	daughter
bull	cow
bullock	heifer

what kinds of lexical semantic features would you set up to differentiate the lexical items? Use as a model the discussion of features for **man-woman, boy-girl**. There is a rather important difference between terms like **bull** or **man** and terms like **father**. The feature analysis we have discussed so far does not capture this difference. What is it?

8. The following prepositions either are or were in earlier English all used as terms indicating place and time relations. There is substantial evidence that time and space should be considered realizations of the same semantic primitive (the criteria are purely linguistic, not philosophical or based on physics). On the basis of the list below, would you designate this primitive as ($\pm$SPACE) or ($\pm$TIME)? Give as many reasons as you can. Before answering this question, use *The Oxford English Dictionary* to check any prepositions that seem surprising to you in either spatial or temporal use.

about	before	in	through
above	behind	inside	throughout
after	below	off	to
ahead	between	on	toward
around	by	out	under
at	down	over	until
away	for	past	up
back	from	since	within

9. In the section on diction, a passage was discussed from Kesey's *Sometimes a Great Notion* in which an old boltcutter disagrees with the rest of the townspeople. The scene ends with this one additional paragraph:

> "What, in your opinion, is the trouble?" The Real Estate Man tilts back his chair and grins up at the intruder, preparing to humor him. But the old fellow beats him to the punch; he laughs sadly, the sudden anger turning as suddenly to pity; he shakes his head and looks about at the citizens—"You boys, you boys . . ."—then places his empty bottle on the table and crooks a long, knob-knuckled forefinger around the neck of a full bottle and shuffles out of the bright sun that slants through the Snag's front window. "Don't you see it's just the same plain old horseshit as always?"[28]

Discuss the diction of this paragraph in as much detail as you can, contrasting the vocabulary of the Real Estate Man with that of the boltcutter, and both with that of the author/narrator. Identify clichés, colloquialisms, solemn and emotive words, and so forth.

10. The juxtaposition of different levels of vocabulary is very striking in Eliot's "Rhapsody on a Windy Night" (quoted on pages 24–26). Latinate, formal terms like **lunar synthesis** coexist in the text with **rancid butter**, for example. Discuss the diction of this poem, and show to what extent particular levels of diction are associated with the narrative of the lamp and of memory as opposed to the narrator.

11. Carroll's "Jabberwocky," based on "A Stanza of Anglo-Saxon Poetry," is one of the most famous "nonsense" poems in English. Here is a less well-known nonsense poem, in which actual words, most of them unfamiliar to the general reader, are used, often with little or none of their original meaning.

"LEPIDOPTERA"

"Polite, polygamous poltroon, 'twas but his retrograde;
Barbel he was, yet barracoon, this limner of Schlazade.
He spoke of scumbled scuppernong, a scutiform corymb—
Too late, his pride to seep along, too late, indeed, for him.

"To outward view conterminous, to inward view adept,
His obfuscation verminous myopic as he wept—
Too late, a gudgeon though it were, in sesquiserried void
Might elevate his soul to her, his chrysoberyloid!"[29]

    a. Look up the words you do not know in a large dictionary, such as Webster's *Third New International Dictionary*, *The American Heritage Dictionary of the English Language*, or *The Oxford English Dictionary*. Discuss what meanings these words actually have, what they convey in the poem, and why.

    b. Quotation marks are purely graphic devices, with no exact correlations in speech. What do they signify here?

12. Many recent works of science fiction, including TV series such as *Star Trek*, tend to use an elevated, somewhat archaic diction. Select a work where this is true, identify clear features of both elevated diction and clear archaism, and suggest why they were chosen for this work.

13. Discuss lexical cohesion and lexical foregrounding in Peter Davison's poem "July," quoted in Exercise 7, Chapter 1.

NOTES

[1] Lewis Carroll, "A Stanza of Anglo-Saxon Poetry," in *The Book of Nonsense*, ed. Roger Lancelyn Green (New York: Dutton, 1965), pp. 118–20.

[2] The following discussion is based on W. Nelson Francis, "Revolution in Grammar," *Quarterly Journal of Speech*, 40 (1954), 299–312. Francis analyzes "Jabberwocky."

[3] Carroll, "A Stanza."

[4] In this respect, we can contrast **deer** with the nouns **pants** and **eyeglasses**. Grammatically, these words are only plural, which is why we have to say **Your pants are ripped** whether we mean one or more pairs. To differentiate nouns like **deer** from nouns like **pants**, then, we say that **pants** is only plural, with plural overtly expressed, while **deer** is either singular or plural, with a $\emptyset$ (zero) plural.

[5] Some of these may vary dialectically, as for example, **ice cream** and **potato salad**, which in some speech communities have the stress of compounds and in others of phrases.

[6] Hans Marchand, *The Categories and Types of Present-Day English Word Formation: A Synchronic-Diacronic Approach*, 2nd ed. (Munich: Beck'sche Verlagshandlung, 1969). Chapter 2 provides extensive discussion of views on the difference between compounds and idioms (he calls the latter "syntactic groups," or "phrases with specified meaning").

[7] Bolinger gives an extensive account of verbal phrases in English. See Dwight Bolinger, *The Verbal Phrase in English* (Cambridge, Mass.: Harvard Univ. Press, 1971).

[8] Leonard Bloomfield, *Language* (New York: Holt, Rinehart and Winston, 1933), p. 137.

[9] For discussion of this distinction, see John Lyons, *Introduction to Theoretical Linguistics* (London and New York: Cambridge Univ. Press, 1968), pp. 424–34; and John Lyons, *Semantics*, Vol. 1 (London and New York: Cambridge Univ. Press, 1977), Chapter 7.

[10] *Funk and Wagnalls Standard College Dictionary* (New York: Funk and Wagnalls, 1972).

[11] Geoffrey Leech, *Semantics* (Baltimore, Md.: Penguin Books, 1974), pp. 96–105.

[12] Manfred Bierwisch, "Some Semantic Universals of German Adjectivals," *Foundations of Language*, 3 (1967), 1–36.

[13] For example, Otto Jespersen, *A Modern English Grammar on Historical Principles* (1909–1949; rpt. London: Allen and Unwin, 1961), VI, 466.

[14] Manfred Bierwisch, "Semantics," in *New Horizons in Linguistics*, ed. John Lyons (Harmondsworth, Mssex.: Penguin, 1970), p. 182.

[15] See Ann Bodine, "Androcentrism in Prescriptive Grammar: Singular 'They,' Sex-indefinite 'He,' and 'He or She,'" *Language in Society*, 4 (1975), 129–46.

[16] Benjamin Lee Whorf, *Language, Thought and Reality* (1940); rpt. in *Selected Writings of Benjamin Lee Whorf*, ed. John B. Caroll (Cambridge, Mass.: The MIT Press, 1956), p. 221.

[17] Whorf, *Language, Thought and Reality*, p. 213.

[18] Also sometimes known as the "Sapir-Whorf hypothesis." The latter name is rather misleading, since, unlike Whorf, Sapir believed that thought influenced language and vice versa, in an endless chain of interaction, cf. Edward Sapir, *Language: An Introduction to the Study of Speech* (New York: Harcourt Brace Jovanovich, Inc., 1921), pp. 12–17.

[19] Whorf, *Language, Thought and Reality*, p. 239.

[20] See, for example, Carl Bereiter and Siegfried Engelmann, *Teaching Disadvantaged Children in the Preschool* (Englewood Cliffs, N.J.: Prentice-Hall, 1966), especially p. 34 and Chapter 8.

[21] George Orwell, *Nineteen Eighty-Four, a Novel* (New York: Harcourt Brace Jovanovich, Inc., 1949), pp. 303–05, 308.

[22] Robert Bridges, *The Poetical Works of Robert Bridges, with The Testament of Beauty, but Excluding the Eight Dramas* (London and New York: Oxford Univ Press, Inc., 1953), pp. 344–45.

[23] John Lennon, "The SinguLARGE Experience of Miss Anne Duffield," in *A Spaniard in the Works* (New York: New American Library, 1964), p. 106.

[24] Gregory Corso, "Bomb," in *The Happy Birthday of Death* (New York: New Directions Publishing Corporation, 1960).

[25] Ken Kesey, *Sometimes a Great Notion* (New York: Viking Press, 1964), pp. 98–99.

[26] Cyra McFadden, *The Serial: A Year in the Life of Marin County* (New York: Alfred A. Knopf, 1977), p. 76.

[27] From Ernest Vincent Wright, *Gadsby, a Story of Over 50,000 Words Without Using the Letter E* (Los Angeles: Wetzel Publishing Co., 1939); cited in *The Codebreakers: The Story of Secret Writing*, David Kahn (New York: Macmillan, 1967), p. 739.

[28] Ken Kesey, *Sometimes a Great Notion*, p. 99.

[29] Gerald Mygatt, "Lepidoptera," in *Such Nonsense!*, ed. Carolyn Wells (New York: George H. Doran, 1918), p. 59.

Syntax

$\mathbf{I}$f language were just "words, words, words," it would do us little good except in the rather limited linguistic function of naming. There are some languages, such as trade languages and pidgins, that have quite small vocabularies, sometimes not more than three or four thousand words. Although they have a narrow range of styles and uses, they are nevertheless languages. And they are languages because they have rules for putting words, or rather, lexical items, together in specific ways. In other words, they have sentence structure, or syntax. This chapter is concerned with outlining some of the basic rules that English language-users have internalized for constructing and understanding sentences. No attempt is made here to cover all the syntax of English—no one has in fact done that yet, as the topic is so vast. Emphasis is laid on rules of a very general sort and, especially, on those structures that will be of use later on in literary analysis. Some basic information is also provided on how syntactic rules can be formalized, both to suggest the kinds of problems that linguists face in thinking about sentence structure and also to make other materials on syntax more accessible to you than they might otherwise be.

While there are disagreements about the exact boundaries between syntax and word formation, or between syntax and semantics, there are some core aspects of language that are clearly syntactic. This is exactly parallel to the situation that holds, say, in defining the novel. Different critics will disagree about where to draw the line between short story and novel or between novel and biography, but no one will dispute that *Wuthering Heights* and *Oliver Twist* are novels.

To begin with some extreme examples, the fact that **I watered the horse** is a likely sentence while **I watered the baby** is not so likely, is a matter of lexical meaning rather than syntax. Specifically, it has to do with our sense of what can be done to horses as opposed to babies. Syntactically, the sentences are well formed because they represent general structures of the type **X did something to Y**. On the other hand, the fact that the sentence ***Watered horses the I** is ill-formed is a syntactic fact—this order of elements is simply not part of the grammar of English. It is also a syntactic fact that a sentence like **I beat the man with a stick** is ambiguous, since what is involved is the hierarchic relation between **with a stick** and **I** or **the man** (in other words, who has the stick). But it is a lexical fact that **The bank was the scene of the crime** is ambiguous, since the relations between the parts of the sentence are the same for both its interpretations, and only the word meanings are different (money bank *versus* river bank).

As we discussed in Chapter 1, the existence of syntactic ambiguities such as we find in **I beat the man with a stick** is one of the main motivations for proposing a distinction between the surface structure of sentences and their underlying structure. The two interpretations of **I ran into the girls with the flowers** correspond to two different underlying structures, one in which **with the flowers** is linked with **girls,** and one in which it is linked with **ran.** These two different underlying structures are manifested by the same surface structure. A further motivation for the distinction between surface and underlying structure comes from look-alike sentences such as:

1. Bill tempted John to go.

2. Bill wanted John to go.

By examining different paraphrases of these sentences we can see that they have different structures:

1. a.	Bill tempted John to go.	2. a.	Bill wanted John to go.
b.	*What Bill tempted was for John to go.	b.	What Bill wanted was for John to go.
c.	John was tempted to go by Bill.	c.	*John was wanted to go by Bill.
d.	Bill tempted John.	d.	*Bill wanted John (this is an acceptable sentence but does not keep the meaning of the original).
e.	*Bill tempted something.	e.	Bill wanted something.

In our grammar, 1a and 2a are described as having different underlying structures. **Bill tempted John to go** is, roughly speaking, the surface manifestation of **Bill tempted John, John should go,** while **Bill wanted John to go** is a manifestation of **Bill wanted something (John should go)**—"roughly speaking" because, as we shall see, underlying structures are actually a good deal more abstract.

Precisely how is this distinction between underlying structure and surface structure to be modeled in a grammar? There are various answers. In the next chapter we will look more closely at the proposal that underlying structure is a semantic/syntactic one. Here, since we are dealing with core syntactic facts, we will outline the proposal developed by Chomsky that the underlying structure is purely syntactic.[1] According to this proposal, there are two major parts to syntax. One part is the "phrase structure," which specifies skeletal structures for sentences. The other is the "transformational component," which modifies the skeletal structures in defined ways to derive well-formed surface structures in the language. It is from this component that the most commonly used name for Chomskyan grammar, "transformational grammar" (or "transformational-generative grammar") is derived. Lexical items are introduced into the phrase structure by "lexical insertion rules," as will be illustrated on pages 140–41. Together, the phrase structure and the lexicon form the "base" of the grammar.

THE BASE

Phrase Structure Rules

Inspection of a vast number of simple sentences in English suggests that, with a few exceptions, the basic English sentence can be broken down into two parts or "constituents" (the units which make up or constitute the sentence),[2] as in:

3.	Bill	laughed.
4.	The men	laughed.
5.	They	just laughed.
6.	The fans	were falling asleep.
7.	Only two of the alligators	battled the mud.
8.	Over a hundred of the employees	might leave work before noon.

On the left-hand side, we find nouns like **Bill**, pronouns like **they**, and sequences made up of article + noun (**the men**), or even a numeral + noun (**over a hundred of the employees**). These and other nominal structures that can occur in this position can be classed together as "noun phrases."[3] On the right-hand side, we find a verb like **laughed**, or an adverb + verb (**just laughed**), or a verb + noun phrase (like **battled the mud**), and so forth; but in each case there is a verb. We will call such sequences "verb phrases." We can then say that all sentences in English basically consist of a noun phrase and a verb phrase.

This rule, or claim, about the structure of the sentence can be abbreviated as:

$$Sentence \rightarrow Noun\ Phrase + Verb\ Phrase$$

or, more shortly:

$$S \rightarrow NP + VP$$

The arrow stands for the relation "consists of/has the structure of/ has as its constituents." Therefore, the rule reads: "A sentence consists of a noun phrase followed by a verb phrase." Some people find that a "tree structure" display such as:

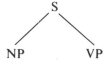

is even more helpful than linear statements like $S \rightarrow NP + VP$, since it shows the hierarchic structure at a glance. Trees will be used where they might clarify the structures under discussion.

Abbreviations like NP and VP are memory devices to help us conceptualize structures. And the rule itself is a shorthand version of what could be expressed in sentences of English or any other language. What particular terms are used does not really matter. We could just as well write

$$A \rightarrow B + C$$

as:

$$S \rightarrow NP + VP$$

but transformationalists have preferred to adapt the traditional vocabulary of grammar rather than use new terms. Whatever a category is called, it represents a distinctly patterned group that has an important function in the language.

The formula $S \rightarrow NP + VP$ tells us not only what a sentence consists of, but by implication, also what it does not consist of. For example, such a formula directly disallows **the man** as a sentence in underlying structure, by requiring that every sentence have both an NP and a VP in underlying structure. **The man** is, of course, a possible utterance. For example, it can serve as the answer to the question **Who did you give it to?**, but we understand it as an abbreviated form of the complete sentence **I gave it to the man.** In our grammar, the truncated sentence will be derived through the transformational component from the complete sentence. Likewise, as we shall see in the section on transformations, imperatives such as **Jump!** that lack an NP in surface structure are derived from underlying structures something like **You jump!** where an NP (**you**) is present.

NP and VP alone are too general to be adequate for a grammar of English. We need to specify exactly what NP and VP can consist of. Later on, we will add additional material to the basic structure of the sentence.

The noun phrase: Consider the kinds of basic nominals that can occur as the subject of a verb like **grin**. They include:

9. a. He   grinned.
    b. Something   grinned.
    c. Isabel   grinned.

10. a. The cat   grinned.
    b. A cat   grinned.
    c. This cat   grinned.
    d. My cat   grinned.
    e. Three of those cats grinned.

and a variety of others. The sentences in 9 exemplify the class of nominals that cannot be preceded by **the, a, three, my,** or similar elements. (**The Isabel I know lives in New York** is a possible sentence, but it means **The person I know called Isabel**, and thus has a rather different structure.) The nominals in 9a and b exemplify "pronouns," short words that substitute for nouns already mentioned (e.g., **he** substitutes for **Billy**), for the speaker (**I**), or hearer (**you**), or for nouns that would be specified were their referent known (e.g., **something** in 9b). The nominal in 9c exemplifies "proper" nouns, nouns that name people and places and that have unique reference (**Isabel** refers to a single person, whereas a noun like **cat** without modifiers like **that** or **my** refers to a class of animals). As the sentences in 10 show, other nouns (known as "common nouns") may be preceded by a variety of elements called DET(erminers). These are the articles **the, a;** the demonstratives (or "pointers") **this, that, these, those;** numerals like **one, hundreds, five of;** and quantifiers like **many, some, some of.** Only the articles and demonstratives will concern us here. In the grammar, a general rule specifies that determiners may occur in underlying structure:

$$NP \rightarrow (DET) \; N$$

The parentheses ( ) indicate that there is a choice at this point; all NP's consist of N, some consist of DET + N.

If we consider the relationship between:

11. a. The panther pounced.
    b. The panthers pounced.

and

    12. a.   A panther pounced.
        b.   Panthers pounced.

we will see that 12b, though it has no surface DET, is not like 9b but actually like 10b. Unlike pronouns and proper nouns, **panther** can take all kinds of DET; the absence of DET in 12b is a surface phenomenon only—the article **a** has the null form (Ø) in the environment of a plural noun, just as the plural has a Ø form in the environment of **deer** (cf. Chapter 3).

    The verb phrase: At a minimum, the verb phrase consists of a main V(erb), as in 9–12. It may also be followed by one NP (usually the traditional "object" relation), as in:

    13.   John saw two bobcats.

    14.   Bill revved his motorbike.

Other sentences like:

    15.   Boris gave a bracelet to Olivia.

    16.   The woman sent a letter to her rival.

involve what are traditionally called a "direct object" (NP) and an "indirect object." The latter is a phrase consisting of a preposition (one of the little function words preceding nouns, like **to, for, with, by, on, at**), usually **to**, and a second NP. These facts can be captured by a rule that states that VP must consist of a V and optionally an NP and a P(repositional) P(hrase):

$$VP \rightarrow V(NP)\ (PP)$$

Then another rule will state that PP has the structure:

$$PP \rightarrow PREP + NP$$

    The lexicon, which specifies individual properties of words as opposed to general properties of sentences, must indicate which particular verbs do or do not allow a following object or indirect object. **Go** does not have a following object, but **eat** does, although the object can be deleted if it is a general term like **food** (he ate = he ate food). **Resemble** requires a following NP, **give** normally requires NP + PP, and so forth (see below).

    The category AUX: If we look once more at all the sentences we have inspected so far, we will notice that the verb is modified in various ways—by a tense-marker at the very least (cf. **she skips** versus **she skipped**) and often by one or more of a set of auxiliary, or "helping," verbs like **may, shall, can, must, have, be.** For various reasons which will become apparent as we go further into the nature of English sentence structure, it is useful to treat these elements as a separate category in underlying structure, although they may be attached to the verb in surface structure. We therefore need to expand our initial characterization of the sentence to include a category which is called AUX.

$$S \rightarrow NP + AUX + VP$$

(Although AUX is short for "auxiliary," it avoids confusion to call it AUX, pronounced [ɔks] (or [aks] by speakers who do not have [ɔ], since it consists of both the traditional auxiliary verbs and the tense-marker.) The following array of English verbal structures illustrates some of the forms taken by AUX:

17. a.   He mutters.
    b.   He muttered.
    c.   He will mutter.
    d.   He would mutter.
    e.   He has muttered.
    f.   He had muttered.
    g.   He is muttering.
    h.   He was muttering.

In a and b, the verb is accompanied only by a tense-marker, the past **-ed** and non-past **-s** morphemes introduced in Chapter 3. In c and d, the verb is accompanied by a M(odal). This is the term used for the set of auxiliary verbs **can, may, must, shall, will** (and their past tenses **could, might, must, should,** and **would**).[4] Notice that in c and d it is the Modal which carries the tense-marker, not the main verb. In e and f, the auxiliary **have** precedes the verb and again carries the tense-marker. As an auxiliary, **have** requires the past participle marker on the following verbal element. For this reason, the **have** auxiliary is referred to in the rules as **have + en**, where **en** stands for the past participle inflection, as in **have eaten.** In g and h, we find the auxiliary **be,** which again carries a tense-marker, and which requires the present participle ending **-ing** on the following verbal element. This construction, referred to in the rules as **be + ing**, roughly corresponds to the meaning "in progress" and is therefore often called the "progressive." **This plane is being hijacked to Morocco** means the hijacking is in progress.

17 illustrates only the simplest AUX constructions. Modal, **have + en**, and **be + ing** can combine with each other to give sentences like:

18. a.   He has been muttering.
    b.   He had been muttering.
    c.   He will have muttered.
    d.   He would have muttered.

    e. He will be muttering.
    f. He would be muttering.
    g. He will have been muttering.
    h. He would have been muttering.

Notice that as in 17, the tense-marker is again carried by the first verbal element. This array shows some further ordering relations among the constituents of AUX. The Modal always precedes **have + en** (hence **He has will eaten*), and **have + en** in turn precedes **be + ing** (hence **He is have eating*). Thus, by abstracting away from the surface structure of the words, we can simplify the highly diverse-looking set of structures in 17 and 18 as in the rule:

$$\text{AUX} \rightarrow \text{TENSE (M) (have + en) (be + ing)}$$

Parentheses indicate that while TENSE is an obligatory part of any verb phrase, the other elements of AUX are optional. As we saw on page 91, TENSE has two possible morphological realizations in English, PAST and non-PAST. A further rule will summarize these facts:

$$\text{TENSE} \rightarrow \left\{ \begin{array}{l} \text{PAST} \\ \text{Non-PAST} \end{array} \right\}$$

Curly brackets are used by convention to indicate that the elements within them are mutually exclusive, that is, either one or the other occurs, but not both. By treating TENSE not as part of the verb, but as an independent element under AUX, we can easily show that it goes with the first element following it. If there is no Modal, **have + en**, or **be + ing**, TENSE will be attached to the verb. This formulation also shows at a glance the relationship of **en** and **ing** to **have** and **be**, respectively. A simple transformation putting TENSE, **en**, and **ing** in their correct positions in surface structure will allow for all the various patterns in 17 and 18. For example, **the + man + PAST + have + en + leave** is transformed into:

    the + man + have + PAST + leave + en (**The man had left**)

This rule will be discussed below in the section on "affix-hopping."

Modals, **have** and **be** (when part of AUX and followed by **en** and **ing**) have been called auxiliary verbs. As opposed to main verbs, which are the core of the VP and must be present, auxiliary verbs are optional, that is, grammatical sentences can be constructed without them. There are a number of other interesting differences between auxiliaries and main verbs.[5] For one, auxiliary verbs form a very small class, while the class of main verbs is very large and easily expanded. Secondly, as their name implies, auxiliaries are "helping verbs," and cannot occur independently of other verbs. Sentences like **He will** are not exceptions, since they assume another sentence in which a main verb is present, such as **Will he leave?**

Auxiliaries may all occur with **not/n't** immediately following them, as in **He can't go, He isn't going, He hasn't gone.** Main verbs have to use **do** to carry **not/n't**. We get **He didn't greet me**, not *****He greetn't me.** Likewise, in so-called "yes-no questions," that is, questions which require **yes** or **no** for an answer, main verbs require **do**, as in **Did he greet you?** (not *****Greeted he you?**). But auxiliaries do not need **do**, and are themselves put at the beginning of the sentence, as in **Might he come?, Has he left?** Furthermore, auxiliary verbs occur in "tags": **He's going, isn't he? He can come, can't he?**, while main verbs other than **be** and **have** require **do** to support the tag: **He let go, didn't he?** not *****He let go, letn't he?** Finally, auxiliary verbs can have very reduced stress, so much so that the first part of the syllable may disappear completely in some cases (**He'll leave, He's going**).

Have and **be** are rather interesting as they may occur not only as "helpers" preceding main verbs, but also independently, as in **I have several rare books** and **He is a phony.** In such cases, they are traditionally called main verbs. However, even as main verbs, they behave much like auxiliaries. For example, the question form of **He is a phony** is **Is he a phony?** not *****Does he be a phony? Have** is like **be** in questions in British English, cf. **Have you a book?**, but more like main verbs in American English: **Do you have a book?** The two verbs, **have** and **be**, therefore, cut across what is otherwise a sharp distinction between auxiliaries and main verbs. The difference between British and American **have** and the existence of Irish constructions like **Does he be here?** suggest that the language is regularizing these verbs and that they will eventually split into two homonymous verbs, one main, one auxiliary.

Some further expansions of the S rule: So far we have introduced some basic rules of English sentence structure that underlie affirmative declarative sentences like those in 9–18. Of course, not all sentences are affirmative. Some may be negative, like **They couldn't bear reading the book any longer.** To capture this, the rule rewriting S can be expanded to:

$$S \rightarrow (NEG)NP + AUX + VP$$

Furthermore, not all sentences are declarative. They may be questions like **Did you hit the jackpot?** or commands like **Leave!, Don't get hurt!** (usually called "imperatives"). Justification for the rules will be given below. It is enough here to indicate that questions and imperative types are marked as such by the abstract constituents Q(uestion) and IMP(erative). Since these constituents are mutually exclusive, they are introduced in curly brackets. Since they are also optional, they are introduced in parentheses as well. The whole S rule, as revised, is:

$$S \rightarrow \left(\begin{Bmatrix} Q \\ IMP \end{Bmatrix} \right) (NEG)NP + AUX + VP$$

Summary of phrase structure rules given so far: Our basic phrase structure rules, as revised, are:

1. $S \rightarrow \left(\left\{ \begin{matrix} Q \\ IMP \end{matrix} \right\} \right)$ (NEG)NP + AUX + VP

2. AUX $\rightarrow$ TENSE(M) (have + en) (be + ing)

3. TENSE $\rightarrow \left\{ \begin{matrix} PAST \\ Non\text{-}PAST \end{matrix} \right\}$

4. VP $\rightarrow$ V(NP) (PP)

5. PP $\rightarrow$ PREP + NP

6. NP $\rightarrow$ (DET)N

These phrase structure rules state three major properties of sentences:

1. The categories (N, V, etc.).
2. The relations between those categories in terms of linear order; for example, VP is to the right of AUX. (In some languages, like Old English, it can be argued that VP should be ordered to the left of AUX.)
3. The relations between those categories in terms of hierarchies. For example, the NP of rule 4 has a different relation to S than that of rule 1. The NP of 4 is directly dominated by VP (in other words, is a direct constituent of VP), and only indirectly by S, whereas the NP of 1 is directly dominated by S.

Phrase structure rules specify possibilities available in the language as a whole. Individual sentences are said to be "derived" from the application of these rules. To derive a sentence, we go through the rules automatically, applying them as often as they are applicable, and making choices wherever there is any kind of bracket or parenthesis. For example, the S rule tells us that S always consists of NP + AUX + VP, and may also consist of NEG and either Q or IMP. In "rewriting" S at the level of rule 1, we have six possibilities:

NP + AUX + VP
   This ultimately underlies such sentences as: He left.

NEG + NP + AUX + VP
   This ultimately underlies such sentences as: He didn't leave.

Q + NP + AUX + VP
   This ultimately underlies such sentences as: Did he leave?

Q + NEG + NP + AUX + VP
This ultimately underlies such sentences as: Didn't he leave?

IMP + NP + AUX + VP
This ultimately underlies such sentences as: Leave!

IMP + NEG + NP + AUX + VP
This ultimately underlies such sentences as: Don't leave!

Having applied rule 1, that is, having rewritten S as one of the six possible sequences or "strings" above, we go on to rule 2 and apply it. This rule tells us what AUX consists of and requires that, while leaving everything else constant, we replace AUX by at least TENSE and, optionally, any combination of auxiliary verbs. Thus, if we had derived

$$NEG + NP + AUX + VP$$

by applying rule 1, we would now have the following choices:

$$NEG + NP + \begin{cases} TENSE \\ or\ TENSE + M \\ or\ TENSE + have + en \\ or\ TENSE + be + ing \\ or\ TENSE + M + have + en \\ or\ TENSE + M + be + ing \\ or\ TENSE + M + have + en + be + ing \\ or\ TENSE + have + en + be + ing \end{cases} + VP$$

Having selected one of these choices, we go on to rule 3, and so forth, rewriting each appropriate category. The specification of a particular sentence structure by applying the rules is called a "derivation."

The derivations can be represented either as a set of strings, or as "trees." To all intents and purposes these two representations are equivalent. A sample derivation, expressed in both ways, is:

1. NEG + NP + AUX + VP
2. NEG + NP + TENSE + have + en + VP
3. NEG + NP + PAST + have + en + VP
4. NEG + NP + PAST + have + en + V
5. Not applicable as PP was not selected in 4.
6. NEG + N + PAST + have + en + V

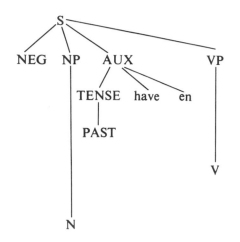

Such a structure underlies sentences of the type **John hasn't arrived**.

There is a third way of providing the same information about constituent structure that is much more concise: by substituting brackets for branches of trees, as in:

$$[\text{NEG } [\text{N}]_{\text{NP}}[[\text{PAST}]_{\text{TENSE}} \text{ have} + \text{en}]_{\text{AUX}}[\text{V}]_{\text{VP}}]_{\text{S}}$$

This bracketed string reads: Everything in the bracket labeled S is a constituent of S; the constituents are NEG, and N, which is itself a constituent of NP; also PAST (which is a constituent of TENSE) and **have + en**, all of which are constituents of AUX; and finally V, which is a constituent of VP. Highly condensed as it is, this kind of display is a great space-saver, and is therefore frequently used instead of a tree structure.

If you try other derivations, you will see how tremendously powerful these phrase structure rules are. They account for but a skeleton of the basic structures of English—no provision is made for Place, Time, Manner, Purpose, or other adverbials, and all subordination has been postponed for later discussion—yet, given these six rules and a few lexical entries, several dozen sentences can be derived.

The Lexicon

Obviously, we do not express ourselves in categories like N + V. Instead, we select particular instances of the category from the lexicon, based on learned information about how these particular instances behave in linguistic contexts. For example, we know that the V in the derivation above can be replaced by the lexical items **fall, come, arrive**, but not by **give, bring, send**, and so forth, because in our derivation nothing follows V. As was discussed in Chapter 3, each lexical item includes information about its syntactic category.

In addition, it includes information about what positions it can occupy in phrase structure. For example, **man** is described in the lexicon as [+N] and also as [+DET___], indicating that it can occur in the position immediately following DET. **Go** can replace V only if V is the sole constituent of VP; therefore, **go** is specified in the lexicon as [+V, +___] (read: the V slot is the only constituent of VP). By contrast, **touch** is [+V, +___NP], since it requires that VP consist of both a V and an NP. And **give, send** are [+V, +___NP, +PP] since they require two objects, the second of which is prepositional.

There are also semantic restrictions on how lexical items may combine, such as the fact that **astonish** requires an animate object, as in **That story astonishes me**, not *That story astonished the cave. Similarly, verbs like **give** that allow indirect objects (PP) require an animate indirect object—if I give a million dollars to the university, it is understood that I give it to the people who administer it, not the building. There has been considerable debate as to whether such facts are syntactic as well as semantic, or semantic only. Here we take them to be semantic only and deal with them apart from syntax.

Deep Structure: Output of Phrase Structure and Lexicon

The phrase structure and lexicon together form the base, or underlying structure. Suppose we have applied the appropriate phrase structure rules and have derived the string $DET + N + PAST + V$ from the phrase structure rules and suppose we have inserted lexical items, along with their phonological and semantic features. Among the many hundreds of possible strings we could have derived, one would be a string that (for our purposes) can be sketched as:

$$\left[\left[[+DET]\begin{bmatrix} +N \\ +DET\text{\_\_\_} \end{bmatrix}\right]_{NP} [PAST]_{AUX}\begin{bmatrix} +V \\ +\text{\_\_\_} \end{bmatrix}_{VP}\right]_S$$

+ Phonological features of the lexical items

+ Semantic features of the lexical items

=   the   man   PAST   run

Note that all the phrase structure information is retained in this string, as indicated by the bracketing.

The string we have just derived is a "deep structure"—a string that gives the skeleton of the sentence with all the information necessary to do three things: to derive a well-formed sentence, to give it a phonological representation, and to give it a semantic interpretation.

We will return to discussion of semantics in Chapter 5.

TRANSFORMATIONS

Obviously strings like **The man PAST run** or **Q NEG John PAST have + en arrive** are not grammatical or "well-formed" surface sentences in English. In this section we will discuss some ways in which surface structures can be derived from the deep structures given here. To derive **Hasn't John arrived?** we need a different kind of rule from phrase structure rules. Phrase structure rules state "A consists of B + C." **Q NEG John PAST have + en arrive** does not "consist of" **Hasn't John arrived?** Rather, it is modified in definite ways to become **Hasn't John arrived?** The rules that specify such modifications are called "transformations."

The purpose of transformational rules is to show relations between deep and surface structures. Transformations are operations which add, delete, or permute (that is, change order and sometimes also hierarchic relationship among) constituents. Some of the transformational processes must apply for a grammatical sentence to be generated (the technical term for this is that they are "obligatory"). Others, however, do not have to apply. For example, it is not necessary, although possible, or "optional," to turn an active sentence like **Bill saw Jeff** into the passive **Bill was seen by Jeff**, but it is obligatory to convert an abstract **NEG I saw someone** into some other sequence, either **I didn't see anyone** or **I saw no one**, because the element NEG cannot turn up in surface structure.

Transformations specify the ways sentences and parts of sentences may be put together while preserving basic meaning. By "preserving basic meaning," we mean that the overall sense is retained. **I saw no one** and **I didn't see anyone** are roughly equivalent in meaning; so are **Bill saw John, John was seen by Bill**; or **I gave the book to Tom, I gave Tom the book**; or **I looked up the word, I looked the word up**. Some slight difference of meaning does usually occur, however. This difference is one of emphasis and focus and will be discussed in Chapter 7.

The transformations to be discussed in this section account for a small but typical subset of possible syntactic processes. They have all been widely discussed, but no consensus has yet been reached on exactly how they should be formulated. Here a relatively traditional view of the processes in question has been taken.

Indirect Object Movement

Any grammar of English needs to account for the relationship between such pairs of sentences as:

19. a. I gave a book to the boy.
     b. I gave the boy a book.

20. a. I sent the petition to the registrar.
    b. I sent the registrar the petition.

In each pair, the a and b sentences have the same basic meaning, and differ in the order of NP's in the VP. While in the a sentences we find NP_1 + to + NP_2, in the b sentences we find reversed NP's but no **to**. Our grammar captures these facts by viewing the b sentences as derived from the a sentences by a transformational rule which deletes **to** and reverses the order of (i.e., permutes) the two NP's. More technically, the transformational rule will transform the phrase-marker that corresponds to the a strings into a new phrase-marker that corresponds to the b strings.

This rule—and all transformational rules—consists of two parts. The first, the structural description (SD), specifies in the most general way possible the relevant structural properties of the a strings. The second part, the structural change (SC), specifies what changes are performed to produce the b strings. Thus, taking the phrase-marker for a:

$$\left[[I]_{NP}[PAST]_{AUX}\left[[give]_V[[a]_{DET}[book]_N]_{NP}[[to]_{PREP}[[the]_{DET}[boy]_N]_{NP}]_{PP}\right]_{VP}\right]_S$$

the relevant parts for the transformation are the object NP (in this case, **a book**), the preposition **to**, and the indirect object NP (in this case, **the boy**). We do not need to specify the rest of the string in the SD, except to indicate that it exists. By convention, the letters X, Y, Z are used to indicate the presence of syntactic materials that do not need specification. Thus, the SD for the rule is:

SD: X NP to NP

For convenience in indicating changes, these elements are numbered, giving:

$$SD: \underset{1}{\underline{X}} \ \underset{2}{\underline{NP}} \ \underset{3}{\underline{to}} \ \underset{4}{\underline{NP}}$$

The structural change is formalized as:

SC: ⇒ 1 ∅ 4 2

The ⇒ means "is transformed into"[6]; thus the SC means that element 3 (**to**) is deleted, and 2 and 4 (the direct and indirect object NP's) are permuted. The SD of indirect object movement and the results of applying the SC can be illustrated in the sample tree shown at the top of p. 144.

To be maximally useful, the SD of a rule has to give neither too much nor too little information. Note that an SD which specified simply PP instead of

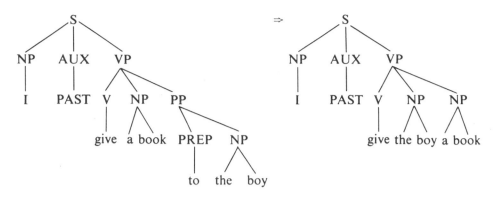

to NP would be inadequate for this rule, since there would then be no way to show in the SC that the preposition **to** is deleted. On the other hand, to specify *to DET N* in the SD would give too much information. (A complete formulation of indirect object movement would have to be a little more complicated than the one given here, since it would have to make clear that the rule does not apply to strings where *to NP* is a Place adverbial, as in **I sent the man to the store**.)

Indirect object movement is an optional transformation in English, that is, grammatical sentences result whether or not it is applied. However, depending on the pragmatics of shared information, it is preferred in some contexts more than in others. For example, it is preferred if the object is indefinite (that is, it has the indefinite article **a**) and the indirect object is definite (as in 19) since indefinite, unshared information usually occurs at the end of the sentence. Thus **I gave the girl a book** is preferred to **I gave a book to the girl** in most unemphatic contexts; however, **I gave the book to a girl** is preferred to **I gave a girl the book**. Since the pronouns **I, you, he, she, it** are always definite, that is, refer to something either known or assumed known, if one of the NP's is one of these pronouns it usually occurs first. So we have **I sent her to Norman**, but **I sent him the book**. Such factors will be discussed in greater detail in Chapter 7.

Passive

The passive is a transformation that captures the relation between pairs like:

21. a. The bobcats were clawing Alex.
    b. Alex was being clawed by the bobcats.

The a-type sentences are traditionally called "active," and the b-type sentences "passive." Again, the pairs are roughly the same in meaning (but not emphasis), and can be treated as variants of each other. There are various formulations of the passive rules in transformational grammar.[7] All must capture the fact that the active sentence and the passive sentence have their NP's (here **Alex** and **the bobcats**) in reverse order, and that both a **be + en** auxiliary and the preposition **by** occur in the passive sentences and not in the active ones. Supposing we have the string:

$$[[[the]_{DET}[man]_N]_{NP}[PAST]_{AUX}[[see]_V [John]_{NP}]_{VP}]_S$$

The relevant parts for our passive rule are the subject NP (here **the man**), the object NP (here **John**, which will change places with **the man**), the V (see) and AUX, since a **be + en** auxiliary will be inserted. Thus the SD for the rule is:

$$\text{SD: } \underset{1}{\underline{NP}} \; \underset{2}{\underline{AUX}} \; \underset{3}{\underline{V}} \; \underset{4}{\underline{NP}}$$

The SC is:

$$\text{SD: } \Rightarrow 4 \quad 2 \quad be + en \quad 3 \quad by \quad 1$$

The following sample trees illustrate the effects of the rule:

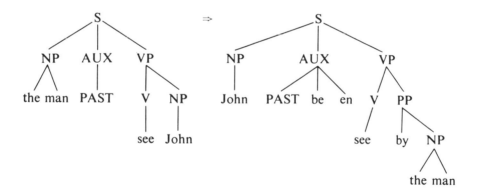

The transformation thus involves both permutation (of the two NP's) and addition (of **be + en** and **by**). Some passive sentences, however, do not contain a **by** phrase, such as **He was kidnapped** or **He was jarred from his thoughts**. These sentences are considered as having an indefinite **by** phrase, **by someone** or **by something**, in underlying structure. This accounts for the meaning relationship which holds between:

22. a.   Someone jarred him from his thoughts.

b. He was jarred from his thoughts by someone.

c. He was jarred from his thoughts.

22c is derived by a rule which, after the application of the passive transformation, optionally deletes **by** + l if l is an indefinite pronoun (usually **someone** or **something**).

Why claim that the passive is a transformation rather than a structure generated directly by the phrase structure rules? One reason is that if both active and passive sentences were generated independently by the phrase structure rules, no relation between them would be expressed by the grammar. They would be viewed simply as random alternatives. In this case, their similarities in form and meaning would be seen as purely coincidental. Such a grammar would also be unable to explain similarities in the distribution of active and passive sentences. For instance, there is a class of verbs, including **frighten, startle,** and **astonish,** which requires animate objects in the active, as illustrated by:

24. a. Too much sincerity frightens me.
    b. *I frighten too much sincerity.

25. a. The statue startled me.
    b. *I startled the statue.

These same verbs require animate subjects in the passive:

24. c. I am frightened by too much sincerity.
    d. *Too much sincerity is frightened by me.

25. c. I was startled by the statue.
    d. *The statue was startled by me.

These distributional facts are not in the least surprising, but in a grammar which treated actives and passives as random alternatives, the fact that active **frighten** requires an animate object and passive **frighten** requires an animate subject would be simply a coincidence.

But why not claim that it is passives which are generated by the phrase structure rules, and actives which are derived by transformation from passives? The reason for claiming that the active is the more basic structure is that passives are limited in various ways that actives are not. For one, passives always involve at least two NP's in underlying structure, and therefore the passive construction must be excluded from all underlying structures of the type $NP + AUX + V$. For another, not all sentences with two NP's actually undergo a passive transformation. Specifically, a class of verbs which includes **have, weigh,** and **resemble** does not have passives—we do not find *A **pink coat is had by me,** *A **ton is weighed by my pet seal** (an exception is the idiom **A good time was had by all**). Such relationships and limitations can be captured by showing that active and passive are not random alternatives, but that the passive is a restricted version of the active.

Imperatives

Now consider sentences like:

26. Jump!

27. Have it finished before I get there!

These sentences are usually called commands or, to use a word borrowed from Latin, "imperatives." How might we go about characterizing these sentences? A very noticeable fact about them is that they have no subject NP. We might consider specifying this fact in a phrase structure rule that allowed for two types of sentences, imperatives (with no subject) and all other types (with subjects), for example:

$$S \rightarrow \begin{Bmatrix} (Q) & (NEG) & NP + AUX + VP \\ (NEG) & AUX + VP \end{Bmatrix}$$

But adding such a rule means losing a lot of generality in the grammar. Moreover, there is ample evidence that imperatives do in fact have a subject **you** in underlying structure. Some of this evidence comes from imperatives in which a person is commanded to do something for him or herself, like **Wash yourself** or **Don't think about yourself**. Note that the pronouns used here are the reflexive ones (those with **-self** added). We do not get plain *Wash you, *Don't think about you. Inspection of other sentences shows that reflexive pronouns occur when subject and object NP's refer to the same person or thing (that is, when they are "in identity"):

28. a.   Jeff saw him in the mirror.

means that there were two different people, but

28. b.   Jeff saw himself in the mirror.

means that the person seen in the mirror was the same as the seer. If we posit an underlying subject NP **you** in imperatives, we can explain the occurrence of reflexive pronouns in imperatives in the same way we explain their occurrence in nonimperative sentences: Underlying **you wash you** is transformed to **You wash yourself**, provided that the **you**'s refer to the same person, just as underlying **Jeff saw Jeff** is transformed into **Jeff saw himself** if the two **Jeff**'s refer to the same person. Otherwise, we have to say that imperatives are an exception to the usual behavior of reflexive pronouns. Notice that the reflexive pronouns also make clear that the underlying subject for imperatives has to be **you**. If it were **I** or **they**, for example, we should get ***Wash myself**, ***Wash themselves**.

Further motivation for positing an underlying **you** is that imperatives can be expressed with a tag **will you/won't you** attached, as in: **Jump, will you!** Again, inspection of the general behavior of tags like **won't you, can't you** shows that the pronoun has to be in identity with the subject:

29. a.   He can swim, can't he?
    b.   *He can swim, can't she?

Furthermore, the auxiliary verbs have to be identical:

29. c.   *He can swim, won't he?
    d.   He will swim, won't he?

To explain **Jump, will you!** in a way that takes these facts into account, we need a **you** subject and also a **will** auxiliary in the deep structure.

We therefore posit for "**Jump!**" a deep and surface structure relationship of the type:

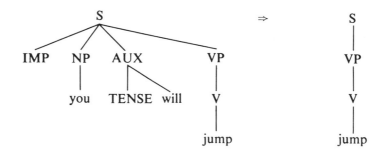

In other words, IMP, **you**, and AUX are deleted, leaving the VP intact. Deep structure strings generated with IMP but some subject other than **you** will be blocked from undergoing the transformation, since they do not conform to the structural description and will be rejected by the grammar as ungrammatical.

Negation

Negation is another example of an obligatory transformation, and also of one that generates strings which themselves need further modification (in this case, by "*do*-support"). Linguists customarily distinguish between two types of negation. One kind operates on the whole sentence as in **He is not happy**. This is often called "sentence negation." Another type operates only on parts of the sentence. For example, the sentence **He is unhappy** is affirmative; it is the adjective which is negative.

Phrase structure rule 1, which introduces NEG to the left of *NP* + *AUX* + *VP*, captures the fact that we can, in formal usage, leave the negative outside the sentence, as in **It is not the case that** .... The possible surface manifestations of this NEG are various. Its most usual form in spoken English is **n't**. In a transformational grammar, NEG is inserted as **n't** into the surface verb phrase and placed directly after the first auxiliary verb (including the **be** introduced by the passive transformation) if there is one:

30. (NEG) John TENSE can↓ leave (John can't leave).

31. (NEG) John TENSE have↓ + en leave (John hasn't left).

32. (NEG) John TENSE be↓ + en hit (John wasn't hit).

If no auxiliary verb is present, then **n't** is introduced after TENSE, and **do** is inserted to support it:

33. (NEG) John TENSE (do) ↓ ↓ leave (John didn't leave).

As discussed earlier in the chapter, the main verbs **be** and in some dialects **have** are exceptions to this *do*-insertion rule.

Certain elements other than the verb are affected by sentence negation, notably indefinite quantifiers, certain indefinite Time adverbs, and certain coordinators. Many of these elements are suppletive (that is, have very different forms in different environments). Consider, for example, **some-any, too-either, already-yet** in:

34. I didn't buy any coffee *versus* I bought some coffee.

35. She doesn't like dancing and Bill doesn't either *versus* She likes dancing and Bill does too.

36. She hasn't left yet *versus* She has already left.

Some of the elements that are affected by negation may attract the negative and absorb it, giving rise to what is known as "negative absorption" or "negative incorporation," for example, **not any** ⇒ **no, not ever** ⇒ **never**.

Besides the negative sentence in 34, we also find:

37.   I bought no coffee.

The negative-incorporated form of **not-any** is **no**, of **not-anybody** is **nobody**, of **not-either** is **neither**; of **many** is **few**, of **much** is **little**. The negative-incorporated form must be used if an indefinite is the subject.

38. a.   Someone is at the window.
    b.   *Anyone is not at the window.
    c.   No one is at the window.

Questions

Questions (also called "interrogatives") are of two kinds. There are "yes-no questions," as in:

39.   Is this the guitar you dropped?

40.   Did they ever come out here to visit you?

Alternatively, yes-no questions are called "truth-questions," as they ask for the truth-value of the sentence.

Instead of asking for a **yes** or **no** answer, one may also ask for specification of some incompletely specified part of the sentence, as in:

41.   **What** are these creatures?

42.   **Who** killed Cock Robin?

43.   **Where** was it done?

41 assumes that the creatures have some identity, and asks what it is. An indefinite answer like **Oh, some bird** is not really a well-formed answer to 42 (although it is partially well-formed insofar as it adds some specification, that is, that the culprit was a bird). A truly well-formed answer would have to give full specification, such as **The sparrow**, in which nothing is left indefinite.

Questions like those in 41–43 involve some surface question pronoun, such as **who** (*wh*-animate N), **what** (*wh*-inanimate N), **where** (*wh*-place), **when** (*wh*-time), **how** (*wh*-manner). They are therefore often called "*wh*-questions." Another name, referring to the type of answer expected rather than to the form of the question, is "content question."

All syntactic questions involve movement of underlying constituents. (Such a sentence as **He left?** is not a question syntactically; although it is one phonologically, because of the rising intonation, and also pragmatically.) The transformation for yes-no questions involves essentially the same phrase structure elements as **n't** insertion. TENSE and the first auxiliary verb are moved to initial position. If only TENSE is present and the main verb is not **be** (or **have**), **do** is introduced.

Wh-questions involve slightly more complex movement rules, since the *wh*-element occurs initially, followed by TENSE and an auxiliary, e.g.,

44. What have you done?

45. Whom did you give it to?

The exact rules will not concern us here, but it should be noted that while several *wh*-elements can occur in the same sentence, only one can be moved to initial position ("fronted," for short):

46. a. Who gave what to whom? (subject fronted)
     b. What did who give to whom? (object fronted)
     c. Whom did who give what to? (indirect object fronted)

The same elements of the sentence that are affected by negation are often also affected by interrogatives. For example, questions often introduce suppletive indefinite quantifiers and adverbs, and so on. In negations, **some-any** suppletion is the norm. In questions it is favored, but not obligatory. Both **Do you have some money?** and **Do you have any money?** occur. The exact conditions under which the **any** form is preferred are not entirely clear, but they seem to be mainly pragmatic. For some speakers, yes-no questions have a strong correlation between the **some** form and the assumption that the answer will be **yes**; with the **any** form the assumption is that the answer will be **no**, or else no assumption is made about the answer. In content questions, **some** usually correlates with positive expectations, **any** with negative expectations or else with absence of expectations.[8] Examples are:

47. a. Would you like some milk? (Expected answer: **yes**)
     b. Would you like any milk? (Either the expected answer is **no** or there is no real expectation)

48. a. Who wants some mustard? (Expectation that some want it)
     b. Who wants any mustard? (Either no expectation; or perhaps the speaker assumes that as he does not want any, no one else will or should)

Do-Support

Where does the **do** in negative sentences like 33 or in questions like 40 come from? There are several **do**'s in English. One of them is a main verb, as in **That is what I do, They do the cleaning once a month.** Another **do** substitutes for a main verb in a sentence much as a pronoun substitutes for a noun, and so it is called a "pro-verb": **Bill works at the market and Gene may do so too in a while.** The **do** that appears in negative and interrogative sentences, but not in the affirmative declarative versions of the same sentence, is an auxiliary verb. Like other auxiliaries, this **do** does not occur independently; it can have **n't** following it, it can be unstressed and it can occur in tags like **He didn't go, did he?** Unlike other auxiliaries, however, auxiliary **do** is very limited in distribution. It is totally predictable in that when no other auxiliary verb is available in the surface form of negatives, questions, and also tag questions and contrastive emphatics, it is introduced to support TENSE, as in:

49. a.   He didn't buy a crowbar.
     b.   Did he buy a crowbar?
     c.   You bought a crowbar, didn't you?
     d.   You díd buy a crowbar, don't you remember?

Because it is totally predictable, **do** in itself has no meaning. **N't** indicates the negative in 49a; word order indicates the question in 49b and c; contrastive stress indicates emphasis in 49d. Since it is totally predictable, **do**, like the **be** + **en** of the passive, is not introduced in the phrase structure, but only by transformational rule.[9] The proposal that TENSE should be introduced as part of AUX, before auxiliary verbs, can now be seen to be justified by more than simplicity of description. Whenever something is inserted between the tense-marker and the next element of the verb phrase, *do*-support is required. What is inserted may be, for example, **n't** as in:

Bill TENSE n't swim $\Rightarrow$ Bill TENSE $\overset{\text{(do)}}{\underset{\downarrow}{}}$ n't swim (Bill doesn't swim)

or it may be the subject NP when the subject is moved in a yes-no question:

TENSE Bill swim $\Rightarrow$ TENSE $\overset{\text{(do)}}{\underset{\downarrow}{}}$ Bill swim (Does Bill swim?)

   Thus a generalization emerges: All negatives and questions have an auxiliary verb in surface structure, whether or not they have an auxiliary verb (Modal, **have** or **be**) in deep structure. Where no deep structure auxiliary occurs, **do** occurs. In earlier English, the surface parallelism was not present. In Old and most of Middle English there was no *do*-support, and so negatives and questions were equivalent to **Bill not swims (or Bill swims not)** and **Swims Bill?** One of the mysteries of the history of English is exactly how and why **do** developed as an auxiliary, but we do know that by the beginning of the seventeenth century **do** was required in yes-no questions where no other auxiliary was present, and that it was required in all negative sentences by the beginning of the twentieth century. Presumably one of the reasons why auxiliary **do** became obligatory was that it established such a neat pattern. There is some evidence that the auxiliary **do** is spreading to affirmative declarative as well, as in the flight attendant's line **At this time we do request that you extinguish all smoking materials.** In this usage, which is becoming increasingly common, **do** occurs where real emphasis is either redundant or clearly not intended.[10]

Affix-Hopping

Given our phrase structure rules, any deep structure has at least a TENSE, and maybe also the **en** and **ing** affixes in the wrong position for surface structure. In imperatives, as we have seen, TENSE and Modal are deleted by transformation. But any other deep structure must undergo a transformation that hops the affixes to their proper place. (Most deep structure strings go through many other transformational rules as well.) The effect of the affix-hopping transformation may be illustrated by:

John (TENSE) may ↓ leave = John may/might leave

(TENSE) have ↓ John (en) leave ↓ = Has/had John left?

John (TENSE) can ↓ n't have (en) be ↓ (ing) leave ↓ =
John can't/couldn't have been leaving

The generalization here is that each affix attaches to the element immediately to its right.

The rules of *do*-support and affix-hopping each capture generalizations about what appear to be disparate phenomena. In that sense they are "explanatory"—they show that the similarities are the result not of chance but of similar linguistic situations, despite different meanings (e.g., negative versus question in the case of *do*-support, the behavior of different kinds of temporal affixes on verbs in the case of affix-hopping). They are among the first rules to have been developed in transformational grammar (they feature large in Chomsky's *Syntactic Structures*, 1957) and are excellent examples of the way in which this approach to language sets out to show relationships in broad terms, at a conceptual level other than the word.

THE RECURSIVE PROPERTY OF LANGUAGE

The rules that we have developed so far account for very basic sentence types in the language. Such single clause sentences are largely confined to very early language acquisition, whether by a child or a second-language learner, and to "simplified" ways of speaking. In writing, they rarely occur except in kindergarten readers. The sentences most speakers use, including children of three or over, are more complex. As we saw in the first chapter, one of the prime characteristics of language is that it is "creative" in the sense that it allows us to construct and understand infinitely long sentences within certain constraints. For example, it allows us to construct and understand a sentence such as the following:

> Similarly, when a girl kisses a boy she may elect to keep her eyes closed so that should he open his he will be unable to see that she is involved in something other than the business at hand, and further, be unable to see that she has seen that he has seen this.[11]

It is the business of a grammar to show what processes are involved in this type of linguistic creativity, otherwise called "recursiveness." Sometimes recursiveness can trap us. We can get totally tied up in knots or let ourselves ad lib along seemingly parallel grammatical paths and lose ourselves entirely. In his parody of those who find a moral in everything and a paradox to boot, Lewis Carroll gives us a mind-boggling example. Alice in Wonderland ventures that mustard is a mineral but corrects herself:

> "It's a vegetable. It doesn't look like one, but it is."
> "I quite agree with you," said the Duchess; "and the moral of that is—'Be what you would seem to be'—or, if you'd like it put more simply—'Never imagine yourself not to be otherwise than what it might appear to others that what you were or might have been was not otherwise than what you had been would have appeared to them to be otherwise.'"[12]

A grammar should either exclude such a sentence because it is not well-formed, or should specify exactly what is deviant about it.

Languages basically have two devices on which linguistic infinity can be based: coordination and subordination.[13] Coordination involves paralleling two or more structures and combining them by **and**, **but**, or **or** under one umbrella structure, as in:

> [[He will be unable to see that she is involved]$_{S_1}$ and further [He will be unable to see that she has seen that he has seen this]$_{S_2}$]$_S$

This is illustrated schematically at the top of p. 155.

Subordination, on the other hand, imposes a hierarchic structure among sentences ("clauses" in traditional grammar) within a sentence. There are var-

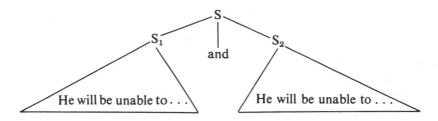

ious kinds of subordination: complementation, as in **he will see [that she has seen [that he has seen this]]**; relativization, as in **this is significant in considering the natural incapacities of gamesmen [who must play their game under the immediate gaze of opponents]**; temporal, as in **[when a subject attempts to conceal his awareness of something at hand] it is nearly certain that . . .**; purposive, as in **she may elect to keep her eyes closed [so that he will be unable to see that she is involved]**, and others. Only the first two, complementation and relativization, will be considered here. In all cases of subordination, otherwise called "embedding," a structural configuration of the following type is involved:

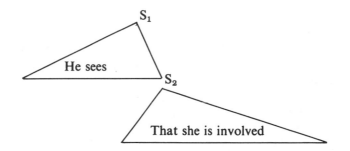

The visual configuration suggests the terminology "higher S" for S_1 and "lower S" for S_2. The highest S is the equivalent to the traditional "main clause."

Since the phrase structure is designed to account for the basic structure of the sentence, its categories and its hierarchies, it must also provide for complex sentences. Recursiveness, therefore, is generated by the phrase structure rules, in ways that are discussed in the relevant sections.

Coordination

In general, any sentence can be coordinated with any other. This can be indicated by the phrase structure rule:

$$S \rightarrow S \ (S)^n$$

where the superscript **n** indicates that the S can be repeated infinitely many times. This may seem to be an overgeneralization if we consider the un-grammaticality of such sentences as: ***We boarded the trains and what do you like? *I destroy trains and someone board them!** Further inspection, however, shows that the constraint on what sentences can be coordinated with what sentences is not a property of sentence types but of the particular meanings involved. It is the business of semantic and pragmatic analysis to show how such sentences fail, and why others such as **I know why I liked it, but why do you?** are grammatical.

Coordinate sentences are, then, syntactically free to combine with **and**. **But**, **or**, and other coordinators are more constrained in that they require negatives of various kinds, as in **I left but you did not**, ***I left but you did**. In surface structure, coordinates are constrained by some very general rules of the language that have to do with identity of reference, that is, reference to the same person or thing. "Second mentions" are typically deleted or modified in some way:

50. The highway follows its northern bank, the trail follows its southern ~~bank~~.

To have repeated **bank** would have suggested some special emphasis, perhaps opposition to **bed**, and the force of the contrast between highway and trail would have been dissipated. The role played by deletion or modification of second mentions in establishing speaker and hearer points of view and emphasis will be discussed far more fully in Chapter 7. Here we consider only some basic syntactic characteristics of this strategy in coordinate sentences.

If two N's are in identity across coordinates or embedded structures, then the second is usually expected to be a pronoun.[14] Thus:

51. Bill sang and Bill played the guitar.

is usually understood to refer to two different Bill's. Preferable is:

51. a.   Bill sang and he played the guitar.

if the two Bill's are in identity, although it is ambiguous (**he** could refer to Bill or some other male person). But even 51a sounds rather strange. We prefer:

51. b.   Bill sang and played the guitar.

This is just one instance of a general rule of "coordination reduction": If certain parts of a sentence (notably N or V) are the same in pairs of coordinate sentences, one of them is normally deleted. If the subjects are in identity, then the second NP is deleted, as in 51b and **He looked in all directions and saw nothing but wilderness**. If the verbs are in identity, then the first is deleted:

52. John and Bill cook well (from underlying **John cooks well and Bill cooks well**).

In some cases, even the first of two object NP's in identity may be deleted:

53. Frances bought and sold books on Saturdays (from underlying **Frances bought books on Saturday and Frances sold books on Saturday**).

Coordination reduction is not obligatory. As with other optional transformations, the fact that there is a choice to use it or not use it is stylistically meaningful. Special effects can be obtained by not using it as we will see in the discussion of a passage from Hemingway below.

In contrast to sentence coordination, there is also NP coordination. Consider again sentence 52. If this can be expanded to:

54. John and Bill cook well together.

or paraphrased as:

55. John cooks well with Bill.

then we have a case of NP coordination. That is, only the NP's **John and Bill** are coordinated in deep structure. If, however, the sentence means:

56. John cooks well and Bill cooks well too.

it implies nothing about togetherness (or even about John and Bill knowing one another), and we have a case of sentence coordination. Similarly, **I met John and Bill yesterday** involves NP coordination if it means **I met John when he was with Bill yesterday**, but sentence coordination if the speaker is reporting having met them separately.

Although sentences like 52 are ambiguous, many are not.

57. Harry and Jean are a couple.

58. Harry and Jean know the answer.

unambiguously illustrate NP coordinates and sentence coordinates, respectively. Sentences like 58 with coordinated subjects of state-of-being verbs expressing inner feelings like **know, like,** and **hate** always involve sentence coordination. The reasons are semantic since the same inner feeling can usually not be held by two people together.

Relative Clauses

Coordinate sentences are basically sentences of the same status strung together in a way that suggests some overall unity. By contrast, relative clauses, which are subordinate clauses, are dependent. That is, they depend for their existence on a higher S. Their function is to describe or particularize an N mentioned in the higher S, as in **The alibi that I gave was false.** Since they essentially function as optional expansions of the NP, they are introduced, according to some analyses, by the phrase structure rule:

$$NP \rightarrow NP \ (S)$$

Relative clauses are of two types: those that are parenthetical or "appositive," as in:

59. a.   They were working on the house, which still had no owner.

and those that are contrastive or "restrictive," as in:

60.   They were working on the house that still had no owner.

The appositive relatives have much in common with coordinate sentences, or even separate sentences that are logically related, and can have paraphrases like:

59. b.   They were working on the house. It still had no owner.
    c.   They were working on the house and/though it still had no owner.

The separateness of these relatives from their NP is highlighted by their separate intonation contours, reflected in writing by commas. Restrictive relatives, on the other hand, are an integral part of an NP and imply some kind of contrast. While 59a presupposes only one house being worked on, 60 presupposes that there were at least two, one of which is identifiable as the one that still had no owner.

The chief requirement on the syntax of relative clauses is that the subordinate sentence contain an N in identity with the N it modifies in the higher sentence. The noun in the higher sentence is called the "head." In appositive clauses, the noun in the subordinate clause is pronominalized by **who** if the N is animate, or **which** if the N is inanimate, as in:

61. a.   I met Bill Cohen, **who** is the janitor at Nicole's school.
    b.   The old barn, **which** we used to hide in, has been torn down.

In restrictive relative clauses the NP may be pronominalized not only by **who** or **which** but also by **that**. Therefore, checking whether **that** is possible is a good test if you are in doubt about which kind of relative is in use. Thus 62a is restrictive, while 62b is appositive:

> 62. a.   The dog which/that attacked you the other day has been caught.
>   b.   John, who/*that is a decoy, makes a lot of money on his job.

There are various kinds of restrictions on the co-occurrence of certain NP's with relatives. For example, appositive relatives, being noncontrastive, may modify nouns with unique reference, such as proper names. They cannot, however, modify generic nouns of the type *any N*:

> 63. a.   I want you to find Sarah, who is in a lot of trouble.
> 64. a.   *Anyone, who has trouble, can call in.

On the other hand, being contrastive, restrictive relatives cannot modify nouns with unique reference, although they can modify any other kind of noun:

> 63. b.   *I want you to find Sarah who is in a lot of trouble.
> 64. b.   Anyone who has trouble can call in.

Like coordinate sentences, relative clauses can be reduced by modification or deletion of elements:

> 65.   I have several pairs of socks ~~which are~~ full of holes.
>
> 66.   I know the little wide-eyed girl ~~who is~~ on the platform.
>
> 67.   He was surprised by the anger ~~which was~~ generated in him by her reply.

Constraints on relative clause reduction vary considerably according to the degree of formality chosen. While more colloquial varieties of English allow a considerable range of deletion, more formal varieties, especially writing, allow reduction only under five main circumstances. These are when the relative clause contains in surface structure:

1. **be** + Adjective
2. **be** + Adverb of place or time
3. auxiliary **be** + **en** or **be** + **ing** + V
4. main verb **have**
5. an object which is relativized

65 to 67 above illustrate the first three cases; and in these cases, if the relative pronoun is deleted, **be** must also be deleted. In the fourth case, **have** is replaced by a prepositional phrase:

68.   Anyone 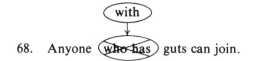 guts can join.

In the fifth case, only the pronoun is deleted:

69.   He read the report ⟨~~which~~⟩ the spy had compiled.

Sentences 65–67 contain **be** followed by some kind of NP or PP, or an adjective followed by an NP or PP. Supposing instead of a sentence like 65 we had:

70. a.   I watched the mayor who was gross

In all likelihood we would prefer:

70. b.   I watched the gross mayor.

Most adjectives that do not have a following PP are moved to a position between the determiner and the head noun. Thus the reduced form of **The man who is old** is not *the man old, but **the old man**. A notable exception is when the head is the pronoun **something** or **someone**:

71. a.   I need something sweet.
    b.   *I need sweet something.

There are several reasons why it is useful to argue that certain prenominal adjectives are derived from relative clauses. For one, **the old man** and (underlying) **The man who TENSE be old** mean the same thing. More significant for syntax is the fact that, in the appropriate circumstances, relative clause reduction can result in ambiguity. Both the following are ambiguous with respect to appositive versus restrictive interpretation:

72.   My cranky brother is coming to stay.
    = a.   My brother, who happens to be cranky, is coming to stay.
      b.   The brother who is cranky is coming to stay (implies I have others who are not cranky).

73. The industrious researchers have developed many different kinds
     of cures.
   = a. The researchers—they are an industrious group—have
          developed many different kinds of cures.
     b. Those of the researchers who are industrious have developed
          many different kinds of cures.

Finally, restrictive relatives do not normally occur with proper nouns as
heads, and neither do prenominal adjectives. We can explain the ungrammati-
cality of:

74. a. *Simon that is happy is a fraud.
     b. *Happy Simon is a fraud (**Happy** is grammatical only if under-
          stood as part of the name).

They can be explained as related rather than coincidental facts if we derive
prenominal adjectives from relatives. There are, of course, some adjectives
that can precede proper nouns; but there are heavy restrictions on the lexical
items available, and also special semantic properties. How many adjectives
can you put before **Simon**? Try **bald, fat, lovable**. They work because they are
epithets—that is, words which are treated as part of a person's name, as in
Blue-eyed Athena, Fat Bertie, and so on, and function as compounds.

Complements

Relative clauses expand an NP. By contrast, complement sentences actually
function rather like NP's themselves. There are three main types of complement, with various subtypes which we will not discuss here: (a) *that*-clauses,
(b) constructions signaled by a possessive marker (-'s) on the subject of the
embedded sentence and **-ing** on the verb, and (c) *for-to* constructions. Some
verbs allow all three, others only two or one. Compare:

75. a. That Bill lies about it is deplorable.
     b. Bill's lying about it is deplorable.
     c. For Bill to lie about it is deplorable.

76. a. I asked that he should be sent.
     b. *I asked his being sent.
     c. I asked for him to be sent.

77. a. *I wanted **that Bill should go**.
     b. *I wanted **Bill's going**.
     c. I wanted **Bill to go**.

Which type of complement is used is determined largely by the verb. This information must therefore be included in the lexical entry of the verb.

We have said that complements function rather like NP's. One example of this is that complements can be replaced by the pronoun **it**. The sentences in 75–77 can be reduced to:

75. d.   It is deplorable.

76. d.   I asked (for) it.

77. d.   I wanted it.

Other evidence suggests, however, that complements are best viewed only as parts of NP's. For instance, 75a is synonymous with:

75. e.   The fact that Bill lies about it is deplorable.

Here the complement S (**Bill lies about it**) is accompanied by DET + N (**the fact**). Moreover, 75e, like 75a, can also be reduced to **It is deplorable**. In other words, the whole *DET + N + S* sequence behaves like an NP. Sometimes both **it** and the complement appear together, as in:

78.   I don't like it that he drives so fast.

These facts can be accounted for if we introduce complements in the phrase structure rules by means of:

$$NP \rightarrow (DET) \; N \; (S)$$

The fact that Bill lies about it is an example of the *DET + N + S* option, while **that he drives so fast** in **I don't like it that he drives so fast** is an example of the *N + S* option. The other structures in 75–77 are derived by transformation in ways that will be discussed shortly.

Because certain nominals such as **fact, hope, idea** can precede complements, it might seem that complements are, like relative clauses, descriptors of NP's rather than sentences which function as NP's. But actually, complements and relatives behave quite differently, as the following sentences show. The a sentences are complements, the b sentences are relatives:

79. a.   The fact that we have discussed this matter is confidential.
    b.   The fact which/that we have just discussed is confidential.

80. a.   That we have discussed this matter is confidential.
    b.   *Which/that we have just discussed is confidential.

81. a.   It is confidential that we have discussed this matter.
    b.   *It is confidential which/that we have discussed.

82. a.   *The facts that we have discussed this matter are confidential.
    b.   The facts which/that we have just discussed are confidential.

***That*-complements:** *That*-complements may be constituents of NP's functioning as subjects, objects, or certain PP's of sentences:

83.   (The fact) that he wanted a lobotomy is significant.

                    subject

84.   I conclude that he had a lobotomy.

                    object

85.   I convinced him that I was from outer space. (I convinced him

    of it.)   PP

The surface complement-introducer **that** is often omitted, especially with objects of verbs like **know, believe, say,** and other verbs having to do with states of mind and with speaking:

86.   I swear ~~that~~ he looks like death warmed over.

87.   I know ~~that~~ it was you.

The form of the complement-introducer **that** is related to the pointer **that** in **that man**. It needs only a slight distortion of English to derive sentences like, **I said that: that he was my idol.** Indeed we find just such constructions in earlier written English, especially Old English, and we find it frequently in spoken language today.

It is a characteristic of many subject *that*-complements that they can be moved from their position in underlying structure to the right of the verb by a rule called *it*-extraposition. The first sentence of this paragraph illustrates this phenomenon. To begin the sentence with **That they can be moved from their position . . .** would have been closer to underlying structure than the actual sentence given. Being whole sentences in underlying structure, complements tend to be long. English is a language which disfavors extensive materials at the beginning of the sentence and favors placement of material at the end of the sentence. This tendency is connected with the fact that English word order is basically subject-verb-object. Languages whose basic order is subject-object-verb, such as Turkish, favor stacking of material at the beginning of the sentence. The *it*-extraposition rule essentially allows for movement of the whole complement to the right of the verb, while marking the original subject position by **it**. The resultant structure is often perceptually more accessible to English speakers than the version without it. The following tree diagrams sketch the possibilities available for:

88. a.   That she is brilliant is obvious.
    b.   It is obvious that she is brilliant.

They show similar pairs of sentences with subject complements extraposed and unextraposed. Elements moved, or deleted, by transformations are circled.

88. a.

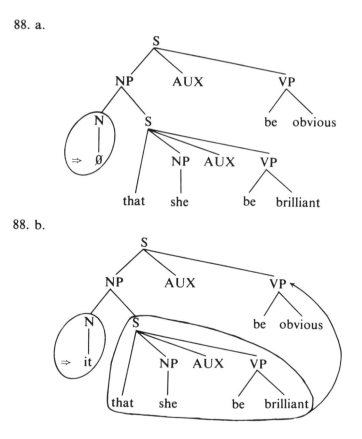

88. b.

Poss-ing **complements**: Besides 83, **The fact that he wanted a lobotomy is significant**, we also find:

89.   His wanting a lobotomy is astounding.

We find a large number of constructions like:

90. His being found guilty surprised me.

91. I regret his having persuaded me to take that course.

92. I blamed him for not drinking the hemlock.

These are characterized by the addition of the possessive marker to the subject NP of the complement and the substitution of **TENSE (M)** by **-ing**. The shorthand name for this phenomenon is the "*Poss-ing* complement," more traditionally known as the "gerund." Only TENSE and M are replaced, not the other auxiliaries, including the **be + en** of the passive, as illustrated by:

93. a. *His maying have left surprised us.
     b. His having left so soon annoyed us.
     c. His being tricked like that came as no surprise.

***For-to* complements**: Among various types of infinitive complements with **to**, the most frequent and best understood is the so-called *for-to* complement. It is called the *for-to* complement because, in many cases, both **for** and **to** introduce the complement (there is some dialect variation here). Consider, for example:

94. My greatest wish is *for* the whole thing *to* be over.

95. I would prefer *for* you *to* go later.

96. *For* you *to* leave so early was wise.

For-to complements involve substitution of **TENSE (M)** by **to**, just as *Poss-ing* complements involve substitution of **TENSE (M)** by **-ing**. This is demonstrated by the array:

97. a. *For him to may refuse would be awful.
     b. For him to have refused would have been dreadful.
     c. For him to be being beaten by a slave in the opening scene seems rather too sensational.

Certain *for-to* complements require a rule which deletes the subject of the complement sentences if that subject is in identity with a subject or object NP in the higher sentence. For example, in the case of verbs like **want, like**, and **arrange**, the subject of the complement sentence is deleted if it is in identity with the subject of the higher S:

98. a. I want you to test yourself against this man.
     b. I want her to test herself against this man.

    c.   I want ⊘me⊘ to test myself against this man.

This kind of deletion-under-identity rule is called EQUI-NP deletion. It is part of the general strategy of the language that we have already noted in reference to reflexivization, coordination reduction, and relative reduction. Redundant material, especially material referring to something already present in the sentence, is modified or even deleted in surface structure.

WHY DO WE NEED TRANSFORMATIONAL RULES?

The study of transformational rules has raised numerous questions of great theoretical interest that we cannot go into here. Just one brief example must suffice: the question whether transformations in addition to phrase structure rules are just a linguist's construct, or whether they have some real function in language, without which language would not be as we know it. The evidence suggests that some transformations, at least, are very closely connected with the communicative function of language. It is unquestionably part of the competence of an English user to produce and understand such sentences as **The rat was white, The cat killed the rat**, and **I chased the cat**. It is also part of the competence of any English user to construct and understand such sentences as **The rat (which) the cat killed was white** or **The cat (which) I chased killed the rat**. In underlying structure these are, approximately:

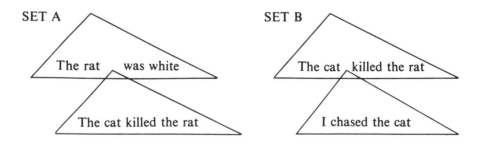

There is no theoretical reason to prevent embedding Set B into Set A, rendering an underlying structure of the sort shown at the top of p. 167.

Yet most people can, in fact, neither produce nor understand:

    99. a.   The rat (the cat (I chased) killed) was white.

Should the grammar prevent the generation of such structures in the phrase structure component? Are such structures not part of our competence?

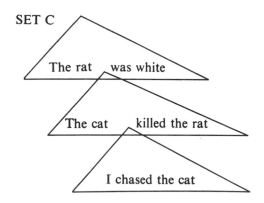

SET C

The rat was white

The cat killed the rat

I chased the cat

Surely they are, because in fact we do get versions of the three-layered structure, such as:

99. b.   The rat was white that the cat that I chased killed.

Much better is the following which has undergone both a passive transformation and movement of the relative:

99. c.   The rat killed by the cat that I chased was white.

In other words, we get versions of 99a that have undergone certain movement transformations, all of which move materials into positions that express the speaker's point of view (on the importance of killing versus chasing), and make the material more accessible to the hearer. It has therefore been proposed that some transformations have the function of rendering materials more informative and comprehensible.[15] Further examples will be discussed in Chapter 7, which is devoted to this aspect of linguistic organization.

SYNTAX AND LITERATURE

Let us now consider how an understanding of syntax can be used in literary analysis. Nontransformational approaches to syntactic stylistics tend to focus on analysis of surface structures. The transformational approach adds further dimensions that have proved useful in stylistic analysis. Particularly fruitful has been the idea that not only the surface sentence structure has significance for a work, but also the deep structure and the degree of difference that may be found between the deep and surface structure.[16] On the one hand, there are texts in which deep structure matches surface structure very closely. In others, there is considerable difference between the two. In this latter case, we may find that deep structures are relatively diverse, while surface structures are relatively uniform and deceptively simple. Or we may find that surface structures are relatively diverse, whereas the deep structures are relatively uniform. And everywhere we find transformations being exploited not only for such essential strategies as making material perceptually available, but also to create structural parallelisms which add cohesion or counteract the potential monotony of overcohesiveness.

Simple Sentences

Examples of passages where little recursiveness is used and where there is very little difference between deep and surface structures are hard to find except in stories for small children.[17] Some experimental writers have recently explored the idea of using highly "simple" language of this sort, largely stripped of optional rules such as passive or coordination reduction, and largely limited to simple sentences. Their purpose is obviously quite different from that of children's literature. Instead of teaching grammar and reading skills, this experimental literature deliberately draws attention to or foregrounds simple language to support, even establish, a particular point of view—that the world is meaningless, disjointed, and doomed by poverty of experience. This kind of stylistic strategy has been developed by Donald Barthelme among others, as a vehicle for expressing the absurd. Consider, for example, the beginning of his short story, "Edward and Pia."

> Edward looked at his red beard in the tableknife. Then Edward and Pia went to Sweden, to the farm. In the mailbox Pia found a check for Willie from the government of Sweden. It was for twenty-three hundred crowns and had a rained-on look. Pia put the check in the pocket of her brown coat. Pia was pregnant. In London she had been sick every day. In London Pia and Edward had seen the Marat/Sade at the Aldwych Theatre. Edward bought a bottle of white stuff for Pia in London. It was supposed to make her stop vomiting. Edward walked out to the wood barn and broke
> 10 up wood for the fire. Snow in patches lay on the ground still. Pia wrapped cabbage leaves around chopped meat. She was still wearing her brown coat. Willie's check was still in the pocket. It was still Sunday.
> "What are you thinking about?" Edward asked Pia and she said she was thinking about Willie's hand. Willie had hurt his hand in a machine in a factory in Markaryd. The check was for compensation.
> Edward turned away from the window. Edward received a cable from his wife in Maine. "Many happy birthdays," the cable
> 20 said. He was thirty-four. His father was in the hospital. His mother was in the hospital. Pia wore white plastic boots with her brown coat. When Edward inhaled sharply—a sharp intake of breath—they could hear a peculiar noise in his chest. Edward inhaled sharply. Pia heard the noise. She looked up. "When will you go to the doctor?" "I have to get something to read," Edward said.[18]

Much of the effect of this passage derives, of course, from the lack of semantic connections. What does Edward's looking at his beard in the tableknife have to do with going to Sweden? Or what in particular does being pregnant have in common with going to *Marat-Sade*? One strains to find significant connections. Pia is physically sick. The characters in *Marat-Sade* are mentally sick. The connection seems appropriate. But we are brought up sharp at every turn, forced to recognize that in Edward and Pia's world, events happen without connection, associative or causal. Even such a possible connective as might exist between Edward's parents' being sick and Pia's and Edward's own sickness is deliberately severed by **Pia wore white plastic boots with her brown coat** (21). At the same time we are asked to find patterns in things we might not expect to be significant: **in London, in Sweden, in Markaryd**—even the exact name of the London theater is given. The places seem to give the only binding force to disjointed activities, other than the co-existence of Edward and Pia.

We must not forget, however, that meaning is expressed by means of syntax. The deliberate choice of simple sentences with only a few connectives and no subordination highlights the discontinuity. So does the choice of proper names as opposed to pronouns in all but a few instances (that is, the preference for using pronouns rather than nouns when referring to the same entity from sentence to sentence is ignored). One of the few exceptions is found in lines 14–15: **"What are you thinking about?" Edward asked Pia and she said she was thinking about Willie's hand**. The whole paragraph in which this occurs is coherent, and, significantly, this paragraph is about a person and events external to Edward and Pia. Others live connected lives; not so our hero and heroine except when thinking about others. This is reflected by the use of the embedded complement in **she said she was thinking about Willie's hand**, where **that** is deleted and the complement is thus more tightly related to the main clause **she said** than if it were not deleted.

It is not only the simple sentence structure that parallels the intended meaning. As we saw, place is semantically important. It is prominent syntactically, too. Place expressions such as **in the mailbox, in London, at the train station** are moved out of their normal position at the end of the sentence to the beginning. This transformation takes on a significance it would not have in ordinary discourse, since place expressions are the only expressions that undergo an optional movement transformation in this passage. (Questions require movement, and therefore movement is stylistically irrelevant in such a question as **What are you thinking about?**).

"Directness," Real and Apparent

Let us turn now to a different writer, Hemingway. His style is well known for its "directness." What evidence does close syntactic analysis give us for this impression? A fairly typical example is the following excerpt from Chapter 13 of *For Whom the Bell Tolls*:

> Because now he was not there. He was walking beside her but his mind was thinking of the problem of the bridge now and it was all clear and hard

and sharp as when a camera lens is brought into focus. He saw the two posts and Anselmo and the gypsy watching. He saw the road empty and he saw movement on it. He saw where he would place the two automatic rifles to get the most level field of fire, and who will serve them, he thought, me at the end, but who at the start? He placed the charges, wedged and lashed them, sunk his caps and crimped them, ran his wires, hooked them up and got back to where he had placed the old box of the exploder and then he started to think of all the things that could have happened and that might go wrong.[19]

The directness is in some sense measurable in the terms we have been using. We may observe a relatively close match between deep and surface structure, despite the use of certain optional transformations, such as subject reduction in coordination (lines 7–8). We may think of an underlying set of simple structures, something like the following, out of which surface sentences have been constructed:

1.   He was walking beside her.
     His mind was thinking of the problem of the bridge now.
     It (the scene) was all clear in a certain way.
     It was all hard in a certain way.
     It was all sharp in a certain way.
     One brings a camera lens into focus.

2.   He saw the two posts.
     He saw Anselmo.
     Anselmo was watching.
     He saw the gypsy.
     The gypsy was watching.

But just to say this is only to scratch the surface. What is striking about Hemingway is that this directness, this "simplicity," actually seems unnatural in written language. Sentences four and five provide especially good examples: **He saw the road empty and he saw movement on it, He saw where he would place the two automatic rifles.** The repetition of **He saw** brings attention to the visual impact; in real life, Jordan could hardly have seen everything simultaneously, but Hemingway is creating a world where everything seems in focus at the same time. The almost machine-gun-like repetition of **he . . . he . . .**, so characteristic of Hemingway, with little modification between deep and surface structure, has the special effect of drawing attention to the person, while at the same time implying an almost automatic response. In other words, nonuse of an optional transformation may foreground and make special the scene being presented. As we said in Chapter 1, style is choice—and choice is a matter both of what is chosen and what is not chosen. This is, of course, an analysis that does not depend on the deep-surface structure hypothesis. However, it is clarified by the hypothesis, since we can show exactly what the choices involved are. Furthermore, the insistence that what is not chosen is as important as what is, given a narrow set of choices, finds particularly active support in generative theory, since this theory depends so heavily on determining what is grammatical on the basis of what is not.

Hemingway's style is not as direct as is sometimes supposed. It is actually a mixture of direct deep-surface structure relations and some very indirect ones. For example, in the main clauses all the deep structure subjects are also subjects in surface structure, and this is true for nearly all the subordinate S's as well, with the notable exception of **camera lens** in line 3, which has been moved into subject position by the passive (the deep structure subject being **someone**). (**As when a camera lens is brought into focus** is exceptional in another way too, being the only simile in the passage.) In the main clauses, the deep structure and surface structure subjects are also extremely simple (**he, his mind, it**), without modification or ambiguity of any sort. NP's that are not subjects of the main clauses, however, tend to be more complex than NP's that are subjects, both in their deep structure and in the transformations needed to derive the surface structures. Many involve modifiers (**two posts, two automatic rifles, the problem of the bridge**). Others, particularly those that are objects of the mental process verbs **see** (here meaning "imagine") and **think**, involve one or more embedded sentences: **Anselmo and the gypsy watching**; **the place [where he would place the rifles [to get the most level field of fire]]**; **the place [where he had placed the old box . . .]**. Particularly interesting is the last sentence, where the subject **he**, whether repeated or not, is a simple pronoun, while objects of actions like **placed** and **wedged** are NP's with determiners like **the charge, his wires**, and the complement of the mental process verb **think** is quite complex: **of all the things that could have happened and that might go wrong**. Throughout the passage, then, the perceiver and doer remain simple; what is done is more complex, and what is thought and seen in the mind is most complex of all. And in terms of syntax as well as content, things are considerably less clear and simple by the end of the passage than they were at the outset.

The passage we have just looked at follows a love scene between Robert Jordan and Maria. The language of this love scene shows some interesting contrasts with the passage just quoted:

> They were walking through the heather of the mountain meadow and Robert Jordan felt the brushing of the heather against his legs, felt the weight of his pistol in its holster against his thigh, felt the sun on his head, felt the breeze from the snow of the mountain peaks cool on his back and, in his hand, he felt the girl's hand firm and strong, the fingers locked in his. From it, from the palm of her hand against the palm of his, from their fingers locked together, and from her wrist across his wrist something came from her hand, her fingers and her wrist to his that was as fresh as the first light
> 10 air that moving toward you over the sea barely wrinkles the glassy

surface of a calm, as light as a feather moved across one's lip, or a leaf falling when there is no breeze; so light that it could be felt with the touch of their fingers alone, but that was so strengthened, so intensified, and made so urgent, so aching and so strong by the hard pressure of their fingers and the close pressed palm and wrist, that it was as though a current moved up his arm and filled his whole body with an aching hollowness of wanting. With the sun shining on her hair, tawny as wheat, and on her gold-brown smooth-lovely face and on the curve of her throat he bent her head back
20   and held her to him and kissed her. He felt her trembling as he kissed her and he held the length of her body tight to him and felt her breasts against his chest through the two khaki shirts, he felt them small and firm and he reached and undid the buttons on her shirt and bent and kissed her and she stood shivering, holding her head back, his arm behind her. Then she dropped her chin to his head and then he felt her hands holding his head and rocking it against her. He straightened and with his two arms around her held her so tightly that she was lifted off the ground, tight against him, and he felt her trembling and then her lips were on his throat,
30   and then he put her down and said, "Maria, oh, my Maria."[20]

The text gives us a sense of urgency, and rapidly accumulating sensations. At the same time it suggests a certain blurredness of perception, which only later will become **clear and hard and sharp as when a camera lens is brought into focus**. The language, although externally simple in ways that resemble the first passage, is actually in deep structure relatively complex and contributes to the total orgasmic effect of the scene. The passage may be divided into two sections, part A, sentences one and two (lines 1–17) and part B, sentences four to six (lines 20–30), with sentence three functioning as a transition. Part A has many of the syntactic characteristics of Hemingway's work, simplicity of the subjects (**they, Robert Jordan, he**) and the coordinate structure including repetition of the connective **and**, and of the verb **felt**, which immediately draws attention to this verb. But in some other respects it is very different from the first passage we looked at. The two sentences in part A are long and involve a complexity not found in the first passage.

On initial inspection the first sentence seems quite direct. It develops a set of parallel objects of feeling.

    a.   Walked through the heather of the mountain meadow.
    b.   Felt the brushing of the heather.
    c.   Felt the weight of his pistol.
    d.   Felt the breeze from the snow of the mountain peaks.

Surface similarities are reinforced by the progression from legs to thigh to head and back. But the syntactic similarities are apparent only. They reflect different underlying structures. All four include the surface . . . N of DET N.

However, a and d have underlying structures of the type N_1 (**heather, snow**) **which was on the** N_2, while b and c have underlying structures of the type **the heather brushed . . . the pistol weighed . . . .** Consider, further, how one might go about breaking the sentences down into simple sub-sentences. Does **against his legs** belong to **the brushing** or to **feel**? Does **against his thigh** belong to **holster, pistol, weighing,** or **feeling**? As readers, we are presumably not required to decide. Both structures can operate at once. Our understanding of the compounding of experience is enhanced not merely by coordinate structures but also by the ambiguity of the end of the sub-sentences. It could be argued that ambiguity is hard to avoid in English and probably of no more significance than in the sentence **He saw Anselmo and the gypsy watching**. Nevertheless, it is clear that the ambiguity in this particular case is structurally important and purposeful, for, toward the end of the sentence, **in his hand** is extracted from its expected position at the end of the sentence, highlighted by its position before **he felt the girl's fingers**, and disambiguated. To test this, one can replace Hemingway's version by an ambiguous one that parallels the preceding coordinates.

> . . . **And he felt the girl's hand firm and strong in his hand**.

Firm and strong could be a quality of the girl's hand everywhere or a quality derived from being in his hand. The effect is quite different from what Hemingway actually wrote. A movement transformation fronting **in his hand** has made a specific place strikingly unambiguous. From this point on in the paragraph, place is fully specified, but the nature of what is in that place takes on a special vagueness rather unusual in Hemingway.

In sentence two, once more we have, on first glance, the typical Hemingway coordination and repetition of elements. But this time the repetition is of elements that cannot be deleted: **from** and **so**. The fact that they are non-deletable makes the repetition stylistically much less important than the repetition of **saw** or **felt**, which we would expect to be deleted. Atypically, we have a long string of Place adverbials in the beginning. The subject, **something**, too, is complex—it is multiply modified by relative clauses that themselves have relatives inside them. Not only is the subject multiply modified, it is indefinite (even though it is definitized later as **her fingers . . . her wrist**)—a truly unusual phenomenon in Hemingway. The deliberate surface reordering and the indefiniteness of the subject help suggest the complexity and ambiguity of the feeling, the wave-on-wave cumulative effect, the movement of the feeling, *and* the all-embracingness of the feeling. This reordering is diagrammed at the top of p. 174.

The cumulative feeling gives way to action in part B. The transition is effected by a sentence with adverb coordination at the beginning, again emphasizing things external to Robert Jordan, but then at the end focusing on him: **With the sun shining on her hair, tawny as wheat, and on her gold-brown smooth-lovely face and on the curve of her throat he bent her head back and held her to him and kissed her.** At the end of this sentence and in part B, we

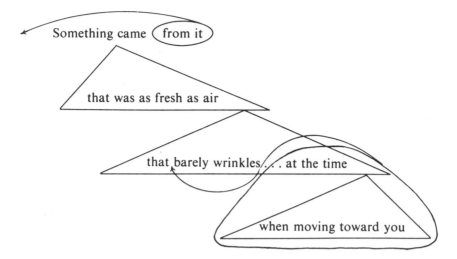

experience a sequence of actions as sharply delineated as the sequence that Robert Jordan later imagines at the guard post. What is striking again is that certain transformations have not been used, specifically not subject deletion. However, a subject deletion is used to great effect in one instance: **he held the length of her body tight to him and felt her breasts against his chest**. This allows an interpretation of simultaneity to the holding and the feeling which **and he felt her breasts** would not. It also permits ambiguity between the action of "feeling" (touching) and the state of sensation. Presence of **he** would emphasize the action interpretation in the context of the actions **he kissed** and **he held**. Absence of the **he** makes greater the likelihood that the sensation is the dominant interpretation intended.

Complexity

Hemingway is often thought of as a relatively direct writer and, more specifically, as one who uses few transformations. We have suggested that the directness is more a matter of surface structure parallelisms than of deep structure simplicity. An author usually considered to be at the other end of the stylistic scale of directness is Henry James, who is well known for indirectness and syntactic complexity. There is no question that his style is vastly different from Hemingway's. If the most striking feature of the latter's style is his use of coordination, James's most striking feature is his use of complementation. Complementation is not only a process of embedding and, therefore, of relative psychological complexity, but also a device for distancing, particularly when the abstract nouns that introduce complements (e.g., **fact, hope, question, idea**) are present in surface structure. What makes James seem so complex, however, is not only his choice of complements and the abstractions attendant on them, but even more the fact that, unlike Hemingway's, his surface structures are very diverse even when his underlying structures are similar. Furthermore, he will, at times, not use a transformation where use of one would aid comprehension. He writes sentences with embeddings inside embeddings that emphasize layers of thoughts and experiences. All these points are illustrated by the following passage from Chapter 29 of *The Portrait of a Lady*.

> "It wouldn't be remarkable if you did think it ridiculous that I should have the means to travel when you've not; for you know everything, and I know nothing."
>
> "The more reason why you should travel and learn," smiled Osmond. "Besides," he added as if it were a point to be made, "I don't know everything."
>
> Isabel was not struck with the oddity of his saying this gravely; she was thinking that the pleasantest incident of her life—so it pleased her to qualify these too few days in Rome, which she might musingly have likened to the figure of some small princess of one of the ages of dress overmuffled in a mantle of state and dragging a train that it took pages or historians to hold up—that this felicity was coming to an end. That most of the interest of the time had been owing to Mr. Osmond was a reflexion she was not just now at pains to make; she had already done the point abundant justice.[21]

(line number: 10)

The beginnings of the first and last sentences both involve complement structures available for *it*-extraposition. The skeletal structure of these sentences is shown on p. 176.

Only sentence one uses extraposition, yet sentence five could well have used it too. Consider the effect of what James might have written: **It was a reflexion (that) she was not just now at pains to make that most of the interest of the time had been owing to Mr. Osmond**. A possibility of partial surface parallelism between sentences one and five seems to have been purposely avoided, adding to the sense of emotional uncertainty.

The fourth sentence, lines 7–13, is a prime example of James's complexity, both in the variation in deep structure and the avoidance of possible surface parallelisms. In this sentence, the complement is interrupted. The interruption contains several layers of relative clauses, the structure of each one being somewhat different. Surface parallelism is avoided, by use first of **which** and then of **that**. James is demanding a degree of concentration in reading which far exceeds what would have been necessary if the underlying structural parallelisms had been preserved on the surface instead of being deformed by a variety of different optional transformations.

There is, of course, much more to James's style in this passage than has been pointed out here, but this preliminary investigation should help suggest paths to more detailed study.

Finally, let us turn again to Carl Sandburg's poem, "The Harbor," discussed in Chapter 2. As we mentioned there, the syntax plays an important

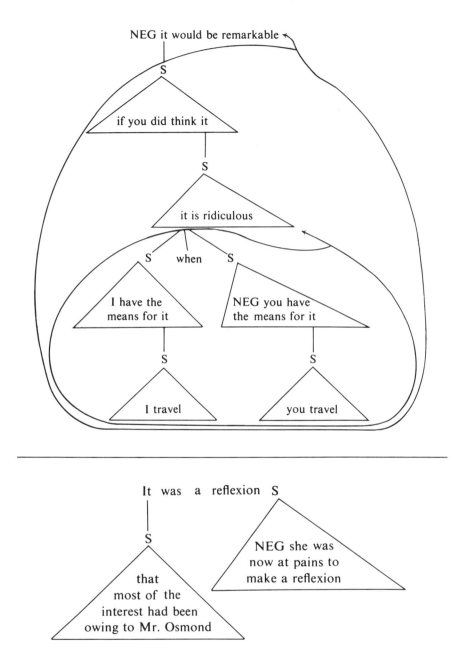

part in conveying the contrasts between the walled-in city and the open lake. Lines 1–5 are not only walled in by the rhyme on **walls** and the repetition of the whole phrase **huddled and ugly walls**, but by the fact that they constitute a subordinate sentence describing the time and manner of the event. Most important of all is the fact that this subordinate clause precedes the subject—

as we have seen, long phrases at the beginning of the sentence are disfavored in English. Line 6, the transitional line, is a simple main clause (S_1 of the complex structure). It is followed by a sequence of coordinate phrases matching the sense of relative independence and, therefore, the freedom experienced in the openness at the edge of the city. The dominant recursive structure in this poem, however, is the relative clause in various reduced and unreduced forms. It is surely hardly irrelevant that the only full relative, showing all its structure, and hence its structural boundaries, is in the part on the enclosed city:

> By doorways **where** (= **in which**) **women**
> **Looked from their hunger-deep eyes**.

Both in the first and the second part we find reduced relatives: **through huddled and ugly walls**; **hunger-deep eyes, haunted with shadows**; **blue burst**; **long lake waves breaking**; **spray-flung curve**; **fluttering storm**; **great grey wings**; **flying white bellies/Veering and wheeling free in the open**. Although the walls are contrasted with openness, with pastness (**looked, haunted, huddled**), and with continuation (**passing, breaking, fluttering, flying, veering, wheeling**), this poem is nevertheless about a vision, a world full of possibilities for rich description. There is an essential cohesiveness to the point of view (though not the evaluation of what is seen), which is indicated by the variously modified underlying relative clauses.

Syntax, then, does a great deal to support meanings, and sometimes even helps create them, especially when a sense of contrast between appearances and reality is at issue.

SUGGESTED FURTHER READINGS

There are a great number of books on English syntax and on syntactic theory in general. Among the major reference grammars, Jespersen's *Modern English Grammar on Historical Principles* remains one of the most widely used. A more recent reference grammar of great value, based on British English, is Quirk et al., *A Grammar of Contemporary English*, which has a useful smaller edition by Quirk and Greenbaum, entitled *A Concise Grammar of Contemporary English*. These grammars approach the subject from a relatively traditional point of view. A reference grammar within the transformational framework, but with some additional features to be discussed in the next chapter (role relationships) is Stockwell et al., *The Major Syntactic Structures of English*. Two journals with a large proportion of articles on generative syntax (and semantics) are *Linguistic Analysis* and *Linguistic Inquiry*. Many of the articles in both these journals are at a very advanced level.

Excellent introductions to transformational syntax are provided by Chapter 5 of Langacker's *Language and Its Structure* and by Postal's article

"Underlying and Superficial Structure." Langacker focuses on complex sentence structure, while Postal focuses on justifications for deep and surface structure and the analysis of imperatives and passives. Thorough accounts of transformational approaches to syntax are to be found in Akmajian and Heny, *An Introduction to the Principles of Transformational Syntax*, Baker, *Introduction to Generative-Transformation Syntax*, and Soames and Perlmutter, *Syntactic Argumentation and Structure of English*.

Fundamental readings on transformational syntax and literature are Ohmann's articles, "Generative Grammars and the Concept of Literary Style" and "Literature as Sentences." In the first of these articles, Ohmann assumes a version of generative grammar preceding the one discussed here, one in which the phrase structure rules specify only simple active declarative sentences; transformations are allowed to change meaning (for example, from affirmative to negative, from statement to question). The principles of transformational grammar remain the same, despite the differences in formulation.

Many nontransformational accounts of syntax and literature focus primarily on surface structure. A topic much discussed within this frame of reference is whether authors or even periods can be characterized as favoring "nominal" as opposed to "verbal" as opposed to "adjectival" styles, and styles exploiting coordinate as opposed to subordinate structures. Miles's *Style and Proportion: The Language of Prose and Poetry* is a classic on this topic. (It also includes extensive discussion of diction.) For an overview of the various issues in the study of syntax and literature, see Section III of Chatman and Levin's *Essays on the Language of Literature*, and Section IV of Freeman's *Linguistic and Literary Style*.

Exercises

1. The sentence: **She made him a good husband because she made him a good wife** consists of two underlying sentences of rather different sort, but nevertheless very similar surface structure (**She made him a good husband, She made him a good wife**). Use this sentence to argue for the difference between underlying and surface structure. You do not have to devise trees to show the difference in underlying structure, but you should consider the possible paraphrases and the possible transformations that are unique to one or the other of the underlying sentences.

2. The sentences below all have similar surface structures; on first appearance it looks as if the VP of each sentence could be diagrammed as shown at the top of p. 179. To say that the VP in each sentence has the same underlying structure is, however, not very revealing. Why not? How can the differences in underlying structure be accounted for?

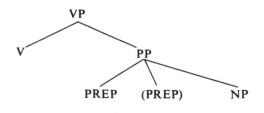

    a. The pilot passed over the house.
    b. The president passed over the peace proposal.
    c. We'll never persuade them to take down those hideous posters.
    d. We read out of the Koran.
    e. They blew up the PGE station.
    f. The ashes blew up the chimney.
    g. The Governor disapproves of pot.
    h. He decided on the boat.
    i. He ran after dinner.
    j. He ran after the cop.

This is primarily an exercise in thinking about the grouping of elements within a sentence, and in developing tests to determine the underlying structure of sentences. As a start, you might like to consider which sentences can have passive variants (for example, is **The chimney was blown up by the ashes** grammatical?), and what the pronoun forms of Prep + NP can be (e.g., **What did the leaves blow up? Where did the leaves blow?** which are related to f, and **What did they blow up?** but not **Where did they blow?** related to e). Other things to consider include pronunciation (stress patterns in particular, see sentences on pages 65–66 in Chapter 2). While you will need to think about each sentence separately to start with (remembering that some of them may be ambiguous), you should deal with groups of sentences in your answer. Hint: There are two main groups, and one of the main groups has two subsets.

3. Use the phrase structure rules on page 138 to derive three strings, one affirmative, one negative, and one imperative. Show each step of the derivation as on page 140, and write trees for each string.

4. Some examples of reflexive sentences have been given in the section on imperatives. Here are some more:

    a. The rabbit tore itself free.
    b. Mary told John that she would look after $\left\{ \begin{array}{l} \text{herself.} \\ \text{him.} \\ \text{*himself.} \end{array} \right\}$

    c. No one must fool himself.
    d. I gave myself a long holiday.

Describe what a "reflexive transformation" would have to account for in the following steps:

    a. State what information must be given in the structural description; that is, state what conditions must apply for T reflexive to be applicable.

    b. State what must be in the structural change; that is, state what the constraints on the surface structures of reflexives are.

    c. Should the transformation be obligatory or optional?

5. a. Give the passive version of:

    (1) Phil watered the garden too heavily.

    (2) Bill expected me to leave soon.

    (3) The doctor expected the technician to develop the X-rays fast. (Note that there are three possibilities for passivizing this sentence, depending on whether the main clause or the subordinate clause is passivized, or both.)

  b. Give the *it*-extraposed version of:

    (1) That there was no publicity was part of the problem.

    (2) That nobody would overcharge them was their prime concern.

    (3) That they would leave seemed obvious by then.

6. Reduce the following relative clauses so that at least the relative pronoun (**who, which, that**) is deleted:

    a. At the station you will see a man who is carrying a large umbrella.

    b. Any coins which are found on this site must be handed in to the police.

    c. This is the day on which he normally goes to San Francisco.

    d. I met a man who has a red moustache.

    e. The children who are tall managed to climb the fence.

    f. They sold the brownies that they had made the day before.

    g. They sold the brownies that were left over.

7. For each of the following sentences state as precisely as you can in what ways it is ambiguous:

    a. The door was closed.

    b. I don't like Bill's painting.

    c. Radical students and workers unite.

    d. I drew the man with the chalk.

8. The following poem was written by a computer. This computer was programmed to produce syntactically correct sentences and syntactically cohesive stanzas.

    A lustful twig can twiddle up the tenderness of a spoon
    And can kill the motion of wisdom.
    But the brain beside gay power heals the action of earth
    While the tenderness of a spoon heals the lustful twig.

A happy muffin shall bask under earth of night
And can ensnare the pond up charity of earth.
But the activity of charity strengthens sorrowful faith
While earth of night beseechs the happy muffin.

A wanton gate may gurgle under the gate of the age of a star
And should worship a gay shovel.
But frail wisdom ensnares the endurance of night
While the gate of the age of a star pursues the wanton gate.

A moody cloud shall ponder over the motion of a shovel
And should beseech the goodness of beauty.
But war over nature worships a wanton goat
While the motion of a shovel strengthens the moody cloud.[22]

a. Write as specific a phrase structure grammar of this poem as you can, assuming for the purposes of this exercise that adjectives and prepositional phrases can be introduced in the phrase structure as follows:

$$NP \rightarrow (DET)(ADJ)N \text{ (of NP)}$$

b. Write some sample lexical entries for N, PREP, ADJ, and V (e.g., **nature** is [+N, +___], while **twig** is [+N, +DET___].

c. What transformation is necessary? You need not formalize it, though you should describe precisely what it does.

d. Using your phrase structure rules, the lexicon you constructed in b, and what you know about the transformation operating in this text, derive one more stanza of the poem. Note that the same phrase structure rules operate in each stanza. Therefore, if you can account for one stanza, you can account for them all. You will obviously generate some strings that are semantically very odd. Do not worry about this—you will have an opportunity to consider the semantic aspect of this poem in an exercise in the next chapter.

9. Robert Bridges's poem "November" (printed on pages 111–12) is as interesting syntactically as it is phonologically and lexically. One often-used transformation is movement of a place-expression to the beginning of the underlying sentence (e.g., **out by the ricks the mantled engine stands** instead of **the mantled engine stands out by the ricks**). Discuss the function of this transformation in the poem, then comment briefly on other important syntactic choices that contribute to the overall meaning. Include comments on the preponderance of intransitive verbs, and on why line 33 is so striking syntactically. Also, why might the first three and the last six lines of the poem be "incomplete sentences" (i.e., sentences without main verbs)?

10. Briefly discuss the major syntactic characteristics of this excerpt from James Joyce's *Ulysses*. What parts of many underlying sentences have been deleted? What effect does Joyce achieve by using this deletion transformation?

> No, not like that. A barren land, bare waste. Vulcanic lake, the dead sea: no fish, weedless, sunk deep in the earth. No wind would lift those waves, grey metal, poisonous foggy waters. Brimstone they called

it raining down: the cities of the plain: Sodom. Gomorrah. Edom, All dead names. A dead sea in a dead land, grey and old. Old now. It bore the oldest, the first race. A bent hag crossed from Cassidy's clutching a naggin bottle by the neck. The oldest people. Wandered far away over all the earth, captivity to captivity, multiplying, dying, being born everywhere. It lay there now. Now it could bear no more. Dead.[23]

11. Ralph Pomeroy's poem "Corner" (printed on page 37) is striking for its syntax. The use of relativization, coordination, simple sentences, and partial sentences is particularly significant. Discuss how these syntactic devices contribute to the overall meaning of the poem. Consider, for example, the fact that most of the longer sentences refer to the cop, while the "I" is referred to in shorter sentences. Punctuation reflects pitch rises and falls and also pauses. These in turn reflect certain sentence types (e.g., question versus statement) and degrees of syntactic closeness. Thus **My ease is fake, and he can tell** is syntactically more cohesive than **My ease is fake. And he can tell**, since in the first case there is one underlying sentence with coordinated sub-sentences, while in the second there are two underlying sentences that are loosely coordinated to each other. In the course of your discussion, discuss the function of the punctuation especially in lines 12–17, 26–27, 36–37.[24]

12. The following is the beginning of the "prelude" to William Faulkner's *Big Woods*. It is a characterization of Mississippi (and the Mississippi) past, present, and future.

   a. What are the main syntactic structures used in this excerpt?
   b. What is the difference syntactically between the description of the land and the description of the land-dwellers, especially the Anglo-Saxons? (Do not look for absolute differences, only for obvious tendencies.)
   c. What is the function of the punctuation, especially colons and semicolons? Include comments on the relative lack of punctuation.
   d. How do syntax and punctuation (or lack of it) contribute to the overall meaning?

MISSISSIPPI:

*The rich deep black alluvial soil which would grow
cotton taller than the head of a man on a horse, already
one jungle one brake one impassable density of brier
and cane and vine interlocking the soar of gum and
cypress and hickory and pinoak and ash, printed now
by the tracks of unalien shapes—bear and deer and
panthers and bison and wolves and alligators and the
myriad smaller beasts, and unalien men to name them*

10 *too perhaps—the (themselves) nameless though
recorded predecessors who built the mounds to escape the
spring floods and left their meagre artifacts: the obsolete
and the dispossessed, dispossessed by those who were
dispossessed in turn because they too were obsolete: the*

> *wild Algonquian, Chickasaw and Choctaw and Natchez*
> *and Pascagoula, peering in virgin astonishment down*
> *from the tall bluffs at a Chippeway canoe bearing three*
> *Frenchmen—and had barely time to whirl and look*
> *behind him at ten and then a hundred and then a thousand*
> 20   *Spaniards come overland from the Atlantic Ocean:*
> *a tide, a wash, a thrice flux-and-ebb of motion so rapid*
> *and quick across the land's slow alluvial chronicle as to*
> *resemble the limber flicking of the magician's one hand*
> *before the other holding the deck of inconstant cards: the*
> *Frenchman for a moment, then the Spaniard for perhaps*
> *two, then the Frenchman for another two and then*
> *the Spaniard again for another and then the Frenchman*
> *for that one last second, half-breath; because then came*
> *the Anglo-Saxon, the pioneer, the tall man, roaring with*
> 30   *Protestant scripture and boiled whisky, Bible and jug*
> *in one hand and (like as not) a native tomahawk in the*
> *other, brawling, turbulent not through viciousness but*
> *simply because of his over-revved glands; uxorious and*
> *polygamous: a married invincible bachelor, dragging*
> *his gravid wife and most of the rest of his mother-in-law's*
> *family behind him into the trackless infested forest,*
> *spawning that child as like as not behind the barricade*
> *of a rifle-crotched log mapless leagues from nowhere*
> *and then getting her with another one before reaching his*
> 40   *final itch-footed destination, and at the same time*
> *scattering his ebullient seed in a hundred dusky bellies*
> *through a thousand miles of wilderness; innocent and*
> *gullible, without bowels for avarice or compassion or*
> *forethought either, changing the face of the earth: felling*
> *a tree which took two hundred years to grow, in order to*
> *extract from it a bear or a capful of wild honey. . . .*[25]

13. In his short story, "The Beast in the Jungle," Henry James explores the psychological trauma experienced by a man called John Marcher who has apparently built around himself a wall of social good manners and of inner detachment, but who discovers that he lacks something. This something, he finally learns, but too late, is the ability to love.

Discuss the major syntactic characteristics of the following passage from the short story. Discuss in particular the chief kinds of transformations used, the degree of difference between underlying and surface structures, and the way in which choice of transformations helps to create the meanings. In the course of your discussion consider what alternative surface structures James might have used in *either* the second or the last sentence, and what different effects these alternative structures would have had.

> It was into this going on as he was that they relapsed, and really for so long a time that the day inevitably came for a further sounding of their depths. These depths, constantly

bridged over by a structure firm enough in spite of its lightness and of its occasional oscillation in the somewhat vertiginous air, invited on occasion, in the interest of their nerves, a dropping of the plummet and a measurement of the abyss. A difference had been made moreover, once for all, by the fact that she had all the while not appeared to feel the need of

10   rebutting his charge of an idea within her that she didn't dare to express—a charge uttered just before one of the fullest of their later discussions ended. It had come up for him then that she "knew" something and that what she knew was bad —too bad to tell him. . . .

*   *   *

He felt in these days what, oddly enough, he had never felt before, the growth of a dread of losing her by some catastrophe —some catastrophe that yet wouldn't at all be *the* catastrophe: partly because she had almost of a sudden begun to strike him as more useful to him that ever yet, and partly by reason of

20   an appearance of uncertainty in her health, coincident and equally new. It was characteristic of the inner detachment he had hitherto so successfully cultivated and to which our whole account of him is a reference, it was characteristic that his complications, such as they were, had never yet seemed so as at this crisis to thicken about him, even to the point of making him ask himself if he were, by any chance, of a truth, within sight or sound, within touch or reach, within the immediate jurisdiction, of the thing that waited.[26]

NOTES

[1] See Noam Chomsky, *Syntactic Structures* (The Hague: Mouton, 1957), *Aspects of the Theory of Syntax* (Cambridge, Mass.: MIT Press, 1965), and "Questions of Form and Interpretation," *Essays on Form and Interpretation* (New York: Elsevier North-Holland, Inc., 1977), et passim.

[2] Note this division is traditional and has affinities with such divisions as subject-predicate, topic-comment, or actor-action, except that the latter are all more or less semantic definitions, whereas the division into noun phrase and verb phrase proposed below is purely syntactic. Criteria for the division include substitutability (the criterion developed in 3–8), the possibility of pausing after the material on the left (a phonological criterion), and meanings such as actor-action. Some other analyses have been proposed that do not subdivide all sentences into two, but allow for a three-way division in sentences like **The men + locked + the door**, cf. M. A. K. Halliday, "Notes on Transitivity and Theme," *Journal of Linguistics*, 3 (1967), 37–81, 199–244, 4 (1968), 179–215. But these analyses will not concern us here.

[3] "Phrase" may suggest a sequence of at least two elements; in transformational grammar, however, "noun phrase" is a cover term for all nominal categories, including single pronouns like **I** or **they**. Similarly "verb phrase" includes single verbs, such as **run**.

[4] These are past tenses in a strictly morphological sense, as discussed in the preceding chapter. Sometimes **can** and **could** (and other Modals) pair semantically with non-PAST and PAST, as in **I can go today, I could go yesterday,** but often they do not, as in **I could go tomorrow.**

[5] The defining characteristics of auxiliary verbs are particularly well outlined in Frank R. Palmer, *A Linguistic Study of the English Verb* (London: Longman, 1965), Chapter 2.

[6] A single-lined arrow ($\rightarrow$) is usually used rather than the double-lined one used here; however, we prefer to distinguish $\rightarrow$, used for phrase structure relations, and $\Rightarrow$, used for transformational relations.

[7] For some alternative suggestions, see Peter W. Culicover, *Syntax* (New York: Academic Press, 1976), pp. 160–72.

[8] See Robin Lakoff, "Some Reasons Why There Can't Be Any *Some-Any* Rule," *Language*, 45 (1969), 608–15.

[9] However, see Culicover, *Syntax*, pp. 69–72, for several proposals that **do** is present in underlying structure.

[10] This **do** is probably influenced not only by **do** in negatives and questions, but also by other auxiliary **do**'s that occur in several nonstandard varieties of English (cf. Chapters 8 and 9). For a sketch of the earlier history of **do**, see Elizabeth Closs Traugott, *A History of English Syntax* (New York: Holt, Rinehart, and Winston, Inc., 1972).

[11] Erving Goffman, *Strategic Interaction* (Philadelphia: Univ. of Pennsylvania Press, 1969), p. 33.

[12] Lewis Carroll, *Alice in Wonderland*, ed. by Donald J. Gray (New York: Norton and Co., 1971), p. 72.

[13] For a number of ground-breaking articles on this area of transformational syntax, see David D. Reibel and Sanford A. Schane, eds., *Modern Studies in English: Readings in Transformational Grammar* (Englewood Cliffs, N.J.: Prentice-Hall, Inc., 1969).

[14] Recently it has been argued widely that identity is a semantic rather than syntactic matter, cf. Ray S. Jackendoff, *Semantic Interpretation in Generative Grammar* (Cambridge, Mass.: MIT Press, 1972).

[15] D. Terence Langendoen, "The Accessibility of Deep Structures," in *Readings in English Transformational Grammar*, eds. Roderick A. Jacobs and Peter S. Rosenbaum (Boston: Ginn and Co., 1970).

[16] See Richard Ohmann, "Generative Grammars and the Concept of Literary Style," *Word*, 20 (1964), 423–39; rpt. in *Linguistics and Literary Style*, ed. Donald C. Freeman (New York: Holt, Rinehart and Winston, Inc., 1970); and rpt. in *Contemporary Essays on Style*, eds. Glen A. Love and Michael Payne (Glenview, Ill.: Scott, Foresman and Co., 1969). See Richard Ohmann, "Literature as Sentences," *College English*, 27 (1966), 261–67; rpt. in *Essays on the Language of Literature*, eds. Seymour Chatman and Samuel R. Levin (Boston: Houghton Mifflin Co., 1967); and rpt. in *Contemporary Essays on Style*, eds. Love and Payne. See also Anne Cluysenaar, *Introduction to Literary Stylistics* (London: Batsford, 1976).

[17] A good example is Dr. Seuss, *Green Eggs and Ham* (New York: Beginner Books, Random House, 1960).

[18] Donald Barthelme, "Edward and Pia," *Unspeakable Practices, Unnatural Acts* (New York: Farrar, Straus and Giroux, 1967), pp. 79–80.

[19] Ernest Hemingway, *For Whom the Bell Tolls* (New York: Charles Scribner's Sons, 1940), p. 161.

[20] Hemingway, *For Whom the Bell Tolls*, p. 158.

[21] Henry James, *The Portrait of a Lady, The New York Edition of Henry James*, vol. II (New York: Charles Scribner's Sons, 1908), pp. 15–16.

[22] James F. Gimpel, *Algorithms in Snobol* (New York: Wiley and Sons, 1976 [Bell Laboratories]), p. 358.

[23] James Joyce, *Ulysses* (Hamburg, Paris, Bologna: Odyssey Press, 1932), p. 62.

[24] For this and subsequent exercises in this chapter, it is important to focus on general issues, with good examples. A two- and three-page paper organized according to topics usually achieves far better results than one which provides line by line analysis or is considerably longer.

[25] William Faulkner, *Big Woods* (New York: Random House, 1955), prelude.

[26] Henry James, "The Beast in the Jungle," *Selected Tales of Henry James* (London: John Baker, 1969), pp. 241–42.

CHAPTER 5

Semantics: How Does
a Sentence Mean?

In Chapter 3 we introduced the idea of describing meaning as bundles of semantic features. But at that point we were talking only about meanings of individual morphemes and lexical items, that is, about "lexical meaning." Here we will be discussing "sentence meaning," that is, meaning relations that hold between morphemes and lexical items in a sentence. In the lexicon, as in a dictionary, we can say that one meaning of **run** is "move fast from here to there," and that another is "organize," but the kind of lexicon that we considered does not tell us how to know which of these meanings is being used in a particular sentence. This is a question that pertains to the study of sentence meaning. When used in sentences, potentially ambiguous words like **run** are often made unambiguous by the other words with which they are combined and related. Thus, when **run** appears with a directional expression as in **He ran into the field**, it means unambiguously "move fast," while **run** in **He ran the boat race** means unambiguously "organize" because boats move on water, while running cannot take place on water (contrast **He ran the egg and spoon race**, which is ambiguous). One might want to argue, however, that what disambiguates **run** in **He ran the boat race** is not linguistic knowledge, but knowledge of the world (that boats have no legs; that it is physically impossible to run on water, and so on). It is true that, especially in questions of disambiguation, the line between knowledge of the world and knowledge of language is thin at certain points. Nevertheless, it is necessary for the grammar to specify in some way that **run** involves movement on land or else we could not account for the oddness of *He ran on land (odd because land is already implied by running) as he opposed to **He ran on the freeway** (not odd because here a special place on land is being specified). Likewise, describing boats in the grammar as vehicles for moving on water gives us a way to account for the ability of **boat** to co-occur with verbs like **sail, dock, land, run aground**, in contrast with verbs like **fly, jump**, or **skip**, where co-occurrence with **boat** necessitates a special interpretation.

Thus the study of sentence meaning directs our attention from individual semantic features to the ways in which they can combine. But sentence meaning involves more than the combined meanings of the individual morphemes and words in a sentence. Suppose we want to account for the meaning of **The man watered the roses**. After a little thought we see that the meaning of this sentence is not just a sum of the lexical features for **man, water**, and **rose**, plus features for the grammatical morphemes **the, PLURAL**, and **PAST**. For we also understand that here the man is the doer of the action, and that the roses are the recipients of the action. Contrast **The roses pricked the man**, where the man is the recipient of the action and roses, or rather their thorns, are the originators of it. These are meaning relationships that hold over and above the individual meanings of the words and morphemes in the sentence. Many such meaning relationships are involved in sentence semantics. Those that will be of main interest to us in this chapter are:

1. Meaning relations that hold between NP's in a sentence, as in **The man watered the roses** versus **The roses pricked the man**. These relations may be thought of as participant or role relations. Is a particular NP functioning as Agent, Experiencer, Location, Instrument, or some other role?
2. Sameness of meaning despite difference in form. Is paraphrase, as in **They concealed the truth** and **The truth was concealed by them**, basically similar to or different from synonymy, as in **They concealed the truth, They hid the truth**?
3. Difference of meaning despite sameness of form. Is ambiguity, as in **Flying planes can be dangerous (Planes which fly can be dangerous, To fly planes can be dangerous)**, basically similar to or different from homonymy, as in **The bill is large (The bird's bill is large, The grocery bill is large)**?
4. Contradictoriness. **The unicorn is not a unicorn** is contradictory whether or not unicorns exist in the world, and whether or not one believes in stories about them.
5. Anomaly. **This book has a toothache** needs special interpretation.
6. Tautology. **This unicorn is a unicorn** gives no information unless a special meaning is inferred.

We will start with the meanings that are most obviously tied to sentence structure—the meaning relations that hold between NP's, and between NP's and verbs.

ROLE RELATIONS

In Chapter 4 we considered several movement transformations: passive, indirect object movement, auxiliary inversion in yes-no questions, insertion of NEG into various parts of the sentence, movement of the relative pronoun to the beginning of the clause, and so forth. Movement transformations are clearly a very important factor in accounting for linguistic competence. Some evidence suggests these transformations may be even more general than was suggested in Chapter 4. What, for example, might we want to say about the relationship between the following three sentences:

    1. a. They broke the icon with an axe.
       b. An axe broke the icon.
       c. The icon broke.

Is there any justification for thinking about the relationship between them as involving movement of the NP's to different positions in the sentence?

In the terms developed in Chapter 4 and in Chomsky's theory of transformational grammar, the answer is no. According to transformational grammar, sentences 1a–c represent three different phrase structure possibilities: 1a represents VP consisting of V + NP + PP, 1b represents VP consisting of V + NP, and 1c represents VP consisting of merely V. The criteria for lexical subcategorization outlined on page 141 further suggest that **break** is three verbs, each associated with a different VP structure, roughly

$$\textbf{break}_1 \ [+V, \ +\underline{\quad}NP \text{ with } NP]$$

$$\textbf{break}_2 \ [+V, \ +\underline{\quad}NP]$$

$$\textbf{break}_3 \ [+V, \ +\underline{\quad}]$$

Such a description is adequate insofar as it indicates the possible structures in which **break** can occur. But it does not express any relationship among the three **breaks**, and thus cannot explain the fact that the class of N's that can be objects of **with** in the case of **break**$_1$ are the only ones that can be subjects of **break**$_2$, while the objects of **break**$_1$ and **break**$_2$ are the only ones that can be subjects of **break**$_3$. These facts suggest that the three **breaks** are very closely related indeed.

If our grammar is to account for the relationships between sentences like 1a, b, c, two different possibilities are open to us. One is to argue, as do transformational grammarians, that syntactically there are indeed three separate verbs, **break**$_1$, **break**$_2$, and **break**$_3$, and that the similarities between them are to be accounted for in terms of identical semantic features and additional information stating the various semantic restrictions on NP's—for example, that objects of **break**$_1$ and **break**$_2$ must have the semantic feature [+RIGID] (only rigid things can be broken, not flabby or soft things like cotton, wool, jelly, hash brown potatoes), and so forth. Furthermore, only those nouns that have the feature [+RIGID] can be subjects of **break$_3$**. Another possibility involves abandoning the kind of base that we discussed in Chapter 4, with its phrase structure rule (S → NP + AUX + VP) and considering a totally different approach. According to this approach, the base includes a verb and a set of associated NP's. These NP's are unordered in the base, but are assigned to particular surface positions by movement transformations according to their role with respect to the verb. For instance, in **They broke the icon with an axe, they** has the role of Agent (doer of action), **axe** that of Instrument (means of action), and **icon** that of Patient (object of action, thing present in the event):

$$\text{break [they]}_{\text{Agent}} \text{ [icon]}_{\text{Patient}} \text{ [axe]}_{\text{Instrument}}$$

According to this analysis, 1a is derived by a transformation which moves Agent into subject position. Patient then becomes the direct object, and the preposition **with** is inserted to introduce Instrument. 1b is derived from an underlying structure in which Agent is indefinite:

$$\text{break [X]}_{\text{Agent}} \text{ [icon]}_{\text{Patient}} \text{ [axe]}_{\text{Instrument}}$$

The indefinite role is deleted, and Instrument is made into the subject. Alternatively, we could get **Someone broke the icon with an axe** from this underlying structure. In 1c, both Agent and Instrument are indefinite in underlying structure, and Patient may thus be moved into subject position. Summing up schematically, we have:

Given this analysis, **break** is only one verb, and movement rules assume an even greater importance in the grammar than was suggested in Chapter 4.

We have moved quite rapidly from the proposal that the base of a grammar is purely syntactic to the proposal that the base of a grammar is a place in which meaning plays a part, and in which no absolute boundary exists between syntax and semantics. The idea of a base in which role relations are realized by NP's gives us a dynamic way of thinking about sentences. Indeed, we can consider the sentence as a kind of miniature drama, expressing in language the drama that we perceive in the interaction of things around us with each other and with ourselves.[1] It is an approach which stresses the fact that, however unconscious we may be about it, every time we speak we express our interpretation of interactions and interrelations among entities and events in the world.

Among several approaches to a syntactic/semantic base, we have selected for discussion in this section the approach called "case grammar" (the name will be explained shortly), developed primarily by Charles Fillmore.[2] It is a controversial model of grammar, but it has provided ways of thinking about the relationship between sentence structure and meaning that have proved very fruitful not only in the analysis of particular languages, but also in cross-linguistic studies. It has also suggested exciting ways of accounting for aspects of the world-view created in literary works, and should prove to be of lasting importance in literary analysis.

According to case grammar, a sentence consists of two parts, one called the "Presentence," the other the "Predication." The Presentence specifies that the whole Predication must be in the PAST or non-PAST (i.e., it includes the category TENSE), and indicates the various ways in which a whole Predication can be negated, questioned, or otherwise modified. Since these properties of sentences have already been discussed, they will not concern us further in this chapter. The Predication consists of a verb (the predicate) and various "arguments." These arguments are NP's functioning in a variety of ways, including Agent, Instrument, Experiencer, Source, Goal, Path, Location, Possessor, Patient, and so forth. Although the terms "predication," "predicate," and "argument" are borrowed from logic, they are used here in a somewhat broader sense. The term "argument" highlights the fact that in this analysis NP's are not considered simply categories but as categories in certain functions or roles relative to the predicate. Similarly, "predicate" highlights the fact that in this analysis we are not speaking just of the category of lexical items called verbs, but also of their function of giving information about the states of affairs, events, and processes in which participants are involved. In underlying structure, then, the sentence is characterized in "case grammar" terms as:[3]

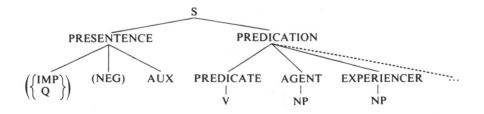

Role Types

There are a number of different role types in languages, probably not more than twenty altogether. Of these only the commonest will be discussed here.

Agent: The "Agent" function is that of the doer responsible for an action or event taking place. In sentences like:

2. a.   **I** hit the boy.

3.   **I** ran away.

4.   **I** laughed.

I is the Agent of the hitting, the running, and the laughing. Since Agents must be able to do something of their own volition, the kind of NP that can fulfill the role of Agent is limited to animates.

Force: There is a difference in role relation between **I** in 2a and **lightning** in:

5. a.   **Lightning** hit the boy.

In the latter, **lightning** is interpreted as a doer, but has no volition—we cannot say, for example:

5. b.   ***Lightning** willingly hit the boy.

(without some very special interpretation), though we can easily say:

2. b.   **I** willingly hit the boy.

Lightning, sun, rain, and man-made things like cars and rockets can function in the role called "Force." This is the role of things that are considered to initiate actions, such as hitting, running, or driving, but that, unlike animals and humans, have no volition.

A word of caution is necessary here. We are now talking about normal expectations, hence the starring of 5b. Special usages, for example, irony, whimsy, or metaphor, are excluded for the moment.

Instrument: "Instrument" is the function expressing the means by which something is done, most explicitly, the thing used to achieve some end. Most often, the Instrument function is expressed by *with NP*, as in:

6. a.   Jake cracked the coconut **with a hammer**.

7. a.   I drew the sketch **with charcoal**.

However, other prepositions are possible, as in **I washed it by hand** and **I went on foot**.

Sometimes the Instrument can occur in subject position without a preposition, depending on the verb. Thus we have:

6. b.   **The hammer** cracked the coconut open.

but not:

    7. b. ***Charcoal** drew the sketch.

With some verbs, most notably **use**, the Instrument becomes the object of the verb in surface structure:

    8. I used **a pencil** to mark the place.

Experiencer: "Experiencer" is the role of the animate being inwardly affected by an event or characterized by a state. For example, if you say:

    9. **I** love Melinda.

you are not claiming that you are an Agent of loving, nor that you are an Instrument of love, but that you are affected by it inwardly. Metaphorically, love is "in" you. It is extremely common in languages for Experiencers to be expressed spatially, the mind being conceived of as a location in which experiences reside, or to which they come. Thus, in English, Experiencers often appear as objects of the preposition **to**:

    10. a. That was obvious **to me**.
       b. That is pleasing **to me**.

or as direct objects of verbs which have an **in-/en-** prefix:

    11. a. The decision **infuriated me**.
       b. The movie **enthralled everyone**.

If Experiencer is the only argument with which a predicate is associated, that predicate will be a nonaction predicate, like **know** or **be angry**, and will not permit the progressive. Thus a sentence like:

    12. I am being angry.

means not that I am experiencing anger, but that I am acting as if I were angry. Here **I** is an Agent, not an Experiencer.

    Source: The place or direction from which something comes is the "Source." Usually, the Source is a location:

    13. I walked home **from the market**.

but it may also be an animate being:

    14. She bought the apples **from the farmer**.

or even a thing:

> 15. **That story** annoyed me.

The Source can also be an NP realized as a complement, that is, another Predication:

> 16. a. **That he left in such a hurry** annoys me.
>   b. **His leaving in such a hurry** suggests that something fishy was going on.

Goal: While the direction from which something comes is the Source, the direction to which something goes is the "Goal." Usually Goal is a location introduced by **to**:

> 17. a. He walked **to school.**

However, with certain locational NP's, **to** is absent:

> 17. b. I walked **home.**

Somewhat archaic now is the derivative suffix **-ward** used to indicate Goals, as in **homeward, westward,** and **skyward.**

Like the Source role, Goal may also be an animate being, often what we have been calling the indirect object.

> 18. a. The farmer sold apples **to her.**
>   b. I handed the knife **to her.**

The Goal is frequently moved to a position immediately following the verb by indirect object movement (see Chapter 4):

> 18. c. I handed **her** the knife.

Unlike the Source role, Goal is not usually realized as a complement.

Path: In moving from one place to another, a "Path" (the route by which something goes) may be contextually assumed, or it may play a significant role.

> 19. a. I walked home from the market **through the field.**
>   b. I walked home from the market **along the river.**
>   c. I drove home **on the freeway.**

The prepositions associated with Path vary far more than they do with the other roles discussed so far. The preposition with the fewest additional location indicators is **via,** but this is stylistically rather formal. All the others, like

around, by, across, over, through, along, on, suggest more than just the Path; these also suggest the dimensionality of the area related to the trajectory (in 19a, the field is thought of as a kind of container; in 19b, the river is a long, linear object; in 19c, the freeway is a kind of line).

Location: The role of place-in-which is "Location." Like Path, this role can be expressed by a variety of prepositions which add extra information about dimensional relations. Location is illustrated by:

20. a. They sat **at home.**
    b. We found the marbles **in the box.**
    c. Your shoes are **under the bed.**

Unlike Path, Location can often become the subject. Thus:

21. a. **The house** smells.

is equivalent to:

21. b. **In the house** it smells.

Similarly:

22. a. **The room** is hot.

means:

22. b. **In the room** it is hot.

In many instances there may be ambiguity between direction and location-in-which, partly because most of our locational prepositions are, or can be, both dynamic (directional) and static (nondirectional). For example, **in** can be used either for putting something in(to) a container (directional) or for being in a container (nondirectional). One can run across the street (directional) or be across the street (nondirectional). This kind of ambiguity was the subject of some discussion in connection with Hemingway's writing at the end of the previous chapter. We can now reanalyze the ambiguity of **Robert Jordan felt the brushing of the heather against his legs** as being a question of whether Jordan's legs are thought of as the Location in which the feeling was registered, or whether they are thought of as the Goal of the heather's movement.

Possessor: A special kind of locative relation is that of possession. For someone to have something, the object must in some sense "be with" the person (at one's disposal, not always physically, but sometimes mentally or legally). All languages have more or less overt markers that indicate that

"Possessor" is a locational role. In English, such expressions include **belong to** (note the **to**), as in:

> 23.   This book **belongs to me.**

or, even more obviously:

> 24.   He has several thousand diamonds **in his possession.**

For this reason, it is far from clear that a separate Possessor role should be set up in underlying structure. However, the distinction seems important enough syntactically and even conceptually (at a fairly superficial level) to introduce a separate role here for ease of analysis.

There are many ways of expressing the Possessor relation. Suppose we consider a Possessor (**he**) and a thing possessed (**car**). We can express these in various surface sentence forms with different surface predicates:

> 25.   a.   He **has** a car.
>   b.   The car **is** his.
>   c.   The car **belongs to** him.

Or, if it is embedded as a relative clause into some other sentence, we find forms like:

> 25.   d.   I saw a man **with** a yellow sports car (= I saw a man who had a yellow sports car).
>   e.   I saw **his** car (I saw a car; the car is his).
>   f.   I saw the car **of** your friend (I saw a car; the car is your friend's).

Such variant forms are dependent on information-conveying strategies, and are not all exactly equivalent in that each cannot be substituted for the other, but the relation of Possessor to Patient (thing possessed) holds in all instances. 25a exemplifies Possessor as subject, while 25b and 25c exemplify the thing possessed (Patient) as subject. The Patient may be the subject only if it is possessed "alienably," in other words, if it is conceived of as something from which one can part, as something which can be owned at one time and not owned at another. Thus:

> 26.   a.   He **has** blond hair.

is normal. On the other hand:

> 26.   b.   That blond hair **is his.**

suggests that the speaker is thinking of the hair as something separable from **him**; for example, it might be a wig. Or someone might say at a party, **Look at**

that shock of blond hair, and someone might answer, **Oh, that blond hair is Phil's**; both speakers are treating the hair as an "alienable," like a piece of clothing. Other examples are gruesome or funny, depending on the way in which one interprets them:

    27. a.   That eye **is** Roger's.

Since inalienable things are so much a part of one's existence, one rarely has occasion simply to state that someone possesses them. Thus, even:

    27. b.   Roger **has** an eye.

is strange (tautological in most contexts), and normally occurs only with modification of the thing possessed, as:

    27. c.   Roger **has** a devilish eye.

Patient: This is the last role to be discussed here, and also the least specific. "Patient" can best be characterized as the role of the being or thing that is affected by the action or event, or that is simply present in it. Thus, if I **have** a car, the car is merely present in my world. If I **see** a person, I experience the seeing, and the person is merely present. If I **kill** a person, that person is present and affected by the action. The car and the persons in these imagined constructions are Patients.

Double roles: Sometimes an NP may have not just one but two functions in a sentence. In

    28.   I rolled down the hill.

the **I** in one interpretation of this sentence is the Agent and also the Patient (cf. **I voluntarily rolled myself down the hill**). It is exclusively Patient in an alternative interpretation, where someone hit the speaker and caused him or her to roll down the hill. To **roll** is to get oneself from one place to another by rolling. Similarly, to **run** is to get oneself from one place to another by running, as to **get up** is to get oneself up. In many languages, including French, the Patient in such sentences often appears on the surface in pronominal form. For example, French **Je me lève** is literally "I myself raise."

    Some other instances of NP's with double functions are illustrated by 14 and 18a. **Buying** is a transaction that involves an Agent responsible for transferring an object from someone else to him- or herself by using money. Thus the buyer is both Agent and Goal. With **selling**, an Agent is responsible for transferring an object from him- or herself to someone else by using money. The seller is both the Agent and the Source. Given this kind of analysis, **buy** and **sell** share the same semantic primitive TRANSFER, but have different surface forms, depending on the alignment of roles:

TRANSFER   Source   Agent   Goal   Patient   Instrument   (= buy)
                 | ‿‿‿ | |
              farmer   she   apples   money

TRANSFER   Source   Agent   Goal   Patient   Instrument   (= sell)
                 ‿‿‿ | | |
                   farmer   she   apples   money

Advantages of Role Structure Analysis

We have seen that when an NP is not moved to subject position, it often appears in surface structure accompanied by a preposition. We have also seen that certain prepositions tend to be associated with certain roles—**with** for Instrument, **to** for Goal and Experiencer, **from** and **off** for Source, and so on. In many languages, role relations are expressed in surface structure not by prepositions but by so-called "case" inflections, that is, inflections added to NP's that indicate relations such as subject, object, and also direction toward a place, movement from a place, place-in-which, experience, possession, and so forth. Languages such as modern Finnish and Russian abound in such cases. For example, among Finnish inflections we find the following ("genitive" is equivalent to "possessive"):

Nominative	subject	**talo** "house"
Genitive	's, of	**talon**
Accusative	object	**talon**
Inessive	in	**talossa**
Elative	out of, from	**talosta**
Illative	into	**taloon**
Adessive	on, at	**talolla**
Ablative	away from	**talolta**
Allative	to	**talolle** [4]

One of the advantages of role structure analysis is that it can systematically relate languages with prepositions, like English or French, with those that have case inflections, like Russian, Latin, or Finnish (hence the name "case grammar").

Role structure analysis can also enable us to account for meaning relations between prepositions and inflections in the same language. For example, English once had case inflections, but most of them have been lost, their function having been taken over by prepositions and word order. Some remnants of the old system remain, however. Thus we have **The man's**

garden with the possessive ("genitive") inflection, and **The garden of the man** with the possessive preposition. According to the analysis proposed here, **The man's garden** and **The garden of the man** would have the same underlying structure, and both the order and the form taken by the possessive would be determined in surface structures.

Furthermore, role structure analysis enables us to account for meaning relations between sentences in which predicates are phonologically dissimilar. Consider, for example:

> 29. a.   I like Utrillo's paintings.
>   b.   Utrillo's paintings please me.
>   c.   Utrillo's paintings are pleasing to me.

In all three sentences **I** is the Experiencer, and the painting is the Source of pleasure. When the Experiencer is the subject, we use the verb **like**; when the Source is the subject, we use either the verb **please** or the adjective **be pleasing**. Here we have an instance of lexical suppletion (that is, phonologically quite distinct forms of the same underlying lexical item). The form of the verb is determined by which role occurs in subject position. It is interesting to note that in Middle English **like** was not suppletive and was used with both Experiencer and Source as subject. **Please** was later borrowed from French, and **like** was restricted to sentences in which the Experiencer was subject. As has been suggested, **have** and **belong to** can similarly be analyzed as suppletive forms of the same predicate, the former being used when the Possessor is the subject, the latter when the Patient is the subject.

PREDICATION ANALYSIS OF LEXICAL ITEMS

Verbs

In a case grammar, the base generates Predications consisting of different configurations of roles associated with predicates. Lexical items are inserted into these Predication structures, just as in a syntax-based grammar they are inserted into the syntactic structures generated by the base. As we have seen, what lexical items may be inserted depends on what roles are present in the Predication.

Predication analysis has given rise to another approach to the lexicon, according to which lexical items themselves are seen as Predications.[5] The motivation for this approach emerges if we turn our attention from the arguments and roles in Predication to the predicates. The following sentences are paraphrases of each other:

> 30. a.   The butter melted.
>   b.   The butter came to be liquid/became liquid.

Here the single lexical item **melt** has the same meaning as the complex syntactic phrase construction **come to be liquid**. Likewise, with

31. a.   What killed him was arsenic.
    b.   What caused him to die was arsenic.

the single lexical item **kill** has the same meaning as the syntactic phrase **cause to die**. In other words, single lexical items may be paraphrased by rather complex Predication structures. In order to account for this fact, it has been proposed that lexical items actually are Predication structures, or rather that they are names for such structures.[6] For example, the sameness of meaning of a and b above can be accounted for by postulating the same underlying structure for them both. In simplified form, this would be:

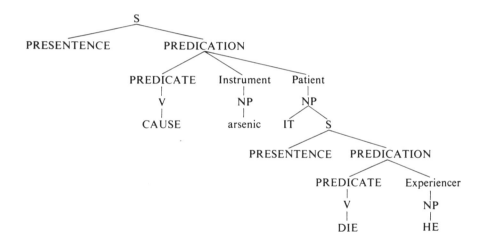

It is fairly easy to see how the surface verbs **cause** and **die** might be inserted into this structure. For the surface verb **kill** to be inserted, **kill** is described in the lexicon as consisting of the Predication: **(someone or something) CAUSE: (someone) DIE**. When an underlying structure is generated that includes this same Predication, **kill** may be inserted, and in effect it replaces this complex structure in the derivation.[7] In linguistic jargon, /kɪl/ is said to be a "conflation" of this larger Predication, that is, it is a surface lexical item that represents the combination of several deeper elements. In a complete analysis, **DIE** would be broken down even further into semantic primitives, and would be something like **CAUSE to COME to BE NOT ALIVE**. In parallel fashion, the verb **melt** will be described in the lexicon roughly as the Predication **(something) COME to BE LIQUID** or **(someone) CAUSE (something) to COME to BE LIQUID**, as in **I melted the butter**.[8]

If we treat lexical items as Predications, we can readily account for a type of ambiguity mentioned in Chapter 1, namely, the kind of ambiguity exemplified by the sentence **I almost killed him**. If **kill** is analyzed as meaning in underlying structure **CAUSE to DIE**, then the two readings of **I almost killed him** come from two different underlying structures, namely, **I cause it: he almost die** and **I almost cause it: he die**. Other examples of lexical items which are conflations of complex Predications are **give** (CAUSE to HAVE), **receive** (COME to HAVE), **persuade** (CAUSE by LANGUAGE (someone) AGREE), **enter** ([someone/something] GO IN), and **arrive** ([someone/ something] COME TO).

In proposing Predication analysis of lexical items, we have moved beyond the bundle-of-feature approach developed in Chapter 3. There we introduced the concept of semantic features as independent elements bundled together without any particular order. Now, however, we have proposed that single lexical items can have the same meaning as ordered sentential structures. Furthermore, we have shown that there are not two kinds of semantics, one having to do with nonrelational meanings (as presented in Chapter 3), the other having to do with syntactic, therefore relational, meanings. Instead, we have shown that there is basically one kind of semantics, which is relational. This suggests that the bundle-of-feature analysis is inadequate, although it still has its usefulness as a preliminary analytic tool.

Nouns and Adjectives

So far we have been looking only at lexical entries for verbs, and indeed, it is for this category that Predication analysis of lexical items has been most studied. Nevertheless, the notion that lexical items may be names for whole Predications does apply to all syntactic categories.[9] To take a fairly obvious case, the entry for any noun derived from a verb will include the Predication associated with the verb. Agentive derivatives such as **talker, farmer, lender, commuter** will be described, roughly, as "one who talks, farms, lends," and so on. Sometimes these agentives can be fairly complex. **Employer**, for instance, will be "one (Agent) who employs someone (Patient)"; **pipefitter** will be "one (Agent) who fits pipes (Patient)." **Bench** in Predication analysis will be, in part, "that which one sits on"; **boy** will be "one who is male, young, human," and so forth. Here, **male** and **young** are not binary features, but predicates.

With adjectives, Predication analysis has some real advantages for making generalizations. In Chapter 4, we discussed deriving the phrase **that gross mayor** from **that mayor, who is/was gross**. These two phrases are essentially equivalent in that either could occur in the place of the other in such a context as **I demand the resignation of that gross mayor/of that mayor, who is gross**. However, there are many prenominal adjectives which are not equivalent to constructions with **be** + **Adj**. For example, the a and b sentences in the following pairs are hardly equivalent:

32. a.   The hard worker.
    b.   The worker who is hard.

33. a.   The criminal lawyer.
    b.   The lawyer who is criminal.

34. a.   The top shelf.
    b.   *The shelf that is top.

33b does correspond to one meaning of 33a, but not the other. As for 34b it is not grammatical in English. Must we abandon the hypothesis developed in Chapter 4 that prenominal adjectives are derived from relative clauses? Not if we analyze nouns like **worker** as **one who works**, in the way just described. Then **hard worker** is, in underlying structure, **one who works hard**, where **hard** is an argument of Manner added to the Predication underlying **worker**. We want to derive 33a and 34a from:

33. c.   The lawyer who deals with crime.

34. c.   The shelf that is at the top.

These relationships can be accounted for readily, if we say in the lexicon that **criminal** and **top** are names for conflations of relative clauses. In the case of:

35.   She's a beautiful soprano.

which is ambiguous (Is she a soprano who is beautiful or one who sings beautifully?), two derivations would be possible. The lexical entry for **soprano** will include, among other things, the Predications **one who is human** and **one who sings**. One of the meanings of **beautiful soprano** derives from **beautiful** being predicated of **one** (one who is human and beautiful and sings). The other derives from **beautiful** being a Manner argument joined to **sing** (one who is human and sings in a beautiful manner).

This sort of analysis also allows us to account for a time-ambiguity common among nouns, and exemplified by the following sentences:

36.   My husband was born in Indiana.

37.   The castle is now a pile of rubble.

In 36, at the time referred to by the verb, the person referred to by the subject of the verb was not the speaker's husband; similarly, in 37, the verb refers to a point in time at which the castle does not exist. Yet both these sentences can be truthfully and appropriately uttered. In the approach we are now considering, this would be explained by claiming that **the one who became my husband** underlies **my husband** in 36, and **that which was a castle** underlies **the castle** in 37. A similar phenomenon is exemplified by the following sentences, both of which are ambiguous:

38.   The painters said my brother-in-law had already paid them.

39.   The idiot called me up at three in the morning.

In the first case, the painters might have said **Your brother-in-law already paid us**, but they might equally well have said **Mr. Adams already paid us** in which case it is the speaker who imposes the information about being Mr. Adams's brother-in-law. In 39, it may be that someone who really was an idiot called up; more probably, however, someone of normal intelligence phoned the speaker, and **idiot** is an epithet added by the speaker to indicate annoyance. Such meaning differences actually correspond to the differences between restrictive and appositive relatives (**The one that is an idiot called me up** versus **X, who I think is an idiot, called me up**). Ambiguities of the type in 38 and 39 are easily exploited rhetorically, as in:

40.   I now present to you the next president of the United States, John Johnson.

This is ambiguous, meaning both "the one who will be the next president and who is named John Johnson" and "John Johnson, who I think will be the next president"; and though the latter meaning is the one usually conveyed, the rhetorical effect of the sentence depends on the fact that the first meaning is nevertheless brought to mind.

SYNONYMY AND HOMONYMY

An interesting conclusion can be drawn from the claim that underlying structures are Predications and that lexical items are collapsed Predications inserted into derivations. This is that insofar as underlying structures are concerned, homonymy is in essence the same phenomenon as ambiguity, and synonymy is the same thing as paraphrase. Traditionally, the terms homonymy and synonymy have been used with reference to lexical items, while the terms ambiguity and paraphrase have been used with reference to sentential structures. For instance, **I hit the girl with the steak/stake** would in a traditional grammar be said to contain homonymy (**steak/stake**) and also ambiguity concerning the relation of the *with NP* phrase either to the subject (the **I** used a steak or stake to hit the girl), or to the object (the girl had a steak or stake).

However, breaking down **steak** and **stake** into propositions, e.g., **something for eating** versus **something for making fences with**, immediately does away with the traditional distinction. Both **steak/stake** and the relation of *with NP* to the NP's in the sentence are cases of ambiguity. Similarly, **The young man fled** and **The youth fled**, which traditionally are called paraphrases because **young man** is a phrase but **youth** is not, are no different in kind from **The thief fled** and **The robber fled**, which in traditional grammars would involve synonymy, not paraphrase, since both sentences involve words with the same meaning.

SELECTIONAL RESTRICTIONS, CONTRADICTION, ANOMALY, AND TAUTOLOGY

There are many constraints on what lexical items can combine with what others. Our internalized knowledge tells us that **tall tower** and **long ribbon** are perfectly good combinations, while **long tower** and **tall ribbon** are somehow deviant. This kind of deviance is called "anomaly." In the terms of our grammar, anomaly results when two semantic primitives which are incompatible are combined in certain ways in a Predication.[10] For example, in our grammar, we specify **tower** and other nouns such as **person, chimney,** and **tree** as being VERTICAL, while others like **ribbon, rug, pencil, snake,** and **platter** are HORIZONTAL, meaning they have length. (Keep in mind that with the approach adopted in this chapter, VERTICAL and HORIZONTAL are not binary features, but parts of Predications, i.e., the lexical entry for **chimney** includes the Predication **that which is vertical.**) Some nouns, like **pencil, spear, platter,** can still combine with **tall** even though they are not intrinsically VERTICAL, but in the case of **tall pencil** or **tall platter** we understand that the objects have been stood up in vertical position. So we say in the grammar that **tall** combines only with inherently VERTICAL nouns or with nouns that can be interpreted as VERTICAL. Such constraints are called "selectional restrictions" because they govern the selection of lexical items for insertion into underlying structures.[11]

Notice that for a noun to be interpreted as VERTICAL, it must have another property, namely, that of being RIGID. Thus we can get **tall pencil/I stood the pencil up** but not ***tall ribbon/*I stood the ribbon up**. Sometimes a noun can be interpreted as RIGID, as with **rug** in **tall rug/I stood the rug up**, which works if the rug is understood as rolled up. Some objects, like **building, fence,** and **grass,** are both HORIZONTAL and VERTICAL linguistically, and thus combine equally well with both **tall** and **long.**

The selectional restrictions on **tall** and **long** overlap in an interesting way with those pertaining to certain verb plus particle forms discussed earlier.

In the section on idioms in Chapter 3, we introduced such idiomatic expressions as

41. a.   The paper burned.
    b.   The paper burned up.
    c.   The paper burned down.

Here the particles **up** and **down** both have a completive meaning, so that b and c both involve total burning, while a involves an unspecified amount of burning. However, 41c contrasts with b in that **down** retains a spatial meaning here—we have to imagine a specialized situation in which paper has been stacked in vertical position. Now compare:

42. a.   The demonstrators burned the fence.
    b.   The demonstrators burned up the fence.
    c.   The demonstrators burned down the fence.

Again, both **up** and **down** retain completive meaning, but unlike 41c, 42c requires no special spatial interpretation. This is because **fence** is intrinsically VERTICAL (as well as HORIZONTAL), while paper is not. The generalization which emerges is that while completive **up** can be used with most Patients, **down**, like **tall**, is restricted to those which are inherently VERTICAL or which can be interpreted as VERTICAL.

Related to anomaly is the phenomenon of "contradiction," in which something is explicitly said to be both X and not-X at the same time. Thus:

44.   This corpse is alive.

is a contradiction, since **corpse**, which is defined as NOT ALIVE, is here being claimed to be ALIVE. A sentence like:

45.   In walked a corpse.

is anomalous rather than contradictory, since no overt claim is made that the corpse is alive. The anomaly involves an implied rather than an explicit contradiction. Notice too that it is not at all contradictory to say **This corpse was alive**, because the past tense allows us to infer that a change has taken place. Expressions like **This corpse is really alive** are also not contradictions, because **really** indicates that a mistake in the designation has been made.

The grammar captures contradiction by a rule that disallows strings which are semantically:

X is not X (or: not X is X)

This rule will apply not only to surface forms like ***This rock is not a rock,** but also to underlying structures. Thus:

46.   My bachelor brother is married to a movie star.

is marked as contradictory because **bachelor** is, among other things NOT
WITH SPOUSE, while **married** is WITH SPOUSE. Thus, the underlying
structure of 46 includes a structure roughly like: **My brother who is not with
(without) spouse is with spouse** (*not X is X*).

Anomaly that borders on contradiction and contradiction itself seem to
be particularly exciting and amusing to children. Of the two children's rhymes
below, notice that the first involves chiefly anomaly and the second contradiction:

'Twas in the month of Liverpool
In the city of July,
The snow was raining heavily,
The streets were very dry.
The flowers were sweetly singing,
The birds were in full bloom,
As I went down the cellar
To sweep an upstairs room.[12]

Ladles and Jellyspoons,
I stand upon this speech to make a platform,
The train I arrived in has not yet come,
So I took a bus and walked.
I come before you
To stand behind you
And tell you something
I know nothing about.[13]

A final kind of violation of selectional restrictions is "tautology," a
violation illustrated by such sentences as **This dog is a dog**, **My husband is
married to me**, **This corpse is not alive**. The problem with tautologies is that
they are Predications which provide no new information; they simply say
X is X. Tautologies are not false or absurd the way contradictions and
anomalies are (in fact, tautologies by definition can never be false: X is
indeed always X). While contradiction and anomaly violate the organization
of sense in a message, tautology seems rather to violate pragmatic rules
requiring that utterances include information which is new and relevant. That
tautology is a pragmatic rather than a semantic kind of deviance is suggested
by the fact that there are contexts in which tautology is not deviant. For
instance, **A dog is an animal** is tautological, but is perfectly well-formed as an
answer to the question **What is a dog?** (Indeed, all definitions are in some sense
tautologies.) Even formulae as tautological as **War is war** or **Boys will be boys**

have a conventional meaning which involves foregrounding the concrete reality of what is referred to as against an unrealistic or overidealized conception of it.

ANOMALY AND METAPHOR

Anomaly provides the basis for one of the most versatile and widely used foregrounding devices, metaphor. The following expressions, taken from literary passages quoted elsewhere in this book, all clearly contain anomalies:

47. The Earth . . . shall dream a dream crept from the sunless pole ("November," page 112).

48. Whispering lunar incantations dissolve the floors of memory ("Rhapsody on a Windy Night," page 24).

49. She . . . plunged at Bourton into the open air (*Mrs. Dalloway*, page 77).

Predication analysis and role structure analysis enable us to state fairly accurately where the anomaly lies in each case. For instance, in 47, **earth** plays the roles of Agent and Experiencer of **dream**, roles that call for an animate noun. In 48, **memory** is predicated as having floors, something that would require that memory be concrete, which it is not.

Though all the expressions in 47–49 contain anomalies, they do not fail to communicate. This is because, when our knowledge of language and the world will not let us take a meaning literally, we do not give up, but rather "make sense" of the anomalies by allowing certain features to override others in the particular context. Thus, we allow the roles associated with **dream** to override the inanimacy normally associated with **earth**. Let us look a little more closely at 49, in which a person **plunges into the air**. When Goal is specified for **plunge into**, then a liquid medium or at least something that resists is assumed. But air is not a liquid medium. One way of describing the effect of this metaphor is to say that by virtue of combination with **plunge**, the concept of liquidness is projected onto **air**. In the passage from *Mrs. Dalloway*, the same projection is repeated a few lines farther down, in the simile **the air . . . like the flap of a wave**, where **wave** again projects liquidness onto **air**. The second simile, **[like] the kiss of a wave**, multiplies the associations. The metaphor of a kissing wave involves projection onto **wave** of the features of physical discreteness, animacy (probably humanness), and capacity for experiencing feelings. Thus, the air at Bourton is liquid, and at the same time animate and full of affection for the young Mrs. Dalloway—like a womb (and yet a **chill** and **sharp** one).

Often these semantic projections from one expression to another can create highly concentrated and unusual meanings, especially when abstract objects are treated as concrete ones. This common type of metaphor is a particular speciality of T. S. Eliot, as illustrated by 48 and:

    50.   His soul stretched tight across the skies.[14]

50 presents a soul as a concrete, pliable object that can be spread out like a blanket. The Path, **across the skies**, lets us know that this object is also a very large one. At the same time, **soul** projects a religious meaning ("heavens") onto **skies** here. According to this projection analysis, we say that in metaphors, anomaly—i.e., semantic incompatibility—is in effect resolved through the projection of semantic characteristics between lexical items. Thus, the soul "becomes" concrete in order that it may be predicated as stretching across the skies, and the sky becomes spiritualized in order that it may accommodate the soul. One problem facing such an approach is that of specifying which semantic characteristics of a particular item get projected and which do not. For instance, the verb **trot** involves quick movement (faster than **walk** and slower than **run** or **gallop**) of a four-footed, normally equine animal. When this verb is used metaphorically of humans, as in **The little boy trotted up with a note in his hand**, the concept of quick movement gets projected, but not the concept of four-footed movement. That is, we do not imagine the child approaching on all fours; only the Manner part of **trot** gets projected. Equally difficult to specify in detail is the fact that often the meaning of a metaphorical expression depends on associations with similar nonmetaphorical Predications. For instance, when Sandburg talks about the **huddled walls** of the city, we think not only of the walls huddling (metaphorically) as if fearful, but also of people huddling (literally) behind the walls. Here, in other words, the act of huddling could be said to have been transferred from the people to the walls. Similarly, when Pope speaks of lines of poetry laboring and words moving slow, he is in part transferring the lines and words from the role of Patient to Agent. Nonmetaphorically, it is the reader (Agent) who labors and utters the words slowly. Such transferral relationships clearly play a role in metaphorical communication, but again it is hard to see how such relations between Predications could be stated formally.[15]

Another difficulty in the linguistic analysis of metaphor is the fact that the effectiveness of a metaphor often depends as much on our knowledge of the world as on our knowledge of language. For example, it is doubtful whether the semantic description of **kiss** would specify that kisses can be wet, but our knowledge of this fact reinforces the association between **kiss** and **wave** in the Woolf passage just discussed. Our knowledge that one can plunge downward into liquids without incurring physical injury contributes to the sense of comfort and security expressed by Mrs. Dalloway's plunging into the air, but again it is unlikely that these facts would be expressed in the semantic description of **plunge**. As a somewhat different example, part of the meta-phorical meaning of Eliot's line **His soul stretched tight across the skies** (50 above) depends on our familiarity with another, older metaphor, the tradi-tional one according to which people's "nerves" are strings which can be stretched or loosened. Thus we use words like tense, uptight, hang loose, or strung out when referring to people. These expressions are now so much a part of the language that we are no longer very much aware of their metaphoric import. They exemplify what is commonly called a "dead metaphor." In 50, Eliot relies on this dead metaphor and, at the same time, brings it back to life by using it in an unfamiliar way.

Though it relies on many kinds of nonlinguistic knowledge, metaphor is at least to some extent a lexical and semantic phenomenon, and the analysis of metaphor as projection of semantic information does capture two im-portant facts about it: first, the fact that metaphor creates cohesion (by making sameness out of difference) and second, the fact that metaphor is a kind of foregrounding, involving deviation from the rules governing how concepts may be combined in Predications.

It is customary to describe metaphor as involving "implied comparison" between two things. We could say, for example, that in 47, Bridges implies a comparison between the earth and a sleeping person, or that Woolf in 49 implies a comparison between air and water. This view of metaphor can be misleading, however. For instance, in 50 above, what could we say the soul was being compared to? Does the metaphor seem to be referring to any particular real object at all? It would seem not. The effect of the metaphor lies not in any particular comparison, but rather in the interaction of the various semantic primitives brought together in the Predication. Similarly, with **a dream crept from the sunless pole** (47 above), we would not want to say that the dream is being compared to any particular creeping creature. The varied semantic interaction between **creep** and **dream** does not depend on an actual comparison.

Nevertheless, comparison is certainly one way of producing the kind of semantic interaction that we are talking about. This is what takes place, notably, in the simile, the device commonly defined as "explicit comparison using **like** or **as**." Here are some examples of similes:

51.   A babel of tongues, **like** running water unceasing ("November," page 112).

52.   Something came from her hand . . . that was **as fresh as** the first light air that moving toward you over the sea barely wrinkles the glassy surface of a calm. (*For Whom the Bell Tolls*, pages 171–72).

Metaphor and simile have traditionally been viewed as closely related devices, and it is true that they bring about similar semantic situations in which features are projected from one expression to another. But there is one important difference between metaphor and simile, which is that similes are not anomalies, nor do they involve any kind of semantic deviance. Rather, similes are normal Predications involving an abstract predicate of comparison, which we can call LIKE. This predicate can appear in surface structures with Agent as subject, as in **I likened (compared) Agrippa to a Venus' flytrap**, or in various formats without Agent, such as **Agrippa is like (resembles) a Venus' flytrap**, **Agrippa and a Venus' flytrap are alike**, **Agrippa is a (veritable) Venus' flytrap**. In other structures, the predicate has no surface realization, as in appositions like **Agrippa, the Venus' flytrap**. Other typical simile constructions involve quantifiers, as in **Agrippa is as affectionate as any Venus' flytrap**.

ROLE STRUCTURES AND LITERARY ANALYSIS

Applying role structure analysis to literary texts can often help us understand the organization of the world conveyed by the narrator. One of the ways writers can set up a particular view of the world is by consistently choosing particular kinds of role structures over others, or consistently selecting certain arguments and not others. Eliot's "Rhapsody on a Windy Night" is a case in point. As noted earlier, two ways of organizing and perceiving the world are contrasted in this poem, the view of the streetlamp, for which everything is dynamic and in motion, and the view of memory, for which everything is static and fixed. Not surprisingly, this contrast manifests itself through contrasting role structures. In connection with the lamp, many Agents are used, and other non-Agent arguments are agentified, as with **the door open on her like a grin** (17–18) where a sense of intention and agency is projected on **door** (Patient) by the Goal **on her** and by the comparison with a **grin**, which requires an animate Agent as subject. In contrast, Patients predominate in connection with memory. Agents and even Forces are downplayed and sometimes, even when present in underlying structure, do not appear in surface structure, as with the adjectives **twisted**, **polished**, **broken** (24–30). The second and third stanzas of the poem show this contrast clearly.

Carl Sandburg's "The Harbor" (see page 71) is also interesting to study from a role structure point of view. In this poem, role structure patterns contribute to establishing distance between the speaker (the **I**) and his surroundings. The poem is reprinted here for your convenience.

> Passing through huddled and ugly walls
> By doorways where women
> Looked from their hunger-deep eyes,
> Haunted with shadows of hunger-hands,

Out from the huddled and ugly walls,
I came sudden, at the city's edge,
On a blue burst of lake,
Long lake waves breaking under the sun
On a spray-flung curve of shore;
10   And a fluttering storm of gulls,
Masses of great gray wings
And flying white bellies
Veering and wheeling free in the open.[16]

In the first four lines, the speaker of the poem is an Agent to whom the city is a Path. He passes through walls and by doorways. The city itself is huddled, a thing turned in on itself, impeding motion. To the women, it is a Location; they are **in** the doorways. For the women, the city is also a Source; they look **from** hunger-deep eyes, toward some dreamed-of Goal, one imagines. For the narrator, too, the city is a Source, **out** from which he emerges (lines 5–6), apparently also toward some envisioned Goal. Thus, both the speaker and the women are oriented away from the city, but for the women this orientation is only perceptual, while the speaker is actually in motion. The opening lines lead us to think of the speaker as being on a kind of quest, moving actively and intentionally toward some predefined Goal. But what he actually arrives at is not a Goal, but a Patient. That is, rather than coming **to** the open, the lake, and the gulls, he merely comes **on** them (lines 7–8). They are the Patients of his accidental discovery rather than the intended Goals of his movement. The lake is presented as an unexpected interruption of the speaker's motion, and in this sense, he is as alienated from it as from the city. Notice once again how lines 7–8 form a transition in role structures, just as they formed a phonological transition.

While the lake puts an end to the speaker's agency and motion, for the waves and the gulls, it is the place within which motion is possible. They are Agents that seem to be in perpetual movement, but their motion, in contrast with the speaker's, is repetitive and circular (**veering, wheeling**), with no Source or Goal expressed or even implied. Thus, while the poem does contrast the freedom of the open and the confinement of the city, the speaker himself is equally distanced from both. He participates in neither; the city is what he is trying to escape, the open is something that he finds but is not looking for. As far as the speaker is concerned, the open does not solve the problem of confinement, and in fact seems to interrupt his quest for a personal solution.

Examining role structures can reveal a lot about how speakers perceive themselves as well as how they perceive the rest of the world. Daniel Defoe's novel *Moll Flanders* is particularly interesting in this respect. First published in 1722, this novel is a fictional autobiography recounted by a woman who was born in London's Newgate Prison and who survives many ups and downs till she ends up a comfortably established, well-to-do, and—so she says—penitent old lady. The book's extended title gives an idea of its contents:

THE
FORTUNES
AND
MISFORTUNES
Of the FAMOUS
Moll Flanders, & C.

Who was Born in NEWGATE,
and during a Life of continu'd Variety for
Threescore Years, besides her Childhood,
was Twelve Year a *Whore*, five times a *Wife*
(whereof once to her own Brother) Twelve Year a *Thief*,
Eight Year a Transported *Felon* in *Virginia*,
at last grew *Rich*, liv'd *Honest*,
and died a *Penitent*,

Written from her own MEMORANDUMS.[17]

One of the interesting things about Moll Flanders is that though her story reveals her to be an extremely dynamic, energetic, and enterprising person, when narrating her life she tends to avoid speaking of herself as an Agent. The reader confronts a kind of discrepancy between form and content. The content reveals a dynamic character who by her own actions moves back and forth between the highest stations in life and the lowest. The language in which Moll describes her life suggests a somewhat passive character whose experience is primarily shaped by outside forces acting upon her. This latter view shows up linguistically in the fact that in her narration, Moll often prefers to place herself in the roles of Experiencer, Possessor, or Patient rather than Agent. Here is an example from the beginning of the book, in which she tells about her time as a servant and companion to the daughters of a well-to-do family:

> Here I continu'd till I was between 17 and 18 Years old, and here I had all the Advantages for my Education that could be imagin'd; the Lady had Masters home to the House to teach her Daughters to Dance, and to speak *French*, and to Write, and others to teach them Musick; and as I was always with them, I learn'd as fast as they; and tho'

the Masters were not appointed to teach me, yet I learn'd by
Imitation and enquiry, all that they learn'd by Instruction
and Direction. So that in short, I learn'd to Dance, and
10   speak *French* as well as any of them, and to Sing much
better, for I had a better Voice than any of them; I could
not so readily come at playing on the Harpsicord or Spinnet,
because I had no Instrument of my own to Practice on, and
could only come at theirs in the intervals, when they left it,
which was uncertain, but yet I learn'd tollerably well too,
and the young Ladies at length got two Instruments, that is
to say, a Harpsicord, and a Spinnet too, and then they
Taught me themselves . . . .
        By this Means I had, as I have said above, all the Advan-
20   tages of Education that I could have had, if I had been as
much a Gentlewoman as they were, with whom I liv'd, and
in some things, I had the Advantage of my Ladies, tho' they
were my Superiors; but they were all the Gifts of Nature,
and which all their Fortunes could not furnish. First, I was
apparently Handsomer than any of them. Secondly, I was
better shap'd, and Thirdly, I Sung better, by which I mean,
I had a better Voice; in all which you will I hope allow me to
say, I do not speak my own Conceit of myself, but the
Opinion of all that knew the Family.[18]

What Moll is describing here are the ways in which she tried to overcome
her subordinate role in the household and take advantage of the family's
prosperity to develop abilities with might eventually enable her to rise out of
her servant role. What is odd is that in describing this undertaking, Moll does
not present herself as the aggressive, enterprising, and upwardly mobile
person that she is. Rather than portray herself as Agent, she describes herself
as a person who happens to **have** certain qualities (Possessor), to **be** on the
premises (Patient), and to **undergo** certain experiences (Experiencer). Others
act: The mother hires the teachers, the teachers teach the daughters, the
daughters teach Moll. Moll **is** always with them, **is** better shaped (Patient),
has a better voice, does **not have** a harpsichord, **has** advantages (Possessor).
Both she and the young ladies, of course, learn (Experiencer). When Moll is
an Agent in a Predication, she seems to try to downplay that fact. The
clearest example is in lines 26–27, where having said **I sung better** (I-Agent),
she corrects herself or "hedges," and recasts herself as a Possessor in **I had a
better voice**. In lines 7–9, the parallel surface structure **I learned by Imitation
and enquiry . . . they learned by Instruction and Direction** downplays the crucial
underlying contrast between Moll's situation and that of the ladies. In underlying structure, Moll is the Agent of **imitate** and **enquire**, while the ladies are
Patients of **instruct** and **direct**. Moll has to actively seek out what the young
ladies receive as a matter of course. Had Moll used the surface verbs **imitate**,
instruct, and so on, this contrast would have been more explicit, since the
Agent and Patient arguments would have had to be present. With the nominal

derivatives, they are not; and the parallel structure conceals at the same time as it reveals the difference between Moll's situation and that of her mistresses.

The same patterns are repeated in this second excerpt, in which the young ladies' older brother finds Moll alone one day and makes advances to her:

30 . . . then having me in his Arms
he Kiss'd me three or four times.

I struggl'd to get away, and yet did it but faintly neither, and he held me fast, and still Kiss'd me, till he was almost out of Breath, and then sitting down, says, *dear Betty* I am in Love with you.

His Words I must confess fir'd my Blood; all my Spirits flew about my Heart, and put me into Disorder enough, which he might easily have seen in my Face: He repeated it afterwards several times, that he was in Love with me, and
40 my Heart spoke as plain as a Voice, that I lik'd it; nay, when ever he said, I am in Love with you, my Blushes plainly reply'd, *wou'd you were* Sir.

However nothing else pass'd at that time; it was but a Surprise, and when he was gone, I soon recover'd myself again. He had stay'd longer with me, but he happen'd to look out at the Window, and see his Sisters coming up the Garden, so he took his leave, Kiss'd me again, told me he was very serious, and I should hear more of him very quickly, and away he went leaving me infinitely pleas'd tho'
50 surpris'd, and had there not been one Misfortune in it, I had been in the Right, but the Mistake lay here, that Mrs. *Betty* was in Earnest, and the Gentleman was not.[19]

Again, we find that Moll just happens to be there to be acted upon by the brother. And again, when she does become an Agent (line 32, **I struggled . . .**), she hedges and denies her own Agency. Her non-Agency appears clearly in the description of her response to the brother's embrace. In order to indicate that she did respond without indicating that she did so voluntarily or actively, Moll segregates the Agent parts of herself off as distinct from her "real" self. Thus the brother's **Words** (Force) fire her **Blood** (Patient), her **Spirits** (Agent) fly about her **Heart** (Location) and put **her** (Patient) into disorder, her **Heart** (Agent) says **she** (Experiencer) liked it, while it is her **Blushes** (Agent) that reply. More generally, especially in the first two-thirds of the book before she becomes a thief, Moll sees herself primarily not as an active participant in the world, but rather as one existing in it and acquiring property, husbands, a "character," and so forth. Rarely is she an actor, and if she becomes engaged in an action of some greater significance than opening doors and everyday household activities, she hedges. It is important to notice that whatever passivity we may associate with Moll is identifiable with the relative semantic passivity of being an Experiencer, Possessor, or Patient, a "passivity" which consists primarily of absence of action, intention, and so forth. It does not derive from syntactic passives, for these are used very rarely in connection with Moll.

Why should Moll Flanders downplay herself as Agent when she is the very epitome of the self-made individual? Many critics view this tendency as a complex rhetorical plot designed to keep the reader from losing sympathy with her despite the sordid aspects of her life. In part this ploy involves encouraging the reader to view Moll as a victim of external forces and circumstances rather than as someone responsible for her actions and for the shape of her life. Thus, it is because she **has** certain attractions that men of higher class pursue her—she is not actively and intentionally threatening the social hierarchy. This is not to say that Moll never sins or does wrong, but to the extent that she is not an Agent, the sins that she commits are not sins of commission, but only sins of omission, such as not struggling hard enough. In this way, Moll can report the worst of her experience and give an impression of complete sincerity without alienating the reader altogether.

Keeping the reader's sympathies is important for Moll, since she is presenting herself as a penitent, reformed sinner whose life story is of value only as an example to others of how not to live and of how one can never be too sinful to be saved. However, there has been considerable debate among critics as to whether Defoe intends his readers to regard Moll's penitence as sincere or not. While it is possible to read the novel "straight" as a moral tale demonstrating the possibilities both for sin and for repentance, it is also possible, and in several ways more plausible, to read the novel ironically. On the ironic reading, Moll feels little sincere regret for the sinfulness that has ultimately brought her such prosperity, and Defoe is using her to exemplify religious hypocrisy. This latter reading is supported by the facts we have been discussing. Moll's reluctance to portray herself as Agent at crucial points in the story suggests that she does not sincerely take responsibility for her past. When she tells of first turning to thieving for a living, for example, she goes on at such lengths about how outside forces drove her to it, that in the end the explanation sounds hollow:

> Let 'em remember that a time of Distress is a time of
> dreadful Temptation, and all the Strength to resist is taken
> away; Poverty presses, the Soul is made Desperate by
> Distress, and what can be done? It was one Evening, when
> being brought, as I may say, to the last Gasp, I think I may
> truly say I was Distracted and Raving, when prompted by I
> know not what Spirit, and as it were, doing I did not know
> what, or why; I dress'd me, for I had still pretty good
> Cloaths, and went out: I am very sure I had no manner of
> Design in my Head, when I went out, I neither knew or
> considered where to go, or on what Business; but as the
> Devil carried me out and laid his Bait for me, so he brought
> me to be sure to the place, for I knew not whither I was
> going or what I did.[20]

Moll's response to the "devil" is a consistent part of her character, the natural outcome of her overall passivity. As such, it takes on a rather special light. The "hardening of her heart" that sets in once she begins to steal is in some sense the willingness to be ruled by her passivity in a situation beyond the bounds of legality.

While a thief, Moll does seem to perceive herself as an Agent, but when she is arrested and condemned for thieving, she returns to her old roles of Experiencer, Possessor, and Patient, almost to the extent of making a monstrous caricature of herself:

> I had a weight of Guilt upon me enough to sink any Creature who had the least power of Reflection left, and had any Sense upon them of the Happiness of this Life, or the Misery of another; then I had at first remorse indeed, but no Repentance; I had now neither Remorse or Repentance: I had a Crime charg'd on me, the Punishment of which was Death by our Law; the Proof so evident, that there was no room for me so much as to plead not Guilty; I had the Name of old Offender, so that I had nothing to expect but Death in a few Weeks time, neither had I myself any thoughts of Escaping, and yet a certain strange Lethargy of Soul possess'd me, I had no Trouble, no Apprehensions, no Sorrow about me, the first Surprize was gone.[21]

Here again, deprived of the power to act, Moll sums up and evaluates her situation in terms of what she has and does not have. She seems to make no connection between the feelings and problems that she **has** and the things that she **did** that brought them upon her. Nor do these feelings seem to be leading her towards any genuine **act** of penitence. Later, after being given a reprieve, and seeing hope of a new life in the New World, Moll becomes an Agent again, this time in an honorable way. Indeed, she becomes the prime mover, organizing her husband's as well as her own transportation as a released convict from England to America, while he becomes the Patient and Experiencer. Although her actions are honorable, there is, however, no evidence of a true change of spirit.

In the case of *Moll Flanders*, role structure analysis has an additional advantage. Not only does it clarify how Defoe intended Moll to be understood by the reader, but it also suggests ways of approaching the longstanding problem of whether the first or second edition of the book is to be taken as the basic text. *Moll Flanders* was first published in January of 1722. A second, "corrected" edition appeared in July of the same year. A "third edition" was published at the end of the year, but the only difference from the second is in the title page. This third edition has been the basis of most modern reprints and critical studies. However, in recent years, evidence has been accumulating that the first edition may be the only one for which Defoe was responsible.

The "corrections" in the second edition in many cases do not improve the text; rather, they remove a few details, and occasionally change the text in such a way that it does not make sense. Such "corrections" as were made were presumably in the interests of economy, as nearly all involved compression of the text. On the other hand, Defoe is known to have revised other writings, so the possibility is not ruled out that Defoe was indeed the author of the revisions in the second edition, unless we look for more specific evidence. The changes made with respect to the role structures discussed here provide linguistic evidence that the "corrector" did not in fact fully understand Moll's character as developed in the first edition, or possibly that he took the tale literally rather than ironically and objected to her denial of responsibility.

As an example, reconsider some of the passages quoted earlier, this time with the corrections of the second edition added. Lines are numbered as above. Deletions are crossed out; changes are indicated in the margin. One additional paragraph, from a little further on in the narrative, is also included here:

> .... I could
> not so readily come at playing on the Harpsicord or Spinnet,
> because I had no Instrument of my own to Practice on, and
> could only come at theirs in the intervals, when they left it,
> 15   ~~which was uncertain,~~ but yet I learn'd tollerably well ~~too,~~   *ℓ*
> and the young Ladies at length got two Instruments, that is
> to say, a Harpsicord, and a Spinnet too, and then they
> Taught me themselves ....

*   *   *

> His Words I must confess fir'd my Blood; all my Spirits
> flew about my Heart, and put me into Disorder enough,
> ~~which he might easily have seen in my Face~~: He repeated it   *ℓ*
> afterwards several times, that he was in Love with me, and
> 40   my Heart spoke as plain as a Voice, that I lik'd it; nay, when
> ever he said, I am in Love with you, my Blushes plainly
> reply'd, *wou'd you were Sir.*
> However nothing else pass'd at that time; it was but a
> Surprise, and ~~when he was gone,~~ I soon recover'd myself   *ℓ*
> again. He had stay'd longer with me, but he happen'd to
> look out at the Window, and see his Sisters coming up the
> Garden, so he took his leave, Kiss'd me again, told me he
> was very serious, and I should hear more of him very
> quickly, and away he went ~~leaving me~~ infinitely pleas'd ~~tho'~~   *ℓ*
> 50   ~~surpris'd,~~ and had there not been one Misfortune in it, I   *ℓ*
> had been in the Right, but the Mistake lay here, that Mrs.
> *Betty* was in Earnest, and the Gentleman was not. ...

It will not be strange, if I now began to think, but alas! it
was but with very little solid Reflection: I had a most un-   — s
bounded Stock of Vanity and Pride, and but a very little
Stock of Vertue; I did indeed cast sometimes with myself   —thing
what my young Master aim'd at, but thought of nothing,
but the fine Words, and the Gold; whether he intended to
Marry me, or not to Marry me, seem'd a Matter of no great   ℓ₁
60   Consequence to me; nor did my Thoughts so much as   I
suggest to me the Necessity of making any Capitulation for   think
myself, till he came to make a kind of formal Proposal to me,
as you shall hear presently.

Thus I gave up myself to a readiness of being ruined with-   ruin
out the least concern, and am a fair *Memento* to all young
Women, whose Vanity prevails over their Vertue.[22]

Modifications significant to the present discussion occur on lines 15, 38,
44, 49, and especially 60, 61, and 64. The omission of **which was uncertain** in
line 15 means that any reference to Moll's inability even to schedule a program
for herself is left out. Although her role is not directly affected by the omission,
the "correction" at least makes it possible that she could actively plan when
to practice. Similarly, the change in line 38 omits reference to Moll's inability
to disguise her emotions actively and therefore leaves open the possibility
that she actually did disguise them. Omission of **when he was gone** in line 44
implies that she took control of herself in his presence (cf. **He had stay'd
longer with me**), whereas the first edition suggests that departure of the source
of "disorder" was a prerequisite to recovery. The change in line 49 suggests a
bungling editor who, in his desire to make Moll seem less culpable (and hence
her "penitence" less suspect in its superficiality), transfers pleasure from her
to the elder brother. As a result, the elder brother, who is elsewhere barely
ever described in terms of emotions, only of actions, is given a new quality,
one that Moll as observer/narrator could hardly have known about (in the
book, she scrupulously avoids the pretence that she knows other people's
emotions). More damagingly, the sense is obscured, since **I had been in the
Right** now has no reference, whereas in the first edition we understand **I had
been in the Right in being pleased**.

Of crucial relevance to the question of whether Defoe was responsible
for the second edition, is line 60. In the first edition, Moll is entirely the passive
recipient of suggestions, the Goal of the suggestions, and the Experiencer of
them, too: **nor did my Thoughts so much as suggest to me the Necessity of
making any Capitulation**. The thoughts are the Source from which these
suggestions could have arisen. By being selected as subject of the sentence,
thoughts become the starting point of our perspective. The change to **nor did I
so much as think of making any Capitulation** downgrades the role of the thoughts
and upgrades that of Moll. She is still the Experiencer, but she is not the
direct Goal of a suggestion. By being made the subject of the sentence, she is
the basis of our perspective, and the possibility arises that she might have

actively set about thinking the issue out. The "correction" has given Moll moral potential that is absent in the first edition, and in doing so has made her receptiveness to suggestion and action elsewhere less consistent, creating problems for our understanding of her character. Line 64 of the first edition delineates Moll's character exactly. She is ready—ready to be influenced by her thoughts, by the elder brother, the devil, indeed anything. The change from **a readiness of being ruined** to **ruin**, like numerous other modifications, shortens, but in doing so dilutes the picture Defoe so carefully drew of her in the first edition. It is hard indeed to believe that he would have made such "corrections" himself.

SUGGESTED FURTHER READINGS

Among recent studies of semantics, with emphasis on the problems discussed in this chapter, Dillon's *Introduction to Contemporary Linguistic Semantics* provides a general survey of the issues; Leech's *Semantics* and Lyons's two-volume book also entitled *Semantics* are comprehensive and in-depth studies of the field, which should prove to be major references for years to come. Two journals that publish important articles on generative semantics are *Linguistic Analysis* and *Linguistic Inquiry*; both assume a fairly advanced knowledge of linguistic theory.

A very clear outline of the aims of case grammar is to be found in Fillmore, "Lexical Entries for Verbs." Two important studies of English sentence structure based on case grammar principles are Langendoen, *Essentials of English Grammar*, and Stockwell et al., *The Major Syntactic Structures of English*. Introductory textbooks on generative grammar using a conceptual but not a specifically case grammar base include Langacker, *Language and Its Structure*, and Stockwell, *Foundations of Syntactic Theory*.

One of the most interesting studies of literature from the point of view of role structure analysis is Halliday's "Linguistic Function and Literary Style: An Inquiry into the Language of William Golding's *The Inheritors*." This article begins by exploring the problems of applying linguistic analysis to literature in general, and then analyzes selected passages from Golding's novel, showing that "the people" (a Neanderthal tribe) are presented as seeing the world in terms of Patients and Experiencers, while the "new people" who conquer them, the first modern tribe, perceive the world in terms of Agency and Cause. While the terminology and theory on which Halliday bases his arguments are not quite the same as those of Fillmore's case grammar, the principle is the same.

A journal devoted to literary aspects of the material under consideration in this chapter is the *Journal of Literary Semantics*. The state of research on metaphor is reflected in *Poetics* IV, 1975.

Exercises

1. The following lexical items are verbs derived from nouns. Part of the meaning of the verbs involves not only the meaning of the noun but also of a role relation in which that noun functions. Group the verbs into two sets according to the understood role of the noun from which they are derived. Do verbs of this sort better support the feature analysis or the predicate analysis of lexical items?

axe	eye	list
bottle	finger	mirror
brake	hammer	pocket
cage	ink	sandpaper
can (fruit, etc.)	knife	screw
chain (someone)	land	X-ray

2. In the course of this chapter it was suggested that verbs could be decomposed into Predications. This approach allowed us to factor out similarities between, for example, **kill** and **cause to die**. In the following sentences it is possible to factor out a basic predicate TRANSFER (of sensations) that is common to **listen to, hear, be audible, look at, see, be visible,** and **taste**. It is also possible to show that the differences between the surface forms of the verbs are a function of assumed (as well as overt) arguments:

   1. a.   John listened to the symphony.
      b.   John heard the symphony.
      c.   The symphony was audible to John.

   2. a.   John looked at the Utrillo.
      b.   John saw the Utrillo.
      c.   The Utrillo was visible to John.

   3. a.   John tasted the fennel (i.e., tried it to see how it tasted).
      b.   John tasted the fennel in the soup.
      c.   The fennel tasted good.

   Suggest a Predication analysis for each sentence using the basic predicate TRANSFER, with the aim of demonstrating similarities between the meanings of the sentences as far as possible. How does predicate analysis help show that the a, b, and c sentences are equivalent in groups 1, 2, and 3, regardless of whether the surface verbs are similar. Also, how does predicate analysis reveal that **He looked at the Utrillo with his eyes** is redundant while **He looked at the Utrillo with watery eyes** is not?

3. In certain respects **tall** and **high** appear to be synonymous; in others they are rather different. Discuss the similarities and differences in the meaning of these two terms with special emphasis on their opposites, **short** and **low**, and on their selectional constraints (for example, **tall building, high building, tall person, *high person**).

4. Supposing all the following lexical items contain the structure *X CAUSE Y to BECOME NOT ALIVE*, what are the selectional restrictions on expressing these underlying predicates as **kill, slaughter, massacre, butcher, assassinate, execute, exterminate, slay**? Support your arguments with examples of anomalous, contradictory, and well-formed sentences.

5. Question 8, Chapter 4 concerned the syntax of a computerized poem. The program included some selectional rules to avoid too much anomaly, while at the same time intentionally introducing some anomaly in order to provide humor. What do you think these selectional rules were? (Again, you need not formalize them, only state precisely what they would try to capture.) If you were writing the program, would you want to constrain the selectional rules even further to achieve other effects? If so, what would you add to the program?

6. The following is a famous sonnet by Gerard Manley Hopkins:

THE WINDHOVER:°

To Christ our Lord

I caught this morning morning's minion,° king-
    dom of daylight's dauphin,° dapple-dawn-drawn Falcon, in
      his riding
Of the rolling level underneath him steady air, and striding
High there, how he rung upon the rein of a wimpling° wing
In his ecstasy! then off, off forth on swing,
    As a skate's heel sweeps smooth on a bow-bend: the hurl and
      gliding
Rebuffed the big wind. My heart in hiding
Stirred for a bird,—the achieve of, the mastery of the thing!

Brute beauty and valour and act, oh, air, pride, plume, here
10   Buckle! And the fire that breaks from thee then, a billion
Times told lovelier, more dangerous, O my chevalier!

No wonder of it: shéer plód makes plough down sillion°
Shine, and blue-bleak embers, ah my dear,
    Fall, gall themselves,° and gash gold-vermilion.[24]

Title **Windhover:** kestrel (a bird rather like a hawk)   **1** **minion:** loved one, favorite of a prince   **2** **dauphin:** prince, usually eldest son of the King of France   **4** **wimpling:** enveloping   **12** **sillion:** ridge between two furrows   **14** **gall themselves:** rub against each other

    a. Transcribe the first eight lines into the broad phonetic alphabet used in Chapter 2. In what ways does sound match sense in these eight lines? Consider consonant alliteration, vowel patterns used in stressed syllables associated with **level air** versus **striding**, and also rhythm.

    b. Look up any words you do not know in your desk dictionary, and then discuss the diction of the poem, and indicate what cohesive lexical sets there are.

c. Hopkins was deeply concerned with contemplating what he saw as a kind of ambiguity in the relation of human beings to God: God creates, but creation is not alive until a person reaches out and responds. An important theme in "The Windhover" is the active and at the same time passive role of individuals, whether the narrator (**I**) or Christ (the bird, God in the form of a man), and this ambiguity is best expressed by **the achieve of, the mastery of the thing**. Discuss in what ways the phrases **the achieve of the thing** and **the mastery of the thing** are ambiguous, and show how **achieve** (as opposed to **achieving** or **achievement**) helps create this ambiguity. (Hint: **the painting of my brother** is ambiguous, meaning both "the painting my brother made" and "the picture which somebody made of my brother.")

7. On pages 115–16, the diction of a short excerpt from John Lennon's "The SinguLARGE Experience of Miss Anne Duffield" was discussed. Here are a few more lines:

> Mary Atkins pruned herselves in the mirrage, running her hand wantanly through her large blond hair. Her tight dress was cut low revealingly three or four blackheads, carefully scrubbed on her chess. She addled the final touches to her makeup and fixed her teeth firmly in her head. 'He's going to want me tonight' she thought and pictured his hamsome black curly face and jaundice. She looked at her clocks impatiently and went to the window, then leapt into her favorite armchurch, picking up the paper she glassed at the
> 10 headlines. 'MORE NEGOES IN THE CONGO' it read, and there was, but it was the Stop Press which corked her eye. 'JACK THE NIPPLE STRIKE AGAIN.' She went cold all over, it was Sydnees and he'd left the door open.
> 'Hello lover' he said slapping her on the butter.
> 'Oh you did give me a start Sydnees' she shrieked laughing arf arfily.
> 'I always do my love' he replied jumping on all fours. She joined him and they galloffed quickly downstairs into a harrased cab. 'Follow that calf' yelped Sydnees pointing a rude
> 20 fingure.
> 'White hole mate!' said the scabbie.
> 'Why are we bellowing that card Sydnees?' inquired Mary fashionably.
> 'He might know where the party' explained Sydnees.
> 'Oh I see' said Mary looking up at him as if to say.
> The journey parssed pleasantly enough with Sydnees and Mary pointing out places of interest to the scab driver; such as Buckinghell Parcel, the Horses of Parliamint, the Chasing of the Guards.[25]

a. Read the passage aloud.

b. Discuss the kinds of linguistic devices Lennon uses to create a nonsense world in this excerpt. In the course of your discussion, show the difference between (1) words which exist in English but are used in the wrong syntactic category (e.g., adverb **revealingly** where progressive **revealing** would be expected); (2) words which exist in English but which are used anomalously, e.g., **chess** for **chest**, **bellowing** for **following** (these are often called "malapropisms"); (3) words which are spelled in new ways to suggest dialect forms (e.g., **white hole mate** for **Right Oh, mate**—very British). Show which syntactic classes (e.g., nouns or verbs) and which noun functions (subject or object) are most likely to be deviant in this passage.

   c. Suppose that Mary and Sydnees continue their cab-ride and find the party. Write a paragraph in Lennon's style, making use of the devices you have noticed in b.

8. Turn to page 172 of Chapter 4, and reread the passage from Hemingway's *For Whom the Bell Tolls*. Identify the linguistic role of each instance of **her** in sentences 3–6. How do the linguistic roles assigned to Maria help us understand the narrator's view of her?

9. The following is a passage from Hemingway's *A Farewell to Arms*:

> In the late summer of that year we lived in a house
>   TIME   PATIENT LOCATION
> in a village that looked across the river and the plain to
>   LOCATION   PATH
> the mountains. In the bed of the river there were peb-
>   GOAL
> bles and boulders, dry and white in the sun, and the
> water was clear and swiftly moving and blue in the
> channels. Troops went by the house and down the road
> and the dust they raised powdered the leaves of the
> trees. The trunks of the trees too were dusty and the
> leaves fell early that year and we saw the troops march-
> ing along the road and the dust rising and leaves, stirred
> by the breeze, falling and the soldiers marching and
> afterward the road bare and white except for the leaves.[23]

   a. Identify the role or roles of each underlined NP in this passage, as exemplified in the first sentence.

   b. Is **the water** the Patient of **be clear, be moving, be blue**, at the end of the second sentence, or is it the Patient of **be clear, be blue**, and the Agent of **be moving**? How would the roles change if Hemingway had written: **and the water was clear and moved swiftly and blue in the channels**? What would **blue in the channels** have been coordinated to if Hemingway had written the sentence this way?

   c. What conclusions do you draw about the perspective on the world that the narrator is developing in terms of role structures?

10. In the passage from William Faulkner's *Big Woods* cited on pages 182–83, the syntax associated with the land is very different from that associated with the Anglo-Saxon invaders. This difference in syntax is obviously related to the different participant roles assigned by Faulkner to the things and people he portrays. Briefly, but as specifically as possible, discuss what these particular roles are and how they affect our attitude toward the various elements that make up Mississippi.

NOTES

[1] Charles J. Fillmore, "Lexical Entries for Verbs," *Foundations of Language*, 4 (1968), 373–93. For a different, but also dynamic approach, see Wallace L. Chafe, *Meaning and the Structure of Language* (Chicago: Univ. of Chicago Press, 1970).

[2] See especially Charles J. Fillmore, "The Case for Case," in *Universals in Linguistic Theory*, eds. Emmon Bach and Robert T. Harms (New York: Holt, Rinehart and Winston, Inc., 1968); and Fillmore, "Lexical Entries for Verbs." For later studies from a more psychological/cognitive point of view, see George A. Miller and Philip N. Johnson-Laird, *Language and Perception* (Cambridge, Mass.: Belknap Press, Harvard Univ. Press, 1976); and Ray Jackendoff, "Grammar as Evidence for Conceptual Structure," in *Linguistic Theory and Psychological Reality*, eds. Morris Halle, Joan Bresnan, and George A. Miller (Cambridge, Mass.: M.I.T. Press, 1979).

[3] Note that there is now no underlying subject, since there is no basic constituent NP + VP; all subjects are therefore surface subjects.

[4] Adapted from Björn Collinder, *Survey of the Uralic Languages* (Stockholm: Almquist and Wiksell, 1957), p. 47.

[5] Linguists who hold the view that the base is syntactic/semantic and also that lexical items are predications in underlying structure are sometimes known as "generative semanticists." The name stems from the fact that they view the base where the structures of sentences are specified ("generated") as in part semantic.

[6] See, for example, James D. McCawley, "Lexical Insertion in a Grammar Without Deep Structure," in *Papers from the Fourth Regional Meeting of the Chicago Linguistic Society* (Chicago: University of Chicago, Linguistics Department, 1968); George Lakoff, "On Generative Semantics," in *Semantics: An Interdisciplinary Reader in Philosophy, Linguistics and Psychology*, eds. Danny D. Steinberg and Leon A. Jakobovitz (London and New York: Cambridge Univ. Press, 1971); Paul M. Postal, "On the Surface Verb 'Remind,'" *Linguistic Inquiry*, 1 (1970), 37–120; Jeffrey S. Gruber, *Lexical Structures in Syntax and Semantics* (New York: Elsevier North-Holland, Inc., 1976). For counterarguments, see Jerrold J. Katz, "Interpretive Semantics Versus Generative Semantics," *Foundations of Language*, 6 (1970), 220–59.

[7] For finer points about lexical insertion, see McCawley, "Lexical Insertion."

[8] Note that capitalized COME is an abstract primitive meaning "change of state" and is different from the surface verb **come**, which is complex and involves movement toward the speaker (cf. Chapter 7).

[9] See especially Emmon Bach, "Nouns and Noun Phrases," in *Universals in Linguistic Theory*, eds. Emmon Bach and Robert T. Harms. Several examples in this section are drawn from Bach.

[10] For issues discussed in this section, see Manfred Bierwisch, "Semantics," in *New Horizons in Linguistics* (Harmondsworth, Mssex.: Penguin, 1970).

[11] Noam Chomsky, *Aspects of the Theory of Syntax* (Cambridge, Mass.: MIT Press, 1965). A somewhat different approach to lexical combinations, called the "collocational" approach, is presented in Angus McIntosh, "Patterns and Ranges," *Language*,

37 (1961), 325–37. The latter approach involves the claim that lexical items belong to sets which have certain "ranges," that is, tolerable extensions. As the terminology suggests, a considerable degree of emphasis is laid on how occurrence patterns can be extended, and why it is, for example, that **steel postage-stamps** calls for modification of one's views about stamps rather than steel, while **hammering weekend** calls for modification of one's views about hammering rather than weekends. Chomsky's approach, on the other hand, is more concerned with restrictions than with extensions of use.

[12] Iona and Peter Opie, *The Lore and Language of Schoolchildren* (London: Oxford Univ. Press, 1959), p. 24.

[13] Opie, *Lore and Language of Schoolchildren*, p. 25.

[14] T. S. Eliot, "Preludes," in *The Collected Poems 1909–1962* (New York: Harcourt Brace Jovanovich, Inc., 1963), p. 25.

[15] For further discussion, see Elizabeth Wissman Bruss, "Formal Semantics and Poetic Meaning," *Poetics*, 4 (1975), 339–63; and Samuel R. Levin, *The Semantics of Metaphor* (Baltimore and London: The Johns Hopkins Univ. Press, 1977).

[16] Carl Sandburg, "The Harbor," in *The Complete Poems of Carl Sandburg* (New York: Harcourt Brace Jovanovich, Inc., 1970), p. 5.

[17] Daniel Defoe, *Moll Flanders*, ed. G. A. Starr (London: Oxford Univ. Press, 1971), title page.

[18] Defoe, *Moll Flanders*, pp. 18–19.

[19] Defoe, *Moll Flanders*, pp. 21–22.

[20] Defoe, *Moll Flanders*, p. 191.

[21] Defoe, *Moll Flanders*, pp. 278–79.

[22] For the additional paragraph, see Defoe, *Moll Flanders*, p. 25. The emendations are taken from Daniel Defoe, *Moll Flanders*, ed. James Sutherland, The Riverside Editions (Boston: Houghton Mifflin Co., 1959), pp. 18, 21–22, 24.

[23] Ernest Hemingway, *A Farewell to Arms* (New York: Charles Scribner's Sons, 1929), p.3.

[24] Gerard Manley Hopkins, W. H. Gardner and H. H. MacKenzie, eds., *The Poems of Gerard Manley Hopkins*, 4th ed. (London and New York: Oxford Univ. Press, 1967), p. 69.

[25] John Lennon, "The SinguLARGE Experience of Miss Anne Duffield," in *A Spaniard in the Works* (New York: New American Library, 1964), pp. 108–09.

6

Speech Acts and Speech Genres

W e now turn to pragmatics, the part of linguistics that deals with language use. While phonology, syntax, and semantics focus on language as a formal system of elements and rules for combining them, pragmatics focuses on language as a purposeful form of behavior and examines how in these respects, too, it is rule-governed. Pragmatics deals with speakers' "communicative competence," [1] the knowledge which enables them to produce and understand utterances in relation to specific communicative purposes and specific speech contexts. As noted in Chapter 1, language use is governed by a wide range of contextual factors, including social and physical circumstances, identities, attitudes, abilities, and beliefs of participants; and relations holding between participants. Among other things, a full description of competence must include an account of how these factors bear on communication. One set of forms that illustrates the impact of these factors especially clearly are the forms used for naming people. [2] Depending on the context, a man named Henry Jones might be addressed variously as **sir**, **Mr. Jones**, **Jones**, **Henry**, **Hank**, **Pinky**, **boy**, **meathead**, **sweetheart**, or **dad**. Some of these forms of address, notably the last two, are associated with specific social relationships, like parenthood, marriage, or courtship. Others, including insult epithets like **meathead** or sexual salutes like **gorgeous**, are primarily distinguished by the emotive attitude they express. Other forms reflect the relative status of interlocutors, such as **sir**, which is for use by Jones's inferiors; **Jones**, for use by his peers or superiors; **boy**, for use only by his superiors. Other forms reflect relative degree of intimacy between participants. Thus, in the list above we can see a continuum from **Mr. Jones** (title plus last name) through the diminutive **Hank** to the private nickname **Pinky**. People of the same relative status as Jones might use any of these depending on how intimate they were with him.

Of course, a factor like relative status itself varies from situation to situation. Someone of low status in the office might have high status in a community organization, and forms of address might vary accordingly. Likewise, the degree of intimacy that one may appropriately express varies from one situation to another. The friend who addresses Jones as **Pinky** in private might address him as **Mr. Jones** in the presence of people of lower status than both of them, or in other settings, by some specialized title like **Mr. Speaker** or **the Honorable Member from Coyote Gulch**. Communicative competence includes the knowledge of what address forms go with what social relationships, what situations, and what attitudes. It also includes knowledge of what communicative purposes these forms can carry out. Forms of address can have many different functions. The simple form **Jones** could be used, among other things, to greet Jones, to get him to pay attention, to warn him of danger, to order him to stop doing something, or to express surprise at something he just did. Knowing how to relate surface forms with particular communicative goals is another central aspect of communicative competence.

One of the most generalized functions performed by terms of address is that of establishing and modifying interpersonal relations. When two people meet for the first time, the terms of address they adopt for each other serve to define their mutual relationship and the situation. Such terms are also used to redefine or alter relationships. Thus the aunt who tells her niece "You're too old to call me Auntie anymore, just make it Helen" is substituting an unequal relationship based on generational hierarchy with a peer relationship based on mutual adulthood. (Notice, however, that it is the hierarchical relation that entitles the aunt to tell the niece to make the change—the niece would have had to ask permission to do so.) Between peers, a shift from title plus last name (e.g., Professor Smith, Mrs. Smith) to first name often only serves as an invitation to redefine a colleagueship as a friendship. Such shifts have important communicative consequences. For instance, they generally redefine what topics may be raised for conversation between the two people, or what personal information they are prepared to share.

In performance, transitions in naming are often difficult, for they mean changing not just a habit, but a whole set of social assumptions that goes along with naming. Between shifts, there will often be a period in which one avoids names and titles altogether, and simply calls the person **you**. This is a convenient option for English speakers, but it is not universally available, for in many languages there is more than one form meaning "you," and the various forms express different relationships between interlocutors (see the discussion of Indonesian on pages 6–7). Such pronoun systems provide a clear and important example of the way in which social structuring is "built into" the linguistic system, and of the kind of complex social and situational information a grammar must incorporate.[3]

We can sum up the idea of communicative competence by saying that it comprises the ability to bring into association surface forms, interpersonal speech functions, and contexts. Terms of address give some idea of just how complex the matching of forms, communicative functions, and contexts can be, but in a way they only scratch the surface, for the study of communicative competence goes beyond the analysis of single words or sentences. Obviously, the ability to use language includes the ability to produce and understand utterances that are many sentences long and to engage in verbal exchanges of great variety and complexity. Part of the job of pragmatics is to describe how longer utterances and verbal exchanges cohere internally, what kinds of communicative functions they perform, and how they are rule-governed. Its domain of analysis, in short, is ultimately discourse, not the sentence.

One of the most important things to be learned from approaching language in terms of its use is that the familiar opposition between saying something and doing something—between word and deed—is not at all clear-cut. Saying is doing, and utterances are acts, capable of producing enormous and far-reaching consequences. For example, the sentence **You are under arrest**, addressed to you by the right person (someone with power to make arrests), can deprive you of your physical freedom and place you under the obligation to respond to some accusation and to be punished if found guilty. By the same token, **Case dismissed**, uttered by the right person in the right circumstances, can restore your physical freedom and relieve you of those obligations. People's lives are shaped by verbally constituted contractual dealings like owning, owing, promising, marrying, or bequeathing. The very name we sign to bind ourselves to such contracts is ours only by virtue of a verbal deed. Politics and government are also to a great extent carried on through verbal action. Elected representatives write bills, legislative bodies vote on them, heads of state sign them into law. International relations are shaped by statements, warnings, protests, diplomatic notes, treaties, and declarations of war or peace. Utterances are also used to perform supernatural deeds like driving away evil spirits (as in exorcism), placing a person in the care of benevolent forces (as in many baptismal and funeral rites), bringing people good fortune or bad (blessings and curses), influencing the weather, the hunt, crops, fertility, health, outcomes of battles and trips—indeed, almost any phenomenon by which humans can be affected. In the Bible, the very creation of the cosmos was brought about through words (uttered, of course, by the appropriate authority): **God said, Let there be light, and there was light**.

Contracts, official pronouncements, and magic formulae are not the only examples of utterances that are deeds. All utterances in fact are acts, and all that are communicative have consequences.[4] If a man comes up to you in the street and asks you what time it is, his question will quite likely have the consequence of getting you to look at your watch and provide a reply. Your reply has the consequence of changing his knowledge of the world (he was uncertain of the time, and now he is certain), and possibly his immediate behavior. Furthermore, both the question and the response are acts that carry social weight. You recognize another as a fellow human being and cooperate with him for his benefit. Notice that to simply ignore the question would constitute an act of social aggression. In accepting and believing your response, the man invests trust in the social pact between you. Hence, you would be offended if after hearing your reply he asked to check your watch just to be sure. Like international relations, interpersonal ones are defined, maintained, and modified chiefly through language.

SPEECH ACT THEORY

Different frameworks have been proposed for describing language use in context. Speech act theory, the approach that we will be outlining here, was developed in the 1960s by a group of British language philosophers, most importantly J. L. Austin, and has more recently been adopted by many linguists on both sides of the Atlantic. As its name suggests, speech act theory treats an utterance as an act performed by a speaker in a context with respect to an addressee. Performing a speech act involves performing (1) a *locutionary act*, the act of producing a recognizable grammatical utterance in the language, and (2) an *illocutionary act*, the attempt to accomplish some communicative purpose. Promising, warning, greeting, reminding, informing, and commanding are all distinct illocutionary acts.[5] While phonology, syntax, and semantics focus on the locutionary act, pragmatics focuses on the illocutionary act, the aspect of the speech act which specifies what the language is being used for on a given occasion. Various attempts have been made to classify illocutionary acts in English. Here is one useful working classification:

> *Representatives*. Illocutionary acts that undertake to represent a state of affairs, for example, stating, claiming, hypothesizing, describing, predicting, and telling, insisting, suggesting, or swearing that something is the case.
> *Expressives*. Illocutionary acts that express only the speaker's psychological attitude toward some state of affairs, for example, congratulating, thanking, deploring, condoling, welcoming, greeting.[6]
> *Verdictives*. Illocutionary acts that deliver a finding as to value or fact, and thus that rate some entity or situation on a scale, such as assessing, ranking, estimating, and all other judgmental acts.
> *Directives*. Illocutionary acts designed to get the addressee to do something, for example, requesting, commanding, pleading, inviting, questioning, daring, and insisting or suggesting that someone do something.
> *Commissives*. Illocutionary acts that commit the speaker to doing something, for example, promising, threatening, vowing.
> *Declarations*. Illocutionary acts that bring about the state of affairs they refer to, such as, blessing, firing, baptizing, bidding, passing sentence, arresting, marrying.

Representatives, expressives, and verdictives are all intended to affect the addressees' mental sets—what they know (representatives), their social attitudes (expressives), their judgments (verdictives)—and are only indirectly intended to modify behavior. Directives, however, are primarily designed to get others to do things. Commissives and declarations are primarily contractual, establishing states of affairs in the world, some with few consequences for the addressee (e.g., vows), others with immediate consequences (e.g., arresting).

A speaker's communicative competence includes not just knowledge of what illocutionary acts can be performed in the language, but also how, when, where, and by whom they can be performed. To take up an earlier example, the act of dismissing a case is performed when:

- certain words are uttered (the conventional formula **Case dismissed**)
- accompanied by a certain gesture (a blow of the gavel)
- by a certain person (the assigned judge)
- who has certain beliefs (e.g., that there really are not sufficient grounds for maintaining the accusation)
- in a certain place (a courtroom)
- at a certain time (after hearing the testimony, and so forth)
- addressed to certain people (the accused and/or his or her representatives)
- in the presence of certain people (a court reporter, a bailiff, and others)

Unless these conditions are met, the act of case dismissal has not taken place or at least has taken place defectively. In speech act theory, conditions such as these on which the accomplishment of an illocutionary act depends are called "appropriateness conditions." [7] Every illocutionary act is subject to a set of such conditions, and if they are all fulfilled in a given instance, the speech act is said to be appropriate; if not, it is considered inappropriate. Not all verbal acts are as heavily restricted as dismissing a case, of course. Nevertheless, all are in some way constrained as to: form(s) the locutionary act may take; surrounding circumstances; identity of the participants; beliefs and attitudes of the participants. Thus the appropriateness conditions on the act of asking a question will include the following:

1. The form of the locutionary act is one that is:
   a. conventionally associated with the illocutionary act of questioning (for example, presence of a question-word like **what**, or auxiliary fronting as in **will you?** or rising intonation)
   b. of a degree of formality appropriate to the occasion (for example, informal **How old are you?** versus formal **What is your age?**).

2. The circumstances are such that:
   a. the question is adequately related to ongoing discourse if any
   b. the question is appropriate in subject matter to the occasion
   c. it is not obvious that the addressee will give the answer at the time without being asked.

3. The participants are such that:
   a. the speaker is entitled to speak at the time
   b. the speaker is entitled to ask a question of this addressee
   c. the addressee is entitled to respond to this speaker at the time
   d. it is possible that the addressee knows the answer to the question
   e. it is possible that the addressee is willing to give the answer at the time.

4. The beliefs and attitudes of the speaker are such that:
   a. the speaker does not know the answer
   b. the speaker wants to know the answer
   c. the speaker believes the conditions in 2 and 3 are met.[8]

So, for example, the question **Has the sun come up yet?** asked of a cellmate in an underground prison violates condition 3d. **Where do you buy your socks?** asked in the question period after a physics lecture would violate condition 2b. 3a would be violated by a question asked while the addressee is in the middle of saying something else. You can easily think of contexts in which the other conditions would be violated. In the grammar, a description of the illocutionary act of questioning will include a specification of these appropriateness conditions, plus a definition of the act itself as an undertaking to elicit information from the addressee.

Many of the appropriateness conditions outlined in 1–4 hold fairly generally. Analogues of 1a–b, 2a–b, 3a–b, and 4c would hold for virtually all illocutionary acts. In addition to these seven conditions, the illocutionary act of giving information, for example, would be subject to the following appropriateness conditions: Speaker believes that the information is true; speaker has evidence for its truth; speaker has some reason for wanting addressee to know it; it is possible that addressee is not aware of the information. These, too, are analogous to some of the conditions attaching to questions. The first two are similar to 4a above, the third is similar to 4b above (these are often referred to as *sincerity conditions*), and the fourth is similar to 2c above (it is often referred to as the *nonobviousness condition*). Again, the grammar's description of the illocutionary act of asserting will specify all these conditions, plus a definition of informing as an undertaking to represent a state of affairs. Notice how such a description expresses relations between surface form, communicative function, and context.

Illocutionary acts can often be differentiated from each other in terms of their appropriateness conditions. Thus pleading and commanding are both directives, but they differ according to the relationship that holds between the speaker and the addressee. Commanding has an appropriateness condition that the speaker is in a position of authority over the addressee; with pleading, the addressee is in authority. Suggesting, insisting, and hypothesizing (that something is the case) all belong to the class of representatives, but they differ in that in each case the speaker is expressing a different degree of belief or commitment towards the truth of what is represented. These distinctions would likewise be stated as appropriateness conditions on the attitude of the speaker. Concluding, replying, and disagreeing are all representatives in this classification, but they each express a different relation between what is being said and the discourse which preceded it.

In the area of pragmatics, the concept of appropriateness plays a role somewhat analogous to the role played in syntax by the concept of grammaticality. The difference is that while grammaticality refers to the surface form of the utterance alone (the locutionary act), appropriateness refers to aspects of the speech act which are not manifested in the surface string. Appropriateness conditions are more like unspoken rules understood to be "in play" when people use the language. When a speaker performs a speech act, the hearer is normally entitled to infer that the speaker believes all the appropriateness conditions on that speech act are met; the speaker normally presupposes that the hearer also takes this for granted.

THE FORMALIZATION OF SPEECH ACTS

Recent linguistic scholarship has been much concerned with how the account of language use suggested by speech act theory can be incorporated into the framework of generative grammar. In one proposal, which involves only a slight modification of the type of semantic-syntactic base described in Chapter 5, Presentence includes: [9]

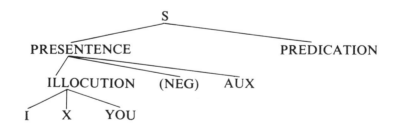

The **I X you** is a way of specifying in underlying structure what illocutionary act the speaker is performing vis-à-vis the addressee. In a given case, the **X** slot would be occupied by an abstract verb denoting the illocutionary act in question, that is, some member of the classes of representatives, expressives, verdictives, directives, commissives, and declarations mentioned earlier. In surface structure, this abstract **I X you** clause can appear in a number of ways.

The abstract verb can be directly realized as a lexical item (the technical term is "lexicalized"). This is the case, for example, in **I insist you return the funds**, whose underlying structure would be something like [I INSIST you [you return the funds]]. **I congratulate you on your victory** is another example of this type. In these examples, the surface verbs **insist** and **congratulate** are said to function as "performative verbs," because they are being used to perform the illocutionary act they refer to. One can often tell whether a verb is being used as a performative verb by checking whether it can co-occur with the adverb **hereby**, as is possible in the above examples.

Sometimes, instead of being lexicalized as a performative verb, the abstract predicate can be realized as an auxiliary verb. PROMISE, for example, can be lexicalized as **I promise to go**, or realized by an auxiliary as in **I will go**. Similarly, we have **I permit you to go** and **You may/can go; I predict he will lose** and **He will lose**. A more idiosyncratic example is SUGGEST, which can be expressed by a performative verb (**I suggest we go to the movies**), or realized by the special constructions **Let's go to the movies, How about going to the movies? Why not go to the movies?** Some abstract predicates allow deletions, so that we can get either **I command you to go** or **Go!** (here there is a direct correlation between I COMMAND YOU and the IMP suggested in Chapter 4). In other cases, deletion is accompanied by word-order transformations. Instead of the lexicalized **I request you state whether or not it is true that Bill failed his exam**, we find **Did Bill fail his exam?** (here there is a direct correlation between I REQUEST YOU STATE WHETHER and the Q suggested in Chapter 4). In other cases, the **I X you** is not realized at all on the surface. The lexicalized **I state that I left at 8 o'clock** has another version, **I left at 8 o'clock**.

Whether a given illocutionary verb is realized as a lexical item or in some other way depends on context. For instance, you have probably noticed that illocutionary acts using a performative verb in the surface structure tend to sound legalistic and impersonal. Stylistically, they are characteristic of formal, often written, discourse of a contractual nature, whereas in normal conversation we tend to avoid them.

INDIRECT SPEECH ACTS

The kind of analysis just proposed applies to a considerable range of speech acts. However, it does not account for another major fact about speech acts— a great many of them are performed indirectly. The form of one may imply another. Consider the following sentences:

1. I {would like you to / want you to / wish you would} turn off the radio.

2. $\left\{\begin{array}{l}\text{Will you}\\\text{Would you}\end{array}\right.$ turn off the radio?

3. $\left\{\begin{array}{l}\text{Can you}\\\text{Could you}\end{array}\right.$ turn off the radio?

All could easily be used as directives, or, in more technical terms, could be used with the "force" of a directive, in this case a request to turn off the radio. Yet none has the exact surface form of a request, such as **Please turn off the radio**. Taken literally, the examples in 1 are assertions (representatives) about the speaker's attitudes and feelings; those in 2 and 3 are questions about the addressee's attitudes and abilities. Yet in context all can (and usually do) function as requests, and speakers of English easily recognize when they are being used as such. How can this be? When we consider the appropriateness conditions on the illocutionary act of requesting, we notice that 1–3 bear a clear relation to them. Requests have an appropriateness condition to the effect that the speaker wants the request to be carried out (this is the sincerity condition on requests). The sentences in 1 assert this condition. Requests also have appropriateness conditions stating that the addressee is able and may be willing to carry out the request. 2 and 3 question these conditions. In fact, 1–3 overtly express certain appropriateness conditions on the act, rather than the act itself.

Many illocutionary acts can be performed indirectly in analogous ways. For example, we have seen that informing includes appropriateness conditions to the effect that (a) the speaker believes the information is true; (b) the speaker has evidence for its truth; (c) the speaker has a reason for wanting the addressee to know it; and (d) it is possible the addressee is not aware of it. The illocutionary act of informing can be performed indirectly by asserting conditions a, b, or c, as in 4, 5, and 6, respectively, or by questioning condition d, as in 7:

4. I believe Smith is leaving tomorrow.

5. It seems Smith is leaving tomorrow.

6. Did you know that Smith is leaving tomorrow?

7. Are you aware that Smith is leaving tomorrow?

The generalization that emerges from 1–7 is that one can perform a speech act indirectly by stating an appropriateness condition that is associated with the speaker (as in 1, 4–6), or by questioning a condition associated with the hearer (as in 2, 3, 7). It has been suggested that such conventions be incorporated into the grammar in the form of rules called "Principles of conversation."[10] Such principles would establish the relations between the speech act literally performed and the one indirectly performed. There appear to be a great variety of such principles in English. For example, one can perform a speech act indirectly by:

A. Stating an obligation to perform it, as in:

    8. I must congratulate you on your work.

    9. I am obliged to object.

B. Stating an emotive attitude to performing it, as in:

    10. I regret to say that you should leave the country.

    11. I'm honored to declare my support for this candidate.

    12. I have the pleasure of revealing that you have won a motorized bobsled.

C. Asking permission to perform it, as in:

    13. May I compliment you on your aquarium?

    14. Allow me to confess my astonishment.

Sometimes these possibilities can be combined, as in:

    15. I'm afraid I'm going to have to ask you to come back tomorrow.

Principles of conversation do not always hold for all illocutionary acts. For example, we do not get:

    16. *May I $\begin{cases} \text{criticize} \\ \text{reprimand} \\ \text{forgive} \end{cases}$ you for your conduct at the game?

    17. *My dear, I am willing to give you some more tea. (as an offer of tea)

The problems with 16–17 arise from the fact that the literal form chosen requires one sort of relation between speaker and hearer while the speech act being performed indirectly requires another conflicting one. In 16, **reprimand**, **forgive**, and **criticize** all have an appropriateness condition that the speaker is in the superior position of judge. The permission-seeking form of the literal speech act, on the other hand, assumes the addressee is in authority. Apparently this contradiction causes the inappropriateness. 17 violates the rule of politeness that requires a host to humbly assume that the guest does not want what is being offered.

    The contextual constraints on indirect speech acts demonstrate once again that though different surface forms may be identical in illocutionary force, they need not be the same pragmatically. For instance, we noted earlier that lexicalized performative verbs like **state** and **request**, which are the most direct means for indicating illocutionary force, are characteristic of formal and written discourse of a contractual nature. There are clear practical and social reasons for this. When a speech act is going to have serious and strictly binding consequences for its participants, as contractual and legal procedures do, it is important that the exact illocutionary force be clear, especially when the speech act has undesirable consequences for the addressee. No one would be willing to consider him or herself under arrest if the sheriff were to say merely **Would you mind if I placed you under arrest?** In written communication, speakers are under a special burden to make themselves clear, because there is no ongoing dialogue to allow for immediate clarification or correction of misunderstandings. Moreover, explicit surface performatives are important in speech situations where there may be no prior basis of friendship or mutual trust among the participants, as in public discourse or dealings with institutions. Friends need not and prefer not to bind each other so explicitly by words, and are more likely to use indirect speech acts. When surface performatives occur in informal discourse, they are often used to add emphasis or express an emotive attitude, as in **I tell you, he had on a red shirt**; **I declare, you look like death warmed over**.

INDIRECT SPEECH ACTS AND THE COOPERATIVE PRINCIPLE

The account of indirect speech acts is made even more complicated by the fact that sentences which can be used to perform indirect speech acts can also be used to perform direct ones. For example, **I want to declare my support for this bill** could be an indirect declaration of support, but it could also be simply a literal statement of the speaker's desires, as in **I want to declare my support for this bill, but party loyalty simply doesn't permit it**; **Could you mow the lawn?** could be an indirect request, or a literal yes-no question accompanying a remark like **What was it like before you got your bionic arm?** In other words, sentences like these are potentially ambiguous in communicative function. The grammar must give an account of this ambiguity. The usual basis for distinguishing between a direct and an indirect speech act is contextual: It seems that indirect speech acts occur only when the context is such that the act literally performed would be obviously inappropriate in some way.[11] For example, **Can you turn down the radio?** taken literally as a question about the addressee's abilities is inappropriate if it is patently obvious that the addressee is capable of turning down the radio. In this context, where the literal act is ruled out by appropriateness conditions, the question can be used to perform some other act which, though different from the one literally performed, is associated with it in some way.

Indirect communication raises an interesting social question. Why doesn't a hearer, on encountering an obviously inappropriate utterance, simply decide that the speaker is using the language inappropriately, and leave it at that? What motivation is there for seeking a message behind the literal message? Indirect communication works only by virtue of a basic, shared assumption that when people speak and listen to each other, they normally do have the intention of accomplishing purposeful and effective communication in the context. This assumption is called the "Cooperative Principle,"[12] and it can be viewed as a large-scale appropriateness condition governing all language use. Basically, the Cooperative Principle represents our knowledge that verbal communication is an activity in which individuals work together to accomplish shared, mutually beneficial goals. The particular goals differ, of course, from speech situation to speech situation, but in the most general terms, being a cooperative speaker means speaking with a viable communicative purpose vis-à-vis the hearer in the context, and speaking in such a way that this purpose is recognizable to the hearer. Being a cooperative hearer means trusting that the speaker has a reasonable purpose in speaking, and doing the necessary work to discern that purpose. The Cooperative Principle is crucial to all communication (imagine a world, for example, in which whenever you asked for the time of day your addressee could never be sure what you wanted to know), but its role comes particularly to the fore in indirect communication, where language-users cooperate to the extent of relying on unspoken inferences to effect the communication. Failure to cooperate at this level gives rise to communicative misfires, as in this well-known joke:

18.   One farmer met another and said, "Hey, Sam, my mule's got distemper. What'd you give yours when he had it?"

"Turpentine," grunted Sam.

A week later they met again and the first farmer shouted, "Sam, I gave my mule turpentine like you said and it killed him."

"Did mine, too," nodded Sam.

Here, **What'd you give yours . . .** is literally a question, that is, a request for information. But the farmer implies that what he is really requesting is advice, that is, information that will help him cure his mule. Sam fails to infer this, and responds only to the literal meaning of the first farmer's utterance. The first farmer, assuming Sam is observing the Cooperative Principle, takes it for granted that Sam is responding to the intended meaning of his question, and is therefore recommending the turpentine. Notice that although Sam uses the language correctly at the literal level, we feel the misunderstanding is chiefly his fault, because making inferences and taking responsibility for creating them are a normal, required part of language use. In other words, we readers make sense of the joke by inferring that Sam is probably deliberately failing to cooperate. The less likely alternative is to infer that Sam lacks full communicative competence.

In thinking about the Cooperative Principle, as with any linguistic rule, it is important to keep in mind the distinction between competence and performance. Obviously, in reality people do not always speak purposefully or reasonably or comprehensibly, and hearers do not always "get" what speakers have in mind. Sometimes communicative breakdowns are unintentional; other times people genuinely choose not to fulfill the Cooperative Principle. People lie, for example, or withhold information, or try to confuse the addressee. Moreover, even at the level of competence, the Cooperative Principle works differently from one speech situation to another. Advertising, for example, often seems to involve a pretense that the communication is primarily for the benefit of the addressee, while the addressee knows that in reality the speaker has his or her own economic interests at heart. Cooperating with advertising, in other words, is quite different from cooperating with friendly advice. There are also speech situations where one might not want to speak of the Cooperative Principle as being in force at all, as, for example, with a prisoner of war under interrogation, where the prisoner's job is supposed to be to reveal a minimum of true information and to deceive if possible.

PRESUPPOSITION

In the previous section we discussed how literal meanings can imply other meanings. Sometimes these relations of implication are highly idiosyncratic and heavily dependent on the specific nonlinguistic context; in other cases they are extremely conventional and generalized. Another kind of meaning relationship whereby utterances convey more than they say is the relationship called "presupposition." Presupposition is illustrated by the following pair:

19. Bill realized that Sheila had borrowed his car.

20. Bill believed that Sheila had borrowed his car.

19 differs from 20 in that in 19 the speaker takes it for granted, or "presupposes" that Sheila did in fact borrow Bill's car, while in 20 this is not taken for granted. When 19 is negated, the presupposition is not affected by the negation:

21. Bill didn't realize that Sheila had borrowed his car.

also presupposes that Sheila had borrowed Bill's car. Hence the contrast between the pair:

22. *Bill didn't realize that Sheila had borrowed his car, and she hadn't.

23. Bill didn't believe that Sheila had borrowed his car, and she hadn't.

While 23 is perfectly acceptable, 22 is not, because what is asserted in the second conjunct (that Sheila did not borrow the car) contradicts what is pre-supposed in the first conjunct (that Sheila did borrow the car). The speaker of 22 is thus committed to two contradictory beliefs, and this produces an un-acceptability. In 23, where there is no such presupposition, there is no contra-diction. Presupposition is usually defined in terms of the property of persisting under negation. In somewhat formal terms, we can say that presupposition is a relation such that anyone who says X takes Y for granted and anyone who says not-X also takes Y for granted. Hence, we say that 24 and 25 below pre-suppose the existence of someone who is the First Lady:

24. The First Lady will propose a toast.

25. The First Lady will not propose a toast.

because the assumption of her existence is the same in both the affirmative and negative versions of the sentence. As these examples suggest, one of the best ways of testing for the presence of a presupposition, in assertions at least, is to negate the sentence and see if the presupposition persists unaffected. Applying this test, we can see that relative clauses systematically involve pre-suppositions. In both

26. The singer (whom) Jan loved was unfaithful.

27. The singer (whom) Jan loved was not unfaithful.

the speaker takes it for granted that Jan loved a singer, though what the speaker asserts in 26 is the opposite of what is asserted in 27. More generally, then, we can say that with relative clauses the speaker always presupposes the truth of the information in the clause.

Sometimes using a particular lexical item involves making a presupposi-tion. This is the case, for example, with **again**, as in:

28. Rita told the joke again.

where it is presupposed that Rita told the joke at least once before. Compare **back** in:

29. I insulted him back.

As 19–23 above illustrate, some of the verbs that take sentential comple-ments involve presupposing the truth of the complement, while others do not. 30 and 31 below give further examples of this contrast. In 30a and b, the truth of the *that*-complement is presupposed, while in 31a and b it is not:

30. a. I am surprised that this papaya is imported.
    b. I am not surprised that this papaya is imported.

31. a.   I suppose that this papaya is imported.
    b.   I don't suppose that this papaya is imported.

Other verbs which pattern with **be surprised** are **be significant, be irrelevant, amuse, comprehend, bear in mind, regret, resent** (all with *that-* and *for-to* complements), and all verbs with *Poss-ing* complements, for example, **annoy** and **flatter**. The truth of the complement is not presupposed, however, with verbs like **be likely, assume, seem, conclude, suggest, doubt, believe, think, be true, want**, and **tempt**.

Particular syntactic constructions may also involve presuppositions. One example is the so-called "cleft" sentence,[13] illustrated by:

32.   It was the marbles that Sheila lost.

33.   It was Sheila who lost the marbles.

In 32 the speaker presupposes that Sheila lost something and asserts that the something was the marbles. In 33 the speaker presupposes that someone lost the marbles and asserts that it was Sheila. Here again, you can test for the pre-supposition by negating the sentences. Another systematic instance of pre-supposition is the content question. The speaker of

34.   Which marbles did you lose?

presupposes that you lost some members of a preexisting set of marbles, and asks you to identify which ones.[14] More generally, all content questions involve presupposing everything except the specific piece or pieces of informa-tion being requested.

Like the other appropriateness conditions we have been discussing,[15] presuppositions can be used to achieve indirect effects. Thus, while the pre-supposition holds that Bill tried to open the door in:

35. a.   Bill managed to open the door.
    b.   Bill didn't manage to open the door.

it does not necessarily hold in:

35. c.   Bill managed to wreck the place all by himself.

In one interpretation, Bill did indeed intend to do the wrecking, but in another this sentence is ironic and implies that he was so inept that he wrecked it without trying. Similarly,

36.   Bill managed to get married within a few months.

can be interpreted literally or ironically. The irony lies in the speaker's implication that whatever Bill did was harmful to himself (or to others) and therefore he could not have intended to do it.

ANALYZING DISCOURSE

The processes discussed in the last few sections demonstrate that a good deal of what gets communicated through language is "unspoken" in the sense that it involves conveying meanings other than or in addition to the literal meaning of what is said. The importance of this fact emerges particularly clearly in the analysis of discourse. Language-users rely so heavily on these processes that almost invariably the ongoing coherence of any verbal exchange or any utterance longer than a sentence cannot be described without them.

The analysis of discourse is one of the least developed branches of linguistics at present, but at least it has been made clear that discourse has many kinds of organization in addition to the specific links between one sentence and the next. Though, at one level, extended discourses and speech exchanges can be viewed simply as sequences of individual illocutionary acts, they must also be seen as wholes structured at levels above that of the individual illocutionary act. Just as there are types and categories of illocutionary acts at the sentence level, so there are types and categories of extended utterances at the discourse level. Some obvious examples are sermons, interviews, prayers, letters, advertisements, oaths, press releases, stories, and speeches. These are referred to as "speech genres."[16] Literary genres will also be identified as speech genres. Though some speech genres may be universal, the repertory of speech genres does vary a good deal from one speech community to another. Like individual illocutionary acts, speech genres are described in terms of their formal characteristics, their communicative function, and their appropriateness conditions. Some involve just one speaker, like presidential addresses; others are structured as exchanges involving more than one speaker, such as the various kinds of debates and verbal duels, question and answer exchanges, and conversations.

Within a given speech genre, subgenres can often be identified. This is obviously true of literature, where the lyric genre, for example, has subclasses like the ode, elegy, and ballad. Likewise, within the category of formal speeches, we would want to distinguish subtypes like the funeral oration and the valedictory address; within the genre of conversation, we would distinguish face-to-face conversation from telephone conversation, and intimate conversation between members of an ingroup from conversation between members of an ingroup and outsiders.

Several speech genres may be included in the structure of one so-called "speech event." Speech events, sometimes considered the basic units of analysis for the study of discourse, are loosely defined as communicative routines that are viewed by the speech community as distinct wholes and characterized by special rules of verbal and nonverbal behavior. One conveniently clear-cut example of a speech event is a church service, which combines several genres in fixed sequence. A typical Protestant church service, for instance, begins with a call to worship followed by invocation, hymn, affirmation of faith, anthem, responsive reading, Scripture reading, pastoral prayer, the Lord's Prayer, dedication of the offering, hymn, sermon, prayer, hymn, benediction. These are associated with particular speakers (priest, congregation, or both) and nonverbal actions such as standing, kneeling, and bowing the head. A fairly recently developed speech event in our culture is the television talk show, made up of a sequence including an introductory monologue, introduction of a guest, and conversation with the guest, interspersed with advertisements and possibly with artistic performance by the guest. A single speech genre may constitute an entire speech event. The lecture as speech event, for example, may consist only of a lecture (one speech genre), or of a lecture followed by a question period (two speech genres).

In the next few pages, we will be examining in further detail the structure of two genres that play a large role in most English-speaking cultures and that are also of particular interest in regard to literary analysis, namely, conversation and narrative.

Conversation

We do not usually think of conversation as being highly organized like a church service. But the fact that conversation is relatively spontaneous does not mean it is unstructured. Here we will take a close look at two aspects of conversational structure, openings and closings, and the system of turn-taking.[17]

Conversations almost always open with an exchange of greetings involving an initiator and a responder. As elsewhere in the linguistic system, styles must be used consistently. Selection of the greeting form by the initiator A immediately establishes degree of formality. Often the responder B will simply repeat A's formula, as in A: **Hi**—B: **Hi**, or A: **Good Morning**—B: **Good Morning**. Or there may be variation, within limits; A: **Hi**—B: **Oh, hello**. But clearly there are boundaries between styles. The sequence A: **Hi, Bill**—B: **Good Morning, Professor Zooks** immediately suggests either a power relationship (B is being respectful) or, if the speakers are peers, unwillingness on the part of B to accept the intimacy A wants to establish. When interlocutors are strangers, they must introduce themselves in certain circumstances. Whether to do so, and how to do so, is also rule-governed. One would not usually introduce oneself when asking directions of a stranger or a policeman. Here the attention-getter **Excuse me** is more appropriate than **Hello**, and B's response will usually be a minimal **uhm uhm** or **yes**?

Conversational endings, like openings, usually involve a paired exchange. Socially, endings are somewhat problematic, because the person initiating the ending is in effect choosing silence over continued talk. In many communities, once a conversation is started, silence is felt to be unwelcome. Silences of more than a few seconds are seen as signs of some problem in the communication, indicating disapproval, irritation, boredom, or incomprehension. This is by no means true of all cultures; in fact Anglo-American culture is somewhat notorious for its intolerance of silence. Given this intolerance, in initiating an ending, A (the initiator) has to find a way to arrange for silence without creating disapproval or a sense of failure on B's part. Endings are usually prefaced by a transition like **Well ... so ... OK ...** followed by such devices as a return to the beginning of the conversation (**Well, I'm really glad I ran into you**; **So, we agree on that election question**), an excuse concerning other obligations (**I have to go, the library closes in an hour**), or an oblique suggestion that B should go do something (**Well, have a good time at the concert tonight** or **Don't work too hard**). B can refuse the closing by initiating again (**Listen, before you go, I must tell you . . .**), or B can agree to close, usually by saying OK and possibly referring to a next encounter (**See you soon**), followed by A: **Good-by**—B: **Good-by**. Conversational endings are particularly difficult to achieve appropriately if the initiator of the ending is not going to physically leave the scene. For example, between adjacent passengers on a train or bus, once a conversation is begun, one usually does not terminate it explicitly until the end of the trip. To arrange for silence in these circumstances, A's usual recourse is to indicate through gesture (looking away, picking up a book) or un-responsiveness that silence is desired, and then hope B will pick up the clues.

Once a conversation is opened, it continues, as a rule, to progress according to the initiator-responder model. A initiates a topic, B acknowledges A's contribution, then assumes in turn the role of initiator. B's obligation to respond to A before initiating helps guarantee the coherence of the exchange. Thus the conversation proceeds by a system of turn-taking, often compared to a game in which players pass a ball from one to another. In conversation, what is passed around is, figuratively speaking, the "floor," that is, the right to speak and have the attention of the other participants. The conversation turn-taking system has a variety of mechanisms whereby the floor is passed from the current speaker, A, to the next speaker, B. One way is for A to initiate a change of turns by asking a question (**Do you know any more about this?**) or by adding an interrogative tag like **don't you think?** or **isn't it?** to a statement. When more than one potential speaker is present, A can even select the next speaker by name (**What do you think, Bill? Bill probably disagrees with me here.**). Sometimes a look is enough. Alternatively, A can simply end his or her turn, and leave the floor up for grabs. In this case, the floor passes to whoever starts talking first. If no one does, A will often pick up the thread again and initiate a new demand for response. Even when the current speaker does not explicitly give up the floor, there are specific points in the utterance where others may legitimately interrupt, such as the break at the end of a clause or sentence. If you listen carefully, you will notice that B, the person who wants to talk next, will often anticipate such a break and start talking before A has finished. This is a way of asking A to give up the floor. You may also notice that A, in anticipation of B's interruption, will often fill pauses with **uh**, or even repeat a phrase in order to retain the floor.

In performance, the turn-taking system does not completely guarantee orderly conversation, of course. For example, when two people start talking in unison there is often a brief period of confusion before it is decided who will defer. In heated or enthusiastic conversation, there are often battles for the floor and relatively long periods with more than one speaker talking. In these cases, a third person is entitled to intervene and decide who will talk first.

The turn-taking system is not unique to conversation. All speech genres and speech events have "floor" rules governing which participants get to talk, and at what points. In some genres, like the lecture, only one participant speaks. In others, like the press conference or questioning of witnesses at a trial, some participants take the floor only to ask questions, others only to respond to the questions. In institutionalized speech situations, a moderator is often appointed to designate who gets the floor. This is often the job of the chairperson in a meeting, for example, who is guided by rules of order.

To illustrate how these rules governing conversation work, we will examine some excerpts from the text of a recorded telephone conversation. In phone calls, the initiator A is the person who places the call, and the ring of the phone substitutes for initiating phrases like **Excuse me** or **Hi**. In situations where secretaries, operators, or other intermediaries intervene, it is they who summon B and identify A to B, so that the sequence opens with B's personal greeting to A. This is the case in the conversation we are going to examine. The participants are two male government officials, personally well-acquainted and of similar rank. They are discussing a government problem. First, the opening sequence:

A1	E	(*places call*)
B1	K	Hi, John
A2	E	Hi, General. How are you?
B2	K	Pretty good, how are you?
A3	E	How was the golf?
B3	K	Half good and half bad.
A4	E	First half good?
B4	K	Well, the middle was good and
A5	E	I want to bring you up to day on what I have been doing. For about the last three weeks. . .[18]

B1 and A2 are the greetings; from A2 **How are you?** to the end of B4 is a transition between the greetings and the information section of the conversation, which the participants use to reestablish friendly contact. In A5, A states his purpose in initiating the conversation, that being to volunteer information to B that A believes B wants or needs. Notice that A interrupts B4 to begin the information section, but does so at an appropriate point, namely the syntactic break at the end of a main clause.

In the exchange that follows this opening, A presents his information and B speaks only to respond to A (e.g., **No kidding?**) or to ask A to confirm or clarify information. When A appears to have completed his task of passing on information, B attempts to initiate a turn:

A16 . . . And I find that I now have very little to add to what Magruder had already given the U.S. Attorney.

B16 K That's not good.

A17 E I felt that I should go forward and at least advise you of this and to—

B17 K John, at this point, it seems to me that you are going to have to be very careful.

A18 E Let me spoil your afternoon completely, will you? One of the things Magruder told me was—[19]

In A16, A is still initiating, with B responding (B16). When A moves to close the topic (A17), B starts a new one at the very first opportunity, the syntactic break at the end of a main clause, and uses A's name to add a sense of urgency and seriousness. B's move into the role of advice-giver and out of the role of information-receiver drastically alters the role structure and the power structure of the situation. A rejects this move by explicitly requesting the floor (A18 **Let me . . . will you?**) at the end of B's first advice-giving clause.

Shortly after, A moves to end the conversation, but B finds a way to re-initiate his advice-giving:

A35 E Yeah. A list. OK, my boy. I just wanted you to have a nice time this evening.

B35 K (*expletive removed*)

A36 E Don't forget my tender that if there is anyway that any of this hearsay of mine that I have collected is in anyway useful, I would be glad to make it available. My present thinking is that it could add very little to what Magruder just told me.

B36 K Thinking of Magruder as a primary witness type. You better be very careful what you do from here on out, John. Don't put yourself in the position of—

A37 E Prejudicing anybody's rights.

B37 K With respect to the Commission—

A38 E That is why I am calling you, my dear.

B38 K Yours is a very goddamn delicate line as to what you do to get information to give to the President and what you can do in giving information to the Department of Justice, you know, to enforce the law.

A39   E   Well you are my favorite law enforcement officer.
B39   K   (*unintelligible*)
A40   E   Do you want me to give you anything additional on Monday?
B40   K   Who did you talk to, John?
A41   E   What do you mean? Mitchell and Magruder.
B41   K   Those are the only two?
A42   E   Well, no I have been talking to people for three weeks. I have
talked to everybody but the milkman.[20]

This exchange is particularly interesting, because here B does succeed in taking over the role of initiator in spite of A's resistance. A35 moves to close with an ironic go-and-do-something-else remark, B35 responds, A36 adds a closing summary of A's position, returning to the opening of the conversation. In B36, rather than moving toward a close, B responds to A36 (**Thinking of M . . .**) and initiates the topic attempted earlier in B17, namely advice. There ensues something of a battle. First A subverts B's advice by interrupting to complete B's sentence himself (A37); when B tries to initiate a new topic (B37), A again interrupts and indicates the topic is not relevant to him. B tries again (B38), avoiding interruption by constructing his utterance without any internal sentence divisions, using the filler **you know** and the intensity marker **God damn**. A's response is a compliment (A39), which is apparently intended to placate B, but which again implies B's advice is superfluous. Notice that A39 and the **my dear** of A38 are devices typical of men's speech when being condescending to women, suggesting that A is subtly treating B as an inferior here. This **my dear** and the **my boy** of A35 contrast markedly with A's initial, flattering address form, **General** (A2).

In A40, A again moves to close, referring back to his role as information-giver. B, evidently annoyed or impatient, ignores the move to close and does not respond to A40 at all. Instead, B simply preempts the role of initiator with a blunt request for information (B40) and remains the initiator for the rest of the exchange.

Before moving on to narrative, we turn briefly to another set of rules that frequently has a great impact on conversation, the rules of politeness. Politeness rules are second nature to most of us because we painstakingly learned them as children—whether or not we ever managed to observe them. But looked at from a sociolinguistic viewpoint, politeness is a complex and curious phenomenon indeed. The basic rule of politeness seems to be: Regardless of the reality, act as if the addressee is superior. One of the most obvious effects of this norm is that it rules out speech acts that require the speaker to be in authority, namely, commands. If one is being polite, one always phrases directives as requests, not commands, and makes them very indirect: not **Hand me that phone book** nor even **Will you hand me that phone book, please?** but **Could I ask you to hand me that phone book?** or **Would you mind handing me that phone book?** These latter forms also illustrate another rule of politeness, namely: Give your addressee options. The indirect requests just quoted do this, at least on the surface of things, by offering the addressee the linguistic option of merely answering the question rather than carrying out the request. The option, of course, is anything but genuine, but it matters nonetheless. Robin Lakoff[21] has pointed out another side to this coin; that is, when being polite, one does use commands to make offers, as in **Have a little of this sherry, Mr. Maelstrom; Do call whenever you like;** or **You must try these kumquats.** Lakoff's hypothesis is that in using such forms, the speaker is still deferring by assuming that what is offered is so inferior that the addressee must be ordered to accept it. The working of these rules is made especially clear when we look at situations where it is inappropriate to be polite, namely, situations in which the speaker is clearly in authority over the addressee. Thus, between a mother and her child, polite forms are inappropriate, and therefore can be used sarcastically, as in **Would you mind wiping your feet?** or **That's right, help yourself to the cookie jar.**

Exchanges in which all participants are being polite can look quite strange from a linguistic point of view, because it means everyone is treating everyone else as his or her superior, that is, everyone pretends equally to be unequal to everyone else. So we get odd exchanges like **May I come in?—Please do,** where a request is answered by another request (compare the bluntness of **Mommy, may I go outside?—Please do**), or **Have some more tea—Thank you, I will,** where a command is answered by a thank-you (contrast the oddness of **Stop this shouting—Thank you, I will**).

In addition to the "act inferior" and the "give options" rules, three other related rules of politeness have been hypothesized: "Do not impose," "Try to make the other person feel good," and "Help the other person save face." These rules particularly affect the content of what is said. Trying to make the other person feel good often involves not saying things one thinks are relevant, or even saying things one doesn't have much faith in. Not imposing involves, among other things, avoiding topics viewed as private or personal, even if information about them is relevant to other matters at hand. From one perspective, cases like these suggest that politeness rules actually override other rules that are otherwise part of cooperative speaking, such as rules about sincerity, or rules about contributing all the relevant information one has, or rules about expressing oneself clearly and avoiding obscurity.[22] Consequently, in certain "business conversations," like the one we just analyzed, politeness rules do not have to be in play.

Narrative

Conversation is typically thought of in nonliterary terms. However, it plays an important role in literature, especially prose fiction and drama, where it is usually termed "dialogue." Conversely, students of literature tend to think of narrative as a literary genre typical of prose fiction or epic poetry. However, narrative is found in a wide number of contexts. In addition to nonfictional narratives such as occur in autobiography and memoirs, narratives also occur in letters, court testimony, news reports, math problems, advertisements, speeches, jokes, interviews, and all manner of conversations. Narration is essentially a way of linguistically representing past experience, whether real or imagined.[23] The basic characteristic of narrative discourse is that the order in which it presents events in speech is the order in which those events are claimed to have occurred in time. As an example, consider this anecdote recounted in *Newsweek* magazine (the sentences have been numbered for convenience).

> [1.] Officials at Pepperdine University, a church-run institution in Los Angeles, had heard that oil-rich nations like Iran wanted to tap U.S. academic resources—and were willing to pay. [2.] So in April, Pepperdine president William Banowsky traveled to Teheran, detailed the virtues of his school and presented an honorary doctor of laws degree to His Imperial Majesty Shah Mohammed Reza Pahlavi. [3.] Last month, Banowsky's diligence paid off. [4.] The Shah gave Pepperdine the largest academic grant it has ever received: $1 million for the university's school of education.[24]

If the order of the clauses in the second sentence is changed to read:

37. In April, Pepperdine president William Banowsky presented an honorary degree to the Shah, detailed to him the virtues of his school, and traveled to Teheran.

a different temporal sequence of events is presented. In the description of narrative, clauses like these, which present the individual events, are the basic units of analysis and are called "narrative clauses." Narrative clauses, as in the above example, are main clauses consisting minimally of a subject NP followed by a verb in the simple past tense (or sometimes, by convention, the simple present), and an object NP if required by the verb. The original passage contains four such clauses, using **traveled, detailed, presented** (sentence 2), and **gave** (sentence 3). The first sentence, however, contains no narrative clauses. Sentence 3 appears to contain a narrative clause, but it does not, since **paid off** is not temporally ordered with respect to **gave**. The function of these two nonnarrative sentences will be discussed in a moment.

Notice that we can easily alter the passage so that it does not meet our definition of a narrative at all:

38. Last month the Shah of Iran gave Pepperdine University a grant of $1 million for its school of education. This grant was apparently the result of a trip to Teheran made by Pepperdine president

William Banowsky last April for the purpose of presenting an
honorary degree to the Shah and detailing the virtues of his
school.

In other words, direct narration is not the only way of representing events
and experience linguistically.

Apart from the minimal definition just given, the form of narrative
utterances varies a great deal according to their function and context. For
example, consider this excerpt from a scholarly historical account:

> [1.] In addition, the United States cut off arms to Villa and Zapata.
> [2.] In retaliation, Villa launched raids against U.S. citizens, some of which
> brought him across the border. [3.] The United States responded with a
> large-scale military buildup along the border and an invasion force led by
> General Pershing. [4.] Finally, the United States threatened armed force
> against Zapata as well, intimidating many of the Zapatistas into seeking
> amnesties from Carranza and into laying down their arms (Womack,
> 1969: 300–317, 346–351).[25]

In addition to narrative clauses, this passage contains many elements emphasizing cause and effect relations among events. In sentence 2, **in retaliation**
explicitly establishes causality, and **some of which brought him across the
border** is there to imply the causal basis for the next sentence. In sentence 3,
the actual events are made objects of **respond**, a verb that asserts an effect and
presupposes a cause. In sentence 4, the final actions of the Zapatistas are
presented in result clauses rather than narrative clauses: The threat causes
intimidation, which causes the seeking of amnesties. This emphasis on
causality within a narrative framework is not surprising in this context, since
one of the historian's main roles is to elucidate causality within chronology.

Much of the time, causal sequence in narrative is simply implied by temporal sequence, so that in a sentence like:

39.   Jesse James held up the stagecoach and then Marshall Dillon
went after him with a posse.

we infer a causal connection between the two clauses, though none is explicitly
made. Even the temporal link can be implied through simple coordination. If
temporal **then** is removed from 39, the temporal and causal connections are
still implied. On the whole, we tend to make such causal and temporal inferences whenever they are plausible, given our knowledge of the world. This
is a tendency advertisers readily exploit, as in **I chose Sorbilex and married this
man**. Notice that in the last sentence of the passage on Villa and Zapata, the
author repeats the preposition **into** expressly to avoid implying temporal and
causal sequence between **seeking amnesties** and **laying down arms**.

We have said that the form of a narrative utterance will vary according to its communicative function and context. In analyzing narratives, we must keep these factors in mind in order to account for those elements that are not part of the minimal narrative structure. For instance, the *Newsweek* text on Pepperdine's president quoted above is the opening paragraph of an article about contributions made to American universities by the oil-producing nations. Its role is both to give a sample case and to excite the attention of readers so they will read the rest of the article. While the narrative clauses begin in sentence 2, sentence 1 provides an "orientation" that identifies the participants in the upcoming narrative and provides the necessary background information. In order to make clear the significance being attributed to the events, the text also provides "evaluation," as, for example, in the last sentence when the Iranian grant is compared with other grants and revealed to be unusually large. Sentence 3 is also part of the evaluation, telling us that the episode is to be viewed as a victory (**paid off**) and, moreover, a victory for the quality of **diligence**. If we change only these evaluative expressions, the whole meaning of the anecdote changes, even though the narrative sequence remains the same. For instance:

40.   . . . Last month, Banowsky's lack of subtlety was soundly re-
    proached. The Shah gave Pepperdine the unexpectedly meager
    sum of $1 million for its school of education.

In both the original and 40, the evaluation functions to show what attitude is being taken toward the events (victory, defeat) and what makes those events worth reporting in the first place (they are unusual or unexpected).

Finally, the attention-getting power of the text depends on its having a dramatic structure or "plot" set in motion by a "complicating action" (the protagonist travels to Teheran to seek favors from the Shah); and closes with a "resolution" (the Shah grants a favor).

Orientation, evaluation, complicating action, and resolution are key components in the structure of a particular category of narrative discourse, namely, the story. Not all narrative utterances are stories. Historical discourse, for example, or courtroom testimony can be narrative, without being stories complete with plots and evaluation (indeed, court witnesses are supposed to narrate without evaluating). The story is distinguished by the fact that it is an utterance type used when one is recapitulating experience for display purposes, rather than for simple information-giving purposes or for some other purpose. The attention-getting anecdote from *Newsweek* has such a displaying function. So do the narratives of personal experience which commonly occur in conversation and letters, and which also have story structure. Particularly important to the displaying function of stories is evaluation. Evaluation serves not only to convey what attitude the speaker is taking to the events being narrated, but also to convey why the speaker believes the events were worthy of display at all.

Narrative in Literature

In narrative literary genres too, the model of the story just outlined holds as the norm. Of course, literary narratives are usually much longer than the anecdotes we have been discussing. Orientations in novels range in length from a few lines to whole chapters, sometimes set apart as prologues. Plots in novels vary widely in degree of complexity. Longer narrative works like novels very often give us stories within stories, as illustrated by this excerpt from the opening chapter of Mark Twain's novel *Pudd'nhead Wilson*:

In that same month of February Dawson's Landing gained a new citizen. This was Mr. David Wilson, a young fellow of Scotch parentage. He had wandered to this remote region from his birthplace in the interior of the State of New York to seek his fortune. He was twenty-five years old, college-bred, and had finished a post-college course in an Eastern law school a couple of years before.

He was a homely, freckled, sandy-haired young fellow, with an intelligent blue eye that had frankness and comradeship in it and a covert twinkle of a pleasant sort. But for an unfortunate remark of his, he would no doubt have entered at once upon a successful career at Dawson's Landing. But he made his fatal remark the first day he spent in the village, and it "gaged" him. He had just made the acquaintance of a group of citizens when an invisible dog began to yelp and snarl and howl and make himself very comprehensively disagreeable, whereupon young Wilson said, much as one who is thinking aloud—

"I wish I owned half of that dog."

"Why?" somebody asked.

"Because I would kill my half."

The group searched his face with curiosity, with anxiety even, but found no light there, no expression that they could read. They fell away from him as from something uncanny, and went into privacy to discuss him. One said:

"'Pears to be a fool."

"'Pears?" said another. "*Is*, I reckon you better say."

"Said he wished he owned *half* of the dog, the idiot," said a third. "What did he reckon would become of the other half if he killed his half? Do you reckon he thought it would live?"

"Why, he must have thought it, unless he *is* the downrightest fool in the world; because, if he hadn't thought it, he would have wanted to own the whole dog, knowing that if he killed his half and the other half died, he would be responsible for that half just the same as if he had killed that half instead of his own. Don't it look that way to you, gents?"

"Yes, it does. If he owned one half of the general dog, it would be so; if he owned one end of the dog and another person owned the other end, it would be so, just the same; particularly in

the first case, because if you kill one half of a general dog there
40   ain't any man that can tell whose half it was, but if he owned one
end of the dog, maybe he could kill his end of it and—"

"No, he couldn't either; he couldn't and not be responsible
if the other end died, which it would. In my opinion the man ain't
in his right mind."

"In my opinion he hain't *got* any mind."

No. 3 said: "Well, he's a lummox, any way."

"That's what he is," said No. 4; "he's a labrick—just a
Simon-pure labrick, if ever there was one."

"Yes, sir, he's a dam fool, that's the way I put him up," said
50   No. 5. "Anybody can think different that wants to, but those are
my sentiments."

"I'm with you, gentlemen," said No. 6. "Perfect jackass—yes,
and it ain't going too far to say he is a pudd'nhead. If he ain't a
pudd'nhead, I ain't no judge, that's all."

Mr. Wilson stood elected. The incident was told all over the
town, and gravely discussed by everybody. Within a week he had
lost his first name; Pudd'nhead took its place. In time he came to
be liked, and well liked, too; but by that time the nickname had got
well stuck on, and it stayed. That first day's verdict made him a
60   fool, and he was not able to get it set aside, or even modified. The
nickname soon ceased to carry any harsh or unfriendly feeling with
it, but it held its place, and was to continue to hold its place for
twenty long years.[26]

In relation to the novel as a whole, this excerpt is part of the orientation
establishing a tone of black comedy and some of the major elements in the
plot: responsibility, the difference between appearance and reality, relationships among pairs (here two halves of a dog, later two boys). At the same
time, the excerpt stands on its own as a self-contained story. It begins with
an orientation (lines 2–13) describing the main character and setting the
scene for the narration. (Notice the verbs in the orientation are typically
descriptive, not narrative: for example, **was**, which describes a state, not
an action, and **had wandered**, which does refer to an action, but not in the
simple past.) The complicating action occurs in the first narrative clause,
a . . . dog began to yelp (15), and the resolution takes place in the last narrative clause, **Mr. Wilson stood elected** (line 55).

In addition, the Twain text illustrates the usual opening and closing
routines for stories. The closing routine is known as the "coda," and takes the
form of a kind of rounding-off statement after the resolution of the plot. In
the Twain passage, the coda consists of the rest of the paragraph after **Mr.
Wilson stood elected** (55). Typical of codas, it describes and evaluates the
ultimate consequences of the events, and moves away from the time of the
narrative back toward the narrator's present, as with the formulaic **They lived
happily ever after**. Such time shifts have obvious similarities to the "go-and-
do-something-else" closings in conversations. Notice too that the shift to

coda is indicated formally in this text by the tense shift in lines 56–57 (**had lost** not narrative **lost**).[27]

The opening routine for stories is illustrated by the first sentence of this passage, which briefly summarizes the whole story before the actual telling takes place. This is called the "abstract," and it commonly consists of a summary of the content, or simply a comment on its tellability, as in **By geez, this was a good one**. In written texts, abstracts often consist only of a title, and perhaps titles of individual chapters. In the early days of the novel, book and chapter titles used to give elaborate plot summaries, as illustrated by the full title of *Moll Flanders* quoted on page 212. Older novels often also have elaborate codas—the traditional epilogue recounting the ultimate fates of all the characters.

If we add the two components, coda and abstract, to the parts of the story already introduced, we can come up with an initial, rudimentary definition of a story as an utterance that begins with an abstract, followed by an orientation, then a narrative sequence that begins with a complicating action and ends with a resolution, then a coda. In addition, all sections of the story may contain evaluative and orientative information. The story conveys a recognizable evaluative stance toward what is reported, and deals with events or experiences the speaker believes to be unusual, unexpected, or otherwise worthy of display. When writers of novels and short stories do not conform to this model of a story, they are understood to be intentionally departing from it. For instance, it is common for written narratives to begin *in medias res*, that is, without an explicit orientation section, and it is also common for them to be open-ended, that is, lacking a resolution of the plot. In such cases, the departure from the model is meaningful in itself; we perceive the author as having intentionally avoided fulfilling our expectations in order to achieve some intended effect. In short, the model of the story itself functions as a kind of generic norm.

Since utterances are acts, they can form part of the plot sequence in a story. In fact, in the *Pudd'nhead Wilson* anecdote just quoted, the events that make up the plot are almost exclusively verbal events. The crisis is provoked by Wilson's "fatal remark," the resolution is the townspeople's act of *naming* him, and the sequence in between consists chiefly of the ordered series of utterances by which the name is arrived at. The only nonverbal events take place in lines 21–23, in the narrative clauses containing **searched**, **fell away**, and **went**, and even these actions are meaningful mainly as sociolinguistic gestures. To make absolutely explicit the workings of this verbal plot, it is helpful to know something about speech acts and the structure of conversation as a genre. What takes place in this story is a communicative mishap whereby Wilson accidentally provokes a breakdown of the Cooperative Principle. Here the speech context is a delicate one, a conversation between members of an ingroup and a stranger who would like to become a member of the ingroup, set in the home territory of the ingroup. Such a situation involves a degree of suspicion if not hostility on the part of the ingroup, and this lack of trust and prior acquaintance makes the Cooperative Principle particularly vulnerable to collapse. The dog's barking adds to the difficulty, and Wilson tries to ease the tension by introducing the dog problem into the conversation as a topic so that all can acknowledge it. Moreover, he tries to do this in a humorous way, to indicate that he does not consider the problem serious and does not want it to put an end to the conversation. Instead, his attempted joke itself puts an end to the conversation by provoking a breakdown of the Cooperative Principle. How does this happen?

Wilson's remark in line 20, taken literally, is appropriate only if Wilson holds the curious belief that it is possible to kill half a dog (provided one owns the half, that is). Of course Wilson does not intend his remark to be taken literally, but rather as an ironic (and humorous) expression of a wish to kill the whole dog in order to make it stop barking. Wilson's interlocutors, however, fail to make the inferences necessary to arrive at this interpretation, and they instead take the remark literally, thus inferring that Wilson sincerely holds these obviously erroneous beliefs about the world. Shocked, no one is able to think of an appropriate response to Wilson's remark, so conversational turn-taking breaks down and, after a ghastly pause, the ingroup "falls away" from the newcomer.

Falling away is the townsmen's way of opting out of one speech situation in order to shift into another, the private conversation among peers, whose purpose here is to arrive at some collective interpretation and evaluation of Wilson's unexpected behavior (which cannot be done in Wilson's presence). As is usual in problem-solving and decision-making gatherings, turn-taking is strictly observed, something Twain stresses by using numbers to refer to the speakers on the second round of turns and by comparing the process to an election (line 55). The conversation can be readily analyzed in terms of initiation and response and in terms of the illocutionary acts performed. Speaker 1 initiates with a *hypothesis*, speaker 2 responds, then initiates, making the hypothesis into a *claim*. Speaker 3 initiates, *recapitulating* Wilson's words, then formulating the *questions* to be discussed; speaker 4 responds to 3's questions, initiates with *arguments* to support his responses, and passes on the floor with an *indirect request* for agreement. Speaker 5 responds by *agreeing*, and initiates with more *arguments*. He is interrupted at the end of a clause by speaker 6, who responds to him by *disagreeing*, initiates with another *argument*, then delivers a *judgment*. After this, each speaker in turn delivers his *judgment* after responding to the previous one.

The townsmen's discussion is a precise parody of the process of conversational inference. Rather than hypothesizing that Wilson might not have been speaking literally, they try to imagine under what circumstances it would be possible for Wilson to believe in his literal remark. The only likely circumstance they can come up with is that Wilson is mentally incompetent, and they record this verdict publicly by selecting a name for him which reflects the kind and degree of incompetence. What the reader has been inferring is, of course, rather different. For the reader, the townsmen's discussion only makes sense if one assumes that their ability to handle indirect communication is abnormally limited. Hence we infer that it is they rather than Wilson who are lacking in intellectual resources.

ANALYZING FICTIONAL DISCOURSE

The preceding analysis was intended to illustrate how speech act theory and discourse analysis can be used to make explicit the internal workings of a text. However, in literary studies, speech act theory and pragmatics have chiefly been applied not to the analysis of specific texts, but rather to large-scale problems in literary theory.[28] Current interest in speech act theory and pragmatics on the part of literary scholars is due mainly to the fact that these approaches give a new perspective on a central concern of literary theory, namely, the relations between reader, author, and text. The discussion in this chapter will focus on these relatively abstract issues rather than stressing textual analysis as in previous chapters. As we have seen, phonology, syntax, and semantics tend to direct attention to the internal structure of a text, and encourage the view of the text as an autonomous object. Such a view provides no way of talking about the author and reader, though it is clear that any adequate theory of literature must provide some such way. Pragmatics corrects this view by requiring that a text be viewed not as an object but as an act of communication between a writer and a public.

Ironically enough, when speech act theory was initially applied to literature, the first thing that was noticed was that it didn't seem to apply at all. Many of the rules governing illocutionary acts did not seem to hold for illocutionary acts in works of literature. For instance, in *Pudd'nhead Wilson*, Mark Twain says **In that same month of February Dawson's Landing gained a new citizen**. This sentence has the form of an assertion, but many of the appropriateness conditions on assertions do not seem to be in force here, in particular, the conditions that the speaker believes what is being asserted is true and that the speaker has evidence for its truth. In the Twain sentence, it does not matter whether Twain believed it was true (though he certainly did not) nor whether he had evidence of its truth. In fact, the sentence doesn't even seem to constitute an assertion. Assertions consist of a speaker making a commitment to the truth of something, and Twain here makes no such commitment. Likewise, when a command is made in a poem, like "Carry me back to old Virginny," it need not be the case that old Virginny exists, or that the poet at the time of writing actually did want to be taken back there, or believed some addressee was in a position to carry out this order, and so on. And again, it would seem that this utterance does not even constitute a command, since its speaker is not actually undertaking to get some addressee to do something. What we are talking about here, obviously, is the nature of fictional discourse.[29] Evidently, in fictional discourse illocutionary acts are appropriate even though their appropriateness conditions may not be fulfilled. This observation has led many linguists and critics to claim that what defines fictional discourse is the fact that appropriateness conditions, and the force of the act itself, are in some way suspended or, put another way, the usual connections between words and the world are severed, and utterances cease to "do" anything at all. Instead, fictional discourses are "mimetic" speech acts; they pretend to do things. Twain in his sentence pretends to make an assertion; the poet in "Carry me back to old Virginny" pretends to issue a command. Another way of putting this is to say that appropriateness conditions are suspended with respect to the author, and transferred to a fictional speaker, or "narrator";[30] the author pretends that someone performs the illocutionary acts. The motivation for this approach is particularly evident in what we call "first person" fictional discourse, such as *Moll Flanders* or Eliot's poem "The Love Song of J. Alfred Prufrock," where a fictional speaker is explicitly identified as a character, is given a name, and refers to him or herself as **I**. Thus, in analyzing a sentence like Moll Flanders's **I sang better, by which I mean I had a better voice**, we have to think of two speakers, the narrator Moll at one level and the author Defoe at another. I in the sentence refers to Moll, and it is Moll who is responsible for fulfilling the appropriateness conditions on the discourse, which include being truthful, not giving too much or too little information, being coherent, being stylistically correct, and so on. Thus when Moll makes claims that seem unlikely to us, or that seem distortive, it is she we suspect of being unreliable, not Defoe.

In "third person" and some first person works (especially lyric poems), the narrator or fictional speaker is not explicitly identified as someone other than the author. The fictional speaker in these cases is often referred to as a "persona" of the author. While we are used to first person narrators being highly individualized, we tend to think of third person ones as being all pretty much the same. But this is quite mistaken. For instance, the fictional speaker narrating Barthelme's "Edward and Pia" (page 168) is a highly individualized one indeed, being either someone whose idea of a story differs markedly from our own, or someone who doesn't know how to tell a story, or someone who is deliberately telling a deviant story, or someone who lives in a world where experience is understood very differently from the way we understand it.

Having claimed that every fictional discourse has a fictional speaker, we may now ask what these fictional speakers talk about and who they talk to. The obvious, and fairly traditional, answers are that they talk about fictional worlds and talk to fictional addressees in a fictional speech situation. Sometimes this situation is highly particularized in a work, as is the case, for instance, in Robert Browning's poem "My Last Duchess," which consists of a monologue uttered by a fictional duke as he shows a portrait of his late wife to a visitor. The job of the real world reader, then, is to "contextualize" the fictional discourse, that is, to infer information about the fictional speaker, speech situation, and world from the text. This is the process by which readers are said to "enter into" or "construct" the fictional world of a novel or poem.[31]

To do this, readers rely on the same processes of deduction and inference they use in conversation. When we read the opening of J. D. Salinger's *The Catcher in the Rye*:

> If you really want to hear about it, the first thing you'll probably want to know is where I was born, and what my lousy childhood was like, and how my parents were occupied and all before they had me, and all that David Copperfield kind of crap, but I don't feel like going into it, if you want to know the truth.[32]

we infer a speech situation in which an **I** is addressing some **you** who has asked the **I** to recount his life. This **I** is distinctly hostile toward the **you**, and is not fully convinced that the **you** sincerely does want to hear about his life (as communicated by the word **really**). Notice that this is virtually the reverse of the typical storytelling situation, where a speaker asks permission to tell a story whose contents he thinks will interest or divert his audience. Here someone else requests the story, and the speaker has grave doubts both about whether the request was sincere and whether his story is really worth hearing about. The passage even more specifically denies the usual model for autobiography, which includes an opening description of the circumstances under which the speaker was born. In fact, the fictional speech situation here is a therapy session in a psychiatric institution. Slightly more difficult to contextualize is this opening, from Henry James's story "The Beast in the Jungle":

> What determined the speech that startled him in the course of their encounter scarcely matters, being probably but some words spoken by himself quite without intention—spoken as they lingered and slowly moved together after their renewal of acquaintance. He had been conveyed by friends an hour or two before to the house at which she was staying; the party of visitors at the other house, of whom he was one, and thanks to whom it was his theory, as always, that he was lost in the crowd, had been invited over to luncheon.[33]

The first clause here presupposes a dialogue in which someone has asked the question, **What determined the speech that startled him?** or its equivalent. The questioner could be an interlocutor in a storytelling situation, or the narrator questioning himself. The word **probably** tells us the narrator does not know the answer to the question, while **scarcely** indicates that the narrator thinks the answer does in fact matter, but not very much. The opening sentence thus sets up the sense of uncertainty and of the presence of hidden knowledge, which is to become a main theme in the story.

In the next chapter we will be looking in detail at some of the specific ways in which fictional situations and fictional worlds are set up in works of literature. Suffice it to say here that both the fictional speech situation and the type of discourse performed by the fictional speaker in a literary work can vary enormously. Novels can consist of fictional autobiographies, confessions, exchanges of letters, diaries, oral narratives, dialogues, streams of consciousness, interior monologues, or even, as in the case of Vladimir Nabokov's *Pale Fire*, a critical edition of a poem. In poetry we find an equally broad range, including many of the types just mentioned as well as others such as prayer (**Oh God our help in ages past . . .**), philosophical commentary (**When I consider how my light is spent . . .**), description (**The sea is calm tonight . . .**), invitation (**Come live with me and be my love . . .**). Conversation and oral narrative are given a special place in poetry by Robert Browning, who used them as the basis for a new literary genre, the dramatic monologue. Robert Frost likewise makes use of conversational speech situations in such poems as "The Witch of Cöos." Many novels, especially relatively contemporary ones, combine a variety of fictional speech acts from different genres and types, including such newcomers as phone calls, tape recordings, newscasts, or psychiatric therapy sessions. Especially with poems, titles are often used to identify the fictional speech act and fictional speech situation. For example, titles like "The Love Song of J. Alfred Prufrock," "Refusal to Mourn the Death, by Fire, of a Child in London," "The Rime of the Ancient Mariner," "Invocation to the Earth," "Stopping by Woods on a Snowy Evening," "Praise for an Urn," and "To His Coy Mistress" give crucial cues to aid the reader in contextualizing the fictional discourse.

The claim that in fictional discourse appropriateness conditions hold with respect to the fictional speaker and not the author raises some obvious problems, however. To begin with, fictional speakers do not exist, so isn't it vacuous to say that they have communicative responsibilities? And anyway, it is the real world author who determines what the fictional speaker says, so isn't the author ultimately the one doing all the communicating? In fact, the author is responsible for what the fictional speaker says, in that the author is creating the fictional speaker and the fictional discourse for a particular communicative purpose of the author's own, namely, the creation in the real world of a work of literature of a particular genre. We could say that Moll Flanders is responsible for the text of *Moll Flanders* insofar as it is an autobiography, and Defoe is responsible for it insofar as it is a novel having the form of a fictional autobiography. So it is Defoe who receives praise or blame for the book's artistic or didactic qualities, and Defoe who is called to task if the work violates obscenity laws or offends public taste or contains material stolen from some other writer. Moreover, since the author is ultimately responsible for the shape of the text, our efforts to contextualize and make sense of the text ultimately refer to the author. Thus when Moll Flanders says something that leads us to believe she is misrepresenting herself, we say that she is violating an appropriateness condition, and then we go on to ask what Defoe's intent might have been in having her violate such a condition at that point in the story.

But once we arrive at the question of author's intent, a whole other batch of problems awaits us. What sort of communication do people undertake to accomplish in novels, poems, and short stories? Some have argued that the communicative act involved in literature is simply that of projecting oneself into an imaginary world; others have said the communicative purpose is to produce pleasure and approval in the audience; still others have said it is to produce shared understanding and evaluations of problematic aspects of existence.[34] And there is always Horace's dictum that literature is to teach and delight. In reality, we are not likely to find a single description of literary communication that will do for all works and all genres. Instead, we must think of the literary context as one that admits a wide range of communicative action.

FICTION VERSUS NONFICTION

Many problems remain unsolved in describing fictional discourse, and the discussion of it here should be taken as tentative. For example, though it is useful to postulate a distinction between author and fictional speaker, the distance between the two can vary enormously, to the extent that the fiction/nonfiction distinction itself is often blurred. Certainly there is no question of identifying Defoe with Moll Flanders or Barthelme with the narrator of "Edward and Pia," but what about works an author presents as highly autobiographical, like James Joyce's *A Portrait of the Artist as a Young Man*, where we are to understand that to some extent the author is presenting his or her own experience via the fictional speaker? Or what about historical novels, where an author tries to explore and reconstruct events that really did happen, and thus also undertakes some truth commitments to what is recounted? The same diversity can be seen in poetry. We do not identify Robert Browning with the fictional duke who speaks in "My Last Duchess," but what about, for instance, Sandburg in "The Harbor"? There, as with many lyric poems, we feel it is quite likely that Sandburg is at least speaking on the basis of a personal experience. We would be surprised if we found he had never seen a lake or a gull. William Wordsworth added to a great many of his lyric poems little introductory descriptions of where they were written and what real world experience inspired them, making it clear that the I of the poem is to be identified with the real world Wordsworth, and the objects and people referred to in the poem with the real world objects and people Wordsworth mentions in his preambles. Yet the speech situation in poetry is such that Wordsworth and Sandburg are not bound to talk only of real people, things, or experiences; and we certainly cannot assume that they do. In this sense we cannot treat their discourse as being entirely nonfictional. Protest poetry provides a similar example. It may have many aspects of a fictional discourse, yet its overall meaning and efficacy as a protest depend on its being a response to specific historical circumstances, and a genuine representation of the speaker's views. Indeed, the tradition of performing protest poetry orally comes from an intention to reduce the possibility of distance, to "defictionalize" the speech situation as completely as possible.

If we look at content alone, we find we must distinguish not only between the real and the fictional, but also between the plausible and the implausible. For instance, we are certain not only that the *Pudd'nhead Wilson* anecdote did not really happen, but also that it could not happen, and that Mark Twain shared this view. We understand Wordsworth in his poem "I wandered lonely as a cloud" to be talking largely about things that did happen and feelings that he did experience. Salinger's *The Catcher in the Rye* can be seen as falling between these two extremes, in that Salinger did not believe the events really happened, but did believe they could happen and were representative of the kind of thing that does happen. James's "The Beast in the Jungle" falls at another place on the continuum in that it involves things that could happen, but which are highly unusual rather than typical. In short, there are infinite possibilities for varying the distance between a fictional speaker and a real speaker, a fictional addressee and a real addressee, a fictional world and the real world. It is thus more useful to think of fiction and nonfiction not as binary categories, but as a complex set of relations. The range of possibilities is attested by the fact that, while no one would ever accuse Defoe of having committed incest on the basis of the fact that Moll Flanders confesses having done so, imprisoned protest poets do not as a rule get out of prison by claiming that the opinions expressed were those of a fictional persona rather than their own.

PRAGMATICS AND WRITTEN DISCOURSE

One of the reasons people have often tended to view literary works as objects rather than communicative acts is that most literary works have the form of written texts, at least in our time. In this sense, they are objects in a way spoken discourses are not. They are visible and tangible, and can be looked at and owned.[35] One of the challenges facing pragmatics is that of developing an approach to written discourse that takes account of its differences from spoken discourse, and that characterizes the varieties of written discourse and the kind of linguistic context writing constitutes. This is another area in which there is no coherent body of research. Here we will do no more than mention some of the points at which the pragmatics of writing differ from the pragmatics of face-to-face speech.

The limitations of our writing system certainly influence the form of written messages, for there is pressure to avoid using forms whose meaning depends on intonational factors or gestures. We have also seen that the rules for degree of formality are not the same for speaking and writing, particularly in that writing tends consistently toward greater formality than speech.

Equally important for many written messages is the fact of their being addressed to a public audience. The speaker who constructs a public discourse does not know or control who will receive it, though the speaker may have a particular group or kind of people in mind as addressees. With public discourse, of which literature and the news media are salient examples, we have the curious situation that the speaker (writer) is unknown or known only by name to the hearers (readers), and the hearers are unknown to the speaker. Speaker/hearer relations are thus extremely depersonalized and abstract in comparison with face-to-face spoken discourse. The publicness of public discourse is doubtless responsible for the formality of the norms in writing and the tendency of written discourse towards standardization.

Also important for literature is the difference between oral and written composition. Oral composition is, as we call it, spontaneous; one composes what one says on the spot, making corrections as one goes, and revising or clearing up misunderstandings as the exchange proceeds.[36] A written utterance, on the other hand, is produced over a much greater and more flexible timespan and is subject to reflection, correction, and revision by the speaker; once it is delivered to the addressee, however, it is fixed, and there is little possibility for clearing up misunderstandings or revising further. These differences in manner of composition and delivery have a great many consequences, one being that the writer regards the written text as more "authoritative" and definitive than spontaneous speech. It is partly because of the possibilities afforded by written composition that, in literary works, weight is given to the smallest particulars of language, and choice is thought of as particularly reflective, careful, and conscious. By the same token, speakers are held very much responsible for what they say in writing. They cannot excuse something by saying they were speaking off the top of their head or in the heat of the moment.

Another factor influencing speaker/hearer relations in written discourse, especially literature, is the selection process that publishing involves. Writers submit manuscripts to publishers, who hire specialists to read them and make recommendations on whether they should be published or not. On the one hand, this selection process increases our trust in the value and communicativeness of the utterance, since it has come to us through winning a kind of competition. On the other hand, we must be skeptical, because the selection procedure is shaped by such factors as the biases of readers, the policies of particular publishers, and above all, economics.

It would be difficult to assess the overall impact of the composition and selection process on reader/author relations in literature. But it does seem that our awareness of these processes plays a role in how we treat deviance in literature. There are a great many literary texts which, in any other context, would be taken as pure gibberish or incompetent communication. The Joyce passage quoted on page 45 is an obvious example; Eliot's "Rhapsody on a Windy Night" is another. Were we to encounter anyone speaking spontaneously in the way these poems do, we would take the person to be mentally impaired—just as the townspeople see Pudd'nhead Wilson. But partly because of what we know of the composition and selection processes, when we encounter such deviance in literature, we assume that it is intentional and connected with some serious communicative intent, and that at least some people other than the author have found the text accessible, meaningful, and generally worthwhile. It is fruitful to think about this situation in terms of the Cooperative Principle. In the literary speech situation, we are prepared to cooperate as hearers to a greater extent than we would in conversation; we are prepared to make more of an effort to "decipher" deviance, to work at understanding beyond the point at which in other contexts the Cooperative Principle would have broken down. Knowing this to be the case, authors are more free to exploit and explore communicative deviance in literature. Thus we could say that the composition and selection processes in literature work to "insulate" the Cooperative Principle. This is surely one of the reasons why literature is so often used to portray and explore the vulnerability of language, as with the *Pudd'nhead Wilson* passage or the Joyce text, where the possibilities of ambiguity, polysemy, and obscurity are explored, or *Moll Flanders*, which looks at the gap between one's real self and the self one presents through language, or Orwell's *Nineteen Eighty-Four*, which speculates on the fate of language in a society where creativity is suppressed.

SUGGESTED FURTHER READINGS

The basic outline of speech act theory is found in Austin's *How to Do Things with Words* and Searle's *Speech Acts: An Essay in the Philosophy of Language.* The papers in Cole and Morgan's anthology *Syntax and Semantics III: Speech Acts* are representative of the initial impact of speech act theory on linguistics, and include many papers on indirect speech acts. The Cole and Morgan collection also includes a substantial excerpt from Grice's work on the Cooperative Principle. For initial consideration of conversational postulates, see David Gordon and George Lakoff's paper "Conversational Postulates."

For further readings on discourse and conversation, Sudnow's anthology *Studies in Social Interaction* is very useful, as are sections one and two of *Directions in Sociolinguistics: The Ethnography of Communication*, edited by Gumperz and Hymes. The latter includes Schegloff's important paper on conversation, entitled "Sequencing in Conversational Openings." See also Gumperz's paper "Sociocultural Knowledge in Conversational Inference." Even more recent are *An Introduction to Discourse Analysis* by Coulthard, and Brown and Levinson's lengthy "Universals in Language Usage: Politeness Phenomena."

Essential reading for the study of narrative is chapter nine of Labov's *Language in the Inner City*, where he works out his model for narrative analysis. See also Sacks's article "On the Analyzability of Stories by Children" in the Gumperz and Hymes volume mentioned above. A great many papers on pragmatics are found in the proceedings of the annual meetings of the Chicago Linguistic Society and the Berkeley Linguistic Society, published every year. Papers in these volumes vary in the amount of background they assume, but they are an indispensable indicator of the state of current research. See also the *Journal of Pragmatics*, the only journal devoted exclusively to pragmatics, where work by both European and American scholars can be found.

For applications of speech act theory to literature, Ohmann's articles "Literature as Act" and "Speech, Literature, and the Space Between" are basic reading. Fish's "How to Do Things with Austin and Searle: Speech Act Theory and Literary Criticism" gives an excellent analysis of Shakespeare's *Coriolanus* from a speech act point of view, and includes theoretical observations questioning the usefulness of speech act theory for literature. Pratt's *Toward a Speech Act Theory of Literary Discourse* considers the applicability to literature of speech act theory as well as Labov's work on narrative and Grice's on the Cooperative Principle. The anthology edited by van Dijk, entitled *Pragmatics of Language and Literature*, has a number of excellent papers, though all tend to be quite advanced. The *Journal of Literary Semantics*, *New Literary History*, *Critical Inquiry*, and *Poetics* frequently contain articles pertaining to pragmatics. For work on conversation in literature, see Garnica's paper "Rules of Verbal Interaction and Literary Analysis" and Page's *Speech in the English Novel*. Discussion of various types of speech genres, literary and nonliterary, and of the issue of fictionality, can be found in Smith's *On the Margins of Discourse*.

For the study of verbal behavior in the wider context of culture and social structure, a basic text is Hymes's *Foundations in Sociolinguistics: An Ethnographic Approach*.

Exercises

1. Choose three of the following illocutionary acts: predicting, hypothesizing, condemning, conceding, denying, demanding, threatening.

    a. State for each one at least two forms the locutionary act may take.
    b. Characterize each one according to its appropriateness conditions governing identity of participants, beliefs and attitudes of participants, and surrounding circumstances, much as the act of asking a question was characterized on pages 230–31.

2. The following is an abstract underlying structure for an illocutionary act of inviting:

    [I INVITE you [you come to a party]]

    a. In surface structure, what are the likely lexicalized versions of this string?
    b. What indirect forms of inviting are possible, based on the appropriateness conditions on inviting?
    c. Are there any indirect forms for inviting deriving from other principles of conversation mentioned in this chapter?

3. Compare the kind of question speech act discussed on pages 230–31 with teachers' questions in the classroom. State as explicitly as you can the difference between the two types of question in terms of appropriateness conditions and communicative function. Then consider why it might be that certain children find teachers' questions hard to understand, and are sometimes downright hostile to them. What similarities and differences obtain in riddles such as the following:

    a. What's the difference between a lion with a toothache and a rainstorm? (**One roars with pain and the other pours with rain.**)
    b. What do you call a gorilla with a Tommy gun? (**Sir.**)
    c. Why does lightning shock people? (**It doesn't know how to conduct itself.**)
    d. What do you get when you cross a jelly with a sheepdog? (**Collie-wobbles.**) (**Collie-wobbles** = American "growling stomach.")
    e. What's red, white, and black? (**A sunburnt penguin.**)[37]

4. For each appropriateness condition on giving information discussed on page 231, make up an example which violates that condition.

5. What two principles of conversation are illustrated by the examples in a and b respectively (treat them all as indirect speech acts):

    a. I can assure you you are not suspected.
        I can defy you to prove otherwise.
        I can reveal that Mr. Jones is somewhere in Central America.
    b. I wish to request a recess.
        I want to apologize for being late.
        I would like to claim it's an optical illusion.

6. What presuppositions might one want to disagree with in:

    a. Have you hugged your kid today? (as a bumpersticker)
    b. Though he has been a widower for years, Mathieu is no ordinary lecher. (from a plot summary of Luis Buñuel's film *That Obscure Object of Desire*)
    c. Jones is a populist, and Smith can't be trusted either.
    d. Make friends with your wife and kids again. (from an advertisement for a luxury resort)
    e. Let them beat you at tennis. (from the same advertisement)

7. On page 239 we suggested that there is a presupposition associated with
    back in **I insulted him back**. Try to state what this presupposition is. You may
    want to take into account the following data:

> Meg hit Paul and he hit her back.
>
> Meg hit Paul and he kicked her back.
>
> Meg hit Paul and Billy hit her back.

8. What presuppositions are made with respect to the complement in the
    following sentences:

    a. I didn't remember that I had parked beside a blue Chevy.
    b. I didn't remember parking beside a blue Chevy.
    c. I didn't remember to park beside a blue Chevy.

    Try to construct examples to substantiate your claims (cf. examples 22–23
    in this chapter). How might this information about **remember** be expressed
    in the grammar?

9. a. In discussing politeness, we stated that the rules for politeness were not
        in force in the telephone conversation quoted in this chapter. What
        evidence do you find in the passages quoted that demonstrates the rules
        of politeness are not being observed?
    b. We noted that linguistic politeness is not appropriate when the speaker
        has great or direct authority over the addressee. Give examples showing
        that politeness is also inappropriate between equals who are close friends.
        What effects can polite forms have in such cases?
    c. Why is the following exchange impolite: **I'm afraid I've got to leave
        now—Yes, please do.**

10. Here are some texts that resulted from a classroom exercise in which a
    group of second-graders were asked to write a story.

    a. Analyze the texts in terms of the categories: orientation, evalua-
        tion, complicating action, and resolution (not all of these will be
        present in all texts; note that abstract and coda are not present at
        all).
    b. Are there any examples here that are not narrative (i.e., that do
        not use temporally ordered narrative clauses)?

    c. Give two examples where causal and/or chronological sequence is
        established by implication.

        (1) One day some people moved in a house. The army ant
             gobbled up the house. So the people had to start all over
             again.
        (2) Once there was a parrot and she laid an egg. The egg didn't
             hatch and the mother parrot, whose name was Sheila,
             started crying. One day Sheila heard a peck-peck and the
             baby bird walked out. The mother bird was very happy.

(3)   Once upon a time there was a lady bug who was busy eating aphids. There are plants in the garden. The lady bug is always in the garden. Every day the lady bug eats aphids. The lady bug is always on plants. The lady bug is always catching aphids.

(4)   Once there was a shark and there was another shark and they ate fishes and they got so fat that they exploded. The sea got so hot that it got on fire and all the fish died and sharks and plants died and the sea was not there.

(5)   One day I planted a seed and I waited and waited and waited until I was an old man. Then it grew a little bit and I died.

11.   Reconsider the initial paragraphs of Barthelme's story "Edward and Pia" quoted on page 168. How does this text conform to and deviate from the model of the story outlined in this chapter? Consider presence or absence of abstract, orientation, complicating action, narrative sequence, and evaluation. How do the deviations contribute to the sense of absurdity in the story? What similarities does this passage have with the children's narratives in Exercise 10?

12.   The following is the opening paragraph from Henry James's short story "The Pupil":

> The poor young man hesitated and procrastinated: it cost him such an effort to broach the subject of terms, to speak of money to a person who spoke only of feelings and, as it were, of the aristocracy. Yet he was unwilling to take leave, treating his engagement as settled, without some more conventional glance in that direction than he could find an opening for in the manner of the large affable lady who sat there drawing a pair of soiled *gants de Suède* through a fat jewelled hand and, at once pressing and gliding, repeated over and over everything but the thing he would have liked to hear. He would have liked
> 10   to hear the figure of his salary; but just as he was nervously about to sound that note the little boy came back—the little boy Mrs. Moreen had sent out of the room to fetch her fan. He came back without the fan, only with the casual observation that he couldn't find it. As he dropped this cynical confession he looked straight and hard at the candidate for the honour of taking his education in hand. This personage reflected somewhat grimly that the first thing he should have to teach his little charge would be to appear to address himself to his mother when he spoke to her—especially not to make her such an improper answer as that.[38]

a.   The speech event underway in this passage is obviously a job interview. Describe the job interview as a speech event, in terms of participants and their roles, degree of formality, restrictions on topic, floor allocation, opening and closing routines, and any other factors you consider relevant.

b. The first two sentences of the text describe a communicative problem that the young man, Pemberton, has. Describe this problem in terms of appropriateness conditions on the speech event. This will require considering in what way Mrs. Moreen's linguistic behavior is deviant or uncooperative in the context. What hypotheses does the reader form here to account for Mrs. Moreen's behavior?

c. How does the child's entrance in the third sentence alter the appropriateness conditions in play? What is "improper" about the child's answer, in terms of appropriateness conditions? Does Pemberton's label of "cynical confession" fit? What is the significance of the child's maintaining eye contact with Pemberton while addressing his mother?

13. Edgar Allan Poe is one writer who uses a variety of fictional speech situations in his works. Below are quoted the opening passages of four of Poe's stories.[39] For each one, as far as is possible, characterize the fictional speech situation in terms of identity of speaker, identity of addressee(s), intentions of speaker, kind of discourse being performed, surrounding circumstances, and preceding discourse, if any. Explain how the text supports your characterization (paying particular attention to presuppositions).

a.   The thousand injuries of Fortunato I had borne as I best could; but when he ventured upon insult, I vowed revenge. You, who so well know the nature of my soul, will not suppose, however, that I gave utterance to a threat. *At length* I would be avenged; this was a point definitively settled—but the very definitiveness with which it was resolved precluded the idea of risk. I must not only punish, but punish with impunity. A wrong is unredressed when retribution overtakes its redresser. It is equally unredressed when the avenger fails to make himself felt as such to him who has done the wrong.

It must be understood that neither by word nor deed had I given Fortunato cause to doubt my good will. I continued, as was my wont, to smile in his face, and he did not perceive that my smile *now* was at the thought of his immolation.

The Cask of Amontillado

b.   True!—nervous—very, very dreadfully nervous I had been and am; but why *will* you say that I am mad? The disease had sharpened my senses—not destroyed—not dulled them. Above all was the sense of hearing acute. I heard all things in the heaven and in the earth. I heard many things in hell. How, then, am I mad? Hearken! and observe how healthily—how calmly I can tell you the whole story.

The Tell-Tale Heart

c.   We had now reached the summit of the loftiest crag. For some minutes the old man seemed too much exhausted to speak.

"Not long ago," said he at length, "and I could have guided you on this route as well as the youngest of my sons; but, about three years past, there happened to me an event such as never happened before to mortal man—or at least such as no man ever survived to tell of—and the six hours of deadly terror which I then endured have broken me up body and soul. You suppose me a *very* old man—but I am not.

A Descent into the Maelström

d.   Of course I shall not pretend to consider it any matter for wonder, that the extraordinary case of M. Valdemar has excited discussion. It would have been a miracle had it not—especially under the circumstances. Through the desire of all parties concerned, to keep the affair from the public, at least for the present, or until we had farther opportunities for investigation—through our endeavors to effect this—a garbled or exaggerated account made its way into society, and became the source of many unpleasant misrepresentations, and, very naturally, of a great deal of disbelief.

It is now rendered necessary that I give the *facts*—as far as I comprehend them myself. They are, succinctly, these:

The Facts in the Case of M. Valdemar

NOTES

[1] This term is taken from Dell Hymes, "Competence and Performance in Linguistic Theory," in *Language Acquisition: Models and Methods*, eds. R. Huxley and E. Ingram (New York: Academic Press, 1971).

[2] See Roger W. Brown and Marguerite Ford, "Address in American English," *Journal of Abnormal and Social Psychology*, 62 (1961), 375–85.

[3] Different languages assign different meanings to these pairs, but there are important generalizations, as suggested in Brown and Gilman's famous article outlining the "power semantic" and the "solidarity semantic" as the two main types of organizations of such pairs. The power semantic is asymmetrical: Inferiors address superiors with "polite" pronouns, while superiors use "familiar" pronouns in return. The solidarity semantic is symmetrical: Members of an in group use familiar pronouns with each other and polite pronouns with outsiders who are not members. See Roger W. Brown and A. Gilman, "The Pronouns of Power and Solidarity," in *Style in Language*, ed. Thomas A. Sebeok (Cambridge, Mass.: MIT Press, 1960); rpt. in *Language in Context*, ed. Pier Paolo Giglioli (Harmondsworth, Mssex.: Penguin, 1972).

[4] There are speech acts which are not communicative, in the sense that they do not involve purposeful communication with an addressee. Examples are sleep-talking and expletives like **Ouch!** Intermediary cases are talking to oneself, for example, when thinking out a problem. Here the speaker in some sense functions in the double role of speaker and listener. Such cases have as yet been studied very little, but it is at least clear that they are acts.

[5] The account of speech act theory given here is based on J. L. Austin, *How to Do Things with Words* (Cambridge, Mass.: Harvard Univ. Press, 1962); John R. Searle, *Speech Acts: An Essay in the Philosophy of Language* (London and New York: Cambridge Univ. Press, 1969); John R. Searle, "A Classification of Illocutionary Acts," *Language*

in Society, 5 (1976), 1–23; and Peter Cole and Jerry L. Morgan, eds., *Syntax and Semantics III: Speech Acts* (New York: Academic Press, 1975). In the original formulation of speech act theory by Austin, a third act, called a "perlocutionary act" was also postulated. This act involved the achievement of certain effects in the addressee by virtue of the illocutionary act. Thus the illocutionary act of arguing has the perlocutionary goal of convincing; the illocutionary act of warning seeks to achieve the perlocutionary effect of frightening, and so on. Very little progress has been made in the study of perlocutions, and we will not be referring further to this category here. For an approach that gives some importance to perlocutions, see Jerrold Sadock, *Towards a Linguistic Theory of Speech Acts* (New York: Academic Press, 1974).

⁶ The expressive function as defined here should not be confused with Bühler's well-known "expressive function." He differentiated the "referential function" (what is said), the "conative function" (effect on addressee), and the "expressive function" (speakers' attitudes to what they say, e.g., whether they are lying or not). In the approach presented here, these three terms have affinities with "underlying structure," "addressee conditions," and "sincerity conditions," and have little direct connection with the classification of illocutionary acts. Karl Bühler's work, *Sprachtheorie; die Darstellungsfunktion der Sprache* (Jena: Gustav Fischer Verlag, 1934), in which the three functions are discussed, is outlined and developed in Roman Jakobson, "Closing Statement: Linguistics and Poetics," in *Style in Language,* ed. Sebeok; rpt. in *Language in Context,* ed. Giglioli. For a recent reconsideration of kinds of illocutionary acts, see Michael Hancher, "The Classification of Cooperative Illocutionary Acts," *Language in Society,* 8 (1979), 1–14.

⁷ This is the term now most commonly used by linguists. Philosophers usually call them "felicity conditions."

⁸ In a more detailed analysis, these rules might not all be considered to be the same type. Clearly the consequences of failure to fulfill a rule differ a great deal from rule to rule. Some linguists and philosophers distinguish rules of verbal politeness or decorum (such as 1b, 2a–b, 3a–c, here) categorically from other rules, and do not view them as appropriateness conditions at all. The basis for this distinction is the claim that politeness rules **regulate** the performance of illocutionary acts, while conditions like those in 4 are part of what **constitutes** the illocutionary act. In this view, a question that violated only 1b would **count as** a fully constituted (appropriate) question, though it would also be **judged** *as* a rude question. This approach has many difficulties, and we are not using it here. For further discussion, however, see Searle, *Speech Acts,* Chapter 2, on the distinction between constitutive and regulative rules.

⁹ Cf. George Lakoff, "On Generative Semantics," in *Semantics: An Interdisciplinary Reader in Philosophy, Linguistics, and Psychology,* eds. Danny S. Steinberg and Leon A. Jakobovits (London and New York: Cambridge Univ. Press, 1971).

¹⁰ This account was first suggested by David Gordon and George Lakoff, "Conversational Postulates," *Papers from the Seventh Regional Meeting of the Chicago Linguistic Society* (Chicago: Univ. of Chicago, Department of Linguistics, 1971). They use the term "conversational postulates" rather than principles of conversation. Other patterns discussed in this section are based on Bruce Fraser, "Hedged Performatives," in *Syntax and Semantics III,* eds. Cole and Morgan. Further studies of indirect speech acts are found in Georgia Green, "How to Get People to Do Things with Words," in *Syntax and Semantics III,* eds. Cole and Morgan; Robin Lakoff, "Language in Context," *Language,* 48 (1972), 907–27; Robin Lakoff, "The Language of Politeness or Minding Your P's and Q's," *Papers from the Ninth Regional Meeting of the Chicago Linguistic Society* (Chicago: Univ. of Chicago, Department of Linguistics, 1973); and John R. Searle, "Indirect Speech Acts," in *Syntax and Semantics III,* eds. Cole and Morgan.

¹¹ H. Paul Grice, "Logic and Conversation," in *Syntax and Semantics III,* eds. Cole and Morgan.

[12] This term was first introduced in Grice, "Logic and Conversation." We are using it in a somewhat more comprehensive way than Grice, since he was discussing only assertive speech acts.

[13] The name "cleft sentence" derives from transformational syntax, in which sentences like 32 and 33 are viewed as derived from the simple sentence **Sheila lost the marbles** by a transformation which "cleaves" the underlying NP V NP sequence, moving an NP to the front and inserting **it was . . . that/who.**

[14] Notice that with these questions the negation test for presupposition does not work. 34 presupposes you lost some marbles, but its negative, **Which marbles didn't you lose?**, presupposes there are some you did *not* lose and asks for specifics.

[15] Originally, linguists and philosophers regarded presuppositions as constant elements in the sentence and therefore part of semantics. However, it soon became clear that presuppositions vary contextually, as illustrated below, and more recently they have been regarded as pragmatic. See John Lyons, *Semantics*, Vol. 2 (London and New York: Cambridge Univ. Press, 1977), Section 14.3; and Lauri Karttunen and Stanley Peters, "Requiem for Presuppositions," in *Proceedings of the Third Annual Meeting of the Berkeley Linguistics Society* (Berkeley, Cal.: Univ. of California, Berkeley Linguistics Society, 1977).

[16] Dell Hymes, "Models of the Interaction of Language and Social Life," in *Directions in Sociolinguistics: The Ethnography of Communication*, eds. John J. Gumperz and Dell Hymes (New York: Holt, Rinehart and Winston, Inc., 1972).

[17] Much of the following discussion is based on Emanuel A. Schegloff, "Sequencing in Conversational Openings," in *Directions in Sociolinguistics: The Ethnography of Communication*, eds., John J. Gumperz and Dell Hymes (New York: Holt, Rinehart and Winston, 1972); Emanuel A. Schegloff and Harvey Sacks, "Opening up Closings," *Semiotica*, 8 (1973), 290–337; and Harvey Sacks, Emanuel A. Schegloff, and Gail Jefferson, "A Simplest Systematics for the Organization of Turn-Taking for Conversation," *Language*, 50 (1974), 696–735.

[18] *The Presidential Transcripts* (New York: Dell Publishing Co., Inc., 1974), p. 340.

[19] *Presidential Transcripts*, p. 342.

[20] *Presidential Transcripts*, pp. 343–44.

[21] This discussion is indebted to Robin Lakoff, "Language in Context," as well as to Robin Lakoff, "The Language of Politeness." See also Penelope Brown and Stephen Levinson, "Universals in Language Usage: Politeness Phenomena," in *Questions and Politeness: Strategies in Social Interaction*, ed. Esther N. Goody (Cambridge: Cambridge University Press, 1978). We are here discussing appropriateness conditions for politeness in American English. These vary considerably from language to language and culture to culture; in Arabic, for example, greater politeness is expected in business transactions than in English; and within English, greater politeness is expected in Britain than in America.

[22] The rules mentioned here requiring clarity, completeness, and relevance are given by Grice, "Logic and Conversation," as subrules of the Cooperative Principle.

[23] The discussion of narrative that follows is based on the approach developed in William Labov, *Language in the Inner City* (Philadelphia: Univ. of Pennsylvania Press, 1972), Chapter 9.

[24] *Newsweek*, 4 July 1977, p. 75.

[25] James D. Cockcroft, "Mexico," in *Latin America; The Struggle with Dependency and Beyond*, eds. Ronald H. Chilcote and Joel C. Edelstein (Cambridge, Mass.: Schenkman Publishing Company, 1974), p. 255.

[26] Mark Twain (Samuel Clemens), *Pudd'nhead Wilson* (New York: Grove Press, 1955), pp. 36–9.

[27] For a study of ending routines in poetry, see Barbara Herrnstein Smith, *Poetic Closure; A Study of How Poems End* (Chicago: Univ. of Chicago Press, 1968).

[28] See, for example, the papers in Teun A. van Dijk, ed., *Pragmatics of Language and Literature* (Amsterdam: North-Holland, 1976).

[29] It should be kept clear, however, that not all fictional discourses are works of literature. Fictional discourse is found everywhere, from advertisements to jokes to mathematical problems of the kind "George was six years old when Henry was born . . ."

[30] Cf. Richard Ohmann, "Speech Acts and the Definition of Literature," *Philosophy and Rhetoric*, 4 (1971), 1–19; and "Literature as Act," in *Approaches to Poetics*, ed. Seymour Chatman (New York: Columbia Univ. Press, 1973). For arguments against the idea of the narrator, see S. Y. Kuroda, "Reflections on the Foundations of Narrative Theory—from a Linguistic Point of View," in *Pragmatics of Language and Literature*, ed. Teun A. van Dijk (Amsterdam: North-Holland, 1976).

[31] Cf. Norman H. Holland, *The Dynamics of Literary Response* (New York: Oxford Univ. Press, 1968) for an excellent literary-psychological account of this process. See also George L. Dillon, *Language Processing and the Reading of Literature: Toward a Model of Comprehension* (Bloomington, Ind.: Indiana Univ. Press, 1978).

[32] J. D. Salinger, *The Catcher in the Rye* (Boston: Little, Brown and Co., 1951), p. 3.

[33] Henry James, "The Beast in the Jungle," in *Selected Tales of Henry James* (London: John Baker, 1969), p. 219.

[34] For the first of these positions, see Samuel R. Levin, "Concerning What Kind of a Speech Act a Poem Is," in *Pragmatics of Language and Literature*, ed. van Dijk; for the second position, see Teun A. van Dijk, "Pragmatics and Poetics," in *Pragmatics of Language and Literature*, ed. van Dijk; for the third, see Mary L. Pratt, *Toward a Speech Act Theory of Literary Discourse* (Bloomington, Ind.: Indiana Univ. Press, 1977).

[35] Of course it is now possible to make speech into an object, in tapes or records, and their invention is having an ever-increasing effect on the distinction between speaking and writing.

[36] Oral composition here does not refer to composition of oral-formulaic poetry, which falls somewhere between writing and spontaneous speech in terms of advance preparation.

[37] From *The Crack-a-Joke Book: Chosen by Children in Aid of Oxfam* (Harmondsworth, Mssex.: Puffin Books, 1978). Examples a and b are from p. 67; Example c is from p. 36; Example d is from p. 48; Example e is from p. 158.

[38] Henry James, "The Pupil," *The New York Edition of Henry James* (New York: Charles Scribner's Sons, 1908), XI, p. 511.

[39] Edgar Allan Poe, *The Collected Works of Edgar Allan Poe* (Cambridge, Mass.: Harvard Univ. Press, 1978), pp. 1256–57, 792, 577–78, and 1233, respectively.

7

Establishing a
Universe of Discourse

In the preceding chapter we considered some of the main principles governing speaker-hearer relations, working from the basic idea that communication is goal-directed and cooperative action. Within this general framework, we discussed some of the particular strategies speakers use to "get the message across," especially strategies whereby more is conveyed than what is literally said. Here we will look at another equally basic set of strategies, those involved in establishing and maintaining a universe of discourse or frame of reference between participants.

"Getting the message across" requires that what is said be anchored in a frame of reference. Suppose someone asks you the question **When are you leaving?** and you reply **Tuesday**. Obviously you are talking about the Tuesday of a particular week, and you assume your interlocutor knows what week you are talking about. Your reply is thus anchored in this shared point of reference. If to the same question you answer **Ten-fifteen**, the effectiveness of your reply depends on shared assumptions about which day and which part of the day you are talking about, while the answer **Mid-February** is anchored in the framework of a particular year. Moreover, the speaker who asks the question **When are you leaving?** also has some time frame in mind, and expects to be answered in terms of that frame. In other words, the question itself is anchored, and answering it successfully involves anchoring the answer in the same time frame as the question. Taking too much for granted makes the message unclear (if you say **Ten-fifteen** in a cross-continent phone call, whose clock time are you talking about?), while taking too little for granted makes it redundant and not worth listening to. (**Do you have the time?—Yes, it's ten-fifteen and thirty-three seconds A.M.**)

In any interaction, speakers make dozens of decisions about what constitutes a relevant and recognizable frame of reference in which to anchor the communication. Time is not the only kind of frame, of course. Space is even more basic. And, insofar as there is a choice, the way in which we put one word after another in a sentence, and one sentence after another in discourse, embodies decisions about where to start, what is important, and what is already known. In the latter part of this chapter, we will discuss the particular relevance of these strategies of organization to what literary critics have long called "narrative point of view."

SPATIAL FRAMES OF REFERENCE

Anchoring in Common-Sense Knowledge of the World

The sociologist Emanuel Schegloff has done extensive work on the strategies people use in locating themselves through language, especially in emergency phone calls to the police. Schegloff has showed that in anchoring messages in terms of space, we work in part with a kind of "common-sense geography" that is organized by levels from largest, least specific spatial frame to smallest and most specific.[1] A useful model of the basic system is an inverted pyramid with layers, each one smaller than the one above. For a person sitting at a desk in Palo Alto, California, the pyramid looks something like this:

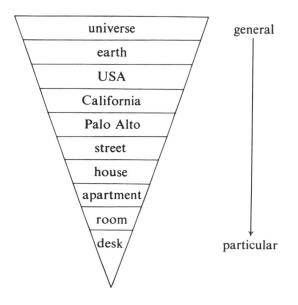

In order to locate yourself verbally, you select an appropriate reference point from the set of layers and assume all less specific locations are known. You then describe where you are in terms of layers more specific than the one in which you anchor yourself. For instance, if the person in the above diagram were asked **Where are you?** he or she might answer **In Palo Alto**. In this case, the reference point or anchor chosen is the state, and all the less specific frames are taken for granted as shared knowledge, while all more specific frames are considered in need of specification. Of these, the speaker chooses the one or ones that are relevant, in this case just the city, rather than, say, the building or room.

The progression from large to small frameworks is clearly conventionalized in the address system used on envelopes. In addressing a letter when in the United States, we omit USA, but specify California, that is, we assume the country and consider the state informative. In terms of the pyramid, we locate ourselves in the US and select the next layer for mention. But if we are in another country, we anchor ourselves in the world and specify the US. On the other hand, when people phone the police in an emergency, they usually assume the town they are in. **Where are you located?** is nearly always answered by a street, not a town specification. Naturally many confusions result, since the speaker's town may not actually lie in the domain of the police called, or the police's domain may contain more than one town.

The inverted pyramid system outlined here, though an important strategy, is not often used on its own, except for purposes of police identification, addresses on envelopes, and similar documents. For example, solely in terms of the diagram above, the most specific answer to the question **Where are you?** would be **I'm at a desk**. But actually, a speaker would be much more likely to be even more precise and say something like **At my desk, At John's desk, At the desk by the window**. In these replies, **desk** is specified not only with respect to the common-sense geography, but also in terms of other relationships, whether by relation to another objective location (**by the window**), or by relation to a person or thing assumed known in the speech situation (**me, John**). Even plain **the**, as in **At the desk**, relates **desk** to the participants by assuming the desk is known to them.

Relational terms that anchor location with respect to speaker, hearer, or some other known object are in fact used in preference to pure common-sense geographical terms whenever possible. So if one asks a stranger where a certain store in San Francisco is, one is likely to get a reply like **Go straight ahead three blocks and it's on your left**, where locational terms are related to location of the hearer, or one might get a reply like **Just off Union Square**, that is, anchored to some landmark presumably known to both parties; or the answer might be prefaced by **Do you know San Francisco?** If the answer is affirmative, a relational anchor will be used; if negative, a plain geographical one like 675 Geary Street. There seems to be a kind of order of preference: Use a term related to speaker and/or hearer if possible; if not, use a term related to a landmark or some other reference assumed known; if this is not possible, in the last resort use pure geographical terms according to the pyramid system. This order of preference reflects the fact that in language the speaker's viewpoint tends to predominate. We turn now to detailed discussion of relational terms based on the speaker's perspective.

Anchoring in the Perspective of the Speaker

The process of anchoring in the spatio-temporal perspective of the speaker is called "deixis," and the linguistic forms that express this perspective are called "deictics" or "shifters."[2] Deixis involves the use of spatial (and temporal) terms like **this** versus **that**, **here** versus **there**, **come** versus **go**, **bring** versus **take**, and others, which can be fully understood only if the hearer reconstructs the position or viewpoint of the speaker. The reference of **this** and **that** (apart from the general notions of "near" and "far") is not constant, but shifts according to the speaker's location (and in some cases speaker's interest), hence the term "shifter." They are also in some sense gestural, pointing to (and indexing)[3] elements, hence their name "deictics," from Greek **deiktos** "able to show directly." If a speech act contains deictic expressions, it is essential to know where the speaker is (or was) and when the speech act is (or was) performed in order to understand it. To use a famous illustration, suppose you found a bottle floating on the ocean containing a note that said **Meet me here tomorrow at noon and bring a stick about this big.**[4] Hardly an effective communication, because we do not have access to the anchors presupposed by the deictics **here, tomorrow,** and **this.** We need either the speaker's presence, or some publicly identifiable reference points like the address and date customarily used in letters and other communications where speaker and hearer cannot be co-present.

As far as modeling our linguistic competence is concerned, we need to specify in the grammar that terms like **here** and **there** presuppose an anchor and assert closeness or distance from that anchor. If in a given situation we cannot surmise what the presupposed anchor is, we will be disoriented, and the utterance will have failed to some extent (unless, of course, disorientation is the intended effect). Given the abstract performative structure **I X you** underlying every speech act, we find in many situations the following alignment of spatial and temporal deictics:

I	X	you
this		that
here		there
now		then

In this basic system, I have **this** and you have **that**, I am **here** and you are **there**. This does not mean that you cannot be here with me, but it does mean that I can hardly be there with you unless I see myself as divided from myself. It is the same with **now** and **then**. You can be present to me now, or you can be present to me then, but I am always present to myself now. And it is the same with the **I-you** pronouns themselves. As we have seen, some languages like Indonesian have special pronouns indicating **we** including you or **we** excluding you; but **you** can never include me, although **you** may include others apart from those immediately addressed.

The alignment proposed above is only a skeleton formula for organizing communication. The speaker's problem is to select appropriate ways for the hearer to orient him or herself in such a way as to recognize and share what is being talked about. Certain spatial relations such as **left-right**, **front-back**, and **up-down** are often interpretable only from the speaker's position. For the first of these pairs, in normal conversational circumstances, hearers live in a reverse world to speakers, since they face each other. Speaker's left is hearer's right, and vice versa, so that the hearer instructed to lift the right side of the table has to step into the speaker's shoes to figure out what to do. However, we do allow for backgrounds. If the table is against a wall, its right and left sides are identified by the lines of vision toward the wall. But if the speaker is talking from behind the wall, or standing on the table facing out from the wall, anchoring reverts back to speaker's position, or further specification is required, like **the side on my right**, or **on your right as you face the wall**.

As already indicated, not all instances of spatial deictics like **left-right** refer to the speaker's body (are "speaker-deictic"). Thus, in **on Bill's left**, the speaker chooses Bill as the anchor; in **to the left of the stove**, the stove is understood to have its own internal orientation irrespective of speaker and hearer. Many objects are linguistically conceived of as having built-in orientations. Desks, cars, chairs, houses, and books, for instance, have their own fronts and backs irrespective of people, and lefts and rights as well. However, many of these are ultimately determined by where we are when we use the object in its basic function, whether sitting in or at it, or holding it in a certain way.

Other spatial terms involve more complex speaker-hearer relations, as is the case with **come** and **go**, **bring** and **take**, relations that clearly depend on language and not on external factors. For **come** and **go**, in their basic directional senses, we can distinguish three meanings. With **come** these are:

Hearer movement toward where speaker is:

1.   Come here. (contrast *Come there)

Speaker movement toward where hearer is:

2.   I'll come over there at six o'clock.

(Past or future) speaker movement toward where speaker is:

3. a.   I came here after the movie.
    b.   I'll come here after the movie.

With **go**, we have the parallel set:

Hearer movement to where speaker is not:

4.   Go there. (contrast *Go here)

Speaker movement to where hearer is not:

5.   I'll go over there at six o'clock.

(Past or future) speaker movement to where speaker is not:

6. a.   I went there after the movie.
   b.   I'll go there after the movie.

Here-there, **come-go**, and the other deictics establish a perspective that is recognizable as that of the speaker (sometimes the hearer too) and sharable even if the specific anchor is not fully known. If we hear an unknown speaker on a tape say:

7.   A bull came charging into the field.

we will still recognize orientation toward the speaker and will be able to visualize the outlines of the action. To the extent permitted by the content of the sentence we will share the speaker's perspective, and will even be able to draw a picture of the scene. How different the drawing would be if the speaker said:

8.   A bull went charging into the field.

In addition to their basic directional meanings, **come** and **go** have an enormous range of extended meanings and appear in dozens of idiomatic expressions. In many of these, we find that **come** (as well as **bring**) involves orientation toward a normal state of affairs, while **go** (as well as **take**) involves orientation from a normal to an abnormal state of affairs. One goes out of one's mind, but comes to one's senses, engines go dead but come alive, one's temperature goes up and comes down, and if it goes down and then comes up we understand it has gone below normal and then returned to normal.[5] This kind of normativity is similar to what we observed in Chapter 3 with **left** and **right**, where **left** in extended senses often has a negative moral connotation and **right** a positive one.

TEMPORAL FRAMES OF REFERENCE

Orientation to speaker's or hearer's place can pose problems in communication, especially when too much is taken for granted. But these problems can very often be solved by pointing to physical objects or drawing diagrams. Orientation to speaker or hearer's time is much more problematic, however, since time is not concrete. We have given ourselves ways of objectifying time—calendars with years, months, weeks, days, hours, minutes, and seconds, to which we can anchor events. Different cultures use different calendars, but all calendars serve the same function of providing "a public time" to which events can be anchored. In speaking we do not have to anchor what we say to this public time, but normally, at least in English, we do anchor Predications to the time of utterance, that is, to the speaker's **now**. The most obvious instance of this anchoring for English speakers is the phenomenon called tense. Tense (in the semantic, not the syntactic sense) involves locating what we talk about on an imaginary time line, of which the speaker is the reference point. The verb inflection **-ed** and the adverbs **yesterday, last week** all refer to points in the speaker's past at the time of utterance. If you read **yesterday** in a letter you have to know what day it was written to know what day is referred to. Tense can be expressed in surface structures by verb inflections (typically **-s, -ed**), auxiliary verbs like **will** and **be going to**, adverbs like **now, then, tomorrow**, or even nothing at all, but it is always part of the underlying semantic structure of the sentence. The ultimate impossibility of using this sort of system purely with reference to the speaker, without any reference to a public time scheme outside of oneself, is the subject of a joke in Lewis Carroll's looking-glass world. The Queen rushes through the woods, her clothes and hair in disarray. Alice tidies her up and suggests that the Queen should have a lady's maid.

> "I'm sure I'll take *you* with pleasure!" the Queen said. "Two pence a week, and jam every other day."
> Alice couldn't help laughing, as she said "I don't want you to hire *me*—and I don't care for jam."
> "It's very good jam," said the Queen.
> "Well, I don't want any *to-day*, at any rate."
> "You couldn't have it if you *did* want it," the Queen said. "The rule is, jam to-morrow and jam yesterday—but never jam *to-day*."
> "It *must* come sometimes to 'jam today'," Alice objected.
> "No, it ca'n't," said the Queen. "It's jam every *other* day: to-day isn't any other day, you know."[6]

It must come to jam today depends on being able to use **today** and **tomorrow** relative not only to oneself but also to some public time scheme in which days come in sequences and consist of twenty-four hours and in which a new day starts at midnight (or is it dawn? or when one gets up?—even these things are sometimes dependent on oneself).

Tense, then, is speaker-deictic in the sense that it is anchored in the perspective of the speaker.[7] We tend to think of tense as a three-way system—past, present, and future—but few languages really treat it that way. Like other orientational systems, it is basically binary: **now** (oriented toward the speaker)—**then** (oriented away from the speaker). Note that **then** is both past and future. In a great many languages we find spatial deictics used for tense, something that is not too surprising when we consider that tense locates events along an imaginary "time line." Thus it is extremely common to find **come** used with reference to past time, **go** with reference to future time. In French we find **Je viens de la faire** "I have just done it," literally "I come from doing it," and **Je vais le faire** "I'm going to do it." In English we do not use **come**, but we do use **go**. The choice of these terms can be explained on grounds of assuming that the present is the normal state; one moves toward it from the past, hence **come**; one moves away from it into the future, hence **go**. We also find such idiomatic expressions as **we look forward to the years ahead, we look back on the past, all that is behind us**. This orientation probably derives from the idea of going along a path facing the unknown. One always knows the path one has already come along; one may or may not know the path to be traversed. Hence the idea of coming from the known and going to the unknown.

It is important to remember that, as was pointed out in Chapter 3 in connection with **-s** and **-ed**, not everything that is commonly called tense is in fact deictic in the sense discussed here. For example, the surface non-past morpheme is not deictic in generic statements like **All men are mortal**. Such statements are generalizations about phenomena in the universe and are not specifically anchored in speaker time. Another example is provided by the so-called "complex tenses." These include the "pluperfect," as in **I had gone**, and the "future perfect," as in **I will have gone**. Both of these are simple as far as tense deixis is concerned. The pluperfect orients things to the speaker's past, the future perfect to the speaker's future. But additionally, both include reference to another point in time. For instance in:

9. a.   I had finished by the time Sam arrived.

10. a.   I will have finished by the time Sam arrives.

the speaker's finishing is located not only with reference to the speaker's present, but also with respect to Sam's arrival. In both cases the finishing precedes (is earlier than) Sam's arrival. Note that if the nondeictic reference time is omitted, we nevertheless understand that there is such a reference point and that the finishing precedes it:

9. b.   I had finished.

10. b.   I will have finished.

Other types of temporal frames of reference will be discussed in the section on narrative tense toward the end of this chapter.

SHARED DOMAINS, COREFERENCE

While **here-there** involve pointable-to, concrete locations, at least part of the time, **now-then** do not (even calendar time cannot be pointed to). **Now-then** point to an imaginary line and positions on it. The notion of pointing can be extended in yet another way, to include "things talked about which are in my purview and that I want to share with you."[8] This kind of deixis is illustrated by:

11.   Put the sculpture on the left of the vase.

In this sentence, **the** is as orientation-controlling as **left**, since to understand which sculpture and which vase are concerned the hearer must figure out which ones the speaker has in mind. Similarly, someone who says:

12.   He left.

either assumes the hearer knows who **he** is, or requires the hearer to figure this out. In other words, we can also speak of the "definite" article **the** and the third person pronouns, in some of their uses, as speaker-deictic expressions which point not to things close or far, but to things within the speaker's world either already shared or to be shared with the hearer. **The** in **I am going to the store**, for example, signals either that the speaker assumes the hearer already knows which store is being referred to or that the speaker assumes the hearer will recognize it as "the store in the speaker's neighborhood," therefore anchored in the speaker but intended to be absorbed into the hearer's universe. By contrast, **I am going to a store**, with the indefinite article **a**, signals that the speaker assumes the store is not already in the universe of discourse.

Personal names, although somewhat more objective and "public" than pronouns, can themselves be used as shared-world creators. A speaker who says:

13.   John left.

demands that the hearer imagine a world in which a John whom the speaker knows figures. Speaker's and hearer's worlds may contain the same Johns, but not necessarily so. The speaker's John may not be the hearer's. Unless the context makes it obvious which John is being referred to, 13 will refer to the speaker's John, and the hearer's John will be referred to some other way, for example:

14.   Your friend John left.

Other creators of shared domains include more obviously deictic constructions like **this man** in **I met this man this morning** and hearer-engaging locutions like **you know** in **He was, you know, selling dope**. This notorious **you know** expresses the speaker's belief that the hearer in fact may not know, but (at least in its origin) demands engagement **as if** the hearer does know.

As stated above, one of the uses of **the** is to refer back to something already shared by speaker and hearer. Indeed, it is one of the commonest uses of **the**. Sometimes the sharedness is a function of nonlinguistic factors, such as co-presence in a room. Of primary linguistic interest is sharedness that results from referring back to something already brought up in the discourse. Such referring back is called "coreference." Out of context it is not always easy to tell whether an NP is coreferential or shared-world creating. For example, if:

> Teddy the bartender peers through his tangled neons at the darkening twist of river past the firehouse.[9]

were to occur at the beginning of a story, we would take the **the**'s as shared-world creating. In the context of the novel *Sometimes a Great Notion*, however, they are coreferential since all have been referred to before. The two uses of **the** differ in that **the** creating shared-worlds is directly deictic to the speaker, while coreferential **the** orients the hearer primarily to the discourse and secondarily to the speaker. Being directly related to the discourse, coreference has far-reaching consequences for syntax. It motivates all the syntactic rules that we have observed involving identity of NP's. One is relative clause formation, whereby we get:

15. a.   Once upon a time there was a farmer who lived with his daughter.

rather than:

15. b.   *Once upon a time there was a farmer. A farmer lived with his daughter.

Another example is EQUI-NP deletion (cf. Chapter 4, page 165), whereby we get:

16. a.   There was once a farmer who wanted to jump over the moon.

but not:

16. b.   *There was once a farmer who wanted the farmer to jump over the moon. (if **farmer** is coreferential)

Failure to use such indicators of coreference can result in apparent incoherence, as discussed with respect to the passage cited on page 168 from Barthelme's "Edward and Pia."

A somewhat different-looking use of **the** can also be subsumed under coreference. This use is illustrated by:

17.   The word "meaning" is defined in many ways.

18.   The crashing of trees hit my ears.

In these sentences, **the** does not refer back to something already mentioned. In 17, the word under discussion is mentioned after it is referred to by **the**; in 18, likewise, the things doing the crashing are mentioned after the crashing is referred to by **the**. Hence **the** seems to be pointing forward in these examples rather than back; it certainly does not appear to be coreferential. However, consideration of underlying structure suggests that in fact what we are dealing with here is a conflation of two or more Predications. Informally, 17 involves something like **We are discussing a word; the word is "meaning,"** and 18 something like **Trees crashed; the noise of the crashing hit my ears.** Similarly, superlative expressions with **the**, such as:

19.   The best singer will get a prize.

can be derived from underlying structures of the sort **A singer will get a prize: The singer must be better than anyone else.**[10]

Not all languages have articles exactly comparable to English **the**. However, all do have terms at least partially similar to **this** and **that**. They also all use strategies of pronominalization and other devices to create shared worlds and to establish coreference. Language cannot be communicative without such devices, for without them there would be no way to indicate sameness and difference among things talked about.

A word of caution is in order. There are many uses of **the**, and it is important not to confuse its deictic and coreferential uses under discussion with others that are essentially nondeictic. Most obvious nondeictic uses are constructions involving place-names such as **The Hague** which is completely fixed. More important is the so-called "generic" **the**, as in **The whale is a mammal.** Here, some idea of shared information is present, but the main function of **the** is that of specifying the set containing all whales, and not any unique whale. In this use, **the** has a relation of near-synonymy with other determiners and with the plural, as in: **A whale is a mammal, Whales are mammals, All whales are mammals.**

POINTS OF DEPARTURE

Every argument in a Predication can be introduced as shared or not shared. Every argument in a Predication can also be coreferential provided identity is established with some previous NP. In discourse we find Predications containing arguments all of which are unshared (**A guy robbed some bank in a city named San Francisco**), others containing arguments all of which are shared (**This guy robbed the bank on the corner**), and others containing a mixture (**Some guy robbed the bank on the corner**). Establishing shared worlds, maintaining coreference, and distinguishing between what information is shared and what is unshared in the context are important factors contributing to the coherence of discourse. Another set of coherence strategies of equal consequence signals which element in a Predication one is focusing on. In English, the signal is often provided by word order. For example, compare:

20. a. He was stroking the cat gently.
    b. The cat was being gently stroked.
    c. Gently the cat was being stroked.

In each case, the order of words in the surface structure communicates a different emphasis or perspective being adopted by the speaker. The first element in surface structure functions as the "point of departure" of the message. In 20a, the sentence is organized from the point of view of the man; it is "about" what the man was doing. In 20b, the perspective shifts to the cat; and the sentence is "about" what the cat is experiencing. In 20c, the focus is on the manner of action, on what someone was doing. If you were making a movie of each of these sentences, you would probably put the camera in a different place in each case. In short, through word order, speakers establish a perspective on what is talked about. Although it is not well understood as yet, this phenomenon has been much discussed by linguists, and various terminologies for it have been used, including topic, functional sentence perspective, and theme, each defined slightly differently according to the precise range of phenomena thought to be involved. We will use the term "theme."[11]

Like other structures discussed so far, thematic structure, the choice of what to put first, is also a kind of deixis, in which a speaker points from one element in the total utterance (the point of departure or "theme") toward the rest.

As we have seen from discussion of syntax (e.g., active versus passive, extraposed versus nonextraposed complements) and of role structures, any argument can in principle occur at the beginning of a sentence, although certain verbs prevent one or more arguments associated with them from becoming subjects. It is a characteristic of English and many other languages that the most unemphatic form of language and the one with the least assumptions makes the following correlations in a sentence:

Theme	Verb	X
Agent	Verb	X
Def NP (shared)	Verb	Indef NP (unshared)
Subject	Verb	X
e.g., The robber	stole	a radio

That is, the shared information (whether coreferential or assumed shared) is often both the Agent and the theme; furthermore, the theme is also the grammatical subject (that is the NP determining number agreement in the verb).[12]

It is not surprising therefore that many traditional grammars associate subject not only with Agent, but also with theme (most often called "topic" in such grammars). It is important to note, however, that there is choice of theme. All sentences have points of departure (the theme), but the theme need be neither Agent, nor definite, nor subject. Various possibilities are illustrated by 20 above and by:

21. a.   Phil rolled a barrel down the hill at lightning speed.
         (Theme = Agent = Definite = Subject)

    b.   A barrel rolled down the hill at lightning speed.
         (Theme = Patient = Indefinite = Subject)

    c.   Down the hill rolled a barrel, at lightning speed.
         (Theme = Direction)

    d.   At lightning speed Phil rolled a barrel down the hill.
         (Theme = Manner)

In English there is a hierarchy among the relationships such that definiteness is dominant over agency, meaning that if an Agent is indefinite, some other argument that is definite will be made into the theme. It is this that gives the passive its important place in English syntax. For example, unless one wants to draw special attention to the fact that the identity of the Agent is not known,

22. a.   My father was hit by a drunk driver.

is preferable in ordinary, unrhetorical ("neutral") contexts in answer to a question like **What happened?** rather than:

22. b.   A drunk driver hit my father.

The definite subject (a Patient) in 22a contributes to the coherence of the discourse by putting shared information as the starting point from which other perspectives are explored. Blanket prohibitions such as "Never use a passive unless you can't help it" are unhelpful because they overlook the fact that in some contexts the passive is exactly what we want. What else can a reporter say when reporting an accident other than:

23. a.   A pedestrian was hit at five o'clock this morning.

when the culprit is not known? Certainly,

23. b.   Someone hit a pedestrian at five o'clock this morning.

is syntactically possible, but it gives quite the wrong perspective since the reporter is interested in the pedestrian, not the anonymous **someone**. As is well known, the passive is also useful in certain types of discourse such as scientific writing, where discoveries, not discoverers, are the focus of attention. The passive is only one among many manifestations of the general tendency in English to disfavor indefinite NP's in initial position, whatever their role. A further example of this tendency is provided by "cleft sentence" constructions beginning with **It is/was**, as in **It was a marble that Sheila lost**. In the "cleft" construction, an indefinite theme is split (or "cleft") into two parts, the first a prenominal form (**it**) pointing forward to the indefinite subject. This split theme has the double function of drawing particular attention to the subject and of putting a definite pronoun in initial position. In this particular construction, stress also falls on the subject, indicating that it is not only theme (the speaker's point of departure), but also new information, that is, what the hearer is to take as truly informative (see the next section). Such constructions imply contrast and are appropriate only if the section of the sentence which is not thematized is presupposed. Thus the exchange:

    24. Q. Who ran over your father?
        A. It was a mobster who ran over my father.

is obviously coherent. But the following is odd:

    25. Q. Why are you in mourning?
        A. It was a mobster who ran over my father.

To make sense of this, we have to imagine that if it had not been a mobster, the speaker would not have been in mourning.

NEW INFORMATION

Closely tied to establishment of shared information and to theme is the strategy of presenting information as either given or new. Every sentence presents at least some of what it says as new information—new in the context, that is, not "new under the sun." New information is signaled by sentence stress.[13] This is most clearly illustrated by contrastive sentence stress, as in:

    26. a. Í did that.
        b. I did thát.

In 26a, the information that someone "did that" is taken as already known or "given," while the information that it was I who did it is new and bears the sentence stress. In 26b, the information that I did something is given, while the heavily stressed **that** (i.e., exactly what I did) is the new information.

Signaling new information by sentence stress seems to be a universal of languages. Exactly how stress is assigned in a sentence is, however, a language-specific matter. In English, as mentioned briefly in Chapter 2, sentence stress in "neutral," noncontrastive sentences falls on the last word if it is an adverb, noun, adjective, or verb; if the last word is not one of these, but is, for example, a pronoun such as **there, that, it,** then the stress falls on the immediately preceding adverb, noun, adjective, or verb:

> 27. a.   He stood on the dóck.
>   b.   He stóod there.
>   c.   He saw the dógs.
>   d.   He sáw them.

In such neutral sentences, either the element stressed is the new information or the whole sentence is new information. These two possibilities are illustrated by **Fido got bitten by a snake** in:

> 28. a.   We went hunting one night and Fido got bitten by a snake. (**Fido got bitten by a snake** is all new information.)
>
>   b.   Q.   I hear Fido got bitten the other day. What by?
>   A.   Fido got bitten by a snake. (**A snake** is new information.)

In 28b, all the information in the answer except **snake** is the same as that in the question, and thus is not presented as new information.

When sentence stress falls on any other element in the sentence, then only the stressed element is new information, and the rest is assumed known in the context. Thus, in neutrally stressed:

> 29. a.   The dish ran away with a spóon.

either **spoon** is new or everything is new, but in nonneutrally stressed:

> 29. b.   The dísh ran away with a spoon.

the speaker presupposes that the hearer knows a spoon was run away with (that is, this information is given); precisely who did it is what is new. All instances of *it*-clefting in English involve assignment of new information to the cleft NP, since the sentence stress always falls on that NP:

> 30.   It was the bóbcats that scratched his face.

It is most important to distinguish between shared information and given information. These may, and often do, coincide, but not necessarily. In 30, **bobcats** are shared or sharable information (hence the definite article **the**), but as the stress indicates, they are also the new information in this sentence, what is new being the fact that it was **the bobcats** who scratched his face and not something else. It is the same in 29b, where **the** (shared) **dish** is the new information in the sentence. In 28, **Fido** is shared information in both cases, as indicated by use of just the proper name. But in 28a, **Fido** is part of the new information, along with everything else in the sentence, while in 28b, **Fido** is part of the given information. Furthermore, although unshared information is most often "new" information, it is not necessarily so, at least in contrastive sentences. Thus in 29b, **a spoon** is given information even though it is indefinite and unshared.

Though there is a clear difference between given and shared information and between new and unshared information, there are tight networks of interrelationship between them. These also involve theme. Since theme is the perspective from which one starts, and since it is normally shared, it is also most typically given information. But just as the theme can be unshared, so it can be new information, as we have seen in the case of *it*-clefted sentences. The constraints on nonneutral sentences are too complex to be gone into here, but the neutral alignments already partially sketched in the preceding section can now be elaborated:

Theme	Verb X
Agent	Verb X
Def NP (shared)	Verb Indef NP (unshared)
Subject	Verb X
Unstressed (given)	Sentence stress (new)
e.g., The robber	stole a rádio

POINT OF VIEW IN NARRATIVE FICTION

The topics we have discussed in this chapter are of particular value for identifying what is often called "point of view" in fiction.[14] Issues often discussed in connection with point of view are the degree of the narrator's authority (from omniscience to incompetence), degree of narrator's presence (from domination to self-effacement), and the way in which our participation as readers is invited. This last issue will be the focus of the following discussions. As we saw in the last chapter, speech act theory is primarily a theory of speakers' linguistic actions and responsibilities. Many speech acts involve direct attempts to modify the hearer's behavior (for example, commands and questions); others involve attempts to modify the hearer's awareness (statements and so forth). To understand a speech act fully, especially an indirect speech act, the hearer has to work to assess the probable intentions of the speaker, given the context of the utterance. In narrative fiction the narrator attempts primarily to modify the reader's awareness, but there are analogues to modification of behavior (for instance, the command **Call me Ishmael** in the opening sentence of *Moby Dick*). The reader, like any hearer, has to work to understand the text correctly, in other words, to interpret not only what is referred to, but also the narrator's intentions vis-à-vis the reader: Is the reader supposed to be at a distance, experiencing the action from afar, or closely involved, for example? Just as speakers require of listeners that they share the same perspective, so narrators do of readers. Authors in some sense "make readers."[15] The process of "making the reader" will be explored here with particular reference to beginnings of fictional works, and within them to the establishment of shared worlds through common-sense geography, spatial and temporal deixis, and thematic organization.

As discussed in the preceding chapter, narrative openings typically orient the reader/audience by giving person, place, and time. These orientations obviously serve to establish a shared universe with the reader. The kind of narrative that presupposes the least shared knowledge and therefore requires the least work on the part of the reader is the kind of tale which starts:

> Once upon a time in a far off country there was a stonemason with great ambitions.

Even this, of course, is more than a totally "indefinite" orientation for a narrative. The **Once upon a time** formula itself signals that this is a fairytale, and brings into play the reader's expectations of this genre. More typical of novelistic practice are the opening lines of William Thackeray's *Vanity Fair*:

> While the present century was in its teens, and on one sunshiny morning in June, there drove up to the great iron gate of Miss Pinkerton's academy for young ladies, on Chiswick Mall, a large family coach, with two fat horses in blazing harness, driven by a fat coachman in a three-cornered hat and wig, at the rate of four miles an hour.[16]

The perspective developed is first of time, then place, and finally participants. Time is anchored to the author/narrator being in his past (**was**), but in **the present century** (*not*, it should be noted, the twentieth century, but the nineteenth). Time is also anchored publicly in the month (**June**), but is not specific to day of the week or hour within the morning. The place is specified as Miss Pinkerton's academy, which we are asked to share as known, on a specific street, Chiswick Mall, which we are also invited to recall as if known. The city is assumed to be so well known as not to need mention. The participants, however, are introduced as unshared, as not yet in our consciousness: **a large family coach, a fat coachman in a three-cornered hat**. How different the effect would be if either the order of orientation or the use of **the** and **a** had been different! For example, had Thackeray wanted to start with the participants and establish them as known in the reader's consciousness, while bringing the place into our consciousness, he might have written:

> At the rate of four miles an hour, the large family coach, with its two fat horses in blazing harness, driven by the fat coachman in his three-cornered hat and wig, drove up to a great iron gate, entrance to an academy for young ladies run by a Miss Pinkerton. It was a sunshiny morning in June while the present century was in its teens.

Vanity Fair starts by assuming no knowledge of the participants. The beginning of Graham Greene's *The Honorary Consul* exemplifies a rather different type of narrator-reader relationship:

> Doctor Eduardo Plarr stood in the small port on the Paraná, among the rails and yellow cranes, watching where a horizontal plume of smoke stretched over the Chaco. It lay between the red bars of sunset like a stripe on a national flag. Doctor Plarr found himself alone at that hour except for the one sailor who was on guard outside the maritime building.[17]

The order of orientation is exactly the reverse of that in *Vanity Fair*: participant (Doctor Plarr), place (the port), and time (sunset). As readers, we are expected to share knowledge of Plarr, the port, the Paraná, the rails and cranes, the Chaco (a region of Argentina), the sailor, and the maritime building. The only thing not presupposed as already known to us is the plume of smoke. Because Plarr is presented first, and because he is presented by proper name as known to us, our tendency in this opening is to assume the narrator is narrating from Doctor Plarr's perspective. We thus assume that it is with Plarr that we share the knowledge of Plarr, the Chaco, the cranes, and so on. Likewise, we suppose that the plume of smoke has also just come into Plarr's consciousness, which would be why he is watching it. Thus, though the narrative is in third person, the narrative point of view here is established as that of one of the characters. It is interesting to note that this tactic also leads us to identify Plarr as the honorary consul referred to in the title, a supposition that is shortly proved wrong.

Again, to test the way we identify with Plarr here, we can toy with the information creating strategies. If we just interchange **the** and **a** where the substitution affects only the shared/unshared relationship, we get:

> Doctor Eduardo Plarr stood in a small port on the Paraná, among rails and yellow cranes, watching where the horizontal plume of smoke stretched over the Chaco.

(**The Paraná** and **the Chaco** have not been changed, since **a** is not a choice here except in a paraphrase such as **over a region called the Chaco**.) Here too we tend to assume that the perspective we are being asked to adopt is Plarr's. In this case, Plarr and the smoke are presented as previously known, everything else as not. The effect here is that we are quite likely to think of Plarr as having just arrived at the small port, from the region where the plume of smoke is; or perhaps the smoke is that of the vessel that has just left him off.

If, however, we alter our link with Plarr, and nothing else, the effect is quite different:

> A man stood in the small port on the Paraná, among the rails and yellow cranes, watching where a horizontal plume of smoke stretched over the Chaco.

Here we are much less likely to assume our perspective is that of the man, simply because the man is not treated as known, whereas nearly everything else is. Instead, in this passage, we and the narrator are sharing a view of the port, the smoke, and so on, and the man is present in that view, rather than sharing with us the familiar place and the unfamiliar sight of the smoke.

So far we have looked only at the briefest of passages, suggesting some of the "work" that authors and readers put into the act of communication in the first sentences of a text. We turn now to two longer passages, each an orientation to a novel, each functioning as an independent unit within a larger whole. The first passage is from near the beginning of F. Scott Fitzgerald's *The Great Gatsby*:

> It was a matter of chance that I should have rented a house in one of the strangest communities in North America. It was on that slender riotous island which extends itself due east of New York—and where there are, among other natural curiosities, two unusual formations of land. Twenty miles from the city a pair of enormous eggs, identical in contour and separated only by a courtesy bay, jut out into the most domesticated body of salt water in the Western hemisphere, the great wet barnyard of Long Island Sound. They are not perfect ovals—like the egg in the Columbus story, they are
> 10 both crushed flat at the contact end—but their physical resemblance must be a source of perpetual confusion to the gulls that fly overhead. To the wingless a more arresting phenomenon is their dissimilarity in every particular except shape and size.
>
> I lived at West Egg, the—well, the less fashionable of the two, though this is a most superficial tag to express the bizarre and not a little sinister contrast between them. My house was at the very tip of the egg, only fifty yards from the Sound, and squeezed between two huge places that rented for twelve or fifteen thousand a season. The one on my right was a colossal affair by any standard—it was a
> 20 factual imitation of some Hôtel de Ville in Normandy, with a tower on one side, spanking new under a thin beard of raw ivy, and a marble swimming pool, and more than forty acres of lawn and garden. It was Gatsby's mansion. Or, rather, as I didn't know Mr. Gatsby, it was a mansion, inhabited by a gentleman of that name. My own house was an eyesore, but it was a small eyesore, and it had been overlooked, so I had a view of the water, a partial view of my neighbor's lawn, and the consoling proximity of millionaires—all for eighty dollars a month.

> 30   Across the courtesy bay the white palaces of fashionable East
> Egg glittered along the water, and the history of the summer really
> begins on the evening I drove over there to have dinner with the
> Tom Buchanans. Daisy was my second cousin once removed, and
> I'd known Tom in college. And just after the war I spent two days
> with them in Chicago.[18]

Appearing some five pages into the novel, this passage serves as a second introduction, and in a highly compressed manner recapitulates the perspectives developed in the beginning. The first introduction is a kind of socio-philosophical orientation, telling how the narrator, Nick, had the intention of reading much that summer, and of making himself

> that most limited of all specialists, the "well-rounded man." This isn't just
> an epigram—life is much more successfully looked at from a single window,
> after all.[19]

This paradox in perspective—a broad view is too limited, a limited one most revealing—is woven in great detail into the formulations of Nick's whereabouts in the second introduction, which provides space and participant orientation.

Consider first a very striking feature here—the use of common-sense geography. There is a systematic movement from a general outer space to a specific, small locus of attention, which is Nick's rented house. We move from North America to New York City, to Long Island Sound, and thence to West Egg. Since our attention is first drawn to North America, we are anchored as citizens of some larger unit, presumably the Western Hemisphere. As it turns out, this anchor is used explicitly as a range of comparison (lines 7–8) and implicitly in line 20, where we are expected to be sufficiently knowledgeable of the Western Hemisphere to compare Gatsby's house with a Hôtel de Ville in Normandy. We are brought to more and more specific points, all presumably recognizable to the general reader, except for the Eggs, which are introduced as unshared, and then referred back to. The geographical locations stand out by their position in sentences. Occurring at the ends of sentences or at points of distinct pause, they carry sentence stress and are structurally among the most important pieces of new information, while at the same time assumed to be recognizable. We feel we are led easily through known spaces by a competent guide to a focal point from which we can view events. In contrast with this strategy, which goes from large to small, is another pattern, which goes from small to large. The central elements in Nick's world are introduced as indefinites and therefore as unshared—**a house** (1), **one of the strangest communities** (2), **a pair of enormous eggs** (5–6). Introduced in mid-sentence as they are, they are neither the theme nor the center of new information, and therefore are given the appearance of being relatively less significant than the known geographical locations. The procedure relating Nick's immediate world of house and island to larger geographical locations appears to permit us to look on without necessarily becoming absorbed into the narrator's point of view. But the distancing is not complete. **That slender riotous island**—is it **that** insofar as it is well-known to citizens of the Western Hemisphere, or is the **that** motivated by Nick's point of view at the time of speaking? The ambiguity is central to the simultaneous distancing and involving of the reader characteristic of the passage under discussion.

The second paragraph goes even further in identifying things in terms of relationships. In fact, it goes so far that we feel we are being told too much for the obvious immediate purposes, so there must be some other purpose as well. More and more specific locations are established, all involving relational terms—the house is fifty yards from the Sound (17), between two enormous mansions (18), one of which is related to the world outside (an imitation of a Hôtel de Ville in Normandy, 20). A deictic relationship brings this latter house into focus and signals that it is a key location: **The one on my right was a colossal affair** (19). The reference of this deictic is no longer clear: Which way is Nick facing when he says Gatsby's house is on his right? The deictic demands that the reader should not only recognize the world created and be willing to share the general experience, but should also participate directly in the point of view.

In the third paragraph, the narrator's house still remains the focal point from which the other houses are seen **across** (a deictic) the bay. How different **I lived across the courtesy bay from the white palaces . . .** would have been, and how jarring. In addition, other kinds of relationships are introduced to orient us, such a kinship: The Buchanans are cousins, though distant. **My second cousin once removed** (32) is interesting in its specificity, in its distance from the narrator, and also in its spatial phrasing. Spatial relations are immediately picked up again: Nick knew Tom at college, and he had visited them in Chicago. Chicago is utterly irrelevant to the narrative at this point, but is textually important in introducing another generally recognizable geographical term. **After the war** brings us to another public anchoring, this time temporal, but also one which is deictic and related to the narrator, since unless we know the date of the composition, we will not know that this is the First World War.

The narrator, then, establishes himself entirely with respect to his surroundings as described in public terms. Even without the first pages of the book, we could surmise a lot about his character from his insistent relational terminology, whether comparing the egg islands to the Columbus story, or Gatsby's mansion to a Hôtel de Ville, or situating himself in his house with its views and its consoling proximity to millionaires. But who are we supposed to be as readers? On the one hand, we are the gulls, flying over the toylike landscape looking objectively and with amusement on the barnyard with its symmetrical eggs and public landmarks. On the other hand, we are the wingless like Nick, who on land perceive asymmetries invisible from the air: Nick's island has a socially asymmetrical relation to its twin, Nick's house is asymmetrical to its neighbors in size and has an asymmetrical view (**a partial** view of my neighbor's lawn, 26–27). Nick's view is identified as a side view, a partial view, always a view from a small to a larger world, or from a private location to a public one.

What is our attitude to Gatsby? It is important to note that nothing whatsoever has been said about him as a person. Yet the narrator invites us to find him suspect by locating him, presumably by choice, not chance, on the wrong island, in a colossal imitation, itself asymmetrical (**with a tower on one side**, 20–21), covered in raw ivy. Character is formulated through formulation of place. If Nick sees himself in relation to his surroundings, he sees Gatsby through that relation to his surroundings. That his view is partial gives us the possibility of inferring that locations may not wholly represent the truth and that Nick (and we as readers) may be judging wrong. Perhaps the most revealing sentence of all is **It was Gatsby's mansion. Or, rather, as I didn't know Mr. Gatsby, it was a mansion, inhabited by a gentleman of that name** (23–24). Again we have the intimate followed by the more objective. Intimacy with Gatsby, both the narrator's, and by extension the reader's, is set up and then retracted. At the same time there is a shift in time-relations. **Gatsby's mansion** is a term appropriate to the narrator as he narrates (having already become acquainted with Gatsby); **Mr. Gatsby** is a term appropriate to the narrator as he arrives in West Egg. We are thus distanced from Gatsby and asked to assume no prior acquaintance. The shift to the impersonal, "impartial" form **Mr. Gatsby** further suggests there is something problematic about Nick's personal relations with Gatsby and raises the question whether that view is partial not only in the sense of "incomplete," but also "biased."

The second passage we will consider is the beginning of Ken Kesey's *Sometimes a Great Notion*. Typographically separated from the immediately following narrative by italic print and a space, this passage is complete in itself. Functionally it is an orientation, giving place and participants (but not time). It sets up the reader first as an observer and then, by a subtle, almost imperceptible shift, as a participant. In this respect it is similar to the passage from *The Great Gatsby*, but the general organizational strategies used are rather different.

> *Along the western slopes of the Oregon Coastal Range... come look: the hysterical crashing of tributaries as they merge into the Wakonda Auga River...*
> *The first little washes flashing like thick rushing winds through sheep sorrel and clover, ghost fern and nettle, sheering, cutting... forming branches. Then, through bearberry and salmonberry, blueberry and blackberry, the branches crashing into creeks, into streams. Finally, in the foothills, through tamarack and sugar pine, shittim bark and silver spruce—and the green and blue mosaic of Douglas fir—the actual river falls five hundred feet... and look: opens out upon the fields.*

10

Metallic at first, seen from the highway down through the trees, like an aluminum rainbow, like a slice of alloy moon. Closer, becoming organic, a vast smile of water with broken and rotting pilings jagged along both gums, foam clinging to the lips. Closer still, it flattens into a river, flat as a street, cement-gray with a texture of rain. Flat as a rain-textured street even during flood season because of a channel so deep and a bed so smooth: no shallows to set up buckwater rapids, no rocks to rile the surface . . . nothing to indicate movement except

20   *the swirling clots of yellow foam skimming seaward with the wind, and the thrusting groves of flooded bam, bent taut and trembling by the pull of silent, dark momentum.*

A river smooth and seeming calm, hiding the cruel file-edge of its current beneath a smooth and calm-seeming surface.

The highway follows its northern bank, the ridges follow its southern. No bridges span its first ten miles. And yet, across, on that southern shore, an ancient two-story wood-frame house rests on a structure of tangled steel, of wood and earth and sacks of sand, like a two-story bird with split-shake feathers, sitting fierce in its tangled

30   *nest. Look . . .*

Rain drifts about the windows. Rain filters through a haze of yellow smoke issuing from a mossy-stoned chimney into slanting sky. The sky runs gray, the smoke wet-yellow. Behind the house, up in the shaggy hem of mountainside, these colors mix in windy distance, making the hillside itself run a muddy green.

On the naked bank between the yard and humming river's edge, a pack of hounds pads back and forth, whimpering with cold and brute frustration, whimpering and barking at an object that dangles out of their reach, over the water, twisting and untwisting, swaying stiffly

40   *at the end of a line tied to the tip of a large fir pole . . . jutting out of a top-story window.*

Twisting and stopping and slowly untwisting in the gusting rain, eight or ten feet above the flood's current, a human arm, tied at the wrist, (just the arm; look) disappearing downward at the frayed shoulder where an invisible dancer performs twisting pirouettes for an enthralled audience (just the arm, turning there, above the water) . . . for the dogs on the bank, for the blinking rain, for the smoke, the house, the trees, and the crowd calling angrily from across the river, "Stammmper! Hey, goddam you anyhow, Hank Stammmmmper!"

50   *And for anyone else who might care to look.*[20]

The spatial orientation again conforms closely to Schegloff's model of formulating place, starting with the most general (the mountain range) and focusing gradually in on the river, the house, and the arm. Here again, the focusing is very gradual. The first paragraph establishes the point of departure: The narrator calls on the reader to come look from some vantage point along the western slopes of the mountain range. In the paragraph that follows, we are stationary, and looking out see the stages whereby the water consolidates into the river. Though these stages are simultaneously present to us, we are asked to see them as a temporal progression: **first** washes (4), **then** creeks and streams (6–8), **finally** the actual river (8–11). Water over time joins the river, our glance over time moves from the near washes to the far river.

Having brought our attention to the river opened out on the fields, the narrator in the third paragraph sets us in motion toward it. **At first** (4) we find ourselves on the highway looking down, but then we start moving **closer** (13), then **closer still** (15)—spatial progression now, not temporal. And as we move, the river transforms itself in our sight, from something very unlike a river (**metallic, an aluminum rainbow,** 12–13) to something a little more like a river (**organic, a smile of water,** 14) to the real thing (**it flattens into a river,** 15–16). But why **a** river in this paragraph and not **the** river as in the previous one? While the first paragraphs engage us by treating the river as known, even by name, this third paragraph distances us again, treating the river as not previously available to our consciousness, something we encounter as we move along **the** (familiar) highway. This estranged view is reinforced by the pileup of metaphors that invite us to think of the river in strange new perspectives. The move from familiarity to estrangement is an important strategy for setting up the particular view of the river that Kesey is after, the one that is finally summed up in paragraph four: The river is something that is not what it seems on the surface. If we know only the familiar surface that opens out upon the fields, we do not really know the river. In paragraph four, between the parallel indefinite phrases **a river smooth and seeming calm** (23) and **a smooth calm-seeming surface** (24) we find **the cruel file-edge of its current** (23–24) (not **a cruel file-edge of current**), which establishes the thing we really need to have in our shared universe in order to understand what follows.

Having elaborately set up this focus, the narrator moves us in along the highway closer to the house and focuses on it as a particular point of interest by shifting to a deictic orientation: **across on that southern shore** (26–27). **Across** is deictic (which side is in view depends on which side the speaker is looking from), while north and south are not deictic. The deictics explicitly locate us on the north river bank looking across at the house on the south bank, and mark the house as the goal of **come, look.**

No other deictics occur until the end of the passage: **and the crowd calling from across the river** (48). As readers we are jolted into realizing that our spatial orientation has shifted. We are no longer looking at the house from the north side, we are now at the house, and others are where we were on the north side. Furthermore, we have been so intent on the house and the arm that we have not really seen the crowd. Now, we discover, we are no longer the sole privileged viewers on a private tour with the narrator. Instead, we are the **anyone else who might care to look** (50), the objects of Stamper's derision. Along with the house, dogs, and crowd, we have become involved in the situation.

In this part of the passage too, the distribution of definites and indefinites is important. Having been brought to **a** river, we follow **the** highway to where we come upon **an ancient . . . house** (27), **a chimney** (32), **a pack of hounds** (37), and **an object** (38) **jutting out of a top-story window** (40–41), an object which is **a human arm** (43). All this is presented as unknown to us, and as somewhat mysterious. Then we are called on to consider **the arm** (43), not as an object, which is what **an arm: look** would imply, but as part of a whole: **just the arm: look. Just** conveys that there should be more than an arm, that something is missing. **The** does not refer back or indicate that the arm should be in the reader's consciousness, rather it refers us to the person of whom this is **the arm** (compare **He was stabbed in the arm** with the rather odd form **He was stabbed in an arm**). Precisely at the point where we become participants in the horror, everything we are asked to think of is made definite, known in our consciousness: **the dogs on the bank, the house, the trees, the crowd** (47–48). But then in the last line comes another jolt, as indefinites (**anyone**) are re-introduced, just as they were in paragraph three. We are made unimportant, merely members of a crowd, and we are again distanced, made to feel that what we see, like the river, conceals some harsh reality unknown to us. As it turns out, the whole novel will be an unfolding of what lies behind this scene and inside this house.

NARRATIVE TENSE

Among the remarkable features of the beginning to *Sometimes a Great Notion* is the absence of verbs in main clauses in the opening and closing sections and the predominance of V-**ing** structures functioning in an adjectival way. For instance, instead of **The first little washes flash like thick rushing winds through sheep sorrel and clover, ghost fern and nettle, sheer, cut . . . form branches**, we find lines 4–6 with **flashing, sheering, cutting**, and **forming branches**. A closer look shows that **falls** (10) is the first verb that is finite (that is, has a tense-marker) in a main clause (**merge** in line 2 is part of a subordinated time/manner clause). Only the river is described in terms of finite verbs (**opens** 11 and **flattens** 15) until line 25, when the highway and then the house, the rain, the sky, the hounds, and the object are all described with finite verbs. Then in the last paragraph, the V-**ing** structures return, with only one finite verb (**perform** 45), which is part of a relative, not main clause.

What effect does this have on the reader's viewpoint? It emphasizes the command **look**, and introduces most elements in the scene as sights, things with dynamic qualities (**rushing, cutting, twisting**) but which are parts of incomplete processes or random sequences of action. The river, which is described with finite verbs (verbs with tense morphemes, like **falls, opens, flattens**), by contrast acts and takes on importance as an entity. We sense that it will have a special role in the action to follow, as will all the other things that appear with finite verbs: the house, the highway, the weather, the dogs, and above all the invisible dancer who **performs** (finite) on the end of the **twisting** (nonfinite, incomplete) arm. Indeed, as it turns out, the owner of this arm is Henry Stamper, patriarch of the Stamper clan, and father of the Hank Stamper at whom the crowd is yelling.

The effect of the alternation between finite verbs and **be** + **ing** verbs is in part a function of the syntax (main clauses versus nominal phrases derived from underlying clauses). But mainly it is a function of the ways in which English in general uses V-ing versus present tense configurations to establish perspectives on actions. In English, **be** + **ing** emphasizes activity in progress, as in **I am/was running**, while the simple forms **I run/ran** do not. The difference between **I ran** and **I was running** is not a difference in tense (both are past), but a difference in what is called "aspect."[21] Verbal aspect involves the view being adopted toward an action, especially whether it is being viewed in terms of completion or duration. In addition to **be** + **ing**, which expresses duration, another aspect-marker in English is **have** + **en**, as in **I have run**, which indicates activity that is completed but has some present relevance (for example, **I have run and therefore I am tired**). While abstractly **be** + **ing** and **have** + **en** are markers of aspect (duration and nonduration) and have little to do with tense, English speakers tend to confuse tense with aspect. This is mainly because tense and aspect normally have to occur together in surface structure since tense is obligatory, as we saw in the discussion of AUX in Chapter 4. Thus in Standard English we say **He was/is/will be fishing**, not **He be fishing**. Furthermore, in discourse, aspect often has extended deictic functions involving foregrounding and backgrounding.[22] As will be shown in more detail below, the progressive **be** + **ing** can have a backgrounding function in contrast with plain tense. In **He was running when he fell**, for example, running is the frame of reference or background for the action of falling. This is particularly clear in the Kesey passage, where -ing without tense presents objects and actions as persisting through time and as incomplete in themselves. These objects and actions form the frame of reference from which the river, house, weather, dogs, and invisible dancer emerge and the background against which they act.

A great deal has been written about the complexities of narrative tense and aspect, and there is no possibility of touching on even the main issues here.[23] However, a few points can be made. One major problem is that in writing, as well as other mechanical ways of preserving speech, the moment of utterance does not coincide with the moment of reading or hearing. Narrator and reader are not co-present in time; narrator's **now** is not reader's **now**, as we so clearly saw in the first line of *Vanity Fair*.

As was discussed in the last chapter, narrative is basically a recounting of something that happened at some earlier time, at a distance from the time of narration. We saw that narration is typically based on narrative clauses that are characterized by finite active verbs in the simple past tense. When other tenses and aspects appear in narrative discourse, they are usually performing some communicative function other than narration proper. For instance, simple present tense, or past progressive, or "pluperfects" are typical of orientation or evaluation, as in **Now, there is no point messing with**

an angry bear, I was working for Ford at the time, or **I had been looking for a job for weeks** (cf. page 250). Although past tense is the norm for narration in both speech and writing, narration can take place in the present tense. In this case, narrative clauses are in the simple present tense, while orientation and evaluation tend to appear as present tense **be** + **ing** or as **have** + **en.** This kind of tense structure is well illustrated by the following passage from Shirley Ann Grau's story "Eight O'Clock One Morning":

My father just grunts and doesn't say anything.

My mother comes back from the phone and says triumphantly: "She didn't know anything about it."

Rosalie asks: "Can we make some fudge?"

"Anything to keep you quiet," my mother tells her.

They both get down on their hands and knees and start looking around in one of the low cupboards for the proper size pan. Taylor has found his kitten and he's feeding it catfood out of the can with a spoon. You can hear him singing to it.

10   Then it happens. I hadn't been looking out, so the first I know of it is when my father says, "Son of a bitch!"

But he says it softly so that my mother and Rosalie, who have their heads inside the cupboard rattling pans, can't hear him. And if Taylor does he pays no attention.

I look out. A diaper service truck (all white and blue painted) has pulled up in front of the Fortiers' across the street. The Negro driver must be awful brave or awful foolish or maybe he just doesn't know.

He has taken the clean diapers into the house and put the
20   dirty ones in the back of the truck and closed the door.

When the kids notice him he is back in the cab. He has just started the motor and he is barely moving when they catch up with him. There are a dozen or so of them, and they dash alongside; some run directly in front and the truck stops. Two of them jump in the open door and grab for the driver, only they keep missing because another kid is beating away with an old mop. He is swinging it with all his strength at the driver but all he hits is the head of one of the boys who have hopped the cab. And all the bits of things, rocks or maybe more ice, are rattling down on the
30   truck.

My old man bangs through the kitchen door.[24]

The father's grunt, the mother's coming back from the phone, the mother and sister getting down on their knees are all part of the narrative sequence. Taylor's finding and feeding his cat, however, are background, not part of the sequence, as tense and aspect indicate. This background-foreground distinction becomes crucial in the description of the attack on the delivery man. The Black driver's actions are presented as background (**a truck has pulled up** (15–16), not **pulls up**), and function as settings for an encounter. These settings are seen either as already established (**he has taken the clean diapers into the** house, 19; **he has just started the motor**, 21–22) or as developing and ongoing (**He is barely moving**, 22). Momentarily the driver's response becomes part of the narrative sequence in **the truck stops** (24), but it is significant that the driver as agent of the stopping is not mentioned. At this point even the children's activities cease to form a narrative sequence, and become simply ongoing, repeated action until the next narrative clause, **My old man bangs through the kitchen door** (31). Thus we get a kind of hierarchy in the passage. The Black man is chiefly seen as background for the children's actions; the children are foreground with respect to the Black man, but act as background with respect to the parents' actions.

This device of transferring narrative into the so-called narrative present tense is of course not restricted to literature. It can also be found in on-the-spot sports-casting, jokes, oral narrative of personal experience, and other genres. In all the purpose is the same: to create a sense of urgency and immediacy. The present tense, as a deictic, indicates proximity to the narrator and implies the narrator's involvement in the action. Working with the Cooperative Principle, the reader allows the tense to establish the events recounted as immediately relevant and involving, even though he or she may be removed by hundreds of years. The Grau passage illustrates the most common form of present tense narration in English. The Kesey passage discussed earlier represents an extension of this. There, instead of a contrast between present, present progressive, and **have + en**, there is a simpler contrast between present and tenseless V-**ing**. To understand both, it is important to recognize that present tense narration is not the same as a description of ongoing action or situation. This latter is almost always expressed in the present progressive. For instance, if you are asked to look out the window and tell what's going on, you will not say **Rain drifts about the windows, a pack of hounds pads back and forth in front of the house, someone goes up and knocks at the door.** Rather you will say **Rain is drifting about the windows, and a pack of hounds is padding back and forth in front of the house, someone is going up to the door, now they're knocking at it**, and so forth.

FREE INDIRECT STYLE

The passages discussed so far have involved relatively simple tense and aspect structures. We will end this chapter with a brief look at one of the more complex types of narrative tense systems, that found in what is known as "narrated monologue" or "free indirect style." Free indirect style is one of a group of techniques used to produce stream of consciousness narrative, in which events are presented through the psyche of a character, while the author/narrator is not distinctly present, and there is no particular appeal to the reader. The following excerpt from Doris Lessing's novel *The Four-Gated City* gives us an example of free indirect style.

Doors slammed. Drawers slammed. A few moments later her voice chided the child, as they descended to the kitchen on the ground floor. From her bed Martha followed the progress of breakfast being made: well, let's hope that Mark was at the factory today and not being disturbed by it.

I shall tell Mark that I'm leaving. Today. I don't want to be involved in all this . . . She meant, this atmosphere of threat, insecurity, and illness. Who would have thought that coming to this house meant—having her nose rubbed in it! Yes, but that wasn't what she had meant, when she had demanded from life that she must have her nose rubbed in it. Something new, surely, not what she had lived through already, was what she ought to be doing? Why was she here at all? If you start something, get on a wavelength of something, then there's no getting off, getting free, unless you've learned everything there is to be learned—have had your nose rubbed in it?[25]

10

This passage illustrates the way in which free indirect style is used: in conjunction with other kinds of narration. The first lines of this passage (from the beginning to the middle of line 4) come to us from the narrator's point of view. Halfway through line 4, we shift into Martha's mind and get her thoughts and perceptions quoted directly as she thinks them. Then in line 8, there is another shift, into free indirect style, made most noticeable by a shift from first to third person pronouns to refer to Martha. The rest of the passage remains in this style.

We can use the sentence **Why was she here at all?** (lines 12–13) to illustrate the most salient characteristics of free indirect style.[26] If Martha's thoughts were still being quoted directly, as they are in line 6, this sentence would read:

31.   She thought, "Why am I here at all?"

If Martha's thoughts were being reported indirectly by the narrator, we would get:

32.   She asked herself why she was there at all.

What we actually get is something that has things in common with both 31 and 32, yet differs from both. Like 32, and unlike 31, the actual sentence uses a third person pronoun and past tense verb. Like 31, and unlike 32, the actual sentence has the syntactic form of a direct question, including inverted AUX NP, and uses the place adverbial **here** rather than **there**. In terms of deixis, then, in Lessing's sentence and in free indirect style in general, tense and person deixis are anchored in the narrator: Martha is a **she** with respect to the narrating **I** and the reading **you**; Martha's present is in the narrator's past. But all other deictic expressions are anchored in the fictional character whose thoughts are being rendered: **Here** means Martha's here, not that of the narrator; **this** in **this house** (8) and **this atmosphere** (7) is also anchored in Martha, not the narrator. Except for tense, all time expressions in this style are likewise anchored in the fictional character. Thus, if in our passage we were to read:

33.   Why was she here at all, and now of all times? Two weeks ago, she had been safe at home. This morning she would spend her last penny on breakfast.

we would automatically understand the time expressions **now, two weeks ago,** and **this morning** as anchored in Martha's present, not that of the narrator. By contrast, narrator's report of 33 would read:

34.   She asked herself why she was there at all, and then of all times. Two weeks before she had been safe at home. That morning she would spend her last penny on breakfast.

Here, all deixis is anchored in the narrator, so that Martha's **now** is narrator's **then**, her **this** narrator's **that**, and so on. Finally, contrast what 33 would look like in direct quotation of Martha's thoughts:

35.   "Why am I here at all?" she thought, "and now of all times? Two weeks ago I was safe at home. This morning, I'm going to spend my last penny on breakfast."

In sum, free indirect style involves a two-way pointing, in which pronouns and verbal inflections are anchored in the narrator and all other deictics in the fictional character. We as readers are placed in a particular vantage point in which we are distanced from the character by pronouns (the character remains a **he** or **she**, that is, an other), and at the same time, the other deictics obliterate the narrator and bring us into the character's immediate purview. This two-way pointing means that often there are co-occurrences of deictic expressions that would be odd indeed in other contexts. For instance, it is hard to think where a sentence like **tomorrow he would be coming** could occur except in free indirect style.

A number of other characteristics in addition to deixis bring us close to the character's viewpoint in this style. For instance, in both 31 and 32 above, the character's thoughts are syntactically embedded in a verb of perception on mental process (**think, wonder, ask oneself**) just as dialogue is typically embedded in a verb of saying. In free indirect style, the verbs of mental process, reminders of the dominating narrator's presence, are absent or very sparse, often occurring only at the beginning to indicate the shift into the character's mind. Another feature approximating us to the character is syntax. As we saw above, the syntax used in free indirect style is that of direct speech, not that of indirect or reported speech. Thus, questions appear with question marks and AUX NP inversion, rather than with periods and uninverted, as they appear in reported speech (in Standard English **He asked what she was doing**, not **He asked what was she doing?**). Other surface forms that normally do not appear at all in reported speech do appear in free indirect style, such as exclamations, interjections like **Oh! For heaven's sake!** and direct reply terms like **No** or **Certainly not**. When we try to incorporate such constructions into reported speech, the results are odd indeed:

36. *She$\begin{cases}\text{thought} \\ \text{exclaimed}\end{cases}$ that who would have thought that coming to that house meant—having her nose rubbed in it!

Another respect in which free indirect style is like directly quoted speech and thought is in its informality. Expressions like **having one's nose rubbed in it** are not usually used by narrators of novels but they are usually spoken or thought by real people, and it is common for switches to free indirect style to be signaled in a text by the appearance of informal, colloquial, or taboo language.

SUGGESTED FURTHER READINGS

The best general introductions to deixis are found in Lyons's *Semantics*, Volume II, Chapter 15, entitled "Deixis, Space, and Time," and in Fillmore's extremely readable *Santa Cruz Lectures on Deixis*. For discussion of the interesting subject of deixis and language acquisition, see H. Clark's "Space, Time, Semantics, and the Child."

Thorough treatment of thematic structure, given-new, and shared-unshared organization is found in Halliday and Hasan's *Cohesion in English*. Chafe's "Givenness, Contrastiveness, Definiteness, Subjects, Topics, and Point of View" and MacWhinney's "Starting Points" are also accessible to the beginner, while Kuno's article "Subject, Theme, and Speaker's Empathy— A Re-examination of Relativization Phenomena" discusses thematic structure in relation to a factor not discussed in this chapter, a factor known as "empathy." Rather advanced but interesting studies of topics discussed in this chapter are found in Givón's *Syntax and Semantics 12: Discourse and Syntax*, and from a psychological point of view, in Miller and Johnson-Laird's *Language and Perception*, especially Chapters 5–7. Basic general readings are found in Giglioli's *Language in Context*, which contains several papers particularly pertinent to this chapter. Also consult the journals suggested in Chapter 6.

There is a very large body of literary criticism and theory on narrative point of view, but surprisingly little with a linguistic orientation. One exception is Scholes and Kellogg's *The Nature of Narrative*, one of the basic texts on literary narrative. More recent is Fowler's *Linguistics and the Novel*, an excellent introductory treatment of topics discussed both here and in Chapter

6. For discussion of deixis and pronominalization in literary texts, see Widdowson's *Stylistics and the Teaching of Literature*, especially Chapters 2–4. Fillmore's "Pragmatics and the Description of Discourse" specifically deals with pragmatic analysis of free indirect style, a topic also discussed in the Fowler text mentioned above, as well as in Page's important book *Speech in the English Novel*.

Hendricks's *Grammars of Style and Styles of Grammar* and Dillon's *Language Processing and the Reading of Literature* have several chapters of interest, notably on discourse analysis, and anaphora. Several pertinent articles are found in *Style and Text*, edited by Ringbom and others. This collection also contains a section on "text linguistics," the approach to discourse analysis now being developed in Europe. European text linguistics shares a great many concerns with the kind of discourse analysis we have been working with here, and focuses heavily on the questions of text cohesion and the role of the reader. For further readings on text linguistics, see the anthologies *Grammars and Descriptions* edited by van Dijk and Petöfi, *Trends in Text-linguistics* edited by Dressler, and van Dijk's book, *Text and Context*.

Exercises

1. Rewrite the following passage from Lincoln's Second Inaugural Address in the most neutral, unemphatic word order, as defined in this chapter. Then discuss the difference in rhetorical effect between your passage and Lincoln's. Include comments on the following:

   a. What arguments (roles) occur as themes in Lincoln's version?
   b. Why might the argument of the theme be rather different in sentence four (**the progress of our arms**) than in the other sentences?
   c. To what extent does the coherence of Lincoln's speech depend on its thematic structure?

   At this second appearing to take the oath of the presidential office, there is less occasion for an extended address than there was at the first. Then a statement, somewhat in detail, of a course to be pursued, seemed fitting and proper. Now, at the expiration of four years, during which public declarations have been constantly called forth on every point and phase of the great contest which still absorbs the attention, and engrosses the energies of the nation, little that is new could be presented. The progress of our arms, upon which all else chiefly depends, is as well known to the public as to myself; and it is, I trust, reasonably satisfactory and encouraging to all. With high hope for the future, no prediction in regard to it is ventured.[27]

2. What is there about the perspective of the locative and directional expressions that makes the a phrase more usual than the b?

> i. a. The money in the box
> b. The box around the money
> ii. a. The rushes beside the lake
> b. The lake beside the rushes
> iii. a. The path along the lake
> b. The lake along the path
> iv. a. The woman by the store
> b. The store beside the woman
> v. a. The paper on the table
> b. The table under the paper
> vi. a. Night over Sorrento
> b. Sorrento under the night.

Using the same locative prepositions, can you think of any pairs where the perspective in both sentences is equally probable, that is, neither sentence requires significantly more contextual information than the other? What makes these sentences different from the ones cited above?

3. In the discussion of spatial deictics, we pointed out some idiomatic expressions in which **come** seemed to mean orientation toward a normal state of affairs and **go** orientation toward an abnormal state of affairs. Using a dictionary, thesaurus, or dictionary of idioms, find some more idioms where these meanings emerge in **come** and **go**. Then do the same for **bring** and **take**. Does **fetch** share the same deictic orientations as **bring**?

4. In this chapter, we mentioned that cars have their own front/back and left/right orientation. Is this always true, or can speaker deixis override it? In thinking about this problem, consider the relative positions of car and speaker (and if relevant, other cars) in such sentences as:

> a. I stood in front of the car.
> b. When he took my picture, I was standing in front of the car.
> c. I stood beside the car.
> d. When he took my picture, I was standing beside the car.

Under what circumstances in a car could you back into the car in front of you? Under what circumstances in a car could you say the driver of the car behind you was in front of you?

5. The following is the famous opening passage of William Faulkner's novel *The Sound and the Fury*. The **I** of the narrative here is a mentally retarded man, who is watching a golf game:

> Through the fence, between the curling flower spaces, I could see them hitting. They were coming toward where the flag was and I went along the fence. Luster was hunting in the grass by the flower tree. They took the flag out, and they were hitting. Then they put the flag back and they went to the table, and he hit and the other hit. Then they went on,

and I went along the fence. Luster came away from the flower tree and we went along the fence and they stopped and we stopped and I looked through the fence while Luster was hunting in the grass.

"Here, caddie." He hit. They went away across the pasture. I held to the fence and watched them going away.[28]

a. Try to draw a sketch of people's positions and paths of movement in this passage. At what places is more information needed in order to contextualize the scene fully?

b. Discuss the use of definites (**the**, third person pronouns, and personal names) and coreference. Do you feel that the definites are being used to create a shared universe of discourse, or do they reflect an assumed universe, or are they being used coreferentially, or some combination of these? Why?

c. In the passage, verbs are either in the past tense or past progressive. We pointed out in this chapter that often in narrative, the progressive is used for backgrounding and orienting the simple past tense for narrative sequence. Is this what is going on here? Give reasons for your answer.

d. Some readers encountering this passage out of context, contextualize it by assuming the **I** is a dog rather than a man who is an idiot. What basis is there in the passage for such an interpretation?

e. Rewrite the passage from the point of view of a person of normal mental capacity.

6. Discuss tense and aspect in T. S. Eliot's "Rhapsody on a Windy Night," quoted on pages 24–26.

7. Discuss how point of view is established in the orientation to the *Pudd'nhead Wilson* anecdote quoted in Chapter 6. From what standpoint are we introduced to Wilson? How is our standpoint made to change in the course of the anecdote?

8. Discuss how Richard Llewellyn creates a shared universe with the reader in these opening lines from *How Green Was My Valley*. Consider, among other things, the use of deictics (**this, that, go**), articles (**the, a**), names, and tense (note that **I am going**, though present in form, refers to the future, and **if I went**, though past in form, refers to a hypothetical future possibility). What age does the narrator appear to be, and why?

I am going to pack my two shirts with my other socks and my best suit in the little blue cloth my mother used to tie round her hair when she did the house, and I am going from the Valley.

This cloth is much too good to pack things in and I would keep it in my pocket only there is nothing else in the house that will serve, and the lace straw basket is over at Mr. Tom Harries', over the mountain. If I went down to Tossall the Shop for a cardboard box I would have to tell him why I wanted it, then everybody would know I was going. That is not what I want, so it is the old blue cloth, and I have promised it a good wash and iron when I have settled down, wherever that is going to be.[29]

9. The text by Virginia Woolf discussed in Chapter 2 (page 77) uses free indirect style.
    a. What characteristics of free indirect style do you find in that passage?
    b. What do **then** and **there** in line 6 refer to?
    c. Rewrite the passage as a direct quotation of Mrs. Dalloway's thoughts. In what case or cases does verb inflection not change, and why?
    d. The following lines are the ones that immediately precede the Woolf text quoted in Chapter 2. They are also the opening lines of the novel:

    Mrs. Dalloway said she would buy the flowers herself.
    For Lucy had her work cut out for her. The doors would be taken off their hinges; Rumpelmayer's men were coming. And then, thought Clarissa Dalloway, what a morning—fresh as if issued to children on a beach.[30]

    (1) At what point do we shift from the narrator's viewpoint to free indirect style, and how do you know?
    (2) How is **And then** in the fourth sentence anchored?

NOTES

[1] Emanuel A. Schegloff, "Notes on Conversational Practice: Formulating Place," in *Studies in Social Interaction*, ed. David Sudnow (New York: The Free Press, 1972); shorter version in *Language in Context*, ed. Pier Paolo Giglioli (Harmondsworth, Mssex.: Penguin, 1972). Much of the present section is based on this work.

[2] See, for example, Roman Jakobson, "Shifters, Verbal Categories, and the Russian Verb," in *Selected Writings* (1957; rpt. The Hague: Mouton, 1971), II; Charles J. Fillmore, *Santa Cruz Lectures on Deixis* (Indiana Linguistics Club, 1971). Much of this section is based on the latter work.

[3] For a study of a wide number of indexicals including those mentioned here, see Michael Silverstein, "Shifters, Linguistics Categories, and Cultural Description," in *Meaning in Anthropology*, eds. Keith H. Basso and Henry A. Selby (Albuquerque: Univ. of New Mexico Press, 1976).

[4] Fillmore, *Lectures on Deixis*, 39.

[5] Eve V. Clark, "Normative States and Evaluative Viewpoints," *Language*, 50 (1974), 316–32.

[6] From Lewis Carroll, *Alice in Wonderland*, ed. Donald J. Gray (New York: W. W. Norton and Co., 1971), p. 149.

[7] Rodney Huddleston, "Some Observations on Tense and Deixis in English," *Language*, 45 (1969), 777–806; John Lyons, *Semantics* (London and New York: Cambridge Univ. Press, 1977), II, pp. 677–90. See also Elizabeth C. Traugott, "Spatial Expressions of Tense and Temporal Sequencing: A Contribution to the Study of Semantic Fields," *Semiotica*, 15 (1975), 207–30.

[8] This and the following two sections owe much to Wallace L. Chafe, "Givenness, Contrastiveness, Definiteness, Subjects, Topics, and Point of View," in *Subject and Topic*, ed. Charles N. Li (New York: Academic Press, 1976).

[9] From Ken Kesey, *Sometimes a Great Notion* (New York: The Viking Press, 1964), p. 207.

[10] See Sandra A. Thompson, "The Deep Structure of Relative Clauses," in *Studies in Linguistic Semantics*, eds. Charles J. Fillmore and D. Terence Langendoen (New York: Holt, Rinehart and Winston, Inc., 1971).

[11] Cf. M. A. K. Halliday, "Notes on Transitivity and Theme," *Journal of Linguistics*, 3 (1967), 37–81, 199–244; 4 (1968), 179–215. Also M. A. K. Halliday and Ruqaiya Hasan, *Cohesion in English* (London: Longman, 1976), Chapter 12.

[12] For several studies of this correlation, see Li, ed., *Subject and Topic*.

[13] The study of intonation (pitch and stress as a factor in establishing textual cohesion) has been studied most extensively in England; cf. Gunther R. Kress, ed., *Halliday; System and Function in Language: Selected Papers* (London: Oxford Univ. Press, 1976); and Geoffrey Leech and Jan Svartvik, *A Communicative Grammar of English* (London: Longman Group Ltd., 1975).

[14] See Charles J. Fillmore, "Pragmatics and the Description of Discourse," *Berkeley Studies in Syntax and Semantics*, 1 (1974), Chapter 5; and Roger Fowler, "The Referential Code and Narrative Authority," *Language and Style*, 10 (1977), 129–61.

[15] Among a number of critical works in which this point of view is adopted, see Wayne C. Booth, *The Rhetoric of Fiction* (Chicago: Univ. of Chicago Press, 1971); Robert Scholes and Richard Kellogg, *The Nature of Narrative* (London and New York: Oxford Univ. Press, 1966); and Walter J. Ong, "The Writer's Audience Is Always a Fiction," *PMLA*, 90 (1975), 9–21. For the complementary view that readers make meanings, see Stanley Fish, "Literature in the Reader: Affective Stylistics," *New Literary History*, 2 (1970), 123–62; and Wolfgang Iser, *The Implied Reader; Patterns of Communication in Prose Fiction from Bunyan to Beckett* (Baltimore: The Johns Hopkins Univ. Press, 1974).

[16] From William Makepeace Thackeray, *Vanity Fair* (New York and London: Harper and Bros., 1898), p. 1.

[17] From Graham Greene, *The Honorary Consul* (New York: Simon and Schuster, 1973), p. 15.

[18] From F. Scott Fitzgerald, *The Great Gatsby* (New York: Charles Scribner's Sons, 1925), pp. 3–4.

[19] Fitzgerald, *Great Gatsby*, p. 3.

[20] From Kesey, *Sometimes a Great Notion*, pp. 1–2.

[21] See John Lyons, *Introduction to Theoretical Linguistics* (London and New York: Cambridge Univ. Press, 1968); and Bernard Comrie, *Aspect* (London and New York: Cambridge Univ. Press, 1976).

[22] See Paul J. Hopper, "Aspect and Foregrounding in Discourse," in *Syntax and Semantics 12: Discourse and Syntax*, ed. Talmy Givón (New York: Academic Press, 1979).

[23] See, for example, Käte Hamburger, *The Logic of Literature*, trans. Marilynn J. Rose (Bloomington: Indiana Univ. Press, 1973) on literary tense; and Nessa Wolfson, "The Conversational Historical Present Alternation," *Language*, 55 (1979), 168–82, on tense in conversation.

[24] From Shirley Ann Grau, "Eight O'Clock One Morning," in *The Wind Shifting West* (New York: Alfred A. Knopf, 1973), pp. 196–97.

[25] From Doris Lessing, *The Four-Gated City* (New York: Alfred A. Knopf, 1974), p. 106.

[26] For two linguistic studies, see Ann Banfield, "Narrative Style and the Grammar of Direct and Indirect Speech," *Foundations of Language*, 10 (1973), 1–39; and Fillmore, "Pragmatics and Description of Discourse."

[27] From Abraham Lincoln, "Second Inaugural Address," in *Abraham Lincoln: Selected Speeches, Messages, and Letters*, ed. T. Harry Williams (New York: Holt, Rinehart and Winston, Inc., 1972), p. 282.

[28] From William Faulkner, *The Sound and the Fury* (New York: Random House, 1956), p. 23.

[29] Richard Llewellyn, *How Green Was My Valley* (New York: The Macmillan Co., 1940), p. 1.

[30] From Virginia Woolf, *Mrs. Dalloway* (New York: Harcourt Brace Jovanovich, Inc., 1925), p. 3.

CHAPTER 8

Varieties of English: Regional, Social, and Ethnic

We have seen how language-users shift their speech habits according to the degree of formality required, the subject about which they are talking, the genre, and medium. All such shifts contribute greatly to the variability of language. There are other types of variation too. Indeed, the phrase "varieties of English" probably makes us think first and foremost of the pronounced differences in the linguistic habits of people from different regions, social classes, and ethnic groups. It is these kinds of variation that we will be discussing in this chapter. In more traditional terminology, this topic would be referred to as "dialects of English," but for reasons outlined below, we adopt the term "variety" as well as the more familiar "dialect."

When you greet someone you don't know and ask formulaic questions, you are not only establishing lines of communication and setting up social roles, you are also finding out something about where the person is from and perhaps also what the person's socioeconomic status is—or at least what he or she would like you to think it is. Dress, style of walk, gesture all indicate such factors too, but language plays a crucial role. Formulaic openings, such as comments on the weather, allow an apparently objective context to reveal delicate differences. Even a formula as simple as

1. a. Hi, how are you?

tells a lot about the speaker, revealing, for instance, that the speaker wants to be informal (**Hi** as opposed to **Hello**), and is from the United States (**Hi** is rarely used in England), and probably from the Southeast United States. In many other parts of the United States the intonation pattern in 1a with rise-fall on **you** can be used only for a real question, not a greeting. Speakers from these regions use an intonation pattern with a rise on **are**:

1. b.   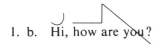 Hi, how are you?

for the greeting. Another greeting formula, **Mornin'**, tells something about regional or social background through presence or absence of **r**, and presence of [ɪn] versus [ɪŋ], where [ɪn] indicates familiarity, casual speech, or lower-class economic status. There are very few utterances that do not give us at least some extra-linguistic information.

In most speech communities, we find language variation along lines of regional or ethnic origin, socioeconomic status, and also sex, age, and education. All speakers have at least some internalized knowledge of how their language varies along these parameters, and in most cases we find culturally shared attitudes to certain varieties. For instance, in England before the Second World War, a social dialect known as the King's or Queen's English was the high prestige variety, mandatory for anybody aspiring to a civil service or academic post, and speakers of this variety were socially approved of while nonspeakers were not. This attitude was immortalized in Shaw's *Pygmalion* and the musical based on it, *My Fair Lady*. Since the 1960s, however, a considerable number of regional and even social varieties have become widely acceptable in England. Indeed, many prospective professors who twenty-five years ago would have cultivated "the Queen's English" now studiously avoid it and announce their social and regional origins proudly (in some cases we may even find a "reverse snobbism," the adoption of a variety typical of a socioeconomic class lower than that into which the speaker was born). This cultural attitude depends for its existence on the knowledge that language varies, and that language varieties can have social meaning. That is, they can function as indicators of social identity.

In sum, when we consider why people speak the way they do, all of the following factors must be considered separately in addition to the structure of the code itself:

1. type of speaker (regional and ethnic origin, socioeconomic status, education, sex, age)
2. type of addressee (as in 1)
3. topic of speech (politics, sex, linguistics, a drunken brawl)
4. genre (sermon, casual talk, interview)
5. medium (spoken, written; radio, television)

6. situation (classroom, bar, a walk in the fields)
7. degree of formality (casual, formal)
8. type of speech act (statement, command, question).

These factors form the basis of study in the discipline called "sociolinguistics." All are essential to a full understanding of language as communication and of the structures that control it. We are concerned with the first of these factors here. Particular attention will be paid to ways in which variation depends on regional or ethnic origin, and social status. Even within these limits, there are dozens of varieties of English on which we could have focused, for example, Irish, Australian, Cockney, Appalachian, or Texan. The one we have chosen is Black American English Vernacular. It has been selected as the focus of this chapter because many recent theoretical and methodological developments in sociolinguistics have been worked out primarily in research on this variety (or rather cluster of varieties), and an extensive, coherent body of research is available on the subject. It is also a language variety that has been used in many highly successful literary experiments.

Before going on to a specific look at some ways in which English varies according to "type of speaker," let us note some of the methodological problems in studying language variation.

THE DATA ON VARIABILITY

Preceding chapters have considered aspects of language that can be established through introspection. However, when we consider the question of variability according to type of speaker or addressee, introspection is no longer of any use. This is because any individual controls only some of all the possible varieties of a language. Also, most people imagine they speak very differently from the way they actually do. People hearing themselves for the first time on a tape recorder are amazed and sometimes shocked by what they hear. Many people think they speak more homogeneously, even more standardly, than they really do. To find out what different kinds of regional or other varieties there are, then, one must use data collected through questionnaires, interviews, tape recordings of free speech, and the like. This method in turn raises problems of its own.

First, one can never be sure the collected data is complete; in fact, one can be pretty sure that it is incomplete, that there are relevant forms that have not shown up. This is particularly true of syntactic structures. A second, related problem is the fact that data is always skewed by the presence of the person collecting it. It is particularly difficult to collect samples of people's most spontaneous, informal speech because people are likely to speak very self-consciously and formally when they know they are part of a linguistic inquiry. Interviews tend to elicit what people think they ought to say, rather than what they do say. Postal questionnaires elicit even more formal and less spontaneous responses, because writing itself triggers formality. Oral questionnaires are more effective, but interviewees are still watchful of their speech in this context. With either medium, material to be elicited often cannot be asked for directly, particularly if it is phonetic. For example, there are some varieties of English in which the vowel in **wash** is [ɔy]. If one wants to investigate presence or absence of [ɔy] in such words, a question like "How do you pronounce **wash**?" would probably make people too conscious of their pronunciation. Their response might be influenced by spelling, by prestige norms, or by the interviewer's own pronunciation—the relevant factor could not be determined. A far better way to approach the problem would be to ask for relevant lexical data: "What is another term for laundry?" If it is lexical variants one wants to study, extensive discussion is often needed to capture stylistic differences or slight meaning differences. For example, a question such as "What is the name of the thing you fry eggs in?" might elicit "A skillet"; only further questioning such as "Do you use or know any other terms?" might elicit **frying pan**, and only a third question would get to appropriate contexts for the two terms.

Various research methods have recently been developed in attempts to overcome such problems, mainly under the inspiration of William Labov. In an early study he investigated a very widespread phenomenon called "*r*-fulness." This has to do with presence or absence of [r] after a vowel in such words as **car**, **barn**, and **farmer**. Brooklynese, for example, is famous for not having [r] in words such as [boyd] "bird." Labov studied the correlation of *r*-fulness with social prestige by asking sales personnel for the location of the shoe department at three large New York department stores. These three stores appealed to very different kinds of clientele, and all had their shoe department on the fourth floor. He jotted down the presence or absence of **r** in the responses, which were almost uniformly "On the fourth floor," and found that the personnel in the highest prestige store used **r** far more frequently than in the middle prestige store, and hardly at all in the lowest prestige store.[1] Such a technique has the advantage of interviewer anonymity (none of the sales personnel knew that this was any other than a shopper's ordinary question), but it has the grave disadvantage of providing only impressionistic results, and no reliable information on the speakers' social or regional background, their education, attitudes to language, and so forth. Although never able to eliminate consciousness of the interviewer and of the tape recorder, Labov found that lengthy interviews, including reading of a passage and casual conversation, tend to relax people, and that questions like "Were you ever in danger of death?" almost always prompt answers in the least self-conscious speech, marked by a switch to a less standard or formal style. The more emotionally involved the speakers, the closer they come to the variety most natural to them. Most recently, Labov has found that one can best collect casual speech by group interviews; this, however, requires extremely fine recording equipment and a group of people who know each other well.[2]

Even when one has collected reasonably reliable data, the task of identifying language varieties is not immediately solved. For one thing, differences between varieties often involve not the bare presence or absence of a form, but the quantitative likelihood of a form being used or not used. Let us take an example from Black American English. It is extremely unlikely that upper-middle-class Black speakers would use multiple negatives in formal speech, such as **Nobody never did nothing** in the sense of **Nobody ever did anything**. At the other end of the scale, working-class Blacks speaking informally are extremely likely to use multiple negatives. But the same upper-middle-class Black speaker who does not use multiple negatives in formal situations will occasionally use them in informal ones. Similarly, the working-class Black speaker who uses multiple negatives most of the time in casual speech will use fewer of them in formal situations. Thus, in distinguishing between middle- and working-class Black English, we would not want to say simply that the former lacks multiple negatives and the latter has them; rather, we would have to talk about the frequency of occurrence of multiple negatives. Moreover, no one feature, such as multiple negation, serves to distinguish one variety from another. A great many varieties of English in fact use multiple negation. It is not a particular feature, but a whole network of features from every aspect of linguistic structure—phonological, morphological, syntactic, lexical, and pragmatic—that make up what is recognized as one variety or another.

That a form is usually not completely present or absent but is used relatively more or less in certain circumstances may at first seem surprising. We have all imitated other varieties of English by selecting certain features that we think are typical. For example, we might characterize a nonstandard speaker by substituting **ain't** for **isn't** in all cases. However, were we to listen closely to such a speaker, we would discover that **ain't** is used only some of the time. The tendency to stereotype certain language varieties may be partly the result of wanting to draw attention to the variety. But it may often be partly determined by ignorance of the factors that control use or nonuse of features like **ain't**. Among literate speakers, the tendency to stereotype is also partly a direct consequence of projecting the relative uniformity of written language onto all varieties of the language other than those with which they are fully familiar.

Stereotyping not only misrepresents what speakers do with their language, but also picks somewhat arbitrary targets. For example, **ain't** and double negatives arouse very bad reactions in standard speakers and even in some nonstandard speakers who recognize that these are socially unacceptable. They are called "stigmatized" forms. On the other hand, other nonstandard forms, such as [ɪn] for [ɪŋ] for the present progressive morpheme, arouse little negative reaction. They are merely the object of condescension, not opprobrium.

Early studies of variation according to type of speaker focused on regional distinctions, sometimes intermixed with social distinctions. Such varieties were called dialects. There has been considerable confusion in the use of this term. Everyone speaks one or more dialects of a language insofar as they use certain regional and social varieties. Yet many people think only other people use dialects. This comes in part from confusion of the term "a dialect," which simply means "a variety," and includes the standard variety, with "dialect," which refers only to nonstandard varieties. People who "speak dialect" are understood to speak with distinct regionalisms, perhaps even with noneducated features. They are often considered quaint, boorish, or in some other way inferior. Another term sometimes confused with "a dialect" is "accent," which refers solely to pronunciation. Although "accent" describes the phonological characteristics of any dialect, in everyday talk, to say someone "speaks with an accent" means they speak with a sound system distinctly different from one's own.

When linguists began to study and establish clear differences between regional and social varieties of English, as well as to study such factors as sex-related differences in language, they found that the term "dialect" used for the first two but not the last obscured the similarity between the different varieties. Many linguists have therefore rejected the term "dialect" and use either "variety" or "lect," with specification of whether the variety is regional, social, ethnic, or sex-related. We prefer the term "variety," but will sometimes use "dialect" too.

REGIONAL VARIETIES

Although there has been an interest in regionalisms from time immemorial, as reflected in jokes about pronunciation, or efforts to imitate regional dialects, little systematic work was done on them until the beginning of this century. Since then, extensive work has been carried out in various countries on regional dialects, and by various methods. The most common methods have been the postal questionnaire and individual interview. Most work has been done on phonetics, inflections, and lexicon, very little indeed on syntax or varieties of discourse.

In all cases of regional studies, maps are made charting the regional distribution of the forms in question. For example, the various phonetic pronunciations of **calf** including [kæf], [kæ·f], [ka·f] (the dot indicates length) would be plotted on one map, the various pronunciations of **path, pass, aunt, farmer**, etc., on others, the various past forms of the verb (e.g., [sɔ·], [sin], [sid] for the past tense of **see**) on others, and the terms used for the wood or metal receptacles in which one carries water (e.g., **bucket, pail**, etc.) on yet others. Such maps are studied for patterns of continuity and discreteness. Boundaries are set by mapping the furthest points to which a form has penetrated, and a line is drawn connecting these boundaries. The line is strictly speaking called an "isophone" if it connects phonetic boundaries, an "isogloss" if it connects lexical or grammatical ones. However, "isogloss" is commonly used for both kinds of lines. Maps marked this way are superimposed and, though the boundaries between forms are usually not identical, they tend to fall into clearly discernible groups or bundles of isoglosses. Large bundles are considered to be the major dialect boundaries. Here only some of the major bundles in America will be illustrated.

The most interesting aspect of dialect differences is the way in which major boundaries tend to reflect earlier stages in the language and political boundaries or migration patterns that may be many centuries old. History is in some sense laid out in geographical space. If one knew nothing about the history of a language or its speakers, one could nevertheless infer changes in the language from contemporary dialect differences. This is particularly true in a country like England where the language has been spoken for a long time (in this case fifteen hundred years), but even when there is little time-depth (only three hundred years in the case of the United States), it is by no means insignificant, as will be shown below.

Work on United States linguistic geography has been going on steadily since the 1930s. At first the focus was on the Eastern States, mainly because the dialect differences are more noticeable there than elsewhere as a result of the longer settlement of the East. However, the whole of the country east of the Mississippi is now covered, either by unedited field work, by partially or fully edited materials, or by published materials.[3] The same is true of some of the country west of the Mississippi, including California and Nevada.

In most countries dialect surveys are based primarily on the criterion of indigenousness—interviewees' families have resided in the area for several generations, and have had largely the same kind of occupations. In the United States, this criterion has to take second place because in certain regions, such as the West, few speakers come from places where their families have resided for several generations; even if they have, there has usually been radical change in occupation over the generations. However, interviewees are normally at least second-generation residents of the area. Usually three age groups are interviewed: people around 70, 60, and 50; and three educational groups: those with little formal education, those with better education (usually through high school), and those with college education (labeled groups I, II, and III, respectively).

Careful plotting of data has shown that the major regional areas are divided as in the map of the dialect areas. The boundaries best established are marked by a heavy continuous line. They represent distinct linguistic differences between the North, Midland, and South of the Eastern United States. The Midland area, starting with the Delaware Valley, fans out in the central United States, and like other less well-defined boundaries, reflects settlement patterns. The earliest immigrants came from England in the seventeenth century and settled all along the Atlantic coast, establishing essentially independent colonies with distinct linguistic and cultural differences. Ties with England were strong, and the seaports were centers not only of trade but of linguistic influence. About 1820 large numbers of Ulster Scots and Palatine

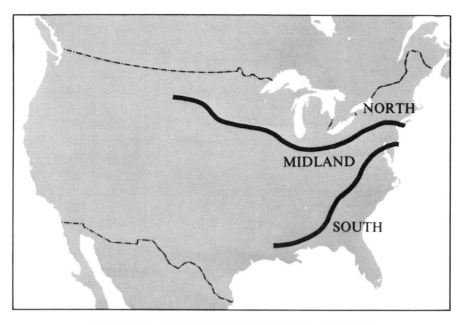

DIALECT AREAS OF THE UNITED STATES
EASTERN DIALECT BOUNDARIES[4]

Germans arrived in the Delaware Bay and spread out to Philadelphia and Ohio. This settlement is reflected by the linguistic boundaries of the Midland area.

A few examples of the distinctions between dialects of the rural North, Midland, and South must suffice here.[5] Of course the areas each have many subareas, each with its own characteristics. The data here are illustrative rather than definitive. However, they clearly demonstrate two facts already mentioned: Dialects are characterized by bundles of characteristics, not single features, and there are degrees of difference between dialects—the Midland and South have more in common with each other than with the North. The characteristics listed here are used by the social groups I, II, and III unless otherwise specified.

Northern Characteristics

Phonology: [r] kept after vowels except in Eastern New England, e.g., in **hoarse, four, cart, father**.

[o] versus [ɔ] in **hoarse** versus **horse**, **mourning** versus **morning**. This distinction is receding in Inland Northern dialects. Also found in Southern dialects.

[s] in **greasy**.

Morphology and Syntax:

dove [dov], past of **dive**.

hadn't ought "oughtn't." (I, II)

clim [klɪm], past of **climb**. (I, II) Also Southern.

Lexicon:

pail. (Midland and Southern "bucket.")

spider "frying pan." (I, II) Receding in Inland Northern. Also Southern.

Midland Characteristics

Phonology: [r] kept after vowels. Also Inland Northern.

[ɔ] in **on**. Also Southern.

[z] in **greasy**. Also Southern.

Morphology and Syntax:

clum [kləm], past of **climb**. (I) Spreading in Inland Northern.

you-all, plural of **you**. Also Southern.

I'll wait on you "for you." (I, II) Also South Carolina.

Lexicon: **skillet** "frying pan." Spreading.

snake feeder "dragon fly." (I, II)

a little piece "a short distance." Also South Carolina.

Southern Characteristics

Phonology: [r] sometimes lost after vowels.

[o] and [ɔ] contrasting in **hoarse-horse, mourning-morning**. Also Northern.

[æw] diphthong in **mountain, loud**. Also Midland.

[ɔ] in **on**. Also Midland.

[z] in **greasy**. Also Midland.

Morphology and Syntax:

        clim [klɪm], past of **climb**. (I, II) Also Northern.

        he belongs to be careful. (I, II)

        he fell outn the bed. (I)

        you-all, plural of **you**. Also Midland.

Lexicon: **spider** "frying pan." Also Northern.

        carry "escort." (I, II)

SOCIAL VARIETIES

The intensive study of social, especially urban, language variation is considerably more recent than that of regional dialects. It gets much of its impetus from a study of English varieties in New York made in the early sixties by William Labov.[6] Although not all the necessary variables have been distinguished in studies of social variation, attempts are usually made to obtain adequate samples from the social spectrum of the urban community, including groups defined by ethnicity, education, age, and sex, as well as socioeconomic status. Among problems still to be rectified in much sociolinguistic work is the tendency to take sociologists' class-scalings as givens, and to assume that language is dependent on them. However, it is conceivable that class stratification actually depends in part on language differences and that language and class do not coincide. Nevertheless, as has often been pointed out, the correlations between social rank and social dialects do seem to hold. Furthermore, in many cases they support the distinctions that sociologists make between working- and middle-class groups. Another problem is that both sociologists and linguists have tended to classify women according to the social status of their husbands. This classification is valueless in predicting networks of linguistic interaction if, for example, a woman works as a domestic and her husband is a road-mender.

    Unlike regional studies, social studies have for the most part been conducted in a very small number of urban areas, most notably New York, Philadelphia, and Detroit in the United States, Montreal in Canada, Glasgow and Norwich in Great Britain. Unlike regional studies, they have been conducted exclusively through verbal (not postal) interaction. Emphasis has been primarily on phonetics, inflections, and function words such as pronouns or forms of the negative. Vocabulary has barely been considered, partly because distinctions in vocabulary are not as great in urban as in rural areas, and partly because the sophisticated recording equipment now used can ensure massive and reliable collection of phonetic data and also of lengthy verbal interactions, something which was impossible in the early days of regional studies. In nearly all studies, the focus is on the interrelation of social stratification with style-shifting from casual to more formal varieties, especially in reading. This has been of central interest because it illustrates not only the variability of individual speakers' usage, but also the general tendency of all speakers in a certain community to shift in similar ways.

It is often said that the modern city is a kind of melting pot where sharp differences of culture, religion, and language disappear. While it is true that regional language differences tend to become minimized in an urban setting, social language differences atypical of rural situations arise. The extent to which regional differences disappear depends on the extent of migration. Broad features of Southern American English persist in the South even in dense urban areas because migration to Southern cities is largely from Southern areas. In Northeastern cities, all but gross regionalisms are less clearly observable because migration to urban areas is from the South as well as the North.

As we saw in the discussion of naming in Chapter 6, social stratification works on two complementary principles—it groups people with similar socio-economic interests together and at the same time it establishes barriers and distances. The groups are, of course, never sharply defined, and therefore there are no absolute distinctions. Studies have repeatedly shown gradation from one group to another, emphasized by speakers' abilities to switch to varieties used by people in neighboring communities. It appears that virtually nobody has a range over the whole spectrum, but most people master a continuous part of the spectrum. Furthermore, there is usually greater skill in mastering varieties higher on the social scale than in mastering those lower on the scale. But even if there is gradation, there are also distinct clusterings of features according to class.

An example of phonetic variability is the well-known case of *r*-fulness in New York City. It has been selected here because it is a very simple example involving only one sound, [r]. In New York, lower-class speakers tend to use postvocalic **r** very little, especially in casual speech, compared to upper-middle-class speakers. All speakers, however, use more **r** in formal speech, particularly in reading, than in informal speech. What is especially interesting is that lower-middle-class speakers who do not use **r** much in casual speech shift when reading word lists to a speech variety in which **r** is not only far more frequent than in their own casual speech, but is also far more frequent than in the variety used by the upper middle class when reading word lists. This suggests that lower-middle-class New Yorkers regard *r*-fulness as highly prestigious. In situations such as in reading, when they are paying a lot of attention to speech, they "hypercorrect" or overdo the *r*-ful forms in an attempt to sound like members of a higher class.

These facts are plotted in Figure 8–1. The vertical axis indicates the percentage of *r*-ful pronunciations of words with postvocalic **r**, such as **guard**, **car**, **beer**, **beard**, **board**. The horizontal axis indicates the degree of attention paid to speech, from most casual on the left to most careful on the right. "Minimal pairs" refers to reading pairs of words that differ primarily or exclusively in one phonemic feature, for example, **guard** and **god**, or **dark** and **dock**, which for most New Yorkers have essentially the same vowel. The designation LC refers to lower class, WC to working class, LMC and UMC to lower- and upper-middle-classes, respectively.[7] Thus the bottom line of the graph reads: Lower-working-class speakers use r-ful forms about 2 percent of the time in casual and careful speech, about 4 percent of the time in reading style, about 10 percent of the time in reading word lists, and over 30 percent of the time when reading minimal pairs like **dark** and **dock**.

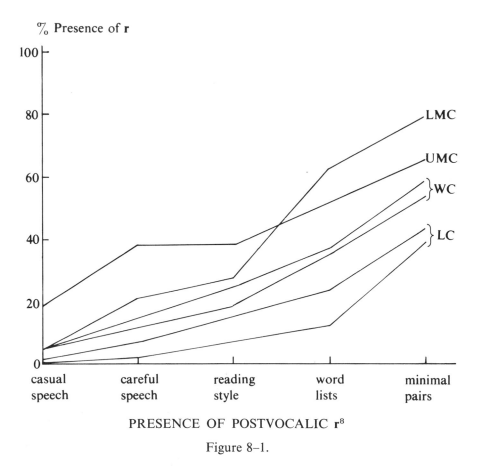

PRESENCE OF POSTVOCALIC r[8]

Figure 8–1.

Comparison of Figure 8–1 with the regional map would readily demonstrate that regional studies are concerned with "horizontal" variation, that is, variation through geographical space, while urban studies are concerned with "vertical" variation, that is, variation through social space. If we think of a model somewhat like:

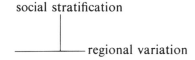

social stratification

regional variation

we can see how the two types of variation study can and indeed must intersect. The influence of social or regional variability is not entirely unidirectional. Migration patterns can affect language, and in the case of New York English, the influx of Midwesterners brought distinct Midwesternisms into speech, such as the use of postvocalic [r]. Nevertheless, in general, innovations spread out from a center of social and cultural importance. Thus we need to think of the relation between the two axes of the model as a dynamic one, each influencing the other, but with the main thrust of change at a social center. Social centers and prestige groups, of course, constantly change, as demonstrated by migration patterns, whether from rural areas to cities, from inner cities to suburbs, from city to city.

Labov and his associates have shown that at least in large urban areas like New York, Philadelphia, and Detroit, the greatest degree of change in speech patterns can be found among those who at the same time have the greatest hope for upward mobility and nevertheless are in the greatest jeopardy of falling back to a lower socioeconomic status. In other words, the greatest change is found linguistically where there is the greatest degree of social insecurity. The group that is linguistically most insecure is the lower middle class, and lower-middle-class teenagers in particular. The lower middle class more than any other demonstrates the phenomenon called "hypercorrection" that we saw in Figure 8-1. Because lower-middle-class speakers, especially teenagers who are just beginning to actively enter the economic system, feel that a linguistic feature such as r-fulness is a marker of social acceptability, they cultivate it so much that in self-conscious speech they actually use it more than the class they are modeling themselves on. That the hypercorrection is actually motivated by a stereotype of prestige and is not a chance phenomenon is strongly supported by evaluation tests in which hearers were asked to listen to recordings and to judge the acceptability of the speech patterns for certain kinds of jobs, such as salespeople in lower-class department stores versus salespeople in upper-class and exclusive stores. Invariably informants in New York rated r-ful utterances higher than r-less ones; if the same speaker had used [ka] in casual speech and [kar] in more formal speech and these two utterances had been spliced in one tape, they were taken to be by different speakers of different social status.[9] A similar kind of test is one where people are asked to evaluate their own speech. Speakers almost always think they speak a more prestigious and consistent variety than they actually do, and New Yorkers were sometimes quite shocked to hear that they actually used r-less forms, while not being at all shocked to hear that they used r-ful forms. In other cities, of course, one might find the reverse.

In language as in other fields of human activity, prestige is a complex factor. Our examples so far have shown prestige accruing to the highest socio-economic class. However, prestige is ultimately a matter of allegiance, not of socioeconomic standing. Positive evaluation may therefore be assigned to features of any social class, given the right conditions. For example, male high school students in South Africa have been shown to evaluate lower-class forms relatively highly, associating them with virility and active life, while their female counterparts evaluate upper-class forms more highly.[10] On Martha's Vineyard in Massachusetts, Labov found linguistic evaluation correlated with lifestyle and values. Groups who associate themselves with mainland culture modify their speech toward upper-class mainland speech, but groups who wish to retain the older fishing culture of the island have adopted certain linguistic habits directly opposed to upper-class mainland English. For example, they have retracted their low diphthongs [ay] and [aw] to something approaching [əy] and [əw] (an archaic pronunciation).[11]

"STANDARD ENGLISH"

What is a "standard" variety? Although most people have intuitive answers, there is often confusion about this question. One of the difficulties is that there are, broadly speaking, two views of what "standard" means, and they frequently get mixed up. One is the view that Standard English is the variety used in formal situations by educated people, especially those commanding local or national respect as leaders. That is, in one view, Standard English is defined descriptively on social and stylistic parameters. It is not conceived as an absolute, but as the appropriate variety for communication, whether spoken or written, in activities of social prestige. It is the variety, then, that is appropriate to a particular intersection of social class (educated, usually but not necessarily upper middle class), topic, style, and medium. Given this view, one could claim that there are a number of Standard Englishes, not only regional varieties such as British and American, but ethnic ones too. Indeed there is considerable evidence that a standard variety of Black English is developing, as used by congressmen, writers, radio and TV reporters, and especially teachers.[12] There is, however, another, very different view of Standard English, which is essentially "prescriptive" rather than descriptive, and which regards the standard as an absolute, as a thing apart, recognizable primarily through the written form of the language. This is the view of the standard as an ideal rather than as a norm, as the repository of refinement in the language, and as something that can be legislated upon. It underlies evaluation of the language of works to be published and of the acceptability of new vocabulary items into the language. In certain countries, such as France and Tanzania, it underlies actual legislation by an academy whose sole or prime function is to pronounce judgment on style and lexicon. For those who hold the prescriptive view of Standard English, the written variety alone is usually considered standard, and the definition is therefore far narrower than for those who hold a descriptive view.

The two concepts of Standard English are largely traceable to the rise of the middle class in the eighteenth century. The upper classes felt threatened in urban communities, especially London, by the growing importance of the lower middle class and the rapid increase in their mobility. At the beginning of the eighteenth century we find grammars that were based on descriptions of the language spoken by educated people. These grammars were aimed primarily at "maintaining caste," that is, establishing for the upper classes a linguistic code based on their own behavior that would, along with moral and other codes, separate them from the threat of middle-class "upstarts." By the end of the eighteenth century, however, we find a new kind of grammar, primarily prescriptive, codifying the language of the upper classes as models or ideals for the social betterment of those with less social status. Such prescriptive grammars dominated thinking about language until this century, when linguists' insistence on the importance of description in analyzing language led to greater interest in the schools in descriptive approaches to English. The prescriptive idea is still markedly present in the average person's expectations of a dictionary—dictionaries are often regarded as Bibles, telling you what you ought to write or say, whereas in fact serious dictionaries simply record the current lexicon as used by educated people. It was the assumption that a dictionary ought to legislate that caused the widespread furor in the sixties over Webster's Third International Dictionary. Painstakingly determined to record more than "educated," "standard" uses of the lexicon, the editors of this dictionary included certain regionalisms and colloquialisms, that is, forms unacceptable in written language, including **ain't**, with explicit indication of the region and style for which such forms were appropriate. But many readers were horrified and wrote outraged reviews.[13]

Another prescriptive approach with very wide currency holds that there is a "best" English, even a "pure" English. There is no intrinsically "best" English, although one can with full justification speak of the more appropriate or effective variety of a language for some particular type of communication. The prime function of standard varieties is public rather than private. Therefore standard language is most appropriate to relatively formal styles and genres, for media addressing large numbers of people, and especially for utterances intended to have some permanence (for example, those that appear in print). Other varieties better fit functions that are private or personal, and expressed in informal genres through impermanent media.

Prescriptive attitudes that regard the standard written language as the only "good" language or regard the language of the educated classes as the "best" language gave rise to the idea that varieties other than the standard were "substandard," in other words, inadequate, sloppy, even unsuitable for logical thought. This, of course, is a judgment based on a feeling of social (even moral or genetic) superiority and on evaluation of different varieties for the *same* function. Since different varieties serve different functions, they cannot be judged fairly by one function alone. Linguists have insisted on the adequacy of different language varieties for their particular functions (they have, however, often been misunderstood as claiming the adequacy of any one variety for all functions, especially those of the standard, which is patently absurd). Clearly a language-user who does not know a standard variety is more limited than one who can use it as the verbal repertoire relevant to public communication and certain types of employment. On the other hand, language-users who know mainly the standard often lack the verbal repertoire relevant to other social activities of the community. "Verbal deficit," about which so much is said in the schools, is not used to refer to inability to use language in structured and effective ways in native settings, but rather to the inability to perform in expected ways in particular formal test situations. Nevertheless, one can say that the fewer linguistic options a speaker has command over, the less power that person has, unless he or she is a member of the standard language-speaking community. Rejection of the prescriptive notion of the standard has led to rejection of the term "substandard" and its replacement by "nonstandard." Less loaded than "substandard," "nonstandard" is still far from an ideal term, since it takes the standard as the norm.

The notion of an English "pure and undefiled" has no basis in the language itself, though it well serves the purpose of those who wish to establish a model for writing and of those who (often dangerously) attempt to equate language with social mores—an idea lurking behind many etiquette books. From the eighteenth century on, it has been traditional to imitate Dr. Johnson, who compiled the first modern dictionary, and to talk of the "decay" of language. As Dr. Johnson himself saw (though with regret), the language necessarily changes since each child has to make his or her hypotheses about the language and develop a grammar. Another reason for inevitability of change is that people change from one social group to another or interact with other groups and are necessarily influenced by those whom they talk to and especially those whom they try to emulate. The sense of decay is primarily due to the fact that the standard language is written as well as spoken, whereas other varieties are usually only spoken. Change in the written language is obviously far more easily perceived than in the spoken.

In both the descriptive and prescriptive sense, Standard English is clearly socially defined. That certain regional varieties such as London British English in England or Middle Western American English tend to become associated with the standard does not change the essential nature of the definition, since all such associations are correlated with the social importance of the region in question. Fundamentally, standard varieties serve a combination of unificational, prestige, and frame of reference (or code of correctness) functions. They tend to obliterate regional associations except of a gross kind and in this sense are unificational. Designed for communication beyond the family, town, state, or even country, they can be learned by speakers of any class, and therefore, although rooted in upper-class language, can even obliterate social distinctions under certain circumstances, resulting in a group defined not so much by class but by education.

ETHNIC VARIETIES: BLACK ENGLISH

There is an enormous mix of ethnic groups in the United States and Great Britain. Members of any one ethnic group will probably speak a variety of English distinct from other varieties. Many speakers have as their native language a language other than English. Others, like Black Americans, speak as their native language varieties that originally derived from other languages in contact with English. Whatever the particular situation, there are gradients from ethnically distinct varieties of English to Standard English.

Because immigrating ethnic groups tend to settle in specific regions, for example, Swedes in Wisconsin, Germans in Pennsylvania, Cubans in Florida, and tend to have similar occupations, it is never possible to make clear distinctions between ethnic, regional, and above all socioeconomic varieties. Should Black English be considered an ethnic variety or a socioeconomic variety? In his extensive studies of speech patterns in New York, Philadelphia, and other urban areas, Labov has treated Black English primarily as a social variety (or rather group of varieties). This approach has led him to stress the view that Black English shows very few absolute differences from White English; the vast majority of differences are quantitative. For example, the speech of Blacks shows greater absence of word-final consonant clusters than the speech of Whites in the same socioeconomic group, but essentially no differences in type. This matter will be discussed further below. Other linguists have treated Black English primarily as an ethnic variety and have concentrated on its differences from White English.[14] The two perspectives can be clearly correlated with different political and pedagogical attitudes. The social approach emphasizes unity, the ethnic approach can be used to promote separatism. Pedagogically, the first approach suggests teaching Standard English as another variety of English, socially more useful in a get-ahead society; the second suggests teaching Standard English as a language so different that it is really a second language. Both perspectives take a stand against traditional prejudices which had branded Black English as an inferior variety, lacking structure and logic and not suitable for complex or abstract communication.[15] This prejudice had a particularly strong effect on pedagogy, leading to a policy that the job of schools was to obliterate Black English and replace it with Standard English in the verbal repertoire of Black speakers. The research of people like Labov refutes this view by demonstrating that though very different in surface structure from Standard English, Black English is a logical and cohesive system, as highly structured as other, more standard varieties. In view of the fact that Black English refers to the type of language spoken by Black Americans in large urban areas, and of the fact that Black leaders, especially politicians and educators, are tending more and more to use a phonetically distinctive pronunciation (accent) when speaking Standard English, it appears appropriate to consider Black English as primarily an ethnic variety, but one that has been largely assimilated into the mainstream of English and that has strong correlatives with socioeconomic varieties in America.

Like other varieties of English, Black English is by no means monolithic. There is a gradation from varieties that are very different from Standard American English (hereafter abbreviated as SAE) to varieties that are very similar. Those that are very different are largely spoken by speakers in the lowest socioeconomic ranges; they are called Black English Vernacular (hereafter abbreviated as BEV), and are the main topic of most research on Black English.

As we have seen, the urban mix tends to wipe out strong regional features, but promotes social stratification. This stratification accounts for many of the characteristics of BEV, although certain features can be related to Southern American characteristics, and others to the historical origins of Black English, specifically the linguistic contact between African slaves in the seventeenth, eighteenth, and nineteenth centuries and British, Spanish, Portuguese, Dutch, and other slave traders or plantation owners. This historical aspect of Black English will be explored briefly in Chapter 9. Here some of the major characteristics of BEV will be reviewed, with some indication of social and stylistic variations, and of characteristics shared with other varieties of English.[16]

Phonology

(1) **Postvocalic r:** Many Black speakers, whatever their regional affiliations, do not have postvocalic r in words like **court** and **core**. This feature can readily be compared with East Midland and Southeastern British English and to Southern American English, but may also have its origins in the phonologies of West Africa. Lack of postvocalic r is also found in SAE in parts of the Northeast. Lack of postvocalic r is therefore not critical for BEV, although it may be distinctive in certain communities, such as Chicago, where White speakers use predominantly r-ful varieties.

(2) **Use of [ɪn]:** The present participle is usually [ɪn], not [ɪŋ]. This is characteristic of most nonstandard varieties of English and of the rapid speech of some standard varieties. However, [ɪn] tends to be found more frequently in the speech of Black than White speakers in comparable regions or social groups.

(3) **Lack of [θ] and [ð]:** SAE [θ] and [ð] tend not to occur in some varieties

of BEV in word-initial and word-final positions. Such varieties are to be found largely among speakers of the lowest socioeconomic ranks and in least formal situations. SAE [θ] corresponds to BEV [t] word-initially as in [tɪŋk] **think**, and to [f] word-finally and sometimes medially, as in [mawf], [nəfɪn] **mouth, nothing**. SAE [ð] corresponds to word-initial and occasionally final BEV [d], as in [dey] and [wid] **they** and **with**, and to word-medial [v] as in [brəvə] **brother**. Such correspondences are characteristic of contact languages —[θ] and [ð] are rare in the languages of the world; and speakers of languages without these interdentals, when in contact with English, tend to reinterpret them as the nearest alveolar stop, or as labiodental fricatives (New Yorkers of Italian origin often demonstrate similar features). However, similar correspondences can be found in the speech of many White Americans, not necessarily as the result of some other contact situation; for example, [v] is common for medial [ð] in the speech of many Whites in Kentucky.

(4) **Deletion of word-final [l]:** Often word-final [l] is deleted, so that **coal** is pronounced [ko]. Again, this is not a criterial feature of BEV. Word-final [l] is lost in various parts of England in contemporary English. During the history of the language it has been lost in many words preconsonantally, as is attested by spellings like **folk** and **talk**. Some regional dialects differ in the United States according to whether a speaker says [kalm] or [kam] for **calm**.

(5) **Reduction of word-final consonant clusters:** Reduction of word-final consonant clusters (as in **walks**) is a widespread phenomenon. It may be a universal of rapid speech, at least when a word ending with two consonants precedes another starting with a consonant (as in **wax seal** [wæks sil, wæksil]). The history of English has seen the reduction of many clusters both initially and finally. The difference between spelling and pronunciation reveals this clearly, since many clusters were reduced after the development of printing with its subsequent fossilization of the spelling system. Consider, for example, Middle English [wrɪŋg] and Modern English [rɪŋ] **wring** or Middle English [lamb] and Modern English [læm] **lamb**. Sometimes the old consonant cluster remains in phonological alternations, such as [yəŋ-yəŋgər] or in related words such as [məlayn-məlɪgnənt].

A characteristic of most word-final consonant cluster reductions is that both members of the cluster share the same feature of voicing—both are voiced, or both are voiceless. Most speakers of English have a rule of the type:

$$-C_1C_2 \Rightarrow -C_1$$

Condition: C_1 and C_2 are both voiced or both voiceless.

Rapid Speech.

Preferred in position preceding word with initial consonant.

BEV, however, has a much more general (i.e., less constrained) rule:

$$-C_1C_2 \Rightarrow -C_1$$

Condition: C_1 and C_2 are both voiced or both voiceless.

Some examples of correspondences are:

SAE   [old]   [maynd]   [ɛnd]   :   BEV   [ol]   [mayn]   [ɛn]

[tɛst]   [wasp]   [lɛft]   [tɛs]   [was]   [lɛf]

but

SAE   [jəmp]   [kræŋk]   :   BEV   [jəmp]   [kræŋk]

Where reduction of a cluster results in retention of a consonant that can itself be reduced, we will find even further modifications. Thus SAE [old] is BEV [ol] by consonant cluster reduction; [l] is in the appropriate position for [l] deletion, and we therefore find [o]. The rules operate systematically like any other rules. We can compare the SAE and BEV forms of **old man** and **old aunt** as follows, assuming rapid speech in both cases:

	SAE	BEV	SAE	BEV
Underlying form	[old mæn]	[old mæn]	[old ænt]	[old ænt]
Cons. Cl. Red.	ol	ol		ol
[l] red.		o		
Surface form	[ol mæn]	[o mæn]	[old ænt]	[ol ænt]

([l]-reduction is disfavored in BEV before a word beginning with a vowel.)

Since the nominal and verbal inflections of English are largely realized by sibilants and alveolars that agree in voicing with the preceding consonant, this difference between BEV and other varieties of English makes BEV appear very different indeed in inflectional structure. This issue will be discussed further in the next section.

(6) **Pitch patterns:** Less extensively studied than the consonant and vowel patterns of BEV are the pitch patterns.[17] These are, however, equally characteristic, and likewise involve questions of tendencies rather than absolute distinctions. In comparable speech situations, pitch contours of Black speakers tend to have a wider range than those used by White speakers. Frequent changes of pitch into high falsetto are characteristic, often indicating ingroup relatedness and friendship. In informal situations, sentences including statements end more often in level or rising contours than do sentences spoken by Whites. The fact that we are speaking here of informal situations is crucial. The tendency to use falling intonations even for yes-no questions seems to be

a feature of formal talk and may be a hypercorrection but is often interpreted as hostile by teachers. Believing that they use rising intonations too much, speakers may compensate by going too far in the opposite direction in not using them when talking to superiors, and say, for example:

2.   You the teacher = "Are you the teacher?"

Intonational patterns play a very important semantic role. Logical connectors like **if** that are so often considered by teachers to be "missing" in BEV are in fact present in the form of intonational contours. Specifically, the subordinate clause often ends in a rise, where in White varieties it would end in a level contour or less of a rise:

3. a.   She wanted proof, I could give her proof.

   b.   She can do me some good, that's cool.

A possible reason for the prevalence of these intonational patterns is the high value set in Black culture on certain interactional genres such as verbal dueling and the call and response components of church services. Middle-class White culture tends to value topic oriented discourse—or at least that is what is most highly valued in school. It also values the written word very highly, a form notorious for its inadequacy in reflecting intonational patterns, and for necessitating substitutes for oral rises and falls in pitch. Although the same kinds of rising intonation patterns can be found in both Black and White speech, they are less highly favored in White speech and tend to be stigmatized, whereas in Black culture they are not.

Inflections

As indicated earlier in this chapter in the fifth part of the section on phonology, the surface absence of consonant clusters in word-final position is not just a phonological phenomenon. It has far-reaching consequences for inflections. For example, BEV [tu kæt] is equivalent to SAE [tu kæts] **two cats**, BEV [də dag lɛg] to SAE [ðə dagz lɛgz] **the dog's legs**, and BEV [ši sɪt] to SAE [ši sɪts] **she sits**. Although final [s] and [z] both function as noun plural, noun possessive, or third person singular present tense-markers, the likelihood of their being absent in surface structure depends on their function. Absence of all three [s, z] morphemes in the variety of BEV spoken in Detroit in an interview situation is noted in Figure 8–2.

% ABSENT

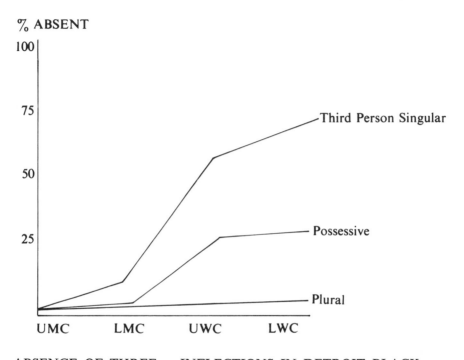

ABSENCE OF THREE -s INFLECTIONS IN DETROIT BLACK ENGLISH[18]

Figure 8–2

Why is this? Since it is used only for the third person singular present (**she walks**, but **I, you, we, they walk**), the verb inflection -s really does not indicate tense so much as number in Standard English. But even here it is redundant. Number is normally a function of nominals and is not needed on the verb to communicate effectively. It appears that some speakers of BEV do not have the third person singular present tense inflection in underlying structure since they never express it. Others have a verb inflection that on first sight corresponds to the Standard English one, but it is used with all persons (e.g., **I walks**) and in fact functions as a present tense-marker, not a number-marker. For these speakers the inflection is sometimes present and sometimes not. In acquiring Standard English, they have to learn not only to use the form more frequently, but also to assign a different function to the inflection.

In the case of the possessive there is considerable redundancy too. Word order alone can indicate the relationship between a possessive and its head; this is common in Standard English compounds such as **table-legs**. The possessive relationship can also be expressed by alternate prepositional phrases such as the **legs of the table**. However, constructions like **taleteller** (where **tale** is the object) render possessive constructions potentially ambiguous in some contexts, and this may account for the greater use of possessive inflections than of third-person-singular-present-markers.

Finally, the plural of the noun is given surface manifestations more often than the other two inflections because, in the absence of quantifiers such as **many**, **some**, or **three**, nothing else indicates number. This explains why the plural-marker is usually absent when some other pluralizer, such as the quantifiers just mentioned, is present that would render the inflection redundant.

While some BEV speakers appear not to have the third person singular present inflection in underlying structure, all seem to have underlying noun possessive and plural, and also underlying past tense (realized as [t, d, əd], etc.). Evidence for this is the use of distinct plural, possessive, and past forms where vowel alternation is concerned (e.g., **man-men, ride-rode**) or where the inflection forms a whole syllable (e.g., **horse-horses, pit-pitted**). Particularly interesting are cases of nouns that have undergone consonant cluster reduction in the singular and then have [əz] added in BEV, where in SAE the plural would be [s], e.g., BEV [tɛs, tɛsəz], equivalent to careful SAE speech [tɛst, tɛsts] (this is usually [tɛss] in less careful speech). The conclusion that we can draw is that BEV speakers learning SAE do not have to learn the possessive and plural noun inflections; what they do have to learn is that consonant cluster deletion should not apply except in rapid, casual speech.

Although past tense inflections are present in deep structure, certain very frequent verbs such as **come** and **say** are treated as invariant (i.e., the past-marker is $\emptyset$), as are **put, cut**, and similar verbs in SAE. Combined with the effect of consonant cluster deletion, this generalization of the $\emptyset$ past can give the casual observer the false impression that past tense is not expressed.

Syntax

(1) Verbal auxiliaries: One of the factors most characteristic of BEV is the system of verbal auxiliaries. Much has been written about them,[19] but there are still some puzzles. Here we will mention only a few major points. Most interesting is the way in which time relations are expressed. In SAE only adverbs, not tense-markers, distinguish something that has happened a long time ago from something that has happened very recently. In BEV, however, the distinction can be made by auxiliary verbs. Thus there is a contrast between:

4. BEV   He done gone.   SAE   He has recently gone.
5. BEV   He bín gone.   SAE   He has been gone a long time.

Bín (where ⎯ signals stress) is currently disappearing, but **done** is widely used. Unlike **bín**, it has counterparts in White dialects, for example, Appalachian English.

Similarly, in SAE, adverbs like **right now** and **often** distinguish states of affairs that are momentary from those that recur at intervals. In some varieties of BEV, however, the first meaning is expressible by an inflected form of the verb **be** (e.g., **am, is, are**), while the second is expressible by an uninflected one. Since the latter **be** never changes according to person or number, it is often called "invariant **be**." Examples are:

6. a.   BEV   She's tired.   SAE   She's tired (right now).

7. a.   BEV   She be tired.   SAE   She's (often) tired.

The invariant **be** is most often used in the context of adverbs like **sometimes, often, always,** and **whenever,** which clearly indicates its iterative nature, as in:

7. b.   Sometime she be angry.
   c.   Whenever she be tired she be cross.

but it is not limited to adverbial contexts.

There is another invariant **be** with quite a different function (that of expressing intention), as in:

8. a.   He say he be going.

This is derived from:

8. b.   He say he will be going.

Constructions of this type are also found extensively in White Southern speech, and so are others like **Be you George's son?** where **be** expresses identity. By contrast, invariant iterative **be** as in 7 is not common in White Southern speech. Indeed, many White speakers do not understand iterative **be** unless they know BEV well. The iterative **be** seems to have its origins in the pidgin and creole languages spoken by Black slaves in the seventeenth and eighteenth centuries and will be discussed further in the next chapter.

(2) Absence of copula: Another characteristic of BEV is that the inflected *be*-verb (frequently called a "copula") is not often present in surface structure if it signals present tense. The form **She's tired** given in 6a is somewhat formal. More often the form is:

6. b.   She tired.

especially in casual speech. As Labov has often pointed out, this "zero copula" occurs where phonologically reduced forms of inflectional **be** occur in SAE; thus:

9. a. BEV   She hungry.   SAE   She's hungry.
   b. BEV   I leaving.   SAE   I'm leaving.
   c. BEV   That where he is.   SAE   That's where he is.
   d. BEV   *That where he.   SAE   *That's where he's.

This suggests that the BEV system essentially parallels the SAE system in this respect. But, because phonological reduction has been carried further, the form disappears in surface structure.

Zero copula in the present tense is actually quite common among the languages of the world. It is attested, for example, in Latin and Russian. In these languages and in BEV, the past tense form appears in surface structure, but often not the present. This is presumably because the present can be inferred from the speech situation, whereas the past cannot be inferred.

(3) Use of *It's a*: Another often mentioned feature of BEV syntax is that where SAE uses **There's a . . .** as a device for thematizing an indefinite NP in certain sentences with locatives. BEV tends to use **It's a . . .**, as in:

10.   It's a boy in my room name John.

Since it is usually pronounced [Iss] (with "long s") this form in fact appears not to be understood as **it** plus **is**, but rather as a unit word the function of which is to shift indefinite nominals from initial position in the sentence.

(4) **Multiple negation:** Multiple negation, while characteristic of most non-standard varieties of English, is particularly common in BEV.[20] In other dialects, multiple negation is largely used for emphasis, as in:

11.   Nobody don't like a boss hardly.

For such speakers it is optional. However, for some speakers of BEV it is nonemphatic and obligatory. Multiple negation is so fundamental to BEV syntax that it can affect not only the main clause but even spread to subordinate ones:

12.   We ain't askin' you to go out and ask no pig to leave us alone.

It should be noted that in these two examples there is one underlying negative which spreads in surface structure to all indefinites (**some, ever,** and so forth). In effect, multiple negation is a kind of agreement rule; it is not fundamentally different from the rule (in languages like Russian) that requires adjectives to agree with the nouns they modify in number, gender, and case, or the English rule that requires the present tense verb to agree with the subject (**He walks** but **They walk**). Those who proscribe multiple negation on the grounds that two negatives make an affirmative (just as two minuses make a plus in mathematics) are confusing surface structure with underlying function.

(5) **Question transformation:** The question transformation in BEV is for many speakers considerably simpler than in SAE. In yes-no questions there is frequently no auxiliary verb shift, and **He left?** rather than **Did he leave?** is typical. Yes-no questions indicated by intonation and not by word-order shifts are of course characteristic of spoken English of all varieties, therefore such question forms in BEV are notable only for their frequency. Content questions, too, tend to remain in the underlying Subject-Auxiliary-Verb order, with only the question word in initial position, as in **Where the white can is?** However, those speakers who do use auxiliary inversion in questions generalize it to subordinate as well as main clauses: **Where did he go? I want to know where did he go?** This, too, is a feature of casual spoken English in general.

Speech Acts

Certain kinds of speech acts may be associated with specific groups of people, not merely particular situations. For example, much reference has been made in recent linguistic studies to certain ritualized speech acts of Black speakers, especially ritual insults, known as "playing the dozens," "sounding," or "signifying." Ritual insulting is highly stylized and forms a significant part of the predominantly oral culture of the BEV speech community. It is a competitive game in which players make up elaborate obscenities with which to describe one another's relatives, especially the opponent's mother, for example:

> Yo mama is so bowlegged, she looks like the bite out
> of a donut.[21]

Playing the dozens involves exchanging insults in a highly formulaic way. The pattern is almost invariably: Speaker A starts with **Your mother (Verb)...** or **Your mother is like ....** Speaker B parries, trying to outdo A. Third parties present evaluate the game.

For example, here is an excerpt from a ritual insult exchange recorded in New York City:

> *Boot:* His mother go to work without any draws on so that she c'd get a good breeze.
> *Money:* Your mother go, your mother go work without anything on, just go naked.
> *David:* That's a lie.
> *Boot:* Your mother, when she go to work and she had—those, you know— open-toe shoes, well her stockings reach her be—sweeping the ground.

Ricky: (laughs)
Roger: Ho lawd! (laughs)
Money: Your mother have holes—potatoes in her shoes.
Boot: Your mother got a putty chest (laugh).
Money: Arrgh! Aww—you wish you had a putty chest, right?[22]

Money loses his first turn because it is less funny than Boot's initiating turn; his loss is confirmed by David's **That's a lie.** Money loses again when he asks a question (**You wish you had a putty chest?**), instead of retorting with a more preposterous claim, and gives up with **Aww!**

As the example suggests, the dozens are well formed only if they are intended and understood to be impersonal, which is usually achieved by making claims so exaggerated as to be obviously false. Among members of a group who can assess the insult's referential truth value or lack of it, such speech acts are acts of friendly verbal dueling. As a ritual they are exempt from consequences other than approval for winning; however, between groups ill-acquainted with each other, they are inappropriate and often meant as (or taken as) acts of aggression, frequently provoking fights.

Age-Grading

All the characteristics we have been discussing here are socially graded, with the greatest differences from SAE being in evidence in the speech of the lower working class (cf. Figure 8–2). They are also heavily age-graded, with young children evidencing the greatest number of forms different from SAE. In particular, it is often noted that in any BEV speech community invariant **be** is used mainly by preteenagers. Comparative studies of the speech of Black and White children of the same class might show similar kinds of stratification, though probably with some statistical differences. Unfortunately, to date most of the acquisitional studies of Black children have focused on school-age children in ghetto communities, especially from the age of eight up, while acquisitional studies of White children have for the most part focused on the speech of preschool children and children up to the age of six, with little emphasis on social stratification. Therefore we know next to nothing about similarities and differences between age-graded social and ethnic groups.

ATTITUDES TO THE USE OF
LANGUAGE VARIETIES IN LITERATURE

The extensive use of colloquialisms or of regional, social, or other varieties in literature to portray character or indicate social meanings is fairly recent. In the early periods of English literature, authors wrote mainly in their own dialect. Whatever social meaning this dialect conveyed derived from the use of English as opposed to Latin, or, in the Middle English period, French. It did not derive from contrast with other varieties of English. Authors simply accepted their variety of English as the norm. Even the most obvious way of indicating social meaning through use of language varieties—interpolation of a passage in one variety within the context of a different one—is rarely found before the sixteenth century. Among the few examples extant is the use of Northern English dialogue by two Cambridge students in Chaucer's "The Reeve's Tale." The advent of printing in the late fifteenth century inevitably had a homogenizing effect on the language. In his famous introduction to the first printed edition of a translation of Virgil's *Aeneid*, published in 1490, Caxton discusses how he agonized over selecting a suitable language variety for use in print, and cites an incident in which a Northerner asking for **egges** "eggs" got into an altercation with a Southern innkeeper who insisted she knew no French. Finally they came to an understanding when she realized that his **egges** were the Northern dialect form for her **eyren**. Caxton selected a fairly Southern variety of English, essentially that of London in the later fifteenth century, setting a precedent for what eventually came to be Standard British English.

In the sixteenth century, a growing interest in people as social and secular beings rather than as moral and religious ones was reflected in new literary forms, particularly the drama and "picaresque" stories telling of wild, often bawdy adventures by characters of less than noble background. These new forms of literature brought attention to various forms of language, including colloquial versus formal, regional versus nonregional. Even so, the prime use of varieties other than the author's own was for comic purposes. In Shakespeare's plays, for example, regionalisms are mainly reserved for rustics and clowns, and verse and prose function as separate varieties, the former being considered more formal than the latter. This distinction extends itself to genre, verse being used for tragedy and prose for comedy. Good examples of all these different language types can be found in the *King Henry IV* plays and in *Henry V*. An additional use of regionalisms can be found in *King Lear*, where Edgar adopts distinctly Southwestern speech when he pretends to be mad.

During the eighteenth century, interest focused on developing a distinctly literary language, and the tradition of an elevated poetic diction became established (for some examples see Chapter 3, page 117). In this context, the derogatory attitude to dialectal varieties that had developed in the preceding centuries naturally became more marked. However, from the late eighteenth century on, a new attitude to nonstandard varieties emerged, beginning with the Romantic movement. Among other things, this movement was characterized by its search for spontaneity and authenticity of feeling, and for a reunion of human beings with the natural world as opposed to the urban industrial one. These ideals, it was believed, were exemplified by primitive peoples (so-called "natural man") and rural peasantry (so-called "common man"). Many Romantics, such as Wordsworth in England and Rousseau in France, took an interest in the language, thought, and customs of such groups and undertook to represent them in literature. Wordsworth's search for the language of human beings in their natural state did not lead him to the use of dialect, but rather to a search for a diction that was not elevated, but that remained poetic. Others after him sought to represent language closer to actual speech, sometimes with great attention to details of language variation. The Scottish poet Robert Burns (1759–96) exemplifies the transition to this new Romantic attitude from the older comic view of nonstandard varieties. Burns, one of the most popular poets of the late eighteenth and early nineteenth centuries, wrote many poems in Standard British English, but is best remembered for his representations of his native Lowland Scots dialect in poetry. Sometimes he used Scots dialect in the traditional way, for comic purposes, as illustrated by the opening stanzas of his poem "To a Louse":

> HA! whare ye gaun, ye crowlin' ferlie°?
> Your impudence protects you sairly:
> I canna say but ye strunt° rarely,
>   Owre gauze and lace;
> Tho' faith, I fear ye dine but sparely
>   On sic° a place.
>
>   Ye ugly, creepin', blastit wonner,
> Detested, shunn'd by saunt an' sinner,
> How dare you set your fit upon her,
>   Sae fine a lady!
> Gae somewhere else and seek your dinner,
>   On some poor body,
>
> Swith°, in some beggar's haffet° squattle°;
> There ye may creep, and sprawl, and sprattle°
> Wi' ither kindred, jumpin' cattle,
>   In shoals and nations;
> Whare *horn* nor *bane* ne'er dare unsettle
>   Your thick plantations.[23]

10

---

1 **ferlie:** wonder (term of contempt)   3 **strunt:** walk sturdily   6 **sic:** such
13 **swith:** get away   **haffet:** head   **squattle:** settle   14 **sprattle:** scramble

This sort of usage is in keeping with the comic tradition. What marks Burns as a Romantic, however, is his use of dialect in serious poetry as well, where it is intended to convey sincerity and emotional fervor, and to give a kind of linguistic authenticity.

> . . . were I in the wildest waste,
>   Sae black and bare, sae black and bare,
> The desert were a paradise,

> If thou wert there, if thou wert there.
> Or were I monarch o' the globe,
> Wi' thee to reign, wi' thee to reign;
> The brightest jewel in my crown
> Wad be my queen, wad be my queen.[24]

Neither Burns nor his nineteenth-century successors succeeded completely in overcoming the traditional condescension toward nonstandard varieties, however. For example, Burns's poems on the whole are clearly more standard the more serious they are. And he as well as other nineteenth-century poets were not above using nonstandard dialects as a comic screen for taboo material (a device still common in contemporary television). Nevertheless, it is important to recognize that Romanticism did show far greater interest in social and regional varieties than was shown in earlier literature.

A major turning point in American writing, the point at which American style came into its own as distinct from British style, is the point at which nonstandard language came to be used not for local color, but for character. Mark Twain's *The Adventures of Huckleberry Finn*, published in 1885, is often thought to signal the beginning of this new idiom. It is the first sustained attempt to break through the leveling force of the standard written language to an individual voice by using a "poor White" boy as the narrator, and hence the boy's language for the frame of reference of the novel. It is also the first major work in which the level of incongruity between standard and vernacular is drastically reduced by rendering the narrative itself (as a first-person narrative) in the vernacular, not just the dialogue.

From then on, the use in American literature of all kinds of linguistic varieties, whether colloquial, ethnic, regional, or other, became very widespread not only in dialogue but also in first-person narrative. It is interesting to consider how radically different a twentieth-century *Moll Flanders* could be. In the eighteenth century, Defoe had no choice but to use Standard English, because Moll would have appeared comic and unsympathetic to a contemporary audience if she had used the vernacular. Had he been writing in this century, Defoe would have had a choice and would probably have used vernacular forms at least in part of the novel. Instead, he has a fictional editor explain in a preface that Moll's language is less vulgar and more modest than would be expected because her penitence led her to alter and purify her speech.

STEREOTYPIC VERSUS VARIABLE REPRESENTATIONS OF LANGUAGE VARIETIES

In studying the use of nonstandard varieties in English literature, it is important to remember that English spelling does not represent any existing dialect phonetically. By convention, therefore, when a writer uses normal

English spellings in dialogue, for example, we infer that the pronunciation intended is the standard of the audience for which the work is written, while special deviant spellings indicate the pronunciation of a dialect that is not the audience's standard. This can lead to some rather unusual variations. For example, a writer representing an Irishman to a predominantly English audience might be inclined to use spelling to indicate Irish pronunciation, while the same writer might not do so when presenting an Irishman to a predominantly Irish audience.

No writer can capture all the features of spoken language. The intonation, all the minute phonetic details, speakers' tendency to leave sentences unfinished, to hesitate and make false starts are naturally omitted. So too, are certain features of any regional, social, or ethnic variety—selection is imperative if the reader's attention is to be held, and if focus is to be placed on meaning rather than form.[25] Nevertheless, it is possible to render a wealth of detail about language varieties in writing; careful evaluation of the language varieties used in a text can be useful to the literary critic. A recognition of the presence and function of variability is a valuable tool in assessing what an author is attempting to do, while knowledge of the variety in question makes it possible to assess how successful and accurate an author is in representing speech.

We have seen that the speech of any individual, far from being consistent, varies a great deal according to such contextual factors as degree of formality, identity of addressee, attitude being conveyed, and speech act being performed. We have also seen that there is unsystematic variation at many points, which is why studies of variation speak of tendencies and probabilities rather than strict presence or absence of a characteristic. Written representations of different language varieties often overlook both these sorts of variability, and simply select a few markers of a particular variety, using them consistently without real attention to the details of the variety in question. This is the kind of representation we speak of as stereotypic. Until the mid-nineteenth century, most attempts to represent language varieties in literature were stereotypic, and many still are. The quality of stereotyping varies, but is often quite thin. At the weakest end of the scale is "eye-dialect," which consists of nothing but the use of "spelling errors" that in fact reflect no distinctive phonological, lexical, or syntactic structure whatsoever, like the familiar **ennything, exkusable, wimmin, thuh**. Truer to linguistic reality, but still far removed is the use of phonological-morphological markers like **runnin'** or of stigmatized lexical forms like **ain't**, which indicate no specific linguistic variety, just "general nonstandard" or "colloquial."

In addition to oversimplifying, writers often make outright mistakes in representing language varieties, especially varieties of which they are not native speakers. Notorious in this regard are the attempts of British mystery writer Agatha Christie to characterize American English. Here is an example from Christie's *The Secret of Chimneys*, in which the American speaker is one "Mr. Hiram P. Fish of New York City":

> "I opine," said Mr. Fish, "that you are seeking for fingerprints?"
> "Maybe," said the superintendent laconically.
> "I should say to that, on a night such as last night, an intruder would have left footprints on the hardwood floor."
> "None inside, plenty outside."[26]

Mr. Fish's language here is distinguished by (a) the archaic verb **opine** and (b) the nonstandard **seeking for**. These forms clearly stand out, but there is nothing particularly American about either of them. Moreover, Mr. Fish uses some very non-American forms, notably the auxiliary **should** rather than **would** in **I should say**. In a slightly later excerpt, some other, more distinctive features are added:

> The American bowed. "That's too kind of you, Lady Eileen."
> "Mr. Fish," said Anthony, "had quite a peaceful morning."
> Mr. Fish shot a quick glance at him. "Ah, sir, you observed me, then, in my seclooded retreat? There are moments, sir, when far from the madding crowd is the only motto for a man of quiet tastes."
> Bundle had drifted on, and the American and Anthony were left together. The former dropped his voice a little. "I opine," he said, "that there is considerable mystery about this little dust up?"
> "Any amount of it," said Anthony.
> "That guy with the bald head was perhaps a family connection?"
> "Something of the kind."
> "These Central European nations beat the band," declared Mr. Fish. "It's kind of being rumored around that the deceased gentleman was a Royal Highness. Is that so, do you know?"[27]

Here again, we find the bizarre **I opine**. In addition, a dash of phonology is added in **seclooded** (as opposed to British [sɪklyudəd]). But what stands out most here are Fish's American colloquialisms: **this little dust up**, **guy**, **beat the band**, and **kind of**. The reason these expressions stand out, however, is not merely that other characters don't use them, but that Hiram Fish uses them in a way that would be most unusual for any American speaker, for in Fish's usage the colloquialisms occur incongruously in a noncolloquial speech situation and in the midst of such formal expressions as **considerable mystery**, **sir**, **family connection**, **deceased gentleman**. Moreover, they clash with marked Britishisms in Fish's speech, like **That's too kind**. Fish's inconsistency here does not make him sound like any real American, but it does make him sound different, and different in a way that lets Christie's well-known biases show through: Fish comes across as a person who, though useful and well-meaning enough, has simply not mastered the manners of polite society—a traditional British stereotype of the American. All these patterns are summed up in Fish's final remarks in the book:

> A little stir of excitement passes round. "That'll do, sonny," says Mr. Fish. "We shall do nicely now." . . .
> "I guess," said Mr. Hiram Fish *sotto voce* to himself and the world at large, "that this has been a great little old week."[28]

Errors like Christie's are common, as are stereotypic representations of regional and social varieties of English. Nevertheless, there are many authors since Twain who have been extremely successful in reflecting the variability of spoken language, despite the limitations of print and English spelling. Before looking at some examples, it may be useful to point out that just as writers often write carelessly and stereotypically, readers often tend to read carelessly and stereotypically, that is, they often notice only a few features of the language they read without paying attention to what particular variety has been chosen, or to how it is represented. Indeed, when critics discuss literary works that reflect speech varieties, they simply tend to speak vaguely about "colloquial" or "nonstandard" or "dialect" English, without distinguishing one variety from another. Yet these three labels refer to quite different phenomena, as we can see by examining a few short passages from prose fiction.

Consider, for example, the first few lines of *The Catcher in the Rye* again (quoted on page 257). We hear a boy who is using a variety without regionalisms and, at least in this part of the text, without nonstandard forms. His language is colloquial, or "vernacular," the variety identified with relatively casual street speech. It is colloquial in its use of **you'll** rather than **you will**, its string of loosely connected coordinate sentences, and in its personal tone: for example, the injection of personal evaluations like **lousy** and **if you want to know the truth**. In addition there are distinctly nonliterary locutions like **that David Copperfield kind of crap**. When *The Catcher in the Rye* was published in 1951, "four-letter words" were taboo in much speech and nearly all writing. To use **crap** was daring in a way that is hard to imagine today, and carried with it a meaning of social insult that contributes to the rejection of the reader even more than **really** and other features already discussed that cast doubt on the reader's supposed interest in the story.

In the first lines from Mark Twain's *Huckleberry Finn* we hear a rather different voice:

> You don't know about me, without you have read a book by the name of "The Adventures of Tom Sawyer," but that ain't no matter. That book was made by Mr. Mark Twain, and he told the truth, mainly. There was things which he stretched, but mainly he told the truth. That is nothing. I never seen anybody but lied, one time or another, without it was Aunt Polly, or the widow, or maybe Mary. Aunt Polly—Tom's Aunt Polly, she is—and Mary, and the Widow Douglas, is all told about in that book—which is mostly a true book; with some stretchers, as I said before.[29]

Huck uses the same kinds of colloquial features as Holden Caulfield in *The Catcher in the Rye*: contraction, tagged-on phrases like **but mainly he told the truth** or **as I said before**. He also uses interpolated explanations such as **Tom's Aunt Polly, she is** and repetition of words like **mainly**. Unlike Caulfield, Huck also uses widely attested nonstandard features like double negatives and **ain't**, as in **that ain't no matter**. **Ain't** was not as stigmatized when Mark Twain was writing as it is now, and was presumably not intended to have the same kind of effect as it has on a modern audience, but there are enough other features like the multiple negation to indicate that Huck's speech is meant to be nonstandard. While the novel contains many regionalisms, particularly in the quasi-phonetic spelling of the dialogue, there is nothing distinctly regional about the first lines, at least not sufficiently so for a reader to identify the "Pike County dialect" that Twain says he is representing.

Contrast the first lines of a novel entitled *Sitting Pretty* by Al Young:

> Maybe it was on accounta it was a full moon. I dont know. It's a whole lotta things I use to be dead certain about—like, day follow night and night follow day—things I wouldnt even bet on no more. It's been that way since me and Squirrel broke up and that's been yeahbout fifteen-some-odd years ago, *odd* years—July the Fourth.[30]

This is colloquial in the same ways as the other two passages: the forms **don't** and **it's**, the tagged-on phrases, and the indicators of hesitation like **maybe**, **yeahbout**. It is also nonstandard, as reflected by the multiple negatives: **things I wouldn't even bet on no more**. We know that the narrator, whose name is the title of the book, is at least middle-aged since he broke up with Squirrel some fifteen years before, just as we can guess that Huck is a child because he refers to Aunt Polly, but the language itself is not distinctly age-correlated in either passage. Sitting Pretty's language is, however, different from Huck's because, in addition to the colloquialisms and nonstandard forms, there are some features that indicate Black English vernacular, such as **It's a whole lotta things I use to be dead certain about**.

Another feature which sharply differentiates Sitting Pretty's language from Huck's is the absence of some apostrophes (**dont**, **wouldnt**) and run-together phrases like **on accounta**, features which are indicators to the reader that the norms of writing are consciously being broken, and the sound, not the written word, is all-important.

Contrast Andrew Lytle's beginning, also with colloquial and nonstandard features, but with distinct regionalisms in addition.

> "I want to speak to Mister McGregor."
>
> Yes, sir, that's what he said. Not marster, but MISTER McGREGOR. If I live to be a hundred, and I don't think I will, account of my kidneys, I'll never forget the feelen that come over the room when he said them two words: Mister McGregor. The air shivered into a cold jelly; and all of us, me, ma, and pa, sort of froze in it. I remember thinken how much we favored one of them waxwork figures Sis Lou had learnt to make at Doctor Price's Female Academy. There I was, a little shaver of eight, standen by the window a-blowen my breath on it so's I could draw my name, like chillun'll do when they're kept to the house with a cold. The knock come sudden and sharp, I remember, as I was crossen a T. My heart flopped down in my belly

and commenced to flutter around in my breakfast; then popped up to my ears and drawed all the blood out'n my nose except a little sack that got left in the point to swell and tingle. It's a singular thing, but the first time that nigger's fist hit the door I knowed it was the knock of death.[31]

This passage is clearly colloquial, as signaled by the contractions **don't** and **I'll**, presence of **-en** for **-ing**, and expressions like **sort of, shaver**. Nonstandard features here include the past tenses **come, drawed**, and the deictic **them**. Among the regionalisms indicating this is a Southern variety of American English are the prefix **a-** on the progressive verb form **a-blowen'**, and the lexical items **out'n**, corresponding to **out of, commenced** and **singular** as nonformal terms, **favored** meaning "preferred," **chillun** for "children." The address form **marster** here gives an interesting example of Southern "eye-dialect." Most Southern varieties are *r*-less, consequently the **r** in **marster** indicates not the pronunciation [marstər], but the pronunciation [mastər], as opposed to standard [mæstər].

Representing the variability of language requires a considerable degree of linguistic attention, since a feature will carry no significance if it is used too sporadically, and will become stereotypic if it is used too consistently and if it is not apparent. An example of remarkably detailed variability is provided by the passage cited below from Zora Neale Hurston's *Their Eyes Were Watching God*. This passage is cited at considerable length, since it is only in extensive materials that one can fully appreciate the details of variability, its function, and its systematization.

Zora Neale Hurston was a Black writer who wrote in the 1930s about the Black experience in the Deep South in the period just after Emancipation and during her own time. An anthropologist as well as a novelist, she was primarily concerned with Black culture, and she saw in the manipulation of language one of its most distinctive characteristics, and one of its great strengths.

> Long before the year was up, Janie noticed that her husband had stopped talking in rhymes to her. He had ceased to wonder at her long black hair and finger it. Six months back he had told her, "If Ah kin haul de wood heah and shop it fuh yuh, look lak you oughta be able tuh tote it inside. Mah fust wife never bothered me 'bout choppin' no wood nohow. She'd grab dat ax and sling chips lak uh man. You done been spoilt rotten."
>
> So Janie had told him, "Ah'm just as stiff as you is stout. If you can stand not to chop and tote wood Ah reckon you can stand not to git no dinner. 'Scuse mah freezolity, Mist' Killicks, but Ah don't mean to chop de first chip."
>
> "Aw you know Ah'm gwine chop de wood fuh yuh. Even if you is stingy as you can be wid me. Yo' Grandma and me myself done spoilt yuh now, and Ah reckon Ah have tuh keep on wid it."
>
> One morning soon he called her out of the kitchen to the barn. He had the mule all saddled at the gate.

10

"Looka heah, LilBit, help me out some. Cut up dese seed taters fuh me. Ah got tuh go step off a piece."

"Where you goin'?"

20

"Over tuh Lake City tuh see uh man about uh mule." . . .

"Ah'll cut de p'taters fuh yuh. When yuh comin' back?"

"Don't know exactly. Round dust dark Ah reckon. It's uh sorta long trip—specially if Ah hafter lead one on de way back."

When Janie had finished indoors she sat down in the barn with the potatoes. But springtime reached her in there so she moved everything to a place in the yard where she could see the road. The noon sun filtered through the leaves of the fine oak tree where she sat and made lacy patterns on the ground. She had been there a long time when she heard whistling coming down the road.

30

It was a cityfied, stylish dressed man with his hat set at an angle that didn't belong in these parts. His coat was over his arm, but he didn't need it to represent his clothes. The shirt with the silk sleeveholders was dazzling enough for the world. He whistled, mopped his face and walked like he knew where he was going. He was a seal-brown color but he acted like Mr. Washburn or somebody like that to Janie. Where would such a man be coming from and where was he going? He didn't look her way nor no other way except straight ahead, so Janie ran to the pump and jerked the handle hard while she pumped. It made a loud noise and also made

40

her heavy hair fall down. So he stopped and looked hard, and then he asked her for a cool drink of water.

Janie pumped it off until she got a good look at the man. He talked friendly while he drank.

Joe Starks was the name, yeah Joe Starks from in and through Georgy. Been workin' for white folks all his life. Saved up some money—round three hundred dollars, yes indeed, right here in his pocket. Kept hearin' 'bout them buildin' a new state down heah in Floridy and sort of wanted to come. But he was makin' money where he was. But when he heard all about 'em makin' a town all

50

outa colored folks, he knowed dat was de place he wanted to be . . . . Where was Janie's papa and mama?

"Dey dead, Ah reckon. Ah wouldn't know 'bout 'em 'cause mah Grandma raised me. She dead too."

"She dead too! Well, who's lookin' after a lil girl-chile lak you?"

"Ah'm married."

"You married? You ain't hardly old enough to be weaned. Ah betcha you still craves sugar-tits, doncher?"[32]

(This passage is not the opening of the novel, but it is the opening section of Janie's story.)

All three speakers in the passage use language variably, but if we look at overall tendencies in the dialogue, it is clear that Janie's husband Logan is being presented as the least standard of the three. When Janie talks back to him, her **first chip** (11) contrasts with his **fust wife** (5), her **can** and **to** contrast with his **kin** and **tuh,** her **If you can stand not to chop and tote wood** (8–9) stands out as markedly standard and formal after his **If Ah kin haul de wood heah and chop it fuh yuh** (4). Hurston thus uses variability to set up a power hierarchy, where Janie's standardness and formality correspond with her power over her husband, while later on Starks's ability to flatter with standard language and condescend with nonstandard (54–58) corresponds with his power over Janie.

It would be tedious to detail all the linguistic variability Hurston has incorporated into this text, but a few examples will illustrate two points: Most features that are currently considered quantitatively characteristic of BEV are present in this text, and where certain features are rare, such as consonant cluster reduction, there appears to be a correlation with anticipated reader difficulty.

In phonology we note: initial and final **d** for SAE /ð/ in function words: **dat** (6), **wid** (13) (this is regular in the dialogue, but variable in the indirectly narrated talk); variable rapid-speech forms of auxiliaries: **kin** (4), but **can** (9); and centralized forms of high back vowels (typical of spoken American): **fuh** (*r*-less) **yuh** (4), **tuh** (5), but **you** (9), **to** (9). There are also variably reduced consonant clusters: **girl-chile** (54), but **old** (57). Consonant cluster deletion is very rare in this novel. In the 1930s BEV would presumably have had fewer rather than more consonant clusters than the contemporary language, considering that BEV developed from a relatively uninflected system (see Chapter 9). Perhaps consonant cluster reduction is absent because it would hamper the reading process; perhaps the reasons are also aesthetic—the number of necessary apostrophes, given the graphic representation adopted here, would establish too much of a barrier between narrator and reader. Finally, we may note monophthongization of diphthongs in function words like **Ah, mah, lak,** but not content words (we do not find **wahf**). It appears that most content words remain standard, even though the function morphology may be nonstandard, because readers need norms on which to peg the variation. This seems to be a common feature of dialect writing, and distinguishes it sharply from bilingual writing and from experiments such as Joyce's in which new forms are created. Examples of these kinds of writing will be discussed in the next chapter.

Several syntactic features are especially noticeable in the Hurston passage. One is the presence of the BEV present tense-marker **-s** for all persons (as opposed to the third person singular present tense-marker of SAE), as in: **you is** (8), **you craves** (58). Hurston appears to be taking this feature as a particularly salient marker of BEV; this may also help explain why consonant cluster deletion is disfavored—it would wipe out the present tense-marker entirely except in the case of verbs like **be.** Another is the variable use of zero copula. While absence of copula is favored, as in **Dey dead** (52), **You married** (57), it is present in the first person **Ah'm married** (56). This is in fact a well-known feature of current BEV, and is just one more example of the care with which the spoken language is represented. Closely connected with absence of copula is the preference for noninverted forms of the question, as in: **When yuh comin' back?** (21). But again this absence is variable, in keeping with spoken BEV, cf. **Who's lookin' after a lil girl-chile lak you?** (54–55).

Noticeably absent among BEV syntactic features is invariant **be**. One can only speculate about the reasons for this—possibly it was not used by Black speakers in Florida at the time Hurston was writing. This, however, is doubtful, particularly in the light of the fact that other BEV-markers like **bín** are also absent. More probable is the constraint mentioned earlier—the variability used is limited to what the author conceived as the potential passive knowledge of her White readers, and she may have felt that it did not include **be** and **bín**. In the case of **bín**, even speakers of BEV have inconsistent responses, and as we have seen, in the case of invariant **be**, White speakers use it as a form of **will be**, but not of the iterative habitual. Therefore use of such forms could cause misunderstandings.

Another very important aspect of this passage is the fact that BEV features are not restricted to the dialogue, but occur also in the language of the narrator. At both the beginning and end of the text, we can see a sharp split between the standard language of the narrator and the BEV of the dialogue, but toward the middle, the narrative shifts into a stream of consciousness mode in which Janie's point of view becomes uppermost, and the language of narration changes accordingly. The first indication of this shift is the appearance of deictics oriented toward Janie: **she heard whistling coming down the road** (line 29) and **that didn't belong in these parts** (31). Then in (36) we hear the so-called free indirect style characterized by **would** in **where would he be coming from?** With these shifts come, first, colloquialisms like **stylish dressed** (30), then nonstandard **nor no** (37). Lines 44–50 give a third person version of Starks's own speech as heard by Janie, and here we get the first nonstandard phonology: **workin'** (45), **hearin'** (47). This section effectively blurs the distinction between narration and dialogue. From 51 on, we shift back to the original pattern of SAE narrative and BEV dialogue.

This shift into Janie's mind in the opening paragraphs of her (Janie's) story is Hurston's way of engaging the reader, particularly the non-Black reader, into Janie's personal and ethnic point of view. Thus though she chooses overall to narrate in SAE, Hurston makes an intricate effort to overcome any incongruity or distancing that may result, and to make clear at the outset that the point of view in the novel is Janie's, even if the narrator's language is generally not the same as Janie's.

Of course, one is immediately led to ask why Hurston didn't simply have Janie tell her own story in the first person, and in BEV. Part of the answer to this question lies in the fact that the reading public for novels in the 1930s in the U.S. was predominantly Whites with little knowledge of BEV, and that the cumbersome typography for writing BEV would have been too hard to read at length. But these facts point to a more general communicative problem confronted by minority writers. Whether they belong to racial, regional, or social minorities, for them the standard language is not the norm of the culture with which they identify and which they are trying to represent. Rather, the standard is a superimposed variety, the language often identified with oppression or defeat. The linguistic problem, then, is essentially how to use the conventions of written language to convey a different set of values, in other words, to break the norms of Standard English writing and establish new ones. In this context, writing becomes in some sense a revolutionary act, a conscious effort to create a dynamics of power. As the Hurston passage exemplifies, the difficulties of such an effort begin with very basic questions like narrator point of view. The first major Black writer in America, Charles Chesnutt, dealt with this problem differently from Hurston. In his first collection of stories, *The Conjure Woman* (1899), Chesnutt used a White Northerner as narrator of tales told him by a former Black slave, in direct imitation of Harris's Uncle Remus stories. On the one hand, such a maneuver sounds like a cop-out and a betrayal of ethnic identity; on the other hand, it should also be thought of as a communicative strategy. Given a White literary tradition in which Blacks were viewed from the outside and from above, as it were, and given an almost exclusively White reading public unaccustomed to the idea of reading a Black writer, one might easily decide that communication would be better effected if the authoritative position of narrator were occupied by a White rather than a Black. Chesnutt's strategy can be compared to that of nineteenth-century women who adopted male pen names (like George Eliot, George Sand, or Ellis Bell) in the hope of being taken more seriously.

It was not until several decades after *Their Eyes Were Watching God* that narrative totally in BEV began to appear. Al Young's novel *Sitting Pretty* (1975), already quoted briefly, is one very successful example. Here is a somewhat longer excerpt from this work:

Well, they sure got a whole lotta colored faces into that promo. He and Patricia ended up passin out one-dollar bills left and right to keep some of the brothers and sisters from clutterin up the set and ruinin everything.

"Yall gon play this flick over television?" one particularly obstreperous teenager come askin Crews just when we bout to do a take.

"That's correct," Patricia answer, runnin interference.

"I wasn't talkin to you, sister," the little dude say. "I was askin this white man that's actin like he in charge."

"I am in charge here," Crews say. "What can I do for you?"

"Yall comin down here in the community, exploitin us to make this picture and we wanna know what's in it for us?"

Crews say, "If you dont mind, sir, I beg to differ with you. Far from exploiting the community, it's our intention to rectify a number of inaccurate and distorted images which have previously been projected by media regarding the community. I should think you would welcome our presence."

"You aint answered my question, faggot. I wanna know what's in it for us."

"You mean what's in it for *you*, dont you?" Crews tell him, noddin at Patricia.

She walk over and hand the joker a five-dollar bill. That's all it took. He break out into a big chesscat grin, rub his chin, cram the money in his pocket and turn to a coupla his buddies and shout, "See, what I tell you? You gotta assert yourself and confront these honkies and bullshit toms. We cant just hang back when our rights is bein violated and have them run all over us."

Kid couldna been more'n thirteen. I couldnt imagine what
30   rights of his was being violated, but I did catch myself thinkin: *Well, more power to you, son, for loudtalkin the man outta five U.S. dollars!* At the same time I'm wonderin whether white folks that be in commercials have to go thru the same kindsa headaches.

The sky cloudin up and it look like it might rain, so we pack up and rush over to do the final commercial which take place down by the ocean on the beach where Playland use to be before it shut down. I still miss all them rides and amusement machines.

I'm perched up on topa one of them giant rocks with waves washin in and out and breakin all around me. My only lines
40   go somethin like this: "As you can see, I'm Sitting Pretty. Just like KRZY Radio, I'm on the scene wherever it's happenin. Set your dial to KRZY and youll be sittin pretty too."[33]

Here, in contrast with *Their Eyes Were Watching God*, the narrative point of view is uniformly first person and the narration uniformly BEV, with little discontinuity between the language Sitting Pretty uses to narrate and the language he uses in dialogue with the other characters. Notice that the BEV narrative does slow down the reading process, something Hurston may have been trying to avoid. Young demands that the reader take time to read and to listen, in part to deliberately counteract the speed and simultaneity of multimedia expression such as is experienced in TV and films. On the other hand, he eases the reader's task typographically by omitting apostrophes and using fewer unusual spellings than Hurston.

Like Hurston, Young is very sensitive to details of language, and there is a lot of variability in his representation of BEV. The advertisement in lines 40–42 is a particularly good example. **I'm Sitting Pretty** (line 40) with **-ing** contrasts with line 42 **you'll be sittin pretty too**. This is not to be understood as a switch from a more standard to a less standard variety in an effort to create camaraderie. Instead, it reflects a fact of BEV—that only the participle **-ing** and **-thing** in indefinite pronouns are normally rendered [ɪn] (or [−θɪn]). To the reader, the variability is an indication of ethnicity, not degree of formality or intimacy.

Rather than analyze the variability in Young's text in detail, we have given you the opportunity to do so in an exercise. Here we will comment instead on the way Young's use of variability differs from Hurston's. In Hurston's text, we saw considerable variation within the language of each character and within the language of the narrator. Moreover this variation was meaningful as an expression of differing relationships between characters and differing relationships between narrator and reader. In Young's text, on the other hand, the narrator's language is consistent and the reader's relationship to the narrator is also stable, the reader's engagement having been assumed. Except for Sitting Pretty, the characters themselves rarely shift in their speech patterns. In the main, the variability in Young's novel lies in two areas: variation within speech that simply reflects the inconsistency of speech, and contrasts between characters that reflect their differing social roles. For instance, Crews and Patricia both speak Standard English. Crews is White, Patricia is Black, but both speak the same way as a function of sharing the same social status. Both are pompous and, by implication in the context of the novel as a whole, so is Standard English in general. The teenager is ridiculous in his own way, like Crews spouting clichés, but the clichés of another social group. In this novel, differences in language, then, are primarily a function of different people, and reflect the enormous disparity of individuals.

The difference between Hurston's use of variability and Young's can be seen in part as indicators of the different narrator-reader relations they establish, and also of the different contexts they portray. Hurston's characters comprise a small range of people in an essentially rural setting where details of phonology and small syntactic differences are all-important in distinguishing social roles. Young writes about a large spectrum of San Francisco Bay Area characters from many walks of life and ethnic backgrounds, and many age groups. The variety of the characters reduces the possibility and the importance of detailed linguistic variability. The latter can only be given full rein in the character of Sitting Pretty who, as the narrator and hero, represents an eclectic but unifying force among the diversity.

There is yet another step from using a variety other than the written standard in first-person narrative to using it in third-person narrative. Relatively speaking, few such narratives exist in any distinctly local, social, or ethnic variety of English. One of the more successful ones in BEV is June Jordan's story, *His Own Where*, about two Black teenagers who make their own world, alienated from the rest of society. It begins:

> First time they come, he simply say, "Come on." He tell her they are going not too far away. She go along not worrying about the heelstrap pinching at her skin, but worrying about the conversation. Long walks take some talking. Otherwise it be embarrassing just side by side embarrassing.[34]

Like Young's *Sitting Pretty*, Jordan's *His Own Where* develops the ethnic perspective over the universal, even though it is in third-person narrative. It is hardly surprising that this is so, since in the current linguistic situation the standard has as its function the public, "objective" mode of expression, while the vernacular, whether merely colloquial or also regional, social, or ethnic, is associated with personal and "subjective" modes of expression.

In writing such as this, the norms of Standard written English have been completely broken. It is far from clear at present whether any new norms are being established. However, partly because of recent successes in using a wide spectrum of linguistic varieties in literature, and partly because of changing attitudes to writing, serious attention has in the last few years been paid to the possibility of using BEV even in nonliterary writings. An example of note is Alex Haley's use of BEV dialogue in *Roots* (1978), an example of a genre which might be called fictionalized history. A far more radical departure is the occasional use, especially for positive evaluation of BEV, of distinctly Black lexical items and exaggerated phonetic spellings such as **baaad** (in the BEV sense of "powerful") in the descriptive prose of Geneva Smitherman's *Talkin and Testifyin; the Language of Black America* (1977), a book on Black language. We can expect to see many more experiments of this type in the future.

SUGGESTED FURTHER READINGS

Among several introductions to "sociolinguistics," Trudgill's *Sociolinguistics: An Introduction* covers the widest range of topics with the greatest clarity for the beginner. Another far-ranging book, with focus on cultural contexts for language, is Burling's *Man's Many Voices: Language in Its Cultural Context.* Useful collections of readings include Allen and Underwood's *Readings in American Dialectology*, Williamson and Burke's *A Various Language: Perspectives on American Dialects*, Bailey and Robinson's *Varieties of Present-Day English*, and Pride and Holmes's *Sociolinguistics: Selected Readings*, all of which focus on both regional and social varieties. Journals with a similarly broad range of interest are *Language in Society*, *Sociolinguistics*, *International Journal of the Sociology of Language*, and with limitation to America, *American Speech*.

Reed's *Dialects of American English* summarizes regional dialect studies in the United States. McDavid's "Dialects of American English," in Francis's *The Structure of American English*, provides an excellent survey of regional distinctions in the Eastern United States, with some discussion of sociological and demographic backgrounds. For British dialects, which we have not been able to discuss here, Wakelin's *English Dialects: An Introduction* is invaluable; it includes some detailed comments on historical backgrounds.

Social variation is the focus of Labov's *Sociolinguistic Patterns.* A series of articles modified into a book, this details the key methodological and theoretical work of one of America's most influential sociolinguists. Less advanced reading is Wolfram and Fasold's *The Study of Social Dialects in American English.* Trudgill's *The Social Differentiation of English in Norwich* is an important study of social variation in eastern England.

Basic reading for Black English is Labov's "The Logic of Non-Standard English." Considerably more advanced is another collection of his papers, *Language in the Inner City*. DeStefano's *Language, Society, and Education: A Profile of Black English* and Stoller's *Black American English: Its Background and Its Usage in the Schools and Literature* are both collections of key articles on Black English, many of them of particular interest to teachers. Both contain Fasold and Wolfram's "Some Linguistic Features of Negro English," which provides an indispensable checklist of BEV features. Other books that pay attention to historical, cultural, and communicative characteristics of BEV are Dillard's *Black English* and *Lexicon of Black English*, and Kochman's *Rappin' and Stylin' Out: Communication in Urban Black America*. As the title of the latter suggests, its particular focus is on the speech act functions of BEV.

One topic that we have not been able to discuss here is sex-correlated language variation. This is well represented in Thorne and Henley's *Language and Sex: Difference and Dominance*, which contains some articles and an extensive annotated bibliography. Particular works on the subject are R. Lakoff's *Language and Woman's Place*, Key's *Male/Female Language*, and Nichols's "Black Women in the Rural South: Conservative and Innovative." Although the latter is a study of a creole-speaking community in South Carolina (see Chapter 9), the findings are valid for a large number of other communities as well.

Language varieties in literature have not been studied extensively from a linguistic point of view. Bridgman's *The Colloquial Style in America* exemplifies a literary approach to language variation, especially colloquial and regional variation. More strictly linguistic is Page's *Speech in the English Novel*, which is a valuable study of the problems facing the writer of dialogue. The section on dialect in literature in Williamson and Burke's *A Various Language: Perspectives on American Dialects* provides several models for discussing details of linguistic variation, including papers on the language of *The Adventures of Huckleberry Finn* and *The Catcher in the Rye*; it also provides easy access to Ives's important paper, "A Theory of Literary Dialect."

Exercises

1. "Translate" a paragraph or so of any well-known historical document, such as the Gettysburg address, or a much-used text, such as The Lord's Prayer, into modern colloquial English. Then discuss the difference in effect between the original version and yours.

2. Examine your own regional dialect or that of a friend with respect to the dialect features for American English mentioned in this chapter. Take your research beyond those features mentioned, if you can.

3. Select a product advertised by one company (e.g., a brand of cigarette or deodorant) in a variety of magazines. Discuss the way in which the language of the advertisements for this product varies according to the audience expected, in terms both of what is said about the product and of how the audience is addressed. Given the right company, you should be able to find differences that correlate with social status, ethnic group, age or sex, or some combination of these.

4. Read the passage from Al Young's *Sitting Pretty* (pages 347–48) very carefully and comment on the variability in the passage. What are the main features of BEV that Young both has and has not selected? Are there any noticeable differences between the BEV of the narrative and that of the dialogue? If so, why might they be present? What is the function, as far as you can tell, of lack of apostrophes in **wasnt, dont,** and so forth?

5. In the manuscript of her novel, *Wuthering Heights*, Emily Brontë represented the servant, Joseph, as speaking with a broad Yorkshire dialect (Yorkshire is in the Northeast of England). One speech assigned to him was:

    > "Noa!" said Joseph ... "Noa! That manes nowt—Hathecliff maks noa 'cahnt uh t'mother, nor yah norther—bud he'll hev his lad; und Aw mun tak him—soa nah yah knaw!"

    Emily Brontë's sister Charlotte, who edited the second edition of the novel, felt that this speech was too inaccessible, and modified it to:

    > "Noa!" said Joseph ... "Noa! that means naught. Hathecliff maks noa 'count o' t'mother, nor ye norther; but he'll hev his lad; une I mun tak him—soa ye knaw!"[35]

    Why do you think Charlotte Brontë made these particular emendations? Might you make any different changes if you were editing the book, and if so, what are they and why would you make them?

6. The following is the beginning of an elegy by Robert Burns:

ELEGY

ON

CAPTAIN MATTHEW HENDERSON,

A GENTLEMAN WHO HELD THE PATENT FOR
HIS HONOURS IMMEDIATELY FROM AL-
MIGHTY GOD!

But now his radiant course is run,
    For Matthew's course was bright:
His soul was like the glorious sun,
    A matchless, Heav'nly light!

O DEATH! thou tyrant fell and bloody;
The meikle° devil wi a woodie°
Haurl thee° hame to his black smiddie,
        O'er hurcheon° hides,
And like stock-fish come o'er his studdie°
        Wi' thy auld sides!

He's gane, he's gane! he's frae us torn,
The ae best fellow e'er was born!
Thee, Matthew, Nature's sel° shall mourn
10   By wood and wild,
Where, haply, Pity strays forlorn,
        Frae man exil'd.

Ye hills, near neebors o' the starnz,
That proudly cock your cresting cairns!
Ye cliffs, the haunts of sailing yearns,
        Where echo slumbers!
Come join, ye Nature's sturdiest bairns,
        My wailing numbers . . .[36]

---

2 meikle: great   **woodie:** rope made of willows   **3 haurl thee:** drag thyself
4 hurcheon: hedgehog   **5 studdie:** anvil   **9 sel:** self

    a. What is the function of the stanza in Standard English?
    b. Why might Burns write more markedly in Scots at the beginning
        of this poem than later on in the poem?
    c. What linguistic features characterize the language of the "Elegy"
        as Scots dialect?

7. The following scene from Harriette Arnow's novel *The Dollmaker* takes place
    in a poor working-class housing development in Detroit. Mr. Daly, a Detroit
    Irishman, and Gertie, a newcomer from the Kentucky hills, are quarreling:

        A sigh of disappointment went up from the alley, then Mr.
    Daly, by her bottom step now, was saying loudly: "Listen, yu
    overgrown hillbilly; yu kid's lyen. He did too beat up on mu
    little kid. My kids don't lie—see."
        Gertie's hand dropped from the door, and she turned and
    looked at him. "Th very first mornen mine went to school, yer
    youngen—"
        "Huh? Youngen, whatcha mean youngen? In Detroit
    youse gotta learn to speak English, yu big nigger-loven com-
10   munist hillbilly. Yu gotta behave. I, Joseph Daly, will see to ut
    yu do. I'm a dacent, respectable, religious good American. See?"
    Gertie opened her mouth, but shut it as he went on, laughing a
    little, one ear cocked for the audience behind him: "Detroit
    was a good town till da hillbillies come. An den Detroit went
    tu hell."

Somewhere down the alley a voice cried, "Oh, yeah?"

Mr. Daly gave it no heed. He came onto the bottom step, and looked up at Gertie, shaking his fist to emphasize his words: "If one a youse touches one a mine, I'll have youse all

20   inu clink, see. Du cops listen tu Joseph Daly, see. I letcha git by wit too much awready." He straightened his shoulders, attempted to make his chest stick out further than his stomach, failed, but continued in his injured-good-citizen tone: "An why for because didjas beat up mu wife, a great big overgrown hillbilly like youse on a little woman like mu wife? Why, because she barred da evil doctrine a communism from her door—yu call yuself a Christian, I prasume."

Gertie gave a slow headshake. "I recken I try tu be, but," she went on in a low, choked voice, "whether I'm a Christian

30   or not is somethin' fer God to decide, not me."

"So yu don't know, huh." He laughed again, and the alley laughed with him.

The laughter somehow loosened her tongue. "I didn't hit yer wife. I kept her from hurten a woman she'd already haf blinded. Th woman was jist tryen to spread some kind a religion, an th Constitution says, 'Congress shall make no—'"

"Communist," he was screaming, waving his fist, and for an instant so choked with wrath he could not go on. "Yu communists allatime yu gotta spout u Constitution. Don'tcha

40   know they's a war? Oh, if u good Father Moneyhan could be President. He'd settle u likes a youse. Yu an yu Constitution, yu commies an heathen hill——"

A soft but dirty snowball splattered the side of his face. He whirled toward Sophronie's coalhouse, now covered with children, including Amos, Enoch, and Wheateye. "Who true dat?" he cried, his grandstand manners lost in fury.[37]

a. The two characters here obviously speak different varieties of English. What dialect features do they have in common? At what points do they contrast? At what points does the text show variability? What significance have the spellings **haf** (line 34) and **true** (45)?

b. In this chapter we pointed out that most of the features that characterize Black English are also found in other varieties of English. What characteristics does Mr. Daly's speech share with BEV?

c. In what ways does Gertie's speech become more standard in lines 28–30, and why?

d. Comment on turn-taking and terms of address in this passage.

e. Comment on the use of progressive versus past tense in the narration here, and in particular on the tense shift in line 37.

8. Discuss the ways in which the reader is invited to share the woman's thoughts in the following passage from Richard Wright's short story "Bright and

Morning Star." Consider not only such factors as the use of **the** and other structures discussed in Chapter 7, but also the way in which Wright gradually shifts from written to spoken language, and then to dialect. Include comments on the difference between the woman's actual words and indirect thought, on the orthographic devices used to reflect dialect, and also on the function of the phrase **with her black face** (line 1). The neutral word "dialect" is used here deliberately. As in Hurston's writing, no criterial feature of BEV is used; but unlike Hurston's White characters, Wright's in this short story speak the same way as the Blacks, using essentially the same nonstandard Southernisms rather than ethnically identifiable linguistic features. This reflects Wright's concern with the essential humanity of all people, overriding ethnic, social, or other groupings.

She stood with her black face some six inches from the moist windowpane and wondered when on earth would it ever stop raining. It might keep up like this all week, she thought. She heard rain droning upon the roof and high up in the wet sky her eyes followed the silent rush of a bright shaft of yellow that swung from the airplane beacon in far off Memphis. Momently she could see it cutting through the rainy dark; it would hover a second like a gleaming sword above her head, then vanish. She sighed, troubling, Johnny-Boys been trampin

10 in his shop all day wid no decent shoes on his feet. . . . Through the window she could see the rich black earth sprawling outside in the night. There was more rain than the clay could soak up; pools stood everywhere. She yawned and mumbled: "Rains good n bad. It kin make seeds bus up thu the ground, er it kin bog things down lika watahsoaked coffin." Her hands were folded loosely over her stomach and the hot air of the kitchen traced a filmy vein of sweat on her forehead. From the cook stove came the soft singing of burning wood and now and then a throaty bubble rose from a pot of simmering greens.

20 "Shucks, Johnny-Boy coulda let somebody else do all tha running in the rain. Theres others bettah fixed fer it than he is. But, naw! Johnny-Boy ain the one t trust nobody t do nothin. Hes gotta do it *all* hissef. . . ."

She glanced at a pile of damp clothes in a zinc tub. Waal, Ah bettah git t work. She turned, lifted a smoothing iron with a thick pad of cloth, touched a spit-wet finger to it with a quick, jerking motion: *smiiitz!* Yeah; its hot! Stooping, she took a blue work-shirt from the tub and shook it out.[38]

NOTES

[1] William Labov, *Sociolinguistic Patterns* (Philadelphia: Univ. of Pennsylvania Press, 1972), Chapter 2.

[2] William Labov, "Some Principles of Linguistic Methodology," *Language in Society*, 1 (1972), 97–120.

[3] These are well represented in Harold B. Allen and Gary N. Underwood, eds., *Readings in American Dialectology* (New York: Appleton-Century-Crofts, Meredith Corporation, 1971).

[4] Adapted from a more detailed map drawn specially for this book by Virginia McDavid, Professor of English, Chicago State University and Associated Editor, Linguistic Atlas of the North-Central States.

[5] Based on Raven I. McDavid, "Dialects of American English," in W. Nelson Francis, *The Structure of American English* (New York: Ronald Press, 1958), with revisions made for this book by Virginia McDavid.

[6] William Labov, *The Social Stratification of English in New York City* (Washington, D.C.: Center for Applied Linguistics, 1966).

[7] Social status in the United States is largely identified according to economic criteria (as well as job classification, etc.). Given this classification, the middle middle class and upper middle class are very small, and usually insignificant linguistically. This is why they do not figure in the statistics in this chapter.

[8] Adapted from Labov, *Sociolinguistic Patterns*, p. 114. The figures are based on a survey made in the early 1960s.

[9] Known as the "matched-guise" technique, this method of subjective evaluation was developed by Wallace E. Lambert, especially in "A Social Psychology of Bilingualism," in *Problems of Bilingualism*, ed. John Macnamara; special issue of *The Journal of Social Issues*, 23, No. 2 (1967).

[10] Peter Trudgill, *Sociolinguistics: An Introduction* (Harmondsworth, Mssex.: Penguin, 1974).

[11] Labov, *Sociolinguistic Patterns*, Chapter 1.

[12] See Orlando Taylor, "Responses to Social Dialects in the Field of Speech," in *Socio-Linguistics: A Cross Disciplinary Perspective*, ed. Roger Shuy (Washington: Center for Applied Linguistics, 1971).

[13] See James Sledd and Wilma R. Ebbitt, eds., *Dictionaries and THAT Dictionary* (Chicago: Scott Foresman and Co., 1962) for a representative sample of arguments for and against Webster's Third International Dictionary.

[14] See J. L. Dillard, *Black English: Its History and Usage in the United States* (New York: Random House, 1972); and William A. Stewart, "Continuity and Change in American Negro Dialects," *The Florida Foreign Language Reporter*, 6, No. 1 (1968); rpt. in *Readings in American Dialectology*, eds. Allen and Underwood.

[15] William Labov, "The Logic of Non-Standard English," *Monograph Series on Languages and Linguistics*, Georgetown University, 22 (1969); rpt. as Chapter 5 of Labov, *Language in the Inner City* (Philadelphia: Univ. of Pennsylvania Press, 1972; rpt. in *Language in Context*, ed. Pier Paolo Giglioli (Harmondsworth, Mssex.: Penguin, 1972); rpt. in *Black American English; Its Background and Its Usage in the Schools and Literature*, ed. Paul Stoller (New York: Dell, 1975).

[16] Materials are largely drawn from Labov, *Language in the Inner City*; and Ralph W. Fasold and Walt Wolfram, "Some Linguistic Features of Negro Dialect," in *Teaching Standard English in the Inner City*, eds., Ralph W. Fasold and Roger W. Shuy (Washington, D.C.: Center for Applied Linguistics, 1970); rpt. in *Language, Society, and Education: A Profile of Black English*, ed. Johanna S. DeStefano (Worthington, Ohio: Charles A. Jones Publishing Co., 1973); rpt. in *Black American English*, ed. Paul Stoller.

[17] This section on intonation is indebted to Elaine Tarone, "Aspects of Intonation in Black English," *American Speech*, 48 (1973), 29–36.

[18] Adapted from Walt Wolfram, *A Sociolinguistic Description of Detroit Negro Speech* (Washington, D.C.: Center for Applied Linguistics, 1969), p. 144.

[19] For example, Ralph W. Fasold, *Tense Marking in Black English; A Linguistic and Sociological Analysis* (Arlington, Va.: Center for Applied Linguistics, 1972).

[20] See especially Labov, *Language in the Inner City*, Chapter 3; and Labov, "Where Do Grammars Stop?" *Monograph Series on Languages and Linguistics*, Georgetown University, 25 (1972), 43–88.

[21] Thomas Kochman, ed., *Rappin' and Stylin' Out; Communication in Urban Black America* (Urbana: Univ. of Illinois Press, 1972), p. 261.

[22] Labov, *Language in the Inner City*, pp. 328–29.

[23] Robert Burns, "To a Louse; on Seeing One on a Lady's Bonnet at Church," in *The Works of Robert Burns; Containing His Life*, ed. John Lockhart (New York: William Pearson, 1835), p. 42.

[24] Robert Burns, "Address to a Lady," in *The Works of Robert Burns*, ed. Lockhart, p. 73.

[25] For further discussion, see Sumner Ives, "A Theory of Literary Dialect," in *A Various Language: Perspectives on American Dialects*, eds. Juanita Williamson and Virginia M. Burke (New York: Holt, Rinehart and Winston, Inc., 1971). Slightly revised version of an article by the same name in *Tulane Studies in English*, 2 (1950), 137–82.

[26] Agatha Christie, *The Secret of Chimneys* (New York, Dell Publishing Co., Inc., 1971), p. 96.

[27] Christie, *Secret of Chimneys*, p. 118.

[28] Christie, *Secret of Chimneys*, pp. 223–24.

[29] From Mark Twain, *The Adventures of Huckleberry Finn*, ed. Henry Nash Smith (Boston: Houghton Mifflin Co., and Cambridge: The Riverside Press, 1958), p. 3.

[30] From Al Young, *Sitting Pretty* (New York: Holt, Rinehart and Winston, Inc., 1975), p. 3.

[31] From Andrew Lytle, "Mister McGregor," *The Virginia Quarterly Review*, 11 (1935), 218.

[32] From Zora Neal Hurston, *Their Eyes Were Watching God* (Philadelphia and London: J. B. Lippincott and Co., 1937), pp. 45–48.

[33] From Al Young, *Sitting Pretty*, pp. 125–26.

[34] From June Jordan, *His Own Where* (New York: Thomas Y. Crowell Company, Inc., 1975).

[35] These two passages are cited in Norman Page, *Speech in the English Novel* (London: Longman, 1973), p. 66.

[36] Robert Burns, "Elegy on Captain Matthew Henderson," in *The Works of Robert Burns*, ed. Lockhart, pp. 49–50.

[37] From Harriette Arnow, *The Dollmaker* (New York: The Macmillan Company, 1954), pp. 282–83.

[38] From Richard Wright, "Bright and Morning Star," in *Uncle Tom's Children* (New York: Harper and Row, 1940), pp. 181–82.

CHAPTER 9

English in Contact

So far we have treated English as a language essentially un-influenced by other languages and without influence on others. No language is ever totally isolated, although political and especially geographical limitations may tend to isolate some languages far more than others. English has had massive contact with other languages as a result first of invasions of England by the Norsemen and the French, later as a result of colonial expansion, and now as the language of world trade. English is the "official," that is parliamentary or administrative, language of a large number of ex-colonial countries, and as such is also developing many new forms as a secondary or tertiary language around the world.[1] Native English speakers in America and England tend to forget that for historical reasons, and especially because of the political power of Great Britain and the United States, the number of English-speakers for whom English is a second language, or even a third, is enormous. Furthermore, they tend to forget that most people in the world are not monolingual but at least bilingual and often multilingual. To understand the nature of English fully, it is necessary to consider English in contact with other languages. Various kinds of contact have led to various kinds of influence, both of other languages on English and of English on other languages. In certain sociopolitical situations, totally new languages that are not English but that have vocabularies largely derived from English, have arisen. Examples include West African Pidgin English and Jamaican Creole. This chapter will pay particular attention to these new languages and to what we can learn about the structure of language from studying them. First we will very briefly sketch the history of English in contact with other languages, mainly to remind readers that English is in its origins a mixed language, and that monolingualism among English-speakers is a relatively recent phenomenon.[2]

Around A.D. 450, a group of Germanic tribes began settling in England. They were later to be called Anglo-Saxons, and their language, based on German dialects, was later to become English. These tribes had been asked to aid a group of Celts in Southern England to fight against Celts in Northern England. Having completed this mission, the Germanic tribes invaded England and during the following centuries eventually pushed the Celts into the least fertile parts of Great Britain: Cornwall in the Southwest, Wales and Ireland in the West, and Scotland in the North. Contact with the Celts appears to have had little impact on the language of the Anglo-Saxons, as its influence was almost exclusively limited to a few vocabulary items. Down through the centuries, Celtic influence on English has continued to be quite small, except in Ireland. During the Anglo-Saxon period, a second influence, mainly on vocabulary, was Latin, the language of Christian missionaries and of education.

Subsequent to the Anglo-Saxon invasion, there were continual invasions by Scandinavians, first Norwegians (Norsemen) and later Danes in the Old English period from 787 on. Apart from a short truce negotiated in 878, fighting with the Scandinavian invaders continued until the eleventh century. Indeed, during a short period, three Danes became kings of England, starting with King Canute, who reigned from 1016–1035. Norse influence on English was rarely studied until recently, but it seems to have been far greater than was assumed, perhaps contributing to the breakdown of the Old English inflectional system. In Old English, nouns, adjectives, demonstratives, and pronouns were inflected not only for number and case, but also for gender, and verbs for first, second, and third person singular and plural, present and past, indicative and subjunctive, rather like the modern verb **to be**, with its forms **am, is, are, was, were, been,** and **be** (as in **If it be so**). Better known influences of Norse on English are vocabulary items including **law, window, call, give, hit, ransack, sky,** and many others. You can be fairly certain that any short, everyday English word with a velar stop ([k] or [g]) or the cluster **sk** before the front vowels [i, ɪ, e, ɛ] is Scandinavian in origin, because in Old English [k] became [č] in this environment, [g] became [y], and [sk] became [š]. Thus **kirk, garden,** and **skirt** are of Scandinavian origin, while **church, yard,** and **shirt** are of Old English origin.

The invasion of England in 1066 by William the Conqueror from what is now Northwest France led to far more extensive changes in English. The Normans who conquered England were, as the name shows, themselves Norse in origin. They had invaded Northwest France in the late ninth century, settled there, and adopted French—a rather unusual phenomenon, since conquerors usually impose their own language rather than adopt that of the conquered people. In this case, the culture of France seems to have had more prestige than the military power of the Norsemen. As a result of the Norman conquest of England, reinforced in the mid-twelfth century by the influence of central and southern French during the reign of Henry II, French became the language of politics and of courtly poetry in England. Rhymed verse as opposed to alliterative verse, romance instead of heroic poem became the literary modes of the Middle English period. French genres in origin, they maintained their popularity in English even after the influence of French waned. It was in this period that English vocabulary was hugely influenced by French. An estimated 40 percent of the words in *Webster's Third New International Dictionary* are French in origin. Much of the borrowed vocabulary was the vocabulary of the court, involving terms for chivalry, morality, government, fashion, and literature (the last five nouns are derived from French), but some were everyday terms like **table, lamp, beast, sandal, purple, age**. With such massive borrowing, there was inevitably going to be influence on the sounds of English. This is most marked in the stress patterns. In Old English, as in Modern German, stress falls on the first syllable of the root. In words borrowed from French, stress falls on different syllables depending on the number of syllables in the word, and for more recent borrowings, depending also on the syntactic function of the word. Some examples were discussed in Chapter 2, like **reálity-réalism, eléctric-electrícity**. French and English stress systems coexisted side by side for a long time, and a full reformulation of English stress did not occur until the eighteenth century. There is still some lack of clarity about stress in English, directly resulting from the coexistence of the two systems. Does one say **cóntroversy, láboratory**, and **córollary**, or **contróversy, labóratory**, and **coróllary**? (The latter set is mainly British.) In any event, the change in stress patterns was sufficient for English to change from a language that favored alliteration in verse to one that favored rhyme (for the correlation of stress and metrical patterns, see page 74).

French lost political, though not literary, prestige early in the thirteenth century when the French king confiscated Norman territory, and even more in the fourteenth century when the English kings unsuccessfully went to war to win back their former lands in France. In 1346, English was used for the first time in the Middle English period as the language of law and education, though by then it had been heavily influenced by French. The pervasive force of French can be seen very clearly in Chaucer's writings (composed in the last quarter of the fourteenth century). We quote the first lines of *The Canterbury Tales* with words of French (and ultimately Latin) origin in boldface type:

> Whan that Aprill with his shoures soote
> When April with his sweet showers
>
> The droghte of **March** hath **perced** to the roote,
> The drought (thirst) of March has pierced to the root,
> (Has completely overcome the dryness of March)
>
> And bathed every **vayne** in swich **licour**
> And has bathed every vein in such liquor (juices)
>
> Of which **vertu engendred** is the **flour**; . . . .
> From whose efficacy the flowers are engendered . . .

Thanne longen folk to goon on **pilgrimages,**
Then people long to go on pilgrimages,

And **palmeres** for to seken **straunge** londes.
And pilgrims (long) to seek out strange countries. [3]

New influences appeared during the Renaissance, when Latin and Greek achieved unprecedented secular prestige. The following few lines from Shakespeare's early play *Love's Labour's Lost* illustrates not only French influence, but also extensive Latin influence (notice there are also some Dutch words; these were borrowed during the late Middle Ages and the sixteenth century, which were times of extensive trade with Holland):

And I, forsooth, in love! I, that have been love's whip; . . .

A **critic**, nay, a night-watch **constable;**
  Lat.   Fr.

A **domineering pedant** over the boy°;
  Dutch   Fr.   ?

Than whom no **mortal** so **magnificent!**
           Fr.   Lat.

This wimpled°, whining, **pur**blind, wayward **boy;**
                  Fr.   ?

This **senior-junior**, **giant**-dwarf, **Dan Cupid;**
  Lat.   Lat.   Fr.   Fr.   Lat.

Regent of love-**rhymes**, lord of folded arms,
 Fr.   Lat.

The **anointed sovereign** of sighs and groans.[4]
  Fr.   Fr.

The word **boy**, surprising though it may be, is obscure in origin, hence the query.
3 **boy**: Cupid   5 **wimpled**: blind-folded

Since most borrowings from Latin and especially Greek were at this time academic, they were called "inkhorn terms" and were the subject of much derision in some quarters (including *Love's Labour's Lost*). However, English speakers went on borrowing new terms from whatever languages they came in contact with, giving English its huge vocabulary and its large range of potential stylistic variants. It is borrowing that has given such triplets as **eat** (English), **dine** (French), **ingest** (Latin), or **smack** (Dutch), **kiss** (English), **osculate** (Latin), with their associated ranges from down-to-earth to polite to scholarly or scientific.

In these days we tend to forget that most educated people in the seventeenth and eighteenth centuries were fluent in at least English, Latin, French, or German, and often were able to write well in at least one language other than English. For example, Jeremy Bentham wrote most of his works in French. Edward Gibbon initially planned to write his *The History of the Decline and Fall of the Roman Empire* in French, since that was culturally the most prestigious language even at the end of the eighteenth century, but changed his mind due to further changes to English: English had become a leading colonial language, no longer absorbing the languages of invaders or prestige cultures, but itself spreading out all over the world. For Gibbon, what mattered most was that it was now the language of America, and he predicted that English would ultimately outdo the other major colonial languages of his time, French, Spanish, and Portuguese. So, for the future generations who would read his book, he chose to write in his native tongue, English.

Colonialism brought the settlement of English-speaking people, largely from very different geographical areas and social backgrounds, in areas remote from England, whether in America, India, Africa, Australia, or elsewhere in the world. In the colonies, British regional dialects soon gave way to a regionally leveled-out kind of speech, often called a **koine**[5] (pronounced [kɔyne]; the term is from Greek **koine** "common, ordinary"). The development of a koine was particularly marked in America, where settlement was greatest. Influence from other languages was small. In America we find a situation rather like that between Anglo-Saxons and Celts. A few Native American words were borrowed, especially to refer to artifacts and foods. Some of these were borrowed directly, such as **moccasin** and **papoose**, more were borrowed from Native American languages via French and Spanish, including **tomato**, **potato**, **tobacco**, **canoe**. But on the whole, as with Anglo-Saxon and Celtic, the influence was much more in the other direction. In India too, although political relations were quite different, only a few native words were borrowed, such as **punch** (originally Hindi **pãc** [pronounced as panch] "five" referring to the five ingredients from which punch was made), **chutney**, **thug**, **bandana**, **bungalow**, and a group of religious terms including **yoga**, **guru**, **nirvana**. On the other hand, the English used by Indians developed its own characteristics as a secondary language, and after India's independence was recognized as a separate variety called Indian English.[6]

Colonialism depended in part on extensive trade, especially slave trade. Trade has, as far as we know, always fostered the development of mixed (or "contact") languages, and the slave trade of the seventeenth and eighteenth centuries did so at an astounding rate, above all along the ocean trade routes (see Map). Contact languages involving English are only a small portion of the contact languages of the world. A trade language known as Sabir, involving Spanish and Portuguese, developed in the Mediterranean in the twelfth century, and was apparently much used during the Crusades. Sabir was in continual use, especially along the African trade routes, until the beginning of the nineteenth century. We can also surmise earlier trade languages at the time of the Greek and Roman empires. We know that Swahili, now a standard language, was once a contact language developed in the Arab slave trade of the Middle Ages. Currently, new contact languages are developing internally within countries. An example is "Gastarbeiterdeutsch," a language mix of German and Turkish, German and Portuguese, or other languages spoken by workers migrating to the factories of modern Germany. During the American intervention in Vietnam, a trade language mixing French, Vietnamese, and English sprang up among American soldiers and Vietnamese. Trade languages and contact languages in general are thus not exclusively products of seventeenth- and eighteenth-century colonialism. But certain social situations created by the slave trade did favor the development of a large number of contact languages at that time, many with remarkably similar structures.

PIDGINS AND CREOLES

Among the contact languages that developed during the slave trade are several known as "pidgins" and "creoles." These terms are used here in their technical linguistic senses. Originally "pidgin" referred to Chinese Pidgin English and was a modification of the word **business**. "Creole" originally meant a White colonist born in the tropical colonies; later it applied to slaves and other residents of these colonies, and later still to the contact languages spoken especially in colonial situations.

A pidgin may be roughly defined as a language that is nobody's native language.[7] It arises in situations where speakers of mutually unintelligible languages come together, typically as social subordinates to a socially dominant minority who speak yet another language. For example, West African slaves were deliberately purchased from different language groups so that they would be unable to communicate and therefore not be able to organize. The slaves had to develop a language for survival, and borrowed words from the prestige language of the slaveholders, while in many cases maintaining features of the grammars of their own languages. In linguistic terminology, people borrowed vocabulary from the "superstrate" while maintaining the grammar of the "substrate." Here "super" and "sub" refer to relative power held by the two groups. Where slavery was maintained, and where there was a regular influx of new slaves, pidgins in some cases met with prolonged use and became highly stabilized. Often vocabulary changed a lot when power passed from one colonizer to another, as in the Caribbean among the Spanish, Portuguese, French, Dutch, German, and English. Pidgins also came into contact with languages other than the superstrate, such as Native American languages, or the languages of Asian workers or merchants. In Hawaii, the pidgin situation involves partial mixing of Indo-European languages (especially English, Spanish, Portuguese) with Malayo-Polynesian languages (Hawaiian, Tagalog), Chinese languages, Japanese, and Korean. Other situations where pidgins arise are exemplified in Nigeria and the Cameroons where West African Pidgin English (abbreviated as WAPE) has been known since the late sixteenth century. Originating as a language of

THE SPREAD OF MARITIME PIDGIN ENGLISH

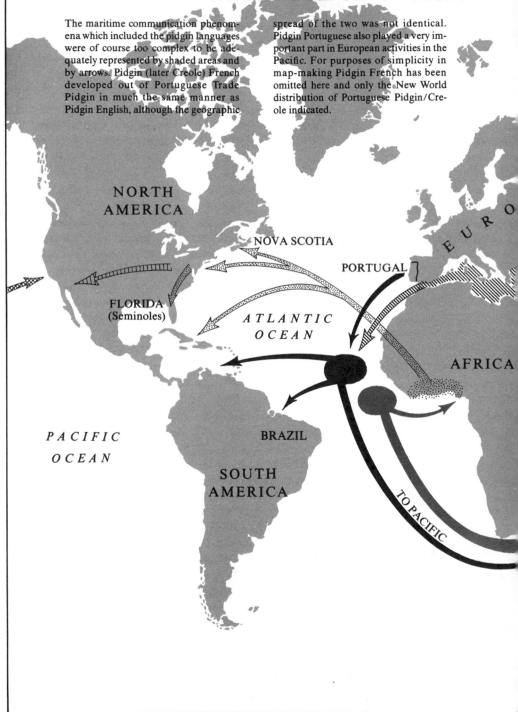

The maritime communication phenomena which included the pidgin languages were of course too complex to be adequately represented by shaded areas and by arrows. Pidgin (later Creole) French developed out of Portuguese Trade Pidgin in much the same manner as Pidgin English, although the geographic spread of the two was not identical. Pidgin Portuguese also played a very important part in European activities in the Pacific. For purposes of simplicity in map-making Pidgin French has been omitted here and only the New World distribution of Portuguese Pidgin/Creole indicated.

NORTH
AMERICA

NOVA SCOTIA

PORTUGAL

EURO

FLORIDA
(Seminoles)

ATLANTIC
OCEAN

AFRICA

PACIFIC
OCEAN

BRAZIL

SOUTH
AMERICA

TO PACIFIC

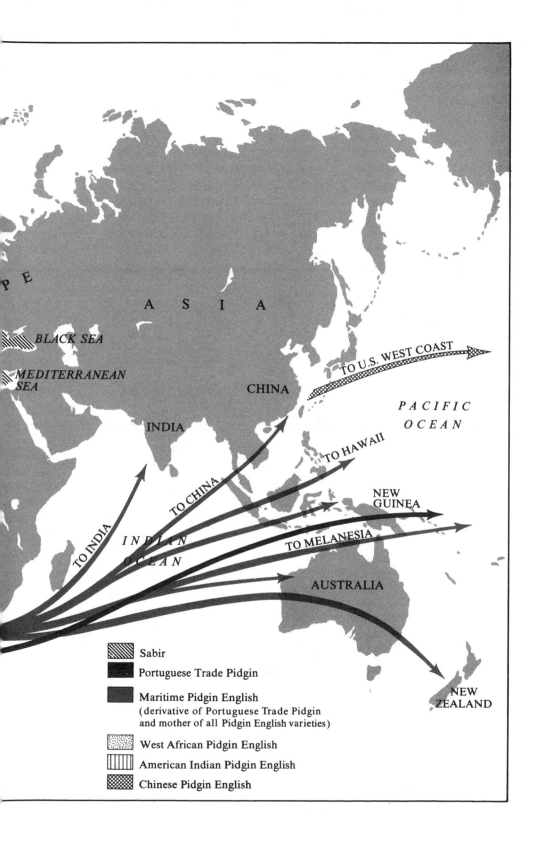

BLACK SEA

MEDITERRANEAN
SEA

E

A S I A

PE

CHINA

INDIA

PACIFIC
OCEAN

TO U.S. WEST COAST

TO HAWAII

NEW
GUINEA

TO CHINA

IN DI AN
OCEAN

TO MELANESIA

TO INDIA

AUSTRALIA

NEW
ZEALAND

Sabir

Portuguese Trade Pidgin

Maritime Pidgin English
(derivative of Portuguese Trade Pidgin
and mother of all Pidgin English varieties)

West African Pidgin English

American Indian Pidgin English

Chinese Pidgin English

slave trade, it has continued to serve an important trade-language function, and since independence of the West African nations, it has become more and more important politically as a "lingua franca" or general language of communication. Its role is vital in a country like Nigeria which has within its boundaries a large number of different languages, including some as un-related to each other as English and Chinese (for example, there are the Niger-Congo languages Yoruba, Ibo, Ewe, and the Hamito-Semitic language Hausa). WAPE also functions as an important vehicle of communication with adjacent countries like the Cameroons. A pidgin has also been main-tained in Papua-New Guinea, where the languages of the island, though related, are nevertheless not mutually comprehensible. Here, Tok Pisin (from Talk Pidgin), also called Neo-Melanesian, has likewise become a lingua franca.

As might be expected, pidgins typically serve limited functions, especially in their early stages. In their simplest form they provide little more than the basic needs of communication. They identify social groupings (who is in and who is out), differentiate speech functions (for example, statement, question, command, request, and naming of trade objects and body parts), and specify immediate local contexts (trading post, ship, harbor, or road). They are often extensively supplemented by gesture. As a pidgin develops, increasingly subtle linguistic distinctions are made. These include modifications specifying the quality or condition of objects (adjectival expressions), or aspectuals, ex-pressions in which events are analyzed as moments without duration or as involving duration, or are designated as completed or not completed. The particular functions of the pidgin, whether used for bargaining, for work orders, or for communicating reports at the end of the day further determine what types of linguistic structure develop.

Pidgins are often regarded as very rudimentary, incomplete languages. To some extent this is true. But, it is less true than one might think, for pidgins are often more complex than they appear on the surface. In the kind of situation in which pidgins thrive, one would not expect complex sentence structure or extensive vocabulary, but rather ingenious use of limited struc-tures to express complex relations. We must always remember that in normal cases, speakers of pidgin bring with them full linguistic competence in their own native languages. Their tacit knowledge of linguistic systems is thus as great as that of speakers of any language. In the pidgin, then, it is likely that complex relations will be understood, though not overtly expressed. To this extent, pidgins are limited in function and surface representation, but not necessarily in cognitive complexity, or "inner form."

Unlike pidgins, creoles are typically native languages. They are usually developed by the children of pidgin speakers. However, they may also develop as the regular home language of adults in situations of intermarriage. As a native or home language, a creole clearly has more linguistic functions than a pidgin and therefore is more varied in structure. More possibilities of sub-ordination are present, and the vocabulary is greater. Various kinds of inflectional structures tend to arise, partly because as native languages, creoles are spoken more rapidly and with an easier flow than most pidgins. This allows for contractions of elements that tend to be separate words or particles in pidgin languages. Creoles thrive where there is a large ethnic mix and clear social stratification such as existed during the colonial period in the Caribbean and in many islands in the Pacific. When there is little access to the superstrate language, the creole will develop relatively independently. This was the case with Sranan, the national language of Surinam. Despite only brief contact with English in the eighteenth century, Sranan nevertheless continued to be characterized by a heavily English-related vocabulary, although undergoing minimal grammatical modification toward English. When access to the superstrate continues, however, we usually find progressive "decreolization," that is, modification in the direction of the superstrate language. Such decreolization is evidenced by Jamaican Creole. The decreolization process may operate so extensively that the creole eventually becomes largely assimilated into the superstrate language, as is the case with Black English, which derives historically from a Caribbean creole. We may then speak of a "post-creole" continuum, from varieties relatively far from the superstrate to varieties indistinguishable from it. Assimilation of the creole does not necessarily mean that all traces of the original creole are lost. On the contrary, as always happens in language change, residues of the earlier structures remain and may become identifying features of particular varieties of the language.[9] Invariant **be** in BEV is an example, as will be discussed below.

As with pidgins, it is often said that creoles are simplified languages. In the sense that they are limited in function, this is true. In the sense that they have small lexicons and few inflections, and tend syntactically to use coordination rather than subordination, this is also true. However, what is not constrained by inflectional representation is constrained by word order and particles. That modifications are expressed coordinately and parenthetically rather than by subordinate clauses does not imply that the cognitive relation of modification is not known. "Simplicity" is a deceptive term. Insofar as it implies "economical," it is useful. But insofar as it is sometimes used to indicate some kind of cognitive deficit, the term is wholly inappropriate.

We will here show English-related pidgins and creoles from two languages that have been studied quite extensively and that have been used in literature: West African Pidgin English and Gullah, a creole which is spoken in parts of Georgia and South Carolina, and which is very far along the post-creole continuum.

Our first example is from a variety of WAPE found in the Cameroons. It is the beginning of a folk narrative and illustrates typical features not only of the language but also of the folk literature in which verbal wit is very highly valued. Each line is given first in pidgin, then with a literal English translation, then with a full-fledged English translation. You will understand the pidgin much more easily if you read it aloud:

SENSE PASS KING

1. som boi i bin bi fo som fan kontri fo insai afrika,
   Some boy he Past be in some fine country in inside Africa,
   There once lived a very clever lad who lived in a beautiful part of Africa,

2. we   i bin get plenti sens. i pas king fo sens   sef,   sow
   where he Past get plenty sense. He pass king in wisdom self,   so
   where he got much wisdom.   He was smarter than the king himself, and so

3. i neym bin bi sens-pas-kinɣ. king i bin feks plenti, ha i bin hia sey,
   he name Past be Sense-pass-k. ɳg. King he Past vex plenty, how he Past hear say,
   his name was Wiser-than-king.   The king was very annoyed, when he heard

4.   dis simol-boi i di   kas eni-man fo sens. ...
   this small boy he Continuative catch any-man for sense.
   how this young boy was outwitting everyone.

   (The king summons the boy, and, planning to trick him,
   demands that he cut his hair) . . .

   sens-pas-king
   Sense-pass-king
   Wiser-than-king

5. i bin don   gri sey, i gow bap king i het. i bigin   kot-am
   he Past Completive agree that he go barb king his head. He began (to) cut-them (i.e., hair)
   agreed to cut the king's hair,

6. bot ha i di   kot-am, i di   sowsow trowwey simol kon
   but how he Continuative cut-them, he Continuative always throw-away small corn
   but as he was cutting   he was also throwing down a little corn for the

7. fo fawu, we   i dey fo king i domot. king i aks i sey, ha yu di
   for fowl, which in there at king his courtyard. King he asks he says, how you Continuative
   chickens in the king's courtyard.   The king asked him, "Why are you

8. sowsow trow   kon? boi ansa i sey, na   lo fo gif   chop
   always throw-away   corn? Boy answers he says, (Is)there law against giv(ing) food
   always throwing down corn?" The lad answered,   "Is there a law against feeding

9. fo fawu?   simol-tam i don   finis i wok. king i het don
   to fowl?   Small-time he Completive finish his work. King his head Completive
   the chickens?" Soon he finished his task.   The king's head looked

10. nyan'ga bat.   king i bigin   hala, sey,   na   wati?
    look-fine very-much. King he begins (to) holler, say(ing), (Is)there what?
    very fine.   The king (then) began to shout, "What's going on here?

11. simol wowwow   pikin klin   het fo bik-man?   meyk yu
    Small good-for-nothing child clean/shave head for elder?   Make yourself
    Can a good-for-nothing youngster cut (shave) the hair of an elder? Put the hair

12. put bak ma biabia wan-tam.   a gow kil yu ifi yu now put-am!
    put back my hair immediately. I go kill you if you not put-them (back)!
    back in place immediately.   I'll kill you if you don't put them back."

13. sens-pas-king tok sey, now keys.   a gri. i bi dasow sey,
    Sense-pass-king talks says, No problem.   I agree. It is just that
    Wiser-than-king replied, "It doesn't matter. I will gladly put your hair back,

14. meyk yu   gif bak ma kon bifo a gow fiks yu biabia agen. king i now
    make yourself give back my corn before I go fix your hair   again. King he not
    if you return the corn I fed to your chickens."   The king was

15. sabi wati fo tok. i mof don   lok.
    know what to say. His mouth Completive lock.
    speechless.   He was dumbfounded.[10]

Three features of the phonology are striking here: tendencies to avoid consonant clusters, to devoice voiced stops, and to reanalyze interdentals. Consonant clusters in general are rare in West African languages; WAPE illustrates the ways in which pidgins tend to modify the sound patterns of the words borrowed from superstrate languages to more native patterns. The only word-final consonant clusters found in this text involve -s, for example, **feks** "vex" (3). All word-final stops are voiceless, e.g., **bap** "barb" (5, cf. **barber**—WAPE is related to British English and is *r*-less), **bat** "badly" (10, "very much," cf. the meaning "powerful" in Black English). Also, as is expected in most contact situations, the equivalents of [θ] and [ð] are [t, f] and [d], respectively, as in **domot** "doormouth" (7), **mof** "mouth" (15), **dey** "there" (7).

Typical of pidgin syntax is the absence of real subordination, in favor of loose connection of the kinds frequently found in narration. Thus we find **we** "where, which," and **sow** "so," but no personal relativizer analogous to **who**. Complements are rare, although some are introduced by **sey**. Originating in constructions in some West African languages that literally translate as **he talked said**, **sey** is mainly found following verbs of speaking, and in this context it means **say**. However, it has been extended to verbs of thinking and other mental activities, as in **gri sey** "agree that" (5) where saying is no longer relevant. In this context **sey** has come to introduce complements with approximately the same function as **that**. It continues into BEV in such structures as **He tell him, say, "This the truth."**

Another common characteristic of spoken language is the use of repeated subjects. These are particularly frequent in pidgins, and probably originate in the need to repeat the subject in difficult communication situations. One of the many examples in the text is **king i bigin hala** "the king, he begins to holler" (10).

Pidgins are typically uninflected, and WAPE is no exception. Relationships expressed in some languages by inflections are expressed in pidgins by word order and grammatical words. Here the possessive is expressed by the formula *N i N*, for example, **king i het** "king his head" (5). There are few prepositions in pidgins, often no more than one or two. Expressions that in English may consist of a preposition, in pidgin are often phrases, many of them involving body parts. The equivalent of **in** is often "at belly," of **on** is "at head," of **behind** is "at back" (cf. English phrases like **in front, in back of**.) An example in the text is **fo insai** (1), with **fo** probably related to a similar preposition in Yoruba.

One of the most striking features of pidgins is their aspectual system. Most frequently we find completive-noncompletive, here expressed by **don** "completive" and **di** "noncompletive, continuative," as in **i mof don lok** "his mouth completely closed" (15) and **ha i di kot-am** "as he was cutting them" (6). **Di** appears to derive from West African languages like Ewe, Twi, and Wolof, where it expresses continuative action. WAPE is unusual in that it also has a past-tense form **bin** as in **king i bin feks plenti** "king he was vexed plenty" (3). Pidgins of shorter duration than WAPE usually do not have tense-markers other than adverbs like **long time ago, tomorrow**. However, they always have aspectual verbs.

Finally, lexical mix is illustrated by **pikin** "small child" (11) and **sabi** "know" (15), which derive from Portuguese, and **nyang'a** "very fine" (10), which derives from Mende **nyanga** "ostentation" (Mende is a Bantu language). Use of English words with new, extended meanings is exemplified by, among others, **domot** "doormouth, door" (13).

Our example of a creole is from Gullah, also known as Sea Island Creole and Geechee. It is taken from an invaluable collection of Gullah material gathered in the 1930s by Lorenzo Dow Turner and published in 1949 in a volume called *Africanisms in the Gullah Dialect*. Turner was one of the first to argue that creoles like Gullah are not just inadequate imitations of English, but rather derive much of their structure from African languages. He gives a detailed list of lexical, phonological, and syntactic equivalences between Gullah and twenty-one West African languages, of which Ewe, Fante, Twi, and Yoruba figure prominently.

The excerpt here is from a story told by an old woman who remembered the time of slavery (**rebel time** as she calls it). The transcription is phonetic and introduces some symbols not previously used in this book. They are:

ʌ	stressed central vowel (signaled by ə in previous chapters)
ɐ	central vowel, slightly lower than ə or ʌ
ɑ	low, vowel, unrounded, as in **father**
ɒ	low back vowel, rounded, as in British **not**
~	nasalization of vowel
ʃ	equivalent of [š]
c	voiceless palatal stop (somewhat like [č], but not affricated)
ɟ	voiced palatal stop (somewhat like [j], but not affricated)
ṛ̥	retroflex flap
ɲ	palatal nasal, close to [ny], except that the palatal is coarticulated with the nasal, not articulated after the nasal

HARD TIMES ON EDISTO

1. unə pɪk ə bɑseɪt ə bin fə fɒɪw n   wʌn sɛnt. tu   bɑseɪt—wɒt ɪt kʌm tu?
   You pick a basket of bean for five and one cent. Two basket—what it come to?

2. dɪ wudn   go dɛ   tɪde; nɒt mi! dɪl it dɪ bin, bʌt dɪ ẽ   gɒɪn go
   I wouldn't go there today; not me! I'll eat the bean, but I ain't going go

3. pɪk nʌn dɛ . . .   bʌkrə   ɟi dɪ pipl kɒn—kʌləd pipl kɒn fə
   pick none there . . . White-man give the people corn—colored people corn to
   The white man give the people corn—colored people corn to

4. mɛk krɒp. ɛnti bʌkrə   wɒt brɑg, sɛ dɪ nɪgə mɛk im krɒp ɒf
   make crop. Ain't-it white-man what brag, that the nigger make him crop off
   make crop. Ain't it the white man what brag that the nigger make crop for him off

5. grɛın kɒn? Ji yu dɪ bɑrɪl ə kɒn n dɪ sak. yu go də
ground corn? Give you the barrel of corn and the sack. You go (and) are
ground corn? (He) give you the barrel of corn and the sack. You go to

6. grɛın əm . . .
grinding them.
grind it.

7. sɛ de mɛk dɪ krɒp ɒf dɪ nɪgə—dɪ kɒn. nɒu de sɛ de had ə
say they make the crop off the nigger—the corn. Now they say they had an
Now they say they had culled

8. ɐɪʃ pətetə kʌl ɑn dɪ pipl hɑ fə pɪk əm in. dɛn de Jɪt ɪt
Irish potato culled and the people have to pick them in. Then they get it
Irish potato and the people have to pick it (cotton) in. Then they get it

9. fərəm. pɪk dɑt kɒtn in fə dɪ ɐɪʃ tetə.
for them. Pick that cotton in for the Irish potato.
(culled potatoes) for them. They pick that cotton in for the Irish potato.

10. ɛnti?— ɛnti rɛbəl tɒɪm kʌmɪn bɑk? ɒl hu nɛwə ʃʌm— ɛnti
Ain't it?—ain't it rebel time coming back? All who never saw them—ain't it
Ain't it?—ain't slavery coming back? All who never saw it—ain't it

11. də kʌmɪn bɑk? dɪ sɛ, "tɒŋk gɒd de ẽ gɒt mi hɑn, ce dɪ cɪn
be coming back? I say, "Thank God they ain't got me hand, because I can
coming back?

12. sɪt dɒuŋ n krɒs mɒɪ fit." nobɒrɪ ẽ wʌrɪ wɛ dɒɪɑnə bɪn, ce
sit down and cross my feet." Nobody ain't worry where Diana is, because

13. mɒɪ tɒɪm dʌn kʌm tru. dɪ dʌn bɪn tru dɑt. nɒu dɪ cɪlən
my time done come through. I done been through that. Now the children

14. də frɛt. dɪ sɛ dɛm bʌkrə gɒt dɛm ɲɒŋ cɪlən fə wʌk fə
are fretting. I say them white people got them young children to work for

15. dɛm—dɛm on.[11]
them—themselves.[11]

Even a cursory glance will show that this passage from Gullah is far more complex both in structure and in its use of variants than the passage from WAPE. This is not a function of the specific texts so much as of the difference between a pidgin and a creole. Creoles begin to develop subordinate structures as part of the requirements of a native language which must indicate hierarchic relations between things, for example, ɛnti bʌkrə wɒt brɑg "Ain't it the white man what brags?" (4). They also begin to develop some inflections, as indicated by the plural form **fit** in line 12 (however, **-s** inflections still do not occur, because of a general avoidance of consonant clusters). The prepositional choices are also greater, including not only [fə], as in kɒn fə mɛk krɒp "corn to make crops" (3–4), which is related to WAPE **fo**, but also [ɒf] "off." This passage does not show it, but the Gullah equivalent for locational **at** and **to** is **to**, for **onto** and **in** it is **on**, and for **into** and **in** it is **in**, showing a considerable expansion of the prepositional system toward English.

Specifically creole features are to be found in the pronoun and verb systems in this passage. Pidgins and creoles in general make a distinction between first, second, and third person singular and plural, but not between genders. In this way, there are both more and fewer forms than in English. Where English uses **you** for singular and plural, pidgins and creoles usually use two forms; here **unə** is a general plural, a form derived from Ibo according to Turner, and also found in WAPE. However, where English distinguishes **he** and **she**, Gullah does not.[12] In "deep creole," that is, at the creole end of the continuum, no distinction is made in pronouns between animate and inanimate (none is made in WAPE either), so that the form **əm** is used for **he**, **him**, **she**, and **it**. Aspects are represented by the completive **dʌn**, as in **mɒI tɒIm dʌn kʌm tru** "my time done come through/my time has come to an end" (13) and the continuative **də**. Both are approximately equivalent in function to WAPE **don** and **di**. Indicative of decreolization is the co-presence of a variety of forms for the continuative. The deep creole **də** is exemplified by **dI cɪlən də frɛt** "the children are fretting" (13–14), coexisting with **ɛnti də kʌmɪn bak** "isn't it coming back?" (10–11), with both **də** and anglicized **-ɪn**. More anglicized is **ɛntɪ rɛbəl tɒIm kʌmɪn bak** "Ain't it slavery coming back?" (10), where there is no recognizable creole morpheme, but also no **be** verb. Later Gullah speakers have in some cases replaced the **də kʌm** expression by **does come**, in other words, by a morpheme that sounds more like English, but does not have the same function. We can hypothesize that in BEV the invariant **be** developed similarly as a replacement of **də**, again with similarity in form to an English word, but not in function.

One item of note in the lexicon is **bʌkrə** (3). This is common creole for "white man" and according to Turner is derived from Ibibio and Efik **m̀bàkárá** "he who surrounds or governs" (the accents signal tones). Another word of wide currency in English-related creoles is **nyung** (phonetically [nɒŋ] in this text, line 14), which is an adaptation of English **young**.

Gullah is rapidly undergoing change. The rapidity of decreolization is a function of many factors, including television and the migration to the cities of young people who then bring back more standard forms of English. It is far from clear now whether Gullah is or is not a separate language from BEV. However, there are still many speakers, among them the children, who have at their command a variety distinctly different from BEV, showing many characteristics of the creole, especially the use of aspectuals, the preposition **fə**, and the third person pronoun **ee**, used for males and females.

We know that Gullah had its origins in the language of field slaves, who presumably had only the barest contact with speakers of English. By contrast, Black English is derived primarily from the language of house slaves who naturally had extensive contact with English. Gullah and BEV thus may never have had a truly common ancestor, but early Black English appears to have had similar features.[13] The speed at which it decreolized is mainly a function of the degree of contact with English rather than a difference in origin. Certain features of BEV still suggest a creole origin, especially the aspectual system, and above all invariant **be**, which seems to have replaced many of the functions of **də**. Also, the quantitatively very high number of instances of consonant cluster deletion in informal speech seems to derive from a time when there were no inflections and few if any consonant clusters (as in WAPE).

The exact history of these languages may forever remain uncertain. But it is now clear that pidgins and creoles cannot be accounted for as they used to be by a theory of superstrate speakers talking down to the natives and being inadequately imitated, since in many instances such contact either did not exist or was minimal. What is most interesting to linguists is not so much the differences from the superstrate languages from which the vocabulary is drawn, but rather the fact that pidgins and creoles around the world are very similar in structure, whatever the superstrate languages in question. Some have argued that this similarity stems from some common ancestral pidgin such as Sabir, but this hardly explains why similarities would be maintained under heavy contact with languages of totally different kinds in all parts of the world. Rather, pidgins, once they are stabilized, and creoles give us a window onto universal properties of language. They raise fascinating questions about what kinds of structure a language must minimally have to be a language, and how it can develop into a far more complex system during the creolization process, not always because of, but also in spite of the influence of some other more prestigious language.

BILINGUAL SITUATIONS

As nonnative languages, pidgins necessarily presume at least a bilingual, usually a multilingual situation. But many bilingual and even multilingual situations do not involve pidgins. Indeed, pidgin speakers make up only a small minority of the hundreds of millions of people in the world who know more than one language. In Great Britain and America it is easy to lose sight of the fact that in a great many parts of the world bilingualism and multilingualism are the norm. Yet even in Great Britain and America, bilingualism was and is a reality for significant numbers of citizens. In Great Britain, bilingualism was common in Old English times (Old English and Scandinavian) and Middle English times (English and French) without, as far as we know, having produced a language that could be identified as a pidgin. Bilingualism has continued for centuries in Wales between Welsh (a Celtic language) and English, and is now growing under nationalist pressures. In Canada, French-English bilingualism is a major political issue. In America, bilingualism has been statistically the norm since the beginning of colonization,[14] but especially since the nineteenth century as different groups, for example, Germans, Spaniards, Italians, Poles, Yiddish-speakers, Chinese, and Filipinos, migrated in large numbers. The languages of these immigrants have always been considered lower in status than English, however, and it is a traditional policy in the United States to view English as essential to good citizenship. Though for awhile on the decline, Spanish is at present the most widely spoken and politically important language in the United States after English, and many Spanish-speaking Americans are working to maintain it and raise its status. Efforts are also underway to revitalize some Native

American languages, such as Navajo in Arizona. All these efforts have had some success, but it is still true that no language in the United States has anywhere near equal status with English. Contrast the situation in Switzerland, where French, German, Romansch, and Italian all are official standard languages and exist alongside a fifth language, Switzerdeutsch (originally a contact language), that is considered nonstandard by most.

Bilingualism has long been a main topic of interest among sociolinguists, and particular attention has been paid to the question of which language, in a bilingual setting, is used when. In bilingual communities, a great deal of switching back and forth from one language to another may be observed. This "code-switching" may at first look random, but is actually highly systematic and based upon particular appropriateness conditions.[15] In most bilingual communities there is a gradient from speakers who know both languages fluently to those who know only one language well and who virtually translate words from this one language into the other. Thus which language is used on a given occasion will in part be determined by the relative competence of the speakers present. But however extensive a person's knowledge of both languages, very rarely will the person use both equally in all situations. This is also true of how the languages are used in the community as a whole. One language (say English) might be used on the job and for writing, another (say Yiddish) might be used at home. One language is nearly always the public, official language, the other the language of intimacy. Since this is the case, the use of one language over another on a given occasion will also depend on the topic and the context.

When drastically different functions are served by two languages in one speech community, they are said to be in a "diglossic" relationship. The term "diglossia" was originally coined by Charles Ferguson to refer to situations where different varieties of the same language were used with markedly different functions.[16] For example, in contemporary Arabic-speaking countries, Classical Arabic and Modern Arabic are both in use, each with a different range of functions. The term diglossia has now been extended to situations where different languages are involved. Typically, one of the two languages is the "high" language, for instance, Classical Arabic. The high language is typically used as the language of religion, parliamentary debate and legislation, university lectures, the news, newspaper editorials, and poetry. On the other hand, the less prestigious, or "low" language (for instance, Modern Arabic) is used for instructions to workers, family conversation, captions on political cartoons, folk literature, and sometimes soap operas. This is also the relationship that exists for some speakers in Hawaii between English and Hawaiian pidgin. Triglossia may occur where three languages are involved. An example is to be found in Nigeria, where English is an official language used for law and education, among other things, while WAPE is used for communication with people of other African languages, especially in trading, and the native language of a region, for example, Yoruba, for most other functions.

While choice of language may be determined by the situation, in the ways just outlined, code-switching from one language to another can also be used to create situations, to establish status relations, and to express attitudes. Spanish-English code-switching among Chicanos provides us with an example of this phenomenon.[17] In public life in the United States, English is the official language, and Chicano Spanish, being considered nonstandard relative both to English and to Standard Spanish, is publicly felt to have low status. As in the case of BEV, Chicano Spanish is not just one variety but a cluster of varieties. Some of its features reflect earlier stages of Spanish. Others show many innovations, especially in slang, sometimes influenced by English. The deep Chicano slang, originally associated with street gangs in Arizona, but now gaining prestige as a vehicle of the Chicano movement, is called "caló." In many families the elder generation, made up of immigrants from Mexico, speak no English. Their children are for the most part bilingual, but with Spanish as their dominant language. The third generation may have learned through the school system and TV to be embarrassed by their Spanish and therefore to use it only at home and to older people who know no English. On the other hand, many third-generation Chicanos are today learning Spanish and using it more and more as a signal of pride in their ethnic identity. In such a context, choice of language has a great deal to do with choice of attitude, as well as with situational factors. Among Chicanos who favor Spanish, one often observes extremely rapid-fire shifts between Spanish and English, often in mid-sentence. This kind of code-switching cannot be explained in terms of situational factors, since these remain constant. But this switching can be shown to correlate very largely with attitude—Spanish is used for evaluation and expressiveness, English for statement and new information. Various studies have shown, for example, that the parts of sentences most likely to be in Spanish, if Spanish is personally highly valued, are the following:

1. Personal names and place names, if associated with Chicano people; thus **Juan** will not usually be switched to **John**, though there may be some flexibility here; terms of endearment, such as **mija** "daughter," and **papá**, pronounced the Spanish way; the term **chicano** is also nearly always pronounced the Spanish way.
2. Tag questions, the function of which is to engage the speaker's attention and reaction, as in **It's about the same, no?**
3. Connectors between sentences, such as **pero** "but," **pues** "then."
4. Interjections and exclamations like **mira** "look," **ándale, pues** "O.K., swell."
5. Evaluative adverbs, as in **'Tá bien easy** "it's real easy."

This kind of code-switching has been called "metaphorical code-switching" or "attitudinal code-switching" in contrast with "situational code-switching." It is in some ways comparable to the pronoun pairs that establish intimacy versus politeness, and to devices for establishing shared worlds, such as the use of **the** versus **a**. Spanish in these contexts, like the pronoun **tu** or **the**, signals involvement and expectation of involvement on the part of the hearer, confidentiality, and intimacy of ingroup bonding. English, like the pronoun **vous** and the article **a**, expresses distance, nonsharing, and lack of bondedness. This kind of phenomenon is obviously not restricted to bilingual situations. It can operate in multilingual ones and in situations that are essentially dialectical ones, where switching between more or less standard varieties occurs. It is a well-known feature of political speeches where a switch, for example, from Standard English to a rural regional variety indicates rejection of urban-centered national values and strong ties with local identity.

LITERARY REPRESENTATION OF OTHER LANGUAGES IN THE CONTEXT OF ENGLISH

In the last chapter we looked at how writers convey different varieties of English against the background of Standard written English. Here we will examine a slightly knottier problem: How does one represent characters speaking an entirely different language from English? The history of this question is similar to the history of dialect representation in literature, especially in that it was not much of a question at all until the nineteenth century. Shakespeare set his plays all over the world, from Denmark to Italy to ancient Rome, and it never seemed incongruous that a Caesar or a Cleopatra or a Romeo should be presented speaking the most eloquent of English. Fictional characters traveled all over the world without ever encountering problems in communication. In the early days of English literature, if more than one language was used, it was primarily for decorative purposes or to show linguistic virtuosity. For example, some medieval religious lyrics and love lyrics use English, French, and Latin, often switching languages for a refrain. Later, as in the case of dialects, other languages were used in an English context for comic purposes. For example, in Shakespeare's *Henry V*, serious Anglo-French politics are discussed in English without any attempt to represent French in English, but there are several comic scenes in which French is used and misunderstood by English soldiers, and in which a French princess tries to speak English. On the whole, writers before the nineteenth century had a kind of "poetic licence" to overlook the reality of language differences, and to more or less pretend that the whole world spoke English. Literary values and conventions changed, however, and with the advent of realism in the nineteenth century, an interest in linguistic realism also began to appear, as we saw in connection with dialects. Under the impetus of making the fictional worlds of literature correspond to the empirical historical world, writers began to feel a need to be specific and plausible about what language was being spoken in a situation, and to explain how characters from different language communities could communicate. This does not mean that writers began actually to use other languages extensively alongside English. It would make poor communicative sense indeed in a novel about American spies in China, for example, to actually write dialogue in Chinese. Literature itself imposes limits on linguistic realism, in the sense that the more languages one uses in a work, the more one limits the audience that will have access to the work. Moreover, it is rare at least for English writers to know another language well enough to compose in it. Yet, we do not believe this limitation should disqualify a writer from writing about another culture altogether. What we do find, in many cases, are elaborate plot manipulations for the sake of linguistic realism. For example, Joseph Conrad's novel *Under Western Eyes* is about Russia and the Russian exile community in Switzerland at the end of the Czarist period. In order to make it plausible that the text is in English rather than Russian, Conrad creates a linguistic intermediary: The text is presented as a reconstruction in English of events recounted in a diary written in Russian by the main character. The reconstruction is the work of an Englishman who, as a teacher of foreign languages, knows Russian and who felt it important that the diary reach the English-speaking world. Another example is provided by D. H. Lawrence's novel *The Plumed Serpent*, whose main character is an Irish woman named Kate Leslie, who goes to Mexico. As it was entirely unlikely that an educated Irish woman in the early twentieth century would know Spanish, Lawrence made her a fluent speaker of Italian (a much more respectable language at the time). This, as he lets us know, enables his protagonist to understand Spanish perfectly, and to speak it well enough to get her message across. The pure-blooded Indian she marries in Mexico is correspondingly given a background which miraculously includes several years of education in England. This kind of attempt at verisimilitude can backfire, of course, as English-speakers handily pop up in the most unlikely corners of the world.

Another common device for maintaining linguistic realism is the use of metalanguage to specify what language is being spoken and how, as in these examples from Lawrence's *The Plumed Serpent*:

> 'What do you think, Mrs Leslie,' cried the pale-faced young Mirabal, in curiously resonant English, with a French accent.[18]

*   *   *

> . . . Her thin, eager figure had something English about it, but her strange, wide brown eyes were not English. She spoke only Spanish—or French. But her Spanish was so slow and distinct and slightly plaintive, that Kate understood her at once.[19]

Another common device is to use little sprinklings of the other language often with accompanying translation, as in:

> He could see that, at the bottom of her soul, it was true.
> '*Puros monos!*' he said to himself in Spanish. '*Y lo que bacen, puras monerias.*'
> 'Pure monkeys! And the things they do, sheer monkeydom!' Then he added: 'Yet you have children!'[20]

Somewhat more interesting from a linguistic point of view are attempts actually to represent another language in English, that is, to make English somehow look or sound like the other language. This is what happens with Gullah in the following excerpt from a Gullah tale by Ambrose Gonzales. A devotee of Gullah lore, Gonzales recorded folktales in the 1920s, and his tales are one of our great sources of Gullah materials. Gonzales worked with delight and concern for authenticity, but nevertheless with a condescending attitude. In the preface to one of his collections he comments on the "grotesqueness" and "laziness" of the Gullah language and wonders how it is that its speakers do not maintain more of their African "jungle-talk."[21] The excerpt we are going to examine is interesting in that it represents Gullah totally stereotypically (indeed it is the only purely stereotypic text investigated either in this chapter or the last), and in that it attempts to treat Gullah as if it were simply a dialect of English. Gonzales uses the narrative structure found in Joel Chandler Harris's Uncle Remus stories and Charles Chesnutt's *The Conjure Woman*—a White narrator reporting the voice of Black people. In this excerpt we witness an old man, terrified by an event involving his daughter and a cat, seeking someone to listen to his sorrows and give advice. He finds someone and asks:

> . . .—"Maussuh, please, suh, tell me ef cat kin git crazy?"
> "Do you mean is it possible for a cat to have rabies?"
> "No, suh, 'taint rabbit, 'tis cat."
> "I apprehend," said the English purist, "that you desire to ascertain whether it is possible for a cat to have the rabies. I may say, for your information, that there are, literally and mathematically speaking, 18 phases of insanity to which humanity is subject, ranging from the emotional insanity of commerce, to the popular *mania a potu*, vulgarly called *delirium inebriosa*. I do not care to give an
> 10   off-hand opinion as to whether or not a cat may have one or more of these kinds of insanity, unless you will accurately describe the symptoms and put your questions categorically. It is manifestly a work of supererogation—"
> "Great Gawd, maussuh!" said the old man, turning appealingly to the tall gentleman. "Please, suh, tell dis juntlemun dat my cat nebbuh had no rabbit, 'e only had kitten. Yaas, suh. My cat name Jane, en' 'e b'long to dis leetle gal chile w'ich is my gran', en' him (dat is de gal) name Jane, en' Jane (dat is de cat) b'long to Jane (w'ich is de gal) en' Jane does use to folluh Jane eb'ryweh 'e go, en'
> 20   Jane does berry lub Jane, en' w'enebbuh Jane does ketch rat, 'e fetch'um een de house, en' w'enebbuh Jane does git 'e bittle fuh eat, 'e always keep some uh de bittle fuh Jane, en' w'en Jane (dat is de cat) had nine kitten' een Mistuh Claa'k' smokehouse on de t'ree Chuesday een dis same berry munt', den Jane (dat is de gal) set up all night fuh nuss Jane (dat is de cat) en', please Gawd, maussuh, jis' as soon as de nyung kitten' eye' biggin fuh op'n, one shaa'pmout' black dog, wid 'e tail stan' like dese bu'd fedduh buckruh 'ooman

> does lub fuh pit on 'e hat w'en Sunday come, dis dog jump obuh de
> fench en' bite'um, en' Jane (dat is de cat en' de gal alltwo) git berry
> 30 agguhnize en' twis' up een alltwo dem min', en' Jane (dat is de cat)
> him jump obuh de fench en' run'way. . . .[22]

In this particular story, both the "English purist" and the "old Negro" are comic. Each serves to highlight the other. Subordination is contrasted with coordination, abstract and ornate vocabulary with commonplace vocabulary, but both characters ramble on, totally oblivious of the fact that they are incomprehensible to each other.

The phonological features of Gullah that Gonzales stereotypes are: r-lessness, e.g., **suh** (3), **nebbuh** (16), **gal** (18), **eb'ryweh** (19); stops for fricatives: **dat** (18), **eb'ryweh** (19), **berry munt'** (20), centralized forms of vowels like **suh** (3), **juntlemun** (15), **folluh** (19), and lack of consonant clusters. This is signaled by orthographic deletion in many cases, cf. **gran'** (17), **en'** (17), **twis'** (30). Exceptions are where the vowel is tense and this tenseness can be indicated by a silent -e, as in **chile** (17), a common orthographic device. No orthographic marking is used to signal the absence of the inflectional tense-markers which suggests that Gonzales (rightly) considered Gullah simply not to have inflections. Some distinctly Gullah pronunciations are captured in **Chuesday** (24), **nyung** (26), and **fench** (29).

Syntactic features of particular note include lack of verbal inflection, as in **cat name Jane** (16–17), **git berry agguhnize** (29–30), and of nominal inflection. Verbal aspect is carefully marked, with completive **done** (not illustrated here) and continuative **does** (20, 21, 28), a form which, as we saw earlier, replaced **də** in some dialects, and was presumably felt by Gonzales to be more comprehensible to his readers. Pronouns do not distinguish gender, but have stressed forms—**him** (17) and unstressed forms—**'e** (19, 27), **'um** (21). They are also distinguished according to function: **'e** and **him** have subject and possessive functions, while **'um** is used in all other functions. Finally, the complement is introduced by **fuh** rather than **to**, as in **set up all night fuh nuss Jane** (24–25).

Comparison with Turner's texts shows that Gonzales is indeed reflecting features of deep creole Gullah. The main structural difference lies in two verbal features: Copulas are typically present in Gonzales, but are only variably present in Turner (cf. the formula **dat is de cat/gal** and other instances like 18, 22–23), and the form of the continuative in Gonzales is **does**, not **do**. As we noted earlier, **does** has replaced **də** in some regions; assuming that it was already present in Gullah speech at the time Gonzales was writing, we can surmise that Gonzales chose it as more likely to be understood by SAE readers.

Despite the similarities between Gullah and English, and despite Gonzales's efforts to make Gullah even more like English than it is, his texts and others like them are extremely hard to read. And of course with languages that have even less in common with English than Gullah, Gonzales's technique becomes impossible. Writers interested in linguistic realism must find other ways of representing the other language. Ernest Hemingway is particularly innovative in this respect in his many works involving the Spanish language. Here we will examine an excerpt from his *For Whom the Bell Tolls*, a novel about the Spanish Civil War. In the passage from this novel discussed in Chapter 4, we saw Robert Jordan and Maria walking through the heather. They make love, and then the two of them must face the irascible, jealous older woman Pilar:

The woman raised her head and looked up at him.

"Oh," she said. "You have terminated already?"

"Art thou ill?" he asked and bent down by her.

"*Qué va,*" she said. "I was asleep."

"Pilar," Maria, who had come up, said and kneeled down by her. "How are you? Are you all right?"

"I'm magnificent," Pilar said but she did not get up. She looked at the two of them. "Well, *Inglés,*" she said. "You have been doing manly tricks again?"

10 "You are all right?" Robert Jordan asked, ignoring the words.

"Why not? I slept. Did you?"

"No."

"Well," Pilar said to the girl. "It seems to agree with you."

Maria blushed and said nothing.

"Leave her alone," Robert Jordan said. . . .

"Maria," Pilar said, and her voice was as hard as her face and there was nothing friendly in her face. "Tell me one thing of thy own volition."

The girl shook her head.

20 Robert Jordan was thinking, if I did not have to work with this woman and her drunken man and her chicken-crut outfit, I would slap her so hard across the face that——

"Go ahead and tell me," Pilar said to the girl.

"No," Maria said. "No."

"Leave her alone," Robert Jordan said and his voice did not sound like his own voice. I'll slap her anyway and the hell with it, he thought.

Pilar did not even speak to him. It was not like a snake charming a bird, nor a cat with a bird. There was nothing predatory.

30 Nor was there anything perverted about it. There was a spreading, though, as a cobra's hood spreads. He could feel this. He could feel the menace of the spreading. But the spreading was a domination, not of evil, but of searching. I wish I did not see this, Robert Jordan thought. But it is not a business for slapping.

"Maria," Pilar said, "I will not touch thee. Tell me now of thy own volition."

"*De tu propia voluntad,*" the words were in Spanish.

The girl shook her head.

"Maria," Pilar said. "Now and of thy own volition. You hear

40 me? Anything at all."

"No," the girl said softly. "No and no."[23]

Hemingway is clearly anticipating an audience who knows no Spanish. He does not attempt to incorporate the Spanish into the English in a way that would make it comprehensible without translation, nor to incorporate the translation into the storyline, but simply gives the translation, at least the first few times an expression is used. **Qué va** and similar expressions of frequent occurrence sometimes stand alone, but longer sentences are regularly translated, usually with the English second. The triad **Tell me one thing of thy own volition** (17–18), **De tu propia voluntad** (37), and **Now and of thy own volition** (39) are not exceptions, for the Spanish in line 37 is not a repetitious translation of lines 35–36, but a more emphatic second attempt on Pilar's part to get an answer from Maria. Line 37 is then translated in line 39. Here we may wonder about the function of **the words were in Spanish** (line 37), as elsewhere in the novel, where the same comment is made. As readers we are obviously aware of the Spanish. Possibly the phrase is an indicator of Jordan's awareness of the cultural differences or is a demand that the reader listen to how it sounds in Spanish and share Hemingway's reverence for it. Alongside the actual Spanish words and phrases, Hemingway attempts to incorporate Spanish by translating it directly and literally into English. The most conspicuous examples of this are, of course, the English pronouns **thou** and **thee**, used to render the Spanish intimate forms **tu, te**. **Thou** and **thee** are not used consistently, however, and alternation with **you** seems to carry no particular social significance in many instances.

In general, the Spanish-in-English is reserved for the dialogue, rendering it quite distinct from the narrative. However, occasionally, as in 28–34, the narrative also takes on the characteristics of translation, most notably **But this is not a business for slapping** (34) and **I wish I did not see this** (33). Narrative distance is abandoned for a while, and Jordan's point of view is taken. Here as elsewhere the suggestion is made that, although an American, he thinks at least part of the time in Spanish. On the whole, however, there is a stylistic disjunction between the English of the narration and the Spanish-in-English of the dialogue. There is also a disjunction between the Spanish-in-English and the pure Spanish of the text. The Spanish is informal (expressions like **Qué va, Qué tal?**) or formulaic (**De tu propia voluntad**), but the Spanish-in-English is formal and sometimes archaic. This is illustrated by the use of Latinate lexical items like **terminate** (2) or **thou**. In Spanish **terminar** is not formal, and **tu** is the intimate address form, but in English these carry different associations.

These characteristics are illustrated again in this second excerpt, taken from earlier in the novel when Jordan visits with El Sordo, one of the Spanish guerrilla leaders. In this passage, there is also an interesting use of what Jordan calls a "pidgin Spanish." The excerpt starts with the end of a quarrel between Pilar and other members of the group on their way to meet Sordo:

> "At times many things tire me," Pilar said angrily. "You understand? And one of them is to have forty-eight years. You hear me? Forty-eight years and an ugly face. And another is to see

panic in the face of a failed bullfighter of Communist tendencies when I say, as a joke, I might kiss him."

"It's not true, Pilar," the boy said, "You did not see that."

"*Qué va*, it's not true. And I obscenity in the milk of all of you. Ah, there he is. *Hola*, Santiago! *Qué tal?*"

The man to whom Pilar spoke was short and heavy, brown-faced, with broad cheekbones.... "*Hola*, woman," he said. "*Hola*," he said to Robert Jordan and shook his hand and looked him keenly in the face. Robert Jordan saw his eyes were yellow as a cat's and flat as reptile's eyes are. "*Guapa*," he said to Maria and patted her shoulder.

"Eaten?" he asked Pilar. She shook her head.

"Eat," he said and looked at Robert Jordan. "Drink?" he asked, making a motion with his hand decanting his thumb downward.

"Yes, thanks."...

"Take drink," Sordo said to Robert Jordan. "I bring mine and four more. Makes twelve. Tonight we discuss all. I have sixty sticks dynamite. You want?"

"What per cent?"

"Don't know."...

"What chance for horses?"

"Maybe. Now eat."

Does he talk that way to every one? Robert Jordan thought. Or is that his idea of how to make foreigners understand?

"And where are we going to go when this is done?" Pilar shouted into Sordo's ear.

He shrugged his shoulders.

"All that must be arranged," the woman said.

"Of course," said Sordo, "Why not?"

"It is bad enough," Pilar said. "It must be planned very well."

"Yes, woman," Sordo said. "What has thee worried?"

"Everything," Pilar shouted.

Sordo grinned at her.

"You've been going about with Pablo," he said.

So he does only speak that pidgin Spanish for foreigners, Robert Jordan thought. Good, I'm glad to hear him talking straight....

"We'll see," Pilar said, her rage gone now. "Give me a glass of that rare drink. I have worn my throat out with anger. We'll see. We'll see what happens."

"You see, comrade," El Sordo explained. "It is the morning that is difficult." He was not talking the pidgin Spanish now and he was looking into Robert Jordan's eyes calmly and explainingly; not searchingly nor suspiciously, nor with the flat superiority of the old campaigner that had been in them before.[24]

Here as above we find a few expressions in Spanish, including informal **Qué va** "Heck no," translated as formal English **It is not true**, plus a lot of

Spanish-in-English, such as Spanish **have forty-eight years** (2) instead of English **be forty-eight years old**. Another Spanish expression, censored by Hemingway, is the taboo phrase **I obscenity in the milk of all of you** (7; in Spanish the obscenity refers to excretion).

It is interesting to note in both these passages and throughout the novel that although the use of Spanish does not indicate code-switching among the characters themselves, the Spanish forms can be classified into the categories typically found in attitudinal code-switching, for example, greetings like **Hola** and forms of address like **Inglés, hombre, guapa**. Other uses of Spanish include fixed phrases, mostly judgmental, many indicating strong reaction; very rarely do they express factual statement. For the most part they are expressions like **Qué va** "Heck no," **Qué tal?** "What's up?" Note **Qué tal?** is written with English not Spanish punctuation. In Spanish it would be **¿Qué tal?** Finally, there are some relatively short sentences that are not fixed phrases, but rather state important points of view or demand some kind of immediate response, for example, the directive implied in **De tu propia voluntad** from the first excerpt.

What Jordan calls a "pidgin Spanish" (39) is not really a pidgin but is more properly called "foreigner talk." None of the social conditions for a pidgin hold here, such as contact with speakers of many languages in a situation of social and ethnic stratification. The situation that does hold here is simply that of a speaker who assumes the addressee does not understand the speaker's language well. But clearly this is only a pretense on Sordo's part here. Obviously he knows Jordan can speak Spanish well, since Jordan is not using the "pidgin." Sordo is using the "pidgin" to establish distance between himself and Jordan. Only when he is satisfied that Jordan is trustworthy does Sordo switch to Spanish. This code-switching, in other words, has clear attitudinal meaning here.

The examples we have discussed so far primarily involve English speakers abroad in the non-English-speaking world. The representation of other languages in the context of English takes on quite a different significance in the case of writers portraying multilingual societies where English is only one of a number of languages in everyday use. One place where this situation arises in American literature is in works dealing with immigrant communities. Here English may be the lingua franca, but also a second language for many people. The language other than English often has enormous sociopsychological importance, serving as a link to the old country and cultural traditions, while at the same time, in many cases, forming a barrier to integration into the new culture and therefore to socioeconomic success (or in some cases even survival). Among many novels taking up the challenge of representing the language of an immigrant community in the United States, one of the most linguistically elaborate and successful is Henry Roth's *Call It Sleep*. Published in 1934, it is about the immigrant Jewish community in New York in the first decade of the twentieth century. The story focuses on one family of which the father, a Polish Jew, speaks Yiddish and Polish as well as English, while the mother, Austrian by birth, speaks only Yiddish and Polish.[25] Both find life in New York extremely hostile. The father is very defensive, and the only language in which he can make any personal contact at all is Yiddish. The mother devotes her whole life to recreating Europe in a tiny clean apartment, a haven in the squalor of Lower East Side tenements, and to raising her son David, the book's protagonist. The main theme of the book is David's struggle to learn to cope with the terrifying urban world outside the family, where different blocks are the territory of different linguistic and cultural groups, Irish Catholics and Italians in particular. As the book progresses, we learn to recognize different voices, only rarely with the help of metalinguistic cues, but rather from increasing familiarity with finely articulated differences in tone and especially linguistic form.

As the only cultural norm in the book, Yiddish is represented in Standard English. Each character has his or her own voice, most distinctly the Rabbi who speaks in hell-fire rhetoric. The children and the few adults who speak English, however, for the most part speak quite differently. Their language is marked phonetically, syntactically, and idiomatically as street speech, with distinct rhythms and sounds. This is the language of manipulation and insult, reflective of the basic cruelty of people to each other, and of a catch-as-catch-can world. David, the boy, remains an outsider, unable to use the street slang in repartee, hence always vulnerable, using, as do the other Jewish boys, a phonetically and idiomatically distinct speech with clearly marked Yiddish features. At the climax of the book, David tries to electrocute himself by inserting the handle of a zinc milk-ladle in a street-car rail, seeking to cleanse himself in fire like Isaiah. The chaos of an unseeing, uncaring society continues around him, peopled by whores, peddlers, and drunken swaggerers in bars. A glimpse of the rottenness of the world contrasted with David's agonized, poetic monologue, marked off in the text by italics, can be caught in the following excerpts.

> "Well." O'Toole puffed out his chest. "He comes up fer air, see? He's troo. Now, I says, now I'll tell yuh sompt'n about cunt— He's still stannin' by de fawge, see, wit' his wrench in his han'. An I says, yuh like udder t'ings, dontcha? Waddayuh mean, he says. Well, I says, yuh got religion, aintcha? Yea, he says. An' I says, yuh play de ponies, dontcha? Yea, he says. An' yuh like yer booze, dontcha? Sure, he says. Well I says, none o' dem fer me! Waddayuh mean, he says. Well, I says, yuh c'n keep yer religion, I says. Shit on de pope, I says—I wuz jis' makin' it hot—an' t'hell witcher
> 10   ponies I says—I bets on a good one sometimes, but I wuzn' tellin' him—an' w'en it comes t' booze I says, shove it up yer ass! Cunt fer me, ev'ytime I says. See, ev'ytime!"
>
> They guffawed. "Yer a card!" said the coal heaver. "Yer a good lad!—"
> *As though he had struck the enormous bell*

of the very heart of silence, he
stared round in horror.

"Gaw blimy, mate!" Jim Haig, oiler on the British tramp
Eastern Greyhound, (now opposite the Cherry Street pier) leaned
20   over the port rail to spit. "I ain't 'ed any fish 'n' chips since the
day I left 'ome. W'y ain't a critter thought of openin' a 'omely place
in New York—Coney Island fer instance. Loads o' prawfit. Taik a
big cod now—"

Now! Now I gotta. In the crack,
remember. In the crack be born. . . .

"Oy, Schmaihe, goy! Vot luck! Vot luck! You should only
croak!"
"Cha! Cha! Cha! Dot's how I play mit cods!"
"Bitt him vit a flush! Ai, yi, yi!"
30   "I bet he vuz mit a niggerteh last night!"
"He rode a dock t' luzno maw jock—jeck I shidda said.
Cha! Cha!"
"He's a poet, dis guy!"
"A putz!"
"Vus dere a hura mezda, Morr's?"
"Sharrop, bummer! Mine Clara is insite!"
Plunged! And he was running! Running!
"Nutt'n'? No, I says, nutt'n'. But every time I sees a pretty
cunt come walkin' up de street, I says, wit' a mean shaft an' a
40   sweet pair o' knockers, Jesus, O'Toole, I says, dere's a mare I'd
radder lay den lay on. See wot I mean? Git a bed under den a bet
on. Git me?"
"Haw! Haw! Haw! Bejeeziz!"
"Ya! Ha! He tella him, you know? He lika de fica 50 stretta!"
They looked down at the lime-streaked, overalled wop
condescendingly. . . .[26]

In the foreground are various speakers, identified stereotypically, as indeed they must to be distinguishable in the frenzied rush of scenes and words.
O'Toole is Irish, we know, because of his name, but also because of his
religious talk, the rhythm of **I says, he says**, phrases like **sweet pair o'knockers**
(40), and phonetic details. We know Jim Haig is English, not only because he
is designated so, but because of his talk of fish and chips and his dropping of
h's. The Italian swears in his native language. Interestingly he is called "a
wop" by the narrator (45), who momentarily adopts the other men's point of
view. We hear also the voices of Yiddish-speakers, some who have very
little command of English and use Yiddish prepositions like **mit** "with" (28)
and the Yiddish possessive in **mine Clara** (36). The address-forms or swearwords are the single most important indicators of the ethnic group involved,
precisely because they create social meanings: **Jesus** (40), **Gaw blimy, mate**

(18), **goy** (26). The passage has to be read aloud to be fully appreciated, not only for the horror of the materialistic society it creates, but for the Babel of tongues that raises a barrier to human understanding and pity.

As a second example of literary representation of a multilingual society, we turn to Nigeria, not an immigrant community but a country emerging from colonialism. Chinua Achebe, the Nigerian author of several novels about conflicts of the old and the new in Nigeria, has expressed himself frequently on the problem of language.[27] For the contemporary Nigerian writer, to use English at all is to use the language associated with colonial power. Yet Achebe sees English as the only viable language for Nigerian literature, because of the possibility of reaching through English a very wide audience within Africa as well as outside it. As we have seen, Nigeria itself is a country of many languages; the educated in Nigeria all know English, but not all know Ibo, Achebe's native language. In choosing to write in English, the task Achebe sets himself is essentially the same one Black American writers face, that of creating from the oppressor's language a medium of expression for the oppressed. In his early works, such as *Things Fall Apart*, Achebe limited himself primarily to using a few Ibo words for cultural terms such as fruit, drums, and customs, with word order giving a slight suggestion of translation. In his later works, he began to explore the importance of different languages in West African society and to write about the politics of language, in particular, the triglossic situation of English, WAPE, and Ibo. In his novel *A Man of the People*, language becomes an important independent factor in the action carrying social meaning through both situational and attitudinal code-switching.

The following is a scene from *A Man of the People*, in which English and WAPE are used both situationally and (to a lesser extent) attitudinally. Chief Nanga, a former teacher at Anata Grammar School, now Minister in the Nigerian government, is making an election speech. He and his staff are welcomed by the pedantic principal of the school, Mr. Nwege, who has made a large crowd attend. The narrator is a teacher at the school and was also a pupil of Chief Nanga when the latter taught at the school.

> Changing the subject slightly, the Minister said, 'Only teachers can make this excellent arrangement.' Then turning to the newspaper correspondent in his party he said, 'It is a mammoth crowd.'
>
> The journalist whipped out his note-book and began to write....
>
> We had now entered the Assembly Hall and the Minister and his party were conducted to their seats on the dais. The crowd raised a deafening shout of welcome. He waved his fan to the different parts of the hall. Then he turned to Mr Nwege and said:
>
> 10   'Thank you very much, thank you, sir.'
>
> A huge, tough-looking member of the Minister's entourage who stood with us at the back of the dais raised his voice and said:
>
> 'You see wetin I de talk. How many minister fit hanswer

sir to any Tom, Dick and Harry wey senior them for age? I hask you how many?' . . .

The Minister's speech sounded spontaneous and was most effective. There was no election at hand, he said, amid laughter. He had not come to beg for their votes; it was just 'a family reunion—pure and simple.' He would have preferred not to
20   speak to his own kinsmen in English which was after all a foreign language, but he had learnt from experience that speeches made in vernacular were liable to be distorted and misquoted in the press. Also there were some strangers in that audience who did not speak our own tongue and he did not wish to exclude them. They were all citizens of our great country whether they came from the highlands or the lowlands, etc. etc.

At the end of his speech the Minister and his party were invited to the Proprietor's Lodge—as Mr Nwege called his square, cement-block house. Outside, the dancers had all come alive again
30   and the hunters—their last powder gone—were tamely waiting for the promised palm-wine. The Minister danced a few dignified steps to the music of each group and stuck red pound notes on the perspiring faces of the best dancers. To one group alone he gave away five pounds.

The same man who had drawn our attention to the Minister's humility was now pointing out yet another quality. I looked at him closely for the first time and noticed that he had one bad eye—what we call a cowrieshell eye.

'You see how e de do as if to say money be san-san,' he was
40   saying. 'People wey de jealous the money gorment de pay Minister no sabi say no be him one de chop am. Na so so troway.'

Later on in the Proprietor's Lodge I said to the Minister: 'You must have spent a fortune today.'

He smiled at the glass of cold beer in his hand and said:

'You call this spend? You never see some thing, my brother. I no de keep anini for myself, na so so troway. If some person come to you and say "I wan' make you Minister" make you run like blazes comot. Na true word I tell you. To God who made me.' He showed the tip of his tongue to the sky to confirm the oath. 'Mini-
50   ster de sweet for eye but too much katakata de for inside. Believe me yours sincerely.'

'Big man, big palaver,' said the one-eyed man.[28]

The narrator always uses SE in the narrative and in his own speeches. The narrative provides a neutral distancing frame of reference against which Achebe plays off the significance of linguistic choice. Corrupt and ridiculous, the Minister always speaks English or pidgin, never his native tongue; his children who attended expensive private schools speak impeccable English, while his wife "stuck to our language"—what "our language" is, is never stated, but the knowledgeable will know that it is Ibo. Speaking English is part of the Minister's front, a signal of his ambition and lack of real concern for Nigeria and especially his own people. But the point is made over and over that his English is not really adequate—for example, "Chief Nanga was one of those fortunate ones who had just enough English (and not one single word more) to have his say strongly, without inhibition, and colourfully." He uses his English to impress, but switches to pidgin to speak with his supporters who know neither Ibo nor English, and to joke with people like the narrator who knows both English and pidgin (45–51). A few pages earlier we have heard that the Minister is a toady of a Prime Minister who expelled two-thirds of his ministers for disagreeing with him. This Prime Minister's policy, we are told, was expressed in the Daily Chronicle as follows: "We are proud to be Africans. Our true leaders are not those intoxicated with their Oxford, Cambridge, or Harvard degrees, but those who speak the language of the people." Chief Nanga, then, is a fraud, who decries English along with the Prime Minister, and yet uses it to address the narrator, journalists, and the crowd (presumably he uses West African Pidgin English to them, although he calls it English) (19–22).

It is interesting to note that a reader familiar with West African, especially Nigerian, culture, would probably recognize immediately that the Minister is speaking English at the beginning of the passage cited. Such a reader would infer this from the academic setting, the presence of the journalist who will no doubt report the election speech in English, and the lack of the specifically African proverbs and attitudes that are prevalent in the Ibo-in-English passages. A less knowledgeable reader, however, may not know that the talk before the speech was English until some twenty pages later when told that Chief Nanga always speaks English or pidgin. In that it involves both situational and attitudinal code-switching, the Achebe passage differs from *Call It Sleep*, which involves almost exclusively situational shifting. The difference is of course not just a question of author's choice. Most of the characters in Roth's book simply do not know English well enough to use it attitudinally, rather than in response to bare necessity.

Concerned as he is to reach a wide audience, Achebe nevertheless uses WAPE quite extensively, and without translation. It is virtually incomprehensible to anyone who doesn't know the pidgin, despite its graphic similarity to English. Achebe expresses the pidgin almost entirely by syntax, lexicon, and discourse types such as proverbs. The phonological markers are few. No attempt is made to represent *r*-lessness or the typical lack of consonant clusters or of final voiced consonants. The word-initial **h**, exemplified by **hanswer** (13) and **hask** (14), appears to be eye-dialect rather than representative of actual speech. Among obvious WAPE syntactic structures are preverbal **no** for the negative: **People . . . no sabi say no be him one de chop am** "the people . . . don't know that it isn't he alone who uses it up" (40–41), the complementizer **say** as in the sentence just quoted, and the polite form of the command: **make you Verb** as in line 47. But above all, the aspectual system is distinctly WAPE, with continuative **de**, as in **You see wetin I de talk** "You see what I am saying" (13). The lexicon is also distinctly WAPE. This is clear from certain English words that have been reanalyzed, for example, **sand** reshaped into **san-san** (39), with repetition indicating that sand is a collective consisting of a great quantity of particles, not one consistent mass. It is also clear from some Portuguese words such as **sabi** "know" (41) and **palaver** (52).

Pidgin is not only used as the language of convenience in multilingual settings. It has a distinct literary function in this novel as the language of humor and especially of evaluative commentary. As the only language in which proverbs are used abundantly, it is the vehicle of common sense and folk wisdom, signaling modes of thought that are intended as distinctly African. As the language of evaluative commentary, WAPE is quite different in function from the native language (presumably Ibo, though this is not stated). Rather than being the language of common sense, this native language is the language of the old order and of limited experience, expressing closeness to nature and implying failure to understand the new post-colonial order. The narrator, speaking to the father of the girl he seeks to marry, hears that the man's wife is sick:

> 'Has your wife been in the hospital a long time?' I asked.
> 'Since three weeks. But her body has not been hers since the beginning of the rainy season.'
> 'God will hear our prayers,' I said.
> 'He holds the knife and He holds the yam.'[29]

The contrast between English and the native-language-in-English is more effective perhaps than the use of Ibo itself might have been, in that it serves to highlight another language through the idioms of that language (**since three weeks**) and another approach to the world.

The formal, archaic English the father uses is not totally unlike the rhetorical Hebraic speech of the Rabbi in *Call It Sleep*. Such elevated, ritualistic, often religious diction seems to be a common feature of literature that represents several languages, as a marker of an older culture, less modernized, but not necessarily more highly valued (for all their virtues, the Rabbi in *Call It Sleep* is ultimately a petty man, and the father in *A Man of the People* is as greedy in his own way as Chief Nanga).

Achebe chooses to make English the basic language of his work, and to use WAPE and Ibo as exceptions against this background. Not all writers from multilingual societies make such a choice, however. Among the rapidly growing literature of the Chicanos in the United States, for example, one finds a wide and varying range of combinations of Standard Mexican Spanish, American English, and Caló, the Chicano street slang, with occasional use of terms from Nahuatl, a language of the Aztecs. All four of these languages are used in the following poem by José Antonio Burciaga, which addresses itself to the workings of multilingualism. The poem ends on a positive note symbolized by the last line: **con o sin safos**, a Chicano slogan associated with the symbol ℂ/ₛ "con safos" meaning approximately "whatever criticism is made will be returned to the criticizer":

> Españotli **titlan** (*entre/between*) Englishic
> **titlan** (*entre/between*) Nahuatl titlan (*entre/between*) Caló
> Que locotl!
> Mi mente spirals al mixtli (*cloud/nube*).
> Buti suave I feel . . . . (4) lenguas in mi boca
> **Coltic** (*torcidos/twisted*) sueños **temostli** (*caen/fall*)
> Y siento una xochitl (*flor/flower*) brotar
> From four diferentes vidas
>
> I **yotl** (*solo/alone*) distinctamentli recuerdotl
> 10   Cuandotl I **yotl** (*solo/alone*) was a Maya
> Cuandotl I **yotl** (*solo/alone*) was a Gachupinchi°
> When Cortez se cogió a mi great bisabuela
> Cuandotl andaba en Pachuc**atlan** (*sobre agua/on water*)°
>
> I **yotl** (*solo/alone*) recordotl el **tonatiuh** (*sol/sun*)°
> En mi boca **cochi** (*dormir/sleep*)
> **Cihuatl** (*mujer/woman*) Nahuatl
> **Teocalli** (*templo/temple*), my mouth
> Tumba de mi querido Nahuatl
> **Micca** (*muerto/dead*) por el English
> 20   E hiriendo mi Español
> Ahora cojo ando en caló°
> Pero no hay pedo
> Porque todo se vale
> Con o sin safos.[30]

---

11 Gachupinchi: a derogatory term used for Spaniards by native Indians   **13 Pachucatlan:** "Pachucos on water"; a pun on Pachucos, early Mexican immigrants to the U.S., and "wetbacks"   **14 tonatiuh:** the sun is a symbol of Aztec history   **21** Burciaga switches to caló in this line, with the slang expression **no hay pedo**; for the last line, see the commentary preceding the poem.

Literally translated, but without the puns and effects of blending languages, this means:

> Spanish between English
> Between Nahuatl and Caló
> How mad!
> My mind spirals to the clouds,
> But suave I feel . . . four tongues/languages in my mouth.
> Twisted dreams fall.
> I sense a flower budded
> from four different lives.

        I alone distinctly remember
10   When I alone was a Maya,
        When I alone was Gachupin,
        When Cortez raped my great grandmother,
        When he went to Pachucoland over the water.

        I alone remember the sun.
        In my mouth sleeps
        The Nahuatl woman
        In the temple of my mouth
        Tomb of my beloved Nahuatl,
        Dead because of the English
20   And wounding my Spanish.
        Now one-legged I go in Caló.
        No sweat,
        For everything goes
        With or without safety.

In this poem, the fusion of Nahuatl, Spanish, and English is observed in the addition of Nahuatl morphemes like **-tl(i)** and **-ic** to both Spanish and English words. Also, the paucity of the English-language experience is reflected in the minimal use of English.

Such experiments with language can tell us a lot about a topic that has been discussed off and on for centuries, namely the possibility of a cosmopolitan future in which human affairs would be conducted in a world language. As the lingua franca of the multinational corporations and, to some extent, international politics, English is the closest thing today to such a language. But as texts like those of Burciaga and Achebe show, there are as many forces working against a world language as there are for it. For a great many people in the world, the more widespread English becomes, the more of an enemy it becomes, threatening to separate people from their cultures, their histories, and their ethnic consciousness, and to merge everyone into a great westernized, anglicized melting pot. From this viewpoint, a multitude of languages, and within them a multitude of dialects, have come to be regarded not as the curse of Babel, but as a source of strength and a key to group autonomy and possibly even survival.

SUGGESTED FURTHER READINGS

Introductory books which focus on linguistic contact, particularly contact between English and other languages, include Fishman's *Sociolinguistics; A Brief Introduction* and *Readings in the Sociology of Language*, Hornby's *Bilingualism; Psychological, Social and Educational Implications,* and Bailey and Robinson's *Varieties of Present-Day English.* The latter provides rich materials on English in former colonial countries and a wealth of excellent exercises. The linguistic journals mentioned at the end of Chapter 8 also cover materials on language in contact, especially the *International Journal of the Sociology of Language.*

Todd's *Pidgins and Creoles* is a good brief introduction, but it barely touches on implications for studies of language universals. Three papers in Valdman's *Pidgin and Creole Linguistics* fill that gap: Bickerton's "Pidginization and Creolization: Language Acquisition and Language Universals," Ferguson and DeBose's "Simplified Registers, Broken Language and Pidginization," and LePage's "Processes of Pidginization and Creolization." Valdman's book ends with a valuable list of pidgin and creole languages around the world. *The Journal of Creole Linguistics* is a new journal specifically devoted to pidgin and creole studies.

There is very little as yet that has been written from a linguistic point of view on experiments with multilingual literature. Ramchand's "The Language of the Master?" on West African and West Indian literatures is a pioneering work in this field, as also is Fallis's paper on "Code-switching in Bilingual Chicano Poetry." Ezekiel Mphahlele and Arthur Delbridge's papers on the language of African and Australian literature in the *Harvard Educational Review* are also valuable contributions to this field.

Exercises

1. If there are different languages used in your area (either at home or at college), find out as much as you can about people's attitudes toward them. Listen to bilingual conversations if you can, and determine whether code-switching is both situational and attitudinal. Ask questions about language functions so as to determine whether there is a diglossic situation or not. Ask people what they think about the non-English language. Find out whether attitudes are positive or negative, whether people approve of the idea of bilingual programs, and so forth.

2. Identify Gullah features in the following passage. What features do you find in the passage in common with BEV, what features are different?

> This about my brother name T. And he was born with—
> I don't know, but he was born with something on ee face and
> he could see ghost when he was little but now he can't. And my
> mother—and he the second oldest in the house—and my mother
> used carry him everywhere she go, because he wouldn't let
> um—my mama—go by eeself. Then one night my mama and
> my brother went to school. And then—big schoolhouse where
> Mrs. N teach right in that—and my brother see—my brother
> see a ghost, but my mother couldn't see it. And then

10   my brother tell my mother say he wasn't scared. But my mother say it might hurt you. And then ee tell um "Let's turn back wait till some other people get there." But my brother he ain't paying no attention to Mama and he went right on. And he come back and Mama ask him if he see anything. And ee say he see a white dog—a white ghost dog. And ee run back there and he say he been gon run behind um but ee been too fast for um. So he turn back and—I forgot. That's all.[31]

3.   In *Nights with Uncle Remus*, Joel Chandler Harris introduces Daddy Jack, an old man, in his eighties, who was brought to the United States as a slave when he was about twenty years old, and who worked all his life in Georgia. He speaks a variety of Gullah, markedly contrasting with Uncle Remus's BEV. Daddy Jack is the first speaker in the following passage:

> . . . "Oona bin know da' 'Tildy gal?"
>
> "I bin a-knowin' dat gal," said Uncle Remus, grimly regarding the old African; "I bin a-knowin' dat gal now gwine on sence she 'uz knee-high ter one er deze yer puddle-ducks; en I bin noticin' lately dat she mighty likely nigger."
>
> "Enty!" exclaimed Daddy Jack, enthusiastically, "I did bin mek up ter da' lilly gal troo t'ick un t'in. I bin fetch 'im one fine 'possum, un mo' ez one, two, t'ree peck-a taty, un bumbye I bin fetch 'im one bag pop-co'n. Wun I bin do dat, I is
> 10   fley 'roun' da' lilly gal so long tam, un I yeddy 'im talk wit' turrer gal. 'E do say: 'Daddy Jack fine ole man fer true.' Dun I is bin talk: 'Oona no call-a me Daddy Jack wun dem preacher man come fer marry we.' Dun da' lilly gal t'row 'e head back; 'e squeal lak filly in canebrake."
>
> The little boy understood this rapidly-spoken lingo perfectly well, but he would have laughed anyhow, for there was more than a suggestion of the comic in the shrewd seriousness that seemed to focus itself in Daddy Jack's pinched and wrinkled face.
>
> 20   "She tuck de truck w'at you tuck'n fotch 'er," said Uncle Remus, with the air of one carefully and deliberately laying the basis of a judicial opinion, "en den w'en you sail in en talk bizness, den she up en gun you de flat un 'er foot en de back un 'er han', en den, atter dat, she tuck'n laff en make spote un you."
>
> "Enty!" assented Daddy Jack, admiringly.
>
> "Well, den, Brer Jack, youer mighty ole, en yit hit seem lak youer mighty young; kaze a man w'at aint got no mo' speunce wid wimmen folks dan w'at you is neenter creep
> 30   'roun' yer callin' deyse'f ole. Dem kinder folks aint ole nuff, let 'lone bein' too ole."[32]

What linguistic features does Harris select to distinguish Daddy Jack's speech from Uncle Remus's? It is fairly widely held nowadays that Harris was not terribly accurate in his selection of linguistic features, especially those of Gullah. From what you have learned about Gullah from the Turner and Gonzales passages in the earlier part of this chapter, which features of Daddy Jack's speech do you think might be misrepresentations of Gullah? What attitude toward Daddy Jack do these features create in the reader?

4. Reread carefully the passage from Hemingway's *For Whom the Bell Tolls* quoted on pages 381–82.

    a. Identify the features of El Sordo's language that could be considered to be "simplified English." What linguistic features might Hemingway have used that he did not?

    b. The reader clearly experiences this passage through Jordan. How is this brought about? Had the narrator commented on El Sordo's reason for using the "pidgin" at the beginning of the passage, what different effect would there have been?

5. At the end of *Call It Sleep*, Henry Roth describes the neighbors crowding round when David is brought back in an ambulance, having survived his suicide attempt with only a shock and a burned foot:

> He turned to leave. A fattish, bare-armed woman stood at his shoulder. David recognized her. She lived on the same floor.
>
> "Ducktuh!" she whispered hurriedly. "Yuh shoulda seen vod a fighd dere vus heyuh!" She contracted, rocked. "Oy-yoy! Yoy-u-yoy! Him, dat man, his faddeh, he vus hittin' eem! Terrible! A terrhible men! En' dere vus heyuh his cozzins—oder huh cozzins—I don' know! En' dey vus fighdingk. Oy-yoy-yoy! Vid scrimms! Vid holleringk! Pwwweeyoy!
> 10   En' den dey chessed de boy all oud f'om de house. En den dey chessed de odder two pipples! En' vee vus listeningk, en' dis man vos crying. Ah'm khrezzy! Ah'm khrezzy! I dun know vod I do! I dun' know vod I said! He ses. Ah'm khrezzy! En' he vus cryingk! Oy!"
>
> "Is that so?" The interne said indifferently.
>
> "Id vus terrhible! Terrhible! En' Ducktuh," she patted his arm. "Maybe you could tell me fah vy my liddle Elix dun eat? I give him eggks vid milk vid kulleh gedillehs°. En he don' vonna eat nottingk. Vod sh'd I do?"
> 20   "I don't know?" He brushed by her. "You'd better see a doctor."
>
> "Oy bist du a chuchim°!" she spat after him in Yiddish. "Does the breath of your mouth cost you something?"[33]

---

20 kulleh gedillehs: everything good   **24 chuchim:** wise guy

How does Roth let the reader know that the woman is speaking English in lines 4–19 and Yiddish in the last sentence (line 23)? What particular signals of a Yiddish accent in the English are used? What is the purpose of spellings like **ducktuh** (instead of, for example, **ductuh**)?

6. As has been suggested in the last two chapters, point of view in fiction can be indicated not only by naming, deictics, tense, and similar devices discussed in Chapters 6 and 7, but also by use of dialect and languages other than English (whether in the original or in translation). Discuss the point of view established between narrator and reader, and the relations of the characters to each other and the narrator in any short work of fiction involving several dialects or languages. The following are some suggestions: Tillie Olsen's "Tell Me a Riddle" in her collection of stories by the same title (Yiddish and English—here the function of the dialogue that is not in quotation marks is particularly interesting); Ron Arias's *The Road to Tamuzanchale*, Chapter 7 (varieties of English and Spanish, including caló); Sam Tagatac's "The New Anak," in *Aiiieeeee: An Anthology of Asian-American Writers*, edited by Frank Chin et al. (Tagalog and English); and Jeffrey Paul Chan's "Jackrabbit" in *Yardbird Lives!* edited by Ishmael Reed and Al Young (Chinese and English).

NOTES

[1] Joshua A. Fishman, Robert L. Cooper, and Andrew Conrad, eds., *The Spread of English; the Sociology of English as an Additional Language* (Rowley, Mass.: Newbury House Publishers, 1977).

[2] See especially Albert C. Baugh and Thomas Cable, *A History of the English Language*, 3rd ed. (Englewood Cliffs, N.J.: Prentice-Hall, 1978); and Mary S. Serjeantson, *A History of Foreign Words in English* (London: Routledge and Kegan Paul, 1935).

[3] Geoffrey Chaucer, "General Prologue," in *The Canterbury Tales*, in *The Works of Geoffrey Chaucer*, ed. F. N. Robinson (Boston: Houghton Mifflin Co., 1957), p. 17, lines 1–4, 12–13. **April** appears to have been borrowed directly from Latin, whereas **March** is borrowed from French. Information on the origins of these and other words can be found in *The American Heritage Dictionary of the English Language* and in *The Oxford English Dictionary*.

[4] William Shakespeare, *Love's Labour's Lost*, III, i, 175–84, in *The Complete Works of Shakespeare*, ed. Hardin Craig (Chicago: Scott, Foresman and Co., 1951), pp. 111–12.

[5] Based on J. L. Dillard, *All-American English: A History of the English Language in America* (New York: Random House, 1975).

[6] For example, see Braj Kachru, "The Indianness of Indian English," *Word*, 21 (1966), 391–410.

[7] This section is based on Elizabeth Closs Traugott, "Pidgins, Creoles, and the Origins of Vernacular Black English," in *Black English: A Seminar*, eds. Deborah Sears Harrison and Tom Trabasso (Hillsdale, N.J.: Laurence Erlbaum Assocs. Publ., 1976). For more detailed studies, see Robert A. Hall, Jr., *Pidgin and Creole Languages* (Ithaca: Cornell Univ. Press, 1966); Dell Hymes, ed., *Pidginization and Creolization of Languages* (London and New York: Cambridge Univ. Press, 1971); Loreto Todd, *Pidgins and Creoles* (London and Boston: Routledge and Kegan Paul, 1974); Albert Valdman, ed., *Pidgin and Creole Linguistics* (Bloomington and London: Indiana Univ. Press, 1977). Derek Bickerton, *Dynamics of a Creole System* (London and New York: Cambridge Univ. Press, 1975) is an important study of one English-based creole, that of Guyana.

[8] From J. L. Dillard, *Black English: Its History and Usage in the United States* (New York: Random House, 1972), pp. 14–15.

[9] The introduction to Cassidy and Le Page gives a good account of seventeenth-century phonological characteristics of English that persist in modern Jamaican Creole. See Frederic Cassidy and Robert Le Page, *Dictionary of Jamaican English* (London and New York: Cambridge Univ. Press, 1967), pp. xxxvi–lxiv.

[10] From Gilbert Schneider, *West African Pidgin-English: A Descriptive Linguistic Analysis with Texts and Glossary for the Cameroon Area* (Athens, Ohio, 1966), pp. 177–79. Reproduced, with literal translation added, from Traugott, "Pidgins, Creoles," in *Black English*, eds. Harrison and Trabasso, pp. 70–71.

[11] From Lorenzo Dow Turner, *Africanisms in the Gullah Dialect* (1949; rpt. Ann Arbor: Univ. of Michigan Press, 1973), pp. 260–63, with literal translation added as in Traugott, "Pidgins, Creoles," in *Black English*, eds. Harrison and Trabasso, p. 82.

[12] Turner actually cites *unə* as both singular and plural; however, in this passage it is plural only, as it is also in Ibo and in WAPE and several Caribbean pidgins and creoles. See Turner, *Africanisms*.

[13] For detailed discussion, see Dillard, *Black English*, especially Chapters 3 and 4. Also see Dillard, *Lexicon of Black English* (New York: The Seabury Press, 1977).

[14] Joshua A. Fishman, *Language Loyalty in the United States* (The Hague: Mouton, 1966). For work on French-English bilingualism in Canada, see Stanley Lieberson, *Language and Ethnic Relations in Canada* (New York: John Wiley and Sons, Inc., 1970).

[15] See John J. Gumperz and Eduardo Hernández-Chavez, "Cognitive Aspects of Bilingual Communication," in *El Lenguaje de los Chicanos; Regional and Social Characteristics of Language Used by Mexican-Americans*, eds. Eduardo Hernández-Chavez, Andrew D. Cohen, and Anthony F. Beltramo (Arlington, Va.: Center for Applied Linguistics, 1975); and Gumperz, "The Social Significance of Code-Switching," in *Papers on Language and Context* (Univ. of California, Berkeley: Working Papers of the Language Behavior Research Laboratory, 1976).

[16] Charles A. Ferguson, "Diglossia," *Word*, 15 (1959), 325–40; rpt. in *Readings in Sociology of Language*, ed. Joshua A. Fishman (The Hague: Mouton, 1968); rpt. in *Language in Context*, ed. Pier Paolo Giglioli (Harmondsworth, Mssex.: Penguin, 1972).

[17] See Hernández-Chavez et al., *El Lenguaje de los Chicanos*, especially papers by Donald M. Lance, "Spanish-English Code-Switching" and by Gumperz and Hernández-Chavez, "Cognitive Aspects of Bilingual Communication."

[18] From D. H. Lawrence, *The Plumed Serpent* (London: Heinemann, 1950), pp. 67–68.

[19] Lawrence, *Plumed Serpent*, p. 166.

[20] Lawrence, *Plumed Serpent*, p. 263.

[21] Ambrose Gonzales, *The Black Border; Gullah Stories of the Carolina Coast* (Columbia, S.C.: The State Printing Co., 1922), p. 17.

[22] Gonzales, *The Black Border*, pp. 227–28.

[23] From Ernest Hemingway, *For Whom the Bell Tolls* (New York: Charles Scribner's Sons, 1940), pp. 172–74.

[24] Hemingway, *For Whom the Bell Tolls*, pp. 141, 146–47, 150–51.

[25] For papers on Yiddish both in the United States and Europe, see Uriel Weinreich, *The Field of Yiddish Language Folklore and Literature* (New York: Linguistic Circle of New York, 1954).

[26] From Henry Roth, *Call It Sleep* (1934; rpt. New York: Cooper Square Publishers, Inc., 1965), pp. 558–59, 562–63.

[27] See several papers in Chinua Achebe, *Morning Yet on Creation Day: Essays* (London: Heinemann, 1975), especially "The African Writer and the English Language."

[28] From Chinua Achebe, *A Man of the People* (London: Heinemann, 1966), pp. 11–12, 15–16.

[29] Achebe, *Man of the People*, p. 102.

[30] José Antonio Burciaga, Untitled poem, *Caracol*, 3, No. 4 (1976), 3. Winner of Caracol Trilingual Poetry Contest. Also published without translation in *Nahualliandoing; Poetry in Espanol/Nahuatl/English*, published by *Caracol*, 1977.

[31] A narrative told by a fifth-grade South Carolina boy; data collected by Patricia C. Nichols in 1974.

[32] From Joel Chandler Harris, *Nights with Uncle Remus* (Boston and New York: Houghton Mifflin Co., 1911), pp. 135–36.

[33] From Roth, *Call It Sleep*, p. 592.

Glossary

Items listed here are lingustic symbols and terms that are used repeatedly, as well as basic literary terms not defined in the text. Terms in boldface are defined elsewhere in the glossary.

SYMBOLS AND ABBREVIATIONS

Phonetic symbols: see Chapter 2, pp. 48–50.

*	"Ungrammatical," i.e., not conforming to the structure of the language in question; see **grammaticality.**
[ ]	Phonetic segment of speech; see **phonetics.**
/ /	Phonemic segment; see **phoneme.**
( )	Optional; may or may not occur, e.g., *(The) N* means a noun must occur but the article is optional.
{ }	One but not both members must be selected, e.g., $\begin{Bmatrix} Sg \\ Pl \end{Bmatrix}$ means "either singular or plural but not both."
→	"Consists of."
⟹	"Is transformed into"; see **transformation.**
S	Sentence.
N	Noun.
NP	Noun phrase.
PP	Prepositional phrase.
DET	Determiner, e.g., *this, the, two.*
V	Verb.
VP	Verb phrase.
AUX	Category term for verbal elements *Tense (Modal) (be + ing) (have + en)*; see each term.
IMP	Imperative.
NEG	Negative; see **negative sentence.**
Q	Question.
Ø	Zero; an element present in underlying structure that has been deleted in surface structure, e.g., in *The woman Ø you saw dancing is from Russia, whom* has been deleted.

TERMS

action/activity verbs and adjectives   Parts of speech that denote actions or activities such as *sing, leap, be noisy, be helpful*. They answer the question *What are you doing?;* usually allow the progressive *be + ing*, as in *I am being helpful;* and contrast with **state-of-being verbs and adjectives.**

active sentence   See **passive.**

adverb   A pronoun or prepositional phrase that answers such question-words as *where* (locative adverb, e.g., *there, at home, in the box*), *when* (temporal adverb, e.g., *then, at two, for a long time*), *why* (reason adverb), *how* (manner adverb).

affix   Any **morpheme** that can be attached to a **root.** "Prefixes" are attached before the root, e.g., *pre-, un-, mis-;* "suffixes" are attached after the root, e.g., *-ly, -ness, -s* (plural).

affix-hopping   A transformational rule that moves underlying affixes (Tense, *-en, -ing*) to their proper place after a verb.

affricate   A consonant articulated with initial stoppage of air followed by a fricative release, e.g., initial and final consonants in *church* and *judge*.

alliteration   Repetition of the initial sound of two or more words, as in *big bat in the belfry*. In alliterative verse, sound-unity is provided in every line by alliteration.

allomorphs   Alternate phonetic forms of a **morpheme,** e.g., noun plural is /rən/ after *child*, /s/ after *cat*, /z/ after *cow*, and /əz/ after *church*. See **complementary distribution.**

allophones   Predictable variants of the same sound class or **phoneme**; e.g., [pʰ] and [p] are both members of /p/. The former occurs initially, the second after /s/. See **complementary distribution.**

alveolar   A consonant articulated by movement of the tip of the tongue toward the hard ridge immediately behind the upper teeth, e.g., [t, d, s, z, n, l] in English.

ambiguity   The property of having two or more distinct interpretations, e.g., *The hunting of the snark* can mean either *somebody hunted the snark* or *the snark hunted something*. This contrasts with "vagueness," where no particular meaning can be assigned.

anomaly   An expression that is semantically or pragmatically odd as a result of the combination of two meanings that are incompatible, e.g., *My desk is weeping*. This violates **selectional restrictions.**

appropriateness conditions   Constraints on the form of the utterance, on the identity, beliefs, and attitudes of the participants, and on the surrounding circumstances that must be met for a **speech act** to have full effect, e.g., *You may come in* is appropriate only if the addressee is or is believed to be socially inferior to the speaker.

arbitrariness   A sound sequence is arbitrarily assigned to a particular meaning, e.g., *rose* is the name given to a certain type of flower arbitrarily, rather than by any natural and necessary condition. These arbitrary relationships are also described as conventional.

archaism   A form that survives from an earlier period of the language and is considered old (and perhaps literary), e.g., *methinks*.

argument   A **noun phrase** in a certain semantic function. See **case grammar.**

aspect   A temporal category that specifies whether an event, process, or state of affairs is viewed in terms of duration or completion. In English, aspect includes (a) "progressive" where action is viewed as being in progress, expressed by *be + ing*, e.g., *He is/was running;* (b) "perfect" where events, processes, or states of affairs are viewed as completed but having some relevance to the time of utterance or to the matter under discussion; expressed by *have + en,* e.g., *He has run;* (c) "habitual," expressed by tense alone, e.g., *He walks to school;* and (d) "iterative," expressed in Standard English by tense-markers alone, e.g., *He jumps every time he hears a noise,* and by invariant *be* in Black English Vernacular, e.g., *Whenever he be tired he be cross.*

aspiration Breathiness in the release of a **stop** consonant before a vowel; symbolized by a raised [ʰ], e.g., [pʰe] "pay."

assonance A resemblance of sounds, usually vowels, in the stressed syllables of a sequence of words, e.g., [e] in *the snail's daily way.*

auxiliary verb A "helping verb" like *may, can, shall, will, must, be, have,* and *do* in *She may leave, He has left, They are leaving, Did she leave?* Auxiliaries may occur in tags, like *He rode, didn't he? She was jogging, wasn't she? You don't really want to study linguistics, do you?,* or sentence-initially in **yes-no questions,** e.g., *Did he ride?, Should she practice?,* and can be followed by *n't.* Verbs that cannot do this are called "main verbs."

base A term referring to the parts of a **transformational grammar** called the **phrase structure** and **lexicon.** Together they model the skeletal structures of sentences and of the words that can occur in these structures.

be + en See **passive.**

be + ing See **aspect.**

caesura Line-internal pause in verse, e.g., pauses marked || in: *Soft is the Strain || when Zephyr gently blows, / And the smooth Stream || in smoother Numbers flows* (Pope).

case grammar Type of analysis focusing on the function that **noun phrases** play with respect to the event, process, or state expressed by the verb. Functions (also called "role relations" or "arguments") include Agent, Patient, Possessor, Source, Goal, Location, Instrument. In *Bobby enjoys disco, Bobby* functions as Experiencer of enjoying, *disco* as the Source of the experience. Case grammar relates languages with prepositions (cf. *the legs of the table*) to those with case inflections (cf. *the table's legs*), hence the name.

causative Type of verb expressing an event in which an Agent purposely manipulates somebody or something to achieve a certain effect, e.g., *Tom lengthened the table.*

channel Medium of expression, e.g., speech, writing, sign language.

clause A group of words with its own subject and predicate. It is analyzed as a sentence in **underlying structure.** The following larger sentence contains two subsentences or clauses: *I was working on the bike, which was badly rusted.* Clauses are "coordinate" (see **coordination**) or "subordinate" (see **subordination**). The clause to which others are attached by coordination or subordination is called the "main clause" (the first clause in the sample sentence). Contrast **phrase.**

cleft sentence A sentence in which a noun is given emphasis by being introduced by *it is/was,* e.g., *It was the cockroaches that bothered me.*

cohesion A property of texts of any length that is supplied by repeated refrains, regular stanzas, rhyme, alliteration, meter, repeated meanings in **lexical items,** similar sentence structure, question-and-answer routines, and so forth.

communicative competence See **competence.**

competence The internalized knowledge about language that language-users have and that they refer to in speaking and understanding. "Grammatical competence" refers to the knowledge that language-users have irrespective of context and communicative intent. "Communicative competence" refers to this knowledge together with the knowledge necessary to produce and understand utterances in relation to specific contexts and specific communicative purposes. Contrast **performance.**

complement   An underlying sentence functioning as a **noun phrase,** e.g., the italicized parts of the following, all of which can substitute for *it;* (1) I believe *that he is from Mars,* (2) I want *to see a UFO,* (3) I liked *his sticking up for her.* "*That*-complements" are introduced in surface structure by *that,* as in the first example; "*for-to* complements" are introduced by *(for) to,* as in the second example and in *I would prefer for you not to leave right now;* and "*Poss-ing* complements," sometimes called "gerunds," are introduced in surface structure by the possessive form of the underlying subject and *-ing* attached to the verb, as in the third example.

complementary distribution   Elements in complementary distribution are predictable variants of each other. Sounds in complementary distribution never occur in the same phonetic contexts, do not change meaning, and are phonetically similar. See **allophone.**

compound   A **lexical item** in which two **roots** combine to make one unit, e.g., *overweight, greenhouse.* Compound nouns have the stress pattern, stressed–less stressed, e.g., rédnèck. Contrast **idiom.**

consonant   A speech sound involving considerable obstruction of the flow of air, e.g., [p, t, f, m, r].

constituent   The units that make up or "constitute" a sentence, e.g., *The three men flipped* is constituted of *the three men* and *flipped, the three men* is constituted of *the* and *three men,* etc. "Constituent structure" models the hierarchy among groups of **morphemes, phrases,** and **clauses** in a sentence.

constraints   Limits on the patterning of language. In English, a constraint on word formation is that no word starts with the sound sequence [mb]. A constraint on the use of imperatives, e.g., *Go!,* is that the addressee is (or is believed to be) socially inferior to the speaker.

content morpheme/word   A **morpheme** or word whose primary function is to name things, concepts, qualities, processes, events and so forth. Contrast **grammatical morpheme/word.**

contradiction   A situation in which something is said to be both X and not-X at the same time, e.g., *My father is not my father, My father is my son.*

cooperative principle   A principle that represents our knowledge that verbal communication is an activity in which individuals work together to accomplish shared, mutually beneficial goals. It accounts for our ability to understand *It's cold in here* as an indirect request to close the window if indeed the room is cold, but as sarcasm if the room is hot.

coordination   A way of combining two or more underlying sentences or **noun phrases** which are approximately on a par with each other, by use of a coordinating conjunction such as *and, or,* or *but.*

copula   The verb *to be* when functioning as the main verb (see **auxiliary**) in a sentence of the type *You are a peach, They may be thirsty.*

coreference   The property of referring back to something already mentioned. In *A man entered. He was wearing a black cloak, he* is coreferential with *a man.*

creativity   Linguistic creativity is the ability to produce and understand utterances that have never been heard before but are possible within the system of the language of the time. See **recursiveness.**

creole   A **pidgin** language that has developed into the primary language of a community.

deep creole   The variety of a **creole** that is closest to the original contact language and farthest from the standard language to which it is assimilated.

deep structure   A technical term in a **transformational grammar** for a syntactic account of a sentence that specifies the skeletal structure of that sentence with all the information necessary to give it a phonological representation and a semantic representation. The output of the **phrase structure** and the **lexicon** before any **transformations** have applied. Contrast **surface structure.**

deixis The part of language involved in locating what is talked about relative to the speaker's point of view, whether in space (*here-there, this-that*), time (*now-then*), discourse (*former-latter*), or social relations (*I-you*). Words effecting this orientation are called "deictics."

derivative morpheme An **affix** that changes the meaning of the **root** when attached at the beginning (e.g., *un-, mis-, re-, co-*) and that changes the syntactic category as well as the meaning of the root when attached after the root (e.g., *-ion, -ness, -ly*).

determiner The cover term for articles (*a, the*), demonstratives (*this, that*), possessives (*her, his*), and quantifiers (*few, three*).

dialect See **variety.**

diction A literary term used to refer to both the totality of lexical choices found in a text and to particular patterns of lexical choice.

diphthong A vowel followed by an upward glide to the front [-y] or back [-w] in the same syllable, e.g., the vowel sounds in *bite* and *bout*.

direct object See **object.**

discourse Any structured stretch of language that is longer than a single sentence.

distinctive sound A sound that can potentially be used to distinguish meaning. /p/ and /b/ are distinctive as they can be used to contrast *pit* and *bit, sip* and *sib*. Classes of distinctive sounds are called **phonemes.** Contrast **allophone.**

elision The running together of two syllables by deletion of a consonant or vowel, e.g., *o'er, th'unbending.*

embedding See **subordination.**

eye dialect Modification of standard orthography to suggest nonstandard pronunciation, without actually signaling any phonetic difference, e.g., *wimmin, wuz.*

feature A term for recurrent components of sound or meaning. Phonological features are components used in classifying speech sounds, e.g., [± nasal], [± labial]. Semantic features are properties of meaning that recur in the **lexicon,** e.g., [+ ADULT] is a property of *man, woman, bull, cow, frog.*

finate verb A verb that in **surface structure** occurs with a **tense-marker,** e.g., *wants* in *He wants to go, has* in *He has left*. Nonfinite verbs occur after the infinitive marker *to* as in the first example, or after **auxiliary verbs** as in the second.

foregrounding Bringing elements to special attention, often by using them in unusual contexts or unusual ways.

free indirect style One of several techniques used to produce stream of consciousness narrative. Tense is based in the point of view of the narrator, but other time and place expressions are based in the consciousness of the character, e.g., *What would she do now?*

fricative A consonant sound resulting from a narrowing, but not total stoppage of the air stream as it passes through the oral cavity, causing a turbulent air flow, e.g., [f, v, s, z].

for-to **complement** See **complement.**

generative grammar A theory of language that aims to characterize what a language-user knows, that is, potentials that a language-user can put to use in producing and understanding language. It accounts in an explicit fashion for (i.e., "generates") all the possible sentences of the language.

genre A type of extended discourse, with identifiable properties, e.g., lecture, prayer, telephone conversation, novel, tragedy, lyric poem.

glide Also called "semivowel." A speech sound ([w] or [y] in English) produced like a vowel (i.e., with minimal obstruction), but unable to take stress and form a syllable on its own. Functions as an onset to a vowel as in [yæm] "yam," or as the end of a vowel as in [flay] "fly."

grammar A "grammar" is a linguist's theory about the structure of a particular language, including sound patterns, sentence and meaning structure. "Universal grammar" is a theory about the structures that are common to all languages.

grammatical morpheme/word   Also called "function morpheme or word." A **morpheme** or word, often unstressed, whose function is to show how words and sentence parts relate to each other (e.g., prepositions, conjunctions) or to indicate definiteness (e.g., articles), **tense, aspect,** and number (e.g., auxiliary verbs, inflection). Contrast **content morpheme/word.**

grammaticality   The property of occurring within the system of a particular language or variety of language at a particular time. *I don't want nothing* is fully gramatical in certain "nonstandard" dialects of English; in "standard" varieties, however, it does not conform to the rules of the community and is "ungrammatical." *You are a thief isn't you?* is, however, ungrammatical in all varieties of English.

have + en   See **aspect.**

higher sentence   An underlying sentence to which some other sentence is subordinated. The subordinated sentence is the "lower sentence." In *I know that you believe that I am guilty, I know it* is the highest sentence, *you believe it* is lower than *I know it,* but higher than *I am guilty.*

homonyms   A term for words with the same sounds but different meanings, e.g., *ear* (for hearing)-*ear* (of corn), *pail-pale.*

hypercorrection   The overuse of a form that has become stereotyped as prestigious, e.g., *I* in *between you and I* or overuse of the **postvocalic r** by lower-middle-class speakers in New York City when emulating the more prestigious speech of upper-middle-class speakers.

idiom   A sequence of two or more words whose meaning cannot be solely determined from the meaning of the parts, and that substitute for a noun, verb, adjective, etc., e.g., *have it out with (someone), sock it to (someone), look up* ("visit").

illocutionary act   An act performed through language for the purpose of accomplishing some communicative goal, such as commanding, promising, stating, or naming.

imperative   A sentence type having a syntactic structure like *Jump!, Do that!* (i.e., no surface subject or Tense), and having the **illocutionary** function of a command.

indirect object   See **object.**

inflection/inflectional morpheme   A suffix (see **affix**) that in English marks grammatical relations such as plurality (-*s*), possession (-*s*), Tense (-*s, -ed*), or comparison (-*er*). Inflections do not alter either the syntactic category or the basic meaning of the **root** to which they are attached.

interdental   A consonant sound articulated by the tongue between the teeth; the first sound in [θay] "thigh" and [ð] "thy."

interrogative   See **question.**

intonation   The pattern of pitch and stress changes that a speaker produces in uttering a phrase or sentence.

***it*-extraposition**   A **transformation** that allows for movement of a whole subject **complement** to the right of the verb, while marking its original position by *it,* e.g., *It was obvious that he was rich* from *That he was rich was obvious.*

jargon   Specialized vocabulary connected with a particular field of knowledge or activity.

labial   A consonant sound formed by contact of both lips with each other; in English [p, b, m, w].

labiodental   A consonant sound formed by contact of the lower lip with the upper teeth; in English [f, v].

laxness   See **tenseness.**

lexical item   An entry in the **lexicon** that specifies the phonological, syntactic, and semantic properties underlying a word.

lexical meaning   The **sense** of individual morphemes or words, e.g., "activity" and "motion by foot" are part of the lexical meaning of *walk*.

lexicon   The component of a grammar that specifies those meaning-sound combinations (**morphemes**) that are nonpredictable in a language. It can be thought of as a dictionary of underlying forms of words.

linguistic relativity   See **Whorfian hypothesis.**

liquid   A cover term for the sounds [l] and [r]. They are consonants produced with very little obstruction of the air stream.

lower sentence   See **higher sentence.**

main clause   See **clause.**

main verb   See **auxiliary verb.**

manner of articulation   One of the main parameters used to characterize speech sounds. A term for the degree of obstruction of the air stream in the production of consonants and for the shape of the lips in the production of vowels, cf. lip spreading or rounding. See **affricate, fricative, glide, liquid, stop.**

metalanguage   A language used for defining and describing objects being studied. Ordinary English is used as a metalanguage for describing languages.

metaphor   A figure of speech whereby semantic transfer is created through anomaly, as in *The kiss of a wave.*

meter   The name for recurring sequences of stressed ($\prime$) and unstressed ($\smile$) syllables in the poetic line; e.g., the pattern $\smile\prime$ is the basis of "iambic" meter, and $\prime\smile$ of "trochaic" meter.

minimal pair   Two words that sound alike in all but one feature, e.g., *sip* versus *zip*. A basic tool for discovering **phonemes** in a language.

modal   The cover term for the set of **auxiliary verbs** *can, may, must, shall,* and *will.* These verbs express the probability, possibility, necessity, or permissibility of the situation named by the main verb.

morpheme   A sound or sound sequence that is conventionally united with a particular meaning or meanings and that cannot be analyzed into simpler elements, e.g., *laugh, -able, -s* (noun plural). See **derivative morpheme, inflection, root.**

narration   A **discourse** presenting events or experiences in the order in which they occurred. "Narrative clauses" are main clauses consisting minimally of a subject followed by a verb in the simple past tense and an object, if required by the verb.

negative incorporation   See **negative sentence.**

negative sentence   Term for a sentence containing *not* or *n't,* or other word into which *n*- has been "incorporated," e.g., *no* (from *not any*), *none* (from *not one*), *neither* (from *not either*). It expresses a denial of something said previously (e.g., *That is not the case*), a rejection (e.g., *We won't go*), or nonexistence (e.g., *There is no wine in the house*).

neologism   A newly invented word. In the 1960s, words like *love-in, be-in,* and *teach-in* were neologisms.

nonstandard   See **standard dialect.**

noun phrase   A **constituent** of a sentence consisting of at least a noun or **pronoun,** and often also a **determiner,** e.g., *Samantha, she, the witch.*

object   A noun phrase that normally follows the verb. "Direct objects" are those that can be made into the subject in **passive** sentences. An "indirect object" is the person or thing to which something is given, done, or said; expressed by a prepositional phrase, usually *to* + **noun phrase.** In *I gave the book to John, book* is the direct object, *to John* the indirect object. "Objects of prepositions" are those noun phrases that follow a preposition in **surface structure.**

onomatopoeia   A literary term for the use of a word that sounds like its referent, e.g., *bang, cuckoo, splat.*

particle   A **grammatical word** like *at, for, up* when it functions as part of a verb **idiom**, e.g., *up* in *look up* (It answers *What did he do?* rather than *Where did he look?*), *look up to* "admire." Contrast **adverb** and **preposition.**

passive   A sentence of the type *The baobab tree was felled by the angry mob.* Contains the **auxiliary verb** *be* + *en* and a *by*-phrase (which may be deleted). It has a counterpart, called an "active sentence," with **noun phrases** in reverse order and no *be* + *en* or *by*-phrase, e.g., *The angry mob felled the baobab tree.*

perfect   See **aspect.**

performance   What we do when we speak or listen; actual language behavior. Contrast **competence.**

performative   A verb in the present tense, with *I* as the subject, used to perform the **illocutionary act** it refers to, e.g., *say* in *I say unto you,* or *name* in *I name you John Jacob.*

permuting   Two or more elements are permuted by a transformational rule if their order is rearranged, e.g., *Give those red socks to Alex* can be permuted to *Give Alex those red socks.*

phone   A sound of language.

phoneme   A distinctive sound class. It consists of phonetically similar sounds that are predictable variants of each other and that can potentially be used, through contrast with other sound classes, to distinguish meaning. /p/ and /b/ are phonemes in English since they alone distinguish *pit* from *bit.*

phonetic alphabet   A linguistic writing system that allows the linguist to write down sounds unambiguously; in principle, one sound is uniquely represented by one letter.

phonetics   The study of the inventory of sounds in languages in general, how they are produced ("articulatory phonetics") and perceived ("acoustic phonetics"). Contrast **phonology.**

phonology   The study of how sounds are organized in a particular language, that is, which sounds can be distinctive in a language, in what position they may occur, and what types of automatic variants of a sound are possible. Also used to refer to the system of sound patterns in a language. Contrast **phonetics.**

phrase   A group of words that is grammatically equivalent to a single word and does not contain its own subject and verb. In *The ball rolled down the hill, the ball, the hill, down the hill,* and *rolled down the hill* are all phrases at different levels of grouping. See **noun phrase, prepositional phrase, verb phrase.** Contrast **clause.**

phrase structure   The part of a grammar that specifies skeletal structures for sentences. It accounts for such categories as noun, verb, etc., and their hierarchic arrangement (e.g., *Bill | turned into a toad,* not *Bill turned into | a toad*).

pidgin   A language that arises from contact between speakers of different languages in a highly stratified social situation, such as slave trade. Usually characterized by simplified sentence structure and a limited and mixed vocabulary. Nobody's native language, a pidgin contrasts with a "creole," which is developed as a first language under similar social and linguistic conditions.

pitch   The rise and fall of the voice in producing an utterance. The "tune" or "melody" associated with particular **speech acts,** e.g., rising pitch associated with **yes-no questions.**

place of articulation   A term for the position of the primary vocal organs (lip position, tongue height and position relative to teeth and the roof of the mouth) in the production of speech sounds. See **alveolar, interdental, labial, labiodental,** and **velar** sounds.

poss-ing **complement**   See **complement**.

postvocalic r   See *r***-less dialect**.

pragmatics   The component of the grammar that deals with how language functions in context. Also used to refer to contextual conditions on language, such as social relations, beliefs, and intentions of speakers and hearers.

predicate   A term used for the verb, especially when viewed in its function as the expression of an event, process, or state of affairs.

predication   In **case grammar**, the part of the sentence consisting of a verb (the predicate) and various **arguments** (**noun phrases** functioning in certain roles).

prefix   See **affix**.

preposition   A **grammatical word** like *at, for, up*, when it is associated with a **noun phrase**, e.g., *He looked up the hill* where *up the hill* functions as a unit (*Where did he look?*). The sequence of preposition and noun phrase is called a "prepositional phrase." Contrast **adverb** and **particle**.

prepositional phrase   See **preposition**.

prescriptive grammar   An account of the **standard variety** of a language aimed at legislating how the language ought to be used. By contrast, a "descriptive grammar" aims at describing any variety of a language at any particular time, without evaluating its propriety. Pedagogical grammars tend to be prescriptive; linguists' grammars are usually descriptive.

presupposition   A **predication** that is taken for granted when a sentence is uttered. In *I resent his leaving the job to me*, it is assumed to be true that there was a job to be done and that someone left the job to the speaker. All the sentence actually says (asserts) is that the speaker resents this fact. The same facts are still assumed to be true in *I don't resent his leaving the job to me*, but the assertion is different.

progressive   See **aspect**.

pronoun   A **grammatical word** that substitutes for a noun. Pronoun subtypes include (a) "personal": *I, we, you, he, she, it, they;* (b) "interrogative": *who, what, why, where, how;* (c) "locative": *here, there, where;* (d) "temporal": *now, then, when;* (e) "relative": *that, who, which;* (f) "indefinite": *someone, anyone, no one;* (g) "demonstrative": *this, that;* and so forth.

psycholinguistics   The study of the relation between language and mind, especially of how language is learned and remembered.

question   Also called "interrogative." A cover term for two types of sentences: (a) yes-no questions, requiring *yes* or *no* for an answer, e.g., *Did you inform the police?*, and (b) content questions requiring a content word for an answer, e.g., *Who informed the police? Who did what to whom?*

*r***-less dialect**   A dialect in which *r* is not pronounced after a vowel and before a consonant or a pause. It is, however, pronounced at the beginning of a word or between vowels, thus: [ka] "car," [kad] "card," but [rɛd] "red," [mɛri] "merry." Characteristic of Standard British English and many Northern and Southern dialects of American English, and of Black English Vernacular.

recursiveness   A type of linguistic **creativity** which allows us to construct and understand infinitely long sentences by principles of **coordination** and **subordination**, e.g., *I know you know he knows that I know and you know that . . .*

reference   The kind of meaning whereby an expression designates real-world entities or states. Contrast **sense**.

relative clause   A type of subordinate clause introduced by the relative pronouns *that, who,* or *which*, the function of which is to describe and particularize the noun it modifies. "Appositive relatives" add descriptive, but incidental, information, e.g., *The president, who arrived only a few minutes ago, will speak in half an hour.* "Restrictive relatives" are contrastive, e.g., *The president who* *arrived only a few minutes ago will speak in half an hour,* which implies that there is at least one other president, and that the defining feature of this one is the time of arrival.

rhyme   Similarity or identity in sound; two words rhyme when the stressed vowel and succeeding sounds are identical, as in *grey-bay, breaking-shaking.*

rhythm   Any sound patterning achieved through the grouping of stressed and unstressed syllables, roughly as in music.

role relations   See **case grammar.**

root   The base of a **content word** to which various **affixes** may be attached, e.g., *real* in *realism* and *unreality,* or *night* in *nights.*

rule   A pattern observed or observable by the investigator of language.

rule-governed   The property of being patterned, not haphazard.

selectional restrictions   Semantic constraints on the co-occurrence of **lexical items** with each other in a sequence.

semantic feature   See **feature.**

semantic primitive   A basic component of meaning that cannot be broken down into smaller meaning components.

semantics   The meaning structure of language. "Lexical semantics" refers to word meaning, particularly the **sense** of words. "Sentence semantics" refers to meanings that hold between parts of the sentence. The noun *boy,* which at the lexical level includes such components of meaning as "human," "male," and "young," functions semantically at the sentence level as the Agent of the action in such a sentence as *The boy squashed the ant,* but as the Patient of the action in *Godzilla squeezed the boy.*

semivowel   See **glide.**

sense   The aspect of meaning that focuses on language-internal concepts. The sense of *cat* consists of the meanings associated with the concept "cat" (including metaphorical extensions, as in *cool cat*). By contrast, the **reference** of *cat* consists of the set of animals to which the word refers.

sibilant   A "hissing" sound; in English [s, z, š, ž, č, ǰ].

sign   An entity that represents or stands for another entity. An "iconic sign" is associated to an object by actual physical resemblance, e.g., an object and its photograph, or some onomatopoetic words (see **onomatopoeia**). An "indexical sign" is associated to an object by a relationship of physical proximity, e.g., smoke is an index for fire; deictic words like *this-that* are linguistic indexicals (see **deixis**). A "symbolic sign" is associated to an object by convention, e.g., a black armband for mourning, or the word *chair* for the objects it represents and the concept of something to sit on.

simile   A literary term for a figure of speech involving an expressed comparison between two relatively unlike things, e.g., *My love is like a rose.*

sociolinguistics   The study of language in its various contexts, particularly social contexts, such as who the speakers and hearers are, what regional, social, ethnic, or other group they come from, or the type of social closeness or distance involved in addressing people, negotiating who speaks when in a conversation, and so forth.

sound-symbolism   Also called "phonesthetics." Association of certain sounds with certain meanings, regardless of actual morpheme boundaries, e.g., *fl-* "rapid movement" in *flash, flick, flip, flop, fly.*

speech acts   Utterances viewed as goal-directed actions. See **illocutionary acts.**

speech community   A group of people who share norms of linguistic behavior with respect to such potential sources of diversity as regional, social, sexual, and educational backgrounds.

standard variety   A dominant **variety** of a language used for public (including international) transactions. In a descriptive sense, the norm used in more formal styles by educated people, and often associated with national broadcasters. In a prescriptive sense, an ideal, the imagined repository of refinement in the language. The term "nonstandard" is applied to any variety that does not have the same social functions as the "standard." Nonstandard varieties are therefore often socially stigmatized, although they have valuable functions in intimate settings and for individual group identity, and are as **rule-governed** as the standard variety.

state-of-being/stative verbs and adjectives   Parts of speech that denote states and experiences, e.g., *like, know, believe, be tall, be delighted (to)*. They typically do not occur with the progressive, cf. **I am liking your book.* Contrast **action/ activity verbs and adjectives.**

stop   A consonant sound made with the air stream momentarily completely stopped at some point in the oral cavity; in English, [p, t, k, b, d, g].

stress   The emphasis given to a vowel in a syllable. Loudest stress (´) is generally associated with higher pitch and respiratory intensity than are characteristic of the surrounding vowels. In English, stress operates at the word level to distinguish word meanings, e.g., *récord-recórd,* and at the sentence level to distinguish new information from shared information, e.g., *Albert will leave sóon* answers *When will Albert leave? (soon* is new information), while *Álbert will leave soon* answers *Who will leave soon? (Albert* is new information).

string   A sequence of elements at some level of grammar. NP + AUX + VP is a string at the phrase structure level, *man* + plural + *go* + Past is a string at the surface syntactic level.

style   A term traditionally used to signify a large number of different things in textual analysis. In this book, style refers to patterned choice, whether at the phonological, lexical, syntactic, or pragmatic level.

subject   This term has been defined in a number of different ways. Here it refers to the **noun phrase** that in the **surface structure** determines the **inflection** of the verb in the present tense (cf. *She trains bloodhounds,* but *They train bloodhounds*), and that in **deep structure** is specified in the rule S → NP + AUX + VP. The surface subject usually functions as the **theme** in English, but not in all cases, e.g., in *Joe likes Amy, Joe* is the subject and the **theme** (the sentence is about *Joe*), but in *It is raining, it* is a subject but not a theme (the sentence is not about *it*). Contrast **object.**

subordination   Also called "embedding." An asymmetrical syntactic relation in which one clause is a constituent or part of another, and thus "dependent" on it. See **complement** and **relative clause.** Contrast **coordination.**

suffix   See **affix.**

suppletion   Occurs when a single **morpheme** is realized in different contexts by sound sequences that have no phonological similarity at all, e.g., *go* versus *went,* where *went = go* + Past.

surface structure   The linear arrangement of words, phrases, and clauses that constitute a sentence as it is actually spoken or as it appears on the page. Contrast **deep structure, underlying structure.**

synonyms   A term for words with the same meaning but different sounds, e.g., *bucket* and *pail.* See **homonyms.**

syntax   The sentence structure of a language.

tense   As a morphological and syntactic category, Tense (note the capital letter) stands for past (*-ed*) and non-past (*-s*). As a semantic category, tense stands for the temporal relationships *now-then,* and past-present-future.

tense-marker   A cover term for the affixes past and non-past, usually represented by *-ed* and *-s* in English.

tenseness   Relative tension of the muscles in the production of vowel sounds. All stressed vowels are tense in word-final position in English, as in *be, bah, boo.*

Tenseness is a feature used to distinguish the [i] in [bit] "beat" from "lax" [ɪ] in [bɪt] "bit." In the latter, the muscles are relatively relaxed.

theme   The initial noun phrase in a sentence, the function of which is to establish a perspective on what is talked about, e.g., in *The crows pecked the plums,* the crows are the point of departure for the message, the rest of which is about them; in *The plums were pecked by the crows,* the fruit are the point of departure. Contrast **subject.**

transformational grammar   A type of **generative grammar** particularly associated with Noam Chomsky. A theory of language that proposes a syntactic **base,** and both **phrase structure** and **transformations** (hence the name).

transformations   Operations that add, delete, or permute syntactic structures. Their purpose is to reveal relations between **underlying** and **surface structures,** e.g., the passive transformation shows the relationship between the active' sentence *Everyone hated the course* and the passive sentence *The course was hated by everyone,* by deriving the second from the first.

underlying structure   The basic semantic-syntactic structure of a sentence, specifying its categories and the hierarchic relations between its parts. Ambiguous sentences like *I pulled it off easily* are understood to have a different underlying structure corresponding to each meaning.

ungrammatical   See **grammaticality.**

variety   Also called "dialect." A version of a language associated with a specific region, social class, ethnic, sex, or age group. It is usually identifiable at all levels of grammar, from sounds to words, sentence structures, and even **speech acts.**

velar   A consonant sound produced by movement of the tongue toward the "velum" or soft palate; in English [k, g, ŋ].

verb phrase   A **constituent** of the sentence consisting of at least a verb and often also associated **noun phrases** functioning as object, indirect object, adverb, etc.

vernacular   The variety of language associated with everyday, casual, or intimate speech, as distinct from learned or literary language.

voicing   A feature of speech sounds made by vibration of the vocal cords during the passage of the air stream through them. Sounds that are characterized by this vibration are "voiced" (cf. all the sounds in *bib*); those not characterized by this vibration are "voiceless" (cf. the initial and final sounds in *pip*).

vowel   A speech sound involving minimal obstruction of the flow of air in its passage through the oral cavity, e.g., [ɪ, ɛ, a, o, ay]. Contrast **consonant.**

Whorfian hypothesis   Also called "linguistic relativity." The hypothesis that language influences thought. "We dissect nature along lines laid down by our native language" (Benjamin Lee Whorf).

yes-no question   See **question.**

Bibliography of Linguistic and Critical Works

For literary works and sample texts, bibliographical information is given in footnotes. References are listed by author, editor, and title in the index of names.

Achebe, Chinua. *Morning Yet on Creation Day: Essays.* London: Heinemann, 1975.

Adams, Valerie. *An Introduction to Modern English Word-Formation.* London: Longman Group Ltd., 1973.

Akmajian, Adrian, Richard A. Demers, and Robert M. Harnish. *Linguistics: An Introduction to Language and Communication.* Cambridge, Mass.: MIT Press, 1979.

————, and Frank Heny. *An Introduction to the Principles of Transformational Syntax.* Cambridge, Mass.: MIT Press, 1975.

Allen, Harold B., and Gary N. Underwood, eds. *Readings in American Dialectology.* New York: Appleton-Century-Crofts. Meredith Corporation, 1971.

Austin, J. L. *How to Do Things with Words.* Cambridge, Mass.: Harvard Univ. Press, 1962.

Babb, Howard S., ed. *Essays in Stylistic Analysis.* New York: Harcourt Brace Jovanovich, Inc., 1972.

Bach, Emmon. "Nouns and Noun Phrases." In *Universals in Linguistic Theory.* Eds. Emmon Bach and Robert T. Harms. New York: Holt, Rinehart and Winston, Inc., 1968.

Bailey, Richard W., and Jay L. Robinson, eds. *Varieties of Present-Day English.* New York: Macmillan, 1973.

Baker, C. L. *Introduction to Generative-Transformational Syntax.* Englewood Cliffs, N.J.: Prentice-Hall, 1978.

Banfield, Ann. "Narrative Style and the Grammar of Direct and Indirect Speech." *Foundations of Language,* 10(1973), 1–39.

Baugh, Albert C., and Thomas Cable. *A History of the English Language.* 3rd ed. Englewood Cliffs, N.J.: Prentice-Hall, 1978.

Beaver, Joseph C. "A Grammar of Prosody." *College English,* 29(1968), 310–21. Rpt. in *Linguistics and Literary Style.* Ed. Donald C. Freeman. New York: Holt, Rinehart and Winston, Inc., 1970.

Bereiter, Carl, and Siegfried Engelmann. *Teaching Disadvantaged Children in the Preschool.* Englewood Cliffs, N.J.: Prentice-Hall, 1966.

Bickerton, Derek. *Dynamics of a Creole System*. London and New York: Cambridge Univ. Press, 1975.

———. "Pidginization and Creolization; Language Acquisition and Language Universals." In *Pidgin and Creole Linguistics*. Ed. Albert Valdman. Bloomington and London: Indiana Univ. Press, 1977.

Bierwisch, Manfred. "Semantics." In *New Horizons in Linguistics*. Ed. John Lyons. Harmondsworth, Mssex: Penguin, 1970.

———. "Some Semantic Universals of German Adjectivals." *Foundations of Language*, 3(1967), 1–36.

Bloomfield, Leonard. *Language*. New York: Holt, Rinehart and Winston, 1933.

Bloomfield, Morton, and Einar Haugen, eds. *Language as a Human Problem*. New York: Norton, 1974.

Bodine, Ann. "Androcentrism in Prescriptive Grammar: Singular 'They,' Sex-indefinite 'He,' and 'He or She.' " *Language in Society*, 4(1975), 129–46.

Bolinger, Dwight. "Around the Edge of Language: Intonation." *Harvard Educational Review*, 34(1964), 121–93.

———. *Aspects of Language*. 2nd ed. New York: Harcourt Brace Jovanovich, Inc., 1975.

———. *The Verbal Phrase in English*. Cambridge, Mass.: Harvard Univ. Press, 1971.

Booth, Wayne C. *The Rhetoric of Fiction*. Chicago: Univ. of Chicago Press, 1961.

Bridgman, Richard. *The Colloquial Style in America*. London and New York: Oxford Univ. Press, 1966.

Brown, Penelope, and Stephen Levinson. "Universals in Language Usage: Politeness Phenomena." In *Questions and Politeness: Strategies in Social Interaction*. Ed. Esther N. Goody. Cambridge: Cambridge Univ. Press, 1978.

Brown, Roger W. *Words and Things*. New York: The Free Press, 1958.

———, and Marguerite Ford. "Address in American English." *Journal of Abnormal and Social Psychology*, 62(1961), 375–85.

———, and A. Gilman. "The Pronouns of Power and Solidarity." In *Style in Language*. Ed. Thomas A. Sebeok. Cambridge, Mass.: MIT Press, 1960. Rpt. in *Language in Context*. Ed. Pier Paolo Giglioli. Harmondsworth, Mssex: Penguin, 1972.

Bruss, Elizabeth Wissman. "Formal Semantics and Poetic Meaning." *Poetics*, 4(1975), 339–63.

Bucher, Justus, ed. *Philosophical Writings of Peirce*. New York: Dover, 1955.

Burling, Robbins. *Man's Many Voices: Language in Its Cultural Context*. New York: Holt, Rinehart and Winston, Inc., 1970.

Cassidy, Frederic, and Robert Le Page. *Dictionary of Jamaican English*. London and New York: Cambridge Univ. Press, 1967.

Catford, J. C. *A Linguistic Theory of Translation: An Essay in Applied Linguistics*. London and New York: Oxford Univ. Press, 1965.

Chafe, Wallace L. "Givenness, Contrastiveness, Definiteness, Subjects, Topics, and Point of View." In *Subject and Topic*. Ed. Charles N. Li. New York: Academic Press, 1976.

———. *Meaning and the Structure of Language*. Chicago: Univ. of Chicago Press, 1970.

Chapman, Raymond. *Linguistics and Literature: An Introduction to Literary Stylistics*. London: Arnold, 1973.

Chatman, Seymour, ed. *Approaches to Poetics*. New York: Columbia Univ. Press, 1973.

———. *Literary Style: A Symposium*. London and New York: Oxford Univ. Press, 1971.

———. *A Theory of Meter*. The Hague: Mouton, 1964.

————, and Samuel R. Levin, eds. *Essays on the Language of Literature.* Boston: Houghton Mifflin Co., 1967.

Chomsky, Noam. *Aspects of the Theory of Syntax.* Cambridge, Mass.: MIT Press, 1965.

————. *Current Issues in Linguistic Theory.* The Hague: Mouton, 1964.

————. *Language and Mind.* 2nd ed. New York: Harcourt Brace Jovanovich, Inc., 1972.

————. "Questions of Form and Interpretation." *Essays on Form and Interpretation.* New York: Elsevier North-Holland, Inc., 1977.

————. *Syntactic Structures.* The Hague: Mouton, 1957.

————, and Morris Halle. *The Sound Pattern of English.* New York: Harper and Row, 1968.

Clark, Eve V. "Normative States and Evaluative Viewpoints." *Language,* 50(1974), 316–32.

Clark, Herbert H. "Space, Time, Semantics and the Child." In *Cognitive Development and the Acquisition of Language.* Ed. Terry E. Moore. New York: Academic Press, 1973.

————, and Eve V. Clark. *Psychology and Language: An Introduction to Psycholinguistics.* New York: Harcourt Brace Jovanovich, Inc., 1977.

Cluysenaar, Anne. *Introduction to Literary Stylistics.* London: Batsford, 1976.

Cole, Peter, and Jerry L. Morgan, eds. *Syntax and Semantics III: Speech Acts.* New York: Academic Press, 1975.

Collinder, Björn. *Survey of the Uralic Languages.* Stockholm: Almqvist and Wiksell, 1957.

Comrie, Bernard. *Aspect.* London and New York: Cambridge Univ. Press, 1976.

Coulthard, Malcolm. *An Introduction to Discourse Analysis.* London: Longman, 1977.

Culicover, Peter W. *Syntax.* New York: Academic Press, 1976.

Culler, Jonathan. *Structuralist Poetics: Structuralism, Linguistics and the Study of Literature.* Ithaca, N.Y.: Cornell Univ. Press, 1975.

Davie, Donald. *Purity of Diction in English Verse.* London: Chatto and Windus, 1952.

Delbridge, Arthur. "The Use of English in Australian Literature." *Harvard Educational Review,* 34, No. 2(1964), 306–11.

Denes, Peter B., and Elliot N. Pinson. *The Speech Chain: The Physics and Biology of Spoken Language.* Garden City, N.Y.: Anchor Books, 1973.

DeStefano, Johanna S., ed. *Language, Society, and Education: A Profile of Black English.* Worthington, Ohio: Charles A. Jones Publishing Co., 1973.

Dillard, J. L. *All-American English: A History of the English Language in America.* New York: Random House, 1975.

————. *Black English: Its History and Usage in the United States.* New York: Random House, 1972.

————. *Lexicon of Black English.* New York: The Seabury Press, 1977.

Dillon, George L. *Introduction to Contemporary Linguistic Semantics.* Englewood Cliffs, N.J.: Prentice-Hall, 1977.

————. *Language Processing and the Reading of Literature: Toward a Model of Comprehension.* Bloomington: Indiana Univ. Press, 1978.

Diringer, David. *Writing.* New York: Praeger, 1962.

Dohan, Mary Helen. *Our Own Words.* Baltimore, Md.: Penguin Books, Inc., 1974.

Dressler, Wolfgang, ed. *Trends in Textlinguistics.* New York: De Gruyter, 1977.

Enkvist, Nils Erik, John Spencer, and Michael J. Gregory. *Linguistics and Style.* London: Oxford Univ. Press, 1964.

Epstein, Edmund L. *Language and Style.* London: Methuen, 1978.

Falk, Julia S. *Linguistics and Language: A Survey of Basic Concepts and Implications.* 2nd ed. New York: John Wiley and Sons, 1978.

Fallis, Guadalupe Valdes. "Code-switching in Bilingual Chicano Poetry." *Hispania,* 59(1976), 877–86.

Farb, Peter. *Word Play: What Happens When People Talk.* New York: Random House, 1973.

Farkas, Donka, Wesley M. Jacobsen, and Karol W. Todrys, eds. *Papers from the Parasession on the Lexicon.* Chicago: Department of Linguistics, Chicago Univ., 1978.

Fasold, Ralph W. *Tense Marking in Black English: A Linguistic and Sociological Analysis.* Arlington, Va.: Center for Applied Linguistics, 1972.

———, and Walt Wolfram. "Some Linguistic Features of Negro Dialect." In *Teaching Standard English in the Inner City.* Eds. Ralph W. Fasold and Roger W. Shuy. Washington, D.C.: Center for Applied Linguistics, 1970. Rpt. in *Language, Society, and Education: A Profile of Black English.* Ed. Johanna S. DeStefano. Worthington, Ohio: Charles A. Jones Publishing Co., 1973. Rpt. in *Black American English: Its Background and Its Usage in the Schools and Literature.* Ed. Paul Stoller. New York: Dell, 1975.

Ferguson, Charles A. "Diglossia." *Word,* 15(1959), 325–40. Rpt. in *Readings in the Sociology of Language.* Ed. Joshua A. Fishman. The Hague: Mouton, 1968. Rpt. in *Language in Context.* Ed. Pier Paolo Giglioli. Harmondsworth, Mssex: Penguin, 1972.

———, and Charles E. DeBose. "Simplified Registers, Broken Language, and Pidginization." In *Pidgin and Creole Linguistics.* Ed. Albert Valdman. Bloomington and London: Indiana Univ. Press, 1977.

Fillmore, Charles J. "The Case for Case." In *Universals in Linguistic Theory.* Eds. Emmon Bach and Robert Harms. New York: Holt, Rinehart and Winston, Inc., 1968.

———. "Lexical Entries for Verbs." *Foundations of Language,* 4(1968), 373–93.

———. "May We Come In?" *Semiotica,* 9(1973), 1–15.

———. "Pragmatics and the Description of Discourse." *Berkeley Studies in Syntax and Semantics,* 1(1974), Chapter 5.

———. *Santa Cruz Lectures on Deixis.* 1971. (Available from the Indiana Linguistics Club).

Fish, Stanley. "How to Do Things with Austin and Searle: Speech Act Theory and Literary Criticism." *Modern Language Notes,* 91(1976), 983–1025.

———. "Literature in the Reader: Affective Stylistics." *New Literary History,* 2(1970), 123–62.

Fishman, Joshua A. *Language Loyalty in the United States.* The Hague: Mouton, 1966.

———, ed. *Readings in the Sociology of Language.* The Hague: Mouton, 1968.

———. *Sociolinguistics: A Brief Introduction.* Rowley, Mass.: Newbury House, 1972.

———, Robert L. Cooper, and Andrew Conrad, eds. *The Spread of English: The Sociology of English as an Additional Language.* Rowley, Mass.: Newbury House Publishers, 1977.

Fowler, Roger, ed. *Essays on Style and Language: Linguistic and Critical Approaches to Literary Style.* London: Routledge and Kegan Paul, 1966.

———. *Linguistics and the Novel.* London: Methuen and Co., 1977.

———. " 'Prose Rhythm' and Meter." In *Essays on Style and Language: Linguistic and Critical Approaches to Literary Style.* Ed. Roger Fowler. London: Routledge and Kegan Paul, 1966. Rpt. in *Linguistics and Literary Style.* Ed. Donald C. Freeman. New York: Holt, Rinehart and Winston, Inc., 1970.

———. "The Referential Code and Narrative Authority." *Language and Style,* 10(1977), 129–61.

Francis, W. Nelson. "Revolution in Grammar." *Quarterly Journal of Speech,* 40(1954), 299–312.

Fraser, Bruce. "Hedged Performatives." In *Syntax and Semantics III: Speech Acts.* Eds. Peter Cole and Jerry L. Morgan. New York: Academic Press, 1975.

Freeman, Donald C., ed. *Linguistics and Literary Style.* New York: Holt, Rinehart and Winston, Inc., 1970.

——. "On the Primes of Metrical Style." *Language and Style,* 1(1968), 63–101. Rpt. in *Linguistics and Literary Style.* Ed. Donald C. Freeman. New York: Holt, Rinehart and Winston, Inc., 1970.

Friedrich, Paul, and James Redfield. "Speech as Personality Symbol: The Case of Achilles." *Language,* 54(1978), 263–88.

Fromkin, Victoria. *Speech Errors as Linguistic Evidence.* The Hague: Mouton, 1973.

——, and Robert Rodman. *An Introduction to Language.* 2nd ed. New York: Holt, Rinehart and Winston, Inc., 1978.

Garnica, Olga K. "Rules of Verbal Interaction and Literary Analysis." *Poetics,* 6(1977), 155–68.

Gelb, I. J. *A Study of Writing: The Foundations of Grammatology.* rev. ed. Chicago: Univ. of Chicago Press, 1963.

Giglioli, Pier Paolo, ed. *Language in Context.* Harmondsworth, Mssex: Penguin, 1972.

Gimson, A. C. *An Introduction to the Pronunciation of English.* London: Arnold, 1962.

Givón, Talmy. *Syntax and Semantics 12: Discourse and Syntax.* New York: Academic Press, 1979.

Gleason, Henry A., Jr. *Linguistics and English Grammar.* New York: Holt, Rinehart and Winston, Inc., 1965.

Gordon, David, and George Lakoff. "Conversational Postulates." *Papers from the Seventh Regional Meeting of the Chicago Linguistic Society.* Chicago: University of Chicago, Department of Linguistics, 1971.

Green, Georgia. "How to Get People to Do Things with Words." In *Syntax and Semantics III: Speech Acts.* Eds. Peter Cole and Jerry L. Morgan. New York: Academic Press, 1975.

Greenberg, Joseph H. *A New Invitation to Linguistics.* Garden City, N.Y.: Anchor Books, 1977.

——, Charles A. Ferguson, and Edith A. Moravcsik, eds. *Universals of Human Language.* 4 vols. Stanford: Stanford Univ. Press, 1978.

Grice, H. Paul. "Logic and Conversation." (Part of the 1967 William James Lectures) In *Syntax and Semantics III: Speech Acts.* Eds. Peter Cole and Jerry L. Morgan. New York: Academic Press, 1975.

Gruber, Jeffrey S. *Lexical Structures in Syntax and Semantics.* New York: Elsevier North-Holland Inc., 1976.

Gumperz, John J. "The Social Significance of Code-Switching." *Papers on Language and Context.* Univ. of California, Berkeley: Working Papers of the Language Behavior Research Laboratory, 1976.

——. "Sociocultural Knowledge in Conversational Inference." *Georgetown University Round Table on Languages and Linguistics,* 1977, pp. 191–212.

——, and Eduardo Hernández-Chavez. "Cognitive Aspects of Bilingual Communication." In *El Lenguaje de los Chicanos: Regional and Social Characteristics of Language used by Mexican-Americans.* Eds. Eduardo Hernández-Chavez, Andrew D. Cohen, and Anthony F. Beltramo. Arlington, Va.: Center for Applied Linguistics, 1975.

——, and Dell Hymes, eds. *Directions in Sociolinguistics: The Ethnography of Communication.* New York: Holt, Rinehart and Winston, 1972.

Hall, Robert A., Jr. *Pidgin and Creole Languages*. Ithaca: Cornell Univ. Press, 1966.

Halle, Morris, "On Meter and Prosody." In *Progress in Linguistics*. Eds. Manfred Bierwisch and Karl Erich Heidolph. The Hague: Mouton, 1970.

————, Joan Bresnan, and George A. Miller, eds. *Linguistic Theory and Psychological Reality*. Cambridge, Mass.: M.I.T. Press, 1979.

————, and Samuel Jay Keyser. "Chaucer and the Study of Prosody." *College English*, 28(1966), 187–219. Rpt. in *Linguistics and Literary Style*. Ed. Donald C. Freeman. New York: Holt, Rinehart and Winston, Inc., 1970.

Halliday, M. A. K. "Linguistic Function and Literary Style: An Inquiry into the Language of William Golding's *The Inheritors*." In *Approaches to Poetics*. Ed. Seymour Chatman. New York: Columbia Univ. Press, 1973.

————. "Notes on Transitivity and Theme." *Journal of Linguistics*, 3(1967), 37–81, 199–244; 4(1968), 179–215.

————, and Ruqaiya Hasan. *Cohesion in English*. London: Longman, 1976.

Hamburger, Käte. *The Logic of Literature*. Trans. Marilynn J. Rose. Bloomington: Indiana Univ. Press, 1973.

Hancher, Michael. "The Classification of Cooperative Illocutionary Acts." *Language in Society*, 8(1979), 1–14.

Hendricks, William O. *Grammars of Style and Styles of Grammars*. New York: Elsevier North-Holland Inc., 1976.

————. "Three models for the description of poetry." *Journal of Linguistics*, 5(1969), 1–22.

Hernández-Chavez, Eduardo, Andrew D. Cohen, and Anthony F. Beltramo, eds. *El Languaje de los Chicanos: Regional and Social Characteristics of Language Used by Mexican-Americans*. Arlington, Va.: Center for Applied Linguistics, 1975.

Herndon, Jeanne H. *A Survey of Modern Grammars*. New York: Holt, Rinehart and Winston, Inc., 1970.

Hill, Archibald A. *Introduction to Linguistic Structures: From Sound to Sentence in English*. New York: Harcourt Brace Jovanovich, Inc., 1958.

Holland, Norman H. *The Dynamics of Literary Response*. New York: Oxford Univ. Press, 1968.

Hopper, Paul J. "Aspect and Foregrounding in Discourse." In *Syntax and Semantics 12: Discourse and Syntax*. Ed. Talmy Givón. New York: Academic Press, 1979.

Hornby, Peter A., ed. *Bilingualism: Psychological, Social and Educational Implications*. New York: Academic Press, 1977.

Hornos, Axel. " 'Ouch!' he said in Japanese." *Verbatim*, 3, No. 1(1976), 1–5.

Householder, Fred W. *Linguistic Speculations*. London and New York: Cambridge Univ. Press, 1971.

Huddleston, Rodney. "Some Observations on Tense and Deixis in English." *Language*, 45(1969), 777–806.

Hyman, Larry M. *Phonology: Theory and Analysis*. New York: Holt, Rinehart and Winston, Inc., 1975.

Hymes, Dell. "Competence and Performance in Linguistic Theory." In *Language Acquisition: Models and Methods*. Eds. R. Huxley and E. Ingram. New York: Academic Press, 1971.

————. *Foundations in Sociolinguistics: An Ethnographic Approach*. Philadelphia: Univ. of Pennsylvania Press, 1974.

————. "Models of the Interaction of Language and Social Life." In *Directions in Sociolinguistics: The Ethnography of Communication*. New York: Holt, Rinehart and Winston, 1972.

————, ed. *Pidginization and Creolization of Languages:* London and New York: Cambridge Univ. Press, 1971.

Iser, Wolfgang. *The Implied Reader: Patterns of Communication in Prose Fiction from Bunyan to Beckett*. Baltimore: The Johns Hopkins Univ. Press, 1974.
———. "The Reality of Fiction: A Functionalist Approach to Literature." *New Literary History*, 7(1975), 7–38.
Ives, Sumner. "A Theory of Literary Dialect." In *A Various Language: Perspectives on American Dialects*. Eds. Juanita Williamson and Virginia M. Burke. New York: Holt, Rinehart and Winston, Inc., 1971. (Slightly revised version of an article by the same name in *Tulane Studies in English*, 2(1950), 137–82.)
Jackendoff, Ray. "Grammar as Evidence for Conceptual Structure." In *Linguistic Theory and Psychological Reality*. Eds. Morris Halle, Joan Bresnan, and George A. Miller. Cambridge, Mass.: MIT Press, 1979.
———. *Semantic Interpretation in Generative Grammar*. Cambridge, Mass.: MIT Press, 1972.
Jacobs, Roderick A., and Peter S. Rosenbaum. *English Transformational Grammar*. Waltham, Mass.: Ginn and Co., 1970.
Jakobson, Roman. "Closing Statement: Linguistics and Poetics." In *Style in Language*. Ed. Thomas A. Sebeok. Cambridge, Mass.: MIT Press, 1960. Rpt. in *Essays on the Language of Literature*. Eds. Seymour Chatman and Samuel R. Levin. Boston: Houghton Mifflin Co., 1967.
———. "Shifters, Verbal Categories, and the Russian Verb." *Selected Writing*. The Hague: Mouton, 1971. Vol. 2 (first published 1957).
Jespersen, Otto. *A Modern English Grammar on Historical Principles*. London: Allen and Unwin, 1961 (orig. published 1909–1949).
———. "Notes on Metre." *Linguistics*. Copenhagen: Levin and Munksgaard, 1933. Rpt. in *Essays on the Language of Literature*. Eds. Seymour Chatman and Samuel R. Levin. Boston: Houghton Mifflin Co., 1967.
Kachru, Braj. "The Indianness of Indian English." *Word*, 21(1966), 391–410.
Karttunen, Lauri, and Stanley Peters. "Requiem for Presuppositions." In *Proceedings of the Third Annual Meeting of the Berkeley Linguistics Society*. Univ. of California, Berkeley: Berkeley Linguistics Society, 1977.
Katz, Jerrold J. "Interpretive Semantics Versus Generative Semantics." *Foundations of Language*, 6(1970), 220–59.
Kempson, Ruth. *Semantic Theory*. London and New York: Cambridge Univ. Press, 1977.
Kenyon, John Samuel. *American Pronunciation*. 10th ed. Ann Arbor: George Wahr Publishing Co., 1966.
Key, Mary Ritchie. *Male/Female Language*. Metuchen, N.J.: Scarecrow Press, 1975.
Kiparsky, Paul. "The Rhythmic Structure of English Verse." *Linguistic Inquiry*, 8(1977), 189–247.
———. "The Role of Linguistics in a Theory of Poetry." In *Language as a Human Problem*. Eds. Morton Bloomfield and Einar Haugen. New York: Norton, 1974.
Kochman, Thomas, ed. *Rappin' and Stylin' Out: Communication in Urban Black America*. Urbana: Univ. of Illinois Press, 1972.
———. "Toward an Ethnography of Black American Speech Behavior." In *Rappin' and Stylin' Out: Communication in Urban Black America*. Ed. Thomas Kochman. Urbana: Univ. of Illinois Press, 1972.
Kress, Gunther R., ed. *Halliday: System and Function in Language: Selected Papers*. London: Oxford Univ. Press, 1976.
Kuno, Susumo. "Subject, Theme, and Speaker's Empathy: A Re-Examination of Relativization Phenomena." In *Subject and Topic*. Ed. Charles N. Li. New York: Academic Press, 1976.
Kuroda, S. Y. "Reflections on the Foundations of Narrative Theory: From a

Linguistic Point of View." In *Pragmatics of Language and Literature*. Ed.
Teun A. van Dijk. Amsterdam: North Holland, 1976.

Labov, William. *Language in the Inner City*. Philadelphia: Univ. of Pennsylvania
Press, 1972.

———. "The Logic of Non-Standard English." *Monograph Series on Languages
and Linguistics*, 22(1969). Rpt. as Chapter 5 in *Language in the Inner City* by
William Labov. Philadelphia: Univ. of Pennsylvania Press, 1972. Rpt. in *Language in Context*. Ed. Pier Paolo Giglioli. Harmondsworth, Mssex: Penguin,
1972. Rpt. in *Black American English: Its Background and Its Usage in the
Schools and Literature*. Ed. Paul Stoller. New York: Dell, 1975.

———. *The Social Stratification of English in New York City*. Washington, D.C.:
Center for Applied Linguistics, 1966.

———. *Sociolinguistic Patterns*. Philadelphia: Univ. of Pennsylvania Press, 1972.

———. "Some Principles of Linguistic Methodology." *Language in Society*,
1(1972), 97–120.

———. "Where do Grammars Stop?" *Monograph Series on Languages and
Linguistics*, Georgetown Univ. 25(1972), 43–88.

Ladefoged, Peter. *A Course in Phonetics*. New York: Harcourt Brace Jovanovich,
Inc., 1975.

Lakoff, George. "On Generative Semantics." In *Semantics: An Interdisciplinary
Reader in Philosophy, Linguistics and Psychology*. Eds. Danny D. Steinberg
and Leon A. Jakobovits. London and New York: Cambridge Univ. Press, 1971.

Lakoff, Robin. *Language and Woman's Place*. New York: Harper and Row,
1975.

———. "Language in Context." *Language* 48(1972), 907–27.

———. "The Language of Politeness or Minding your P's and Q's." *Papers from
the Ninth Regional Meeting of the Chicago Linguistic Society*. Chicago: University of Chicago, Department of Linguistics, 1973.

———. "Some Reasons Why There Can't Be Any *Some-Any* Rule." *Language*,
45(1969), 608–15.

Lambert, Wallace E. "A Social Psychology of Bilingualism." In *Problems of
Bilingualism*. Ed. John Macnamara; special issue of *The Journal of Social
Issues*, 23, No. 2 (1967).

Lance, Donald M. "Spanish-English Code-Switching." In *El Lenguaje de los
Chicanos: Regional and Social Characteristics of Language Used by Mexican-
Americans*. Eds. Eduardo Hernández-Chavez, Andrew D. Cohen, and Anthony
F. Beltramo. Arlington, Va.: Center for Applied Linguistics, 1975 (paper originally published 1969).

Langacker, Ronald W. *Language and Its Structure*. 2nd ed. New York: Harcourt
Brace Jovanovich, Inc., 1973.

Langendoen, D. Terence. "The Accessibility of Deep Structures." In *Readings in
English Transformational Grammar*. Eds. Roderick A. Jacobs and Peter S.
Rosenbaum. Waltham, Mass.: Ginn and Co., 1970.

———. *Essentials of English Grammar*. New York: Holt, Rinehart and Winston,
1970.

Leach, Edmund. "Anthropological Aspects of Language: Animal Categories and
Verbal Abuse." In *New Directions in the Study of Language*. Ed. Eric H.
Lenneberg. Cambridge, Mass.: MIT Press, 1966.

Leech, Geoffrey. *Semantics*. Baltimore, Md: Penguin Books, 1974.

———, and Jan Svartvik. *A Communicative Grammar of English*. London: Longman Group Ltd., 1975.

Leiber, Justin. *Noam Chomsky: A Philosophic Overview*. Boston: Twayne Publishers, 1975.

LePage, Robert. "Processes of Pidginization and Creolization." In *Pidgin and*

Creole Linguistics. Ed. Albert Valdman. Bloomington and London: Indiana Univ. Press, 1977.

Levin, Samuel R. "Concerning What Kind of a Speech Act a Poem Is." In *Pragmatics of Language and Literature*. Ed. Teun A. van Dijk. Amsterdam: North Holland, 1976.

——. *Linguistic Structures in Poetry*. The Hague: Mouton, 1962.

——. *The Semantics of Metaphor*. Baltimore and London: The Johns Hopkins Univ. Press, 1977.

Li, Charles N., ed. *Subject and Topic*. New York: Academic Press, 1976.

Lieberson, Stanley. *Language and Ethnic Relations in Canada*. New York: John Wiley and Sons, Inc., 1970.

Lodge, David. *The Language of Fiction: Essays in Critical and Verbal Analysis of the English Novel*. New York: Columbia Univ. Press, 1966.

Love, Glen A. and Michael Payne, eds. *Contemporary Essays on Style*. Glenview, Ill.: Scott, Foresman and Co., 1969.

Lyons, John. *Introduction to Theoretical Linguistics*. London and New York: Cambridge Univ. Press, 1968.

——. *Noam Chomsky*. New York: Viking Press, 1970.

——. *Semantics*. 2 vols. London and New York: Cambridge Univ. Press, 1977.

McCawley, James D. "Lexical Insertion in a Grammar Without Deep Structure." In *Papers from the Fourth Regional Meeting of the Chicago Linguistic Society*. Chicago: Univ. of Chicago, Linguistics Department, 1968.

McDavid, Raven I. "Dialects of American English." In *The Structure of American English*. Ed. W. Nelson Francis. New York: Ronald Press, 1958.

McIntosh, Angus, "Patterns and Ranges." *Language,* 37(1961), 325–37.

MacWhinney, Brian. "Starting Points." *Language,* 53(1977), 152–68.

Marchand, Hans. *Categories and Types of Present-Day English Word Formation: A Synchronic-Diachronic Approach*. 2nd ed. Munich: Beck'sche Verlagshandlung, 1969.

Mencken, H. L. *The American Language: An Inquiry into the Development of English in the United States*. 4th ed. New York: Alfred A. Knopf, 1936.

Miles, Josephine. *Style and Proportion: The Language of Prose and Poetry*. Boston: Little, Brown and Co., 1967.

——. *The Vocabulary of Poetry: Three Studies*. Berkeley and Los Angeles: Univ. of California Press, 1946.

Miller, George A., and Philip N. Johnson-Laird. *Language and Perception*. Cambridge, Mass.: Belknap Press, Harvard Univ. Press, 1976.

Mphahlele, Ezekiel, and Arthur Delbridge. "The Languages of African Literature." *Harvard Educational Review,* 34, No. 2 (1964), 298–305.

Mukařovský, Jan. "Standard Language and Poetic Language." In *A Prague School Reader on Esthetics, Literary Structure, and Style*. Ed. Paul Garvin (trans. from the original Czech by Paul Garvin). Washington, D.C.: Georgetown Univ. Press, 1964. Rpt. in *Linguistics and Literary Style*. Ed. Donald C. Freeman. New York: Holt, Rinehart and Winston, Inc., 1970.

Nager, Rae Ann. "A Selective Annotated Bibliography of Recent Work on English Prosody." *Style,* 2(1977), 136–70.

Nichols, Patricia C. "Black Women in the Rural South: Conservative and Innovative." In *The Sociology of the Languages of American Women*. Eds. Betty Lou Dubois and Isabel Crouch. San Antonio, Texas: Trinity Univ. 1976.

Nowottny, Winifred. *The Language Poets Use*. London: The Athlone Press, 1972.

Ohmann, Richard. "Generative Grammars and the Concept of Literary Style." *Word,* 20(1964), 423–39. Rpt. in *Linguistics and Literary Style*. Ed. Donald C. Freeman. New York: Holt, Rinehart and Winston, Inc., 1970. Rpt. in *Contem-*

porary Essays on Style. Eds. Glen A. Love and Michael Payne. Glenview, Ill.: Scott, Foresman and Co., 1969.

————. "Literature as Act." In *Approaches to Poetics.* Ed. Seymour Chatman. New York: Columbia Univ. Press, 1973.

————. "Literature as Sentences." *College English,* 27(1966), 261–67. Rpt. in *Essays on the Language of Literature.* Eds. Seymour Chatman and Samuel R. Levin. Boston: Houghton Mifflin Co., 1967. Rpt. in *Contemporary Essays on Style.* Eds. Glen A. Love and Michael Payne. Glenview, Ill.: Scott, Foresman and Co., 1969.

————. "Speech Acts and the Definition of Literature." *Philosophy and Rhetoric,* 4(1971), 1–19.

————. "Speech, Literature, and the Space Between." *New Literary History,* 4(1973), 47–63.

Ong, Walter J. "The Writer's Audience is Always a Fiction." *PMLA,* 90(1975), 9–21.

Page, Norman. *Speech in the English Novel.* London: Longman, 1973.

Palmer, Frank R. *A Linguistic Study of the English Verb.* London: Longman, 1965.

Partridge, Eric. *Slang Today and Yesterday.* 2nd ed. London: George Routledge and Sons Ltd., 1935.

Postal, Paul M. "On the Surface Verb 'Remind.' " *Linguistic Inquiry,* 1(1970), 37–120.

————. "Underlying and Superficial Structure." *Harvard Educational Review,* 34(1964), 246–66.

Pratt, Mary L. *Toward a Speech Act Theory of Literary Discourse.* Bloomington: Indiana Univ. Press, 1977.

Premack, Ann James, and David Premack. "Teaching Language to an Ape." *Scientific American,* 227, No. 4 (1972), 92–99.

Pride, J. B., and Janet Holmes, eds. *Sociolinguistics: Selected Readings.* Harmondsworth, Mssex.: Penguin, 1972.

Pyles, Thomas. *The Origins and Development of the English Language.* 2nd ed. New York: Harcourt Brace Jovanovich, Inc., 1971.

Quirk, Randolph, and Sidney Greenbaum. *A Concise Grammar of Contemporary English.* New York: Harcourt Brace Jovanovich, Inc., 1973.

————, Sidney Greenbaum, Geoffrey Leech, and Jan Svartvik. *A Grammar of Contemporary English.* New York and London: Seminar Press, 1972.

Ramchand, Kenneth. "The Language of the Master?" In *Varieties of Present-Day English.* Eds. Richard W. Bailey and Jay L. Robinson. New York: Macmillan, 1973.

Reed, Carroll. *Dialects of American English.* New York: World Publishing Co., 1967.

Reibel, David D., and Sanford A. Schane, eds. *Modern Studies in English: Readings in Transformational Grammar.* Englewood Cliffs, N.J.: Prentice-Hall, Inc., 1969.

Ringbom, Haakan et al., eds. *Style and Text: Studies Presented to Nils Erik Enkvist.* Stockholm: Skriptor, 1975.

Sacks, Harvey. "On the Analyzability of Stories by Children." In *Directions in Sociolinguistics: The Ethnography of Communication.* Eds. John J. Gumperz and Dell Hymes. New York: Holt, Rinehart and Winston, 1972.

————, Emanuel A. Schegloff, and Gail Jefferson. "A Simplest Systematics for the Organization of Turn-Taking for Conversation." *Language,* 50(1974), 696–735.

Sadock, Jerrold. *Towards a Linguistic Theory of Speech Acts.* New York: Academic Press, 1974.

Sapir, Edward. *Language: An Introduction to the Study of Speech*. New York: Harcourt Brace Jovanovich, Inc., 1921.

Schegloff, Emanuel A. "Notes on Conversational Practice: Formulating Place." In *Studies in Social Interaction*. Ed. David Sudnow. New York: The Free Press, 1972. Shorter version in *Language in Context*. Ed. Pier Paolo Giglioli. Harmondsworth, Mssex: Penguin, 1972.

————. "Sequencing in Conversational Openings." In *Directions in Sociolinguistics: The Ethnography of Communication*. Eds. John J. Gumperz and Dell Hymes. New York: Holt, Rinehart and Winston, 1972.

————, and Harvey Sacks. "Opening up Closings." *Semiotica*, 8(1973), 290–337.

Schneider, Gilbert. *West African Pidgin-English: A Descriptive Linguistic Analysis with Texts and Glossary for the Cameroon Area*. Athens, Ohio, 1966.

Scholes, Robert, and Richard Kellogg. *The Nature of Narrative*. London and New York: Oxford Univ. Press, 1966.

Scott, Charles T. "Toward a Formal Poetics: Metrical Patterning in 'The Windhover.' " *Language and Style*, 7(1974), 91–107.

Searle, John R. "A Classification of Illocutionary Acts." *Language in Society*, 5(1976), 1–23.

————. "Indirect Speech Acts." In *Syntax and Semantics III: Speech Acts*. Eds. Peter Cole and Jerry L. Morgan. New York: Academic Press, 1975.

————. *Speech Acts: An Essay in the Philosophy of Language*. London and New York: Cambridge Univ. Press, 1969.

Sebeok, Thomas A., ed. *Style in Language*. Cambridge, Mass.: MIT Press, 1960.

Serjeantson, Mary S. *A History of Foreign Words in English*. London: Routledge and Kegan Paul, 1935.

Shapiro, Michael. *Asymmetry: An Inquiry into the Linguistic Structure of Poetry*. New York: North-Holland Publishing Co., 1976.

Silverstein, Michael. "Shifters, Linguistic Categories, and Cultural Description." In *Meaning in Anthropology*. Eds. Keith H. Basso and Henry A. Selby. Albuquerque: Univ. of New Mexico Press, 1976.

Sledd, James, and Wilma R. Ebbitt, eds. *Dictionaries and THAT Dictionary*. Chicago: Scott Foresman and Co., 1962.

Sloat, Clarence, Sharon Henderson Taylor, and James E. Hoard. *Introduction to Phonology*. Englewood Cliffs, N.J.: Prentice-Hall, 1978.

Smith, Barbara Herrnstein. *On the Margins of Discourse: The Relation of Literature to Language*. Chicago: Univ. of Chicago Press, 1978.

————. *Poetic Closure: A Study of How Poems End*. Chicago: Univ. of Chicago Press, 1968.

Smitherman, Geneva. *Talkin and Testifyin: The Language of Black America*. Boston: Houghton Mifflin, 1977.

Snow, Catherine E., and Charles A. Ferguson, eds. *Talking to Children: Language Input and Acquisition*. London and New York: Cambridge Univ. Press, 1977.

Soames, Scott, and David M. Perlmutter. *Syntactic Argumentation and the Structure of English*. Los Angeles and Berkeley: Univ. of California Press.

Stewart, William A. "Continuity and Change in American Negro Dialects." *The Florida Foreign Language Reporter*, 6, No. 1 (1968). Rpt. in *Readings in American Dialectology*. Eds. Harold B. Allen and Gary N. Underwood. New York: Appleton-Century-Crofts. Meredith Corporation, 1971.

Stockwell, Robert P. *Foundations of Syntactic Theory*. Englewood Cliffs, N.J.: Prentice-Hall, 1977.

————, Paul Schachter, and Barbara Hall Partee. *The Major Syntactic Structures of English*. New York: Holt, Rinehart and Winston, 1973.

Stoller, Paul, ed. *Black American English: Its Background and Its Usage in the Schools and Literature*. New York: Dell, 1975.

Strang, Barbara M. H. *A History of English*. London: Methuen, 1970.

Sudnow, David, ed. *Studies in Social Interaction*. New York: The Free Press, 1972.

Tarone, Elaine. "Aspects of Intonation in Black English." *American Speech*, 48(1973), 29–36.

Taylor, Orlando. "Responses to Social Dialects in the Field of Speech." In *Socio-Linguistics: A Cross Disciplinary Perspective*. Ed. Roger Shuy. Washington, D.C.: Center for Applied Linguistics, 1971.

Thompson, Sandra A. "The Deep Structure of Relative Clauses." In *Studies in Linguistic Semantics*. Eds. Charles J. Fillmore and D. Terence Langendoen. New York: Holt, Rinehart and Winston, 1971.

Thorne, Barrie, and Nancy Henley, eds. *Language and Sex: Difference and Dominance*. Rowley, Mass.: Newbury House, 1975.

Thorne, James Peter. "Stylistics and Generative Grammar." *Journal of Linguistics*, 1(1965), 49–59. Rpt. in *Linguistics and Literary Style*. New York: Holt, Rinehart and Winston, Inc., 1970.

Todd, Loreto. *Pidgins and Creoles*. London and Boston: Routledge and Kegan Paul, 1974.

Traugott, Elizabeth Closs. *A History of English Syntax*. New York: Holt, Rinehart and Winston, Inc., 1972.

————. "Pidgins, Creoles, and the Origins of Vernacular Black English." In *Black English: A Seminar*. Eds. Deborah Sears Harrison and Tom Trabasso. Hillsdale, N.J.: Laurence Erlbaum Assocs., Publ., 1976.

————. "Spatial Expressions of Tense and Temporal Sequencing: A Contribution to the Study of Semantic Fields." *Semiotica*, 15(1975), 207–30.

Trudgill, Peter. *The Social Differentiation of English in Norwich*. London and New York: Cambridge Univ. Press, 1974.

————. *Sociolinguistics: An Introduction*. Harmondsworth, Mssex.: Penguin, 1974.

Turner, G. W. *Stylistics*. Harmondsworth, Mssex.: Penguin, 1973.

Turner, Lorenzo Dow. *Africanisms in the Gullah Dialect*. Ann Arbor: Univ. of Michigan Press, 1973 (rept. of 1949 ed.).

Ullmann, Stephen. *Semantics: An Introduction to the Science of Meaning*. Oxford: Basil Blackwell, 1964.

Valdman, Albert, ed. *Pidgin and Creole Linguistics*. Bloomington and London: Indiana Univ. Press, 1977.

van Dijk, Teun A. "Pragmatics and Poetics." In *Pragmatics of Language and Literature*. Ed. Teun A. van Dijk. Amsterdam: North Holland, 1976.

————, ed. *Pragmatics of Language and Literature*. Amsterdam: North Holland, 1976.

————, and Jan Petöfi, eds. *Grammars and Descriptions*. Berlin: W. de Gruyter, 1977.

————. *Text and Context: Explorations in the Semantics and Pragmatics of Discourse*. London: Longman Group Ltd., 1977.

Wakelin, Martyn. *English Dialects: An Introduction*. London: Athlone Press, 1972.

Watt, Ian. "The First Paragraph of *The Ambassadors*." *Essays in Criticism*, 10(1960), 250–74.

Weinreich, Uriel. *The Field of Yiddish Language Folklore and Literature*. New York: Linguistic Circle of New York, 1954.

Whorf, Benjamin Lee. *Language, Thought and Reality*. In *Selected Writings of*

Benjamin Lee Whorf. Ed. John B. Caroll. Cambridge, Mass.: The MIT Press, 1956.

Widdowson, H. G. *Stylistics and the Teaching of Literature.* London: Longman Group Ltd., 1976.

Williamson, Juanita, and Virginia M. Burke, eds. *A Various Language: Perspectives on American Dialects.* New York: Holt, Rinehart and Winston, Inc., 1971.

Wolfram, Walt. *A Sociolinguistic Description of Detroit Negro Speech.* Washington, D.C.: Center for Applied Linguistics, 1969.

————, and Ralph W. Fasold. *The Study of Social Dialects in American English.* Englewood Cliffs, N.J.: Prentice-Hall, 1974.

Wolfson, Nessa. "The Conversational Historical Present Alternation." *Language,* 55(1979), 168–82.

Zimmerman, Don H., and Candace West. "Sex Roles, Interruptions and Silences in Conversations." In *Language and Sex: Difference and Dominance.* Eds. Barrie Thorne and Nancy Henley. Rowley, Mass.: Newbury House, 1975.

Index

Note: Numbers in italics indicate references to exercises.

A. AUTHORS, EDITORS, AND TITLES OF LITERARY WORKS AND SAMPLE TEXTS

B. AUTHORS OF LINGUISTIC AND CRITICAL WORKS

C. SUBJECTS

COPYRIGHTS AND ACKNOWLEDGMENTS

The authors wish to thank the following publishers and copyright holders for their permission to reprint the material listed below:

HARRIETTE SIMPSON ARNOW for the excerpt from *The Dollmaker* by Harriette Simpson Arnow. Copyright 1954 by Harriette Simpson Arnow. Reprinted by permission of the author.

BELL TELEPHONE LABORATORIES for the excerpt from *Algorithms in Snobol* by James F. Gimpel. Copyright 1976 Bell Telephone Laboratories. Reprinted by permission.

BASIL BLACKWELL PUBLISHERS for the figure adapted from *Sociolinguistic Patterns* by William Labov. Reprinted by permission of Basil Blackwell Publishers.

THE BODLEY HEAD for the excerpt from *The Great Gatsby* by F. Scott Fitzgerald. Reprinted by permission of The Bodley Head.

JOSÉ ANTONIO BURCIAGA for "Españotli titlan Englishic" by José Antonio Burciaga. Reprinted by permission of the author.

JONATHAN CAPE LTD for the excerpt from "Edward and Pia" from *Unspeakable Practices, Unnatural Acts* by Donald Barthelme. Reprinted by permission of Deborah Rogers Ltd Literary Agency; for the excerpt from *For Whom the Bell Tolls* by Ernest Hemingway. Reprinted by permission of the Executors of the Ernest Hemingway Estate; and for the excerpt from "The SinguLARGE Experience of Miss Anne Duffield" from *In His Own Write and A Spaniard in the Works* by John Lennon. Reprinted by permission of the author.

CENTER FOR APPLIED LINGUISTICS for the figures adapted from *A Sociolinguistic Description of Detroit Negro Speech* by Walter A. Wolfram. Reprinted by permission of the Center for Applied Linguistics.

CHATTO AND WINDUS LTD for the excerpt from "Prelude" to *Big Woods* by William Faulkner. Reprinted by permission of the author's estate and Chatto and Windus.

COOPER SQUARE PUBLISHERS, INC. for the excerpt from *Call It Sleep* by Henry Roth. Reprinted by permission of Cooper Square Publishers, Inc.

E. P. DUTTON & CO., INC. for "A Stanza of Anglo-Saxon Poetry" by Lewis Carroll. From *The Book of Nonsense* by Roger Lancelyn Green. Reprinted by permission of E. P. Dutton & Co., Inc.

LAWRENCE ERLBAUM ASSOCIATES, INC. for "Sense Pass King" and "Hard Times on Edisto" in *Black English; a Seminar* by Deborah Sears Harrison and Tom Trabasso. Reprinted by permission of the publisher. "Hard Times on Edisto" reprinted by permission of Lois Turner Williams and the publisher.

FABER AND FABER LIMITED for "Rhapsody on a Windy Night" by T. S. Eliot. Reprinted by permission of Faber and Faber Ltd. from *Collected Poems 1909–1962* by T. S. Eliot; and for an excerpt from "Carnal Knowledge" from *Fighting Terms* by Thom Gunn. Reprinted by permission of Faber and Faber Ltd.

FARRAR, STRAUS & GIROUX, INC. for the excerpt from "Edward and Pia" from *Unspeakable Practices, Unnatural Acts* by Donald Barthelme. Copyright © 1965, 1968 by Donald Barthelme. Reprinted with the permission of Farrar, Straus & Giroux, Inc. This selection appeared originally in *The New Yorker*.

GRANADA PUBLISHING LIMITED for "love is more thicker than forget," from *Complete Poems 1923–54* by E. E. Cummings. Reprinted by permission of MacGibbon & Kee Ltd/Granada Publishing Ltd.

GROVE PRESS, INC. for the excerpt from *Murphy* by Samuel Beckett. Reprinted by permission of Grove Press, Inc. First published in 1938.

HARCOURT BRACE JOVANOVICH, INC. for "love is more thicker than forget" by E. E. Cummings. Copyright 1939 by E. E. Cummings, renewed 1967 by Marion More-

J
K 2
L 3
M 4
N 5
O 6
P 7